BRITISH WARPLANES
OF WORLD WAR II

WORLD AIR POWER JOURNAL | WINGS OF FAME

BRITISH WARPLANES OF WORLD WAR II

EDITED BY DANIEL J. MARCH

BARNES & NOBLE BOOKS
NEW YORK

This edition published by Barnes & Noble, Inc.,
by arrangement with Amber Books Ltd
2000 Barnes & Noble Books

M 10 9 8 7 6 5 4 3 2 1

ISBN: 0-7607-2275-7

Jacket design by
Amber Books Ltd
Bradley's Close
74–77 White Lion Street
London N1 9PF

Managing Editor: David Donald
Editor: Daniel J. March
Illustrations: Mike Badrocke, Chris Davey, John Weal, Keith Fretwell

Printed in Italy

CONTENTS

Airspeed AS.5 Courier/AS.6 Envoy

Formed in the spring of 1931, the Airspeed company produced a number of unsuccessful prototypes before designing the **AS.5 Courier**. Intended as a light transport, the Courier introduced a number of novel features including retractable tailwheel landing gear, which was dismissed at the time as useless although later proved to significantly improve performance.

Powered by either an Armstrong Siddeley Lynx or Cheetah engine, the AS.5 was of low-wing monoplane layout and handled well except during approach and landing. In 1934 the RAF acquired an **AS.5A** for use as a communications aircraft and in 1935 returned the aircraft to Airspeed for the fitting of drag and high-lift devices to improve low-speed handling. This example, along with nine civilian impressed aircraft, went on to serve the RAF in the transport role during World War II. In 1933 Airspeed began developing a larger twin-engined aircraft based on the Courier. Designated **AS.6 Envoy**, the aircraft, like the AS.5, was of all-wood construction with fabric-covered surfaces and was intended mainly for the civilian market.

The Envoy proved adaptable in the choice of powerplant and no fewer than seven different engines from four manufacturers could be fitted. The later **Series II** and **Series III** featured split flaps which continued from wingroot to wingroot beneath the centre-section. First flown in June 1934, the Envoy entered RAF service as the first type to equip the King's Flight, when a civilian AS.6 was converted for the task. In 1938 the RAF received seven **Envoy Mk III**s for communications duties at home and in India. One of these was taken over by the FAA and used throughout the war. The only other military operator was the South African Air Force, which acquired seven in 1936.

This AS.6 Envoy was one of three armed versions which were delivered to the South African Air Force. Armament consisted of a forward-firing machine-gun and a dorsal gun turret. Four civilian AS.6s operated by South African Airways could be converted for use in a military role.

G-ABXN, an AS.5A Courier, was impressed into military service in the spring of 1940 and served with No. 3 Ferry Pilot's Pool, RAF, whilst retaining its civil identity. It was retired from service in September 1940.

Specification
AS.5B Courier
Type: five/six-seat light transport
Powerplant: one 305-hp (227-kW) Armstrong Siddeley Cheetah V radial piston engine
Performance: maximum speed 165 mph (266 km/h) at sea level; cruising speed 145 mph (233 km/h) at 1,000 ft (305 m); service ceiling 17,000 ft (5180 m); range 640 miles (1030 km)
Weights: empty 2,328 lb (1056 kg); maximum take-off 4,000 lb (1814 kg)
Dimensions: span 47 ft 0 in (14.33 m); length 28 ft 6 in (8.69 m); wing area 250 sq ft (23.23 m^2)

Envoy Mk III
Type: seven-seat light transport
Powerplant: two 350-hp (261-kW) Armstrong Siddeley Cheetah IX radial piston engines
Performance: maximum speed 210 mph (338 km/h) at 7,300 ft (2225 m); service ceiling 22,500 ft (6860 m); range 650 miles (1046 km)
Weights: empty 4,057 lb (1840 kg); maximum take-off 6,300 lb (2858 kg)
Dimensions: span 52 ft 4 in (15.95 m); length 34 ft 6 in (10.52 m); height 9 ft 6 in (2.90 m); wing area 339 sq ft (31.49 m^2)

Airspeed AS.10 Oxford

In 1936 the Airspeed company was given the opportunity of submitting a proposal to meet Air Ministry Specification T.23/36, which called for a twin-engined trainer. Airspeed's design for this was based on the successful AS.6 Envoy, of which about 24 were already in civil use and earning a reputation for reliability which, possibly, may have helped the Air Ministry's decision to order an initial quantity of 136 **AS.10**s.

The prototype AS.10, by then bearing the name **Oxford**, made its first flight on 19 June 1937, and token deliveries began in November of that year, with four of the first six going to the RAF's Central Flying School, the other two to No. 11 Flying Training School. Very similar in overall proportions and configuration to the AS.6 Envoy, it also shared that type's wooden construction, tailwheel-type retractable landing gear and basic airframe. The variations came in powerplant, internal layout and, in the **Oxford Mk I**, provision of an Armstrong Whitworth gun turret with one machine-gun for the training of air gunners.

The Oxford was to be built in large numbers and used extensively for the Commonwealth Air Training Scheme when World War II began, and the considerable thought which Airspeed had put into its internal layout undoubtedly had a bearing on the demand for this aircraft. Normal accommodation was for a crew of three at any one time, but in addition to seats for a pilot/pupil and co-pilot/instructor, there were positions for the training of an air-gunner, bomb-aimer, camera operator, navigator and radio operator. Dual controls were standard, making the Oxford suitable for use as a twin-engined trainer; with the dual-control set removed from the co-pilot's position a bomb-aimer could take up a prone position and drop smoke practice bombs, which were carried in the centre-section well; or the seat could be

This Oxford Mk I, L9703 of No. 3 Flying Training School, was based at RAF South Cerney from June 1938. In September 1939 the unit was renamed No. 3 Service Flying Training School.

Aircraft of the RAF's No. 4 FTS at Habbaniyah, such as this Oxford Mk I of 'B' Squadron, were hastily equipped with underwing bomb racks at the outbreak of war.

The sole Oxford Mk III was first flown in March 1940 and was fitted with Armstrong Siddeley Cheetah XV engines and Rotol constant-speed propellers. It was not placed into production.

Affectionately known to its crews as the 'Ox-box', the Oxford was the RAF's first twin-engined, monoplane advanced trainer, and nearly 400 were in service by the outbreak of war. By 1945 8,586 had been built.

slid back and a chart table, hinged to the fuselage side, erected for use by a trainee navigator; an aft-facing seat behind the co-pilot position was available for a radio operator. A hood was also available so that the Oxford could be used for instrument training.

Powerplants varied according to mark. The **Mk I**, a general-purpose, bombing and gunnery trainer, and the **Mk II** pilot, radio operator and navigator trainer were both powered by two 375-hp (280-kW) Armstrong Siddeley Cheetah X radial engines, with fixed-pitch propellers. The **Mk V**, equipped for the same role as the Mk II, had two 450-hp (336-kW) Pratt & Whitney R-985-AN6 radial engines, driving constant speed propellers. The **Oxford Mk III**, of which only a single example was built, had two 425-hp (317-kW) Cheetah XV radials and Rotol constant-speed propellers. Odd variants included an early Oxford Mk I equipped with special McLaren landing gear, the main units of which could be offset to cater for a reasonable degree of crosswind at both take-off and landing.

As mentioned above, the outbreak of World War II created an enormous demand for these trainers, not only for use by the RAF, but by those nations which were involved in the Commonwealth Air Training Scheme. Examples went also to the Free French air force and, under reverse Lend-Lease, a number were used by USAAF units in Europe. In addition to their use for training purposes, a number were equipped to serve as air ambulances, for radar calibration and for communications. Many served with anti-aircraft co-operation squadrons, these including Nos 285, 286, 289, 290, 567, 577, 598, 631, 667 and 691. The FAA also had one training unit, No. 758 Instrument Flying Squadron, equipped with Oxfords from June 1942.

The demand for Oxfords was beyond Airspeed's productive capacity, the company building a total of 4,411 at Portsmouth, Hants and 550 at Christchurch, Hants. Other construction was by de Havilland at Hatfield (1,515), Percival Aircraft at Luton (1,360) and Standard Motors at Coventry (750), to give a grand total of 8,586. Airspeed built its last example in July 1945, and the Oxford remained in service with the RAF at No. 10 Advanced Flying Training School, Pershore, until 1954.

Specification
Oxford Mk V
Type: two-seat general-purpose trainer
Powerplant: two 450-hp (336-kW) Pratt & Whitney R-985-AN6 Wasp Junior radial piston engines
Performance: maximum speed 202 mph (325 km/h) at 4,100 ft (1250 m); service ceiling 21,000 ft (6400 m); range 700 miles (1127 km)
Weights: empty 5,670 lb (2572 kg); maximum take-off 8,000 lb (3629 kg)
Dimensions: span 53 ft 4 in (16.26 m); length 34 ft 6 in (10.52 m); height 11 ft 1 in (3.38 m); wing area 348 sq ft (32.33 m²)
Armament (Oxford Mk I): one 0.303-in (7.7-mm) machine-gun in dorsal turret.

Airspeed AS.30 Queen Wasp

In 1935 the de Havilland Queen Bee entered service as the RAF's first controlled pilotless aircraft. However, by 1936 this aircraft's performance was considered unrepresentative of contemporary service aircraft and the Air Ministry issued Specification Q.32/35 for a higher-speed and more effectively controlled replacement.

Airspeed submitted its **AS.30** design, and two prototypes were built: a wheeled example for the RAF and a float-equipped version for the Royal Navy. Of all-wood construction with fabric-covered control surfaces the **Queen Wasp**, as it had become named, first flew in landplane form in June 1937. The Queen Wasp's enclosed cabin was equipped with a single seat for a pilot allowing the aircraft to be flown independently of its radio control system.

Although the AS.30 featured full-span slotted flaps along the entire trailing edge of the upper wing and slotted ailerons on the lower wing which interconnected with the flaps to droop when they were lowered, flight tests revealed that low-speed control and handling characteristics were poor. Despite successful catapult trials of the naval version, the service never placed a production order. The first two production examples flew in March and May 1940, respectively, and despite an RAF order for 65 examples only three more were delivered before the order was cancelled. Another five examples which had been partially completed by the Airspeed company were abandoned.

Specification
AS.30 Queen Wasp
Type: pilotless target aircraft
Powerplant: one 350-hp (261-kW) Armstrong Siddeley Cheetah IX radial piston engine
Performance: maximum speed (landplane) 172 mph (277 km/h) at 8,000 ft (2440 m); cruising speed (landplane) 151 mph (243 km/h) at 10,000 ft (3050 m); service ceiling 20,000 ft (6100 m)
Weights: maximum take-off (landplane) 3,500 lb (1588 kg), (seaplane) 3,800 lb (1724 kg)
Dimensions: span 31 ft 0 in (9.45 m); length (landplane) 24 ft 4 in (7.42 m), (seaplane) 29 ft 1 in (8.86 m); height (landplane) 10 ft 1 in (3.07 m), (seaplane) 13 ft 0 in (3.96 m)

The second Queen Wasp prototype, fitted with floats, was successfully catapulted from the aircraft-carrier HMS Pegasus *during the evaluation period. It is seen here taking off during handling trials near Gosport.*

Airspeed AS.51/AS.58 Horsa

Early deployment by Germany of gliders carrying airborne troops or supplies had been seen by the British to be tactically advantageous. It was considered essential in Britain that its armed forces should be similarly equipped.

In December 1940 Airspeed received an Air Ministry specification which called for a troop-carrying glider which was to have almost double the capacity of the Waco CG-4A Hadrian which was developed for the US Army during 1941. Following acceptance of Airspeed's design proposal, the Air Ministry ordered seven prototypes. Two of these, when fabricated, were assembled at Fairey's works, these being the flight test examples. The remaining five were assembled at Airspeed's factory at Portsmouth, and these were for use by the British Army to carry out trials in the loading and unloading of typical equipment that they would be expected to carry.

One would expect the construction of Airspeed's **AS.51** to be simple. This would have been true if it had not been an essential requirement that the glider must be composed of a number of easily assembled units, instead of being built conventionally on a production line. Thus, it consisted of 30 separate assemblies built mainly by woodworking sub-contractors, such as furniture manufacturers. These were subsequently assembled and test flown at RAF Maintenance Units, with some 3,000 of these gliders being constructed in this way. Only about 700 of all the AS.51s that were built were manufactured, assembled and test flown in one place, and these originated from Airspeed at its Christchurch, Hants, factory. Produced simultaneously with the AS.51, which became designated **Horsa Mk I**, was the **AS.58** with a hinged nose for the direct loading of vehicles and guns, and this was designated **Horsa Mk II**.

Almost entirely of wood construction, the cantilever high-set wing was built in three sections, had ailerons, split trailing-edge flaps, and underwing dive brakes. The fuselage was also in three sections, and provided accommodation for two pilots and a maximum of 25 troops. Landing gear was of the fixed tricycle type, and there was provision to jettison the main units for landing on very rough areas, when the nosewheel and sprung landing skid on the underfuselage centre-line had to suffice.

The first prototype, towed by an Armstrong Whitworth Whitley, was flown from Fairey's Great West Aerodrome on 12 September 1941, and soon after this date the Horsa began to enter service with the RAF, towed for operational purposes by powered aircraft of RAF Transport Command. They were used to carry men and equipment of the Air Landing Brigades of the 1st and 6th Airborne Divisions piloted mainly by men of the British Army's Glider Pilot Regiment but also, as and when necessary, by RAF pilots.

Towed airborne from their base at RAF Brize Norton, these three Horsa Mk Is are from the Heavy Glider Conversion Unit which was equipped with up to 50 Horsas. This unit became No. 21 HGCU in October 1944.

The first significant operational use of the Horsa was on 10 July 1943 when 27 survivors of 30 air-towed from Britain to North Africa were deployed during the invasion of Sicily. Horsas subsequently played an important part in the Normandy invasion of June 1944, operated by the RAF and the USAAF, in the invasion of southern France in August 1944, at Arnhem in September 1944, and during the Rhine crossing in March 1945.

It is impossible to quote accurate production figures for the Horsa. The totals agreed by several researchers, however, cannot be too far out, and are as near as possible to the true number. These comprise 470 Mk Is and 225 Mk IIs by Airspeed, plus the original seven prototypes; 300 Mk Is and 65 Mk IIs by the Austin Motor Company; and 1,461 Mk Is and 1,271 Mk IIs by sub-contractors in the woodworking industry, the majority produced by the furniture manufacturer Harris Lebuis.

Specification
Horsa Mk I
Type: troop and cargo combat glider
Powerplant: none
Performance: maximum towing speed 150 mph (241 km/h); normal gliding speed 100 mph (161 km/h)
Weights: empty 8,370 lb (3797 kg); maximum take-off (Horsa Mk I) 15,500 lb (7031 kg), (Horsa Mk II) 15,750 lb (7144 kg)
Dimensions: span 88 ft 0 in (26.82 m); length (Horsa Mk I) 67 ft 0 in (20.42 m), (Horsa Mk II) 67 ft 11 in (20.70 m); height (Horsa Mk I) 19 ft 6 in (5.94 m), (Horsa Mk II) 20 ft 4 in (6.20 m); wing area 1,104 sq ft (102.56 m²)

Below: Normandy fields were littered with Horsas after the Allied airborne assault. The rear fuselage easily separated to allow rapid egress by the troops.

Above: 'Vee' struts were fitted to the tailplanes of later Horsas allowing steep descents into small landing areas to be made, as demonstrated here. The supplementary landing skid can be seen beneath the fuselage.

Armstrong Whitworth A.W.38 Whitley

Above: Crews flying with No. 4 Group Bomber Command Whitley squadrons, based in Yorkshire, flew many freezing sorties during the first winter of the war. As well as making limited bombing raids, many propaganda leaflet dropping missions were flown all over Germany.

Left: A 2,000-lb (907-kg) armour-piercing bomb is prepared for loading onto a Whitley Mk V. The Mk V could carry 7,000 lb (3175 kg) of bombs, which was significantly more than the RAF's other heavy bombers of the period, the Hampden and the Wellington.

Designed to Air Ministry Specification B.3/34, which was circulated in July 1934, the Armstrong Whitworth **A.W.38 Whitley** was the most extensively built of the company's designs, production reaching a total of 1,814 aircraft. It also marked a departure from Armstrong Whitworth's traditional steel tube construction, the Whitley's fuselage being a light alloy monocoque structure.

Production was authorised while the aircraft was still in the design stage, an order for 80 aircraft being placed in August 1935. Alan Campbell-Orde flew the first prototype at Whitley Abbey on 17 March 1936, the machine's two Armstrong Siddeley Tiger X engines turning the then-new three-bladed, variable-pitch de Havilland propellers. A second prototype built to Specification B.21/35 had the more powerful Tiger XI engines and was flown by Charles Turner Hughes on 24 February 1937.

Trials at the Aircraft and Armament Experimental Establishment at Martlesham Heath were undertaken in the autumn of 1936, and the first production **Whitley Mk I**s were delivered early in 1937, including the second aircraft which was flown to RAF Dishforth on 9 March for No. 10 Squadron. Thirty-four Mk Is were built before the **Whitley Mk II** was introduced. This mark had Tiger VIII engines with two-speed superchargers, the first fitted to an RAF aircraft; 46 Mk IIs completed the initial order for 80.

Mk I and Mk II Whitleys had Armstrong Whitworth manually-operated nose and tail turrets, each with a 0.303-in (7.7-mm) Vickers machine-gun, but in the **Whitley Mk III** the nose turret was replaced by a power-operated Nash and Thompson turret, and a retractable ventral turret with two 0.303-in (7.7-mm) Brownings was added. The 80 Whitley Mk IIIs also had modified bomb bays to accommodate larger bombs.

By far the most numerous of the Whitley variants were those with Rolls-Royce engines. A Whitley Mk I was fitted with Merlin IIs and

Finished in day bomber camouflage, this Whitley Mk V is fitted with a glider-towing yoke on the rear of the fuselage beneath the gun-less turret.

This Whitley Mk V flew with No. 78 Squadron at RAF Croft in late 1941. It was painted in a non-standard Bomber Command all-black scheme adopted for night operations. Mission markings have been applied to the nose of the aircraft.

Left: ***Fitted with two Rolls-Royce Merlin X engines, the Whitley Mk V offered much improved performance over the earlier Armstrong Siddeley Tiger-powered versions. This example of No. 78 Squadron has 36 mission markings applied to its nose.***

Below: ***Powered by two Armstrong Siddeley Tiger IX radial engines, the Whitley Mk I was the first variant to enter production, and entered service in March 1937. Tiger-powered Mk IIIs conducted the first operational Whitley sorties of World War II, but by late 1940 most of the Tiger-engined Whitleys had been replaced by Merlin-engined Mk IVs and Mk Vs.***

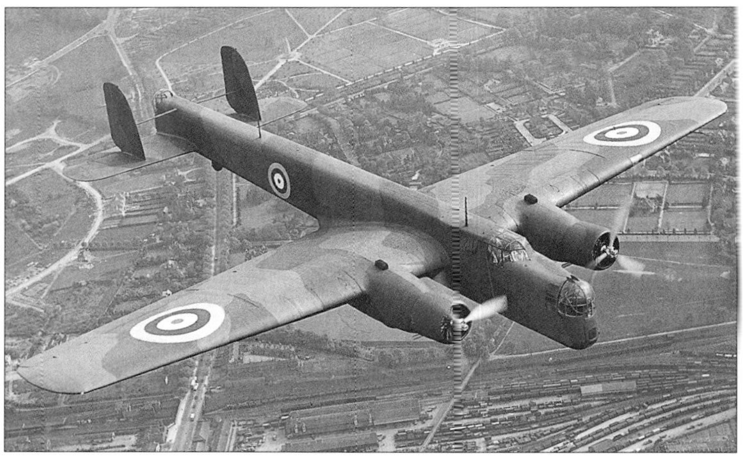

Above: ***Whitley Mk Vs of No. 102 Sqn are seen landing at RAF Driffield during the 'phoney' war. A Whitley from this squadron was the first RAF aircraft to deliberately drop bombs on German soil, in March 1940.***

test-flown at Hucknall on 11 February 1938, although engine failure prematurely concluded the second flight. The programme was quickly resumed, however, and during April and May the aircraft carried out trials at Martlesham Heath.

Merlin IVs of 1,030 hp (768 kW) were installed in production **Whitley Mk IVs**, the first of which flew on 5 April 1939. Other changes incorporated in this version included a power-operated Nash and Thompson tail turret with four 0.303-in (7.7-mm) Browning guns, a transparent panel was added in the lower nose to improve the view for the bomb-aimer, and two additional wing tank were fitted to bring total capacity to 705 Imp gal (3205 litres). Production totalled 33, together with seven **Mk IVA**s which had 1,145-hp (854-kW) Merlin X engines.

The same engines were retained for the **Whitley Mk V**, which incorporated a number of improvements. The most noticeable of these were modified fins with straight leading edges, and an extension of 1 ft 3 in (0.38 m) to the rear fuselage to provide a wider field of fire for the rear gunner. Rubber de-icer boots were fitted to the wing leading-edges, and fuel capacity was increased to 837 Imp gal (3805 litres), or 969 Imp gal (4405 litres) if extra tanks were carried in the bomb bay. Production totalled 1,466 aircraft.

The **Whitley Mk VI** was a projected version with Pratt & Whitney engines, studied as an insurance against short supply of Merlins. It was not built, however, and the ultimate production Whitley was the **Mk VII**, which was essentially a Mk V with auxiliary fuel tanks in the bomb bay and in the rear fuselage to bring the total capacity to 1,100 Imp gal (5001 litres), increasing the range to 2,300 miles (3701 km) for maritime patrol duties. Externally the Mk VIIs could be distinguished by the dorsal radar aerials of the ASV Mk II air-to-surface radar. Production reached 146, and some Mk Vs were converted to the later standard.

As noted above, No. 10 Squadron at RAF Dishforth was the first to equip with the Whitley, which replaced the Handley Page Heyford in March 1937. Nos 51 and 58 Squadrons at RAF Leconfield soon followed and, during the night of 3 September 1939, 10 Whitley Mk IIIs from these two squadrons flew a leaflet raid over Bremen, Hamburg and the Ruhr. Just under a month later, during the night of 1 October, No. 10 Squadron flew a similar mission over Berlin. The first bombs were dropped on Berlin during the night of 25 August 1940, the attacking squadrons including Nos 51 and 78 with Whitleys. To mark the entry of the Italians into the war, 36 Whitleys drawn from Nos 10, 51, 58, 77 and 102 Squadrons were tasked to raid Genoa and Turin during the night of 11 June 1940, although only 13 actually reached their targets, weather and engine troubles taking their toll. The Whitley was retired from Bomber Command in April 1942, the last operation being flown against Ostend during the night of 29 April, although some aircraft from operational training units were flown in the '1,000 Bomber' raid on Cologne on the night of 30 May 1942.

Coastal Command's association with the Whitley began in September 1939 when No. 58 Squadron was transferred to Boscombe Down to operate anti-submarine patrols over the English Channel.

Right: ***Based at RAF Linton-on-Ouse, Yorkshire, this No. 58 Squadron Whitley Mk V departs at dusk for a night raid over Germany. In September 1939 Whitleys of this unit, along with No. 51 Squadron, on a leaflet dropping raid, became the first RAF aircraft to penetrate into German airspace during the World War II. Departing RAF Leconfield, they dropped nearly six million leaflets weighing over 13 tons (13200 kg) on the Ruhr, Hamburg and Bremen.***

Left: After being superseded as a front-line bomber, many Whitleys were converted to the glider-towing role. This example from No. 21 Glider Conversion Unit tows a Horsa glider aloft on a training mission. Close co-operation between the Whitley pilots and the trainee glider pilots was essential to prevent accidents.

Right: The Whitley Mk V's duties included the dropping of propaganda leaflets, supplies and clandestine agents by parachute. T4149 is shown here with a large supply canister mounted under each wing.

Left: The Whitley Mk V, with two Rolls-Royce Merlin X engines, was the most numerous variant, a total of 1,466 being built. Many Whitleys found their way into conversion units teaching fledgling pilots the art of bomber flying. Shown here is N1503 'M' of No. 19 OTU, based at Kinloss, during the summer of 1940.

This lasted until February 1940, when the unit returned to Bomber Command, but during 1942 it took up patrol duties once again, flying over the Western Approaches from St Eval and Stornoway. Other units similarly occupied at that time included Nos 51 and 77 Squadrons, the latter operating in the Bay of Biscay area.

Mk V Whitleys replaced the Avro Ansons of No. 502 Squadron at RAF Aldergrove in the autumn of 1940 and a second Coastal Command Whitley unit, No. 612 Squadron, formed in May 1941. The Mk Vs were replaced by the ASV Mk II-equipped Whitley Mk VII, and an aircraft of No. 502 Squadron sank the type's first German submarine when it attacked *U-206* in the Bay of Biscay on 30 November 1941.

Whitleys were also used at No. 1 Parachute Training School at Ringway, Manchester, and were adapted for use as glider tugs, becoming attached to No. 21 Glider Conversion Unit at Brize Norton for the training of tug pilots. The paratroop raid on the German radar site at Bruneval used Whitleys of No. 51 Squadron, and the aircraft of 'special duty' units at RAF Tempsford (Nos 138 and 161 Squadrons) flew numerous sorties, dropping agents into occupied territory and supplying Resistance groups with arms and equipment. Fifteen Whitley Mk Vs were handed over to BOAC in May 1942 and, stripped of armament but with additional fuel tanks in the bomb bays, flew regularly from Gibraltar to Malta carrying supplies for the beleaguered island.

Specification
Whitley Mk V
Type: five-seat long-range night-bomber
Powerplant: two 1,145-hp (854-kW) Rolls-Royce Merlin X inline piston engines
Performance: maximum speed 230 mph (370 km h) at 16,400 ft (5000 m); cruising speed 210 mph (338 km/h) at 15,000 ft (4570 m); service ceiling 26,000 ft (7925 m); range 1,500 miles (2414 km)
Weights: empty 19,350 lb (8777 kg); maximum take-off 33,500 lb (15195 kg)
Dimensions: span 84 ft 0 in (25.60 m); length 70 ft 6 in (21.49 m); height 15 ft 0 in (4.57 m); wing area 1,137 sq ft (105.63 m^2)
Armament: four 0.303-in (7.7-mm) machine-guns in powered tail turret and one similar gun in nose turret, plus up to 7,000 lb (3175 kg) of bombs

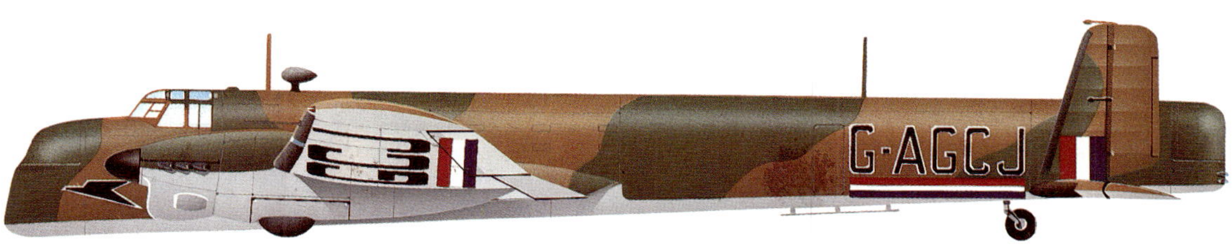

Modified for passenger carrying with the British Overseas Airways Corporation during 1942, this Mk V originally served with the RAF as BD383 before attaining the civilian identity G-AGCJ. Fifteen Whitleys were used by BOAC in 1942, one of their main tasks being the transportation of urgent supplies to Malta.

Whitley Mk VII Z9190 of No. 502 Squadron, RAF Coastal Command, in the colours adopted in late 1942. Equipped with ASV Mk II radar, this elderly warplane gave valuable service on patrols over the Bay of Biscay. The sinking of U-boat U-206 on 30 November 1941 was the first confirmed kill achieved by the use of ASV Mk II.

Armstrong Whitworth A.W.41 Albemarle

Twenty-four Albemarles took airborne troops to Normandy before the D-Day landings commenced on 6 June 1944. A further 20 were used during the day, including this Albemarle Mk V V1823 of No. 297 Squadron based at Brize Norton in June 1944.

The **Albemarle** originated as a Bristol Aeroplane Company design to meet an Air Ministry specification for a twin-engined bomber. With a change in the official specification, however, design responsibility was transferred to Armstrong Whitworth, under a team led by John Lloyd, who was set the difficult task of taking over another company's creation and adapting it as a reconnaissance bomber. The resulting Armstrong Whitworth **A.W.41** was given the name Albemarle.

Designed for mixed composite steel and wood construction, the prototype flew in 1939, but was destroyed in a crash before the flight of the second prototype on 20 March 1940. The Albemarle's form enabled wide use of sub-contracting, even to small companies outside the aircraft industry (one source mentions almost 1,000 sub-contractors), and an additional bonus came from conservation of light alloy and other strategic materials.

The first 32 aircraft were built as bombers, although not used as such, and there was considerable delay in establishing production lines. The first three production Albemarles left the factory in December 1941, by which time the decision had been made to adapt the aircraft as a glider tug and airborne forces transport.

Deliveries to the RAF began in January 1943 when No. 295 Squadron received its first aircraft the type was blooded with Nos 296 and 297 Squadrons, part of No. 38 Wing operating from North Africa, in the invasion of Sicily in July 1943. On D-Day (6 June 1944) six No. 295 Squadron Albemarles, operating from Harwell, served as pathfinders for the 6th Airborne Division, dropping paratroops over Normandy.

In the glider-tug role, four squadrons of Albemarles were used to tow Airspeed Horsas to France in support of ground operations, while in September 1944 two of No. 38 Group's squadrons participated in the ill-fated Arnhem operation, towing gliders carrying troops of the 1st Airborne Division.

Production of the Albemarle, apart from the prototypes, was undertaken by A.W. Hawksley Ltd, part of the Hawker Siddeley Group; production came to an end in December 1944 when 600 Albemarles had been built. Original orders had covered 1,080.

Deliveries to the RAF consisted of 359 transport versions (78 **Mk I**, 99 **Mk II**, 49 **Mk V** and 133 **Mk VI**) and 197 glider tugs (80 Mk I and 117 Mk VI). Additional to these were the original 42 bombers which were subsequently converted to transports.

All production Albemarles used the 1,590-hp (1186-kW) Bristol Hercules XI engine, and differences in the marks were primarily in equipment. The bomber versions were fitted with a four-gun Boulton Paul dorsal turret.

Designed as a bomber, the Albemarle never entered service in this role, but achieved notable success in glider-towing and special transport duties.

Specification
Albemarle Mk VI
Type: transport and glider-tug
Powerplant: two 1,590-hp (1186-kW) Bristol Hercules XI radial piston engines
Performance: maximum speed 265 mph (426 km/h) at 10,500 ft (3200 m); cruising speed 170 mph (274 km/h); service ceiling 18,000 ft (5485 m); range 1,300 miles (2092 km)
Weight: maximum take-off 22,600 lb (10251 kg)
Dimensions: span 77 ft 0 in (23.47 m); length 59 ft 11 in (18.26 m); height 15 ft 7 in (4.75 m); wing area 803.5 sq ft (74.65 m²)
Armament (glider tug and transport): twin 0.303-in (7.7-mm) Vickers 'K' machine-guns in dorsal position

Avro 621 Tutor/626 Prefect

At the start of the 1930s it had become apparent that the excellent, but ageing, Avro 504N would have to be replaced as the RAF's basic trainer. Roy Chadwick of the Avro company used welded steel-tube in the construction of the **Avro 621** which was submitted in December to the Aircraft and Armament Experimental Establishment for evaluation.

Following its service trials against designs submitted from a number of other companies, the **Tutor**, as it was by then named, was selected by the RAF. An original trial batch of 21, powered by the Armstrong Siddeley Mongoose IIIA engine, was ordered. The RAF quickly placed further orders to be powered by the Armstrong Siddeley Lynx engine, and by the time production ceased in 1936 the service had received 394 production examples. During the late 1930s the Tutor equipped a number of different training units and by the outbreak of war around 50 per cent remained on charge with these establishments. As the war progressed the Tutor was relegated to the training role, serving with various station flights and the Auxiliary Air Force.

The Avro **626 Prefect** was basically a redesign of the Tutor airframe and was intended primarily for the export market. It was offered with a number of conversion kits, making it suitable for a variety of roles including gunnery training, bombing or wireless training.

The RAF's seven Prefects were configured for navigation training and were allocated to the Andover School of Air Navigation, replacing the Armstrong Siddeley Mongoose-engined Tutors, in 1935. The remaining Prefects were still in service in this role at the outbreak of World War II.

The Tutor was a manoeuvrable training aircraft, this view clearly shows the Frise ailerons fitted to both upper and lower wings giving an excellent rate of roll.

Specification
Tutor Mk I
Type: two-seat single-engined elementary trainer
Powerplant: one 240-hp (179-kW) Armstrong Siddeley Lynx IVC radial piston engine
Performance: maximum speed 122 mph (196 km/h); cruising speed 105 mph (169 km/h) at 1,000 ft (305 m); service ceiling 16,200 ft (4940 m); range 250 miles (402 km)
Weight: empty 1844 lb (836 kg); maximum take-off 2,458 lb (1115 kg)
Dimensions: span 34 ft 0 in (10.36 m); length 26 ft 6 in (8.08 m); height 9 ft 7 in (2.92 m); wing area 301 sq ft (27.96 m²)

Avro 652A Anson

***Right:* At the outbreak of World War II the Anson was the RAF's primary coastal reconnaissance aircraft. This Anson Mk I was flown by a Royal Netherlands Navy crew (note triangle on tail) attached to No. 217 Squadron based at RAF St Eval between October 1939 and November 1940.**

***Below:* The Anson Mk I's primary task in the first two years of the war was protecting the vital supply convoys heading for British ports. Bombs were carried to attack marauding German E-boats and U-boats.**

The **Avro Anson** enjoyed one of the longest production runs of any British aircraft, this status being maintained from 1934 until 15 May 1952 when the last Anson T.Mk 21 completed its acceptance trials. Its origin lay in an Imperial Airways specification, sent to A. V. Roe in April 1933, which required that the resulting aircraft should be capable of transporting four passengers over 420-mile (676-km) sectors at a cruising speed in excess of 130 mph (209 km/h). Other requirements were that the stalling speed should not exceed 60 mph (97 km/h) and that the machine should be capable of maintaining 2,000 ft (610 m) on one engine.

In August 1933, a design team headed by Roy Chadwick produced a study, bearing the Avro type number **652**, for a low-wing monoplane with retractable landing gear, to be powered by two Armstrong Siddeley Cheetah V engines, and with a design gross weight of 6,500 lb (2948 kg). A change in the Imperial Airways specification to enable the aircraft to fly the Karachi-Bombay-Colombo night mail service resulted in modifications which raised the gross weight to 7,650 Ib (3470 kg) .

On 7 May 1934 the Director of Contracts at the Air Ministry notified A. V. Roe of a requirement for twin-engined landplanes for use as coastal reconnaissance aircraft, and requested information as to the possibility of adapting existing designs. A new design study, based on the Imperial Airways machine, was designated **Type 652A**. This was completed within the month and selected for prototype development together with the militarised de Havilland DH.89.

The resulting Air Ministry contract called for delivery in March 1935, giving the company fewer than six months to complete detail design and prototype construction for the military version of an aircraft which had not then flown in civil form. External changes included rectangular rather than the round windows on the 652, and the addition of an Armstrong Whitworth dorsal turret with a single Lewis gun.

The prototype was flown on 24 March 1935 and delivered to Martlesham Heath for official trials in the following month. After minor modifications to tailplane and elevators, the machine was transferred to the Coastal Defence Development Unit at Gosport for a competitive fly-off with the DH.89M. A fleet exercise provided a practical test of the capabilities of the contenders, and the superior range and endurance of the Avro 652A enabled it to win the competition.

Specification 18/35 was written to cover production aircraft, designated **Anson GR.Mk I**, and the first was flown on 31 December 1935. On 6 March 1936 No. 48 Squadron at Manston became the first operational RAF Anson unit; it also proved to be the last to use the type in front-line service, converting to the Lockheed Hudson in January 1942. Twenty-one Coastal Command squadrons used Ansons in general reconnaissance, and search and rescue roles.

The Anson Mk I was armed with a fixed forward-firing Vickers gun

Featuring an Armstrong Whitworth dorsal turret and a forward-firing Vickers gun in the nose, the Anson Mk I could adequately defend itself from aerial attack. This No. 217 Squadron aircraft served with Coastal Command until replaced by the Beaufort at the end of 1940.

Anson Mk I K8754 joined No. 206 Squadron at Bircham Newton in 1937 and served on North Sea patrols until 1940, when the squadron re-equipped with Hudsons. This particular Anson went to No. 1 OTU, where it crashed on 29 August 1940.

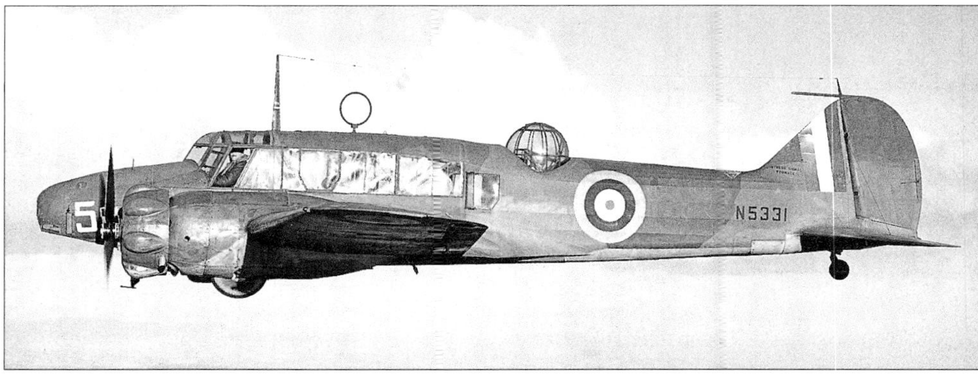

***Left:* After retirement from frontline service many Anson Mk Is found secondary roles. N5331 served with No. 10 Radio School based at Carew Cheriton in 1943-44. As with most training versions the armament has been removed.**

***Below:* Many of the later Anson Mk Is were completed as trainers with the addition of landing flaps and twin landing lights. Gunnery trainers, such as this example were fitted with a hydraulically operated Bristol B.1 Mk VI turret.**

***Below:* Although considered obsolete when the war commenced, the Anson fulfilled the maritime patrol role with great credit. As well as claiming a number of U-boat and E-boat kills, Ansons also managed to down some hostile aircraft, including Messerschmitt Bf 109 and Bf 110 fighters.**

Avro Anson military variants

Avro 652A prototype: single prototype (K4771) powered by Cheetah VI engines which flew service trials in 1935
Anson Mk I: main wartime production variant with Armstrong Whitworth turret and Lewis machine-gun. Many later converted to training roles with a variety of equipment fits; a number had the turret removed; total 6,708 including aircraft for the Commonwealth Air Training Plan and exports
Anson Mk II: constructed in Canada with revised windows and hydraulic flap system, and powered by Jacobs L6MB engines; total 1,050
Anson Mk III: British-built version of Mk II with Jacobs engines
Anson Mk IV: constructed in Britain then fitted with Wright Whirlwind R-760-E1 engines in Canada; total 223
Anson Mk V: Canadian all-wooden version made from Vidal plywood and powered by Pratt & Whitney Wasp Junior R985-AN12B or AN14B engines, with trainees increased to five and 'greenhouse' windows' replaced by circular portholes; total 1,070
Anson Mk VI: single gunnery trainer fitted with Mk V engines and Bristol B.1 Mk VI turret
Anson Mk X: same as Mk I with strengthened cabin floor for heavy freight, and smoothed engine cowlings; total 103 plus 18 converted from Mk I
Anson Mk XI: raised cabin roof and revised window layout with hydraulic flaps and landing gear, and Armstrong Siddeley Cheetah 19 engines; total 90
Anson Mk XII: same as Mk XI except fitted with Cheetah 15 engines and Rotol constant-speed airscrew; total 271
Anson Mk 18: general-purpose version for Royal Afghan Air Force; also similarly equipped Mk 18C with opaque nose caps for Indian government; total 24
Anson C.Mk 19: post-war VIP transport with five oval windows and up to nine seats; Series 1 with wooden wings and Series 2 with metal wings; total 263
Anson T.Mk 20: post-war navigation trainer with metal wings and tailplane; total 60
Anson T.Mk 21: navigation trainer with crew of six, externally identical to Mk 20 except metal nose cap; total 252
Anson T.Mk 22: radio trainer similar to Mk 21 but without astrodome and addition of D/F loop above the fuselage; total 54
Federal AT-20: 50 Canadian-built Anson Mk IIs diverted to the USAAF as bomber crew trainers

in the nose, mounted on the port side, and the Armstrong Whitworth dorsal turret with its single Lewis gun. A bomb-aimer's position was provided in the nose and bomb load comprised two 100-lb (45-kg) bombs carried in the wing centre-section and eight 20-lb (9-kg) bombs under the wings. No. 500 Squadron at Detling fitted its aircraft with a swivel mounting for a 0.303-in (7.7-mm) Vickers 'G' gun on each side of the main cabin and, later in the war, to improve the Anson's effectiveness against E-boats, a 20-mm cannon was installed in the commanding officer's Anson, firing downward through a hole in the floor between the wing spars. On 1 June 1940 one of the squadron's Ansons was attacked by three Messerschmitt Bf 109s, one being shot down by the pilot using the nose gun, while another was despatched by the turret gunner.

Further RAF orders followed, together with export contracts which included aircraft for Australia, Egypt, Eire, Estonia, Finland and Greece, and almost 1,000 had been manufactured by the outbreak of war in September 1939. Some of these were training aircraft, and it was in this role that the Anson was to make its greatest contribution to the war effort. Although A. V. Roe had proposed a trainer version as early as November 1936, there was some delay before the first **Anson Trainers**, with dual controls and trailing-edge flaps, made their appearance. They were to serve in various forms with Operational Training Units, Pilots Advanced Flying Units, Schools of Air Navigation and Army Co-operation, Air Observer Schools and Air Gunnery Schools, the last using Ansons with Bristol B.1 Mk VI power-operated turrets. Total Mk I production was 6,742, of which 3,935 were built at Woodford and the balance at Yeadon.

On 18 December 1939 the British Commonwealth Air Training Plan was instituted, and the Anson was selected as one of the standard training aircraft.The production contract was placed in Britain, engineless airframes being shipped to Canada from Woodford, to be fitted on arrival with either Jacobs L-6MB or Wright Whirlwind R-975-E3 radial engines. The former were designated **Mk III** and the latter **Mk IV**; Mk IIIs were later modified to incorporate Dowty hydraulically actuated flaps and landing gear. Those British airframes which had turrets when delivered retained them, although most Ansons used in Canada did not have this equipment.

As the situation in Britain deteriorated, and after 223 airframes had been delivered, production was initiated in Canada, with Federal Aircraft Ltd set up to co-ordinate a multi-company manufacturing programme. The first version produced entirely in Canada was the **Anson Mk II**, with Jacobs engines, a moulded plywood nose, and hydraulically-actuated flaps and landing gear. The first of them was flown on 21 August 1941, and production totalled 1,832, 50 of which were supplied to the US Army Air Force as crew trainers under the designation **AT-20**.

The use of moulded plywood in the Mk II led to adoption of this material for the entire fuselage, in which the familiar 'glasshouse' or square window gave way to circular portholes. With standard Mk II components fitted to this new fuselage, the aircraft became the **Anson Mk V**, powered by 450-hp (336-kW) Pratt & Whitney R-985-AN-12B engines, and able to accommodate five trainee crew members instead of three as in earlier versions. Mk V navigation trainers were built to the number of 1,050, and a single example of a gunnery training version, with a Bristol B.1 Mk VI dorsal turret, was produced in 1943. The designations **Mk VII**, **VIII** and **IX** were allocated for Canadian versions which were not built.

Subsequent marks were developed and manufactured in Britain, commencing with the **Anson X**, a Mk I with a strengthened cabin floor for freight/passenger use, which saw service with the Air Transport Auxiliary as a communications aircraft for ferry pilots. It retained the 350-hp (261-kW) Cheetah IX engines of the later Mk Is and the manually-operated landing gear, but the fluted cowlings were replaced by smooth ones, as used on the two Avro 652s. Gross weight was increased to 9,450 lb (4286 kg), and 103 of this version were built at Yeadon.

The raising of the roofline, to provide more headroom in the cabin for passenger operations, led to the introduction of the **Mks XI** and **XII**, which had hydraulically-operated flaps and landing gear, and three large square windows on each side of the fuselage. The Anson XI was powered by 395-hp (295kW) Cheetah XIXs, driving fixed-pitch Fairey-Reed metal propellers, and the Mk XII by 420-hp (313-kW) Cheetah XVs with variable-pitch Rotol propellers. Later Mk XIIs were designated **Series 2**, to denote the provision of an all-metal wing in place of the standard wooden assembly. Ambulance versions of both marks were produced, first flights having taken place on 30 July and 27 October 1944 respectively. Yeadon manufactured 91 Mk XIs and 254 Mk XIIs.

The **Anson Mks XIII** and **XIV** were to have been gunnery trainers, with Cheetah XI or XIX, and Cheetah XV engines respectively, but these, like the **Mks XV** and **XVI** which were to have been navigation and bombing trainers, were not produced. The Mk XVII designation was not allocated. Early in 1945, with the end of the war in sight, the company produced a **Mk XI** airframe with five oval windows on each side of the fuselage and a furnished interior, meeting the requirements of the Brabazon Committee's civil transport Specification 19; it acquired the designation **Avro 19**. It was operated over British internal routes, at that time administered by the Associated Airways Joint Committee, and then put into production as a civil feederliner. Among early customers was Railway Air Services, with a fleet of 14 aircraft, which were flown on routes from Croydon to the north of England, the Isle of Man and Dublin until replaced by Douglas Dakotas, when the company was nationalised and absorbed into British European Airways.

The same aircraft in RAF service became the **Anson C.Mk 19**, and 264 of these were built between 1945 and 1947. Twenty were converted Mk XIIs, and 158 were Series 2 aircraft with metal wings and tailplanes. The production line at Woodford was reopened, producing three Series 1s and 167 Series 2s, while 137 Series 1s and 18 Series 2s were built at Yeadon. Developed from the Avro 19 were 12 specially equipped Ansons for police patrol, communications and aerial survey duties, and this version, designated **Mk 18**, was ordered by the Royal Afghan Air Force. In addition, 13 **Anson 18C**s with Cheetah 15 engines were ordered by the Indian government for civil aircrew training, and all 25 of these aircraft were built at Woodford.

The **Anson T.Mk 20** was developed from the Anson 19 Series 2 to Specification T.24/46, for service as a bombing and navigation trainer in Southern Rhodesia. This was fitted with a transparent nose for the bomb-aimer and with racks for 16 practice bombs under the fuselage and wings. The prototype flew on 5 August 1947 and a further 59 production T.20s were manufactured at Woodford. Specification T.25/46 covered the Anson **T.Mk 21** navigation trainer, which lacked the transparent nose and bomb racks of the T.20, but was otherwise similar. Following the maiden flight of the prototype on 6 February 1948, the Yeadon factory built 252.

The Anson's long service career, spanning 22 years, ended officially on 28 June 1968 when six aircraft of the Southern Communications Squadron carried out a formation flypast at their Bovington, Hampshire, base.

Above: Starting off life as an Anson Mk I, MG159 was converted to a Mk XII, with two Armstrong Siddeley Cheetah engines, before again undergoing conversion as the prototype Mk XIX to satisfy the Brabazon feederliner specification of 1943. The model became known as the Avro 652A Nineteen.

Right: In 1944 a modernised version of the Anson replaced the Mk I in production. Built in two versions, Mk XI and Mk XII, the aircraft featured a raised cabin roof, new window layouts and hydraulically operated flaps and undercarriage, as well as new engines.

Below: Anson Mks II-VI were built or re-engined in Canada. In 1941 R9816 was fitted with two Wright Whirlwind engines to become the prototype Mk IV. A total of 223 airframes was subsequently sent to Canada to be similarly equipped.

Specification
Anson Mk I

Type: three/five-seat maritime patrol or conversion, navigation, bombing, gunnery and radio trainer
Powerplant: two 350-hp (261-kW) Armstrong Siddeley Cheetah IX radial piston engines
Performance: maximum speed 188 mph (303 km/h) at 7,000 ft (2135 m); cruising speed 158 mph (254 km/h); service ceiling 19,000 ft (5790 m); range 790 miles (1271 km)
Weights: empty 5,375 lb (2438 kg); maximum take-off 8,000 lb (3629 kg)
Dimensions: span 56 ft 5 in (17.20 m); length 42 ft 3 in (12.88 m); height 13 ft 1 in (3.99 m); wing area 410 sq ft (38.09 m^2)
Armament: one Vickers 0.303-in (7.7-mm) fixed forward-firing machine-gun and one 0.303-in gun in Armstrong Whitworth dorsal turret, plus up to 360 lb (163 kg) of bombs

Avro 671 Rota

Twelve Avro Rota Mk Is were delivered between August 1934 and May 1935, serving with the School of Army Co-operation at Old Sarum prior to September 1939. Early in the war they were based at Duxford with No. 74 (Signals) Wing for coastal radar calibration flying.

In 1925 Juan de la Cierva was invited to England by the Air Ministry to demonstate his unique autogyro concepts, and in October of that year he flew his C.6A design at Farnborough. Finance from the British government enabled him to initiate a series of designs in Spain.

The first production variant was the C.19, of which two were obtained by the RAE for trials. The success of these trials prompted the RAF, in 1934, to order 10 Cierva C.30As to be built under licence by Avro. Given the Type number **671** and the designation **Rota Mk I**, these aircraft were evaluated in the army co-operation role. Powered by an Armstrong Siddeley Civet I engine, the type continued trial flying until early 1939 when RAF interest waned and the remaining Rotas were struck off charge.

However, the outbreak of war in September 1939 encouraged the RAF to return the aircraft to service and the surviving aircraft, along with several impressed civilian examples, were allocated to No. 74 (Signals) Wing and conducted radar calibration duties.

In June 1943 the **Rota Mk IA**s which by then were flying with No. 1448 Flight at RAF Halton, were joined by a **Rota Mk II** (Cierva C.40) and formed No. 529 Squadron. This was the first RAF squadron to use a rotary-wing aircraft operationally and continued in the radar calibration role until it was disbanded in October 1945.

This Cierva (Avro) Rota Mk IA of No. 529 Squadron was based at RAF Halton, and later Henley-on-Thames, for radar calibration duties from June 1943 to October 1945.

Specification
Rota Mk IA (C.30A)
Type: two-seat radar calibration autogyro
Powerplant: one 140-hp (104.4-kW) Armstrong Siddeley Civet I piston engine
Performance: maximum speed 110 mph (177 km/h); cruising speed 95 mph (153 km/h); range 285 miles (459 km)
Weights: empty 1,220 lb (553 kg); maximum take-off 1,800 lb (816 kg)
Dimensions: rotor diameter 37 ft 0 in (11.28 m); length 19 ft 9 in (6.02 m)

Avro 679 Manchester

Seldom has the marriage between a new airframe and new engines been satisfactory, and the Avro **679 Manchester** was no exception. Designed to Specification P.13/36 as a twin-engined medium bomber with the new Rolls-Royce Vulture 24-cylinder engine, the Manchester would have been in competition with the Handley Page H.P.56. Plans for this were abandoned in 1937, however, leaving a clear field for the Avro design, while Handley Page concentrated its efforts on the four-engined Halifax, itself to become a rival to the Lancaster when the latter eventually replaced the Manchester.

The first of two Manchester prototypes flew on 25 July 1939, to be followed by the second on 26 May 1940. A production contract had been placed for 200 aircraft to meet another Air Ministry Specification, 19/37, on 1 July 1937, and this was later increased to 400.

Following flight trials the wing span was increased by 10 ft (3.05 m) and a central fin was added to supplement the small twin fins and rudders. Later, after a number of Manchesters had been delivered as **Mk I**s, the central fin was deleted and the twin fins increased in area; in this form it became the **Mk IA**. The prototype and first two production aircraft were delivered to the Aircraft and Armament Experimental Establishment, Boscombe Down, for tests, while the second prototype went to the Royal Aircraft Establishment, Farnborough. The first squadron delivery was to No. 207, which reformed at Waddington on 1 November 1940, and six Manchesters of the 18 on squadron strength carried out their first operational flight, to Brest, on the night of 24/25 February 1941.

As deliveries built up, so squadrons became equipped with the new bomber, and others to receive Manchesters included Nos 49, 50, 57, 61, 83, 97, 106, 408 and 420, while No. 144 Squadron of Coastal Command received enough aircraft to form one flight.

The Manchester proved to be a failure mainly because of the unreliability of the Vulture engines, and the inability of these powerplants to deliver their designed power; there were also a number of airframe defects. It was with great relief that squadrons began to relinquish their Manchesters from mid-1942 as Lancasters began to replace them. The last Bomber Command Manchester operation took place

Coinciding with the entry into service of the Stirling, the new twin-engined Manchester joined the RAF in November 1940, but by 1942 was ready for withdrawal. This is an early Mk I with the additional (third) central fin.

Left: Manchester Mk I L7427 'OL-Q' 'Queenie' of No. 83 Squadron operated from RAF Scampton in December 1941. This aircraft was lost on a raid against the Blohm und Voss shipyards at Hamburg on its 15th operation. The squadron operated Manchesters until May 1942, when the ill-fated aircraft were replaced by Lancasters.

on 25/26 June 1942 against Bremen, and in the final tally it was found that the type had flown 1,269 sorties, dropping 1,826 tons (1855 tonnes) of HE plus incendiaries. Some 202 aircraft were built, of which about 40 per cent were lost on operations and 25 per cent were written off in crashes. However, on the credit side, the Manchester paved the way for the Lancaster, and without the earlier aircraft one must conjecture whether or not the RAF's finest bomber would have seen the light of day. One Victoria Cross was awarded to a member of a Manchester crew. Flying Officer L. T. Manser, a pilot of No. 50 Squadron, for his actions on 30 May 1942.

Specification
Manchester Mk IA
Type: seven-seat twin-engined medium bomber
Powerplant: two 1,760-hp (1312-kW) Rolls-Royce Vulture inline piston engines
Performances: maximum speed 265 mph (426 km/h) at 17,000 ft (5180 m); cruising speed 185 mph (298 km/h) at 15,000 ft (4570 m); service ceiling 19,200 ft (5850 m); range 1,630 miles (2623 km) with 8,100-lb (3674-kg) bomb load
Weights: empty 29,432 lb (13350 kg); maximum take-off 56,000 lb (25401 kg)
Dimensions: span 90 ft 1 in (27.46 m); length 69 ft 4 in (21.13 m); height 19 ft 6 in (5.94 m); wing area 1,131 sq ft (105.63 m²)
Armament: eight 0.303-in (7.7-mm) machine-guns (two each in nose and dorsal turrets, and four in tail turret) plus up to 10,350 lb (4695 kg) of bombs

Above: Two hundred production Manchesters were built, 157 by Avro and 43 by Metropolitan-Vickers. Despite the aircraft's shortcomings, the airframe formed the basis of the Avro Lancaster which was to become the RAF's premier heavy bomber of World War II.

Below: The Manchester was a failure, largely due to the protracted teething problems with its Vulture engines. This is Manchester Mk IA L7515 of No. 207 Squadron, showing the larger twin-fin layout that was subsequently adopted for the bomber.

Shown in the camouflage scheme which was applied to No. 207 Squadron aircraft in early 1942, this Manchester Mk I features the mid-upper gun turret which was added in January of that year.

Avro 683 Lancaster

Above: A fine head-on view of a Rolls-Royce Merlin-powered Lancaster – the mainstay of the RAF's night bombing offensive. Britain's greatest bomber of World War II, it was by far the most important instrument of Arthur Harris's policy of undertaking night attacks by massed bombers on German cities.

In response to the RAF's specification P.13/36 for a twin-engined medium bomber, Avro and Handley Page proposed designs powered by the Rolls-Royce Vulture, a 24-cylinder development of the successful 12-cylinder Kestrel and Peregrine engines. Such were the new engine's shortcomings, however, that Handley Page abandoned it and its twin-engined design (the H.P.56) in 1937. Avro persevered, the result being the Manchester Mk I which was to enter production and RAF service in 1940. But, with the Vulture's problems far from solved, the Manchester was destined for a short career.

From both the Handley Page and Avro designs were eventually derived new aircraft, each powered by four Rolls-Royce Merlins: from the HP.56 came the HP.57 Halifax and from the Manchester, the **Manchester Mk III**, later renamed the **Lancaster**. The Halifax was initially the RAF's preferred type; in fact, the Air Ministry wanted Avro to establish a Halifax production line of its own. In reply, Avro suggested that it would simpler and quicker to start Lancaster production, given that this would mean merely adapting the Manchester production line. So it was that the Lancaster was built in the greater numbers and reigned as the Bomber Command's

Above: Pictured at Boscombe Down in 1941 during trials with the A&AEE, the Manchester Mk III (prototype Lancaster) BT308/G had the distinctive three-fin layout and 22-ft tailplane of its predecessor, the Manchester. This aircraft, which first flew on 9 January 1941, carried a black serial and its undersurfaces were painted yellow to denote its non-operational status.

Left: A formation of Pathfinder Force Lancasters of No. 405 Squadron, photographed en route to its assigned target. No. 405 was the first Canadian heavy bomber unit to join Bomber Command and operated Lancasters from August 1943. The squadron took part in the strategic bomber offensive until the war ended.

Avro 683 Lancaster

Below: To guard against a possible shortage of Rolls-Royce Merlin engines, the Lancaster Mk II was produced with 1,650-hp (1230-kW) Bristol Hercules VI or XVI radial engines. The Lancaster Mk II had good performance but high fuel consumption. Eventually, only 301 of this variant were built, as Merlins remained in plentiful supply and Hercules engines were needed for other types in production. All Mk IIs had an enlarged bomb bay.

Left: Seen over Lincolnshire, this is a vic formation of Lancaster Mk Is of No. 207 Squadron, which was based at Bottesford in June 1942. It had converted from Manchesters three months earlier. The nearest aircraft, R5570 'EM-F', was eventually lost over Turin on 8/9 December 1942.

most successful aircraft of the period, largely due to its load-carrying capacity and versatility. By the end of the war, over 7,300 had been constructed and by March 1945, 56 squadrons were equipped with 745 examples of the type, another 296 serving with Operational Conversion Units.

The Lancaster shared many of the Manchester's features; in fact, the prototype, first flown on 9 January 1941, used a number of Manchester Mk I components. The latter's fuselage, centre-section and tail were retained (along with the nose, tail and mid-upper gun turrets) and new outer wing sections were fitted to incorporate the extra engines. The three-fin tail was soon altered to a twin-fin layout, as applied to the Manchester Mk IA.

The Air Ministry drew up a specification around the 'new' Avro design (**Lancaster I/P1**), requiring a 250-mph (402-km/h) cruising speed at 15,000 ft (4575 m) and a 7,500-lb (3405-kg) bomb load capacity over a 2,000 mile (3218 km) range. Maximum range would be 3,000 miles (4827 km). The large bomb bay inherited from the Manchester was able to carry a variety of bomb types, the largest being a single 4,000-lb (1816-kg) Cookie high-capacity device.

Impressed with the prototype's performance during testing, the Air Ministry cut Manchester production from 300 to just 100, ordering 454 **Lancaster Mk I**s instead. The first production example made its first flight on 31 October 1941. On Christmas Eve, No. 44 Squadron at RAF Waddington became the first unit to receive four of these new heavy bombers and on 3 March 1942 flew the type's first operational sortie – a mine-laying mission over the Heligoland Bight. On the night of 10/11 March, two of No. 44's aircraft took part in a bombing raid on Essen. The Lancaster's existence was not publicly revealed until 17 August 1942, when 12 aircraft from Nos 44 and 97 Squadrons carried out an unescorted daylight raid on Augsburg. Flown at low level, the raid inflicted considerable damage on a factory producing U-boat diesel engines, but the cost was high, seven aircraft being lost. Squadron Leaders Nettleton and Sherwood each received the Victoria Cross, the latter posthumously, for leading the operation. The British Air Staff realised such high loss rates could not be sustained and switched permanently to night operations. It was to be more than two years before the Royal Air Force resumed such attacks.

Certain modifications to the Lancaster were deemed necessary after an initial period of service. These included deletion of a ventral gun turret fitted to early production aircraft, a larger perspex bomb-aimer's blister in the nose of the aircraft, an increase in fuel capacity and, most significantly, changes to the aircraft's bomb support system to allow the carriage of an 8000-lb (3632-kg) Blockbuster bomb.

This early Lancaster Mk I (W4113 'J') was operated by No. 1661 Conversion Unit (using code letters 'GP'), which was formed at RAF Waddington in November 1942 to provide crews for the rapidly building Lancaster force in Bomber Command.

This Lancaster B.Mk III ED912/G served with No. 617 Squadron at RAF Coningsby in May 1943. This aircraft was specially modified to carry the Upkeep dam-busting mine developed by Barnes Wallis. On 17 May 1943, it was one of the Lancasters involved in the daring attack on the Möhne, Eder and Sorpe dams in Germany and it remained with the squadron until December 1943, when it was sent to a Maintenance Unit. It was eventually scrapped in 1946.

Avro 683 Lancaster

Below: The Lancaster B.Mk IIIs of No. 617 Squadron that took part in the dams raid of May 1943 were extensively modified to enable them to carry the top-secret 'bouncing' bomb. The dorsal turret was removed and the lower fuselage cut away to enable the fitting of the special trapeze from which the spinning cylindrical bomb was released.

Above: To enable more precise bombing a number of Lancaster Mk Is, such as this example, were fitted with H_2S radar bombing equipment. The mapping radar in the large blister took up the position of the ventral guns. By this time the vital Gee navigational aid was also being carried.

Below: A Lancaster drops a mixed bomb load comprising a 4,000-lb (1814-kg) bomb and incendiaries during an early morning raid over eastern Germany on 14 October 1944.

Bulged bomb bay doors were fitted and, later, further internal changes were made to allow a 12,000-lb (5448-kg) bomb to be carried. The maximum bomb load for a Lancaster was increased to 14,000 lb (6350 kg). To cope with these new demands on the design, more powerful Merlin engines were fitted. While the first Mk Is were equipped with Merlin XXs rated at 1,390 hp (1037 kW), later production aircraft had 1,610-hp (1201-kW) Merlin 24s, though these new Merlin variants did not bring a change in aircraft designation.

Concerns regarding the supply of Rolls-Royce engines prompted the development of the **Lancaster Mk II**, first flown in November 1941. This differed from the Mk I in having more powerful Bristol Hercules radial powerplants. In all, 301 Mk IIs were built, but their speed and altitude performance was always inferior to those of the Mk I, the extra drag and fuel consumption of the Hercules outweighing their power advantage. Once Merlin supplies were secured, repeat orders for Mk IIs were cancelled. The last Lancaster Mk II operation was flown by No. 514 Squadron on 23 September 1944.

The engine supply problem was ultimately solved by setting up Merlin production overseas. In August 1942, the **Lancaster Mk III** was introduced, with American-built Packard Merlins, though these aircraft were, in most other respects, identical to the Mk I. In fact, it was not unknown for Mk Is to be re-engined with Packard engines in service (thus becoming Mk IIIs) and *vice versa*.

The aircraft's defensive armament was also the focus of improvements. Various alternative Frazer-Nash mid-upper turrets were introduced, while some aircraft carried a Rose-Rice rear turret, armed

Based at Waterbeach, Cambridgeshire, this Armstrong Whitworth-built Lancaster Mk I carried H_2S radar and the codes of 'C' Flight of No. 514 Squadron. In a span of 18 months from September 1943, Lancasters from this squadron flew 3,675 operational sorties, dropping 14,652 tons (14888 tonnes) of bombs and laying 70 mines.

This Canadian-built Lancaster Mk X of No. 431 (Iroquois) Squadron, Royal Canadian Air Force was based at Croft, County Durham in early 1945 as a component of No. 6 (RCAF) Group. Constructed by the Victory company, it featured Packard engines and the Martin electrically-driven mid-upper turret with 0.50-in (12.7-mm) guns. This turret was further forward than the British FN type.

Left: On 23 March 1945, Lancasters of No. 617 Squadron dropped the first 22,000-lb (9979-kg) Grand Slam bombs on the Bielefeld viaduct. They fell onto nearby ground and caused such violent tremors that much of the viaduct subsequently collapsed.

Below: The female form was without doubt one of the most popular adornments to feature on the noses of operational Lancasters. Crew decorations were common and the bomb symbols denoted the number of missions undertaken. This particular aircraft has over 60 missions to its credit.

with two 0.5-in (12.7-mm) Browning machine-guns in place of the usual quartet of 0.303-in (7.7-mm) guns. Towards the end of the war, other aircraft were fitted with the AGLT (Automatic Gun-Laying Turret) in the rear position. Codenamed 'Village Inn', this incorporated a small radar set for automated aiming and twin 0.5-in (12.7-mm) Brownings.

Only the Hurricane and Spitfire fighters were built at a higher rate than the Lancaster during World War II (though the Halifax production rate was higher than that of the Lancaster until mid-1943). By the end of 1942, 91 Lancasters a month were being produced by five manufacturers in Britain (Avro, Metropolitan-Vickers, Vickers Armstrong, Austin Motors and Armstrong Whitworth) and planning was well advanced for production in Canada, by Victory Aircraft of Malton, Ontario, of the **Lancaster Mk X**. Essentially a Mk III with minor equipment changes, the first of these aircraft arrived in Britain in September 1943, many being issued to the Canadian units within Bomber Command.

From mid-1942 until VE-Day, the Lancaster was to be RAF Bomber Command's main weapon in its nightly assault on German targets. From March 1943, the Battle of the Ruhr focused attention on the industrial centres of this region; cities like Hamburg and Berlin would soon be added to the target list. In early 1944, lines of communication in northern France were bombed in preparation for the D-Day landings, Lancasters switching to tactical targets in support of the Allied ground forces once a beachhead had been established. In

Above: Installed on a number of bomber airfields, the Fog Investigation and Dispersal Operation (FIDO) system was used to disperse fog and act as a landing aid for bombers returning from night raids. Hazardous weather conditions were often encountered in eastern England, especially in the winter months. Here a returning Lancaster finds the runway at Ludford Magna. It was remarkable that such large flames were produced from the frail-looking pipes that were used.

Left: Mission markings were testimony to the Lancaster's durability on night bombing sorties. The Lancaster had the highest tonnage of bombs dropped per loss of aircraft ratio of all the RAF's heavy bombers.

Grand Slam
The heaviest bomb dropped in anger during World War II was the 22,000-lb (9979-kg) Grand Slam, which fell to earth faster than the speed of sound and destroyed its targets by the shock waves created when it hit the ground.

Avro Lancaster B.Mk I (Special) No. 617 Squadron, Woodhall Spa, 1945

No. 617 Squadron received modified Lancaster B.Mk Is in the spring of 1944 in preparation for attacks on high-value point targets. These aircraft had no bomb doors, enabling them to carry Tallboy and Grand Slam bombs.

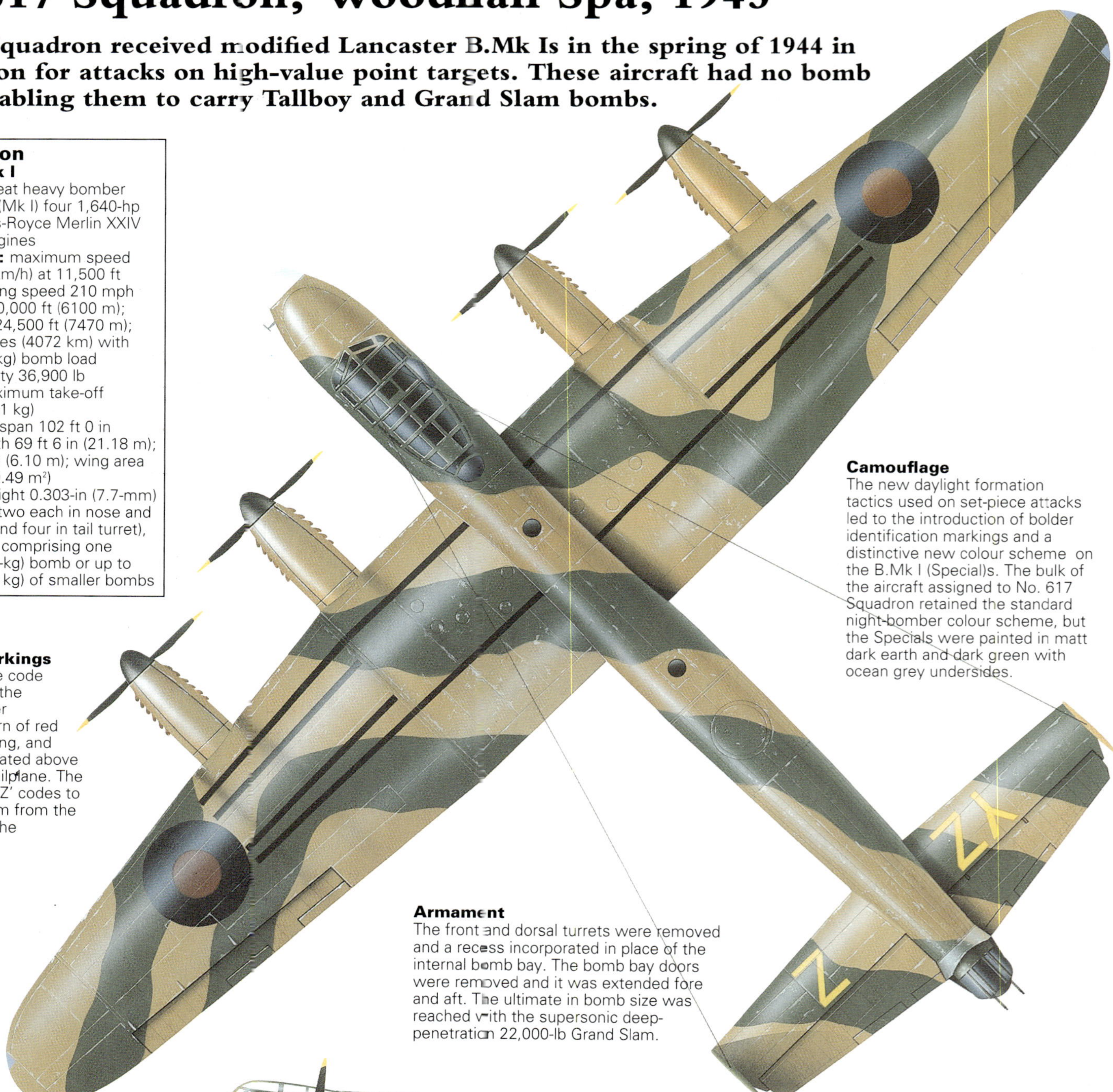

Specification
Lancaster Mk I
Type: seven-seat heavy bomber
Powerplant: (Mk I) four 1,640-hp (1223-kW) Rolls-Royce Merlin XXIV inline piston engines
Performance: maximum speed 287 mph (462 km/h) at 11,500 ft (3505 m); cruising speed 210 mph (338 km/h) at 20,000 ft (6100 m); service ceiling 24,500 ft (7470 m); range 2,530 miles (4072 km) with 7,000-lb (3175-kg) bomb load
Weights: empty 36,900 lb (16738 kg); maximum take-off 70,000 lb (31751 kg)
Dimensions: span 102 ft 0 in (31.09 m); length 69 ft 6 in (21.18 m); height 20 ft 0 in (6.10 m); wing area 1,297 sq ft (120.49 m^2)
Armament: eight 0.303-in (7.7-mm) machine-guns (two each in nose and dorsal turrets, and four in tail turret), plus bomb load comprising one 22,000-lb (9979-kg) bomb or up to 14,000 lb (6350 kg) of smaller bombs

Camouflage
The new daylight formation tactics used on set-piece attacks led to the introduction of bolder identification markings and a distinctive new colour scheme on the B.Mk I (Special)s. The bulk of the aircraft assigned to No. 617 Squadron retained the standard night-bomber colour scheme, but the Specials were painted in matt dark earth and dark green with ocean grey undersides.

Individual markings
The colour of the code letters reversed the common Bomber Command pattern of red with yellow edging, and these were repeated above and below the tailplane. The Specials wore 'YZ' codes to differentiate them from the other aircraft in the squadron.

Armament
The front and dorsal turrets were removed and a recess incorporated in place of the internal bomb bay. The bomb bay doors were removed and it was extended fore and aft. The ultimate in bomb size was reached with the supersonic deep-penetration 22,000-lb Grand Slam.

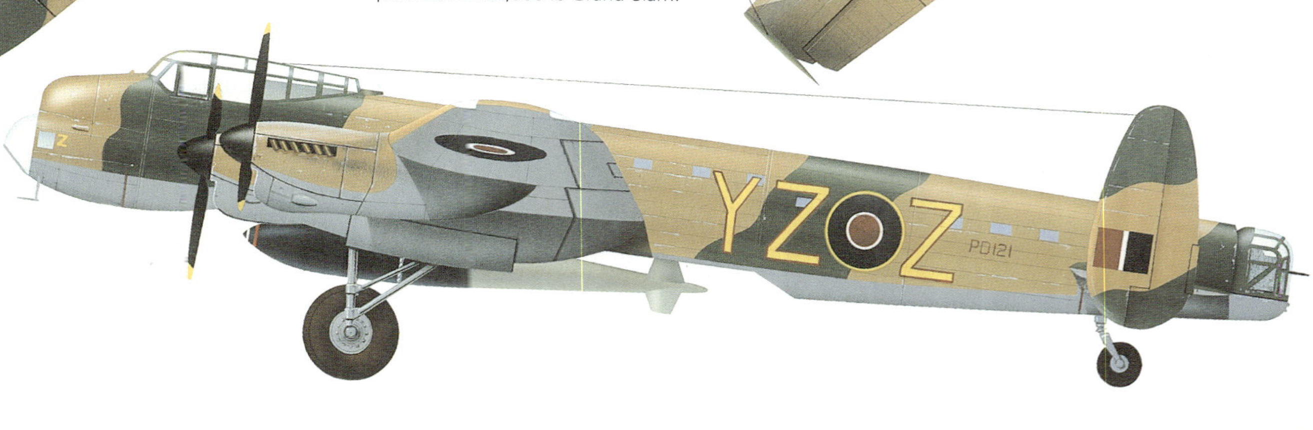

Daylight tactics
Although the threat of enemy day fighters had reduced by late 1944, a vertically-staggered formation of three vics of four, known as the 'gaggle', was adopted for mutual defence during Tallboy and Grand Slam attacks.

Above: At the war's close, the Lancaster was retained as the standard Bomber Command aircraft. Most of those in service were B.Mk I(FE)s, which had been modified for operation in the Far East, but the Japanese surrender ensured the aircraft would not see operational service in that theatre. They were painted in a white and black colour scheme.

Right: Back from Berlin in the early hours, Lancasters of No. 106 Squadron based at Syerston in January 1943 are silhouetted against the rising sun. The squadron operated Lancasters from May 1942 until the unit was disbanded in February 1946.

order to take some of the pressure off the Atlantic convoys, U-boat pens and shipyards were also attacked by the bomber squadrons. Contemporary statistics showed how Lancasters were proving their worth; by July 1943, 132 tons of bombs were dropped for every Lancaster lost on operations. The corresponding figures for Bomber Command's other four-engined 'heavies' were 56 tons for each Halifax and 41 tons for each Stirling. Some aircraft survived to successfully complete over 100 sorties.

More specialised operations were also undertaken, taking advantage of the Lancaster's adaptability. Perhaps the best known of these was the raid on a series of dams in western Germany, on the night of 16/17 May 1943 (Operation Chastise). Modified aircraft of No. 617 Squadron, each armed with a 9250-lb (4196-kg) mine, succeeded in breaching two of the three dams targeted in a daring low-level sortie, thus cutting power supplies to industry on the Ruhr and, above all, providing a tremendous propaganda and morale boost for the Allies.

In 1944, No. 617's Lancasters undertook raids using a streamlined 12,000-lb (5448-kg) 'Tallboy' bomb on Saumur railway tunnel and, with No. 9 Squadron, on the German battleship *Tirpitz*, anchored in a Norwegian fjord. Further raids on the ship eventually achieved success, the battleship capsizing on 12 November. Many of these modified aircraft had their mid-upper gun turrets removed to save weight.

The heaviest bomb of all entrusted to the Lancaster was the 22,000-lb (9988-kg) Grand Slam. With one of these giant bombs aboard, the suitably modified aircraft had a maximum take-off weight of 72,000 lb (32688 kg), compared to the 57,000 lb (25878 kg) of the Lancaster prototype. On 13 March 1945, the Bielefeld Viaduct was destroyed in a raid in which Tallboys and a single Grand Slam were dropped. Another 40 of the latter were delivered by Lancasters to targets in Europe before the end of the war.

However, it was as the main weapon of Bomber Command's Main Force and Pathfinder Force (PFF) that the Lancaster was most utilised and best known. The first operations by the Pathfinder Force were made on the night of 18/19 August 1942 when Lancasters from No. 83 Squadron marked the target areas for a raid on Flensberg. In the PFF (later No. 8 Group, Bomber Command) Lancasters were equipped with pyrotechnic bombs for target marking and carried

Lancaster B.Mk I NG128 of No. 101 Squadron was based at Ludford Magna, Lincolnshire in 1944. This aircraft carried 'Airborne Cigar' (ABC) jamming equipment. The dorsal aerials passed misinformation to attacking German fighter crews.

Operating with the Royal Australian Air Force, this Lancaster B.Mk I of No. 463 Squadron was based at Waddington, Lincolnshire in spring 1945. This aircraft was lost to night-fighters during the last Lancaster night attack of the war on an oil refinery at Vallø in Norway on 25/26 April 1945.

Avro 683 Lancaster

G-AGJI was the Lancaster Mk I testbed and is seen in its original form with Merlin 22 engines. It was delivered to BOAC's Development Flight at Hurn on 20 January 1944, and with neat fairings replacing the front and rear turrets (but initially retaining wartime camouflage), it was first used for developing equipment for new transport aircraft. Later, the Merlin 22s were replaced by 102s with annular radiators for test under operational conditions, before their installation in the new Avro 688 Tudor Is.

Wartime Avro Lancaster variants

Manchester Mk III: 2 aircraft; Avro Type 683 prototypes with four Merlin Xs
Lancaster Mk I: 3,440 aircraft; first production variant of Type 683, with Merlin XXs, 22s or 24s
Lancaster Mk I(Special): Mk Is modified to carry stores in excess of 12,000 lb (5443 kg)
Lancaster Mk I(FE): Mk Is tropicalised for Far East service
Lancaster Mk II: 302 aircraft including prototypes; four Bristol Hercules VIs or XVIs
Lancaster Mk III: 3,020 aircraft; improved production variant with Packard-Merlin 28s, 38s or 224s
Lancaster Mk III(Special): Mk IIIs modified to carry Upkeep mine
Lancaster Mk VI: 9 conversions from Lancaster Mk IIIs with Merlin 85s for improved performance and RCM gear
Lancaster Mk VII: 180 aircraft; repositioned Martin mid-upper turret and FN82 tail turret; all built by Austin Motors with Packard-Merlins
Lancaster Mk VII(FE): Mk VIIs tropicalised for Far East service
Lancaster Mk X: 430 aircraft built by Victory Aircraft, Canada; Packard-Merlin 38s or 224s

A Lancaster from No. 101 Squadron drops bundles of Window (chaff) over Duisburg on 14 October 1944. The most interesting features of this particular aircraft are the two ABC aerials on top of the fuselage. Such features were normally deemed too secret to be photographed. Whenever these Lancasters landed away from base, the aerials were covered over and an armed guard was placed on the aircraft.

Avro Lancaster B.Mk III cutaway key

1 Two 0.303-in (7.7-mm) Browning machine-guns
2 Frazer-Nash power-operated nose turret
3 Nose blister
4 Bomb-aimer's panel (optically flat)
5 Bomb-aimer's control panel
6 Side windows
7 External air temperature thermometer
8 Pitot head
9 Bomb-aimer's chest support
10 Fire extinguisher
11 Parachute emergency exit
12 F-24 camera
13 Glycol tank/step
14 Ventilator fairing
15 Bomb-bay doors forward actuating jacks
16 Bomb-bay doors forward bulkhead
17 Control linkage
18 Rudder pedals
19 Instrument panel
20 Windscreen sprays
21 Windscreen
22 Dimmer switches
23 Flight-engineer's folding seat
24 Flight-engineer's control panel
25 Pilot's seat
26 Flight-deck floor level
27 Elevator and rudder control rods (under floor)
28 Trim tab control cables
29 Main floor/bomb-bay support longeron
30 Fire extinguisher
31 Wireless installation
32 Navigator's seat
33 Canopy rear/down-view blister
34 Pilot's head armour
35 Cockpit canopy emergency escape hatch
36 D/F loop
37 Aerial mast support
38 Electrical services panel
39 Navigator's compartment window
40 Navigator's desk
41 Aircraft and radio compass receiver
42 Wireless-operator's desk
43 Wireless-operator's seat
44 Wireless-operator's compartment window
45 Front spar carry-through/fuselage frame
46 Astrodome
47 Inboard section wing ribs
48 Spar join
49 Aerial mast
50 Starboard inboard engine nacelle
51 Spinner

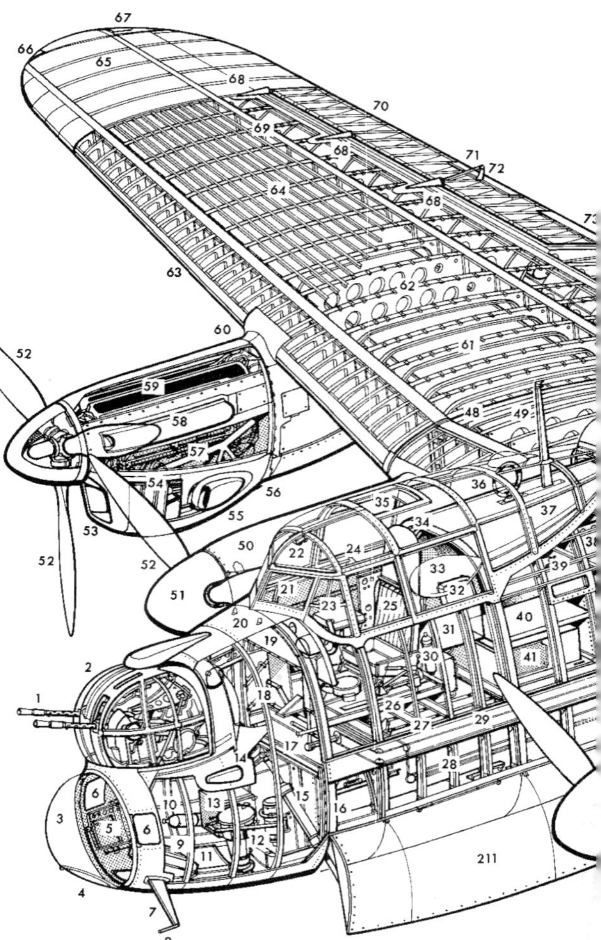

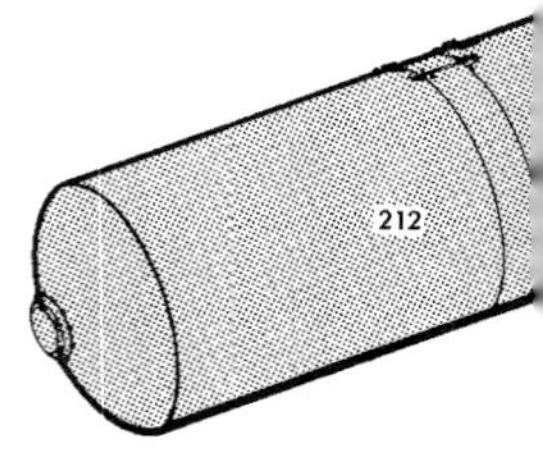

52 Three-bladed de Havilland constant-speed propellers
53 Oil cooler intake
54 Oil cooler radiator
55 Carburettor air intake
56 Radiator shutter
57 Engine bearer frame
58 Exhaust flame damper shroud
59 Packard-built Rolls-Royce Merlin 28 liquid-cooled engine
60 Nacelle/wing fairing
61 Fuel tank bearer ribs
62 Intermediate ribs
63 Leading-edge structure
64 Wing stringers
65 Wingtip skinning
66 Starboard navigation light
67 Starboard formation light
68 Aileron hinge fairings
69 Wing rear spar
70 Starboard aileron
71 Aileron balance tab
72 Balance tab control rod
73 Aileron trim tab
74 HF aerial
75 Split trailing-edge flap (outboard section)
76 Emergency (ditching) exit
77 Crash axe stowage
78 Fire extinguisher
79 Hydraulic reservoir
80 Signal/flare pistol stowage
81 Parachute stowage box/spar step
82 Rear spar carry-through
83 Bunk backrest
84 Rear spar fuselage frame
85 Emergency packs
86 Roof light
87 Dinghy manual release cable (dinghy stowage in starboard wingroot)
88 Mid-gunner's parachute stowage
89 Tail turret ammunition box
90 Ammunition feed track
91 Emergency (ditching) exit
92 Flame floats stowage
93 Sea markers stowage
94 Roof light
95 Dorsal turret fairing
96 Frazer-Nash power-operated dorsal turret
97 Two 0.303-in (7.7-mm) Browning machine-guns
98 Turret mounting ring
99 Turret mechanism
100 Ammunition track cover plate
101 Turret step bracket
102 Header tank
103 Oxygen cylinder
104 Fire extinguisher
105 DR compass housing
106 Handrail
107 Crew entry door (starboard)
108 Parachute stowage
109 First-aid pack
110 Starboard tailplane
111 Rudder control lever
112 Starboard tailfin
113 Rudder balance weights
114 Starboard rudder
115 Rudder datum hinge
116 Rudder tab actuating rod
117 Rudder tab
118 Starboard elevator
119 Elevator balance tab
126 Four 0.303-in (7.7-mm) Browning machine-guns
127 Cartridge case ejection chutes
128 Rear navigation light
129 Elevator trim tab
130 Fin construction
131 Rudder balance weights
132 Port rudder frame
133 Rudder trim tab
134 Rudder tab balance weight
135 Rudder tab actuating rod
136 Rudder horn balance
137 Trim tab actuating jack
138 Tailplane construction
139 Elevator torque tube
140 Tailplane carry-through
141 Non-retractable tailwheel
142 Elsan closet
152 Reserve ammunition boxes
153 Main floor support structure
154 Flap operating hydraulic jack
155 Flap operating tube
156 Flap toggle links
157 Flap tube connecting link
158 Rear spar
159 Split trailing-edge flap (inboard section)
160 Split trailing-edge flap (outboard section)
161 Aileron control lever
162 Aileron trim tab control cable linkage
163 Aileron trim tab
164 Aileron balance tab control rod
165 Aileron balance tab
166 Aileron hinge fairings
167 Port aileron
168 Port wingtip
169 Port formation light
170 Port navigation light
181 Outboard engine oil tank
182 Firewall/bulkhead
183 Carburettor air intake
184 Outboard engine support frame
185 Port mainwheel
186 Undercarriage oleo struts
187 Flame-damper shroud
188 Outboard engine support frame/main spar pick-up
189 Undercarriage retraction jacks
190 Oleo strut attachment pin
191 Undercarriage support beam (light-alloy casting)
192 Centre-section outer rib/undercarriage support
193 Location of port intermediate (No. 2) fuel tank (383 Imp gal/1741 litres)
194 Main wheel well
195 Emergency retraction air valve
196 Retraction cylinder attachment

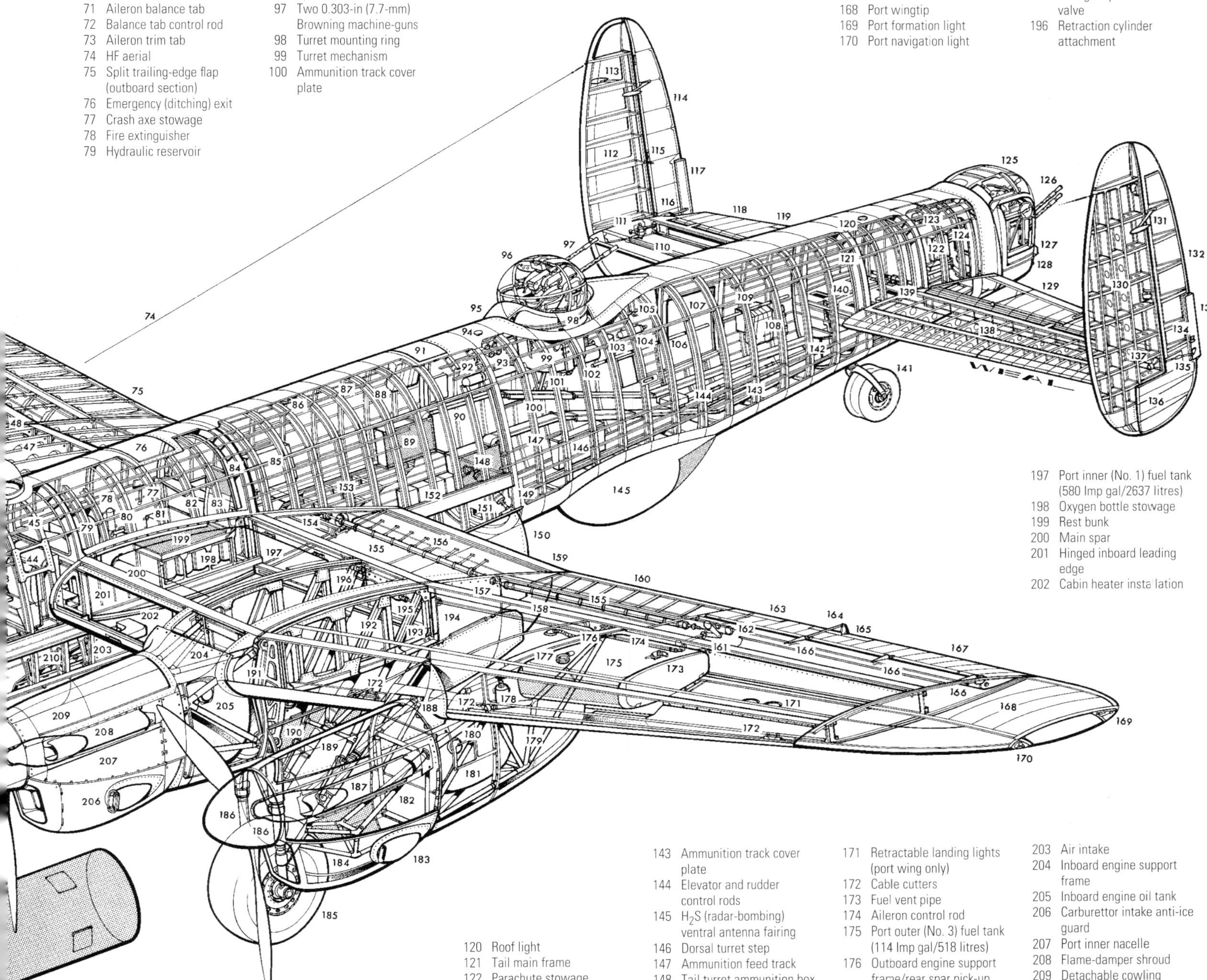

197 Port inner (No. 1) fuel tank (580 Imp gal/2637 litres)
198 Oxygen bottle stowage
199 Rest bunk
200 Main spar
201 Hinged inboard leading edge
202 Cabin heater installation

120 Roof light
121 Tail main frame
122 Parachute stowage
123 Fire extinguisher
124 Tail turret entry door
125 Frazer-Nash power-operated tail turret
143 Ammunition track cover plate
144 Elevator and rudder control rods
145 H_2S (radar-bombing) ventral antenna fairing
146 Dorsal turret step
147 Ammunition feed track
148 Tail turret ammunition box
149 Bomb-bay aft bulkhead
150 Bomb-bay doors
151 Bomb-bay doors aft actuating jacks
171 Retractable landing lights (port wing only)
172 Cable cutters
173 Fuel vent pipe
174 Aileron control rod
175 Port outer (No. 3) fuel tank (114 Imp gal/518 litres)
176 Outboard engine support frame/rear spar pick-up
177 Fuel booster pump
178 Fire extinguisher
179 Engine sub-frame
180 Filler cap
203 Air intake
204 Inboard engine support frame
205 Inboard engine oil tank
206 Carburettor intake anti-ice guard
207 Port inner nacelle
208 Flame-damper shroud
209 Detachable cowling panels
210 Bomb shackles
211 Bomb-bay doors (open)
212 8000-lb (3632-kg) bomb

navigation and bombing aids, on occasions with extra crew members to operate them, with which to guide Main Force aircraft. From August many of the latter (though only those without bulged bomb bay doors) had been equipped with H2S, a navigation and target location device in a prominent fairing under the rear fuselage. A Pathfinder unit, No. 635 Squadron, was equipped with a few examples of the **Lancaster Mk VI** in 1944. Converted from Mk IIIs, these machines were fitted with Merlin 85s which, thanks to their two-speed, two-stage supercharging, boasted greatly improved performance at altitude. Radio countermeasures equipment was fitted to these machines, distinguishable by the removal of their mid-upper and nose gun turrets.

After D-Day Lancasters not only continued their night assaults on major German cities, but also helped Allied ground forces by bombing German armies in the field during tactical daylight sorties near Caen. One of the last Lancaster raids of the war was a daylight attack on Hitler's retreat at Berchtesgaden on 25 April 1945.

The last wartime Lancaster variants were the tropicalised **B.Mk I(FE)** and **B.Mk VII(FE)**, the latter boasting a repositioned Martin mid-upper gun turret and an FN82 tail turret, both with 0.5-in (12.7-mm) machine-guns in place of the 0.303-in (7.7-mm) guns fitted hitherto. Both these variants would have joined Tiger Force, the RAF's very-long-range bomber force, in the bombing of Japan had the war continued. In an attempt to improve the type's range for these missions, trials were carried out with large 'saddle' fuel tanks (which increased fuel capacity by 50 per cent) fitted to two Lancaster Mk Is. These aircraft were flown to India for testing in mid-1945. These were not the first Lancasters to reach the Far East; two aircraft had already flown to India in 1943 for tropicalisation trials and were additionally flown with Horsa and Hamilcar gliders in tow with a view to utilising gliders in the India-Burma theatre.

Another type intended for Tiger Force was the Avro Lincoln, effectively an enlarged version of the Lancaster, first flown in June 1944 as the **Lancaster Mk IV**. Of the over 7,300 Lancasters built, 3,345 were reported missing on operations, such was the intensity of their operation between 1942 and 1945, when 156,000 sorties were flown and 608,612 tons of bombs dropped. The last bombing missions of the war were flown by Lancasters in April 1945. During April and May, Lancasters were employed in Operation Manna, the air-dropping of urgently needed food to the starving Dutch population, while the last Lancaster operations of the war saw the type used to transport 74,000 prisoners of war back to the UK during May. Though troop-carrying had been considered as a secondary role for the Lancaster, investigations initiated in 1944 had failed to bear fruit before VJ-Day, but served as the basis for post-war transport conversions, like the Avro Lancastrian. Post-war a number of Lancasters were supplied to the French navy, these serving into the 1960s. The Lancaster's legacy also continued in the Avro York transport which used Lancaster wings and engines, plus a central fin in addition to the twin endplate fins.

Shown in Tiger Force colours, the Lancaster B.Mk VII saw operational service during the war only in that force. This example flew with No. 9 Squadron which, along with No. 617, was based at Salbani, India. The B.Mk VII was normally fitted with the Martin mid-upper turret, but this example has the Bristol B.17 turret with twin 20-mm guns.

Avro 685 York

One of the wartime agreements concluded between Britain and the United States allocated to the Americans responsibility for building all transport aircraft for Allied use, enabling the British industry to concentrate on fighters and bombers. Despite this, at Avro's Chadderton factory in February 1942, designer Roy Chadwick and his team completed the drawings for a four-engined long-range transport. This united the wings, tail assembly, engines and landing gear of the Lancaster with a new square-section fuselage.

Shortly before the **York Mk I** prototype flew at Ringway, Manchester, on 5 July 1942, an official order was placed for four aircraft, the first two to have Rolls-Royce Merlin XXs and the others Bristol Hercules VIs. All four were in fact ultimately flown with the former engines, the sole Hercules-powered aircraft being the prototype, which was re-engined with Hercules XVIs late in 1943 to become the **York Mk II**. To compensate for the additional side area forward of the centre of gravity, a central third fin was added from the third aircraft which, named *Ascalon*, was delivered to No. 24 Squadron at RAF Northolt in March 1943. Equipped as a flying conference room, principally for the use of Prime Minister Winston Churchill, it carried him to Algiers in May and, just a few days later, His Majesty King George VI used it for his visit to troops in North Africa.

The first two production aircraft were delivered to No. 24 Squadron for VIP duties. Other VIP-configured Yorks included those allocated for official duties to Louis Mountbatten, Field Marshal Smuts and the Duke of Gloucester. Five early aircraft were delivered to BOAC for the operation of a UK-Morocco-Cairo service from April 1944 and a further 25 were delivered from August 1945 for joint operation with Transport Command.

During 1945 No. 511 Squadron at Lyneham became the first to receive a full complement of Yorks; 10 squadrons were eventually to fly the aircraft in RAF service, and seven of these squadrons were equipped in time to take part in the Berlin Airlift from 1 July 1948. Production ceased with the delivery of the 257th York to RAF Honington on 29 April 1948.

Yorks were produced in three variants: all-passenger, all-freight and mixed passenger/freight. When superseded by Handley Page Hastings transports in RAF Transport Command service, Yorks continued in their accustomed roles when operated by civilian firms with government contracts for troop carrying. The last York in RAF service was retired in 1957.

Specification

Type: long-range passenger and cargo transport

Powerplant: four 1,280-hp (954-kW) Rolls-Royce Merlin XX inline piston engines

Performance: maximum speed 298 mph (480 km/h) at 21,000 ft (6400 m); cruising speed 210 mph (338 km/h); service ceiling 23,000 ft (7010 m); range 2,700 miles (4345 km)

Weight: empty 42,040 lb (19069 kg); maximum take-off 68,597 lb (31115 kg)

Dimensions: span 102 ft 0 in (31.09 m); length 78 ft 6 in (23.93 m); height 17 ft 10 in (5.44 m); wing area 1,297 sq ft (120.49 m²)

The third prototype York, LV633* Ascalon*, (the first of the type with triple fins) was used by Prime Minister Winston Churchill and had square windows instead of the usual round ones. Although allocated the civil registration G-AGFT, it was never applied.

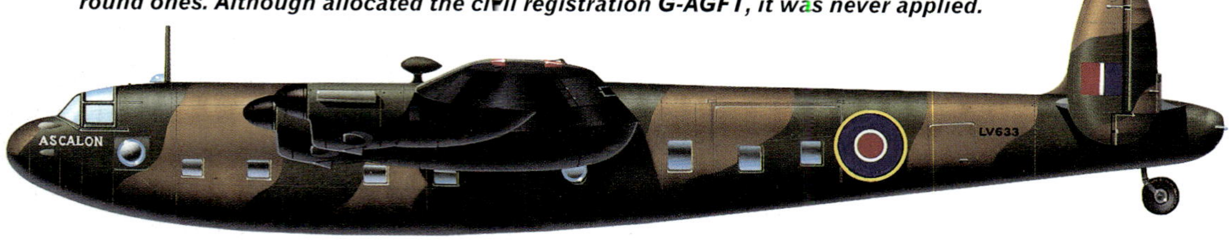

Beech Expeditor

Developed by Beech Aircraft in the late 1930s, the **Model 18** was a light twin-engined aircraft arranged to seat six passengers with a crew of two. It achieved only modest pre-war success, but spawned a multitude of military variants for the USAAF and USN, with production eventually totalling 6,326 (including post-war civil versions). Lend-Lease supplies to the UK totalled 429.

The Beech 18 served, in military guise, primarily in the communications/light transport role, but the first for Britain were in fact examples of the **AT-7** navigation trainer (known in US service as the **Navigator**). In a complex deal, five AT-7s were supplied to the Royal Navy in place of five Grumman OA-9 Goose amphibians diverted to the US Army from a British contract.

Two of these AT-7s, delivered in 1943, remained in the USA – one later going to the Dutch government for the use of HRH Prince Bernhardt – while the other three went to No. 742 Sqn based in Ceylon. Principal supplies comprised 121 **Expeditor Mk I**s, equivalent to the UC-45B, and 303 **Expeditor Mk II**s, similar to the UC-45F.

The latter differed only in small details, with a revised seven-seat interior and a slightly lengthened nose. Apart from the diversion of 48 Expeditor Mk Is (and seven Mk IIs) to the RCAF, the Expeditors served primarily with RAF units in the Middle and Far East, providing a vital service in the communications role. Six Mk Is and 68 Mk IIs went to the Royal Navy, and these also served extensively in the Far East, particularly with No. 742 Sqn at Ceylon. In the UK, No. 782 Sqn, FAA, was the principal user, at Donibristle, several of its aircraft bearing the name *Merlin*.

Expeditor Mk II HB275 of No. 353 Squadron was based at Palam, India in early 1945, where the type replaced Ansons in the communications role for the last seven months of the war.

About 200 examples of the Expeditor were supplied to the RAF under Lend-Lease. The type served with RAF units mainly in the Middle and Far East theatres for essential communications flying.

Beech Traveller

This distinctive and elegant biplane, with its retractable undercarriage and back-staggered wings, first appeared in British military markings in 1941, when two civil-registered Beechcraft Model 17s were impressed, one to serve with the ATA and the other with the Allied Flight of No. 24 Sqn at Hendon, where it was often flown by HRH Prince Bernhardt.

Two more were purchased in the US in July 1941 for use by the British Purchasing Commission based in Washington. These four aircraft remained known as **Beechcraft 17**s, but the acquisition of 107 through the Lend-Lease arrangement led to the adoption of the USAAF name, albeit Anglicised with a double 'l' to **Traveller Mk I**. The Traveller Mk I provided comfortable seating for four passengers and the pilot, and was a welcome addition to both the RAF and the FAA for communications duty. Deliveries to Britain comprised a batch of 75 for the Admiralty; these were US Navy **GB-2**s. Aircraft for the RAF were delivered direct to the Middle East, 12 of the first 18 being lost at sea in May 1943. Delivery of 14 more gave the RAF a strength of 20 of the type. In the Middle East, the Traveller Mk Is served with the communications flights of Nos 201 and 205 Group, and with the Aden Communications Flight, the latter flying daily reconnaissance flights along the coast. In the Fleet Air Arm, Travellers were dispersed through seven squadrons, principally those providing communications within the UK. These comprised No. 701 Sqn at Heathrow; No. 712 at Hatston in the Orkneys; No. 725 Sqn at Eglinton; No. 730 at Ayr; No. 740 Sqn at Machrihanish; No. 781 Sqn at Lee-on-Solent and No. 782 Sqn at Donibristle. Others flew as 'hacks' with station flights. Upon the end of hostilities, the great majority of the Navy's Travellers were returned to the US under the Lend-Lease terms, but most of those serving the RAF remained in British hands until they were sold into the civil market in 1946.

Among the 105 Beechcraft Model 17 aircraft supplied under Lend-Lease, some 25 were ex-US Navy GB-2s for use by the Royal Navy. They were named Traveller Mk II, including F7461 seen here.

The thirty Travellers Mk Is destined for the RAF were to be shipped in batches from New York to Suez in the Middle East between March and October 1943, aboard* SS Tabian, Augumonte *and* Philip Schugler. *However, 12 of the aircraft were lost at sea when the* Augumonte *was torpedoed by a U-boat on 29 May 1943.

Bell Airacobra

Flown by the A&AEE at Boscombe Down, AH573 was the first of four Airacobras to undergo flight trials. Performance tests were disappointing, especially in climb and level flight. The type only served briefly with one RAF front-line unit.

Only a single prototype of the Bell **Model 14** had flown when, in April 1940, the British Purchasing Commission placed a contract for 675 of this advanced all-metal, stressed-skin single-seat fighter. Claims of a top speed in excess of 400 mph (644 km/h), operating altitude above 36,000 ft (10973 m) and a range of more than 1,000 miles (1610 km) – based on trials with the XP-39 prototype – would be found to be greatly exaggerated when fully-laden and armed production aircraft became available. Difficulties would also derive from the buried engine installation with its long drive shaft to the propeller, and with the armament, which included a 20-mm cannon firing through the spinner.

Before delivery of the British aircraft began, the USAAC made available four **P-39C Airacobras** from its own stocks; these were in the UK by July 1941 for early evaluation at the A&AEE and AFDU. These tests recorded a disappointing performance, soon to be confirmed with the arrival of the British-contract aircraft, starting in mid-1941. By that time, the original proposed name of **Caribou** had been dropped in favour of the USAAC's Airacobra. The **Airacobra Mk I** was similar to the P-39D, other than having the export-model 1,150-hp Allison V-1710-E4 engine and British-specified armament.

No. 601 Sqn began to receive Airacobras in August 1941 and flew the first operational sorties in September, but problems dogged the deployment and the unit was pulled back in October to begin re-equipment on Spitfires. No further operational use was made of the type by the RAF. Of the total ordered by Britain, at least 54 were lost at sea on delivery; 212 were diverted to the Soviet Union and 179 were repossessed by the USAAF in December 1941 for urgent use (as P-400s) in the South Pacific. The planned delivery of 494 Airacobra Mk Is (P-39D-1s) through Lend-Lease did not take place.

Specification
Airacobra Mk I
Type: single-seat fighter
Powerplant: one 1,150-hp (858-kW) Allison V-1710-E4 piston engine
Performance: maximum speed 358 mph (576 km/h) at 15,000 ft (4572 m); cruising speed 335 mph (539 km/h); service ceiling 35,000 ft (10668 m); range 1,098 miles (1767 km)
Weights: empty 5,360 lb (2431 kg); maximum take-off 7,380 lb (3347 kg)
Dimensions: span 34 ft 0 in (10.36 m); length 34 ft 2 in (10.41 m); height 9 ft 3 in (2.82 m); wing area 213 sq ft (19.79 m²)
Armament: one 20-mm cannon firing through the airscrew boss, plus two 0.303-in (7.7-mm) machine-guns in nose and four in the wings

This is a line-up of Airacobra Mk Is of No. 601 Squadron at Duxford in 1941, the only RAF fighter squadron to be equipped with the type. They were used for only a few months before the squadron converted to Spitfires.

Blackburn B-6 Shark

Coming at the end of a distinguished line of Blackburn torpedo biplanes which had served with the Fleet Air Arm, the Shark upheld the high reputations of its predecessors, the Dart, Ripon and Baffin.

Begun as a private venture, the Shark prototype, known as the **B-6**, flew on 24 August 1933 at Brough and was flown to the Aircraft and Armament Experimental Establishment, Martlesham Heath, for testing in November 1933. Deck landing trials aboard HMS *Courageous* early the following year were successful and a contract for 16 aircraft was placed for the Fleet Air Arm in August 1934.

The prototype was fitted with twin floats and flown at Brough the following April, and successful sea trials took place from Felixstowe. Further contracts fol-lowed, and during the three-year production run Blackburn delivered 238 Sharks to the Fleet Air Arm, with which the type served in both seaplane and landplane configurations.

Shark Mk Is, like the prototype, used the 700-hp (522-kW) Armstrong Siddeley Tiger IV engine, but the last aircraft in the first production batch was used for development flying with the uprated Tiger VI. This engine was used in the **Shark Mk II**, production of which began in 1936. An alternative engine was available for the next production variant, the **Shark Mk III**, in the form of the 800-hp (597-kW) Bristol Pegasus III engine. Ninety-five Shark Mk IIIs were delivered between April 1937 and the end of the year.

The Shark's front-line service was brief and in 1938 they were replaced by the Fairey Swordfish. However, by the outbreak of World War II more than 20 Shark Mk IIs and Mk IIIs had been reconfigured as target-tugs and were stationed at target-towing units around the country.

During the Dunkirk evacuation a number of Gosport-based Sharks towed lighted flares to illuminate German E-boats in the English Channel.

At least 17 Sharks were dispatched to Seletar for target-towing duties and four of these were detached to Batu Pahat in January 1943 to attack Japanese army columns.

Canada also operated licence-built Shark Mk IIIs which served until August 1944. In June of that year five of these aircraft were transferred to the British Air Observers School at Trinidad, where they served faithfully if without distinction.

Twin-float versions of the Shark were operated by No. 705 (Catapult) Flight, aboard HMS Repulse and HMS Warspite.

Specification
Shark Mk II
Type: two/three-seat torpedo/reconnaissance biplane
Powerplant: one 760-hp (567-kW) Armstrong Siddeley Tiger VI radial piston engine
Performance (torpedo landplane): maximum speed 150 mph (241 km/h) at sea level; cruising speed 118 mph (190 km/h); service ceiling 16,000 ft (4875 m); range 625 miles (1006 km)
Weights: empty 4,039 lb (1832 kg); maximum take-off 8,050 lb (3651 kg)
Dimensions: span 46 ft 0 in (14.02 m); length 35 ft 3 in (10.74 m); height 12 ft 1 in (3.68 m); wing area 489 sq ft (45.43 m²)
Armament: one fixed forward-firing 0.303-in (7.7-mm) machine-gun and one 0.303-in (7.7-mm) gun on flexible mount in rear cockpit, plus one 1,500-lb (680-kg) torpedo or equivalent weight in bombs

Blackburn B-24 Skua

Left: *With its arrester hook down, a Skua of No. 801 Squadron lands on the flight deck of HMS* Furious. *During the Dunkirk evacuation No. 801's Skuas flew with RAF Coastal Command from Detling.*

Below: The Blackburn B.24 Skua was designed around a pair of irreconcilable requirements – fighter and dive bomber. The aircraft illustrated are from No. 803 Squadron, one of the four carrier squadrons that operated the Skua from 1939 until mid-1941.

Designed to Specification 0.27/34, the all-metal Blackburn **B-24 Skua** broke away from the Royal Navy's long tradition of biplanes with fabric covering: it was Britain's first naval dive-bomber and the country's first deck-landing aircraft to have flaps, retractable landing gear and a variable-pitch propeller.

The Skua competed with designs from Avro, Boulton Paul, Hawker and Vickers for the naval contract, and two prototypes were ordered in April 1935, the first of which flew at Brough on 9 February 1937, powered by an 840-hp (626-kW) Bristol Mercury IX.

After appearing in the New Types Park at the RAF Display, Hendon, on 26 June 1937 and the SBAC Display at Hatfield two days later, the prototype was sent to the Aircraft and Armament Experimental Establishment, Martlesham Heath, for the customary handling trials. Favourable reports were given on the Skua's handling qualities, and it subsequently carried out gunnery trials at Martlesham and, later, ditching experiments at Gosport.

Orders for 190 Skuas had been placed six months before the flight of the prototype and some sub-contract work was awarded to speed up production. Because all Mercury engines were required for Bristol Blenheims, production Skuas were given the 890-hp (664-kW) Bristol Perseus XII sleeve-valve engine, in which form they became **Skua Mk II**s.

The first production aircraft flew at Brough on 28 August 1938 and few modifications to the basic design were required apart from fitting upturned wingtips and a modified tailwheel oleo to cure juddering. The entire production run of 190 aircraft was delivered between October 1938 and March 1940, no mean feat at that period, although the programme was about a year behind schedule.

The first Fleet Air Arm squadrons to receive Skuas late in 1938 were Nos 800 and 803, for service on HMS *Ark Royal* where they replaced Hawker Nimrods and Ospreys. No. 801 Squadron aboard HMS *Furious* was also re-equipped and Skuas also joined No. 806 Squadron, then at Eastleigh, before the outbreak of war.

As a fighter, the Skua was already obsolete, but it made its mark in the dive-bombing role early in the war when 16 aircraft from Nos 800 and 803 Squadrons, flying from Hatston in the Orkneys, sank the German cruiser *Königsberg* in Bergen harbour at dawn on 10 April 1940. Although at the very limits of their range, all but one Skua returned from this long night flight. The squadron suffered a severe setback 11 days later, however, losing most of its Skuas during an attack on Narvik.

Skuas from No. 801 Squadron flying from Detling covered the Dunkirk evacuation, but the type was withdrawn from operational service in 1941 when Nos 800 and 806 Squadrons re-equipped with Fairey Fulmars, while Nos 801 and 803 received Hawker Sea Hurricanes.

The remaining Skuas ended their days comparatively peacefully as target tugs and on general training duties.

Specification

Skua Mk II

Type: two-seat naval fighter/dive-bomber

Powerplant: one 890-hp (664-kW) Bristol Perseus XII radial piston engine

Performance: maximum speed 225 mph (362 km/h) at 6,500 ft (1980 m); cruising speed 165 mph (266 km/h) at 15,000 ft (4570 m); service ceiling 20,200 ft (6160 m); range 760 miles (1223 km)

Weights: empty 5,490 lb (2490 kg); maximum take off 8,228 lb (3732 kg)

Dimensions: span 46 ft 2 in (14.07 m); length 35 ft 7 in (10.85 m); height 12 ft 6 in (3.81 m); wing area 312 sq ft (28.98 m^2)

Armament: four 0.303-in (7.7-mm) forward-firing machine-guns in wings and one Lewis gun on flexible mount in rear cockpit, plus one 500-lb (227-kg) bomb beneath fuselage and eight 30-lb (14-kg) practice bombs on underwing racks

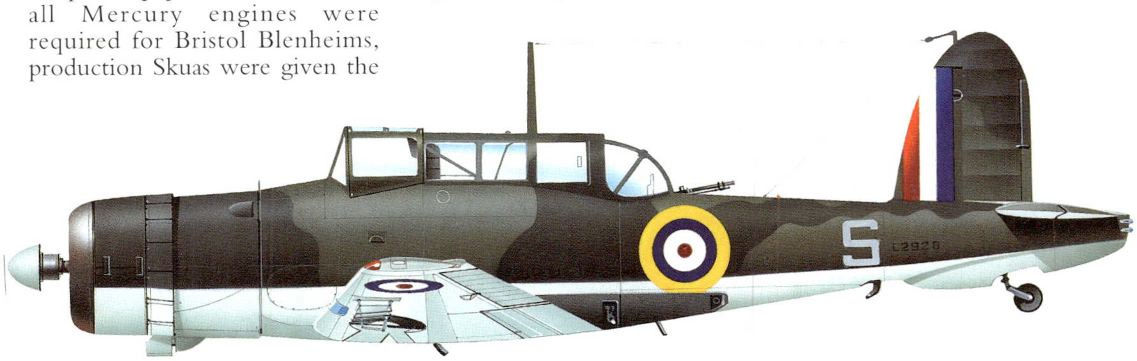

The Skua has a place in Fleet Air Arm history as its first operational monoplane, and also the first British aircraft specifically designed for dive bombing. It first entered service with No. 800 Squadron in November 1938.

Blackburn B-25 Roc

Developed from the Skua dive-bomber, the Blackburn **B-25 Roc** was the first Fleet Air Arm aircraft to have a power-driven gun turret. The idea was that four guns could be brought to bear in broadside attacks on enemy bombers, but with a maximum speed of less than 200 mph (322 km/h) it is doubtful if the Roc could have caught an enemy bomber, and the idea was dropped.

Orders for 136 Rocs to Specification 0.15/37 were received on 28 April 1937 and, because of Blackburn's involvement with the Skua programme, production was undertaken by Boulton Paul at Wolverhampton, the first aircraft flying on 23 December 1938. Following trials at Brough, the Roc went to the Aircraft and Armament Experimental Establishment, Martlesham Heath, in March 1939, and was joined there by the next two aircraft so that simultaneous handling and armament trials could be undertaken. As expected, the heavy turret penalised the Roc by comparison with the Skua, but the former could still be held steady in a steep dive with the use of dive brakes. An enlarged propeller was fitted, and various other means of improving performance were tried, without much success.

Four Rocs were flown as seaplanes, fitted with Blackburn Shark floats, and these reduced the already low speed by another 30 mph (48 km/h). Stability was rather poor and low altitude turns had to be avoided.

After familiarization with several Fleet Air Arm units, the first four Rocs to go into service were delivered to No. 806 Squadron at Eastleigh in February 1940 to serve alongside eight Skuas. Six Rocs went to join No. 801 Squadron's Skuas at Hatston, Orkney, four months later. No. 2 Anti-Aircraft Co-operation Unit at Gosport received 16 Rocs to replace its Blackburn Sharks and supplement its Skuas in June 1940.

Perhaps the most unusual role for the Roc fell to four which had been damaged in a Junkers Ju 87 raid on Gosport and were used as ground-based machine-gun posts with their turrets permanently manned.

Other Rocs were dispersed to various locations in the UK and even to Bermuda. The type gradually faded away until the last two aircraft were withdrawn from service in August 1943 for lack of spars, after an distinguished career.

Above: *The Blackburn Roc was designed to do for the Fleet Air Arm what the Boulton Paul Defiant had done for the RAF, but both aircraft suffered from the same failings – a lack of performance, agility and firepower.*

Left: *Tests with the Roc floatplane were undertaken at MAEE at Helensburgh, down the Clyde from the Dumbarton factory. Directional instability was apparent during testing of L3059 and it subsequently crashed on 3 December 1939.*

It had been quickly realised that the Roc was entirely unsuitable as a fighter and it was quickly relegated to second-line duties. This example was delivered to No. 6 Maintenance Unit before seeing service as a target tug with No. 2 AACU based at Gosport.

Specification

Type: two-seat naval fighter/target-tug

Powerplant: one 905-hp (675-kW) Bristol Perseus XII radial piston engine

Performance (landplane): maximum speed 223 mph (359 km/h) at 10,000 ft (3050 m); cruising speed 135 mph (217 km/h); service ceiling 18,000 ft (5485 m); range 810 miles (1304 km)

Weights: empty 6,124 lb (2778 kg); maximum take-off 7,950 lb (3606 kg)

Dimensions: span 46 ft 0 in (14.02 m); length 35 ft 7 in (10.85 m); height 12 ft 1 in (3.68 m); wing area 310 sq ft (28.80 m^2)

Armament: four 0.303-in (7.7-mm) machine-guns in electrically actuated Boulton Paul turret

Blackburn B-26 Botha

When the Air Ministry issued Specification M. 15/35 for a three-seat twin-engined reconnaissance bomber with the ability to carry a torpedo, it attracted submissions by Blackburn and Bristol. Both envisaged 850-hp (634-kW) Bristol Perseus engines, but a change in the requirement increased the crew to four, leading to the new Specification 10/36, and both types were ordered, respectively, as the **Botha** and Beaufort.

Because of the greater weight of the revised designs the Beaufort was given 1,130-hp (843-kW) Bristol Taurus radials, but these were in short supply and Blackburn was accordingly committed to using 880-hp (656-kW) Bristol Perseus X engines in the initial production version of the Botha.

Orders for 442 were received in 1936, and the first production aircraft flew at Brough on 28 December 1938. Trials at the Experimental Establishment, Martlesham Heath, resulted in an increase in tailplane area and fitting of a horn balanced elevator to provide better elevator control. Tests at the Torpedo Development Unit at Gosport began late in 1939 and production lines were established at Brough and Dumbarton. The first Botha to be delivered to the RAF was the third aircraft off the Dumbarton line, which arrived at No. 5 Maintenance Unit, Kemble, on 12 December 1939.

The Blackburn B.26 Botha was seriously underpowered, and therefore totally unsuited to its intended operational role as a torpedo bomber. It was soon relegated to general reconnaissance and operational training duties until declared obsolete in August 1943.

A number of unexplained fatal accidents occurred in the first half of 1940 and the Botha came in for considerable criticism in view of its shortcomings and the fact that it was underpowered. Bristol managed to squeeze a little more power out of the Perseus engine, the Mk XA producing 930 hp (694 kW), and some other improvements were incorporated.

The fact that the Botha was underpowered and unfit for operational duties gave the Air Staff the idea that it could be relegated to training units where, not surprisingly, it continued to suffer fatal accidents. Probably the most appropriate, and certainly the safest Botha deliveries, came in late 1942 when some time-expired airframes went to RAF Schools of Technical Training. A few Bothas were fitted with winch gear and used by the Target Towing Unit at Abbotsinch as TT.Mk Is.

A total of 580 Bothas was built, 380 at Brough and 200 at Dumbarton, and the type was finally withdrawn from service in September 1944.

Specification
Type: four-seat reconnaissance/ torpedo-bomber/ trainer
Powerplant: two 930-hp (694-kW) Bristol Perseus XA radial piston engines
Performance: maximum speec 249 mph (401 km/h) at 5,500 ft (1675 m); cruising speed 212 mph (341 km/h) at 15,000 ft (4570 m); service ceiling 17,500 ft (5335 m); range 1,270 miles (2044 km)
Weights: empty 11,830 lb (5366 kg); maximum takeoff 18,450 lb (8369 kg)
Dimensions: span 59 ft 0 in (17.98 m); length 51 ft 2 in (15.58 m); height 14 ft 7 in (4.46 m); wing area 518 sq ft (48.12 m²)
Armament: one fixed forward-firing 0.303-in (7.7-mm) machine-gun and two 0.303-in (7.7-mm) guns in dorsal turret, plus an internal torpedo, bombs or depth charges up to 2,000 lb (907 kg) in weight

Boeing Fortress

Among the best known of all warplanes used by any of the combatants in World War II, the Boeing **B-17 Flying Fortress** originated in 1934 in response to a USAAC requirement. Designed to have an eight-man crew and an armament of five defensive machine-guns, the prototype made its first flight on 28 July 1935. Three weeks later it gave a foretaste of its capabilities when it flew 2,100 miles (3380 km) from Seattle to Wright Field, Ohio, at an average speed of 232 mph (373 km/h). Small-scale production allowed service trials to continue and, by the time the RAF found itself at war, Boeing was producing the **B-17C** variant, featuring heavier armament (10 machine-guns in all) that dispensed with the large lateral blisters but introduced a large ventral 'bathtub'.

Committed to the development of heavy bombers for night operation, the RAF was unsure that the B-17 would be useful for European operations, but was ready to put it to the test. In an unusual deal concluded in March 1940, the US government agreed to release 20 B-17Cs to Britain in exchange for detailed information on their operation in combat. Known as the **Fortress Mk I**, these aircraft arrived early in 1941 and were used to equip No. 90 Sqn based at West Raynham, a unit that had previously operated Blenheim Mk IVs. Moving to Polebrook for operations, the squadron took the Fortress into battle for the first time on 8 July 1941, when three of the bombers attacked Wilhelmshaven.

One of the first Fortress Mk IIAs to be used by No. 220 Squadron was FK185, with an experimental installation of a Vickers 'S' gun. This large-calibre weapon was sighted from the nose gondola and was intended to silence the anti-aircraft guns on U-boats when attacked on the surface.

Fortress Mk IIA FK186 was one of many B-17Es allocated to Coastal Command. Arriving in Britain during March 1942, it joined No. 220 Squadron. Together with the Liberator, the B-17s were able to close off part of the 'Atlantic Gap'.

The USAAC believed that the B-17s should be used in multi-ship formations to benefit from mutual defensive fire; the RAF missions, however, were flown mostly on an individual basis, operating in daylight at heights up to 30,000 ft (9144 m). By the end of September, 26 raids had been launched, totalling 51 sorties, but half of these had been aborted with no bombs dropped. Many difficulties were encountered, particularly with guns freezing up and with the operation of the Sperry bomb-sight (use of the more advanced Norden sight had been denied

Twenty B-17C Fortress Mk Is were delivered to the RAF, entering service with No. 90 Squadron. After a series of unsuccessful bombing raids they were transferred to Coastal Command for patrol duties.

This Fortress Mk III, KJ109, of No. 223 (Special Duties) Squadron operated from Oulton, Norfolk, in 1944-45. It was employed on clandestine electronic jamming of German radar and other radio countermeasures duties.

Above: AN521 was the first of the 20 B-17C Fortress Mk Is to arrive in Britain. It commenced operations with No. 90 Squadron on 8 July 1941, taking part in a raid on Wilhelmshaven. It crashed in Egypt in 1942.

Left: Fortress Mk II FL459 'J' of No. 206 Squadron is seen in formation with a second Coastal Command Fortress, while based at Lajes in the Azores in late 1943. It was fitted with underwing- and nose-mounted ASV radar antennas for its Atlantic convoy patrol duties.

to Britain). Seven aircraft had been lost – four to enemy fighters and three to other causes.

The RAF concluded, not unreasonably, that the Fortress, at least in the form in which it was then operating, was unsuitable for the European theatre. A detachment of No. 90 Sqn was sent to Shallufa, Egypt – losing another Fortress Mk I in January 1942 – but was then redesignated No. 220 Sqn; the existing No. 220 Sqn, flying Hudsons in Coastal Command, moved to Nutts Corner, took over the remainder of the Fortresses and took them to Northern Ireland to fly anti-submarine patrols. Joined there by the detachment from Egypt, No. 220 Sqn's strength grew to eight Fortress Mk Is, which remained in service until July. In preparation for operations with later marks of the Fortress, No. 206 Sqn, also in Coastal Command, briefly had four of the Mk Is, and No. 214 – which as noted later would eventually

This view clearly shows the radar aerials fitted underneath the wings and above the nose to Coastal Command's B-17F Fortress Mk IIAs . This aircraft was operated by No. 220 Squadron based at Ballykelly, Northern Ireland.

Below: Brand-new B-17C Fortress Mk Is are seen lined up in the USA awaiting delivery to the RAF. These aircraft have the ventral 'bathtub', which was inadequately armed with a single 0.50-in (12.7-mm) machine-gun.

specialise in radio countermeasures with Fortress Mk Is and **Mk III**s – also used a couple of Mk Is for training.

The unpropitious debut of the B-17 in Europe notwithstanding, the RAF sought the inclusion of substantial numbers of later, improved, models in the Lend-Lease programme, initially calling for 300 **B-17F**s which it designated **Fortress B.Mk II**. In the event, only 19 of this batch materialised as the USAAF's needs had by this time become paramount and production could not keep pace with demand. They were preceded during 1942 by 46 **Fortress B.Mk IIA**s (of 84 requested), these being the **B-17E** variant. Differences between the B-17E and **B-17F** were minimal, but both represented a considerable improvement over the Fortress Mk I, with two-gun dorsal and ventral ball turrets and better mounts for the tail and beam guns. A longer rear fuselage with a large dorsal fin was a ready identification feature.

In the RAF, the new Fortresses were dedicated to Coastal Command service – designations changing to **GR.Mk II** and **GR.Mk IIA** – their long range and heavy armament making them especially suitable for overwater patrols. Already flying the Fortress Mk I, No. 220 Sqn was first to operate the Mk II/IIAs, from Ballykelly. It was soon joined by No. 206 Sqn at Benbecula, and then by No. 59 Sqn at St Eval to cover the Western Approaches. In the hands of these units, the Fortresses made a major contribution to closing the mid-Atlantic 'gap' where U-boats were operating with relative ease. To combat the U-boat, the Fortress relied largely – in common with other aircraft in Coastal Command – upon the standard Torpex-filled Mk VII or Mk VIII depth charge, and the 'Mk I eyeball', the latter being eventually complemented by ASV Mk III radar with its distinctive 'stickleback' aerials on the fuselage and underwing Yagi aerials.

As part of No. 15 Group, the Fortress squadrons sank 10 U-boats between 27 October 1942 and 11 June 1943, the first success being scored by No. 206 Sqn. Both this unit and No. 220 Sqn then moved to the Azores and scored three more kills. With a decline in the U-boat threat, and the availability of Liberators and Sunderlands in

Left: Two squadrons of No. 100 (Bomber Support) Group operated the Fortress Mk III. Their task was to protect the main force of heavy bombers by disrupting enemy radar using the dedicated jamming equipment they carried.

Below: This is a radio countermeasures Fortress Mk III in all-black finish, carrying an H_2S scanner beneath its nose. Visible below the waist gun hatch on the port side is a special chute for dispensing radar disruptive Window, the codename for chaff.

larger numbers, other roles were found for the Fortress. In particular, No. 519 Sqn at Wick and No. 521 at Docking flew the type on long-range weather reconnaissance and No. 251 Sqn used it for air-sea rescue patrols out of Iceland.

Another important role was found for the type when deliveries began to the RAF of the **B-17G** version, identified as the **Fortress B.Mk III**. From an initial batch of 60, deliveries of which began in March 1944, 13 were diverted to the USAAF; another 38 followed later in 1944 and 1945. After appropriate modification – by Scottish Aviation at Prestwick – these aircraft were issued to No. 214 Sqn to operate in the new role of Special Duties in No. 100 Group, based at Oulton. To allow this unit to begin training, 14 B-17Fs were transferred to the RAF from 8th Air Force stocks in the UK; these became **Fortress Mk II(SD)**s after modification, matched by the **Fortress Mk III(SD)**. Externally, the modifications were characterised by the variety of aerials required for the radio countermeasures role, with a number of different standards being adopted. The basic modification included a Monica Mk IIIA tail-warning receiver, a Jostle Mk IV VHF jammer, four Airborne Grocer AI jammers, Gee and Loran navigation aids and an H_2S navigation radar. Other jamming devices, such as the anti-V2 Big Ben Jostle, were introduced later. The H2S scanner was contained in a large perspex fairing under the nose, replacing the chin turret of the standard B-17G bomber.

No. 214 Sqn flew its first operational sortie, with a Fortress Mk II, on 20/21 April 1944. From then until the end of the war it flew more than 1,000 sorties, losing eight aircraft. In May 1945, No. 223(SD) Sqn at Oulton converted from B-24s to B-17s, but flew only four sorties. No. 1969 Flt, also at Oulton, provided conversion training for the Special Duties Fortresses.

The RAF promptly retired its Fortresses at the end of the war under the terms of Lend-Lease, with the survivors being scrapped in the UK.

Specification
Fortress Mk III
Type: eight-seat heavy bomber
Powerplant: four 1,200-hp (895-kW) Wright Cyclone GR-1820 radial piston engines
Performance: maximum speed 280 mph (451 km/h) at 20,000 ft (6096 m); service ceiling 31,500 ft (9601 m); maximum range 2,740 miles (4410 km)
Weights: empty 35,800 lb (16239 kg); maximum take-off 64,000 lb (29030 kg)
Dimensions: span 103 ft 9 in (31.62 m); length 73 ft 0 in (22.25 m); height 15 ft 6 in (4.72 m); wing area 1,486 sq ft (138.05 m²)
Armament: two 0.5-in (12.7-mm) machine-guns in nose, chin turret, dorsal turret, ventral turret and tail turret plus two 0.5-in (12.7-mm) machine-guns in waist positions and one in radio compartment, plus up to 12,800 lb (5806 kg) of bombs

In the markings of No. 214 Squadron, No. 100 (Bomber Support) Group, based at Sculthorpe, Norfolk in 1944-45, this Fortress Mk III was used to jam the enemy's early warning and AI radar, fighter control and VHF/HF radio communications.

Boulton Paul P.75 Overstrand

First flown in 1933, the **Overstrand** was a five-seat medium bomber developed from the successful Boulton Paul Sidestrand. The Overstrand benefitted from increased power provided by its Bristol Pegasus engines, allowing a greater bomb load and improved performance.

It was the first RAF bomber to be equipped with a power-operated, enclosed gun turret which was mounted in the nose and also featured a fully enclosed cockpit and a large protective windshield for the mid-upper gunner.

No. 101 Squadron was the only RAF unit to operate the Overstrand in front-line service and only 24 production examples were built at the company's Norwich factory. In 1937 No. 101 Sqn re-equipped with the Bristol Blenheim, bringing to an end the aircraft's front-line career; however, the power-operated turret was viewed as a major success, helping to markedly increase the gunners' firing accuracy. The excellence of the turret persuaded the RAF to keep the surviving Overstrands in service and the aircraft was used as a gunnery trainer. Surviving aircraft were mostly allocated to the Armament Training Camps, which were re-named Armament Training Schools in 1938, and also the Air Observer Schools (AOS). Five Overstrands were concentrated at No. 2 AOS at Dumfries in Scotland, which by the outbreak of war had become No. 10 Bombing and Gunnery School.

In July 1940 an Overstrand broke up in mid-air and all but two examples were subsequently relegated to ground instruction. One of these remaining airworthy Overstrands was allocated to the Balloon Development Unit at Cardington, where it provided a slipstream to test the strength of barrage balloon cables. The other example was transferred to the Army Co-operation Development Unit where it remained in service until mid-1941.

The Overstrand was the last biplane design by the Boulton Paul company, but the power turret was used in a number of subsequent designs, most notably the Defiant.

Originally finished in RAF 1930s standard silver colour scheme, the remaining Overstrands were camouflaged in 1937 and, after retiring from front-line service, remained in this colour scheme when operated by the Air Observer Schools for gunnery training duties.

Specification
Overstrand Mk I
Type: five-seat medium bomber and gunnery trainer
Powerplant: two 580-hp (433-kW) Bristol Pegasus II.M3 radial piston engines
Performance: maximum speed 153 mph (246 km/h) at 6,500 ft (1981 m); service ceiling 22,500 ft (6858 m); range 545 miles (877 km)
Weights: empty 7,936 lb (3600 kg); maximum take-off 12,000 lb (5443 kg)
Dimensions: span 72 ft 0 in (21.95 m); length 46 ft 0 in (14.02 m); height 15 ft 6 in (4.72 m); wing area 980 sq ft (91.04 m²)
Armament: one 0.303-in (7.7-mm) Lewis machine-gun in power-operated nose turret and one 0.303-in (7.7-mm) Lewis machine-gun in dorsal and ventral positions plus up to 1,500 lb (680 kg) of bombs

Boulton Paul P.82 Defiant

A trio of No. 264 (Madras Presidency) Squadron Defiant Mk I day-fighters, comprising L7026 'V', N1535 'A' and L6967 'T' is seen just prior to the Battle of France. The squadron's main duty at the time was fighter patrols in the English Channel area.

Below: No. 264 Squadron moved to Martlesham Heath to receive its first Defiants on 8 December 1939. There were numerous teething troubles with engine malfunctions and problems. The squadron did not attain operational status until 22 March 1940.

Fighters were fighters not just for the reason that they were the fastest and most manoeuvrable of aircraft, but because they carried offensive weapons to attack and destroy other aircraft. This had been a slowly developing process, originating with such weapons as the revolvers which had first been used in anger by pilots or observers of reconnaissance aircraft that took to the skies over the Western Front during World War I. From that point development was rapid, leading first to rifles and then to a variety of machine-guns. By the end of that war, twin machine-guns firing forward and provided with synchronising gear to 'time' the moment of fire of each cartridge so that the bullet passed between the revolving propeller blades, was considered to be the best form of armament for a fighter aircraft.

There was to be little change until the 1930s and the introduction of monoplane fighters. This factor, coupled with the greater reliability of machine-gun mechanisms, made it possible to dispense with the synchronising gear, and to mount the guns in the wing to fire forward, well clear of the propeller disc. So far as the UK was concerned, the ultimate appeared to have been reached with the Hawker Hurricane, which first entered service with the RAF in December 1937. This 40-ft (12.19-m) span fighter carried eight machine-guns, and it can be appreciated that with these eight guns harmonised to concentrate their fire at an optimum aiming point the Hurricane represented a formidable weapon. It was not long, of course, before the fighter aircraft of other nations became similarly equipped, and the tactical advantage held initially by the Hurricane and Supermarine Spitfire was of comparatively short duration.

A new tactical concept, first conceived in 1935, proposed the use in fighters of a power-operated multi-gun turret. This appeared to have more than one advantage: firstly, it relieved the fighter pilot of the dual task of flying the aircraft and concentrating on finding, holding and hitting a target; secondly, the weapons could be used offensively, or defensively, over a far greater field of fire than that possible for a fixed battery. The use of a power-operated turret was not entirely new, however, for a Hawker Demon biplane had been so equipped in 1934, but for a very different reason. The high performance of this two-seat fighter made it almost impossible for the observer/gunner in the aft cockpit to sight and fire the single Lewis gun with sufficient accuracy. A total of 59 Demons was manufactured for Hawker by Boulton Paul Aircraft under sub-contract, and each had a Frazer-Nash hydraulically operated turret installed; in addition, many Demons of Hawker manufacture were modified retrospectively.

Thus, when the Air Ministry issued Specification F.9/35, calling for a two-seat fighter with a power-operated gun turret, both Boulton Paul and Hawker made submissions. The Hawker Hotspur prototype was not, however, to compete against the two which were ordered from Boulton Paul, primarily because the Hawker factories had no productive capacity available, and consequently the Hotspur prototype was abandoned .

Named Defiant, the first of Boulton Paul's prototypes made its initial flight on 11 August 1937. It was a low-wing cantilever monoplane of all-metal construction, provided with retractable tailwheel-type landing gear, and powered by a 1,030-hp (768-kW) Rolls-Royce

Seen in standard 1940 RAF camouflage, this Defiant Mk I, coded 'PS-A' of No. 264 Squadron, was based at RAF Kirton-in-Lindsey in August 1940. It carries the CO's pennant of Sqn Ldr Philip Hunter, who with his gunner Pilot Officer King was killed on 24 August the same year during an engagement with a Junkers Ju 88.

Boulton Paul P.82 Defiant

Above: Defiant NF.Mk II AE370 underwent airborne interception radar trials at A&AEE Boscombe Down in August 1941, equipped with AI Mk IV radar. Note the 'broad arrow' aerials projecting forward from the wing.

Left: Night-fighter Defiants were fitted with flame-dampening exhaust shrouds to make them less visible to the enemy during night operations.

Merlin I inline engine; the second prototype had a Merlin II engine. Both, of course, had the large and heavy four-gun turret mounted within the fuselage aft of the pilot's cockpit. Its weight, and the high degree of drag imposed by the protruding section of the turret, no matter how cleverly faired in, was to impose limits on speed and manoeuvrability.

The first production **Defiant Mk I** day fighter was flown on 30 July 1939, and deliveries to No. 264 Squadron began in December of that year. It was this squadron which first deployed the type operationally, on 12 May 1940 over the beaches of Dunkirk, achieving complete tactical surprise. Fighters making conventional attack on the tail of the Defiants were met with an unprecedented burst of fire from the four machine-guns: on one day they claimed 38 enemy aircraft destroyed, and a total of 65 by the end of May, with most of these successes coming against German bomber formations. It was, however, only brief air superiority, for it did not take long for Luftwaffe fighter pilots to discover that they could attack head-on, or against the belly of the Defiant, with complete immunity. The days of these fighters

In the markings of No. 277 Squadron in December 1941, Defiant Mk I AA326 was based at Stapleford Tawney for air-sea rescue duties. It was used to cover the busy area between southeast England and northern France until May 1943. After retirement from front-line duties it was converted as a TT.Mk III target-tug.

Built as a Mk II, this Defiant TT.Mk I target-tug of No. 286 Squadron was based at Exeter in 1944. It is finished in a day-fighter disruptive camouflage with yellow and black stripes on the undersides. The aircraft was principally flown over the Bristol Channel and southwest England on Army Co-operation duties.

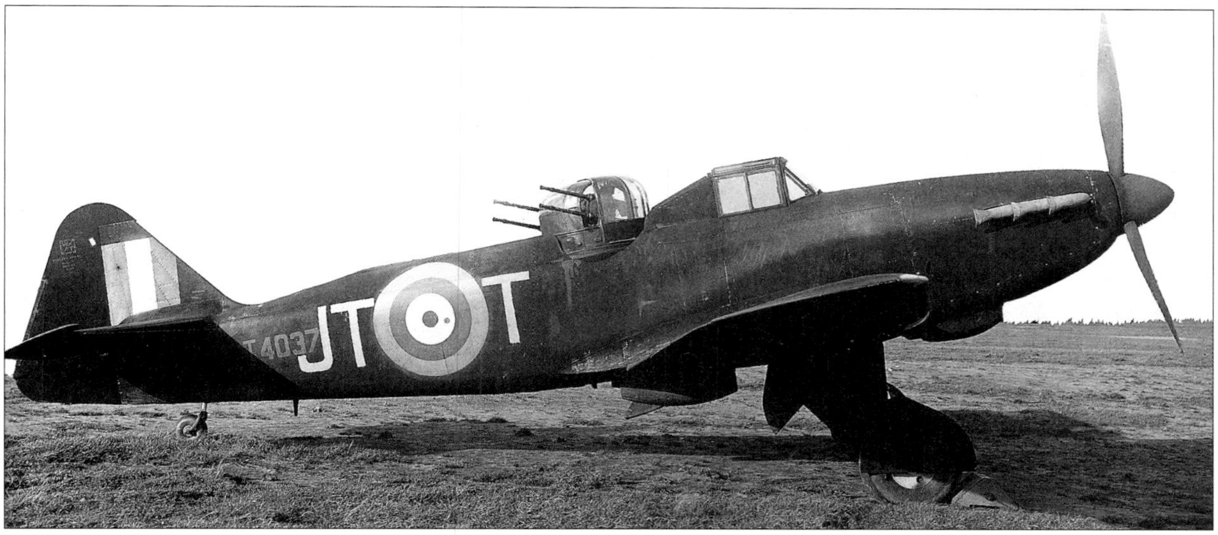

Above: After the initial success and then drastic losses incurred as a day-fighter, the Defiant operated with some success as a night-fighter. This example of an NF.Mk II is shown here in the markings of No. 151 Squadron at RAF Wittering.

Right: No. 256 Squadron at RAF Squires Gate was responsible for the night defence of Liverpool. The squadron operated Defiant Mk I night-fighters from December 1940 until 1942. This view clearly shows how the fuselage top panels retract to give a clear field of fire for the gunner.

were numbered, and they were withdrawn from daylight operations in August 1940.

It was instead decided to use the Defiant in a night-fighter role, and the comparatively new and highly secret AI radar was installed in many of the Mk I aircraft, comprising either AI Mk IV or Mk VI, aircraft so fitted being designated **NF.Mk IA**. With this equipment they were to prove a valuable addition to Britain's night defences in the winter of 1940-41, and during this period they were to record more 'kills' per interception than any other contemporary night-fighter.

In an attempt to improve the performance of the Defiant, two Mk Is served for conversion as prototypes of a new **Mk II** version. Apart from the installation of a more powerful Merlin XX engine, fuel capacity was increased, a rudder of greater area was provided, and there were modifications to the engine cooling and fuel systems. First flown on 20 June 1940, the Defiant Mk II was built to a total of 210 examples, of which many were later converted as **TT.Mk 1** target tugs. In addition, 150 Mk Is were converted to **TT.Mk III**s, and 140 new production TT.Mk Is were built to bring total construction, including prototypes, to 1,065 when production finally ceased in February 1943.

At the peak of its deployment as a night-fighter, Defiants equipped 13 RAF squadrons. They were used subsequently at home, and in the Middle and Far East, as target-tugs, and in addition about 50 Mk Is were modified for use in air/sea rescue role, serving with Nos 275, 276, 277, 280 and 281 Squadrons. The Defiant was also tested in the army co-operation role by No. II(AC) Squadron between August 1940 and August 1941, but was found to be totally unsuitable.

Below: Fitted with target-towing equipment (beneath the rear fuselage) this Defiant TT.Mk III operated in Fleet Air Arm service with No. 776 FRU (Fleet Requirements Unit), flying from Woodvale during the last months of the war.

Specification

Defiant Mk II

Type: two-seat night-fighter
Powerplant: one 1,280-hp (954-kW) Rolls-Royce Merlin XX inline piston engine
Performance: maximum speed 313 mph (504 km/h) at 19,000 ft (5790 m); cruising speed 260 mph (418 km/h); service ceiling 30,350 ft (9250 m); range 465 miles (748 km)
Weights: empty 6,282 lb (2849 kg); maximum take-off 8,424 lb (3821 kg)
Dimensions: span 39 ft 4 in (11.99 m); length 35 ft 4 in (10.77 m); height 11 ft 4 in (3.45 m); wing area 250 sq ft (23.23m^2)
Armament: four 0.303-in (7.7-mm) machine-guns in power-operated dorsal turret

Brewster Bermuda

In 1939 the US Navy ordered a single prototype of a new scout bomber from the Brewster company. Designated **XSB2A-1**, the aircraft was developed from Brewster's first aircraft design, the SBA scout-bomber which was, at the time, entering US Navy service.

Before the prototype had taken to the air the company was extolling the virtues of its new aircraft, claiming that it was a potent combat dive-bomber. The prototype eventually flew on 17 June 1941, and by that time orders stood at 140 for the US Navy, 162 for the Netherlands and 750 for the RAF.

Of all-metal construction and mid-wing monoplane layout, it was proposed that the US version, named Buccaneer, would have an internal bomb bay capable of carrying a 1,000-lb (454-kg) bomb, a powered turret with a 0.5-in (12.7-mm) machine-gun, along with two machine-guns and two cannon firing forwards. The Dutch and RAF versions were to be land-based and incorporated many changes to reflect European wartime experience, including a fixed instead of folding wing and removal of the arrester gear fitted to the US Navy version.

The first examples to arrive in the UK underwent dive-bombing trials with the Aeroplane & Armament Experimental Establishment. This example is carrying a 250-lb (113-kg) bomb beneath each wing pylon.

Designated **Bermuda Mk I** in RAF service, the first examples arrived in Britain under Lend-Lease in July 1942 and underwent evaluation at the A&AEE. It was discovered that the aircraft did not live up to its reputation, and was regarded as entirely unsuitable for combat operations. Being underpowered and overweight, with poor manoeuvrability and handling, the Bermudas were allocated a new role as target-tugs. As examples arrived from the US they were converted with a target drogue attachment fixed to the lower rear fuselage for their new tasking.

Deliveries continued throughout 1943, with 468 Bermudas along with 302 Buccaneers completed by the time production ceased in early 1944. By mid-1944 the US Navy had removed the aircraft from operational service and most of the RAF's examples had been grounded as instructional airframes.

Specification
Bermuda Mk I
Type: two-seat dive-bomber and target-tug
Powerplant: one 1,700-hp (1268-kW) Wright Double Row Cyclone GR-2600 radial piston engine
Performance: maximum speed 284 mph (457 km/h); service ceiling 23,000 ft (7010 m); range 1,675 miles (2696 km)
Weights: empty 9,924 lb (4501 kg); maximum take-off 14,289 lb (6481 kg)
Dimensions: span 47 ft 0 in (14.33 m); length 39 ft 2 in (11.94 m); height 15 ft 5 in (4.70 m); wing area 379 sq ft (35.21 m^2)
Armament: eight 0.3-in (7.62-mm) machine-guns, four in the wings, two in the cowl and two in the rear cockpit on a flexible mounting

Brewster Buffalo

Arising from a US Navy requirement for a carrier-based single-seat fighter, the Brewster **XF2A-1** first flew in December 1937. The type entered production and service in December 1939 as the Navy's first monoplane fighter. It was also the Brewster company's first production programme, and during 1939 it attracted the attention of Belgium, with a contract for 40, followed in 1940 by an order for 170 placed by the British Purchasing Commission. Further large orders were placed by Australia and the Netherlands East Indies.

Belgium's **B-339B**s, similar the US Navy **F2A-2** but devoid of all carrier-specific gear, proved to be the first of the type to enter service in Britain. Deliveries had begun in the spring of 1940, but Belgium had fallen by the time the first aircraft arrived in Europe. Consequently, Britain took over the balance of the Belgian contract, and the first examples were under test at the A&AEE by July 1940. Meanwhile, the name **Buffalo Mk I** had been selected for the British-bought **B-339E**s, delivery of which did not begin until April 1941.

The RAF allocated serial numbers to 39 Belgian Brewsters, but 30 or fewer actually arrived. Three were used briefly to assist

Above: In a scramble to buy as many aircraft as possible after the start of hostilities, Buffaloes were bought from the USA. Because their performance was too poor for the European theatre, they were sent to the Far East, where they were also found to be of limited combat value.

Making a show of strength over Singapore Island before the Japanese attacks began are these Brewster Buffaloes of No. 243 Squadron. Based at Kallang, the squadron received its first Buffalo Mk Is in March 1941. They were found to be no match for the superior Japanese fighters.

the formation of the American-manned No. 71 (Eagle) Squadron before all the available examples were transferred to Admiralty ownership. At least 12 were then used operationally by No. 805 Sqn at Dekheila, in Egypt, and briefly in the defence of Crete.

Only three of the British contract Buffalo Mk Is were brought to the UK (for flight testing), as it had been decided to allocate the type to the Far East, where it was thought it would be "eminently satisfactory for the task". In the event, the Buffalo proved sadly inadequate in combat with Japanese forces. To operate the Brewster fighters, two RAF squadrons, Nos 67 and 243, were stood up at Kallang, Singapore, during 1941, while British aircraft were also used to equip Nos 21 and 453 Sqns of the Royal Australian Air Force, and No. 488 Sqn, Royal New Zealand Air Force, in the same area.

By December 1941, three Buffalo squadrons were in Singapore, No. 21 was in northern Malaya and No. 67 had moved to Burma. All quickly became involved in the attempt to repel the Japanese invasion down the Malayan peninsula and air attacks on targets in Burma. Although the Buffaloes demonstrated useful manoeuvrability in the air, they lacked the speed to pursue bomber formations and to meet Japanese fighters on equal terms. More significantly, their serviceability – operating in conditions far removed from those for which they had been designed – proved extremely poor, the accident rate was high, and major losses were suffered on the ground in bombing raids on their airfield bases. Some 130 Buffaloes were lost in Malaya and Singapore, and of 32 in Burma with No. 67 Sqn, only three were serviceable by the end of February 1942. Of this trio, just one reached Calcutta after passing to No. 146 Sqn at Assam. Possibly the best service rendered to the RAF by the type was given by just two aircraft, flown by No. 4 PRU Flight. With cameras replacing all armour and armament, these aircraft flew more than 100 sorties from Singapore through December and January, providing vital information on the movement of Japanese forces.

Specification
Buffalo Mk I
Type: single-seat fighter
Powerplant: one 1,100-hp (820-kW) Wright Cyclone GR-1820-G 105A radial piston engine
Performance: maximum speed 292 mph (470 km/h) at 20,000 ft (6096 m); cruising speed 255 mph (410 km/h); service ceiling 30,500 ft (9296 m); normal range 650 miles (1046 km)
Weights: empty 4,479 lb (2032 kg); maximum take-off 6,840 lb (3101 kg)
Dimensions: span 35 ft 0 in (10.67 m); length 26 ft 0 in (7.92 m); height 12 ft 1 in (3.68 m); wing area 209 sq ft (19.42 m²)
Armament: four 0.5-in (12.7-mm) or 0.303-in (7.7-mm) machine-guns, two in the fuselage and two in the wings

These Buffaloes, belonging to No. 453 Squadron, RAAF, were based at Sembawang in Singapore in November 1941. They fought briefly in the disastrous campaign against the invading Japanese forces.

Bristol Type 130 Bombay

Designed as a replacement for the Vickers Valentia serving in the Middle East and India, the Bristol **Type 130 Bombay** was intended as a troop or cargo carrier. It had also to be capable of self-defence and to double as a long-range bomber. The prototype made its first flight from Filton on 23 June 1935 flown by Cyril Uwins. Military trials at the A&AEE, Martlesham Heath, were undertaken by Flt Lt 'Bill' Pegg, later to join the company and become its chief test pilot. Development testing resulted in various improvements being made, including the installation of the more powerful Bristol Pegasus XXII engines.

A production contract for a batch of 50 was awarded, but with Filton's production lines geared to the Blenheim it was decided that production would be undertaken by Short Brothers & Harland in Belfast.

The first production Bombay flew in March 1939, and the initial squadron to receive the type was No. 216 in Egypt the following September. Other deliveries followed to Nos 117, 267 and 271 Squadrons, and Bombays fulfilled their dual transport and bomber roles during the Libyan campaign of 1940. Although few in number, the Bombays were very active, and among their achievements was the evacuation of the Greek royal family from Crete to Egypt. A few UK-based aircraft ferried supplies across the English Channel before the collapse of France.

As the bomber/transport idea became outdated, Bombays were eventually replaced by more modern types and the type passed out of service in the mid-1940s.

Specification
Bombay Mk I
Type: bomber-transport with a crew of 3 and up to 24 troops
Powerplant: two 1,010-hp (753-kW) Bristol Pegasus XXII radial piston engines
Performance: maximum speed 192 mph (309 km/h) at 6,500 ft (1980 m); cruising speed 160 mph (257 km/h) at 10,000 ft (3050 m); service ceiling 25,000 ft (7620 m); range 880 miles (1416 km) or 2,230 miles (3589 km) with fuselage tanks
Weights: empty 13,800 lb (6260 kg); maximum take-off 20,000 lb (9072 kg)
Dimensions: span 95 ft 9 in (29.18 m); length 69 ft 3 in (21.11 m); height 19 ft 11 in (6.07 m); wing area 1,340 sq ft (124.49 m²)
Armament: two 0.303-in (7.7-mm) Vickers 'K' machine-guns (one each in nose and tail turrets) plus up to 2,000 lb (907 kg) of bombs

Left: A trio of No. 216 Squadron's Bombays dispatches soldiers from what was to become the SAS regiment, during November 1941. Bombays participated in the first operational airborne deployment of paratroops in North Africa.

Flown as a transport and night bomber carrying 24 troops or a 2,000-lb bomb load, this Bombay Mk I of No. 216 Squadron was based at Heliopolis, El Khanka and Cairo West, Egypt in 1940-41. The squadron finally replaced its Bombays in May 1943.

Bristol 142M, 149 & 160 Blenheim

Great Britain's *Daily Mail* newspaper had championed the cause of aviation from the very beginning of powered flight, with Lord Northcliffe ever ready to remind his readers that the world was on the threshold of a new era of scientific and technical progress that would affect the lives of all its citizens. It was he who, in 1906, engaged one Harry Harper to become the world's first aviation journalist and, between them, the idea of the famous *Daily Mail* prizes for progress in aviation was born. The first of those prizes went to A. V. Roe in 1907, his elastic-powered biplane proving an easy winner of the Model Aeroplane Competition held at London's Alexandra Palace. A whole series of 'encouragement' prizes followed, highlighting such powered aircraft flights as the first 'all-British', the first London-to-Manchester, the first Channel crossing, the first circuit of Britain, and the first non-stop Atlantic crossing.

Such a background will help to explain to the uninitiated why in 1934 Lord Rothermere, who was then proprietor of the *Daily Mail*, should have expressed a desire to obtain for his personal use a fast and

Top: The Blenheim's progenitor, the original Type 142, was named* Britain First *and was instrumental in disrupting the complacency of the time, with its phenomenal performance. This performance, which revolutionised official thinking, bettered by some 30 mph (48 km/h) the highest speeds then attainable by fighters in service with the RAF.

Left: The air component of the British Expeditionary Force in France boasted two squadrons of Blenheim Mk IVs, Nos 53 and 59 both based at Poix, for long-range tactical reconnaissance and bombing. A formation of nine Blenheims of No. 59 Squadron is seen flying low over their base.

Below: The Blenheim Mk IF was the RAF's only practical night-fighter at the beginning of the war. It 1940 already equipped No. 25 Squadron operating from North Weald and Martlesham Heath, and No. 29 Squadron at Debden and Wellingore.

***Left:** At a desert strip in Egypt, ground crew of No. 113 Squadron bomb-up a Blenheim Mk I for a sortie over the Western Desert in 1940. The Blenheim Mk I was almost entirely replaced by the Blenheim Mk IV in the desert campaign during 1941-42.*

***Below:** Serving with No. 54 Operational Training Unit based at RAF Church Fenton in the summer of 1941, Blenheim Mk IF 'YX-N' was one of many former front-line Mk Is which were relegated to training duties as the war progressed. The aircraft's code letter is outlined in yellow and the outer circle of the roundel is overpainted. It later passed to No. 12 (PA) AFU, with whom it crashed on 6 May 1943.*

spacious private aircraft, for this aviation-minded organisation had then appreciated the potential of what is today called the business or corporate aircraft. Lord Rothermere envisaged his requirements as a fast aircraft that would accommodate a crew of two and six passengers, and it just so happened that the Bristol Aeroplane Company had already drawn up the outline of a light transport in this category.

The brain-child was the doyen of Bristol's designer, Frank Barnwel. The new aircraft had been designed originally to be powered by two 500-hp (373-kW) Bristol Aquila I engines which were then under development. Lord Rothermere's interest in a high-speed transport resulted in Barnwell's proposal to mount a couple of 650-hp (485-kW) Bristol Mercury VIS engines in his embryo airframe, and this was to result in the Bristol **Type 142**. First flown at Filton on 12 April 1935, it was to spark off a hubbub of comment and excitement when, during its initial trials, it was found to be some 30 mph (48 km/h) faster than the prototype of Britain's most-recently procured fighter. Named *Britain First*, it was presented to the nation by Lord Rothermere after the Air Ministry had requested that it might retain it for a period of testing to evaluate its potential as a light bomber. This, then, was the sire of the Bristol Blenheim which was to prove an important interim weapon at the beginning of World War II.

Aware of Air Ministry interest in the Type 142, Bristol busied itself with homework to evolve a military version (**Type 142M**) of this aircraft, and in the summer of 1935 the Air Ministry decided to accept the company's proposal, placing a first order for 150 aircraft to Specification 28/35 in September. The new aircraft was very similar to the Type 142, but there had, of course, been some changes to make it suitable for the military role, primarily to accommodate a bomb-aimer's station, a bomb bay and a dorsal gun turret. Little time was lost by either the Bristol company or the Air Ministry, for, following the first flight of the prototype on 25 June 1936, initial deliveries to RAF squadrons began in March 1937, and in July 1937 the Air Ministry placed a follow-on order for 434 additional **Blenheim Mk I**s, as the type had by then been named.

***Above:** In September 1940, No. 84 Squadron was transferred to Egypt. Subsequently, in November its Blenheim Mk Is were sent on to Greece for operations against the Italians in Albania.*

***Right:** As war in Europe loomed, more squadrons were equipped with the Blenheim. This Blenheim Mk I of No. 90 Squadron was based at RAF Bicester in 1938. It became a training squadron for No. 6 Group on the outbreak of war in September 1939.*

Bristol Blenheim Mk IF

This is a Blenheim Mk IF of No. 25 (Fighter) Squadron based at Hawkinge, Kent, immediately prior to the outbreak of World War II. Points of interest include the black-and-white undersurfaces, the squadron codes 'RX' (changed to 'ZK' in September 1939) and the squadron badge (obliterated when hostilities started) on the fin. The four-gun belly pack was a feature of most Blenheim fighters (including the Mk IVF), but the single gas-operated Lewis gun in the semi-retractable dorsal turret was a relic of the inter-war conviction that single dorsal gun armament constituted adequate tail protection for 'fast' aircraft.

Powerplant
The switch from Bristol Aquila to Bristol Mercury engines during design work on the Type 142 proved to be one of the more important factors in the success of the Blenheim. The Mk I was powered by Mercury VIIIs which developed 840 hp (627 kW). The engine proved to have good reliability and was used in subsequent variants.

Raised wing
Although largely based on the Type 142, the production Blenheim Mk I had its wings, along with the engine nacelles and landing gear, raised about 16 in (41 cm). This allowed internal bomb-storage inside the fuselage below the wing spars, making the aircraft practically a 'middle-wing'. The wing itself was built along standard lines, with two large spars with heavy but widely spaced ribs.

Left: A formation of Blenheim Mk IVs of No. 139 Squadron are seen flying a combat mission over France in 1940. This unit went across the Channel in September 1939 and, flying from Plivot, sustained heavy losses while making unescorted daylight attacks on German infantry columns as the invasion advanced westward towards the Channel ports.

Below: Like its predecessor, the Mk I, many Mk IVs were used by Operational Training Units to train fresh bomber crews. No. 13 OTU formed at Bicester in April 1940 and initially retained the codes of the two formative squadrons, Nos 104 and 108. However, it soon introduced its own 'FV' code letters for its Blenheim Mk IVs.

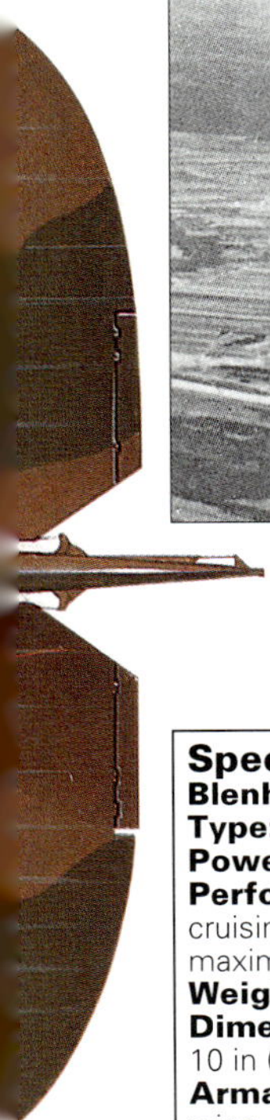

Specification
Blenheim Mk IV
Type: three-seat light bomber
Powerplant: two 905-hp (675-kW) Bristol Mercury XV radial piston engines
Performance: maximum speed 266 mph (428 km/h) at 11,800 ft (3595 m); cruising speed 198 mph (319 km/h); service ceiling 27,260 ft (8310 m); maximum range 1,460 miles (2350 km)
Weights: empty 9,790 lb (4441 kg); maximum take-off 14,400 lb (65.32 kg)
Dimensions: span 56 ft 4 in (17.17 m); length 42 ft 7 in (12.98 m); height 9 ft 10 in (3.00 m); wing area 469 sq ft (43.57 m²)
Armament: five 0.303-in (7.7-mm) machine-guns (one forward-firing in port wing, two in power-operated dorsal turret, and two remotely controlled in mounting beneath nose and firing aft), plus up to 1,000 lb (434 kg) of bombs internally and 320 lb (145 kg) of bombs externally

Below: At the outbreak of World War II production of the Blenheim Mk IV at Bristol's main factory at Filton had reached maximum capacity. A total of 312 of this variant was built there along with 2,860 built elsewhere by licensees or other contractors.

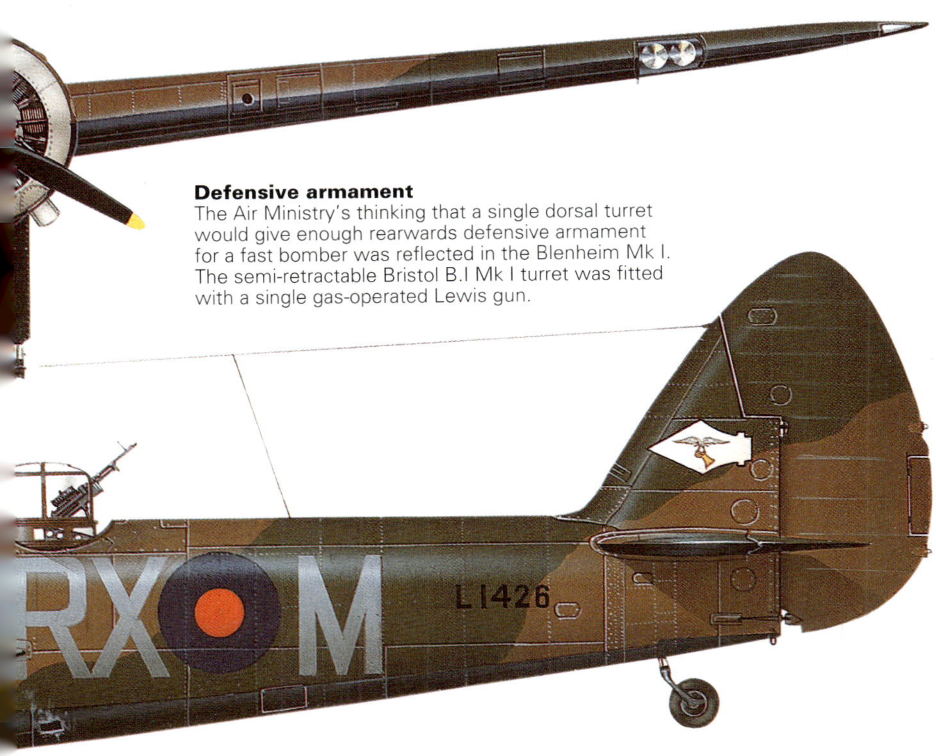

Defensive armament
The Air Ministry's thinking that a single dorsal turret would give enough rearwards defensive armament for a fast bomber was reflected in the Blenheim Mk I. The semi-retractable Bristol B.I Mk I turret was fitted with a single gas-operated Lewis gun.

Undercarriage
The fixed tailwheel was originally designed to be retractable, but this offered no notable increase in performance. As operations were mainly from grass airfields, the tailwheel was fitted with a strong shock absorber. The single mainwheels were mounted on sturdy twin-strut units, retracting backwards to lie semi-recessed in the rear of the engine nacelles.

Bristol 142M, 149 & 160 Blenheim

The first 68 Blenheim Mk IVs produced were actually modified Mk I airframes, and to distinguish true production aircraft from these hybrids, they were designated as Blenheim Mk IVLs. This Mk IVL flew with No. 18 (Burma) Squadron in Egypt during 1942.

Of all-metal construction, except for fabric-covered control surfaces, the Blenheim Mk I was a cantilever mid-wing monoplane, with the wing having Frise mass-balanced ailerons and split trailing-edge flaps. The fuselage nose extended only slightly forward of the engines, and both fuselage and tail unit were conventional light alloy structures. Landing gear was of the retractable tailwheel type. The tailwheel of the prototype had also been retractable, operated by cables linked to the main landing gear but, wisely, this feature was not carried forward into the production aircraft. The powerplant comprised two 840-hp (626-kW) Bristol Mercury VIII engines, mounted in nacelles on the wing leading edge, and driving three-bladed variable-pitch propellers. Accommodation was provided for a pilot, navigator/bomb-aimer, and air gunner/radio operator. A bomb bay in the wing centre-section could contain a maximum 1,000 lb (454 kg) of bombs, and standard armament comprised a 0.303-in (7.7-mm) machine-gun in the port wing, plus a Vickers 'K' gun in the dorsal turret.

The first RAF squadron to receive Blenheim Mk Is was No. 114, then based at RAF Wyton, and it was this unit which first demonstrated the new type officially to the public at the RAF's final Hendon Display in the summer of 1937. The Blenheims were to arouse excited comment with their high speed and modern appearance, being launched on their career in an aura of emotion created by the belief that, in an unsettled Europe, the RAF was armed with the world's most formidable bomber aircraft. Production contracts soared, necessitating the establishment of new construction lines by A. V. Roe at Chadderton and Rootes Securities at Speke and at Meir, both these factories being in Lancashire. Between them, the three lines built a total of 1,552 Blenheim Mk Is which, at their peak, equipped no fewer than 20 RAF squadrons at home and overseas. The Blenheim's first overseas deployments was with No. 30 Squadron in Iraq and No. 11 Squadron in India, in January and July 1938, respectively.

However, by the outbreak of World War II few Blenheim Mk Is remained in service with home-based bomber squadrons, having been superseded in the bombing role by the **Blenheim Mk IV**, which incorporated the lessons learned from the experience which squadrons had gained in operating the Mk I. But their usefulness was by no means ended, many continuing to serve as conversion trainers and, initially, as crew trainers in OTUs. More valuable by far were some 200 which were converted to serve as night-fighters, pioneering the newly conceived technique of AI (Airborne Interception) radar, carrying AI Mk III or Mk IV. The single forward-firing machine-gun was totally inadequate for this role, of course, and a special underfuselage pack to house four 0.303-in (7.7-mm) machine-guns was produced. So equipped, **Blenheim Mk IF**s scored the first AI success against an enemy aircraft on the night of 2-3 July 1940.

Export versions of the Blenheim Mk I were sold before the war to Finland, Turkey and Yugoslavia and were also built under licence by these first two nations. In addition, a small number had been supplied to Romania as a diplomatic bribe in 1939, but this proved to be unsuccessful. The result, of course, was that Blenheim Mk Is fought for and against the Allies.

When, in August 1935, the Air Ministry had initiated Specification

Blenheim Mk IV, L8756 'XD-E', operated with No. 139 Squadron based at RAF Horsham St Faith in 1940. The Blenheim-equipped daylight bombing squadrons suffered major losses during the early stages of World War II. However, one survivor was this aircraft, which was relegated to training duties until it was withdrawn from service in 1944.

Based at Aqir, Palestine in April 1944, this Blenheim Mk IV served with No. 84 Squadron. The squadron returned to Habbaniyah in Iraq for a short time before resuming bombing raids in the Western Desert in November 1941. The squadron was posted to the Far East in early 1942.

Blenheim Mk IVs played a significant part in the first years of the desert campaigns, particularly during Operation Crusader when seven squadrons and a detachment were involved. The nearest aircraft, Z5893, displays its rear-firing machine-gun located under the nose, to counter attacks from behind.

G.24/35 to find a successor to the Avro Anson for use in a coastal reconnaissance/light bomber role. Bristol had proposed its **Type 149**. Very similar to the Blenheim Mk I, this was based on the use of Bristol Aquila engines to confer long range with the existing fuel capacity, but proved unacceptable to the Air Ministry. Subsequently, renewed interest was shown in the Type 149 for use in a general-reconnaissance role, and a prototype was built, by conversion of an early Blenheim Mk I, this retaining the Mercury VIII engines and being provided with increased fuel capacity. The fuselage nose was lengthened to provide additional accommodation for the navigator/observer and his equipment, and this was to be finalised as that which graced the Blenheim Mk IV.

The Air Ministry then had misgivings about the Type 149, fearing that its introduction and manufacture would interfere with the production of urgently needed Blenheims. Instead, the Type 149 was adopted by the Royal Canadian Air Force for production in Canada as the **Bolingbroke Mk I**, the Bristol prototype being shipped to Canada to help in the establishment of a production line by Fairchild Aircraft at Longueuil, Quebec. The first Bolingbroke Mk Is had Mercury VIII engines and came off the production line in the second half of 1939. After 18 of these had been built production changed to the definitive Canadian version, the **Bolingbroke Mk IV** with Mercury XV engines, and equipment from Canadian and US manufacturers. Later variants included a small number of **Bolingbroke Mk**

In late 1940, this Blenheim Mk IVF was used by Coastal Command for reconnaissance flights off the Norwegian coast and attacks on enemy shipping from the Shetlands, where No. 248 Squadron was based on detachment.

Below: The nose of the Blenheim Mk IV was redesigned to bring the windscreen closer to the pilot. The scalloping (on the port side only) gave the pilot a better view, but gave the nose a characteristic asymmetric appearance.

Below: This is a late-production Rootes-built Blenheim Mk IV in 1941, carrying the code letters of No. 13 OTU. The Bristol mid-upper turret and nose turret were both equipped with a pair of Browning machine-guns. This aircraft features a modified leading edge with balloon cable-cutters.

In RAF desert-style camouflage, this Blenheim Mk V, BA491 'L', served with No. 614 (County of Glamorgan) Squadron, based at Canrobert, Algeria in January 1942. Sorties included attacks on the German-held ports of Bizerta and Tunis as well as airfields and lines of communication.

After the withdrawal of the Blenheim Mk V from combat status in Europe, the type was relegated to advanced pilot training duties. The aircraft shown here, AZ959 '48', served with No. 12 (P)AFU at Grantham during 1944.

IVWs with 1,200-hp (895-kW) Pratt & Whitney R-1830 Twin Wasp engines, a single **Bolingbroke Mk IVC** with Wright R-1820 Cyclone G3Bs, and a number of **Bolingbroke Mk IVT** multi-purpose trainers.

There was a sudden renewal of interest in the Type 149, primarily as an interim measure until the Type 152 torpedo-bomber, derived from the Blenheim, should become available. The decision was taken, therefore, to introduce the longer nose and stepped windscreen of the Bolingbroke, and to make provision for longer range by the introduction of increased wing fuel capacity. The Bristol designation Type 149 was retained for this changed configuration, the new RAF designation being Blenheim Mk IV. This change took place quietly on the production lines towards the end of 1938, although the first 68 Blenheim Mk IVs were built without the 'long-range wing'. The powerplant comprised two more-powerful Mercury XV engines, and these allowed gross weight to be increased eventually by 16 per cent.

No. 90 Squadron was the initial unit to be equipped with Blenheim Mk IVs in March 1938, the first of more than 70 squadrons to operate these aircraft, consisting of units from Army Co-operation, Bomber, Coastal, Far East Bomber, Fighter and Middle East Commands, both at home and overseas. Inevitably, such extensive use brought changes in armament and equipment, but especially the former, for the armament of the first Blenheim IVs was unchanged from the initial two-gun armament of the Mk I. As finalised, the number became five, the single forward-firing gun in the wing being retained, a new dorsal turret carrying two guns being adopted, and a completely new remotely-controlled Frazer-Nash mounting being added beneath the nose to hold two aft-firing machine-guns. Protective armour was also increased, but, while it was not possible to enlarge the capacity of the bomb bay, provision was made for an additional 320 lb (145 kg) of bombs to be carried externally, under the inner wings, for short-range missions.

With so many squadrons operating the type it was inevitable that Blenheims should notch up many wartime 'firsts' for the RAF. These included the first reconnaissance over German territory, made on 3 September 1939 by a Blenheim Mk IV of No. 139 Squadron. The type was the first to drop bombs on German targets, on 4 September 1939, when 10 aircraft from Nos 107 and 110 Squadrons made an attack on the German fleet in the Schillig Roads, off Wilhelmshaven. From the beginning of the war, until replaced in home squadrons of Bomber Command by Douglas Bostons and de Havilland Mosquitoes in 1942, Blenheim Mk IVs were used extensively in the European theatre. Although vulnerable to fighter attack, they were frequently used for unescorted daylight operations and undoubtedly the skill of their crews and the aircraft's ability to absorb a great deal of punishment were the primary reasons for their survival, for high speed and heavy firepower was certainly not their *forte*. In the overseas squadrons Blenheims continued to serve long after their usefulness had ended in Europe, and, except in Singapore where they were no match for the Japanese fighters, they proved a valuable weapon. A total of 1,930 had been built when production ended, and in addition to serving with the

The Blenheim Mk V gave valuable service in the Malayan campaign where the damp climate prooved unsuitable for the wooden Mosquito.

Bristol Blenheim Mk IV cutaway drawing key

1 Starboard navigation light
2 Starboard formation light
3 Wing rib construction
4 Aileron control rod
5 Starboard aileron
6 Aileron tab
7 Starboard outer flap
8 Outboard, long-range fuel tank, capacity 94 Imp gal (427 litres)
9 Fuel tank filler cap
10 Starboard nacelle fairing
11 Main inboard fuel tank, capacity 140 Imp gal (636 litres)
12 Oil tank, capacity 11.5 Imp gal (52 litres)
13 Engine bearers
14 Oil cooler exhaust duct
15 Engine cooling flaps
16 Cowling blister fairings
17 Bristol Mercury XV nine-cylinder radial engine
18 Oil cooler ram air intakes
19 Propeller hub mechanism
20 De Havilland three-bladed propeller
21 Nose compartment glazing
22 Cabin air intake
23 Navigator/bombardier's instrument panel
24 Bomb aiming windows
25 Pitot tube
26 Rearward-firing, ventral machine-gun cupola
27 Browning 0.303-in (7.7-mm) machine-gun
28 Fireman's axe
29 Nose companment escape hatch
30 Fire extinguisher
31 Chart table
32 Fixed foresight
33 Back of instrument panel
34 Foot boards
35 Rudder pedals
36 Compass
37 Control column
38 Windscreen panels
39 Pilot's gunsight
40 Navigator/bombardier's seat
41 Pilot's seat
42 Engine throttles
43 Venturi tube
44 Pilot's blister observation window
45 Armoured headrest
46 Cockpit roof sliding hatch
47 Parachute stowage
48 Wing centre-section construction
49 Sliding hatch rails
50 Aerial mast
51 Parachute stowage
52 Wing centre-section attachment frame
53 Pneumatic system compressed air bottle
54 Three-man dinghy
55 First aid box
56 Fuselage double frame
57 Rear gunner's entry/emergency escape hatch
58 Rear gunner's seat
59 Gun turret
60 Two Browning 0.303-in (7.7-mm) machine-guns
61 Aerial cable
62 Fuselage skin plating
63 Starboard tailplane
64 Starboard elevator
65 Fin construction

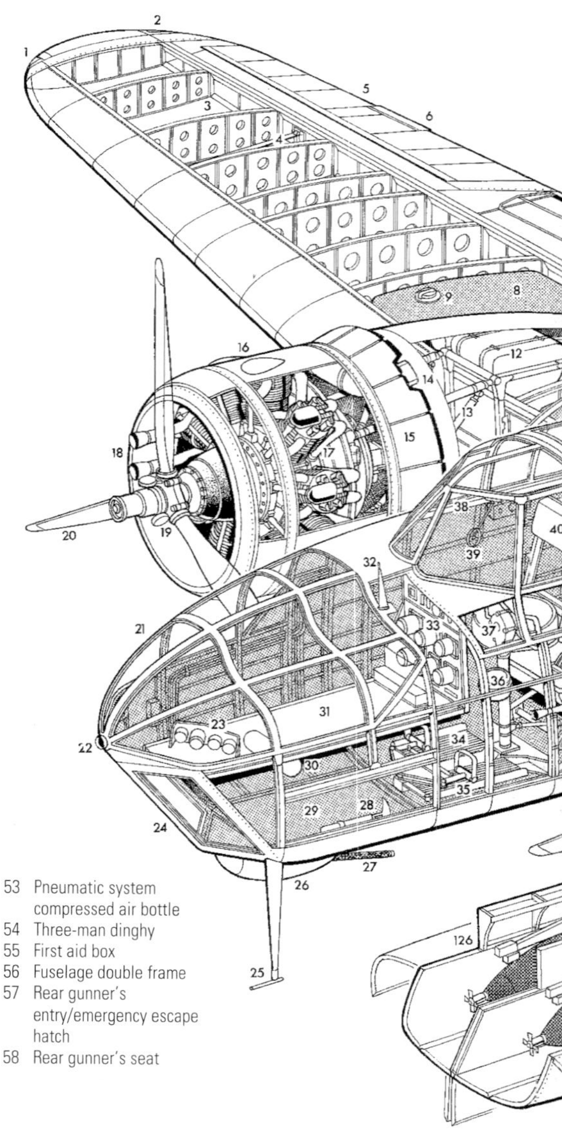

No. 248 Squadron of RAF Coastal Command operated seven Blenheim Mk IVFs from February 1940 to July 1941 based at North Coates. The Mk IVF was adapted from the standard Mk IV bomber by the addition of four fixed 0.303-in (7.7-mm) Browning machine-guns in a self-contained battery under the bomb cell.

RAF they had been used by the French Free and South African air forces, and supplied in small numbers to Finland, Greece and Turkey.

Last of the direct developments of the Blenheim design was Bristol's **Type 160**, known briefly as the **Bisley**, which was to enter service in the summer of 1942 as the **Blenheim Mk V**. Envisaged originally as a low-altitude close-support bomber, it was in fact to be built for deployment as a high-altitude bomber, powered by Mercury XV or XXV engines. Except for a changed nose, some alterations in detail and updated equipment, these aircraft were basically the same as their predecessors. Some 940 were built, all produced by Rootes at its Speke and Stoke-on-Trent factories, and the first unit to receive Blenheim Mk Vs was No. 18 Squadron. The type was to equip six squadrons in the Middle East and four in the Far East, where they were used without distinction. This resulted from an increase in gross weight of over 17 per cent which, without the introduction of more powerful engines, had brought about a serious fall in performance. It was only when the Blenheim Mk Vs were deployed in the Italian campaign, contending with the advanced fighters in service with the Luftwaffe, that losses rose to quite unacceptable proportions, and the Blenheim Vs were withdrawn from service.

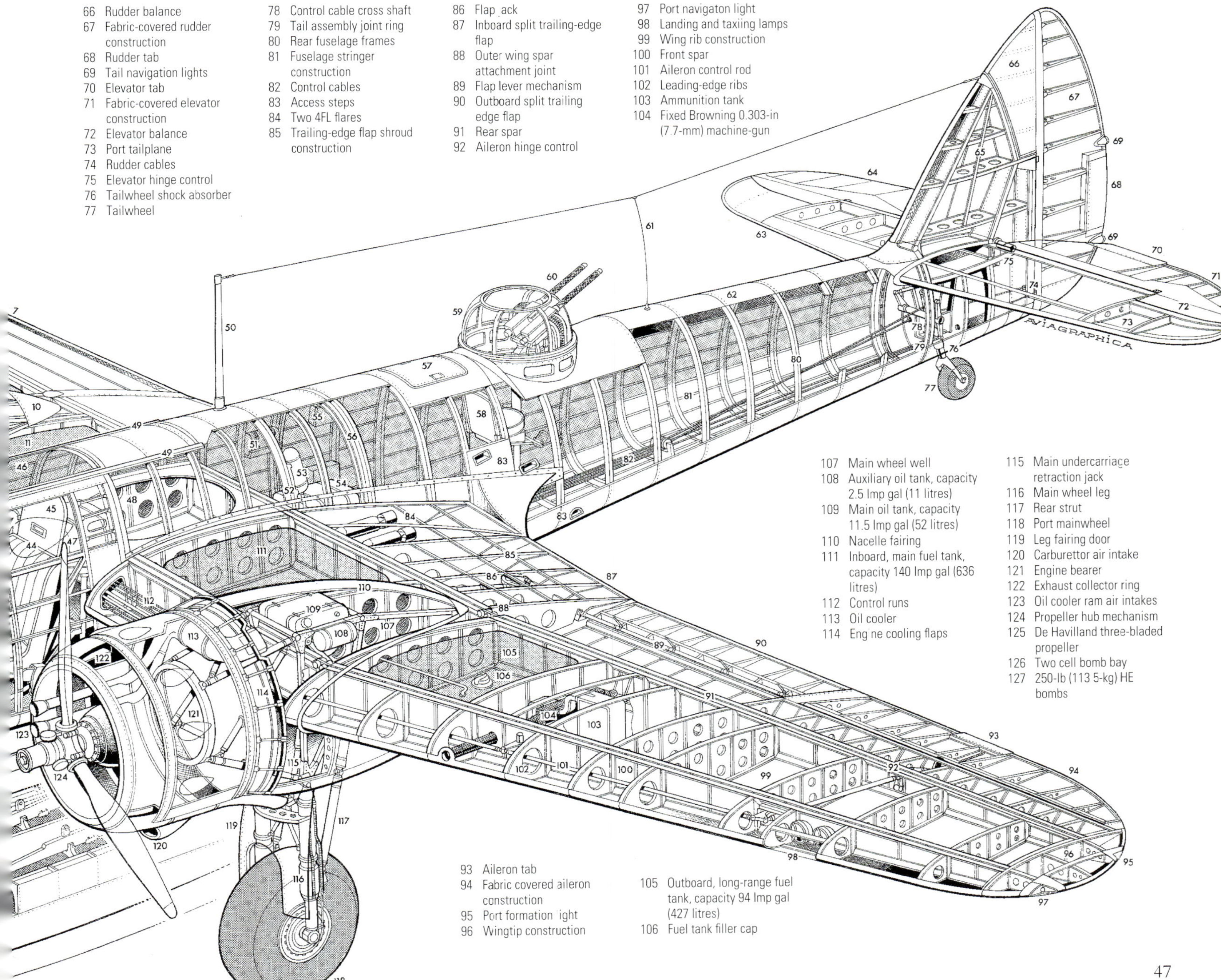

66 Rudder balance
67 Fabric-covered rudder construction
68 Rudder tab
69 Tail navigation lights
70 Elevator tab
71 Fabric-covered elevator construction
72 Elevator balance
73 Port tailplane
74 Rudder cables
75 Elevator hinge control
76 Tailwheel shock absorber
77 Tailwheel
78 Control cable cross shaft
79 Tail assembly joint ring
80 Rear fuselage frames
81 Fuselage stringer construction
82 Control cables
83 Access steps
84 Two 4FL flares
85 Trailing-edge flap shroud construction
86 Flap jack
87 Inboard split trailing-edge flap
88 Outer wing spar attachment joint
89 Flap lever mechanism
90 Outboard split trailing edge flap
91 Rear spar
92 Aileron hinge control
93 Aileron tab
94 Fabric covered aileron construction
95 Port formation light
96 Wingtip construction
97 Port navigaton light
98 Landing and taxiing lamps
99 Wing rib construction
100 Front spar
101 Aileron control rod
102 Leading-edge ribs
103 Ammunition tank
104 Fixed Browning 0.303-in (7.7-mm) machine-gun
105 Outboard, long-range fuel tank, capacity 94 Imp gal (427 litres)
106 Fuel tank filler cap
107 Main wheel well
108 Auxiliary oil tank, capacity 2.5 Imp gal (11 litres)
109 Main oil tank, capacity 11.5 Imp gal (52 litres)
110 Nacelle fairing
111 Inboard, main fuel tank, capacity 140 Imp gal (636 litres)
112 Control runs
113 Oil cooler
114 Engine cooling flaps
115 Main undercarriage retraction jack
116 Main wheel leg
117 Rear strut
118 Port mainwheel
119 Leg fairing door
120 Carburettor air intake
121 Engine bearer
122 Exhaust collector ring
123 Oil cooler ram air intakes
124 Propeller hub mechanism
125 De Havilland three-bladed propeller
126 Two cell bomb bay
127 250-lb (113 5-kg) HE bombs

Bristol Type 152 Beaufort

Showing the aircraft's substantial forward fuselage section which housed the crew, radio office, defensive armament and semi-recessed torpedo, this Beaufort Mk I L9878 flew with No. 217 Squadron, RAF Coastal Command.

Below: The size of the 1,605-lb (728-kg) torpedo carried by Coastal Command's Beauforts is apparent as ground crew manhandle 11 such weapons towards aircraft from No. 22 Squadron based at Thorney Island.

In 1935 the Air Ministry had issued two specifications, M.15/35 and G.24/35, which detailed requirements for a torpedo-bomber and a general reconnaissance/bomber, respectively. The latter was required to replace the Avro Anson in service for this role and, as mentioned in the Bristol Blenheim entry, was to be met by the Bristol Type 149 which was built in Canada as the Bolingbroke. To meet the first requirement, for a torpedo-bomber, Bristol began by considering an adaptation of the Blenheim, identifying its design as the **Type 150**. This proposal, which was concerned primarily with a change in fuselage design to provide accommodation for a torpedo and the installation of more powerful engines, was submitted to the Air Ministry in November 1935.

After sending off these details of the Type 150, the Bristol design team came to the conclusion that it would be possible to meet both of the Air Ministry's specifications by a single aircraft evolved from the Blenheim, and immediately prepared a new design outline, the **Type 152**. By comparison with the Blenheim Mk IV, the new design was increased slightly in length to allow for the carriage of a torpedo in a semi-exposed position, provided a navigation station, and seated pilot and navigator side-by-side; behind them were radio and camera positions which would be manned by a gunner/camera/radio operator. The Type 152 was more attractive to the Air Ministry, but it was considered that a crew of four was essential, and the accommodation was redesigned to this end. The resulting high roof line, which continued unbroken to the dorsal turret, became a distinguishing feature of this new aircraft, built to Air Ministry Specification 10/36, and subsequently named Beaufort.

Right: In November 1939 No. 22 Squadron, based at Thorney Island, replaced its Vickers Vildebeests with the Beaufort Mk I. In April 1940 the squadron moved to North Coates, and during March 1941 the squadron destroyed 16,500 tons (16765 tonnes) of enemy shipping for the loss of two aircraft.

In March 1942 No. 22 Squadron left the UK, and its Beaufort Mk Is, such as this example, were shipped to Ceylon. The squadron continued to fly its Beauforts on anti-shipping patrols and convoy escort duties until it re-equipped with the Beaufighter in June 1944. The squadron remained in the Far East until it disbanded at the end of the war.

Detail design was initiated immediately, but early analysis and estimates showed that the intended powerplant of two Bristol Perseus engines would provide insufficient power to cater for the increase of almost 25 per cent in gross weight without a serious loss of performance. Instead, the newly developed twin-row Taurus sleeve-valve engine was selected for the Beaufort, the only concern being whether it would be cleared for production in time to coincide with the construction of the new airframe. The initial contract, for 78 aircraft, was placed in August 1936, but the first prototype did not fly until just over two years later, on 15 October 1938. There had been a number of reasons for this long period of labour, one being overheating problems with the powerplant, and another the need to disperse the Blenheim production line to shadow factories before the Beaufort could be built.

Test flying of the prototype revealed a number of shortcomings, leading to the provision of doors to enclose the main landing gear units when retracted, repositioning of the engine exhausts, and an increase to two machine-guns in the dorsal turret. These, and other items, added to the continuing teething problems with the new engine, delayed the entry into service of the **Beaufort Mk I**s, these first equipping No. 22 Squadron of Coastal Command in January 1940. It was this unit which, on the night of 15-16 April 1940, began the Beaufort's operational career by laying mines in enemy coastal waters, but in the following month all in-service aircraft were grounded until engine modifications could be carried out.

Earlier, the Australian government had shown interest in the Beaufort, and following the visit of a British Air Mission in early 1939, it was decided that railway and industrial workshops could be adapted to produce these aircraft, resulting in the establishment of two assembly plants (at Fishermen's Bend, Melbourne, and at Mascot, Sydney) with the production backing of railway workshops at Chullora, Islington and Newport. Twenty sets of airframe parts and the eighth production aircraft as a working sample were shipped out, but at an early stage the Australians decided they did not want the Taurus powerplant. Accordingly, they obtained a licence from Pratt & Whitney to build the Twin Wasp, and these were to power all Australian-built Beauforts, which eventually totalled 700.

Australian production began in 1940, the first Australian **Beaufort Mk V** making its initial flight in May 1941. These were generally similar to their British counterparts except for the change in engines and an increase in fin area to improve stability with the powerful Twin Wasp engine. In fact, engine and propeller changes accounted for most of the different variants produced by the Australian factories. These included the Beaufort V (50) and **Beaufort Mk VA** (30), both with licence-built Twin Wasp S3C4-G engines; **Beaufort Mk VI** (60 with Curtiss propellers) and **Beaufort Mk VII** (40 with Hamilton propellers), all 100 being powered by imported SlC3-G Twin Wasps due to insufficient licence-production; and the **Beaufort Mk VIII** with licence-built S3C4-Gs. This last mark was the definitive production version, of which 520 were built, and had additional fuel tankage, Loran navigation system and variations in armament, with production ending in August 1944. Some 46 of the last production batch were subsequently converted to serve as unarmed transports; designated **Beaufort Mk IX**, this variant had the dorsal turret removed and the resulting aperture faired in. The powerplant rating of all the Australian versions was 1,200 hp (895 kW). The Beaufort was used extensively by the Royal Australian Air Force in the Pacific theatre, serving from the summer of 1942 until the end of the war.

The early trials of the Australian Beaufort Mk V with Twin Wasp engines induced the Air Ministry to specify this powerplant for the next contract, and a prototype with these American engines was flown in November 1940. The first production **Beaufort Mk II** flew in September 1941, and by comparison with the Beaufort Mk I revealed

Above: Seen flying low over choppy Channel waters is a Beaufort of No. 22 Squadron. It was from this squadron that the only Beaufort VC was won when F/O Campbell carried out a daring attack on Brest, damaging the German battleship* Gneisenau*, from which he did not return.

Below: These Beaufort Mk IIs of No. 39 Squadron are seen flying near their base at Luqa, Malta, from where they flew mine-laying and anti-shipping missions from August 1942 until the unit re-equipped with Beaufighters in June 1943.

Bristol Type 152 Beaufort

A pair of No. 42 Squadron Beauforts is seen on patrol. Nearest aircraft is L9965, with the name* Mercury *painted on the side of its nose. The squadron operated Beauforts from April 1940 to February 1943, flying them on anti-shipping and mine-laying missions around the North Sea coast for the first year, then in the Mediterranean, before arriving in the Far East in December 1942.

Bristol Beaufort Mk I

1 Starboard navigation light
2 Formation-keeping light
3 Starboard aileron, fabric-covered
4 Aileron tab
5 Aileron hinge control
6 Starboard ASV Mk II radar aerial
7 Oil cooler intake
8 Starboard outboard fuel tank
18 Bristol Taurus VI 14-cylinder sleeve valve radial engine
19 Engine cowlings
20 Exhaust collector ring
21 de Havilland three-bladed propeller
22 Spinner
23 Twin Vickers K-type 0.303-in (7.7mm) nose guns
24 Windproof sealing apertures
25 Ammunition drums
26 Bomb aiming windows
27 Bomb sight
32 Navigator's chart table
33 Nose glazing
34 Chart case
35 Navigator's instrument panel
36 Forward end of semi-recessed torpedo housing
37 Rudder pedals
38 Pilot's instrument panel
39 Windscreen panels
40 Pilot's fixed gun sight
41 Control column
42 Compass
43 Pilot's floor
44 Autopilot controller
45 Control cable runs
52 Pilot's armoured backplate
53 Cockpit roof escape hatch
54 Sliding sun blind
55 Parachute stowage
56 Radio equipment
57 Hydraulic fluid tank
58 Aerial mast
59 D/F loop aerial
60 Cabin side window
61 Radar viewfinder
62 Radio console
63 Radio operator's seat
64 Rear spar step
65 Radio equipment racks
66 Flush mounted roof aerial
67 Fuselage double frame
68 Wing spar attachments
69 Oxygen bottles
70 Top of flare launch tube
71 Cabin bulkhead
72 Fuselage skin plating
73 Entry hatch
74 Vickers K-type 0.303-in (7.7-mm) beam gun (in hatch door)
75 Toilet
76 Gunner's seat
77 Turret mechanism
78 Aerial mast
79 Turret fume extractor
80 Rotating Bristol B.IV Mk I turret
81 Twin Vickers K-guns
82 Fuselage upper longeron
83 Radar equipment racks
84 Fuselage frame construction
85 Divebrake de-icing fluid tank
86 Carburettor de-icing tank
87 Vertical control cable shaft
88 Rear fuselage joint frame
89 Dust-proof fabric bulkhead
90 Fin root fairing
91 Fin spar attachment

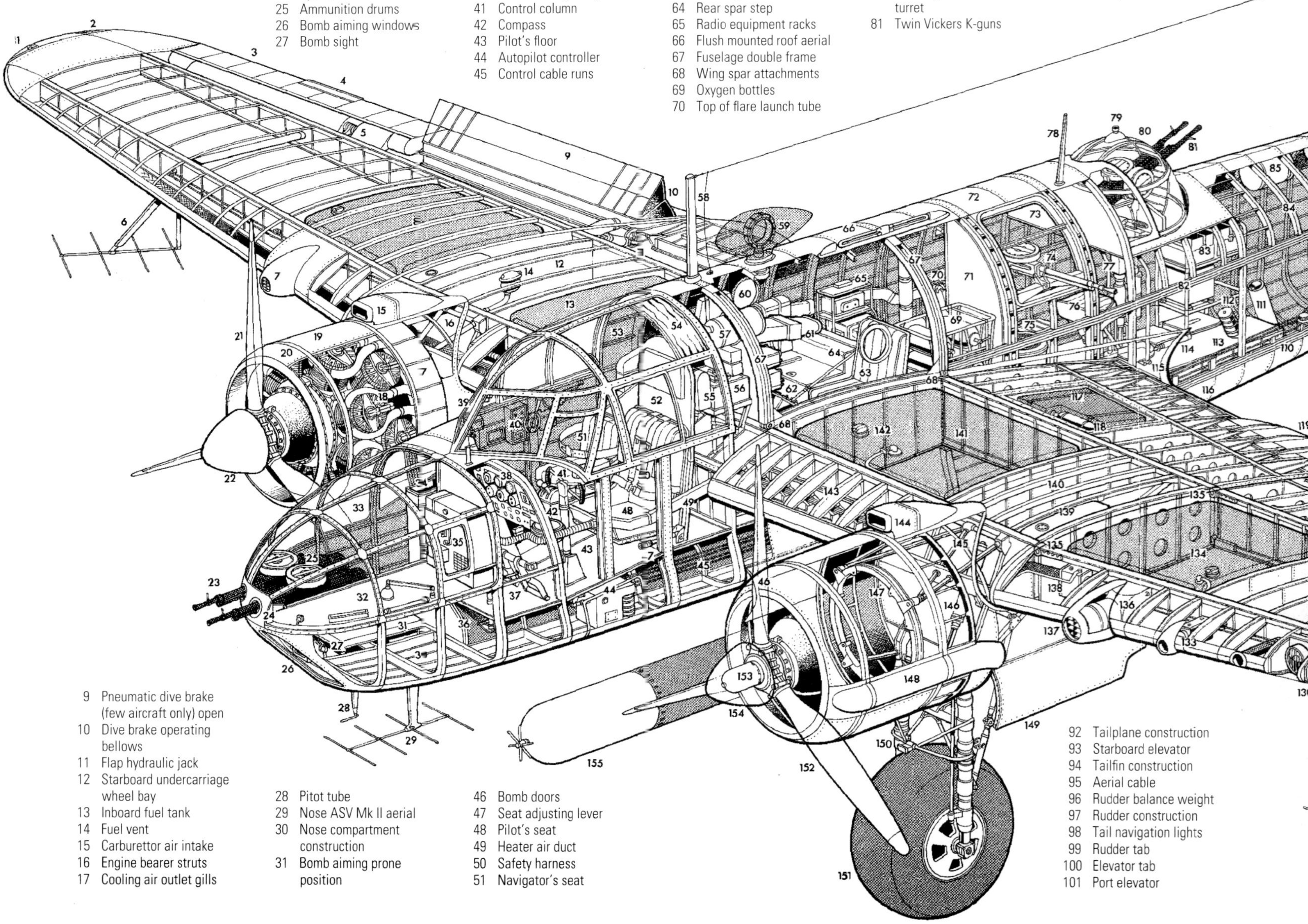

9 Pneumatic dive brake (few aircraft only) open
10 Dive brake operating bellows
11 Flap hydraulic jack
12 Starboard undercarriage wheel bay
13 Inboard fuel tank
14 Fuel vent
15 Carburettor air intake
16 Engine bearer struts
17 Cooling air outlet gills
28 Pitot tube
29 Nose ASV Mk II aerial
30 Nose compartment construction
31 Bomb aiming prone position
46 Bomb doors
47 Seat adjusting lever
48 Pilot's seat
49 Heater air duct
50 Safety harness
51 Navigator's seat
92 Tailplane construction
93 Starboard elevator
94 Tailfin construction
95 Aerial cable
96 Rudder balance weight
97 Rudder construction
98 Tail navigation lights
99 Rudder tab
100 Elevator tab
101 Port elevator

102 Port tailplane
103 Rudder control horn
104 Elevator hinge controls
105 Tailplane fixing double frames
106 Tailwheel retraction mechanism
107 Lockheed tailwheel unit
108 Tailwheel housing, fixed tailwheel on early aircraft
109 Tailplane control cables
110 Fuselage lower longeron
111 Emergency landing flare chute
112 Ballast weights
113 Walkway
114 Turret rotating jack
115 Wingroot trailing-edge fillet
116 Inboard split flap
117 Dinghy stowage
118 Inflation bottle
119 Airflow deflectors
120 Port upper surface dive brake
121 Outboard flap housing
122 Port aileron construction
123 Aileron tab
124 Formation-keeping light
125 Port navigation light
126 Wing rib construction
127 Aileron cable duct
128 Leading-edge nose ribs
129 Port ASV Mk II radar aerial
130 Landing and taxiing lamps
131 Ammunition box
132 Fixed Browning 0.303-in (7.7-mm) machine-gun (port wing only)
133 G45 gun camera
134 Port outboard fuel tank, capacity 91 Imp gal (413 litres)
135 Outer wing panel spar joints
136 Oil cooler
137 Ram air intake
138 Cabin heater
139 Engine oil tank
140 Main undercarriage wheel bay
141 Port inboard fuel tank, capacity 194 Imp gal (882 litres)
142 Filler cap
143 Engine control ducting
144 Carburettor air intake
145 Engine bearer struts
146 Undercarriage hydraulic retraction jack
147 Engine mounting ring frame
148 Exhaust pipe fairing
149 Mainwheel doors
150 Vickers oleo-pneumatic undercarriage leg struts
151 Port mainwheel
152 de Havilland three-bladed propeller
153 Propeller pitch change mechanism
154 Spinner
155 18-in (45.7-cm) torpedo

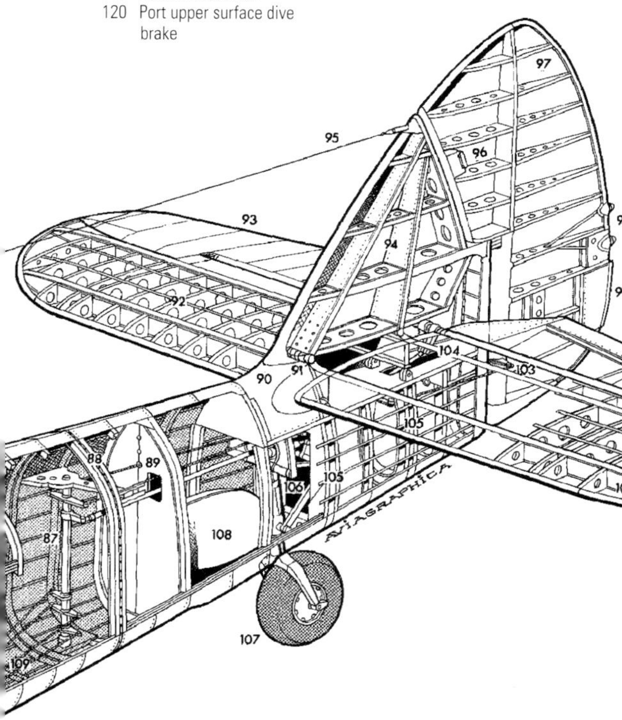

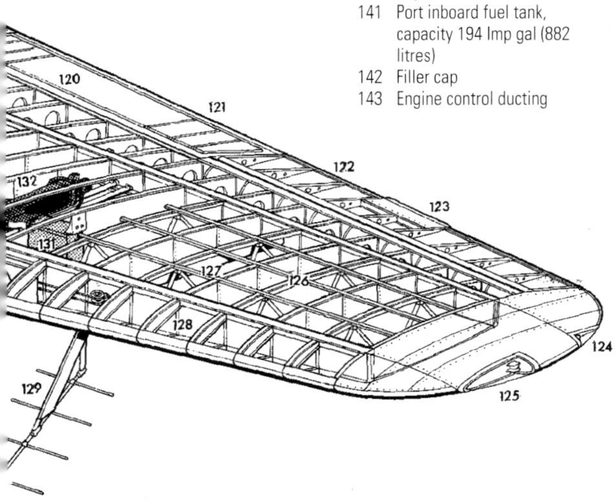

much improved take-off performance. However, because of a shortage of Twin Wasps in the UK, only 164 production Mk IIs were built before Mk Is with improved Taurus XII engines were reintroduced on the line. In addition to the powerplant change, this version had structural strengthening, a changed gun turret and ASV radar with Yagi aerials. When production of this version ended in 1944, well over 1,200 Beauforts had been built in Britain.

The final two Beaufort designations, **Mk III** and **Mk IV**, related respectively to a version with Rolls-Royce Merlin XX engines, of which none was built, and a version with two 1,250-hp (932-kW) Taurus XX engines of which only a prototype was built.

Beauforts were the standard torpedo-bomber in service with Coastal Command during 1940-43, equipping Nos 22, 42, 86, 217, 415 and 489 Squadrons in home waters, and Nos 39, 47 and 217 in the Middle East. They were to acquit themselves well until superseded by the Beaufighter, and were involved in many of the early and bloody attacks against – the German battlecruisers *Gneisenau* and *Scharnhorst*, and the heavy cruiser *Prinz Eugen*, three vessels which often seemed to be invincible, at least to aircraft carrying conventional weapons.

Specification
Beaufort Mk I
Type: four-seat torpedo-bomber
Powerplant: two 1,130-hp (843-kW) Bristol Taurus VI, XII, or XVI radial piston engines
Performance: maximum speed 260 mph (418 km/h) at 6,000 ft (1830 m); cruising speed 200 mph (322 km/h); service ceiling 16,500 ft (5030 m); normal range 1,035 miles (1666 km)
Weights: empty 13,107 lb (5945 kg); maximum take-off 21,230 lb (9630 kg)
Dimensions: span 57 ft 10 in (17.63 m); length 44 ft 7 in (13.59 m); height 12 ft 5 in (3.78 m); wing area 503 sq ft (46.73 m²)
Armament: four 0.303-in (7.7-mm) machine-guns (two each in nose and dorsal turrets) and (in some aircraft) three additional 0.303-in (7.7-mm) guns (one in blister beneath the nose and two in beam positions), plus up to 1,500 lb (1680 kg) of bombs or mines, or one 1,605-lb (728-kg) torpedo

The Beaufort was designed specifically as a torpedo-bomber, and it carried a semi-recessed torpedo as seen here. It was used to attack enemy shipping around the coasts of Britain, and later in the war became even more effective in the Middle East.

Bristol Type 156 Beaufighter

Top: The first squadron to be equipped with the Beaufighter Mk IC was No. 252 Squadron at Bircham Newton in November 1940. In the following April the squadron moved to Aldergrove, Northern Ireland for convoy patrols in the North Atlantic.

Above: A deceptively peaceful scene at Cassibile, Sicily, in August 1943 with No. 600 Squadron's Beaufighters dispersed among the almond trees. Second figure from the right is the squadron commander Wg Cdr 'Paddy' Green DSO, DFC. From this base the Beaufighter Mk VIFs provided bridgehead cover for the Allied landings at Salerno, Italy.

Developed as a private venture by the Bristol Aeroplane Company, the **Type 156** was a two-seat, all-metal fighter using components (wings, rear fuselage, tail unit and landing gear) from the Beaufort torpedo-bomber. This unlikely evolution produced one of the most successful aircraft of World War II. Adopted by the RAF and first flown on 17 July 1939, the Beaufighter, as the aircraft was soon named (from Beaufort, fighter), eventually equipped 52 operational RAF squadrons and gave outstanding service during World War II, in particular as a night-fighter and maritime strike aircraft.

In its original production form, the **Beaufighter Mk I** was powered by two 1,400-hp (1044-kW) Bristol Hercules III radial engines and was capable of 309 mph (497 km/h) at 15,000 ft (4572 m), some 26 mph (42 km/h) slower than the 335 mph (539 km/h) expected of the aircraft. Thus, with a top speed inferior to that of the RAF's Hurricane, the Beaufighter was judged unsuitable for the home-based day fighter role. However, with Luftwaffe night bombing raids on the increase, the Beaufighter was soon adapted to carry AI Mk IV radar as a night-fighter, replacing the first of the radar-carrying fighters, the makeshift Blenheim Mk IF.

The first radar-equipped Beaufighter Mk Is entered service experimentally with RAF Fighter Command's Fighter Interception Unit in August 1940 and flew their first operational sorties in September. That month, five squadrons received examples, No. 604 Squadron scoring the first victory by a Beaufighter using AI Mk IV radar on the night of 19/20 November. (The pilot was Squadron Leader John Cunningham and this was the first of 20 confirmed kills by the night-fighter ace.)

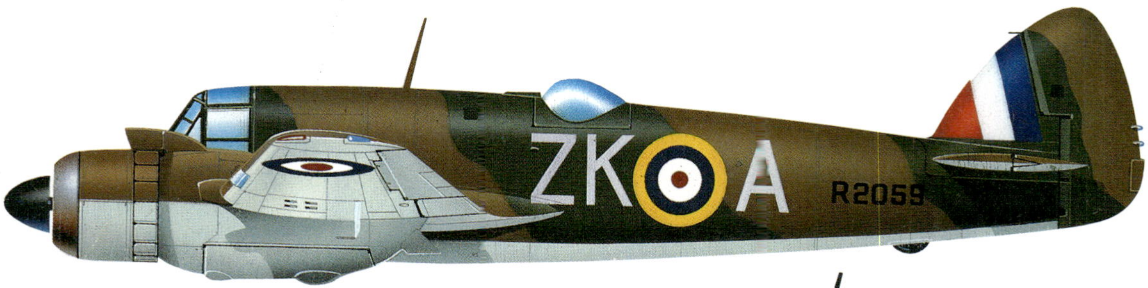

This Beaufighter Mk IF night-fighter was employed by No. 25 Squadron at RAF North Weald in October 1940, scoring its first victory on 15 November. This squadron and No. 29 Squadron (at Wellingore) were the first units to receive Beaufighters.

An expected lack of Hercules engines resulted in the Beaufighter Mk II which was fitted with Rolls-Royce Merlins. Painted in overall Special Night matt black with dull red codes and serial, this aircraft served with No. 307 (Polish) Squadron (note Polish national emblem) at RAF Exeter from April 1941 to April 1943.

T4638 was the 16th Beaufighter Mk IF night-fighter built by the Fairey Aviation Company, and was equipped with AI Mk IV airborne interception radar, characterised by the broad arrow nose aerial and outer wing arrays. It joined No. 604 (County of Middlesex) Squadron at Middle Wallop in 1941. At this time the squadron, commanded by Wg Cdr John Cunningham, was the top-scoring night-fighter unit in the RAF.

Below: Fitted with AI Mk IV radar, this Beaufighter Mk IIF is seen during trials in 1940. Note the gas warning patch on the upper rear fuselage. The longer Merlin powerplants increased the tendency to swing on take-off and a new tailfin and rudder were fitted, but this resulted in little significant improvement.

The Mk I's armament comprised four 20-mm cannon in the forward fuselage and six 0.303-in (7.7-mm) machine-guns in the wings. By the end of 1941, 10 UK-based squadrons operated AI-equipped Beaufighters.

The German invasion of Crete in April 1941 highlighted the need for a long-range day-fighter and prompted the development of the **Beaufighter Mk IC** (the 'C' indicating Coastal Command; the Mk I night-fighter was retrospectively redesignated **Mk IF**, the 'F' indicating Fighter Command). This variant entered service with a detachment of No. 252 Squadron, Coastal Command from Malta the following month. Many were modified locally to carry two 250-lb (114-kg) or 500-lb (227-kg) bombs under the fuselage for ground attack duties. Such was the success of the type against enemy aircraft, shipping and ground targets in the Mediterranean theatre, and later in Italy, that RAF Coastal Command became the major operator of the Beaufighter, the type replacing Blenheim Mk IVs and Beauforts.

Meanwhile, as insurance against engine shortages (Hercules engines being in heavy demand for medium and heavy bombers, like the Wellington and Stirling), the Air Ministry had stipulated that a **Beaufighter Mk II** be developed, powered by Rolls-Royce Griffons. In the event, the need to divert Griffon production to the

This battle-worn Beaufighter Mk VIC is from No. 272 Squadron, which was based at Ta Kali and Luqa, Malta, from November 1942. The Mk VIC achieved great success in the Mediterranean, attacking enemy shipping, ground targets and aircraft.

Below: The RAF's most potent strike weapon was the Beaufighter. Here Mk VIF 'F' of No. 272 Squadron taxis out from its dispersal area at Luqa, with Valetta in the background. The racks under the wings could take two 250-lb (113-kg) bombs, with later versions able to carry eight rocket projectiles.

Equipped with a 200-Imp gal (909-litre) drop tank on the torpedo rack, this Beaufighter TF.Mk X underwent operational trials in 1944. The long-range rocket projectile-equipped aircraft were operated by the RAF over the Aegean Sea and with the Balkan Air Force in support of Marshal Tito.

Bristol Beaufighter Mk I

1 Starboard navigation light (fore) and formation-keeping light (aft)
2 Wing structure
3 Aileron adjustable tab
4 Starboard aileron
5 Four Browning 0.303-in (7.7-mm) machine-guns
6 Machine-gun ports
7 Starboard outer wing fuel tank, capacity 87 Imp gal (395 litres)
8 Split trailing-edge flaps, hydraulically actuated
9 Starboard flap
10 Flap operating jack
11 Starboard nacelle tail fairing
12 Oil tank capacity 178 Imp gal (77 litres)
13 Starboard inner wing fuel tank, capacity 188 Imp gal (855 litres)
14 Cabin air duct
15 Hinged leading-edge sections
16 Engine bulkhead
17 Engine bearers
18 Auxiliary intake
19 Supercharger air intake
20 Engine cooling flaps
21 1,560-hp Bristol Hercules III radial engine
22 de Havilland Hydromatic propeller
23 Propeller spinner
24 Lockheed oleo-pneumatic shock absorber
25 Starboard mainwheel, with Dunlop brakes
26 Forward identification lamp in nose cap
27 Rudder pedals
28 Control column
29 Cannon ports
30 Seat adjusting lever
31 Pilot's seat
32 Instrument panel
33 Clear vision panel
34 Flat bullet-proof windscreen
35 Fixed canopy (sideways-hinged on later aircraft)
36 Spar carry-through step
37 Nose centre-section attachment point
38 Fuselage/centre-section attachment point
39 Pilot's entry/emergency escape hatch
40 Underfloor cannon blast tubes
41 Fuselage/centre-section attachment points
42 Centre-section attachment longeron reinforcement
43 Cabin air duct
44 Cannon heating duct
45 Rear spar carry-through
46 Bulkhead cut out (observer access to front hatch)
47 Bulkhead
48 Hydraulic header tank
49 Aerial mast
50 Monocoque fuselage construction
51 Starboard cannon (two 20-mm)
52 Floor level
53 Steps
54 Observer's swivel seat (normally forward facing)
55 Radio controls and intercom
56 Observer's cupola
57 Hinged panel
58 Aerial
59 Oxygen bottles
60 Vertical control cable shaft
61 Sheet metal bulkhead
62 Control cables
63 Tailplane structure
64 Elevator
65 Elevator balance tab
66 Fin structure
67 Rudder balance
68 Rudder framework
69 Tail formation keeping (upper) and navigation lamps
70 Rudder
71 Rudder trim tab
72 Elevator trim tab
73 Elevator balance tab
74 Elevator structure
75 Port tailplane (12° dihedral on later aircraft)
76 Rudder hinge (lower)
77 Tailwheel retraction mechanism
78 Retracting tailwheel
79 Tailwheel bay
80 Tail unit joint ring
81 Control cables
82 Parachute flare chute
83 Fuselage skinning – flush riveted Alclad
84 Observer's entry/emergency escape hatchway
85 Lower fuselage longeron
86 Entry ladder/emergency exit chute
87 Wing root fairing fillet
88 Port cannon breeches and magazine drum
89 Dinghy location – multi-seat 'H' or 'K' type in blow-out stowage
90 Flap (inner section)
91 Flap operating jack

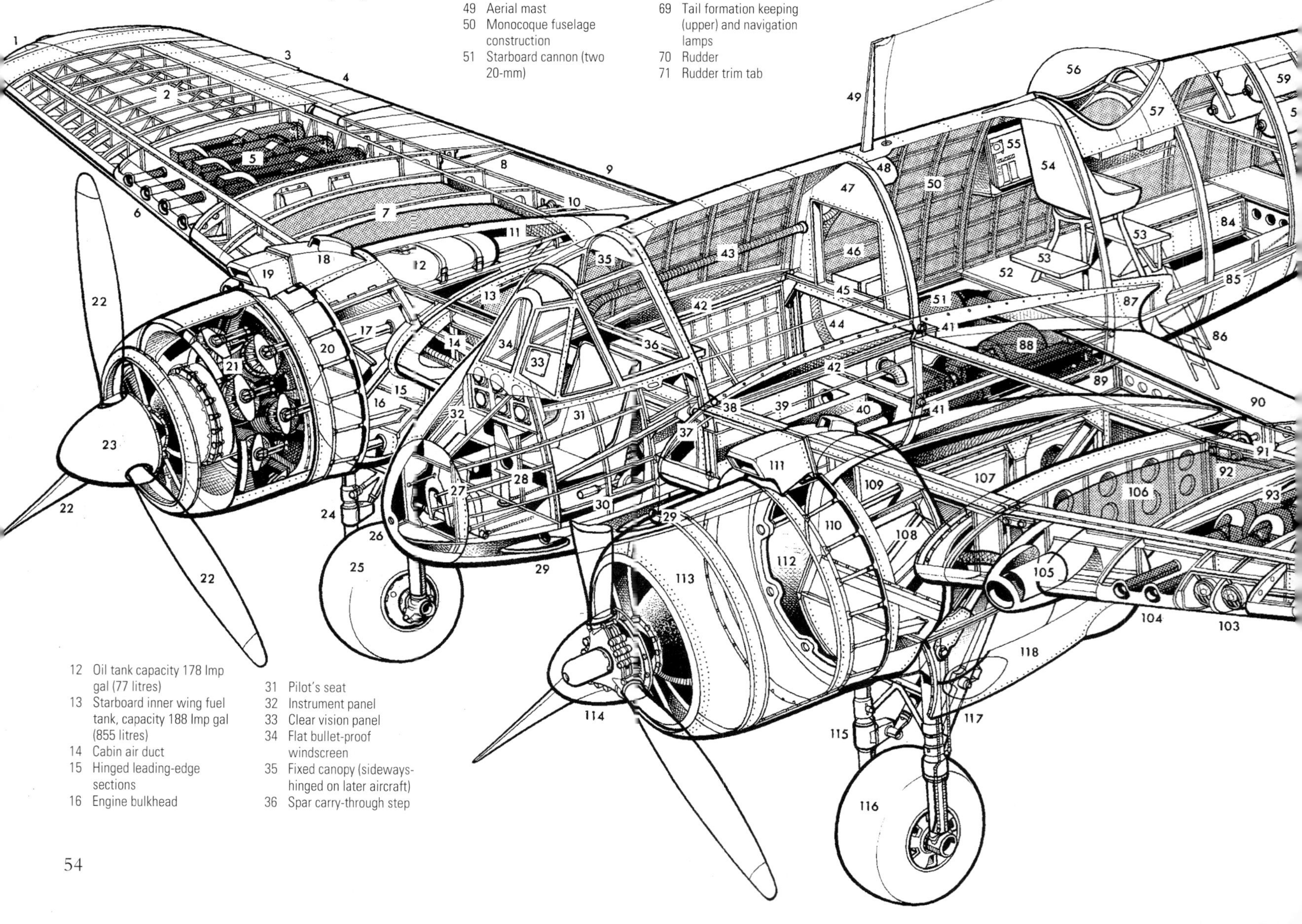

Bristol Type 156 Beaufighter

Equipped with Beaufighter TF.Mk Xs, No. 404 Squadron was manned by Royal Canadian Air Force personnel. Seen here in June 1944 while based at RAF Davidstow Moor, Cornwall, the aircraft covered the western Channel during the D-Day invasion of Normandy.

92 Wing centre/outer-section attachment point
93 Two 0.303-in (7.7-mm) machine guns
94 Flap (outer section)
95 Rear spar
96 Aileron control rod and linkage
97 Port aileron

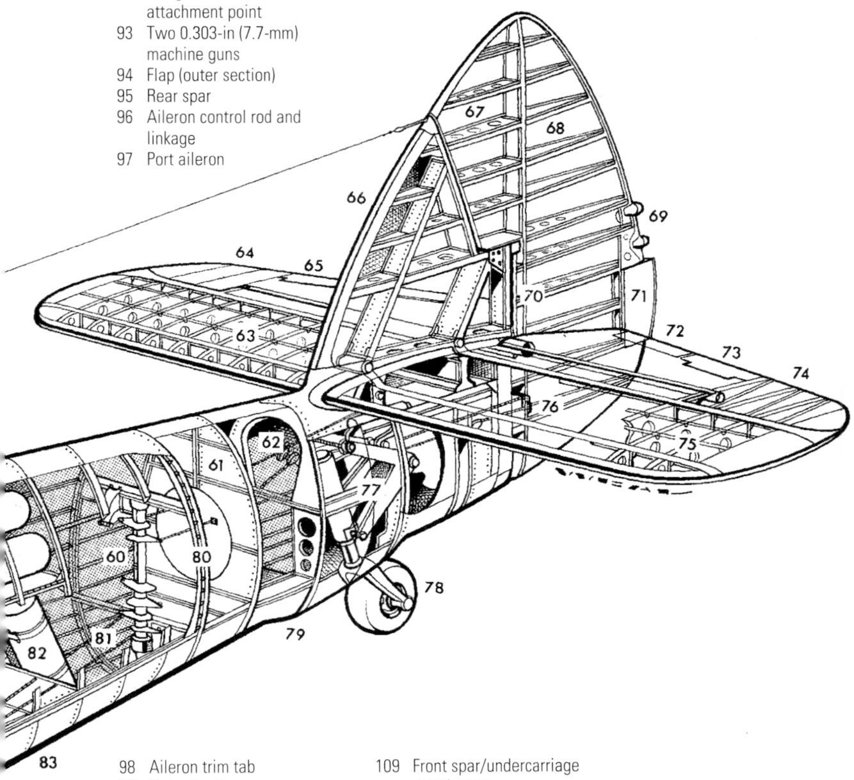

98 Aileron trim tab
99 Port wingtip
100 Port navigation light (forward) and formation-keeping lamp (rear)
101 Front spar
102 Pitot head
109 Front spar/undercarriage attachment
110 Engine cooling flaps
111 Supercharger air intake
112 Engine mounting ring
113 Cowling nose ring
114 Non-feathering (early) or feathering constant speed (late) propellers

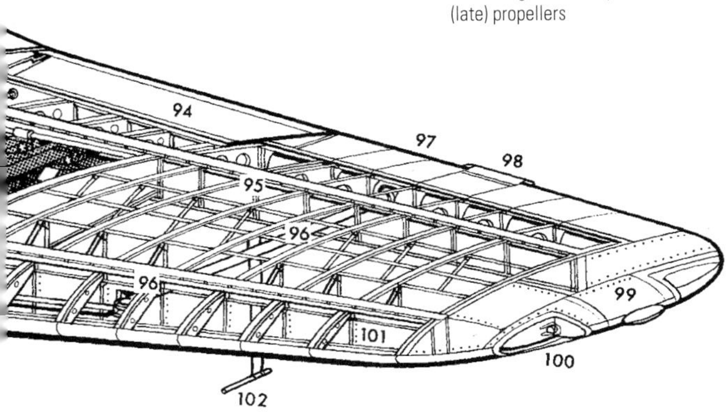

103 Twin landing lights (port wing only)
104 Machine-gun ports
105 Oil cooler
106 Port outer wing fuel tank
107 Mainwheel well
108 Engine bearers
115 Mainwheel leg
116 Port mainwheel
117 Retraction jack
118 Undercarriage door

Bristol Beaufighter variants

Type 156 Beaufighter: four prototypes (R2052-R2055)
Beaufighter Mk IF and Mk IC: powered by Hercules III, X or XI engines; Mk IF employed as night-fighter and Mk IC as maritime strike fighter; total 910 built by Bristol and Fairey including 54 for Australia
Beaufighter Mk II: two prototypes powered by Rolls-Royce Merlin X
Beaufighter Mk IIF: night-fighter powered by Merlin XX; total 448
Beaufighter Mk V: two aircraft with dorsal turrets and Merlin XX engines
Beaufighter Mk VI: three converted from Mk IFs; Hercules VI engines
Beaufighter Mk VIF and Mk VIC: powered by Hercules VI or XVI engines, rear Vickers machine-gun, underwing stores; Mk VIF ground-attack fighter and Mk VIC maritime strike fighter; total 1,832 including 60 ITF torpedo fighters
Beaufighter Mk X: prototype with Hercules XVII engines
Beaufighter TF.Mk X and XC: anti-shipping strike fighter and torpedo bomber equipped with AI Mk VIII radar, rear Browning machine-guns and dorsal fin; total 2,205
Beaufighter TT.Mk 10: target-tug version converted from TF.Mk X; total 36
Beaufighter F.Mk XIC: similar to TF.Mk X but without torpedo gear; total 163
Beaufighter Mk XX: Australian-built version for RNZAF similar to TF.Mk X
Beaufighter Mk XXI: Australian-built version for RAAF (same as Mk XX); total 364 including Mk XXs

Fleet Air Arm's Barracuda saw the Mk II enter service powered, instead, by Rolls-Royce Merlin XXs taken from Lancaster bomber production and housed in nacelles designed for the four-engined bomber. All were completed as **Mk IIF** night-fighters, but were never particularly popular with their crews. Though faster than the Hercules-engined Mk IFs at altitude, they had less power for take-off and consequently needed a longer run in which to get airborne.

The Beaufighter's distinctive 12° dihedral tailplane made its first appearance on the Mk II. This was introduced to cure longitudinal instability in the climb, from which the type had always suffered, but which was more pronounced in the tail-heavy Mk II. This became a standard feature of late-production Mk I and Mk II aircraft and all subsequent Beaufighters, in some cases as a retrofitted feature. Ironically, Fighter Command units preferred the original 'flat' tail, taking the view that the revised tailplane made their aircraft too stable for night fighting.

Beaufighters of **Mks III**, **IV** and **V** all failed to see service. The Mk III and Mk IV were so-called 'sports model' fighter variants of the Mk I and Mk II, respectively, with redesigned, slimmer rear fuselages; neither was built. The Mk V reached prototype stage and was essentially a Mk II fitted with a four-gun Boulton Paul turret, of the type fitted to the Boulton Paul Defiant, behind the cockpit. However, this

A potent addition to RAF Coastal Command's strike capability was provided by the Beaufighter Mk VIC and TF.Mk X torpedo-bombers, which carried a single Mk XII torpedo with the usual battery of four 20-mm cannon. The first Beaufighter Strike Wing was formed at RAF North Coates in November 1942. The Perspex bulge immediately behind the cockpit covered the D/F loop for the radio compass.

Bristol Type 156 Beaufighter

ungainly conversion was ultimately rejected, as the turret offered few benefits over the original armament fit and, additionally, impaired the pilot's emergency exit from the aircraft.

By mid-1941, as the Luftwaffe's night attacks were scaled down, Beaufighter night-fighter units had begun intruder sorties ('Rangers') over France and Belgium, attacking road and rail communications. In a daring raid on 12 June 1942, to boost public morale, an aircraft of No. 263 Squadron dropped a *tricolore* flag over the Arc de Triomphe in Paris and strafed the German Admiralty headquarters. Other aircraft were engaged in bomber escort duties at this time, acting as decoys for German night-fighters.

Coastal Command was taking delivery of **Beaufighter Mk VIC**s by the spring of 1942, these aircraft featuring improved 1,650-hp (1230-kW) Hercules VI engines. The anti-shipping role was becoming an increasingly important one for the type, Beaufighters seeing action against shipping and submarines in the North Sea and Bay of Biscay, in particular.

The Hercules VI engine produced peak power at a higher altitude than the Hercules III and was therefore better suited to the Beaufighter's night-fighter role. A night-fighter version of the Mk VI, the **Mk VIF**, with AI Mk VIII radar, was issued to night-fighter units from March 1942, two squadrons taking their aircraft to North Africa in the spring of the following year. Four USAAF units in the Mediterranean also flew Mk VIFs pending the availability of Northrop P-61 Black Widows.

In the Far East, Beaufighter Mk VIFs arrived in 1942, three squadrons operating the type, mainly in the night interdiction role from bases in India. Favoured targets were Japanese lines of communication in Thailand and Burma, these low-level, high-speed attacks earning the Beaufighter the Japanese nickname 'Whispering Death'. Though these operations were effective, losses were high, largely due to the adverse weather and poor ground facilities in the region.

By the end of 1942, Mk VICs were being completed with torpedo-carrying gear to replace Coastal Command's Beauforts. These weapons (of either British 18-in/45.7-cm or American 22.5-in/57.2-cm type)

Top and above: Wearing D-Day invasion stripes, these Beaufighters of RAF Coastal Command are seen attacking heavily armed German ships in the Heligoland Bight in September 1944. The rocket attack sank one ship while the other was left blazing. Once the rockets had been expended, the ships were strafed with cannon fire.

Above: A Beaufighter launches a salvo of what was one of the aircraft's most destructive weapons, the 90-lb (41-kg) rocket projectile. The photograph was taken by a following Beaufighter flying close enough to be struck by expended cannon cases.

were mounted externally and first employed successfully from a Beaufighter on 4 April 1943, when aircraft of No. 254 Squadron sank two supply ships off Norway. Mk VICs modified in this way were designated **Mk VIC (ITF)** 'interim torpedo fighters'. It was in conjunction with torpedo fighter developments that dive brakes were tested and soon introduced as an aid to the low-level tactics used by the crews of these machines.

To make the Beaufighter more suitable for this low-altitude work, a Hercules engine variant (the **Mk XVII**) was developed to produce peak power, 1,735 hp (1294 kW) at 500 ft (152 m). With these engines installed, the torpedo-carrying Mk VIC became the **Beaufighter TF.Mk X** (or 'Torbeau'); a strike variant of the **Mk X** without a torpedo-carrying capability was known as the **Mk XIC**.

Wing-mounted machine-guns had been deleted from Coastal Command Beaufighters (to make way for extra fuel tanks), but production TF.Mk Xs featured a 0.303-in (7.7-mm) Browning or Vickers 'K' machine-gun firing to the rear from in the observer's position. To help compensate for the lack of wing guns, the Mk X also carried 283 20-mm rounds instead of the 240 of earlier marks.

The Mk X was to be the main Beaufighter production variant and generally flew with a crew of two, though a third crew member could be accommodated to assist in torpedo aiming. Using a gyro-angling device and a radio altimeter, the Beaufighter could make accurate attacks using rockets and torpedoes at wave-top height. To help in finding targets for their weapons, early examples carried ASV (air-to-surface vessel) radar, but this was eventually replaced with AI Mk VIII adapted successfully for air-to-surface use and housed in a 'thimble' nose radome.

Eight rockets or two 250-lb (114-kg) bombs under the wings had been introduced on modified Mk VICs; these weapons became standard on the Mk X. It was the extra weight of the radar and weapons that prompted the fitting of a dorsal fin (originally tested on a Mk II to correct take-off swing) to improve the handling of an aircraft that was, operating at weights 50 per cent higher than originally envisaged.

Radar
Coastal Command Beaufighters often carried ASV radar to find shipping targets. Shown fitted to this aircraft is the initial form (ASV Mk III), which was of limited effect due to the blanking effect of the engine nacelles.

Bristol Beaufighter TF.Mk X

Beaufighter TF.Mk X NE429 was Bristol (Weston)-built and served with No. 489 (RNZAF) Squadron based at RAF Dallachy, Moray. Part of the special Beaufighter wing of Coastal Command, the Beaufighters flew strikes against shipping in the fjords and among the islands of Norway in 1944. They concentrated on convoys carrying supplies to the *Tirpitz* and returning with Swedish iron ore.

Strike fighter
The Beaufighter was a two/three-seat anti-shipping strike fighter. This Mk X is carrying a torpedo, but other squadron Mk Xs could be equipped with eight 60-lb (27-kg) rockets. Rocket aircraft would go in first to sweep the decks and silence the guns, followed by the second wave launching their torpedoes.

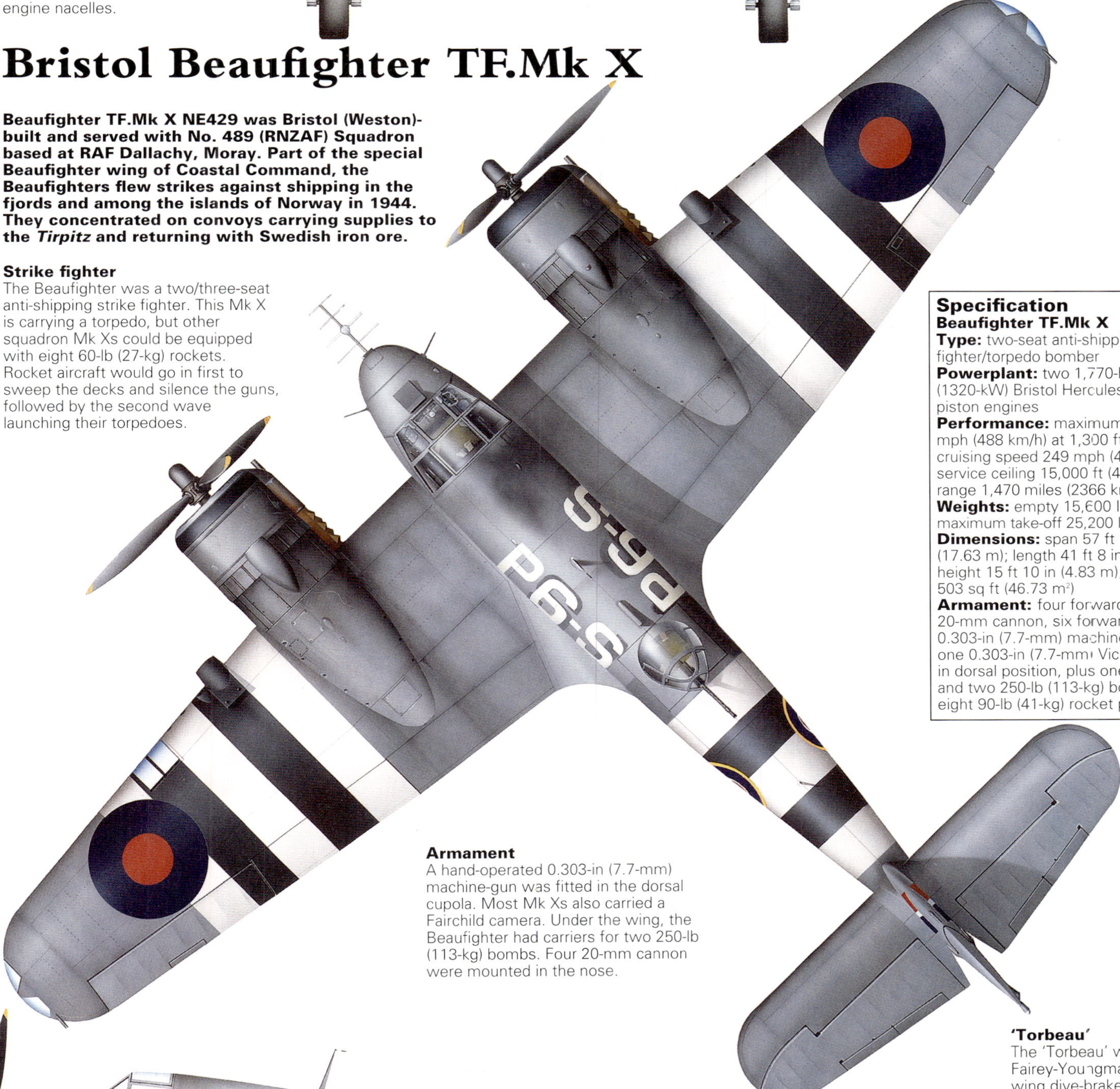

Specification
Beaufighter TF.Mk X
Type: two-seat anti-shipping strike fighter/torpedo bomber
Powerplant: two 1,770-hp (1320-kW) Bristol Hercules XVIII radial piston engines
Performance: maximum speed 303 mph (488 km/h) at 1,300 ft (395 m); cruising speed 249 mph (401 km/h); service ceiling 15,000 ft (4570 m); range 1,470 miles (2366 km)
Weights: empty 15,600 lb (7076 kg); maximum take-off 25,200 lb (11431 kg)
Dimensions: span 57 ft 10 in (17.63 m); length 41 ft 8 in (12.70 m); height 15 ft 10 in (4.83 m); wing area 503 sq ft (46.73 m²)
Armament: four forward-firing 20-mm cannon, six forward-firing 0.303-in (7.7-mm) machine-guns and one 0.303-in (7.7-mm) Vickers 'K' gun in dorsal position, plus one torpedo and two 250-lb (113-kg) bombs or eight 90-lb (41-kg) rocket projectiles

Armament
A hand-operated 0.303-in (7.7-mm) machine-gun was fitted in the dorsal cupola. Most Mk Xs also carried a Fairchild camera. Under the wing, the Beaufighter had carriers for two 250-lb (113-kg) bombs. Four 20-mm cannon were mounted in the nose.

'Torbeau'
The 'Torbeau' was fitted with the Fairey-Youngman bellows-type wing dive-brakes – a modification originally intended for Beaufighter night-fighters. Gyro-angling gear and radio altimeters were fitted, and a third crew member behind the pilot helped him to aim the torpedo. The aircraft carried a 1,700-lb (771-kg) 18-in (45.7-cm) torpedo complete with Mono Air Tail (MAT). The MAT stabilised the torpedo's flight, and was released upon impact with the water.

Above: On its way to attack another German target in the autumn of 1943 is Beaufighter TF.Mk X LZ293 of No. 236 Squadron based at RAF North Coates. The rails under the wings are loaded with 25-lb (11.3-kg) SAP-headed rockets. The squadron operated the Beaufighter Mk X until it was disbanded in May 1945.

Left: In Burma, Beaufighters of Nos 176 and 217 Squadrons went into action against the Japanese and earned the sobriquet of 'Whispering Death'. In their sorties against railways and river boats, Beaufighter pilots often flew so low that the enemy retaliated by setting up trip-wires above dummy targets in the valleys.

Below: Beaufighter detachments were made to Palestine to cover a wide sweep of the eastern Mediterranean on convoy patrols and attacks on ground and sea targets. From 1942, airfields increasingly became the targets for the Beaufighters. This example carries an AI Mk VIII in a 'thimble-nose' fairing. This equipment could locate surfaced submarine targets, notably increasing the aircraft's effectiveness.

By early 1944, Beaufighter Strike Wings (made up of a mixture of RAF, RCAF, RAAF and RNZAF units) were harrying enemy shipping from bases in the UK, initially in Scotland, but later on the east and south coasts. These squadrons supported the D-Day landings with the earlier Beaufighters of other units, modified to carry bombs under their fuselage and wings. Other TF.Mk Xs were assigned to the South African squadrons of the Balkan Air Force, which had a number of notable successes with the type. Though Mk Xs arrived in the China-Burma-India theatre before VJ-Day, their numbers were too small to have a significant effect on operations in the region.

The RAAF's urgent need for more Beaufighters with which to attack Japanese shipping to the north of Australia (54 Mk ICs were already in service) led to plans for a Hercules-engined Mk VII to be built by the Department of Aircraft Production, then engaged in Beaufort production. However, fears that Hercules supplies could be interrupted resulted in the proposed **Mk VIII** and **Mk IX** with Wright Double Cyclone engines. In the event, Hercules availability was maintained, the Hercules XVIII powering the **Beaufighter Mk 21**, which entered service in 1944 and played a prominent part in the RAAF's support of the Allied advance on the Netherlands East Indies.

The last British-built wartime 'Beau' variant was to be the **Mk XII**, with wings strengthened to carry a 1,000-lb (454-kg) bomb each, but suitable engines were unavailable. Instead, the new wings were incorporated in late Mk X production, the bomb racks additionally allowing the carriage of external fuel tanks.

Beaufighter Mk IC T9068 'V', painted in the RAF's desert camouflage, was one of the aircraft used by No. 272 Squadron in 1942. The squadron was very active in North Africa and the Mediterranean, flying convoy escorts, fighter patrols and ground-attack sorties.

A sizeable part of Coastal Command's strike force consisted of Beaufighter TF.Mk Xs, of which RD351 is typical. It served with No. 254 Squadron in the North Coates Strike Wing. With the cessation of hostilities, this force was reduced to a single squadron (No. 254), which moved to Thorney Island and was renumbered No. 42 Squadron.

Bristol 163 Buckingham/166 Buckmaster

Following on from the success of its Blenheim light bomber, the Bristol company began design work on a replacement. It had no means of knowing that their design, the **Type 163** Buckingham, would be rendered obsolete by the superlative Mosquito before it had even flown.

Problems with the new Bristol Centaurus engine, along with official delays in finalising requirements, resulted in the prototype not flying until February 1943. The first production example flew the following year, and although outclassed by the Mosquito in the European theatre it was felt that the Buckingham's superior range would be an asset in the Far East. However, by the time production examples were ready the war was at a close. It was decided that the last batch of 65 airframes was to be completed as **Buckingham C.Mk 1** transports but they were uneconomical to operate and all examples had been retired by 1949.

Derived from the Buckingham, the **Type 166 Buckmaster** had considerable commonality with its predecessor, and in fact the last 110 Buckinghams on the production line were converted to Buckmasters. Deliveries began at the end of the war and several examples served with No. 8 Squadron on communications duties. However, most Buckmasters were delivered to Operational Conversion Units to train Bristol Brigand crews. The type was retired in the mid 1950s.

Above: Designed as a light day-bomber, the Bristol Buckingham did not see service in this role – just a handful were used as high speed transports by the Transport Command Development Unit.

Left: First flown in October 1944, the Buckmaster was a three-seat advanced trainer. This aircraft, RP246, was delivered in 1945 to the Empire Central Flying School to train flying instructors. It is seen here, flying for this unit, in post-war markings.

Specification

Buckingham B.Mk 1

Type: four-seat tactical day bomber/ courier transport

Powerplant: two 2,250-hp (1879-kW) Bristol Centaurus VII or XI radial piston engines

Performance: maximum speed 330 mph (531 km/h) at 12,000 ft (3660 m); cruising speed 285 mph (459 km/h); service ceiling 25,000 ft (7620 m); range 3,180 miles (5118 km)

Weights: empty 24,042 lb (10905 kg); maximum take-off 38,050 lb (17259 kg)

Dimensions: span 71 ft 10 in (21.89 m); length 46 ft 10 in (14.27 m); height 17 ft 6 in (5.33 m); wing area 708 sq ft (65.77 m²)

Armament: ten 0.303-in (7.7-mm) machine-guns (four each in fixed forward position and dorsal turret and two in ventral cupola), plus up to 4,000 lb (1814 kg) of bombs

Buckmaster T.Mk 1

Type: three-seat advanced trainer

Powerplant: two 2,520-hp (1879-kW) Bristol Centaurus VII radial piston engines

Performance: maximum speed 352 mph (566 km/h) at 12,000 ft (3660 m); service ceiling 30,000 ft (9145 m); range 2,000 miles (3219 km)

Weights: empty 23,000 lb (10433 kg); maximum take-off 33,700 lb (15286 kg)

Dimensions: span 71 ft 10 in (21.89 m); length 46 ft 5 in (14.15 m); height 17 ft 6 in (5.33 m); wing area 708 sq ft (65.77 m²)

Consolidated Catalina

More Catalinas were built than were any other flying-boats in the annals of aircraft production, and in the RAF this twin-engined patrol bomber was second only to the Short Sunderland in importance in the 'boat-equipped' squadrons of Coastal Command. As the **XP3Y-1**, the first of the 'Cats' was built as the Consolidated **Model 28** and was flown, at NAS Norfolk, for the first time on 21 March 1935. Demonstrating a range of some 2,000 miles (3218 km) with four 1,000-lb (454-kg) bombs or two Mk XIII torpedoes, the new 'boat quickly gained US Navy acceptance and some 15 squadrons were flying **PBY-2**, **PBY-3** and **PBY-4** versions by the end of 1939. By that time Consolidated was busy developing the **PBY-5** and an amphibian variant as the **PBY-5A**, destined to become the most-produced and most effective of all the Catalinas.

Britain's first experience of the Consolidated flying boat came with the arrival, in July 1939, of a single **Model 28-5** purchased by the British Purchasing Commission in order to evaluate US hull design trends rather than the performance of the aircraft itself. Testing of this aircraft ended in February 1940 when it crashed and sank at Dumbarton. Another single example, a **Model 28-3**, was purchased in 1940 (named *Guba II*) from the explorer Dr Richard Archbold, and served briefly, October to December, with No. 209 Sqn before passing to BOAC – thus giving the RAF its first experience of the type at an operational level.

Meanwhile, the British Purchasing Commission had been busy ordering the Model 28-5, a total of 59 on direct contract being supplemented by 40 similar aircraft that had been ordered by France but not delivered before the surrender. These 100 aircraft (including *Guba II*) took the designation **Catalina Mk I**; deliveries were spread from March 1941 to January 1942. They were preceded by seven similar **Catalina Mk II**s, released by the USN for early delivery, from January to April 1941. The RAF also received 17 **Catalina Mk IIA**s, this being the designation for 36 examples purchased by Canada in

This Catalina Mk I was flown by No. 209 Squadron for general reconnaissance, the squadron receiving its first aircraft, replacing Saro Lerwicks, in April 1941 at Castle Archdale.

Consolidated Catalina

Above: The success of the Catalina with the US Navy attracted the attention of the Air Ministry as early as 1938, the first example reaching Britain in July 1939 for trials with the MAEE at Felixstowe. From an initial order for 30 aircraft, the RAF eventually received over 500.

Right: In October 1944 No. 240 Squadron, based in the Far East, began special operations dropping and picking up secret agents along the Burmese and Malayan coastline. Three complete crews and aircraft (SD Flight) were assigned to this task. This Catalina Mk IB, from the flight, is seen here on the first trial dropping of a special agent by parachute.

1941, the others going to the RCAF and RAAF.

Full service use of the Catalina began in March 1941 with No. 240 Squadron stationed at Stranraer, closely followed by Nos 209 and 210. More than a year would pass before any of the squadrons could claim the destruction of a U-boat, but Catalinas from all three units took part in the discovery and shadowing of the *Bismarck* in the 24 hours before it was sunk, in May 1941, by ships of the British Home Fleet. A further squadron to use Catalina Mk Is, No. 413 (RCAF), formed in the UK in mid-1941 and moved to Ceylon in March 1942 to fly anti-submarine patrols over the Indian Ocean.

The advent of Lend-Lease arrangements allowed a steady build-up of the RAF's Catalina force, starting with the allocation of 225 **Catalina Mk IB**s (of which 55 were retained by the US Navy). These were basically similar to the Catalina Mk I but built to the PBY-5 standard, as were 97 **Catalina Mk IVA**s built by Consolidated and 200 **Catalina Mk IVB**s built by Boeing Aircraft of Canada. Not all of these allocated aircraft actually reached the RAF, there being some diversions to the RCAF (which called the aircraft the **Canso**), RAAF and RNZAF. In the RAF, the Catalina Mk I and **Mk IV** variants served in the Coastal Command squadrons already mentioned, being heavily committed to the Battle of the Atlantic and flying from bases in the UK, Gibraltar and Iceland.

As more Catalinas became available further squadrons were equipped: No. 202 was primarily Gibraltar-based; Nos 212 and 191 flew principally from Indian bases; and Nos 209, 259, 262, 265 and 270 were Africa-based. No. 205 Sqn, flying Catalina Mk Is from Singapore by October 1941, was virtually wiped out within three months, but later reformed in Ceylon to operate Mk IVs with great success, alongside the Dutch-manned No. 321 Sqn. Because of its light defensive armament – six machine guns in all – the Catalina was susceptible to attacking fighters and was therefore not best suited to patrols close to enemy shore bases. Its long range, on the other hand, permitted sorties of up to 20 hours' duration, allowing it to search far out to sea, although, with only four Mk VII or Mk VIII depth charges, pinpoint accuracy was needed to attack submarines successfully.

The effectiveness of the Catalina in the anti-submarine role was enhanced with the introduction of ASV radar, initially in the Mk II form with its array of Yagi aerials on the fuselage and beneath the wing. More effective was the ASV Mk III and, eventually, ASV Mk VI, with its dish scanner contained in a pod mounted above the cockpit. During 1943, No. 210 Sqn alone flew Catalina Mk IVAs with an underwing Leigh Light installation, but this displaced two of the depth charges usually carried, and therefore required the operation of aircraft in pairs, one with the light and one fully armed.

The Catalina's role was extended when No. 357 Squadron flew agents into and out of Burma and Malaya, and No. 210 Squadron, flying from the Shetlands, flew similar sorties supporting clandestine Norwegian forces. In India, No. 628 Squadron was flying air-sea

Based at Pembroke Dock, this Catalina Mk IIA was allocated to No. 209 Squadron. This unit first received the Catalina in April 1941 at Castle Archdale, before moving to South Wales in October of that year. Leaving for East Africa in March 1942, No. 209 continued to fly Catalinas over the Indian Ocean until April 1945, being largely occupied as a Flying-Boat Conversion Unit.

Carrying an ASV aerial under the port wing and a Leigh Light for illuminating surface targets at night under its starboard wing, this Catalina Mk IVA, JX574, of No. 210 Squadron was based at RAF Sullom Voe, Shetland in 1944. The squadron flew Catalinas from April 1941 until the end of the war, sinking a confirmed total of eight U-boats.

Below: A Catalina Mk IB of No. 265 Squadron flies from Tulear in southern Madagascar in 1943. The squadron operated Catalinas over a wide area from South Africa to the Red Sea until it was disbanded in April 1945.

rescue and weather reconnaissance before the end of the war. This role led to the designation **Catalina ASR.Mk IVB**.

The advent of an amphibian version of the Catalina further enhanced its usefulness, although the RAF found less need for this type than did the US Navy and the RCAF. The adaptation was simple, with a nosewheel and mainwheels retracting into watertight bays in the hull. As the PBY-5A, the amphibious version entered US Navy service at the end of 1941 – by which time the RAF name had also been adopted by that service. The designation **Catalina Mk IA** was given to 14 of the amphibians bought by Canada, but these saw no service with the RAF. Through Lend-Lease, the RAF received 14 **Catalina Mk III**s, similar to the USN PBY-5A. These were used almost wholly in Iceland, in the hands of No. 119 Squadron and Norwegian-manned No. 330 Squadron. Another of the Norwegian squadrons, No. 333, also used Catalinas (Mk IVs) during the final months of the war in Europe. Two Catalina Mk IBs helped to maintain an important passenger, mail and freight link across the Indian Ocean from July 1943 to July 1945 in the hands of BOAC; three Mk IVs added for this service were, however, little used.

Below: The Catalina was operated by Coastal Command on long-range, extended endurance patrols in the Atlantic and Bay of Biscay. Here a Catalina releases a depth charge close to a diving U-boat.

Left: Early in 1942 Catalina Mk I AH545 of No. 209 Squadron was based at Pembroke Dock. A total of 89 Catalina Mk Is was built for the RAF, including 30 taken over from a French order.

Consolidated Catalina

Final designations allotted to the Consolidated flying-boats were **Catalina Mk V** and **Catalina Mk VI**. The Mk V was reserved for Lend-Lease supply of tall-tailed **PBN-1** versions, but none of these was in fact delivered. The Mk VI was another tall-tailed version, the **PB2B-2** produced by Boeing Aircraft of Canada. The RAF expected to receive 77 Catalina Mk VIs, but only 67 **PB2B-1**s had been built when production was terminated with the ending of hostilities, and only five of these actually reached Britain. They saw no service with the RAF, but were later transferred to the RAAF.

For the most part, Britain's Catalinas were scrapped wherever they happened to be when the war ended, the US government having no need for their return. Small numbers were, however, transferred to other nation's air forces, including those of South Africa, Norway and the Netherlands.

Right: The Catalina had a longer range and endurance than the Sunderland, but could not carry such a heavy warload. It was also able to operate in more extreme weather conditions, both temperature and sea state proving less of a problem for the Catalina. This Mk IVB operated in the Pacific theatre with No. 205 Squadron.

Above: Fitted with ASV Mk II radar, this Catalina Mk IB of No. 202 Squadron was based at Gibraltar, where it received the first of the amphibians in June 1941, replacing Saro Londons and Fairey Swordfish floatplanes. The squadron remained with its Catalinas at Gibraltar until September 1944, when it relocated to the Shetland Isles.

Below: As the war progressed the Catalina was fitted with the more effective ASV Mk VI radar (mounted above the cockpit). In July 1944 F/O Cruickshank of No. 210 Squadron sank a U-boat found by this equipment. Despite receiving 72 wounds in the attack he guided the Catalina back to base, receiving the Victoria Cross for his bravery.

Specification
Catalina Mk IB
Type: eight/nine-seat general reconnaissance flying-boat
Powerplant: two 1,200-hp (895-kW) Pratt & Whitney R-1830 radial piston engines
Performance: maximum speed 190 mph (306 km/h) at 10,500 ft (3200 m); cruising speed 179 mph (288 km/h); service ceiling 24,000 ft (7315 m); range 4,000 miles (6437 km)
Weights: empty 14,240 lb (6459 kg); maximum take-off 27,080 lb (12283 kg)
Dimensions: span 104 ft 0 in (31.70 m); length 65 ft 2 in (19.86 m); height 17 ft 11 in (5.46 m); wing area 1,400 sq ft (130.06 m^2)
Armament: one 0.303-in (7.7-mm) machine-gun in bow and two 0.303-in (7.7-mm) machine-guns in each side blister and in ventral position, plus up to 2,000 lb (907 kg) of bombs or depth charges

Consolidated Coronado

Although Coronado Mk Is were intended for Coastal Command, they were switched in September 1944 to Transport Command for transatlantic operations with No. 231 Squadron between North America, West Africa and Britain.

As the **XP2Y-1**, the prototype of this large maritime patrol flying-boat first flew on 17 December 1937. Production for the US Navy followed, with service entry on the last day of 1940. Well-armed with nose, dorsal and tail turrets in addition to beam guns, the Coronado in its production form had a crew of nine, and carried bombs, torpedoes and/or depth charges in weapon bays incorporated in the thick wing. Stabilising floats retracted to form wingtip fairings, a feature well proven on the company's earlier Catalina.

Through Lend-Lease, plans were made to provide 32 of the big Consolidated flying-boats to the RAF, with the designation **Coronado GR.Mk I**, but in the event only 10 were taken on charge; the first delivery was made on 16 April 1943. Evaluation of the Coronado at the MAEE, Helensburgh, showed a tendency to 'skip' on take-off, later cured by the introduction of a ventilated step, and heavy controls which became tiring on long flights. The RAF found no requirement for the Coronados in the GR role, and instead allocated them as transports to No. 45 Group's No. 231 Squadron, based at Boucherville, Montreal. Turrets, without guns, were at first retained, but later were faired over; as well as a 44-seat passenger cabin, the Coronado provided a VIP cabin and a large cargo bay.

Between September 1944 and January 1946, the Coronados flew regularly out of Montreal to Scotland, Iceland, Baltimore and Bermuda. Unwanted by the USN after the war ended, five were scrapped in 1945; one had been lost in a collision with a Mariner, and the final four were scuttled off the coast of Bermuda in 1946.

Specification
Coronado GR.Mk I
Type: patrol/transport flying-boat
Powerplant: four 1,200-hp (895-kW) Pratt & Whitney R-1830 Twin Wasp radial piston engines
Performance: maximum speed 223 mph (359 km/h); service ceiling 20,500 ft (6250 m); range 2,370 miles (3814 km)
Weights: empty 40,935 lb (18568 kg); maximum take-off 68,000 lb (30844 kg)
Dimensions: span 115 ft 0 in (35.05 m); length 79 ft 3 in (24.16 m); height 27 ft 6 in (8.38 m); wing area 1,780 sq ft (165.36 m²)
Armament: two 0.5-in (12.7-mm) machine-guns in bow, dorsal and tail turrets, and one 0.5-in (12.7-mm) machine-gun in two beam positions, plus up to 12,000 lb (5443 kg) of bombs, depth charges or torpedoes

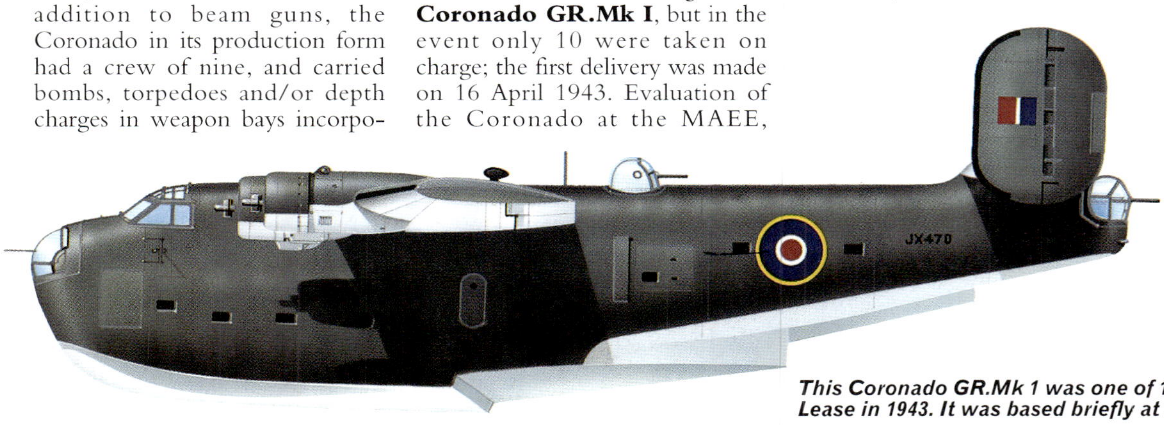

This Coronado GR.Mk 1 was one of 10 delivered to the RAF under Lend-Lease in 1943. It was based briefly at Beaumaris with Coastal Command.

Consolidated Liberator

Perhaps the most important of all the American aircraft that served with the RAF during World War II, the Liberator fulfilled three distinct roles – those of transport, bomber and overwater patrol. As the **Model 32**, the aircraft that would become known as the Liberator had been designed by Consolidated Aircraft during 1939 and obtained a USAAC contract for a prototype **XB-24**. Built in 10 months, it flew on 29 December 1939 and sired the largest production run of any US combat type, with a total of 18,431 built in all versions. Of the total, some 2,340 came to Britain, although, as with several other important additions to Britain's armoury, it was French interest that brought the first Liberators to the UK. As late as April 1940, France had optimistically ordered 165 of the Consolidated bombers, under the designation **LB-30MF**. This contract was taken over by Britain, resulting in the designation **Liberator Mk II** for 86 aircraft actually received by the RAF between August and December 1941 – the balance being taken over by the USAAC immediately following Pearl Harbor. The shortfall was made up in part, however, by the delivery between March 1941 and May 1942 of six **YB-24**s from USAAF stocks, which remained known as the Consolidated **LB-30A**, and 20 ex-USAAF **B-24A**s in April to August 1941, which became **Liberator Mk I**s. The six LB-30As, lacking armour and self-sealing fuel tanks, were used to open the ATFERO Atlantic Return Ferry Service, starting on 4 May 1941. Flying mail and cargo eastwards between St Hubert, Montreal, and Prestwick, Ayr, they performed the vital role of returning to Canada the ferry pilots who were regularly delivering Hudsons and other types to Britain via Iceland. A few of the Liberator Mk Is were also assigned to this role, and for training, while the remainder of this mark were developed for use by Coastal Command, which urgently needed aircraft with the Liberator's long range and striking power.

Entering service with No. 120 Squadron at Nutts Corner, the Liberator Mk Is were operational from 20 September 1941 onwards, 15 of the 20 Mk Is serving with this unit at some time. To supplement the Liberator's offensive armament, a semi-retractable pack of four 20-mm cannon was developed in Britain to fit in the forward end of the bomb-bay, which could also carry four 500-lb (227-kg) and two 250-lb (113.5-kg) bombs, or up to six depth charges. The cannon were to be used to attack ships or submarines; defensive armament comprised single machine-guns in the nose and tail, and single or paired beam guns. ASV Mk II 'stickleback' radar was added during the

Delivered in 1942 this Liberator Mk III was one of 11 in this Lend-Lease batch. Soon after this picture was taken it was fitted out with maritime reconnaissance equipment and delivered to RAF Coastal Command for anti-U-boat operations over the North Atlantic.

Consolidated Liberator

This Liberator GR.Mk VI, KG869, served with No. 547 Squadron at RAF Leuchars, Fife in late 1944. Developed from the American B-24H, the Mk VI had a maximum endurance of 12.5 hours with a 907-kg (2,000-lb) load of depth charges.

Used for anti-submarine operations over the Bay of Biscay and attacks on shipping off the coast of France, this Liberator GR.Mk V flew with No. 224 Squadron. The squadron was based at St Eval, Cornwall, from April 1943 to September 1944.

time the Liberator Mk Is were in service. The first recorded 'kill' of a U-boat by a Liberator Mk I of No. 120 Sqn came on 16 August 1942; there was another two days later, after which the Mk Is began to give way to Mk IIs and Mk IIIs.

The (ex-French order) Liberator Mk II introduced Boulton Paul four-gun dorsal and tail turrets, as well as the beam and nose guns – although turret production lagged behind aircraft deliveries and some Mk IIs operated without the dorsal turret. While some of the Mk IIs went to Coastal Command, delivery of this variant allowed Bomber Command to introduce the Liberator, earlier plans to issue Mk Is to No. 150 Sqn having been thwarted by Coastal's more urgent needs. At Kabrit in Egypt, No. 108 Sqn became the first to fly the Liberator as a bomber, in November 1941, while Nos 159 and 160 Sqns arrived at Fayid in June 1942 to join in the fight to stem the Axis advance into Egypt. A Special Liberator Flight was formed to support SOE operations in the Middle East, and No. 178 joined the fray early in 1943, staying on to receive **Liberator Mk III**s at the end of the year. Nos 149 and 160, meanwhile, took Liberator Mk IIs to India, where operations began in November 1942 – and it was from Indian bases that later marks would see most action. Some Mk IIs adapted in later life as transports became designated **Liberator C.Mk II**.

Deliveries to the RAF continued through Lend-Lease contracts,

Among the first Liberators to arrive in the UK was AM261. This LB-30A Liberator was diverted along with six others for transport duties, and was the first Liberator to carry royalty when it conveyed the Duke of Kent to Canada on 28 July 1941. This was also the first time any member of the British Royal Family had flown across the Atlantic.

Below: A RAF Liberator Mk VI of Strategic Air Force, Eastern Air Command is seen landing after taking part in a successful attack on Rangoon. Far East bomber squadrons of the RAF used different patterns of markings on the rudders to denote the different units.

***Left:** One of the original LB-30 transport versions of the Liberator bomber,* **Commando** *became the personal transport of Prime Minister Winston Churchill, who used it to travel to many of his World War II conferences worldwide. Modifications included a longer fuselage and a large single fin and rudder.*

***Below:** The Liberator became the principal RAF maritime reconnaissance aircraft for patrols over both the Atlantic and Indian Oceans. This Liberator GR.Mk VI, the most numerous variant operated by the RAF, has its centrimetric radar antenna lowered to scan the ocean for shipping.*

Seen returning from an attack on Japanese oil installations is this Liberator B.Mk VI of No. 356 Squadron. The squadron operated from Salbani, India and the Cocos Islands from its formation in January 1944 until it was disbanded in November 1945. In that time it dropped a total of 2,540.8 tons (2581.6 tonnes) of bombs and mines.

starting with 382 **B-24Ds** (of which 249 had initially been earmarked as a British Direct Purchase). These became **Liberator B.Mk III** or, when converted for Coastal Command, **GR.Mk III** (without ASV radar) and **GR.Mk V** (with ASV). Some were also converted for transport duty as **C.Mk V**s. The B-24D versions all differed from the earlier models in having the dorsal turrret (by Martin) moved forward to a position just aft the cockpit, and were the first of the Liberators to have exhaust-driven turbosuperchargers.

In Coastal Command, the Liberator GR.Mk IIIs and, mostly, GR.Mk Vs served with Nos 53, 59, 86, 130 and 311 Squadrons over the North Atlantic and No. 354 in India. In the latter mark, ASV Mk III had been introduced, with aerial scanners in a chin fairing and a

An unsung role for the Liberator in RAF service was radio countermeasures. No. 223 Squadron reformed at Oulton in August 1944, flying specially-equipped Liberator B.Mk VIs on electronic spoofing and Window dropping missions. For the last month of the war No. 223 operated Fortresses alongside the Liberators.

Consolidated Liberator

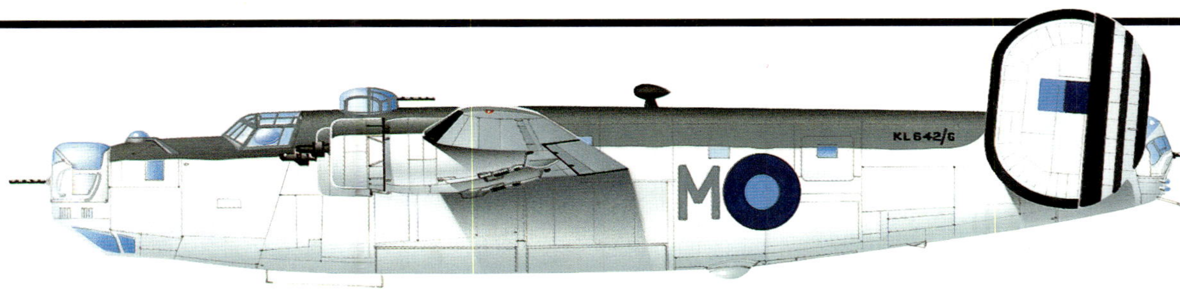

This Liberator Mk VI was assigned to No. 355 Squadron in India. The squadron painted black and white vertical stripes on the rudders of its aircraft as an identification feature. Attacks were made against enemy airfields, harbour installations and shipping which often involved round trips of over 2,000 miles (3219 km).

retractable ventral radome, providing a less drag-inducing addition than the ASV Mk II used in Liberator Mk IIs. Some Mk Vs also had their armament supplemented by eight forward-firing rocket projectiles on racks each side of the forward fuselage.

In the bomber role, the Liberator B.Mk IIIs served wholly in the Far East, where Nos 159 and 160 Sqns were already flying the Mk IIs. They were joined in August 1943 by No. 355 in the offensive against Japanese targets in Burma.

Transport operations were continuing with No. 511 Sqn which, initially as No. 1425 Flight, had been using Liberator Mk Is and C.Mk IIs between the UK and Gibraltar, and by No. 45 Group, which had grown out of Ferry Command for the ATFERO operation and was to evolve into No. 231 Sqn. BOAC also flew several Liberators in support of the Transatlantic Ferry.

The **Liberator B.Mk IV** (and **C.Mk IV**) designations were applied to the planned Lend-Lease acquisition of the **B-24E**; none was delivered. Instead, the RAF received a total of 1,648 **B-24J**s which, depending on role and equipment standard, became the **Liberator B.Mk VI**, **C.Mk VI**, **GR.Mk VI**, **B.Mk VIII**, **C.Mk VIII** and **GR.Mk VIII** (and included the final 40 of what had been the original British purchase). Deliveries continued up to March 1945. The B-24J, which was the basis for all these British versions, featured an Emerson nose turret, Martin dorsal and Sperry ventral 'ball' turret; after delivery, the British aircraft received a Boulton Paul four-gun rear turret and, in the GR versions for Coastal Command, were fitted with ASV in a ventral radome in place of the ventral turret. Starting in October 1943, No. 53 Sqn Liberators had an underwing Leigh Light installation, as later did those of Nos 206 and 547 Sqns. While several squadrons continued to operate bomber Liberators in the Middle East, the great majority of the Mk VI and Mk VIII bombers went straight to the Far East, there to equip some 15 squadrons for the RAF's final campaign in Burma through 1944/45. From the Cocos Islands, eight Liberators of No. 99 Sqn and No. 356 Sqn mounted the RAF's last bombing raid of the war, on 7 August 1945.

Equivalent of the unarmed **C-87** transport version of the Liberator that had been developed for and put into service with the USAAF, 24 **Liberator C.Mk VII**s were delivered to Britain from June to September 1944, and were used by Transport Command's Nos 511, 246 and 232 Squadrons between the UK and the Far East. Finally, the RAF received 22 **Liberator C.Mk IX**s, these being the **RY-3** version with a large, single fin and rudder. Such a tail unit was also fitted retrospectively to one of the original LB-30 transports that, with the name *Commando*, was used for a time as the personal transport of Prime Minister Winston Churchill.

Extended overwater reconnaissance and anti-submarine operations were provided for Coastal Command by Liberators from June 1941. This GR.Mk III was flown by No. 59 Squadron from Aldergrove in 1943, helping to close the mid-Atlantic 'gap' where German submarines had been causing heavy losses to shipping convoys.

Specification
Liberator B.Mk VI
Type: eight-seat heavy bomber
Powerplant: four 1,200-hp (895-kW) Pratt & Whitney R-1830 Twin Wasp radial piston engines
Performance: maximum speed 270 mph (435 km/h) at 20,000 ft (6096 m); service ceiling 28,000 ft (8534 m); range 1,470 miles (2366 km)
Weights: empty 15,600 lb (7076 kg); maximum take-off 25,200 lb (11431 kg)
Dimensions: span 57 ft 10 in (17.63 m); length 41 ft 8 in (12.70 m); height 15 ft 10 in (4.83 m); wing area 503 sq ft (46.73 m^2)
Armament: four forward-firing 20-mm cannon, six forward-firing 0.303-in (7.7-mm) machine-guns and one 0.303-in (7.7-mm) Vickers 'K' gun in dorsal position, plus one torpedo and two 250-lb (113-kg) bombs or eight 90-lb (41-kg) rocket projectiles

Liberator GR.Mk V FL927 operated with No. 59 Squadron at Ballykelly in 1944. Note the rocket projectile rack on the side of the fuselage and underwing Leigh Lights. Delivered as a Liberator Mk III, it was subsequently converted to GR.Mk V standard as a Very Long Range (VLR) aircraft.

Curtiss Cleveland

Known to the US Navy as the Helldiver, the Curtiss SBC scout-bomber biplane had begun life as early as 1932 as a two-seat carrier-based fighter. Subsequently considered as a purely scouting biplane, it finally emerged in definitive form as the **XSBC-1** in 1934.

Evolution of the Helldiver led to production of the **SBC-4** variant by 1939, this proving to be the last combat biplane produced for and put into service with the US Navy; 124 were procured. In addition, France placed a contract early in 1940 for 90 examples of the essentially similar Curtiss Hawk 77. To meet the urgent French need in 1940, the US Navy released 50 of its SBC-4s for direct delivery to France, allowing Curtiss to add a similar quantity at the end of the production run to make good the US Navy's contract.

Most of the aircraft destined for France were aboard the carrier *Béarn* and were en route when France fell. They were unloaded, and eventually scrapped, at Martinique. Five of the French-destined SBC-4s, however, were still in the US and, transferred to the RAF, arrived in Britain in August 1940. Given the name **Cleveland Mk I**, these five aircraft were assembled at Burtonwood and transferred to Little Rissington, where deciding their potential value no doubt proved somewhat elusive.

Two of the Clevelands were issued to No. 24 (Communications) Squadron at RAF Hendon, to serve in the communications role. However, one was soon destroyed (on 8 September 1940) in an air raid. The survivor was subsequently retired to become, with two more, ground instructional airframes. The fifth Cleveland Mk I saw useful service as a 'hack' with several different units until it was finally retired early in 1944.

Specification
Cleveland Mk I
Type: two-seat scout-bomber
Powerplant: one 950-hp (708-kW) Wright R-1820 Cyclone radial piston engine
Performance: maximum speed 237 mph (381 km/h) at 15,200 ft (4635 m); cruising speed 127 mph (204 km/h); service ceiling 27,300 ft (8320 m); range 855 miles (1376 km)
Weights: empty 4,841 lb (2196 kg); maximum take-off 7,632 lb (3462 kg)
Dimensions: span 34 ft 0 in (10.36 m); length 28 ft 4 in (8.64 m); height 12 ft 7 in (3.84 m); wing area 317 sq ft (29.45 m²)
Armament: one forward-firing 0.3-in (7.62-mm) machine-gun and one 0.3-in (7.62-mm) machine-gun on flexible mounting in the rear cockpit, plus one 500-lb (227-kg) or 1,000 lb (454-kg) bomb

This is one of the five Clevelands that were delivered to the RAF in August 1940. This aircraft (AS469) is seen taking off from RAF Little Rissington, where it had been delivered for ground instructional duties, but was kept flying in 1944 as a station hack.

Curtiss Helldiver

Urgently needing both to modernise and to expand its force of carrier-based strike-bombers, the US Navy endorsed a massive production programme for the Curtiss Model 84, the **XSB2C-1** prototype of which had entered flight test on 18 December 1940. Sadly, initial expectations of the Helldiver were never wholly fulfilled, and the type was dogged throughout the war by a high incidence of crashes, carrier landing accidents and in-flight break-ups. Nevertheless, production continued at a high rate while efforts were made to overcome the problems.

Initially enthused by US Navy expectations for the Curtiss bomber, the Admiralty called up a requirement for 450 to be supplied through Lend-Lease. Named **Helldiver DB.Mk I**, the British aircraft were to be supplied from the Canadian Car & Foundry production line at Fort William (this being one of the three companies building the type), and would therefore be **SBW-1B**s, similar to the parent company's **SB2C-1C**.

Deliveries to the UK began at the end of 1943, but ceased at a total of 26 aircraft in April 1944 even before the unsatisfactory characteristics of the type had been fully appreciated during testing at the A&AEE. To operate the Helldiver, the FAA established No. 1820 Sqn at Brunswick, Maine, and this unit eventually received 18 of the total delivered. It transferred to Burscough, Lancashire, via HMS *Arbiter* in July 1944, but by the end of the year had lost four Helldivers and seriously damaged three others. Unsurprisingly, interest in the Curtiss bomber waned and the squadron was disbanded at Burscough in December 1944. Other than two aircraft at the A&AEE, and one in the hands of the Empire Central Flying School's Handling Squadron for the preparation of the Pilot's Notes, no other use was made of the Helldiver.

Specification
Helldiver Mk I
Type: two-seat scout-bomber
Powerplant: one 1,700-hp (1268-kW) Wright R-2600-8 Double Row Cyclone radial piston engine
Performance: maximum speed 273 mph (439 km/h); service ceiling 21,200 ft (6462 m); range 1,375 miles (2213 km)
Weights: empty 10,114 lb (4588); maximum take-off 16,607 lb (7533 kg)
Dimensions: span 49 ft 9 in (15.15 m); length 36 ft 8 in (11.18 m); height 13 ft 1 in (4.00 m); wing area 422 sq ft (39.20 m²)
Armament: two 20-mm cannon, two flexible 0.3-in (7.62-mm) machine-guns plus up to 2,000 lb (907 kg) of bombs

Although 26 Helldiver Mk I dive-bombers were delivered under Lend-Lease in 1944 and equipped No. 1820 Squadron, they did not enter operational service with the Fleet Air Arm.

Curtiss Mohawk

Acquired by the RAF more by default than specific intention, the Mohawk was a member of the extended family of Curtiss Hawk fighters, and the first of the monoplane Hawks. Developed for the USAAC as the **P-36**, the Curtiss **Hawk 75** became available for export from 1938 onwards, and attracted the interest of several nations, not least France. In urgent need of large-scale expansion and modernisation, the Armée de l'Air ordered 100 of the **Hawk 75A-1** version in mid-1938 and 250 **Hawk 75A-2**s in March 1939. Swiftly thrown into action, these French Hawks gave valuable service up to the time of the Armistice in June 1940.

Deliveries had just begun by then against an order for 135 **Hawk 75A-3**s, with uprated 1,200-hp (895-kW) Pratt & Whitney R-1830-S1C3G engines, and 285 **Hawk 75A-4**s with 1,200-hp (895-kW) Wright GR-1820-G205A Cyclones.

With the fall of France, it was agreed that Britain should take over all of the undelivered French Hawks. The RAF assigned the name **Mohawk**, and designations **Mk I**, **Mk II**, **Mk III** and **Mk IV** were allocated to the Hawk 75A-1, A-2, A-3 and A-4, resepectively. In fact, though, all the A-ls and A-2s, and most of the A-3s and a handful of A-4s, had already gone to France. Most of the 229 ex-French Mohawks for which the RAF assigned serial numbers were therefore Mk IVs, plus a few Mk IIIs and 'escapee' Mk Is and IIs.

Having arrived in Britain, the ex-French Hawks were modified to have British throttle movement (the reverse of French), six Browning 0.303-in (7.7-mm) machine-guns, and British radio and gunsights. None, however, was issued to any operational squadrons in the UK. At least 72 Mohawks were transferred to the SAAF in 1941; they served briefly in No. 3 Squadron against Italian forces in Somalia but were primarily used for home defence and as fighter trainers.

Another 74 Mohawk Mk IVs went to India, where they equipped No. 5 Sqn, RAF, and saw operations from June 1942 to June 1943, particularly around Imphal. In this same area, No. 155 Sqn also used Mohawks, which it retained until the end of 1944, despite considerable problems in keeping aircraft serviclable. In any case, Mohawks dive-bombing with 20-lb (9-kg) bombs did not make very effective close support fighters.

Plans to produce the Hawk 75A-1 in India (by Hindustan Aircraft) appear not to have come to fruition, but HAL did assemble nine **Hawk 75A-9**s that had been supplied to Iran and were captured, when British forces occupied Iran in August 1941. Similar to the Mohawk Mk IV, these aircraft served with No. 1 OTU (India), later No. 151 (Fighter) OTU, at Risalpur, until early 1944. Britain also supplied 12 of the ex-French Mohawk Mk IVs to Portugal in October 1941.

The only operational service RAF Mohawk Mk IVs saw during World War II was in India. The RAF's examples had originally been ordered by the French Air Force.

Specification
Mohawk Mk IV
Type: single-seat fighter
Powerplant: one 1,200-hp (895-kW) Wright GR-1820-G205A radial piston engine
Performance: maximum speed 302 mph (486 km/h) at 14,000 ft (4267 m); cruising speed 248 mph (399 km/h); service ceiling 32,700 ft (9967 m); range 603 miles (970 km)
Weights: empty 4,451 lb (2019 kg); maximum take-off 6,662 lb (3022 kg)
Dimensions: span 37 ft 4 in (11.38 m); length 28 ft 8 in (8.74 m); height 11 ft 8 in (3.56 m); wing area 236 sq ft (21.92 m^2)
Armament: six 0.303-in (7.7-mm) forward-firing machine-guns plus up to 400 lb (181 kg) of bombs

Curtiss Seamew

Designed for the US Navy as a replacement for the SOC Seagull shipboard biplane scout, the **XSO3C-1** prototype, first flown on 6 October 1939, could operate as a landplane or a floatplane, in the latter case with a single central float and wingtip stabilisers. Production, as the **SO3C-1 Seagull** was delayed by protracted flight development to overcome serious instability, while the competing Vought-Sikorsky Kingfisher proved much more successful.

Britain requested 250 **SO3C-2C Seagulls** through Lend-Lease, with deliveries commencing in March 1943. To avoid confusion with the Supermarine Seagull, the name **Seamew Mk I** was adopted (and was later taken up by the US Navy also) and plans were made in January 1943 for an FAA squadron, No. 850, to equip with the type at Quonset Point, Rhode Island, in order to provision escort carriers. Testing of an early example at the A&AEE, however, cast serious doubt on its suitability for operational use, and No. 830 Squadron was 'disbanded' (having only existed on paper). Use of the Seamew was then limited to the training role: in the UK, No. 755 Sqn at Worthy Down flew Seamews as part of No. 1 Telegraphist Air Gunner's School, and a similar function was performed by Nos 744 and 755 Sqns at Dartmouth, Nova Scotia, as part of No. 2 TAG School.

Finding little use for its SO3Cs, the US Navy had meanwhile adapted the type for use as a radio-controlled target drone. The Admiralty requested 30 such drone conversions to be delivered as the **Queen Seamew**, but these did not materialise. Neither did the **Seamew Mk II** (**SO3C-4B** with centre-section fuel tanks) or the **Seamew Mk III** (the Ryan-built **SOR-1**). In the training role, British Seamews were out of service before the end of 1944 and all were scrapped in the UK – even the Canadian examples were shipped to Worthy Down for this purpose.

Specification
Seamew Mk I
Type: two-seat maritime reconnaissance/trainer
Powerplant: one 600-hp (447-kW) Ranger SGV-770-8 inline piston engine
Performance: (floatplane) maximum speed 172 mph (277 km/h) at 8,100 ft (2470 m); cruising speed 125 mph (201 km/h); service ceiling 15,800 ft (4815 m); range 1,150 miles (1851 km)
Weights: (floatplane) empty 4,284 lb (1943 kg); maximum take-off 5,279 lb (2599 kg)
Dimensions: (floatplane) span 38 ft 0 in (11.58 m); length 36 ft 10 in (11.23 m); height 15 ft 0 in (4.57 m); wing area 290 sq ft (26.94 m^2)
Armament: one forward-firing 0.3-in (7.62-mm) machine-gun and one 0.5-in (12.7-mm) machine-gun on a flexible mount plus two 100-lb (45-kg) bombs or two 325-lb (147-kg) depth charges

The Seamew saw no combat operational service with the Royal Navy, and from 1943 was relegated to training. FN473 was one of only 13 examples delivered.

Curtiss Tomahawk/Kittyhawk

Equivalent to the USAAC P-40B, this Tomahawk Mk I, AH660, was from the first RAF batch of Tomahawks the RAF received. Originally configured to a French order, the RAF used this model briefly at home (mainly for army co-operation) and, more significantly, in the Middle East before the improved Tomahawk Mk IIA and Mk IIB arrived.

Below: On the Tomahawk Mk IIA, the wing armament was increased from two to a total of four 0.3 in (7.62 mm) calibre machine-guns. Unlike the Mk I, these aircraft were fitted out with British radio equipment and instrumentation and after testing in the UK most were shipped directly to the Middle East.

Essentially, the aircraft known to the RAF (but not to the USAAC) as the Tomahawk was a Curtiss **Hawk 75** (the **P-36 Mohawk**) with an Allison V-1720 inline liquid-cooled engine replacing the Twin Wasp or Cyclone. As the **XP-40**, the prototype of this new single-seat fighter was actually a conversion of the **P-36A**, and first flew on 14 October 1938. It was powered by a 1,160-hp Allison V-1710-19 and armed with two machine-guns in the nose. Performance was modest for a fighter of its era, but in April 1939 the USAAC ordered 524 **P-40**s – the largest single aircraft order placed by the War Department since 1918 – and the future of the **Hawk 81** was assured.

Already flying the Hawk 75, France's Armée de l'Air was quick to order the improved **Hawk 81A-1**, with a contract for 230 in October 1939. Deliveries had to wait for USAAC priorities to be fulfilled, and the first of the French machines was not ready for despatch until the end of May 1940. With the French collapse imminent, the entire contract was taken over by the British Purchasing Commission, which also then placed an order for another 630 aircraft.

The first 140 of the Hawk 81A-1s were completed to the original French specification, which included French radio, instrumentation and throttle operation, and armament of two 0.50-in (12.7-mm) Colt-Brownings in the fuselage plus provision for four 7.5-mm FN-Brownings in the wing. Reaching Britain in this guise, but without the 'Zing' guns, from November 1940 onwards, these aircraft were fitted with 0.303-in (7.7-mm) Brownings in the wing, and the minimum of changes to suit them for RAF use. Named **Tomahawk Mk I**, they lacked self-sealing fuel tanks and armour protection and were judged unsuitable for use by RAF day-fighter squadrons.

The same might have been said of their suitability for low-level tactical reconnaissance and army co-operation duties, but this was the role to which the Tomahawk Mk Is were applied. With improved variants known to be in the pipeline, the Tomahawk Mk Is were issued, for training and preliminary operations, to Nos 2, 26, 171, 231, 239, 268 and 613 Squadrons of the RAF, and the UK-based Nos 400 and 403 (RCAF) Sqns. The first operation was flown by No. 26 Sqn from Gatwick in February 1941.

Next to appear was the **Hawk 81A-2**, designated by the RAF **Tomahawk Mk IIA**, which had a measure of armour protection for the pilot, self-sealing fuel tanks and 0.3-in (7.62-mm) Colt-Browning machine-guns in the wing. A total of 110 was delivered, representing the conclusion of the original French contract and the first 20 of the

Based at RAF Odiham in late 1941, this Tomahawk Mk I served with No. 400 Squadron flying Rhubarb missions over northern France, followed by Poplar missions over the English Channel. It features a bright yellow strip along the wing leading edge for head-on identification purposes.

Delivered to No. 414 Squadron RCAF at RAF Croydon in late 1941 for army co-operation duties was this Tomahawk Mk IIB. Operating alongside Lysanders on low-level reconnaissance work, it saw action over Dieppe in August 1942. In the UK, the Mk IIB was used principally for tactical support duties at low altitude.

Curtiss Tomahawk/Kittyhawk

Below: No. 403 Squadron, RCAF was formed at Baginton on 1 March 1941 as a fighter squadron. It operated Tomahawks in the army co-operation role between March and July 1941 before the squadron re-equipped with the more suitable Spitfire.

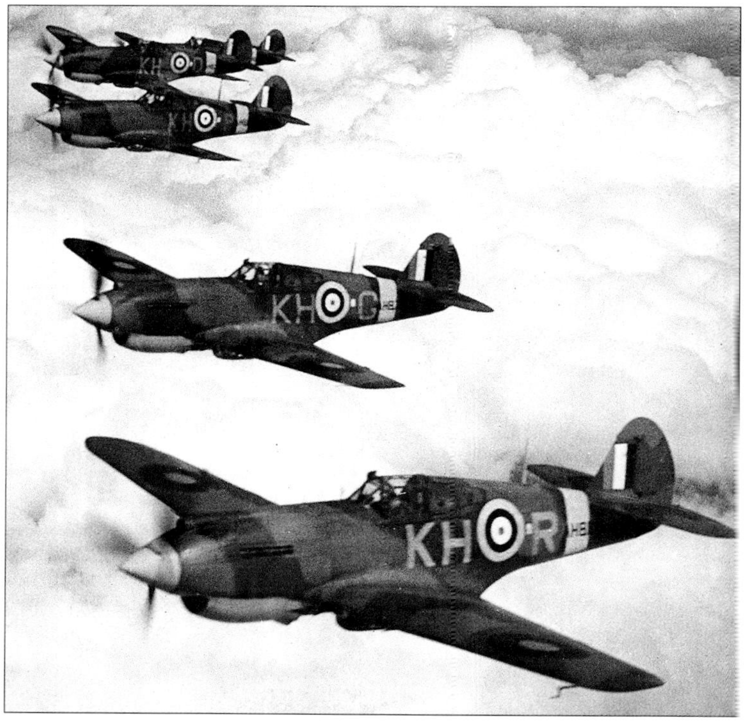

Above: While the Tomahawk proved a failure as a fighter in Europe, it served the RAF well in the deserts of North Africa. These shark-mouthed examples operated with No. 112 Squadron at Sidi Haneish in late 1941. The type had mastery over Italian fighters, but was outclassed by the Luftwaffe's Messerschmitt Bf 109Es.

British contract. Deliveries proceeded through the early months of 1941 and then continued with the **Tomahawk Mk IIB**, which differed in having British rather than US radio and oxygen equipment and the British-standard 0.303-in (7.7-mm) wing guns. The British contract had meanwhile been increased by a further 300 aircraft: these were **Hawk 81A-3**s, with provision for a 43-Imp gal (197-litre) belly drop tank. Delivery of these aircraft in the second half of 1941 brought the total of Tomahawk Mk IIBs to 910 and of all Tomahawks to 1,160.

In the UK, the Tomahawk Mk IIA and Mk IIB supplanted the Mk Is in Nos 2, 26, 231, 239 and 241 Sqns and the two RCAF units. Of these, No. 239, at Gatwick, was the first to fly armed reconnaissance Rhubarbs with the Tomahawk Mk IIs. With the availability of more aircraft and the reduction in the threat of an early German invasion of the UK, the RAF was able to assign some 300 of its Tomahawks for service in the Middle East, where No. 250 Sqn became the first to convert to the Curtiss fighter, in May 1941, followed by No. 3 (RAAF) and No. 2 (SAAF) Squadrons. The Tomahawk force in

Above: The P-40D model brought a major redesign of the nose with the introduction of the Allison V-1710-39 engine. The radiator was moved forward and deepened, and the main landing gear shortened. The RAF ordered this model as the Kittyhawk Mk I.

South Africans were predominant on the personnel roster of No. 250 Squadron which flew Tomahawks in North Africa. It was a truly cosmopolitan unit, with pilots from Rhodesia, Australia, New Zealand, Canada, India, Malaya, Great Britain and Norway, plus some Free French and one American.

In February 1943, this Tomahawk Mk IIA, 'GE-H', flew defensive fighter patrols with No. 349 (Belgian) Squadron from Ikeja in Nigeria. A Belgian-manned fighter squadron, it subsequently re-equipped with Spitfire Mk Vs in June 1943.

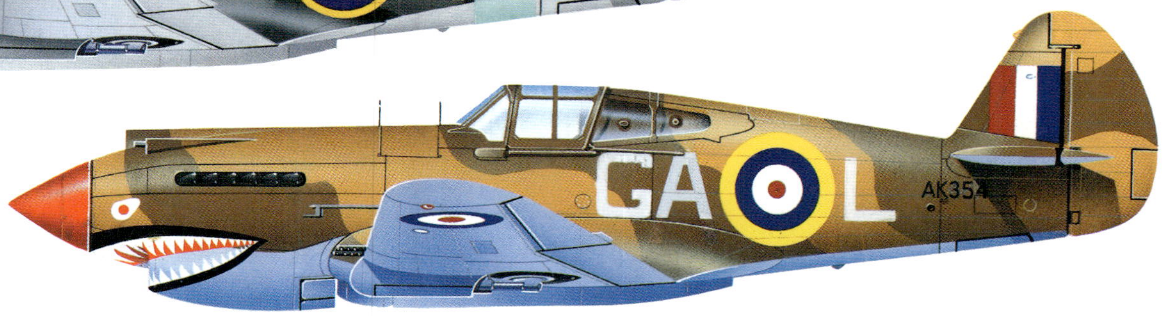

One of the most famous 'desert' P-40 squadrons was No. 112, which operated Tomahawks and Kittyhawks in this theatre from June 1941 until June 1944. This No. 112 Tomahawk Mk IIB flew from Sidi Haneish in October 1941. The squadron was famous for adorning its aircraft with sharks-mouth nose decorations.

North Africa grew with the addition of Nos 112 and 260 Sqns, RAF, and Nos 4, 5 and 40 of the SAAF, providing the basis for later introduction of the Kittyhawk into the area.

Britain also released 100 of its Tomahawk Mk IIBs to the Chinese National Government for use by the American Volunteer Group (AVG) 'Flying Tigers', and 195 were transferred to the Soviet Union in 1941; small numbers also went to the Royal Egyptian Air Force and the Turkish Air Force.

While production of the Hawk 81s continued apace for the USAAC and the RAF, Curtiss was busy developing improved versions of its fighter. In particular, introduction of the Allison V-1710-39 engine – which required some recontouring of the front fuselage and radiator, with consequent elimination of the nose guns – gave the aircraft a much improved performance, especially at higher altitudes than those at which the Tomahawk had become performance-limited. As

Above: Seen taxiing at a desert strip is one of the 616 P-40M Kittyhawk Mk IIIs supplied for service in the Middle East. This aircraft, from No. 112 Squadron, has the squadron's famous shark-mouth paint scheme that was 'borrowed' from the Luftwaffe's II./ZG 76 'Shark' Gruppe which flew Messerschmitt Bf 110s.

Left: Kittyhawk Mk IIs from No. 260 Squadron are lined up in a typical massed take-off pattern on a desert landing ground (LG) in 1942. They were tasked, on this occasion, with escorting a bomber formation on a raid against German bases in Libya.

Below: As well as fighter duties, the Kittyhawks were used extensively in the ground-attack role. These Kittyhawk Mk IIIs of No. 260 Squadron are seen landing on a captured airfield in Sicily after providing fighter-bomber support for the Army.

Curtiss Tomahawk/Kittyhawk

This Tomahawk Mk IIB is from No. 112 Squadron operating from Sidi Haneish, North Africa in late 1941. Shark-mouth markings were in existence before World War II, but it is believed that this unit was the first Allied fighter squadron to formally adopt this distinctive artwork.

Although it proved to be a mediocre fighter at higher altitudes, the Kittyhawk was useful in the low-level fighter and ground-attack roles. This Kittyhawk Mk III is from No. 250 (Sudan) Squadron, which was based in southern Italy in the latter part of 1943.

Serving with No. 112 Squadron, No. 239 Wing at RAF Cutella, Italy in 1944 was this Kittyhawk Mk III. The 'Kittybomber' was capable of carrying a 250-lb (113-kg), 500-lb (227-kg)(as shown here), or 1,000-lb (454-kg) bomb beneath the fuselage. The squadron used this latter weapon on 'bridge-felling' sorties in the spring of 1944.

A highly decorative Kittyhawk Mk II of No. 112 Squadron taxis through desert scrub. The ground crewman on the wing is seen here directing the pilot, whose view ahead was hindered by the steep attitude of the aircraft's nose when taxiing on the ground.

Below: This Kittyhawk Mk I of No. 250 Squadron is equipped with a long-range tank. The squadron was based at Aqir in Palestine, in early 1942, for offensive fighter sweeps over Syria. In May the squadron's Kittyhawks downed 10 Junkers Ju 52s and two Messerschmitt Bf 110s on one sortie.

the **Hawk 87A-1**, this new version was first ordered by the British Purchasing Commission, in May 1940; the USAAC soon followed with an order for the basically similar **P-40D**. These aircraft had only four wing guns, but the **Hawk 87A-2** and **P-40E** quickly followed, with six wing guns, and provision for a 500-lb (227-kg) bomb in place of a drop tank under the fuselage and, later, wing racks for two 100-lb (45-kg) bombs.

Britain's order was for 560 Hawk 87s, of which the first 20 had only four wing guns and the remainder six wing guns; all were designated **Kittyhawk Mk I**. The USAAC, having used early P-40s without a name, adopted the name Warhawk for all versions from the P-40E onwards. With the advent of the Lend-Lease programme, large quantities of later Hawk 87 variants were added to the RAF inventory, comprising 1,500 **Kittyhawk Mk IA**s, which were essentially the same as the Kittyhawk Mk I and the **P-40E-1**; 330 **Kittyhawk Mk II**s similar to the **P-40F**; 616 **Kittyhawk Mk III**s, of which 21 were **P-40K-1** equivalents and the remainder **P-40M**s; and finally 536

Left: Kittyhawks of No. 450 Squadron, RAAF, based initially at Luqa, Malta in July 1943, were involved in the attacks which accompanied the Allied invasion of Sicily. They later moved onto captured airfields as they were taken from the Germans.

Above: A line-up of Kittyhawk Mk IIIs of No. 3 RAAF Squadron is seen in Libya in early 1943. These aircraft were mainly engaged on anti-shipping patrols along the Libyan coast.

Kittyhawk Mk IVs similar to the **P-40N**.

Development of the P-40 to meet USAAF needs had produced a profusion of variants, accounting for these changes of designations for the RAF aircraft. The significant features of the P-40E and P-40E-1 had been the six-gun wing armament and ability to carry bombs. The P-40F made use of the 1,300-hp (970-kW) Packard-built V-1650-1 Merlin but was otherwise generally similar to the P-40E until the introduction, during the production run, of a lengthened rear fuselage that moved the vertical tail surfaces aft in relation to the tailplane with benefit to directional stability. The P-40K reverted to the Allison engine in the 1,325-hp (988-kW) V-1710-73 version; early models introduced a small dorsal fin and later batches had the lengthened rear fuselage. The P-40M, intended specifically for the Lend-Lease programme and supply to Commonwealth Air Forces, was identical with the P-40K apart from use of the 1,200-hp (895-kW) V-1710-81 engine. Finally, the P-40N, on which the long fuselage was standard, introduced a new lightweight structure and an improved frameless sliding hood over the cockpit.

Apart from examples brought to the UK for evaluation at the A&AEE and other assessments, the Kittyhawk was wholly excluded from British skies, with deliveries going straight to RAF and Commonwealth squadrons in the Middle East. Substantial numbers of the British direct-purchase and Lend-Lease Kittyhawks were also transferred to the RAAF (159 Kittyhawk Mk IAs), the RNZAF (62 Kittyhawk Mk Is) and the RCAF (72 Kittyhawk Mk Is, 12 Kittyhawk Mk IAs, 15 Kittyhawk Mk IIIs and 35 Kittyhawk Mk IVs), as well as to the SAAF. Others went to the Soviet Union and 81 were retained by the USAAF.

From early 1942 onwards, Kittyhawks replaced Tomahawks in Nos 112, 260, 250 and 94 Sqns of the RAF, Nos 3 and 450 Sqns of the RAAF and Nos 2, 4, 5 and 11 Squadrons of the SAAF, of which No. 3 (RAAF) was the first to convert to the Kittyhawk Mk I and commence operations, soon followed by No. 5 (SAAF) using Kittyhawk Mk IAs. Operating the Kittyhawks as fighter-bombers (the so-called 'Kittybombers'), these squadrons flew intensively in the Western Desert campaigns of 1942/43, responding to calls for close support from Army units on the ground. No. 260 Sqn, RAF, retained its Kittyhawks until August 1945, moving with them from North Africa to Italy, as did Nos 112 and 250 Sqns. Among the squadrons flying Kittyhawks in the Western Desert, one became particularly well-known for the shark-mouth marking that it adopted; this was No. 112 Sqn, RAF, which under the command of Sqn Ldr Clive 'Killer' Caldwell was among the first and most successful to use the 'Kittybomber' with 250-lb (113.5-kg) bombs for strafing and ground-

To help increase operational range, Kittyhawks were often fitted with an underfuselage fuel tank. These could be jettisoned in combat to improve manoeuvrability. This Kittyhawk Mk II is one of 330 which were powered by a Packard-built Rolls-Royce Merlin engine distinguishable by the lack of an intake above the engine.

The Kittyhawk's most productive period was with the Desert Air Force in 1942-43. The key to its success was its versatility, being capable of ground-attack or fighter duties. In air-to-air combat the Kittyhawk proved a better match for the Messerschmitt Bf 109F than the Hurricane, especially at lower altitudes.

attack. Combining these operations with bomber escort duties, pilots of this and other Kittyhawk units flew three or four sorties a day at the height of the North African campaign.

Although the RAF did not use its Kittyhawks in other war theatres, the aircraft transferred to the Commonwealth countries did see extensive action – particularly with the RAAF and the RNZAF in the Pacific and with the RCAF in the defence of Alaska.

Production of the P-40 in all its variants, including the Tomahawks and Kittyhawks, totalled 16,802. It is remarkable that of this total, Britain purchased, or was allocated through Lend-Lease, no fewer than 4,702, or 28 per cent of all built. The operational success of the P-40s may not have justified such large-scale production, but there is no doubt that the RAF's Tomahawk Mk IIs and Kittyhawks did make a significant contribution to the ultimate success of the Allied forces in the Western desert.

RAF Curtiss Tomahawk/Kittyhawk variants

Tomahawk Mk I (Hawk 81A-1): export version of the P-40 diverted from French order; total 140
Tomahawk Mk IIA (Hawk 81A-2): RAF version of the P-40B with armour and increased armament; total 110 plus 100 diverted from RAF order to AVG
Tomahawk Mk IIB (Hawk 81A-3): RAF version of P-40C which introduced self-sealing fuel tanks; total orders of 820 of which approximately 600 served with RAF, others being lost at sea or diverted to other air arms
Kittyhawk Mk I (Hawk 87A-2): RAF version of P-40D powered by Allison V-1710-39 with deepened radiator and increased all-up weight; total 560 of which 24 went to RCAF and 17 to Turkey
Kittyhawk Mk IA (Hawk 87A-3): RAF version of P-40E with wing armament increased to six machine-guns; total 1,500 of which 911 served with the RAF
Kittyhawk Mk II/Mk IIA: converted for RAF from US P-40F stocks fitted with Packard-built Merlin engine; total 330 of which 80 returned to USAAF, seven lost at sea and seven transferred to Free French
Kittyhawk Mk III: RAF version of P-40M with Allison V-1710-81 engine; total 616 delivered to RAF in the Middle East
Kittyhawk Mk IV: RAF version of P-40N with Allison V-1710-99 engine; total 588 of which seven were lost at sea during delivery

Specification
Kittyhawk Mk III
Type: single-seat fighter-bomber
Powerplant: one 1,600-hp (1193-kW) Allison V-1710-81 inline piston engine
Performance: maximum speed 362 mph (583 km/h) at 5,000 ft (1524 m); service ceiling 30,000 ft (9144 m); range 1,190 miles (1915 km)
Weights: empty 6,400 lb (2903 kg); maximum take-off 8,500 lb (3856 kg)
Dimensions: span 37 ft 4 in (11.38 m); length 31 ft 2 in (9.50 m); height 10 ft 7 in (3.23 m); wing area 236 sq ft (21.92 m^2)
Armament: six wing-mounted forward-firing 0.5-in (12.7-mm) machine-guns plus up to 1,000 lb (454 kg) of bombs

de Havilland DH.82 Tiger Moth

The success of the de Havilland Moth as a civil trainer led inevitably, to the development of a military version. Known as the **DH.60T Moth Trainer**, this was supplied to a number of overseas air forces, including those of Brazil, China, Egypt, Iraq and Sweden, though not to the Royal Air Force which was already using the DH.60G Gipsy Moth for training and communications. Compared with the earlier civil machine, the DH.60T was strengthened to allow it to operate at a higher all-up weight, and could carry four 20-lb (9-kg) practice bombs under the fuselage. It could also be fitted with a camera gun, or reconnaissance cameras, and was therefore suitable for various training roles.

To aid escape from the front cockpit in emergency, the rear flying wires were angled forward to the front wingroot fitting, and the cockpit doors were deepened. The centre-section struts still surrounded the front cockpit, however, and in the new trainer which was developed to Specification 15/31, these were moved forward to provide improved egress. To lessen the effect of centre of gravity changes caused by this staggering of the wings, the mainplanes were given 19 in (0.48 m) of sweepback at the tips. The 120-hp (89-kW) Gipsy III inverted inline engine was installed, the sloping line of the engine cowling providing improved visibility from the cockpit.

Eight pre-production aircraft were built, still designated D.H.60T, but bearing the name **Tiger Moth**. These were followed by a machine with increased lower wing dihedral and sweepback and this, redesignated **DH.82**, was first flown at Stag Lane on 26 October 1931. An order for 35 was placed to Specification T.23/31, and first deliveries were made to No. 3 Flying Training School at Grantham in November 1931. Others went to the Central Flying School in May 1932, and a team of five CFS pilots displayed their skill and the inverted flying capability of this new trainer at the 1932 Hendon display. Similar machines were supplied to the air forces of Brazil, Denmark, Persia, Portugal and Sweden, and two, with twin floats supplied by Short Brothers, were built to specification T.6/33 for RAF evaluation at Rochester and Felixstowe.

De Havilland then developed an improved version, with a 130-hp (97-kW) Gipsy Major engine, and plywood rear fuselage decking in place of the fabric covering of the initial production aircraft. This was designated **DH.82A** and named **Tiger Moth II** by the RAF, which ordered 50 to Specification T.26/33. They were fitted with hoods which could be positioned over the rear cockpit for instrument flying instruction, and were delivered to Kenley between November 1934 and January 1935. Others were supplied to the Bristol Aeroplane Company, the de Havilland School of Flying, Brooklands Aviation Ltd, Phillips and Powis School of Flying, Reid and Sigrist Ltd,

The Tiger Moth provided initial flying experience for most wartime RAF and Commonwealth pilots, who regarded it with great affection. It was not simple to fly, but this was no bad thing for a trainee who would soon be flying a front-line combat aircraft.

de Havilland DH.82 Tiger Moth

The main users of the Tiger Moth were civilian-operated Elementary and Reserve Flying Training Schools, and later their wartime counterparts at home and overseas, the Elementary Flying Training Schools. Tiger Moths were also used to train instructors.

Below: A radio-controlled pilotless target derivative of the Tiger Moth was the Queen Bee, which was first flown on 5 January 1935. A total of 380 was built for the RAF, mainly for live-target gunnery practice on various AA ranges. These had wooden, plywood-covered fuselages, in contrast to the Tiger Moth's metal fabric-covered structure. The Queen Bee was declared obsolete in May 1947.

Airwork Ltd and Scottish Aviation Ltd for the Elementary and Reserve Flying Schools which these companies operated under the RAF expansion scheme.

Pre-war licence-manufacture of the Tiger Moth included aircraft built in Norway, Portugal and Sweden, and by de Havilland Aircraft of Canada, whose pre-war output included 227 DH.82As. The company was later to build 1,520 of a winterised version, designated **DH.82C**, which had a 145-hp (108-kW) Gipsy Major engine with a revised, easy-access cowling, sliding cockpit canopies, cockpit heating, Bendix wheel brakes and a tailwheel in place of the standard skid. Skis or floats could also be fitted if required, and some were powered by a Menasco Pirate engine when Gipsy Majors were in short supply. A batch of 200 DH.82Cs was ordered by the US Army Air Force, with the designation **PT-24**, although they were diverted for use by the Royal Canadian Air Force.

The outbreak of war saw civil machines impressed for RAF communications and training duties, and larger orders were placed. A further 795 were built at Hatfield, before the factory was turned over to de Havilland Mosquito production and the Tiger Moth line was re-established at the Cowley works of Morris Motors Ltd, where some 3,500 were to be manufactured. De Havilland Aircraft of New Zealand built a further 345, and in Australia de Havilland Aircraft produced a total of 1,085.

On 17 September 1939, just two weeks after war had been declared, 'A' Flight of the British Expeditionary Force Communications Squadron (later No. 81 Squadron) was despatched to France. Throughout the winter and the following spring, the unit's Tiger Moths operated in northern France, providing valuable communications facilities until the Dunkirk evacuation, when surviving aircraft were flown back to Britain.

Preparations were also made for the Tiger Moth to be used in an offensive role, to combat the threatened German invasion. Racks designed to carry eight 20-lb (9-kg) bombs were fitted under the rear cockpit or, more suitably, beneath the wings. Although some 1,500 sets of racks were made and distributed to the flying schools, none was used operationally. Earlier, in December 1939, six coastal patrol squadrons were formed, five of them equipped with Tiger Moths. However futile this may seem, it was considered that despite an inability to attack, the sound of any engine might deter a U-boat commander from running on the surface or at periscope depth, and thus reduce his capacity to attack shipping.

In the Far East a small number of Tiger Moths were converted for use as ambulance aircraft with No. 224 Group Communications Squadrons, the necessary modification being effected at Comilla, East Bengal in late 1944. The luggage locker lid was enlarged and a hinged lid cut into the rear fuselage decking, providing a compartment some 6 ft (1.83 m) long, which could accommodate one casualty. Flying in and out of small strips, they performed valuable service until replaced by Stinson Sentinels.

It was in its primary trainer role, however, that the Tiger Moth made its greatest contribution the war effort. The type equipped no fewer than 28 Elementary Flying Training Schools in Britain, 25 in Canada (plus four Wireless Schools), 12 in Australia, four in Rhodesia (plus a Flying Instructors' School), seven in South Africa and two in India.

Specification
DH.82A Tiger Moth
Type: two-seat elementary trainer and communications aircraft
Powerplant: one 130-hp (97-kW) de Havilland Gipsy Major inline piston engine
Performance: maximum speed 109 mph (175 km/h) at 1,000 ft (305 m); cruising speed 93 mph (150 km/h); service ceiling 13,600 ft (4145 m); range 302 miles (486 km)
Weights: empty 1,115 lb (506 kg); maximum take-off 1,770 lb (8013 kg)
Dimensions: span 29 ft 4 in (8.94 m); length 23 ft 11 in (7.29 m); height 8 ft 9 1/2 in (2.68 m); wing area 2.39 sq ft (22.20 m²)
Armament: none normally, but see text

Like the majority of the RAF's Tiger Moths, this Mk II in 1940s markings served with an RAF Elementary and Reserve Flying Training School. One of the world's most famous training aircraft, the Tiger Moth remained in service with the RAF for over 15 years. It was fully approved for aerobatics and suitable for blind-flying instruction, using a hood over the rear cockpit.

de Havilland DH.89 Dominie

Designed in the light of experience gained in the production and operation of the de Havilland DH.84 Dragon and DH.86 Express light transports, the prototype **DH.89 Dragon Six**, powered by two 200-hp (149-kW) de Havilland Gipsy Six engines, was flown at Stag Lane by Hubert Broad on 17 April 1934. Production aircraft, which were named **Dragon Rapide**, were delivered from July 1934, the first customers including Hillman's Airways Ltd, Railway Air Services and Olley Air Service Ltd. From March 1937 small trailing-edge flaps were fitted to the lower wings, outboard of the engine nacelles, and the type was redesignated **DH.89A**.

A militarised version, designated **DH.89M**, was developed to meet Air Ministry Specification G.18/35, which called for a general reconnaissance aircraft for service with Coastal Command. A forward-firing gun was fitted in the nose, to the right of the pilot's seat, and a gun mounting ring was installed in the roof, aft of the cabin door. Although the competition was won by the Avro 652A Anson, armed Rapides were supplied to the Spanish government in 1936, for operation in Morocco. Although the DH.89M did not gain a production contract, the Dragon Rapide was selected as a communications aircraft, a single example having been purchased for the use of the Air Council and operated by No. 24 Squadron at Hendon; two more were delivered in November 1938. Civil Rapides were used to supply British forces in France in the spring and early summer of 1940, and many were impressed for communications duties, particularly with the Air Transport Auxiliary.

In 1939, three DH.89s had been acquired as wireless trainers, to Air Ministry Specification T.29/38, followed by a further 14 for use by No. 2 Electrical and Wireless School. The first two DH.89As, also for No. 2 E & WS, were delivered in September 1939. The trainer version was identified by the direction-finding loop in the cabin roof, later being designated **Dominie Mk I**, the communications version becoming the **Dominie Mk II**.

Of 728 Rapides built before production ended in July 1946, 521 were to British military contracts, mostly as **DH.89B**s. Some 186 were built at Hatfield before pressure of work on other aircraft resulted in the transfer of production to Brush Coachworks Ltd at Loughborough, Leicestershire. The military DH.89 figure includes 65 aircraft used by the Royal Navy between 1940 and 1958, when the last was retired; some were impressed civil machines, some supplied new, and others transferred from the RAF.

The Dominie Mk II communications variant gave particularly useful service with the Air Transport Auxiliary. This Mk II was built by Brush Coachworks Ltd, Loughborough.

Left: These two Dominie Mk Is, '209' and '205', both flew with the RAF's No. 2 Radio School at Yatesbury during 1943. The training variant was identifiable by the direction-finding loop which was mounted above the forward cabin.

Specification
Dominie Mk II
Type: five/six-seat radio or navigation trainer, and eight/10-seat communications aircraft
Powerplant: two 200-hp (149-kW) de Havilland Gipsy Queen inline piston engines
Performance: maximum speed 157 mph (253 km/h) at 1,000 ft (305 m); cruising speed 132 mph (212km/h); service ceiling 16,700 ft (5090 m); range 570 miles (917 km)
Weights: empty 3,230 lb (1465 kg); maximum take-off 5,500 lb (2945 kg)
Dimensions: span 48 ft 0 in (14.63 m); length 34 ft 6 in (10.52 m); height 10 ft 3 in (3.12 m); wing area 340 sq ft (31.59 m²)

de Havilland DH.93 Don

L2391 was the fifth DH.93 to be built and was the first to be converted, by the removal of the turret, as a three-seat communications aircraft.

Originally designed as a three-seat general-purpose trainer to meet the Air Ministry Specification T.6/36, the **DH.93 Don** was an extremely clean low-wing monoplane with retractable main landing gear and a manually-operated gun turret for gunnery training. The prototype first flew in June 1937 and the RAF promptly ordered 250 examples. However, a change in official policy resulted in the cancellation of the training version, and the aircraft was assigned as a communications type.

The DH.93 underwent trials at Martlesham Heath where several modifications, including the removal of the turret and other heavy equipment, were identified. The production order for the resulting communications version was cut to 50 examples, with the fifth airframe being the first to be converted to this standard.

Of the 50 aircraft ordered around 20 were delivered unassembled, or as engineless airframes for use by the Schools of Technical Training. The first in-service examples were allocated to the Central Flying School, Upavon, No. 11 Group Station Flight, Northolt and to No. 24 Squadron based at Hendon, which used the aircraft for communications flights around the UK. Other examples were delivered in late 1938/early 1939 to Station Flights at Abingdon, Andover, Brize Norton, Eastchurch, Mildenhall, Netheravon, South Cerney and Wyton, as well as to the Electrical and Wireless School at Cranwell.

During 1939 the RAF's Dons were gradually allocated to Schools of Technical Training or to Air Training Corps squadrons as ground instructional airframes, joining the incomplete examples. The last airworthy examples were withdrawn from service in 1940 and relegated to No. 24 Maintenance Unit at Ternhill.

Specification
DH.93 Don
Type: three-seat communications aircraft
Powerplant: one 525-hp (391-kW) de Havilland Gipsy King I supercharged inline piston engine
Performance: maximum speed 189 mph (304 km/h) at 8,750 ft (2665 m); service ceiling 23,300 ft (7100 m); range 890 miles (1432 km)
Weights: empty 5,050 lb (2291 kg); maximum take-off 6,860 lb (3112 kg)
Dimensions: span 47 ft 6 in (14.48 m); length 37 ft 4 in (11.38 m); height 9 ft 5 in (2.87 m); wing area 304 sq ft (28.24 m^2)

de Havilland DH.95 Flamingo

The ability to fly two new airliner prototypes of such completely different design within 19 months, from the same factory, was a remarkable achievement, the all-metal de Havilland **DH.95 Flamingo** following the wooden Albatross on 23 December 1938. Like the Albatross, however, the Flamingo's promise was stifled by the war.

Its initial performance trials attracted the attention of military and civil customers alike, and the Air Ministry evaluated the prototype as a military transport in March 1939.

Proving flights from Heston and Eastleigh to the Channel Islands in May 1939 were carried out by Guernsey and Jersey Airways Ltd, but the outbreak of war put a stop to these operations and the two Flamingoes ordered by the airline were delivered, along with the prototype, to No. 24 Squadron at Hendon, for use as VIP transports.

Of the remaining 13 Flamingoes completed, 10 were built to civil standards and three went to the RAF. The first two of these were delivered to the King's Flight at Benson on 7 September 1940, to be joined by a third later, for possible emergency evacuation of the Royal Family.

A contract for 30 aircraft to military specifications under the name **Hertfordshire** was placed, but cancelled after the first had been delivered and tested at Boscombe Down. The only visible difference in the single Hertfordshire was the substitution of portholes for windows.

Seven Flamingoes were operated by BOAC in the Near East on a number of routes radiating from Cairo and including Asmara, Aden, Addis Ababa, Adana, Jeddah and Lydda. Of these aircraft, two were lost in 1943 in separate crashes at Asmara, one crashed at Adana in 1942 and the other four were brought back to the UK, being scrapped at Redhill in 1950.

A single Flamingo, the 11th aircraft, was impressed by the Admiralty in 1940 and based with the Fleet Air Arm's No. 782 Squadron at Donibristle, from where it served the Orkneys, Shetlands and Northern Ireland. It was joined in 1945 by an ex-RAF Flamingo.

The former aircraft was the last survivor of the breed; after demobilisation in 1945 it flew for a while in its original civil marks, but was eventually scrapped in May 1954 at Redhill.

Specification
DH.95 Flamingo
Type: 17-passenger transport aircraft
Powerplant: two 930-hp (694-kW) Bristol Perseus XVI radial piston engines
Performance: maximum speed 243 mph (391 km/h); cruising speed 204 mph (328 km/h); service ceiling 20,900 ft (6370 m); range 1,345 miles (2165 km)
Weights: empty 11,325 lb (5137 kg); maximum take-off 18,000 lb (8165 kg)
Dimensions: span 70 ft 0 in (21.34 m); length 51 ft 7 in (15.72 m); height 15 ft 3 in (4.65 m); wing area 651 sq ft (60.48 m^2)

Flamingo R2766 served with No. 24 Squadron at Hendon on VIP transport duties. The Flamingo was unusual for a pre-war de Havilland design in being of all-metal construction.

de Havilland DH.98 Mosquito

The yellow-painted prototype DH.98 Mosquito, W4050, flew for the first time on 25 November 1940, four days short of 11 months from the beginning of detailed design work.

Below: Mosquito PR.Mk I W4051 'LY-V' of No. 1 PRU at Benson was the last of the three prototypes to fly. It had the shorter engine nacelles as fitted to W4050. Ten Mosquito PR.Mk Is were eventually built.

The all-wooden de Havilland Mosquito was possibly the most useful single type of aircraft produced by the Allies in World War II. Like so many other great aircraft, it owed nothing to any official specification and was created in the teeth of often fierce opposition by officialdom. Even after a prototype had been ordered, the limited nature of the programme (a mere 50 aircraft) caused it to be removed entirely from future plans three times after the Dunkirk evacuation. Each time it was daringly put back by a single believer, Patrick (later Sir Patrick) Hennessy, brought in from Ford Motors by Lord Beaverbrook to help run British aircraft production. So in November 1940 a single prototype at last took to the air. Once that had happened, the fantastic performance of the Mosquito carried all before it.

The de Havilland Aircraft Company was famed chiefly for lightplanes and rather primitive mixed-construction light transports, but in 1936 it designed the aerodynamically superb (but technically disastrous) DH.91 Albatross airliner with a structure entirely of wood. A few months later, work was started on a military derivative with two Merlin engines to meet the requirements of Specification P.13/36, but this was not accepted, largely because of the wooden structure which was not taken seriously. Undeterred, the project staff under R. E. Bishop, R. M. Clarkson and C. T. Wilkins continued to study a new high-speed bomber able to evade hostile fighters and thus dispense with gun turrets. The concept appeared to make sense. Doing away with turrets reduced the crew from six to two, comprising a pilot on the left in the nose cockpit with the navigator/bombardier on his right. Either could work the radio. Thanks to the scale effect, in that saving weight enabled the aircraft to be smaller and burn less fuel, it was calculated that the twin-Merlin unarmed bomber could carry 1,000 lb (454 kg) of bombs 1,500 miles (2400 km) for a weight of just over 15,000 lb (6800 kg), so that, with good streamlining, the speed could reach almost 400 mph (655 km/h), nearly double the speed of other British bombers.

The first Mosquito night-fighter (NF.Mk II) prototype was W4052, which was first flown on 15 May 1941. Fitted with AI Mk IV radar and a nose armament of four 20-mm cannon and four 0.303-in (7.7-mm) machine-guns, production examples entered service in April 1942.

This Mosquito Mk I served with No. 1 Photographic Unit in 1941. The ninth production aircraft, W4055 operated with this unit until it was lost on operations on 4 December 1941. It was finished in PRU blue camouflage with pale grey codes.

The night-fighter Mosquitos of No. 157 Squadron were painted in 'Lamp Black' RDM 2A matt non-reflective Special Night Finish camouflage and red code letters, adopted by the RAF in November 1940. This Mosquito NF.Mk II served with the squadron at Castle Camps in mid-1942.

Left: Mosquito NF.Mk IIs of No. 23 Squadron operated from RAF Luqa, Malta, flying intruder missions over southern Italy in the autumn of 1943. These were the first Mosquitos to serve in the Mediterranean. The squadron was detached to Sigonella, Sicily, later in the year and flew 'roving commissions' over enemy positions, attacking trains, transport columns and airfields.

The aircraft could have flown in early 1939 but officials, including the Air Staff, showed either disinterest or hostility. Dozens of objections were raised to show that an unarmed bomber would be useless, that a crew of only two could not fly the mission, and that the company's proposals were pointless. At a major meeting at the Air Ministry just after the Munich crisis, in October 1938, the officials declined to study the proposals but asked if de Havilland would build wings for one of the existing bomber programmes. Even after the outbreak of war, no member of the Air Staff saw in the proposals anything but a pointless diversion. It was not until long after the outbreak of war that, partly because of support by Air Marshal Sir Wilfred Freeman, the Air Staff began to concede that a twin-Merlin aircraft, provided it was built solely for reconnaissance, might possibly be unarmed and might even be made of wood. With great efforts the point was reached on 1 March 1940 at which a contract could be signed for a prototype plus 49 production machines.

The first **D.H.98 Mosquito** (W4050) was secretly built at Salisbury Hall, close to the Hatfield works, to which it was taken by road on 3 November 1940. Geoffrey de Havilland Jr made the first flight on 25 November. It had been estimated that, with twice the power of a Spitfire, twice the skin area and more than twice the

Right: Mosquito Mk II 'RX-X' of No. 456 Squadron, RAAF at RAF Colerne in mid-1943 was used for intruder patrols over France and sweeps over the Bay of Biscay coast to catch enemy fighters attempting to interfere with Coastal Command's anti-submarine aircraft.

Below: The Mosqutio FB.Mk VI had a powerful mixed armament of cannon and machine-guns which could be used against ground or aerial targets. This example is seen test-firing a newly-fitted gun before an early morning sortie.

weight, the Mosquito would be 20 mph (32 km/h) faster. Nobody in the Air Ministry believed this; they were amazed when the prototype was officially tested at Boscombe Down in February 1941 and found to reach 392 mph (631 km h), over 20 mph (32 km/h) faster than any RAF fighter.

The basic design was a streamlined monoplane, with the sharply tapered wing mounted in the mid position above a bomb bay for four 250-lb (113-kg) bombs. The pilot sat just ahead of the leading edge, where he had an excellent field-of-view except where blocked by the engine cowlings, which extended aft to the trailing edge. Almost the entire structure was of wood, the wing having two spars and ply skins (double on the upper surface) with spruce stringers, while the fuselage was made in left and right halves moulded on concrete formers from a sandwich structure which comprised light balsa between inner and outer skins of plywood. Flying-control surfaces were light alloy, with metal skin on the ailerons and fabric on the tail, but the hydraulic plain flaps were wooden. Unusual features included coolant radiators occupying the wing leading edge between engines and fuselage, which with development could give positive thrust in cruising flight, and simple landing gears with twin shock struts filled with rubber blocks. This eliminated much need for precision metalwork, and the total weight of castings (250 lb/113 kg) and forgings (30 lb/13.6 kg) was less than for any other twin-engined combat aircraft of its day.

Flight development showed the need for an increase in span from 52 ft 6 in (16.00 m) to 54 ft 2 in (16.51 m), a larger tailplane, improved cowlings and exhaust systems, and lengthened nacelles which divided the flaps into four small sections joined by torque tubes. The leading-edge slats were judged unnecessary and eliminated. Though the aircraft had only managed to survive by being a reconnaissance machine, its brilliant performance now opened the way to

de Havilland Mosquito NF.Mk II cutaway drawing key

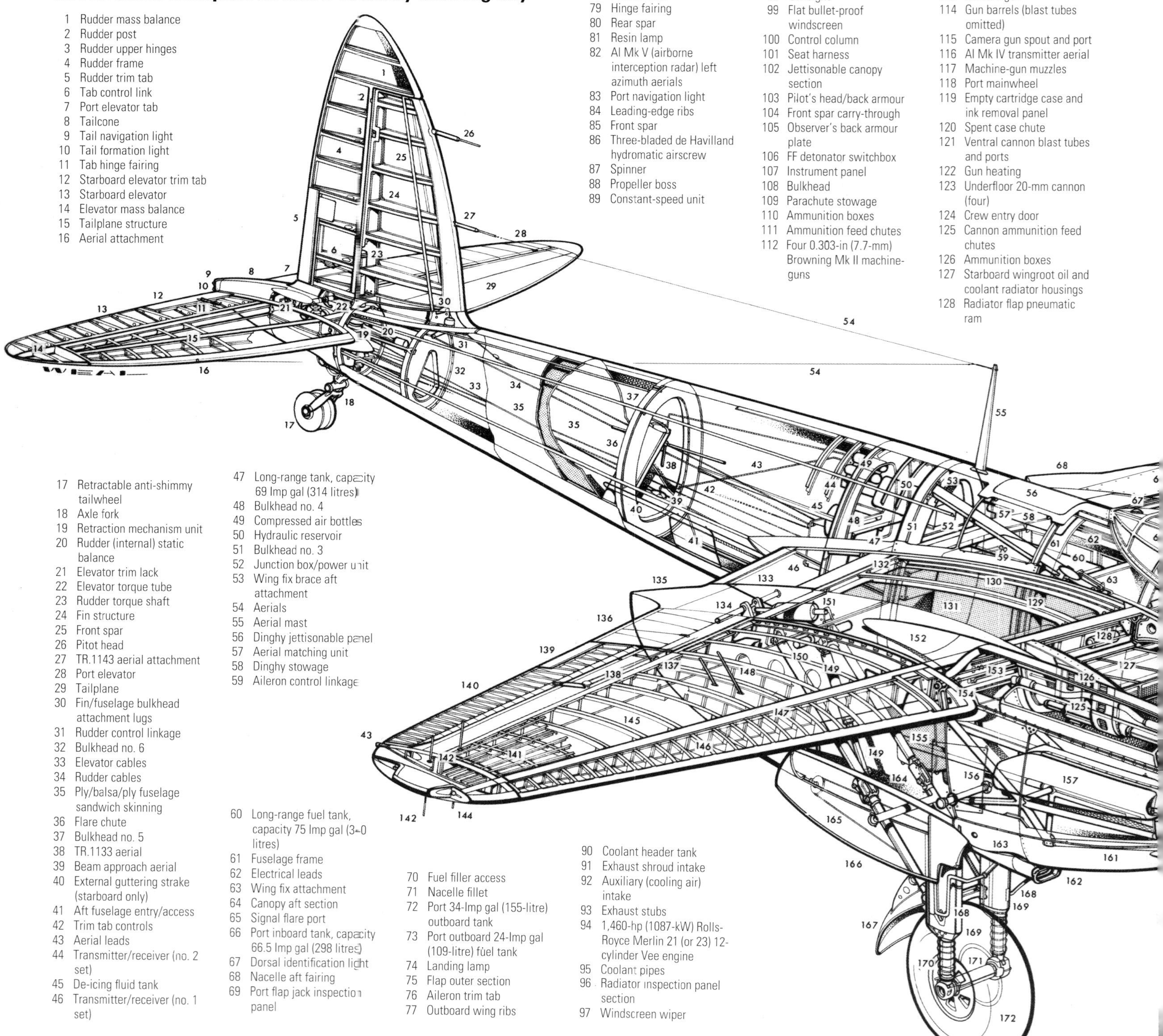

1 Rudder mass balance
2 Rudder post
3 Rudder upper hinges
4 Rudder frame
5 Rudder trim tab
6 Tab control link
7 Port elevator tab
8 Tailcone
9 Tail navigation light
10 Tail formation light
11 Tab hinge fairing
12 Starboard elevator trim tab
13 Starboard elevator
14 Elevator mass balance
15 Tailplane structure
16 Aerial attachment
17 Retractable anti-shimmy tailwheel
18 Axle fork
19 Retraction mechanism unit
20 Rudder (internal) static balance
21 Elevator trim lack
22 Elevator torque tube
23 Rudder torque shaft
24 Fin structure
25 Front spar
26 Pitot head
27 TR.1143 aerial attachment
28 Port elevator
29 Tailplane
30 Fin/fuselage bulkhead attachment lugs
31 Rudder control linkage
32 Bulkhead no. 6
33 Elevator cables
34 Rudder cables
35 Ply/balsa/ply fuselage sandwich skinning
36 Flare chute
37 Bulkhead no. 5
38 TR.1133 aerial
39 Beam approach aerial
40 External guttering strake (starboard only)
41 Aft fuselage entry/access
42 Trim tab controls
43 Aerial leads
44 Transmitter/receiver (no. 2 set)
45 De-icing fluid tank
46 Transmitter/receiver (no. 1 set)
47 Long-range tank, capacity 69 Imp gal (314 litres)
48 Bulkhead no. 4
49 Compressed air bottles
50 Hydraulic reservoir
51 Bulkhead no. 3
52 Junction box/power unit
53 Wing fix brace aft attachment
54 Aerials
55 Aerial mast
56 Dinghy jettisonable panel
57 Aerial matching unit
58 Dinghy stowage
59 Aileron control linkage
60 Long-range fuel tank, capacity 75 Imp gal (340 litres)
61 Fuselage frame
62 Electrical leads
63 Wing fix attachment
64 Canopy aft section
65 Signal flare port
66 Port inboard tank, capacity 66.5 Imp gal (298 litres)
67 Dorsal identification light
68 Nacelle aft fairing
69 Port flap jack inspection panel
70 Fuel filler access
71 Nacelle fillet
72 Port 34-Imp gal (155-litre) outboard tank
73 Port outboard 24-Imp gal (109-litre) fuel tank
74 Landing lamp
75 Flap outer section
76 Aileron trim tab
77 Outboard wing ribs
78 Port aileron
79 Hinge fairing
80 Rear spar
81 Resin lamp
82 AI Mk V (airborne interception radar) left azimuth aerials
83 Port navigation light
84 Leading-edge ribs
85 Front spar
86 Three-bladed de Havilland hydromatic airscrew
87 Spinner
88 Propeller boss
89 Constant-speed unit
90 Coolant header tank
91 Exhaust shroud intake
92 Auxiliary (cooling air) intake
93 Exhaust stubs
94 1,460-hp (1087-kW) Rolls-Royce Merlin 21 (or 23) 12-cylinder Vee engine
95 Coolant pipes
96 Radiator inspection panel section
97 Windscreen wiper
98 Gunsight
99 Flat bullet-proof windscreen
100 Control column
101 Seat harness
102 Jettisonable canopy section
103 Pilot's head/back armour
104 Front spar carry-through
105 Observer's back armour plate
106 FF detonator switchbox
107 Instrument panel
108 Bulkhead
109 Parachute stowage
110 Ammunition boxes
111 Ammunition feed chutes
112 Four 0.303-in (7.7-mm) Browning Mk II machine-guns
113 Camera gun
114 Gun barrels (blast tubes omitted)
115 Camera gun spout and port
116 AI Mk IV transmitter aerial
117 Machine-gun muzzles
118 Port mainwheel
119 Empty cartridge case and ink removal panel
120 Spent case chute
121 Ventral cannon blast tubes and ports
122 Gun heating
123 Underfloor 20-mm cannon (four)
124 Crew entry door
125 Cannon ammunition feed chutes
126 Ammunition boxes
127 Starboard wingroot oil and coolant radiator housings
128 Radiator flap pneumatic ram

129 Wing inboard rib
130 Starboard inboard fuel tank, capacity 78 Imp gal (355 litres)
131 Starboard inboard fuel tank, capacity 65.5 Imp gal (298 litres)
132 Rear spar fixing
133 Starboard flap section
134 Flap jack and crank
135 Nacelle aft fairing
136 Flap outer section
137 Aileron tab chain drive
138 Aileron balance and actuating cables
139 Aileron trim tab
140 Starboard aileron
141 Wing stringers
142 AI Mk V right azimuth aerials
143 Resin lamp
144 Starboard navigation light
145 Wing outer ribs
146 Leading-edge ribs
147 Front spar
148 AI Mk IV elevation aerials (above and below starboard wing only)
149 Undercarriage retraction jack
150 Undercarriage radius rod/rear spar attachment
151 Flap hydraulic actuator
152 Nacelle fillet
153 Control lines
154 Undercarriage jacking lug
155 Starboard oil tank
156 Engine bearer supports
157 Exhaust flame damper shroud
158 Spinner back plate
159 Starboard spinner
160 de Havilland hydromatic airscrew
161 Starboard engine nacelle
162 Carburettor air intake (with anti-ice guard)
163 Intake fairing
164 Radius rod hinge
165 Undercarriage door elasticated cord and drum
166 Main undercarriage doors
167 Mudguards
168 Wheel door guides
169 Undercarriage compression legs
170 Rubber shock pads (cuffed)
171 Mainwheel axle
172 Starboard mainwheel

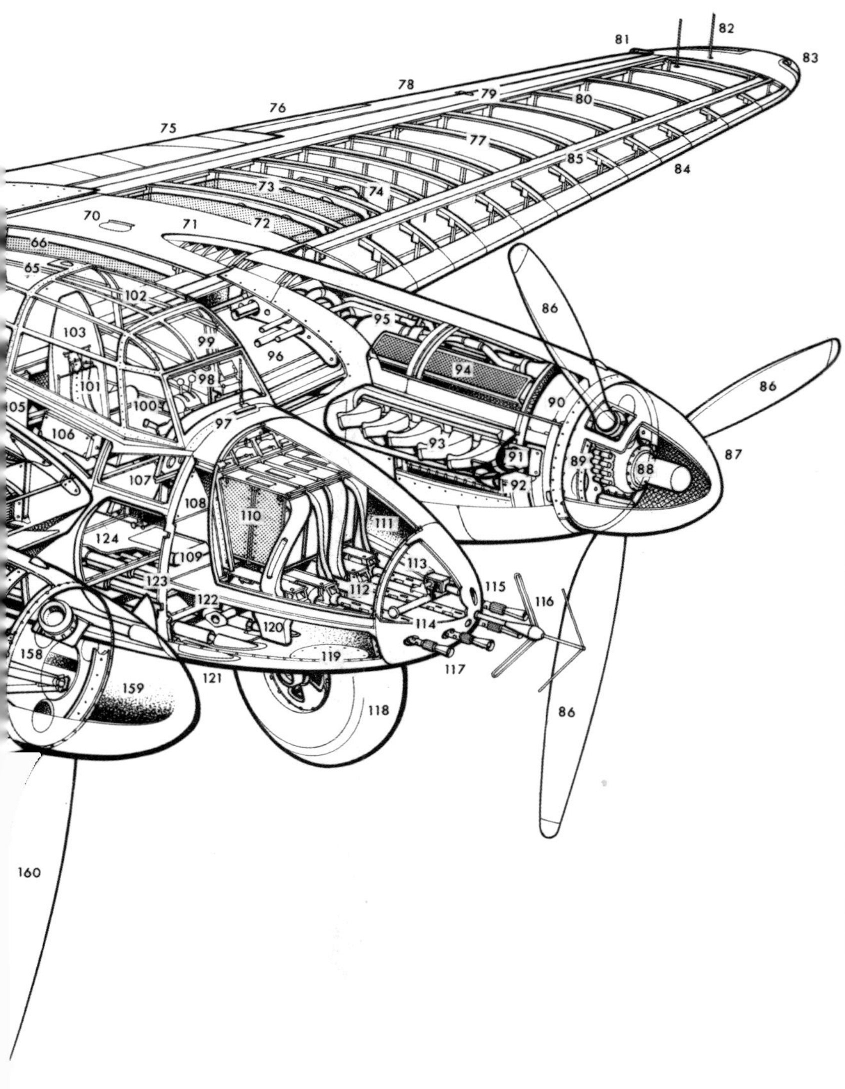

The T.Mk III was a dual-control trainer version. HJ880 was built at Leavesden and was one of over 300 delivered to the RAF from September 1942 for conversion training.

de Havilland Mosquito variants of World War II

D.H.98: prototype with two 1,280-hp (955-kW) Rolls-Royce Merlin RM.3SMs, and short engine nacelles
PR.Mk I: Merlin 21 engines, short nacelles, 54-ft 2-in (16.51-m) span, larger tailplane, three vertical and one oblique cameras; total 1 prototype and 10 production
F.Mk II: Merlin 21, 22 or 23 engines, AI Mk IV radar, four 20-mm cannon and four 0.303-in (7.7-mm) machine-guns, side door, flat windscreen, long nacelles; total 467
T.Mk III: dual trainer with Merlin 21, 23 or 25 engines, drop tanks; total 343
B.Mk IV Series I: converted from PR.Mk I, 2,000-lb (907-kg) bomb load, short nacelles; total 38
B.Mk IV Series II: first production bomber with Merlin 21 or 23 engines, drop tanks, some with bomb bay for 4,000-lb (1814-kg) bomb: some converted as PR.Mk IV, others for Highball (Wallis skipping bomb); total 235, including 32 PR.Mk IV
FB.Mk VI: fighter-bomber with Merlin 21, 23 or 25 engines, F.Mk II guns plus two 500-lb (227-kg) bombs internal plus drop tanks/bombs/rockets; total 2,248
B.Mk VII: Canadian-built B.Mk IV Series II with Merlin 31 engines; total 25
PR.Mk VIII: photographic version of PR.Mk IV with Merlin 61 engines; total 5
B.Mk IX: high-altitude bomber with Merlin 72/73 or 76/77 engines, up to 4,000 lb (1814 kg) of bombs, some with H2S Mk VI radar/Oboe/drop tanks: **PR.Mk IX** photo version, increased fuel fitted with Rebecca/ Boozer; total 4 B.Mk IX and 90 PR.Mk IX
NF.Mk XII: night-fighter with Merlin 21 or 23 engines, AI Mk VIII in thimble nose, four 20-mm cannon; total 97 conversions from Mk II
NF.Mk XIII: night-fighter with Merlin 21, 23 or 25 engines, Mk VI wings suitable for tanks/bombs/rockets, AI Mk VIII or SCR-720 in universal 'bull' nose; total 270
NF.Mk XV: high-altitude fighter with long-span 59-ft 2-in (18.03-m) wing, Merlin 73 or 77 engines, four 0.303-in (7.7-mm) guns in ventral pack, reduced fuel, pressure cabin; total 5 conversions from B.Mk IV
PR.Mk XVI, B.Mk XVI: photo and bomber models with Mk IX engines but pressure cabin, increased fuel as PR.Mk IX, very wide range of electronic fits; total 433 PR.Mk XVI and 1,200 B.Mk XVI
NF.Mk XVII: Merlin 21 or 23 engines, SCR-720 or 729 (AI Mk X) radar, some with tail warning; total 100 conversions from Mk II
FB.Mk XVIII: 'Tse Tse Fly', Merlin 25 engines, FB.Mk VI with Molins 57-mm cannon with 25 rounds plus four 0.303-in (7.7-mm) guns and eight rockets; total 25
NF.Mk XIX: Merlin 25 engines, night-fighter based on Mk XIII; total 220
B.Mk XX: Canadian B.Mk IV Series II, Packard Merlin 31 or 33 engines; total 145, including 40 F-8
FB.Mk 21: Canadian-built FB.Mk VI; total 3
T.Mk 22: Canadian T.Mk III
B.Mk 25: improved B.Mk XX, Merlin 225 engines; total 400
FB.Mk 26: improved Mk 21 with Merlin 225 engines; total 338
T.Mk 27: improved T.Mk 22 with Merlin 225 engines
T.Mk 29: trainer conversion of Mk 26
NF.Mk 30: high-altitude night-fighter with Merlin 72 or 76 engines, AI Mk X; total 526
PR.Mk 32: photographic aircraft with Merlin 113/114 engines, pressurised; total 5
PR.Mk 34: long-range photographic aircraft with Merlin 114 (Mk 34A Merlin 114A) engines, pressurised, exceptional fuel capacity; total 50
B.Mk 35: long-range bomber with Merlin 113A/114A engines, pressurised, could carry 597 Imp gal (2714 litres) plus 4,000-lb (1814-kg) bomb load, post-war conversions to PR.Mk 35 and TT.Mk 35; total 122
FB.Mk 40: Australian Mk VI with Packard Merlin 31 or 33 engines; total 178
FB.Mk 41: Australian photographic aircraft based on Mks XVI and 40, Packard Merlin 69 engines
FB.Mk 42: Australian Mk VI with Merlin 69 engines; total 1 conversion from FB.Mk 40
T.Mk 43: Australian T.Mk III with Packard Merlin 33 engines

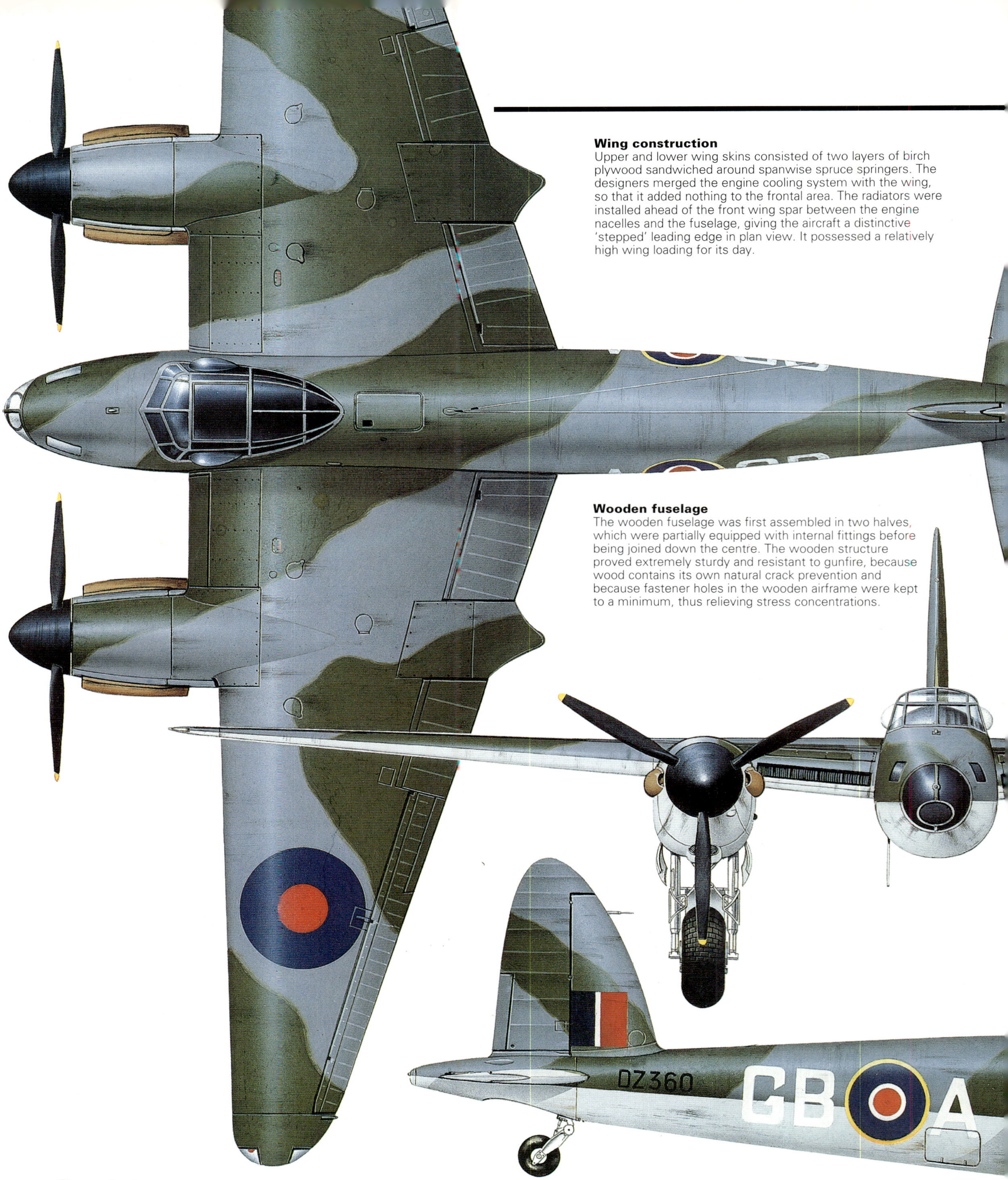

Wing construction
Upper and lower wing skins consisted of two layers of birch plywood sandwiched around spanwise spruce springers. The designers merged the engine cooling system with the wing, so that it added nothing to the frontal area. The radiators were installed ahead of the front wing spar between the engine nacelles and the fuselage, giving the aircraft a distinctive 'stepped' leading edge in plan view. It possessed a relatively high wing loading for its day.

Wooden fuselage
The wooden fuselage was first assembled in two halves, which were partially equipped with internal fittings before being joined down the centre. The wooden structure proved extremely sturdy and resistant to gunfire, because wood contains its own natural crack prevention and because fastener holes in the wooden airframe were kept to a minimum, thus relieving stress concentrations.

Powerplant
The Mosquito was a delightful aircraft to fly under most circumstances but it was also a demanding machine. Like most contemporary high-powered twin-engined aircraft, the Mosquito could be a handful with asymmetric power. The loss of an engine just after a high-weight take-off could be highly dangerous. The aircraft was designed with the most advanced version of the Rolls-Royce Merlin available in 1939-40, the XX series, with a single-speed supercharger. By 1942, the two-stage Merlin 61 was available, which enabled the Mosquito to attain an altitude of 40,000 ft (12195 m).

Early bombers
Some Mosquito B.Mk IVs were converted for Highball operations involving the skipping bomb designed by Barnes Wallis. A total of 235 Series IVs was built, including 32 PR.Mk IVs. The crew sat well forward, which gave good visibility on landing but made rearward visibility something of a problem in later years. A flat windscreen was fitted, but no airbrake was installed. The lack of enthusiasm for the Mosquito within Bomber Command accounted for the fact that the reconnaissance and night-fighter versions were deployed earlier than the bomber versions and took the larger share of production in 1942-43.

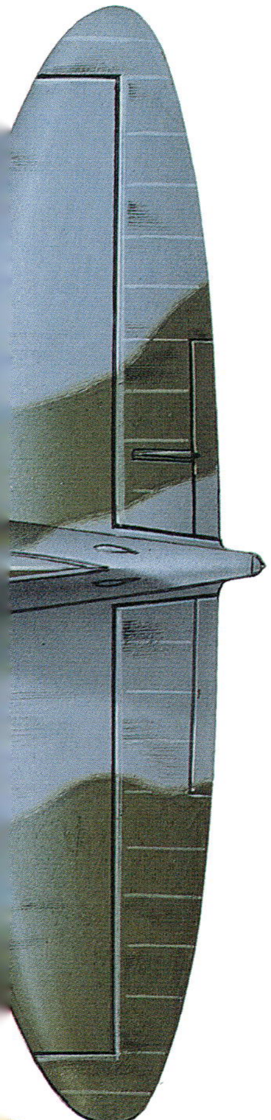

Mosquito B. Mk IVs of No. 139 Squadron, Bomber Command based at RAF Horsham St Faith are seen in echelon formation in February 1943. This view shows the Mosquito's remarkably clean, curved lines in its fuselage shape.

Mosquito B.Mk IV Series II, No. 105 Squadron, RAF Marham, December 1942

The Mosquito B.Mk IV Series II was tremendously well received when it was delivered to the first two squadrons, Nos 105 and 139 at RAF Marham in 1942. These squadrons pioneered unescorted high-speed bombing missions over Germany.

Specification
Mosquito B.Mk IV Series II
Type: high-speed day-bomber
Powerplant: two 1,230-hp (918-kW) Rolls-Royce Merlin 21 inline piston engines
Performance: maximum speed 380 mph (612 km/ h) at 21,000 ft (6400 m) with multi-stub exhausts, or 366 mph (589 km/h) with ducted saxophone exhausts; service ceiling 31,000 ft (9449 m); range 1,220 miles (1963 km)
Weights: empty 13,100 lb (5942 kg); maximum take-off 22,380 lb (10152 kg)
Dimensions: span 54 ft 2 in (16.51 m); length 40 ft 10 in (12.43 m); height 15 ft 3 in (4.65 m); wing area 454 sq ft (42.18 m^2)
Armament: normal internal bomb load 2,000 lb (907 kg)

bomber and fighter roles. By summer 1941 many ideas were being drawn or tested, including the fitting of Merlin 60 series two-stage engines; four-bladed propellers; span increased to pointed tips at 65 ft 0 in (19.81 m), though in fact only half this extension was the limit, flown on the high-altitude version in 1942 and leading to the **F.Mk XV**; and, most importantly, fitting guns and bombs. Bishop had always ensured there was room under the floor for four 20-mm Hispano cannon, and in 1942 the **F.Mk II** night-fighter went into production with these guns plus four 0.303-in (7.7-mm) Browning machine-guns in the nose, plus the new AI Mk IV radar. The fighter had a side door instead of a hatch in the underside of the nose, and a flat armoured windscreen.

In October 1941 it was suggested that the 500-lb (227-kg) bomb should have short or retractable tailfins, so that four could be carried. This was at first rejected, but after prolonged tests it was found to be perfectly feasible and the standard bomb was made with shorter fins. Thus, the bomb load was doubled at a stroke, and the **B.Mk IV** went into production alongside the fighter in 1942. The **T.Mk III** dual trainer flew in January 1942 but was mainly built post-war, such was the demand for operational Mosquitos. Meanwhile, the original 49 short-nacelle aircraft entered service in summer 1941 as photo-reconnaissance **Mosquito PR.Mk I**s or as conversions to B.Mk IV

de Havilland DH.98 Mosquito

Mosquito B.Mk IVs are seen at their home base of RAF Marham in 1942. These light bombers of No. 105 Squadron had been on strength since December 1941 and were used for high-speed, long-range bombing raids. Their speed allowed them to fly without fighter escort.

Below: The Mosquito was renowned for its speed and bomb load relative to its size. The bomber version, the Mk IV, entered service in the summer of 1942. This example, DK338, is seen during a test flight in September that year before it was delivered to No. 105 Squadron at RAF Marham. It served with the squadron until it crashed on approach to its home base on 1 May 1943.

bombers, all with the 2,000-lb (907-kg) bomb load. The first mission was a camera trip to Bordeaux and La Pallice on 17 September 1941 by W4055 of No. 1 PRU (Photographic Reconnaissance Unit).

Full-scale RAF service began with the **B.Mk IV Series II**, the first definitive bomber version, which entered service with No. 105 Squadron of No. 2 Group at Swanton Morley in November 1941. Next came No. 139 Sqn at Marham. The first bomber mission was flown by just one aircraft, W4072 (a Series I) of No. 105 Sqn at the end of the '1,000-bomber' raid on Cologne on 30-31 May 1942. After various ineffective sorties, a daring attack was made on the Gestapo HQ in Oslo, thwarted by the performance of the bombs: one failed to explode, though inside the building, while three others passed through the far wall before detonating. For the rest of the war the B.Mk IV, usually with 50-Imp gal (227-litre) underwing drop tanks, made daring

The Mosquito B.Mk IV was the first version to enter service with Bomber Command, in November 1941. DZ464 'XD-C' joined the second squadron to be formed, No. 139, at RAF Marham nearly a year later and flew on low-level raids.

This Mosquito FB.Mk VI served with No. 464 Squadron, RAAF at RAF Thorney Island in late 1944. The squadron was engaged mainly on night intruder missions, but also undertook daylight operations. In February 1945, No. 464 moved to France to extend the range of its night patrols.

Right: Operational experience with the Mosquito Mk II in its day-fighter and intruder roles led to the development of the FB.Mk VI, a potent fighter-bomber which came into service during the early months of 1943. This Mosquito FB.Mk VI, MM417 'EG-T' of No. 487 (RNZAF) Squadron, was based at RAF Gravesend, shortly before D-Day.

Above: One of the Mosquito's most effective and spectacular roles was to supplement Coastal Command Beaufighters on shipping strikes, employing cannon, bombs and rockets against mainly coastal targets.

Above: The Coastal Command strike offensive was pursued until the very end, exemplified by this attack by Mosquitos of No. 143 Squadron on enemy shipping on 4 May 1945 – only days before the ceasefire in Europe.

Right: At Banff in Scotland, armourers load rockets under the wings of a Mosquito FB.Mk VI of No. 143 Squadron in preparation for a strike against German shipping off the Norwegian coast early in 1945. The rockets were to prove highly effective against enemy shipping and ground targets.

precision attacks throughout Europe from tree-top height. More important even than this, 'Mossies' were fitted with the precision navigation aid known as Oboe and used as Pathfinder target markers, or on occasion to drop bombs with great accuracy on point targets. No. 109 Squadron was the first Oboe-equipped Mosquito unit in No. 8 Group (PFF, or Pathfinder Force), later joined by nine other squadrons. They marked the targets for Bomber Command's 'Main Force' on all subsequent heavy night raids, and formed the Light Night Striking Force

de Havilland DH.98 Mosquito

This Mosquito B.Mk IX of No. 105 Squadron was based at RAF Marham in March 1944, equipped with Oboe for Pathfinder missions. It features an extension of the black Smooth Night finish to cover the fin. It could carry a 2,000-lb (907-kg) bomb load and had an operational ceiling of 36,000ft (10975 m).

Operating as part of No. 8 (Pathfinder Force) Group Light Night Striking Force, this Mosquito B.Mk XVI, ML963 '8K-K', flew with No. 571 Squadron at RAF Oakington in late 1944. The bulged bomb-bay could carry a 4,000-lb (1814-kg) bomb.

Most of the FB.Mk VI versions were equipped to take two 500-lb (227-kg) bombs internally, plus another pair on the wing pylons – a 2,000-lb (907-kg) total load – in addition to the four 20-mm cannon and quartet of 0.303-in (7.7-mm) machine-guns.

Below: The Mosquito B.Mk XVI, with a pressurised cockpit, could fly at an altitude of 40,000 ft (12192 m). This aircraft was flown by No. 571 Squadron, which formed at Downham Market in April 1944 as a light bomber unit with No. 8 (Pathfinder) Group.

for damaging nuisance raids on German cities.

By 1943 bomber production switched to the high-flying **B.Mk IX** with two-stage Merlins, paddle-bladed propellers and much increased high-altitude performance. In 1944 the B.Mk IX and **B.Mk IV Special** were fitted with modified bomb beams and bulged bomb bays to carry a 4,000-lb (1814-kg) bomb, four times the design bomb load. The **Mosquito B.Mk XVI**, first flown in November 1943, was a high-altitude bomber designed to carry this bomb from the start, and was also fitted with a pressure cabin for routine operations at up to 35,000 ft (10670 m).

The Mosquito was also exceptional in the photographic reconnaissance and fighter-bomber roles. The **Mosquito PR.Mk IV** was a camera variant of the B.Mk IV Series II (32 delivered), but the **B.Mk V** bomber was not built. Next came the **FB.Mk VI** fighter-bomber, built in larger numbers (2,584) than any other of the 43 marks. First flown in June 1942, it had single-stage engines, the guns of the F.Mk II, a short bomb-bay for two 113-kg (250-lb) bombs and wing racks for two more 250-lb (113-kg) bombs or two 50-Imp gal (227-litre) drop tanks. With the **FB.Mk VI Series II** the bomb size in the bomb-bay and under the wing was doubled, and other wing loads could include 100-Imp gal (455-litre) fuel tanks or eight rockets. The versatile FB.Mk VI ranged throughout Europe, hitting such point targets as the walls of Amiens prison, the Gestapo HQ at The Hague, the Gestapo HQ at Copenhagen, and numerous V-weapon sites; they were among various Mosquitos that destroyed 428 V-1 flying bombs in the air, and this mark, backed up by the **FB.Mk XVIII** with a 57-mm gun, was the chief attack weapon of Coastal Command against surface ships from mid-1943, using guns, bombs and rockets.

After the F.Mk II the chief night-fighters were the **NF.Mk XII** and **NF.Mk XIII**, in which the harpoon-like aerials of AI Mk II were replaced by bluff radomes on the nose, requiring the removal of the machine guns. In the NF.Mk XII the radar was the British AI Mk VIII, while the NF.Mk XIII had a blunter 'bull nose' which alternatively could accommodate American AI Mk X (SCR-720). A handful were built of the long-span F.Mk XV already mentioned, and the designation **NF.Mk XVII** was allotted to 100 NF.Mk XIIIs with SCR-720. The **NF.Mk XIX** was an improved but heavier NF.Mk XIII (230 built in late 1944). A big jump in performance came when a

Right: A Mosquito B.Mk XVI fitted with long-range tanks demonstrates the confidence of the crew in having one engine 'feathered out' despite the large bomb load carried in its bulged bomb-bay.

Left: In the mid-war years, the Mosquito joined the Spitfire for longer-range photo-reconnaissance missions. LR412 is a PR.Mk IX from No. 540 Squadron based at RAF Leuchars in 1943.

Below: The Mosquito PR.Mk XVI became the standard model for high-altitude photographic reconnaissance. NS777 served only with No. 140 Squadron, which operated from B.58 (Melsbroek), Belgium, during the last seven months of the war in Europe.

fighter Mosquito was fitted with two-stage engines, the resulting **NF.Mk 30** becoming extremely important and effective in the final year of the war in Europe. Though weighing up to 23,650 lb (10730 kg), it reached 424 mph (682 km/h) and carried many EW (electronic warfare) devices such as Perfectos and Airborne Cigar jamming gear; six squadrons of NF.Mk XXXs operated with No. 100 Group on bomber support missions, as well as with night-fighter units.

Following on from the successful sorties flown by the few PR.Mk Is the RAF had on strength, it was decided to develop further photographic reconnaissance versions. The **PR.Mk IV** and **PR.Mk VIII** were limited-nimber conversions from the B.Mk IV bomber and it was not until the **PR.Mk IX** entered service in mid-1943 that Mosquitos made a significant contibution to Allied intelligence gathering over the continent. Based at RAF Benson, PR.Mk IXs kept the whole of Europe under daily surveillance, flying 3,000 sorties in four months at the end of 1943. Early in 1944 the type went into service in the Far East, completing vital survey work over the whole of Burma as well as photographing all enemy seaports in the Dutch East Indies and Malaya.

The other significant photographic reconnaissance variant operated by the RAF was the **PR.Mk XVI**, of which 432 were built. These aircraft took over the main PR responsibility from the PR.Mk IX for the last year of the war in Europe. Thanks to more powerful Merlin engines and a pressurised cabin, the Mk XVI could operate unmolested over western Europe, providing vital information on German defences as the Allies advanced through France and the Low Countries. PR.Mk XVIs also served with the USAAF in Europe. The ultimate PR version of the Mosquito developed during the war was the **PR.Mk 34**. Developed for Far East service, the size of the wing tanks was doubled and an extra fuel tank fitted in the bomb-bay to give the aircraft a range of over 3,500 miles (5633 km). Fifty examples were built by Percival Aircraft before the end of the war resulted in the cancellation of further orders.

Many marks flew with all Allied air forces, including the Russian air force and the USAAF, the latter acquiring Canadian-built aircraft as the **F-8** reconnaissance version as well as the British-built T.Mk III and PR.Mk XVI. De Havilland Aircraft of Canada at Downsview built a series of variants from Mks 21 to 29, with Packard engines (see variants list), while DH Australia at Bankstown built the Mks 40 to 43. All these were based on the FB.Mk VI. At home, production was

Above: Allied photographic reconnaissance aircraft played a vital part in plotting the movements of enemy supplies and reinforcements, allowing them to be targeted by tactical air units. NS502, a PR.Mk XVI of No. 540 Squadron, flew a sortie over Berlin on D-Day. Both the RAF and USAAF used Mosquitos in the PR role.

Right: Mosquitos in the tropics suffered serious problems due to their wooden construction – the plywood webs of the spars would shrink or swell in the humid air. This is a PR.Mk 34.

de Havilland DH.98 Mosquito

Mosquito PR.Mk XVI NS777 was one of 433 of this version built. The PR.Mk XVI was a photo-reconnaissance and bomber model with Mk IX engines, pressurised cabin, increased fuel capacity and a wide range of electronic equipment.

Above: This Mosquito FB.Mk XVIII of No. 248 Squadron, based at RAF Portreath, was fitted with a 57-mm Molins gun in the forward fuselage in place of the four 20-mm cannon. Although only 27 were produced, the 'Tse Tse' proved effective against shipping, submarines and shore targets.

Below: The underside of invasion-striped Mosquito FB.Mk XVIII NS502 shows the retractable landing lights under the wings inboard of the long-range tanks.

supported by a vast array of sub-contractors, furniture- and piano-makers, and even tiny groups in cottage back rooms, with assembly lines at de Havilland Hatfield, de Havilland Plant 2 at Leavesden, Percival Aircraft at Luton, Standard Motors at Canley, Coventry and Airspeed at Portsmouth.

In addition to 10 civil Mosquitos (a B.Mk IV Series II and nine FB.Mk VIs) used by BOAC on urgent services with cargo and passengers between the UK and Sweden (and occasionally other places), there were various later marks that did not see war service. There were also numerous Sea Mosquito variants, of which the most important was the TR.Mk 33. The last of 7,781 Mosquitos was VX916, an NF.Mk 38 delivered from Chester on 28 November 1950. It was the 6,439th built in England; Canadian production totalled 1,034 and Australian 212. Post-war air forces using Mosquitos included those of Belgium, China, Czechoslovakia, Denmark, Dominica, France, Israel, New Zealand, Norway, South Africa, Sweden, Turkey and Yugoslavia.

Above: The Mosquito NF.Mk XV was developed in 1942 to counter the Luftwaffe's high-altitude Junkers Ju 86Ps that were flying unchallenged over Britain at over 40,000 ft (12192 m). This high-altitude version had an extended wing and machine-guns in a ventral blister.

Left: The last wartime night-fighter version of the Mosquito was the NF.Mk 30, introduced in 1944. A total of 270 was built, with the more powerful Merlin 25 engines.

Douglas Boston/Havoc

Built as a private venture by the Douglas Aircraft Company, albeit with the encouragement of the USAAC, the **Model 7B** provided the basis for a family of versatile light attack bombers that would serve throughout the war with several Allied air forces. First flown on 26 October 1938, it was followed by the more definitive **DB-7** prototype on 17 August 1939 – by which time production orders had been placed by both the USAAC and the French Armée de l'Air.

French orders were placed for 100 in February 1939, 270 more in October 1939 and finally 480 in May 1940, embracing several different versions. The first of several British Purchasing Commission orders were placed in February and April 1940, for 300 **DB-7B**s, for which the name **Boston** was selected. By May 1940, three French escadrilles were working up on the Douglas twins, but only about 70 aircraft were actually on French territory at that time. With the collapse of France a few weeks later, all outstanding orders, and those aircraft in the delivery pipeline, were taken over by Britain.

Because of the piecemeal manner in which they were acquired – some at the factory, some from shipments already at sea and some flown to Britain from France by escaping Armée de l'Air crews – the number of earlier (ex-French) Bostons in the RAF is uncertain. Those with R-1830-S3C-G engines and single-stage superchargers took the designation **Boston Mk I** and probably totalled only 20; those with R-1830-S3C4-G engines and two-stage superchargers were **Boston Mk II**s and totalled 183. Having arrived in Britain, they were brought up to minimum RAF standard, with modified throttles and British 0.303-in (7.7-mm) machine-guns; two dorsal and two in the nose.

Considered unsuitable for use as bombers, the Boston Mk IIs in the RAF became **Havoc Mk I** night-fighters, while 100 ex-French **DB-7A**s became **Havoc Mk II**s, distinguished by longer nacelle tails. With eight machine-guns in the nose and AI Mk IV or Mk V radar, Havoc Mk Is were operating with No. 85 Squadron by March 1941, followed by Nos 25 and 600 Sqns. No. 23 Squadron, meanwhile, began using Havoc Mk Is that retained the original nose transparencies, dorsal guns and three-man crews for night intruder operations. These aircraft were known for a time as **Havoc Mk IV**s before becoming the **Havoc (Intruder)**, and were also used in the intruder role by No. 605 Sqn.

About 20 of the night-fighters were also modified as the **Havoc Mk I (LAM)** and used by No. 93 Sqn to operate, albeit with scant

The first Boston Mk IIIs were shipped to the UK during the autumn of 1941. They were used by No. 2 Group as replacements for the Blenheim. Many were converted from bomber to intruder versions.

Most of the DB-7 Boston Mk IIs, powered by Pratt & Whitney Twin Wasps, were converted for use by the RAF as Havoc Mk I night-fighters. The aircraft shown here (BD112) was operated on intruder duties from April 1941.

Carrying the pilot's personal emblem below the cockpit, this Boston Mk III of No. 107 Squadron operated from Great Massingham, Norfolk in March 1942. The squadron made a number of daring low-level daylight raids including a disastrous attack on the Philips radio and valve factory at Eindhoven.

This Havoc Mk I, BD112, operated with No. 23 Squadron from Ford in 1941. The squadron replaced its Blenheim Mk IF night-fighters with the American twin in April that year and added Boston Mk IIIs in February 1942. Note the badly flaking matt black night finish.

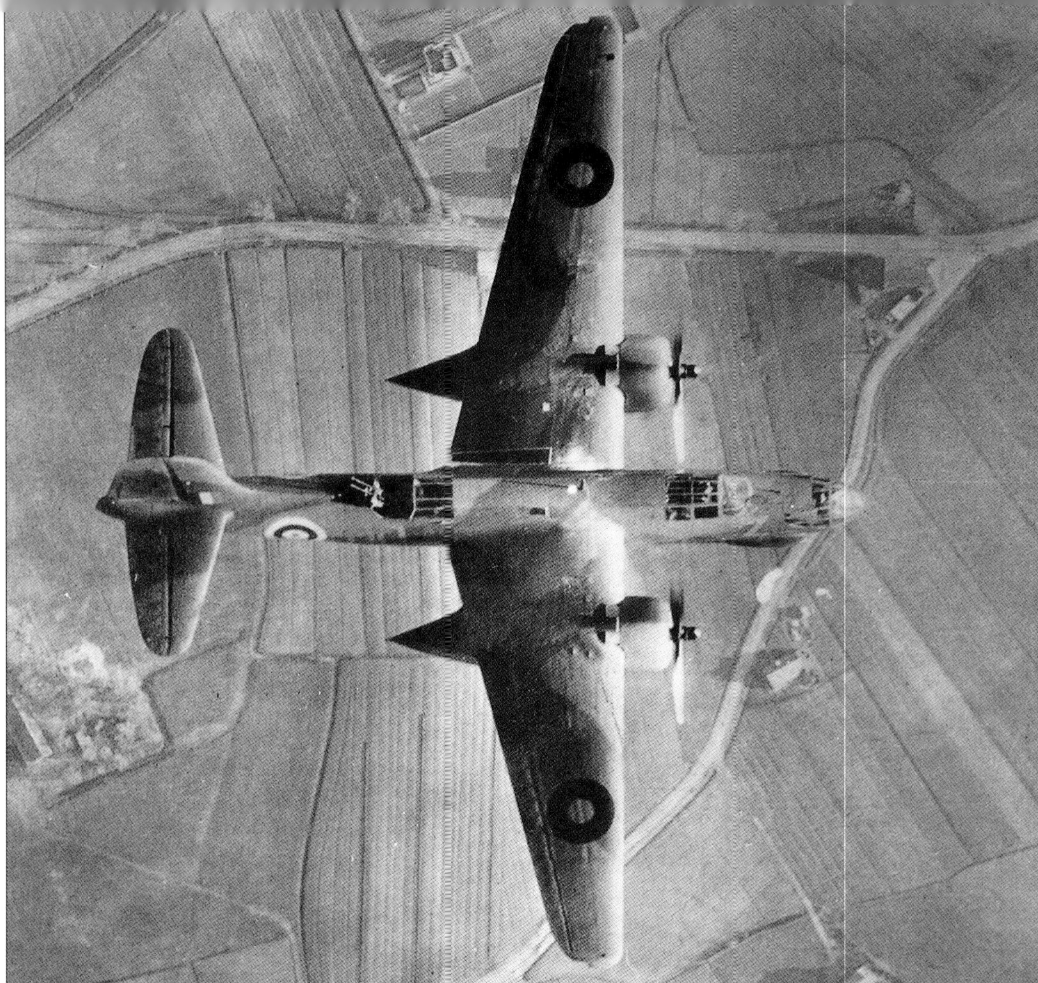

A Boston Mk III from No. 88 Squadron is photographed from another of the squadron's aircraft making a low-level bomb run during a sortie over northern France. A total of 540 Boston Mk IIIs entered service with the RAF and equipped 15 squadrons.

Below: While the Boston was viewed with suspicion at the beginning by RAF pilots, it was soon accepted by the crews on the squadrons with which it served and became a highly regarded and successful light bomber. This formation of three Boston Mk IIIs from No. 107 Squadron demonstrates the aerodynamically clean lines of the type.

success, with the Long Aerial Mine, a weapon trailed on a 2,000-ft (610-m) length of wire in the path of enemy raiders. This variant was also known as the **Havoc Mk III** or **Havoc Mk I (Pandora)**. Other Havoc Mk Is, and 39 of the Havoc Mk IIs, were fitted in the nose with a 2,700 million-candlepower Helmore/GEC searchlight and, as **Havoc Mk I (Turbinlite)** were used by 10 flights (later, squadrons) to operate alongside Hurricane night-fighters and attempt to illuminate enemy raiders. The other Havoc Mk II night-fighters were fitted with a 'solid' nose containing 12 machine-guns, and operated with AI Mk V radar but no dorsal guns. The planned introduction of a four-cannon armament led to the designations **Havoc Mk IIC-B** and **Havoc Mk IIC-D**, indicating belt feed or drum feed, respectively, but no such conversions reached the squadrons, and may not have been made at all.

Britain's 'own' Boston deliveries began in the early summer of 1941, introducing the **Boston Mk III** light bomber, in which role it entered service later that year as a Blenheim replacement in No. 88 (Hong Kong) squadron, followed by No. 226 Sqn. Flying intensively to attack a variety of targets, including Channel shipping, these squadrons were joined in due course by No. 107 and No. 342 (Free French) 'Lorraine' Sqns. The inventory of Boston Mk IIIs was increased by the 480 French-ordered DB-7Bs, these being similar to the British version, with R-2600-A5B engines, a lengthened nose (compared with the Boston Mk I and Boston Mk II) and the broad fin first seen on the Boston Mk II. They had a crew of three, four 0.303-in (7.7-mm) guns in the nose and two each in dorsal and ventral positions.

With some of the planned French DB-7Bs eventually being diverted to serve with the USAAF, Britain actually received 568 Boston Mk IIIs. Almost identical were 200 **Boston Mk IIIA**s supplied through Lend-Lease, from October 1942 onwards, and a further 55 that were 'swapped' for RAF Spitfires while passing through the Middle East en route to the Soviet Union. The Boston Mk IIIA was equivalent to the

Unarmed Havoc 'Turbinlite' fighters carried AI radar and a large searchlight in the nose to illuminate potential targets for accompanying Hurricane night-fighters. The system achieved only limited success.

Above: The RAF received 165 A-20J Havocs, which were known as Boston Mk IVs. Depicted here is BZ403, the fourth RAF Boston Mk IV, which entered service in August 1944 and operated with the 2nd Tactical Air Force in Europe until the end of the war.

USAAF **A-20C** and had greater fuel capacity than the Boston Mk III.

Two squadrons, Nos 605 and 418 (RCAF), used the **Boston Mk III (Intruder)**, carrying a ventral tray with four 20-mmm cannon and having an overall black finish like the Havoc night fighters. Also painted black for night operation were three Boston Mk IIIs fitted with Turbinlites and designated **Boston (Turbinlite)**.

Final Lend-Lease supplies to Britain comprised 169 **Boston Mk IV**s and 90 **Boston Mk V**s, the equivalent, respectively, of the USAAF **A-20J** and **A-20K**. These both had a Martin electric dorsal turret with two 0.50-in (12.7-mm) machine-guns, in a widened rear fuselage, and could carry four 500-lb (227-kg) underwing bombs. The A-20J/Boston Mk IV had R-2600-23 engines, and the A-20K/Boston Mk V had -29 engines; in virtually all other respects the two types were similar.

The Boston Mk IV and Mk V were used in North Africa and the Mediterranean area to supplement Boston Mk III/IIIAs already being flown there by Nos 13, 18, 55 and 114 Sqns of the RAF, alongside Nos 12 and 24 Sqns (SAAF). Bostons remained a useful component of the RAF right up to the end of the war, participating in the D-Day landings by laying smoke screens over the Normandy beaches, and serving with Nos 88 and 342 Sqns in 2nd TAF until April 1945.

Above: In March 1943 the Blenheim was augmented in the desert campaign by the Boston. It played a significant part in the final sweeping of the Axis powers out of Africa, and then on through Sicily and Italy. They remained in service after the war with several squadrons.

Specification
Boston Mk III
Type: light bomber
Powerplant: two 1,600-hp (1193-kW) Wright GR-2600-A5B radial piston engines
Performance: maximum speed 304 mph (489 km/h) at 13,000 ft (3962 m); cruising speed 250 mph (402 km/h); service ceiling 24,250 ft (7391 m); range 1,020 miles (1642 km) with maximum bomb load
Weights: empty 12,200 lb (5534 kg); maximum take-off 25,000 lb (11340 kg)
Dimensions: span 61 ft 4 in (18.69 m); length 47 ft 0 in (14.33 m); height 15 ft 10 in (4.83 m); wing area 465 sq ft (43.20 m^2)
Armament: four fixed forward-firing 0.303-in (7.7-mm) machine-guns in nose, two 0.303-in (7.7-mm) manually-operated machine-guns in dorsal and ventral positions plus up to 2,000 lb (907 kg) of bombs

On their arrival in Britain, the first Boston Mk IIIs were modified for use by No. 2 Group squadrons (Nos 88, 107, 226 and 342) on anti-shipping strikes in the English Channel and the North Sea, and for daylight raids on continental fringe targets.

Douglas Dakota

This Dakota Mk III (named Kwicherbichin UK) was from No. 233 Squadron. After the D-Day landings, two Dakotas from this squadron were the first Transport Command aircraft to land in France on 13 June 1944. This Dakota is seen returning from Normandy on 1 August 1944 with wounded servicemen. It survived the war and went on to serve with BOAC.

Any list of the 10 most significant aircraft of World War II would almost certainly include the Douglas Dakota (one of its several appellations, others including **DC-3**, **C-47**, **Skytrain** and **Skytrooper**). As the DC-3, this ubiquitous aircraft began life as the third 'Douglas Commercial' twin-engined transport, for use primarily on the rapidly developing air transport network in the US. A progressive evolution of the DC-1 and DC-2, the DC-3 (or **DST**, **Douglas Sleeper Transport**) first flew on 17 December 1935. While production proceeded apace for a variety of airlines, the US military was quick to place orders (having already bought DC-2s), and once America was at war, also impressed large numbers of the civil transport under several different 'C for Cargo' designations.

The RAF's first experience of the DC-3 was obtained with some of these impressed aircraft (as well as some similarly ex-civil DC-2s). From April 1942 onwards, 10 of these aircraft – which were known in

Above: Dakota transports from No. 271 Squadron, part of No. 46 Group based at Down Ampney, line-up at an airstrip in Belgium after bringing in supplies from the UK. On the return flight, they carried casualties or prisoners of war.

Above: These Dakota Mk IIIs of No. 44 Squadron, SAAF, were among the aircraft that dropped partisans in Yugoslavia in February 1945. They flew from Bari, Italy.

Left: Lend-Lease Dakota deliveries included a number of these former C-53 Skytroopers, that had a single fuselage door and small cargo door aft. These Dakota Mk IIs were mainly used for paratroop drops but were also tasked with passenger and VIP duties.

Formations of Dakotas dropped supplies at Arnhem in September 1944. This operation cost Nos 38 and 46 Groups a total of 55 Dakotas destroyed, 320 damaged by flak and seven by fighters.

British service as DC-3 and later Dakota with no mark number – were flown out the US to India to serve with No. 31 Squadron, becoming engaged in operations in Burma, including support for the first Wingate expedition in 1943.

Meanwhile, provision had been made for Britain to receive substantial numbers of the Douglas twins through Lend-Lease; eventually, the total would grow to more than 1,900, from wartime production of just over 10,000 military examples in three US centres. The Lend-Lease aircraft were designated in four variants, comprising the **Dakota Mk I**, equivalent of the USAAF C-47; **Dakota Mk II**, equivalent to the **C-53**; **Dakota Mk III**, being the **C-47A**; and **Dakota Mk IV**, the **C-47B**. Of these versions, the C-53, known as the Skytrooper to the USAAF, was the dedicated troop and paratroop transport, having a 26-in (66-cm) door in the port side of the rear fuselage, rather than the C-47's double door for freight loading, and 28 troop seats. The 'basic' C-47 Skytrain had Pratt & Whitney R-1830-92 radial engines, bucket-types seats along the cabin walls and a gross weight of 29,300 lb (13290 kg). The C-47A differed, primarily, in having the 12-volt electric system of the C-47 changed to a 24-volt system; and the C-47B switched to R-1830-90 or -90B engines with high-altitude blowers and extra fuel capacity, making it suitable in particular for the China-Burma-India theatre. Totals delivered to the RAF were 51 Dakota Mk Is; four Dakota Mk IIs (of 40 planned); 950 Dakota Mk IIIs; and 894 Dakota Mk IVs. These Lend-Lease totals were swelled by some 20 transfers from USAAF stocks towards the end of the war, for particular needs that arose 'in the field'; these

Camouflaged Dakotas of No. 267 Squadron are seen parked at Bari, Italy during 1944. Dakota Mk IIIs KG496, FL586 and FD857 are in the foreground. The airfield was heavily utilised by RAF and USAAF aircraft. Types seen in the background include USAAF P-47 and P-38 fighters and B-24 and B-17 bombers.

No. 24 Squadron operated solely as a communications unit based at RAF Hendon during World War II. This Dakota Mk III was delivered to No. 24 Sqn in February 1944. The Dakotas were used for mail and VIP services to Malta from 1943 onwards.

Joining the squadron in spring 1943, this Douglas Dakota Mk III of No. 267 Squadron was based at Araxos in Greece, 1944. In October of that year the squadron was busy inserting troops behind enemy lines in Greece.

Douglas Dakota

A Dakota comes in at low level to 'hook' an American-designed Waco glider during training. This technique was used to recover the valuable gliders in Burma during the 2nd Chindit expedition.

Below: Carrying the 'Flying Elephant' insignia of No. 194 Squadron, a Dakota from 'The Friendly Firm' unloads Ghurkha troops somewhere in Burma. The Dakota became the most valuable transport asset for the Allied forces in the Far East.

included an additional Dakota Mk. I and four more Dakota Mk IIs.

The Lend-Lease Dakotas began to arrive in Britain in February 1943, several of the earliest Mk Is going immediately to BOAC to operate the route from the UK to Gibraltar and Africa, in RAF camouflage but with civil registrations replacing the military serial numbers. Other early users of the Dakota Mk I, supplemented later by Dakota Mk IIIs in 1943, were No. 216 Squadron in Cairo, for use on the regular run between Egypt and West Africa, and casualty evacuation from the Western Desert; No. 117 Squadron, taking part in the invasion of Sicily; No. 31 Squadron, to continue the supply missions in Burma started with DC-3s; and in the UK No. 24 Squadron began to standardise on the Dakota in April 1943, giving up a miscellany of short-range aircraft in order to fly regular services to Gibraltar and other destinations – a service in which it was soon joined by No. 511 Squadron.

No. 24 Squadron was one of several Dakota squadrons supporting the D-Day landings. In this they were joined by Nos 48 and 271 Squadrons at Down Ampney and Nos 512 and 575 at Broadwell, these being heavily engaged in dropping paratroops and towing Horsa gliders for the Normandy landings and later at Arnhem and the Rhine crossing. For a resupply mission to Arnhem, the pilot of a Dakota Mk III of No. 271 Sqn, Flt Lt D. S. A. Lord, DFC, was awarded a posthumous VC. Formed in the UK too late for D-Day, No. 437 Sqn, RCAF, also participated in Operation Market Garden to Arnhem. Nos 147 and 525 Squadrons flew Dakotas on supply flights to Europe for the final few months of the war.

Farther afield, the work of Nos 31, 117 and 216 Squadrons in the Middle East has already been mentioned. Also in Egypt, No. 267 Sqn was among the first to fly Dakotas, operating throughout the Mediterranean theatre.

Dakotas also played an important role in the fight against Japan, several squadrons receiving the Douglas aircraft in India. At Lahore, No. 194 Sqn received its first two Dakotas at the end of May 1943 and joined with No. 31 Squadron to support the Chindit incursions into Burma. No. 62 Squadron from 1943 and No. 52 from 1944 both flew Dakotas from Indian bases, including flights over 'the Hump' into China, and two RCAF squadrons, Nos 435 and 436, were similarly engaged from 1944. Further squadrons were in the process of working up on Dakotas in India when the war came to an end, but the Dakota was destined to remain in service with the RAF for several more years – notably with No. 216 Squadron at home and No. 267 Squadron in the Malayan conflict.

Specification
Dakota Mk I
Type: cargo and 28-troop transport
Powerplant: two 1,200-hp (895-kW) Pratt & Whitney R-1830-92 Twin Wasp radial piston engines
Performance: maximum speed 230 mph (370 km/h) at 8,500 ft (2591 m); cruising speed 185 mph (298 km/h); service ceiling 23,200 ft (7071 m); maximum range 2,125 miles (3420 km)
Weights: empty 16,865 lb (7650 kg); maximum take-off 31,000 lb (14061 kg)
Dimensions: span 95 ft 0 in (28.96 m); length 64 ft 6 in (19.66 m); height 16 ft 11 in (5.16 m); wing area 987 sq ft (91.69 m²)

This Dakota Mk III of No. 257 Squadron is seen flying over the Greek islands near Missolonghi on its way back to its base at Araxos during October 1944.

Douglas Dauntless

JS997 was one of nine SBD-5 Dauntless DB.Mk 1s delivered for evaluation by the RAF and Royal Navy in December 1943. It was rejected for use by both services, neither of which saw any requirement for a dedicated dive-bomber.

Destined to play an important role in the hands of US Navy squadrons in the first year or so of the war in the Pacific, the Douglas **SBD** had its origins in a design by the Northrop corporation in 1938. After Northrop became the El Segundo division of Douglas, its **BT-1** two-seat low-wing dive-bomber monoplane evolved into the **XSBD-1** prototype, successful testing of which led to acceptance for large-scale production in 1939.

The Dauntless, as the SBD was named, was designed to deliver its 1,000-lb (454-kg) bomb in a dive at angles of up to 70° – a technique already effectively demonstrated in Europe by the Luftwaffe's Ju 87 Stuka squadrons. In Britain, neither the RAF nor the FAA was convinced that the specialised dive-bomber had a role to play in the conflict. The procurement of a small batch of SBDs through Lend-Lease provided an opportunity for the evaluation of the dive-bombing role. The nine **Dauntless DB.Mk I** aircraft received in Britain, in late 1943 and early 1944, were **SBD-5** versions, almost 3,000 of which had been built for the US Navy. They were used, as planned, at several test establishments in the UK, including, in particular, the IAD Flight at RAE Farnborough for dive-bomb sight tests. No. 787 Squadron, the FAA Fleet Fighter Development Unit at Wittering, had two of the Dauntlesses for a time; one reached No. 700 Squadron, then serving as a Maintenance Test Pilot Training Squadron, at Donibristle, in February 1945. Three were taken onto RAF strength, but only for storage at a Maintenance Unit. Whatever conclusions may have been reached through evaluation of the Dauntless, they came too late to influence the acquisition of further examples before the war had come to an end.

Specification
Dauntless DB.Mk I
Type: two-seat dive-bomber
Powerplant: one 1,200-hp (895-kW) Wright R-1820-60 Cyclone radial piston engine
Performance: maximum speed 252 mph (406 km/h) at 10,000 ft (3050 m); service ceiling 25,200 ft (7681 m); normal range 773 miles (1244 km)
Weights: empty 6,533 lb (2963 kg); maximum take-off 10,700 lb (4854 kg)
Dimensions: span 41 ft 7 in (12.67 m); length 33 ft 2 in (10.10 m); height 13 ft 7 in (4.14 m); wing area 325 sq ft (30.19 m^2)

Douglas Skymaster

First flown on 7 June 1938, the Douglas **DC-4** was intended to be a 'big brother' for the DC-3 in the commercial market. Before airline use could begin, however, America was at war, and the DC-4 was adapted for military service as the **C-54**. Several hundred were built in different versions for the USAAF and USN, to serve as freight and personnel transports, particularly in the China-Burma-India theatre of operations.

A Lend-Lease allocation of 24 of these aircraft was made to Britain late in the war, being given the RAF name **Skymaster C.Mk I**. First to arrive, in June 1944, was a single **C-54B** intended for the personal use of the Rt Hon. Winston Churchill, Britain's Prime Minister. To this end, it was fitted out by Armstrong-Whitworth Aircraft with a special 10-seat VIP cabin and was based at RAF Northolt for operation by No. 24 Squadron. It was later operated by the VIP Flight of No. 246 Squadron and was returned to America in November 1945.

A further 10 Skymasters arrived between February and July 1945, the balance of 13 remaining undelivered. These were built as **C-54D**s to USAAF specification, differing from the C-54B only in the engine version fitted and other small details. Training was in the hands of No. 1332 Conversion Unit, and the aircraft were operated briefly by No. 246 Squadron in No. 47 Group, before being used to equip No. 232 Squadron at Palam, from where this unit maintained a regular service between Ceylon and Australia.

All 10 aircraft were returned to the US in July 1946, and were then taken on strength by the US Navy with the designation **R5D-3**.

Specification
Skymaster C.Mk I
Type: cargo, troop and VIP heavy transport
Powerplant: four 1,350-hp (1007-kW) Pratt & Whitney R-2000-7 radial piston engines
Performance: maximum speed 265 mph (426 km/h) at 14,000 ft (4265 m); service ceiling 26,600 ft (8108 m); maximum range 3,800 miles (6115 km)
Weights: empty 38,000 lb (17237 kg); maximum take-off 73,000 lb (33112 kg)
Dimensions: span 117 ft 6 in (35.81 m); length 93 ft 11 in (28.63 m); height 27 ft 6 in (8.39 m); wing area 1,463 sq ft (135.91 m^2)

Ten examples of the Douglas Skymaster were obtained by RAF Transport Command for its trunk routes to the Far East. These sorties were flown by Nos 232 and 236 Squadrons. One further example, and the first Skymaster delivered to the UK, was fitted out in VIP configuration for use by the British Prime Minister, Winston Churchill.

Fairchild Argus

A wartime production version of the Fairchild **Model 24W** four-seat touring monoplane, the Argus was notable in that the greater part of total production against USAAC/USAAF contracts was transferred to Britain through Lend-Lease arrangements. Early experience of the type was obtained through the purchase in February 1937 of a **Model F.24** for use by the British Air Attaché in Washington, and then the impressment for the RAF of a single civil example in the UK in July 1941. It was, however, the needs of the Air Transport Auxiliary that led to Britain's request for substantial numbers of the militarised **C-61** (later **UC-61**), known to the USAAF as the **Forwarder**. The ATA was heavily engaged in ferrying military aircraft between production and repair centres, and operational units throughout the UK; getting the ferry pilots to and from their departure and arrival airfields required a large fleet of small transports. The Fairchild F.24 met this need most effectively.

First deliveries, starting in January 1942, totalled 97 **Argus Mk I**s (a few of these being lost at sea in transit), and these were used almost exclusively by the ATA. The **Argus Mk II**, deliveries of which began almost simultaneously, was the **UC-61A**, which differed by having a 24-Volt electrical system. Britain received 307 Mk IIs, some two-thirds of total production, and allocated this variant almost exclusively to bases in the Middle and Far East for local communications duty.

Starting in June 1944, the RAF received 306 Argus Mk IIIs, representing the entire production of **UC-61K**s. This version differed in having the 175-hp (130-kW) Ranger L-440-7 inline engine replacing the 165-hp (123-kW) Warner Super Scarab R-500 air-cooled radial. Argus Mk IIIs were shared between the ATA at home, and overseas bases in the Middle and Far East to supplement the Argus Mk IIs.

Specification
Argus Mk II
Type: four-seat liaison and communications aircraft
Powerplant: one 165-hp (123-kW) Warner R-500 Super Scarab radial piston engine
Performance: maximum speed 132 mph (212 km/h); cruising speed 117 mph (188 km/h); service ceiling 15,700 ft (4785 m); range 640 miles (1030 km)
Weights: empty 1,613 lb (732 kg); maximum take-off 2,562 lb (1162 kg)
Dimensions: span 36 ft 4 in (11.07 m); length 23 ft 9 in (7.24 m); height 7 ft 7 in (2.32 m); wing area 193.3 sq ft (17.96 m²)

The Argus was one of the RAF's most important aircraft in the light communications role. The Mk I variant was used mainly by the Air Transport Auxiliary ferry organisation.

Fairey Albacore

As a replacement for the antiquated Fairey Swordfish, the Fairey **Albacore** appeared to have everything going for it. Neat in appearance, and with an enclosed cabin providing such luxuries as heating, a windscreen wiper and automatic emergency dinghy ejection, the Albacore nevertheless failed to come up to expectations. Far from supplanting the Swordfish, it merely complemented the older biplane and, ironically, was outlived by the latter in service.

Above: The Fairey Albacore was operational with 15 Fleet Air Arm squadrons at its peak, but failed to fully live up to its designers' expectations, having an operational life of less than four years.

Right: A formation of Albacores from No. 828 Squadron, based at Hal Far, departs the Maltese coastline for a sortie against enemy shipping in the Mediterranean. The squadron operated from Malta between October 1941 and July 1943, using bombs and mines as well as torpedoes against targets in Italy, Sicily and North Africa.

Above: Fitted with underwing bomb racks, Albacores were tasked with attacking ground targets as well as shipping. Unlike in its predecessor, the Swordfish, the crew was fully enclosed, making winter operations much more bearable.

Right: Seen on board HMS* Formidable*, this Albacore is typical of those which operated from this carrier when playing a major part in the Battle of Cape Matapan in March 1941. During the battle, a formation of Albacores from Nos 826 and 829 Squadrons succeeded in severely damaging the Italian battleship* Vittorio Veneto*. This was the first occasion Albacores had used torpedoes against an enemy warship.

Designed to Specification S.41/36, the Albacore was ordered off the drawing board in May 1937, the Air Ministry placing a contract for two prototypes and 98 production aircraft. The first prototype flew on 12 December 1938 from Fairey's Great West Aerodrome (now part of London's Heathrow Airport), and production began in 1939. The prototype was tested on floats at Hamble in 1940, but the results did not justify further development along these lines.

Later in the same year the first production aircraft underwent tests at the Aircraft and Armament Experimental Establishment at Martlesham Heath, and it was this source that first reported all was not well with the Albacore. Elevators and ailerons were said to be very heavy, the stall with slots free was 'uncomfortable', the front cockpit was too hot in normal summer weather, and the rear cockpit was cold and draughty. There were a few things on the credit side: the Albacore was steady in a dive, with a smooth recovery when carrying a torpedo, and the pilot's view was excellent. Despite this rather unpromising background, Albacores began to roll off the production line after a hold-up caused by engine development problems: the 1,065-hp (794-kW) Bristol Taurus II installed in early aircraft was replaced by the Taurus XII of 1,130 hp (843 kW).

No. 826 Squadron was formed at Ford, Sussex, specially to fly the Albacore, and received 12 aircraft on 15 March 1940. The squadron went into action on 31 May, attacking E-boats off Zeebrugge and road and rail targets at Westende, Belgium. The squadron moved to Bircham Newton, Norfolk the following month, operating under the direction of Coastal Command until November, making night attacks, laying mines and bombing shipping. Three more Albacore squadrons formed before the end of 1940: No. 829 at Lee-on-Solent, No. 828 at Ford and No. 827 at Yeovilton, the last moving to Stornoway for anti-submarine patrols.

Albacores finally went to sea when Nos 826 and 829 Squadrons joined HMS *Formidable* on 26 November 1940, for convoy escort duty to Cape Town. Aircraft from these squadrons took part in the Battle of Cape Matapan in March 1941, pressing home their torpedo attacks in the true Swordfish tradition against the Italian battleship *Vittorio Veneto*, the first occasion on which they had used torpedoes in action.

By mid-1942 some 15 Fleet Air Arm squadrons were equipped with

This Albacore Mk I strike and torpedo-bomber wears the markings of No. 826 Naval Air Squadron that operated the type from March 1940 to August 1943. The squadron flew from HMS* Formidable *from November 1940 to April 1941 on convoy escort duties. It was subsequently shore-based in the eastern Mediterranean and the Western Desert.

Fairey Albacore

Above: Mid-1942 saw the peak of Albacore operations, when no fewer than 15 squadrons were equipped with the type aboard carriers protecting convoys to Russia, as well as in the Indian Ocean and Mediterranean. Within a year, the Albacore was being replaced in service by the more modern monoplane Fairey Barracuda.

Left: Fairey designed the Albacore as a replacement for the Swordfish, but the 'Stringbag' was to outlive its intended successor. These Albacores served with the Royal Naval Air Torpedo School. Training was carried out under mock-combat conditions; techniques taught included the correct methods of launching torpedoes, and the vulnerable points of a ship at which the torpedo should be aimed.

Albacores, operating from the Arctic Circle on Russian convoys, to the Western Desert, the Mediterranean and the Indian Ocean, and in November of that year Albacores of Nos 817, 820, 822 and 832 Squadrons were in action during the Allied invasion of North Africa, flying anti-submarine patrols and bombing enemy coastal guns. Albacores had reached their zenith in 1942, and the next year Fairey Barracudas began to replace them in all squadrons except No. 832, which was to be equipped with Grumman Avengers. The last two squadrons to give up their Albacores were Nos 820 and 841 in November 1943, aircraft from the latter squadron being passed to No. 415 Squadron, Royal Canadian Air Force, at Manston for use in English Channel operations on D-Day.

Total Albacore production between 1939 and 1943 amounted to 800 including two prototypes, all built at Fairey's Hayes factory and test-flown at what became Heathrow Airport.

Below: The technique of launching the torpedo was crucial to the success of an attack. If a torpedo was launched from too great a height it was likely to dive too deep or break its back. Launched from too low, it had a tendency to 'skip' off the surface.

Specification

Type: three-seat torpedo-bomber
Powerplant: one 1,130-hp (843-kW) Bristol Taurus XII radial piston engine
Performance: maximum speed 161 mph (259 km/h) at 4,500 ft (1370 m); cruising speed 116 mph (187 km/h) at 6,000 ft (1830 m); service ceiling 20,700 ft (6310 m); range 930 miles (1497 km) with 1,600-lb (726-kg) weapons load
Weights: empty 7,250 lb (3289 kg); maximum take-off 10,460 lb (4745 kg)
Dimensions: span 50 ft 0 in (15.24 m); length 39 ft 10 in (12.14 m); height 14 ft 2 in (4.32 m); wing area 623 sq ft (57.88 m^2)
Armament: one forward-firing 0.303-in (7.7-mm) machine-gun in starboard wing and twin 0.303-in (7.7-mm) Vickers 'K' guns in rear cockpit, plus one 1,610-lb (730-kg) torpedo beneath the fuselage, or six 250-lb (113-kg) or four 500-lb (227-kg) bombs beneath the wings

Fairey Barracuda

Aircrew converting from antiquated Fairey Swordfish and Albacore biplanes to the Fairey Barracuda must have thought their new mount an extremely complicated machine. It was at least more streamlined than its predecessors, although with landing gear down and a full radar array its appearance was distinctly odd.

The Barracuda originated with Specification S.24/37 to which six companies (Bristol, Blackburn, Fairey, Hawker, Vickers and Westland) tendered designs, and an order for two prototypes to be built at Hayes was placed with Fairey in July 1938. The original engine selected was the 1,200-hp (895-kW) Rolls-Royce 24-cylinder 'X' engine, but when the makers stopped work on the new engine in favour of Merlins, Peregrines and Vultures, the decision was taken to use the 1,300-hp (969-kW) Merlin 30 in the **Barracuda Mk I**.

The first prototype flew on 7 December 1940, and differed from later aircraft in having an Albacore-type tail unit with low-set tailplane on top of the fuselage, but flight testing showed that the Fairey-Youngman flaps at negative angle created an air wake which caused tail buffeting, loss of elevator effectiveness and vibration at high speeds. The result was a redesigned tail in which the tailplane was strut-braced high up on a taller, narrower fin.

Large flaps were provided to give additional wing area when set in the neutral position, and for take-off these were lowered 20° to increase lift. In the landing configuration they were lowered to provide maximum drag, while for diving attacks they adopted a negative angle of 30°. Prototype testing soon confirmed the vast performance increase of the Barracuda over its biplane ancestors: speeds of 269 mph (433 km/h) were reached in level flight at 9,000 ft (2745 m) in 'clean' configuration, and this was lowered by about 20 mph (32 km/h) when an underslung torpedo was carried. In this condition, the Barracuda prototype could climb at 1,100 ft (335 m) per minute.

Priority construction of fighters and bombers inevitably slowed work on the prototype, until the Admiralty intervened with the Ministry of Aircraft Production and managed to get full production of aircraft for the Royal Navy reinstated.

***Top:** Prototype Barracudas flew in 1940 and 1941, but production versions did not fly until May 1942. These versions incorporated several improvements, including a high-set tailplane rather than the more conventional layout of the prototype aircraft.*

***Above:** An early production Barracuda Mk I demonstates the configuration of the Fairey-Youngman flaps when deployed for dive-bombing. The slipstream created when the flaps were at a negative angle necessitated a high-set tailplane.*

***Left:** A Barracuda departs the deck of HMS Indomitable. The aircraft's 'stalky' undercarriage was a weak point, being susceptible to damage during heavy landings.*

A Barracuda Mk II of No. 769 Squadron manoeuvres carefully on the deck of a Royal Navy aircraft-carrier. ASV radar was carried to provide surface target detection for anti-shipping patrols. The aerials mounted above the wings.

The second prototype flew with the new tail unit on 29 June 1941, and in the meantime the first prototype, on loan to No. 778 Squadron, had carried out deck-landing trials aboard HMS *Victorious* on 18/19 May 1941, following which it was returned to Fairey for the new tail to be fitted. Handling trials at the Aircraft and Armament Experimental Establishment at Boscombe Down commenced in October that year, but some unserviceability and modifications delayed their completion until February 1942.

It was at this point that a problem arose which was to remain with the Barracuda for the rest of its career – it was overweight. Strengthening of the airframe and addition of equipment not included in the original specification played havoc with the take-off and climb performance. The result was that after the first 30 production aircraft had been built, subsequent aircraft, known as **Barracuda Mk II**s, had the 1,640-hp (1223-kW) Merlin 32 engine installed, this providing an increase of some 30 per cent in rated output over the earlier powerplant. No changes were made to the airframe of the Mk II, but a four-bladed propeller was substituted for the three-bladed version of the Mk I.

The Mk II, ordered in quantity, was the main production version and other companies were selected to build the type, these including Blackburn, Boulton Paul and Westland. By November 1941, 1,050 Barracudas had been ordered, but Westland was to build only five Mk Is and 13 Mk IIs before the remainder of its order (for another 232) was cancelled to allow the company to build Supermarine Seafires.

Barracudas built by Blackburn and by Boulton Paul began to enter service in spring 1943 and, although additional orders were placed, some of these were cancelled with the end of the war in Europe. In all, 1,688 Mk IIs were built, plus 30 Mk Is and two prototypes.

The **Barracuda Mk III** was evolved to take a new ASV radar installation, with a blister radome beneath the rear fuselage. The prototype, converted from a Boulton Paul-built Mk II, flew first in 1943. Following orders placed that year, production of this version began in early 1944 alongside Mk IIs. A total of 852 Mk IIIs was manufactured by Boulton Paul and Fairey.

The final production variant was the **Barracuda Mk V** (the **Mk IV** being an unbuilt project), and this differed considerably in appearance although the basic structure was unchanged. The shortfall of power of the Merlins available in 1941 made the designers consider alternatives, and the decision was taken to use a Rolls-Royce Griffon. Initial development was slow and the first Griffon-powered aircraft, converted from a Fairey-built Mk II, did not fly until 16 November 1944.

In its production form, the Barracuda Mk V had a longer, square wing than earlier versions, enlarged fin area to counteract the greater torque of the 2,030-hp (1514-kW) Griffon 37, and increased fuel capacity. However, this development had come too late and, of the 140 Mk Vs ordered, only 30 were delivered before the end of the war brought cancellation of the outstanding balance. The Barracuda's operational service life began when No. 827 Squadron received 12 Mk IIs on being reformed at Stretton, Cheshire, on 10 January 1943. Its companion squadron, No. 810, was re-equipped the following month and by January 1944 there were 12 Barracuda squadrons, first into action being No. 810 from HMS *Illustrious* in September 1943.

Fairey Barracuda Mk II cutaway

1 Spinner
2 Four-bladed Rotol propeller
3 Coolant header tank
4 Generator cooling intake
5 Radiator intake
6 Oil cooler radiator (centre)
7 Engine coolant radiators (left and right)
8 Debris guard
9 Carburretor air intake filter fairing
10 Starboard mainwheel
11 Mainwheel door
12 Exhaust outlet
13 Engine bearer assembly
14 Coolant pipes
15 Exhaust shroud
16 Rolls-Royce Merlin 32 engine
17 Angled firewall
18 Oil tank
19 Engine bearer/bulkhead attachment
20 Entry foot/handholds
21 Strengthening plate
22 Rudder pedal bar
23 Throttle lever quadrant
24 Control column grip
25 Down view panel
26 Pilot's seat
27 Windscreen hot-air/de-icing pipe
28 Windscreen
29 Wing skinning
30 Gun camera housing
31 Wing main front spar
32 Starboard navigation light
33 Outer wing section locking plunger
34 Starboard recognition light
35 Starboard aileron
36 Aileron hinge box covers (3)
37 Aileron trim tab control linkage
38 Starboard outer fuel cell
39 Bomb gear access panels (3)
40 Hinged trailing edge
41 Scrap view showing underwing panels
42 Hinged (Fairey-Youngman diving brake) flap
43 Outer wing section handling rail (stowed)

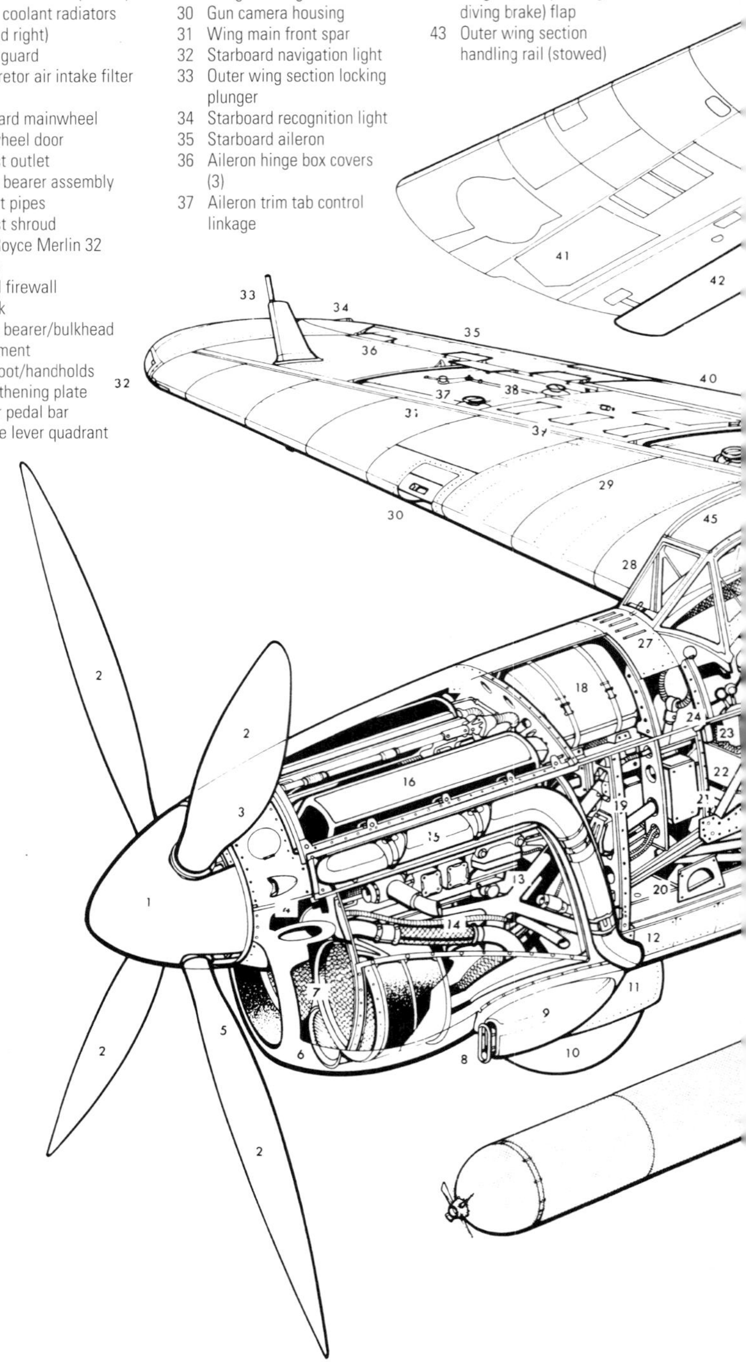

This Barracuda Mk II, MX613, was used for experiments and demonstration while carrying an air-sea rescue lifeboat underneath the fuselage. This configuration was not adopted for operational use.

44 Starboard inner fuel cell
45 Pilot's sliding canopy
46 Pilot's head rest
47 Incendiary bomb
48 Frame members
49 Seat frame mounting
50 Underfloor control runs
51 Mainwheel unit operating jack
52 Mainwheel unit torsion box well
53 Main spar centre-section carry-through
54 Navigator's Vickers gun (stowed)
55 Decking cut out
56 Main slinging point
57 Navigator's tilting canopy
58 Aileron control linkage
59 Radio equipment
60 Aerial mast
61 Radio operator's tilting canopy section
62 Sliding decking section
63 Radio operator's twin Vickers guns (stowed)
64 Track
65 Ammunition stowage
66 Dinghy stowage
67 Detachable fairing
68 Tail surface control runs
69 Decking
70 Tailfin/fuselage fillet
71 Tailfin structure/access panel
72 Tailplane bracing struts
73 Elevator control linkage
74 Tailplane
75 Aerials
76 Tailplane catches
77 Starboard elevator
78 Tail fin upper section
79 Rudder balance
80 Rudder upper hinge
81 Elevator trim tabs
82 Tab control linkage
83 Port elevator
84 Rudder trim tabs
85 Tab control mechanism (starboard side)
86 Rudder post
87 Rear navigation light
88 Fuselage aft frame
89 Tailwheel shock-absorber
90 Fixed tailwheel
91 Dinghy external release cable
92 Lifting tube
93 D/R compass
94 Deck arrester hook (extended)
95 Deck arrester hook damper
96 Hook housing pivot
97 Aft catapult spool
98 Smoke-float internal stowage
99 Launching chute
100 Trailing aerial winch
101 T.1115/R.1116 radio transmitter receiver
102 Radio operator's window
103 Radio operator's seat
104 Accumulators
105 Bomb gear access panels (3)
106 Rear spar station
107 Hinged (Fairey-Youngman diving-brake) flap
108 Port outer fuel cell
109 Aileron tab control linkage
110 Aileron trim tab
111 Port aileron framework
112 Port formation light
113 Port recognition light

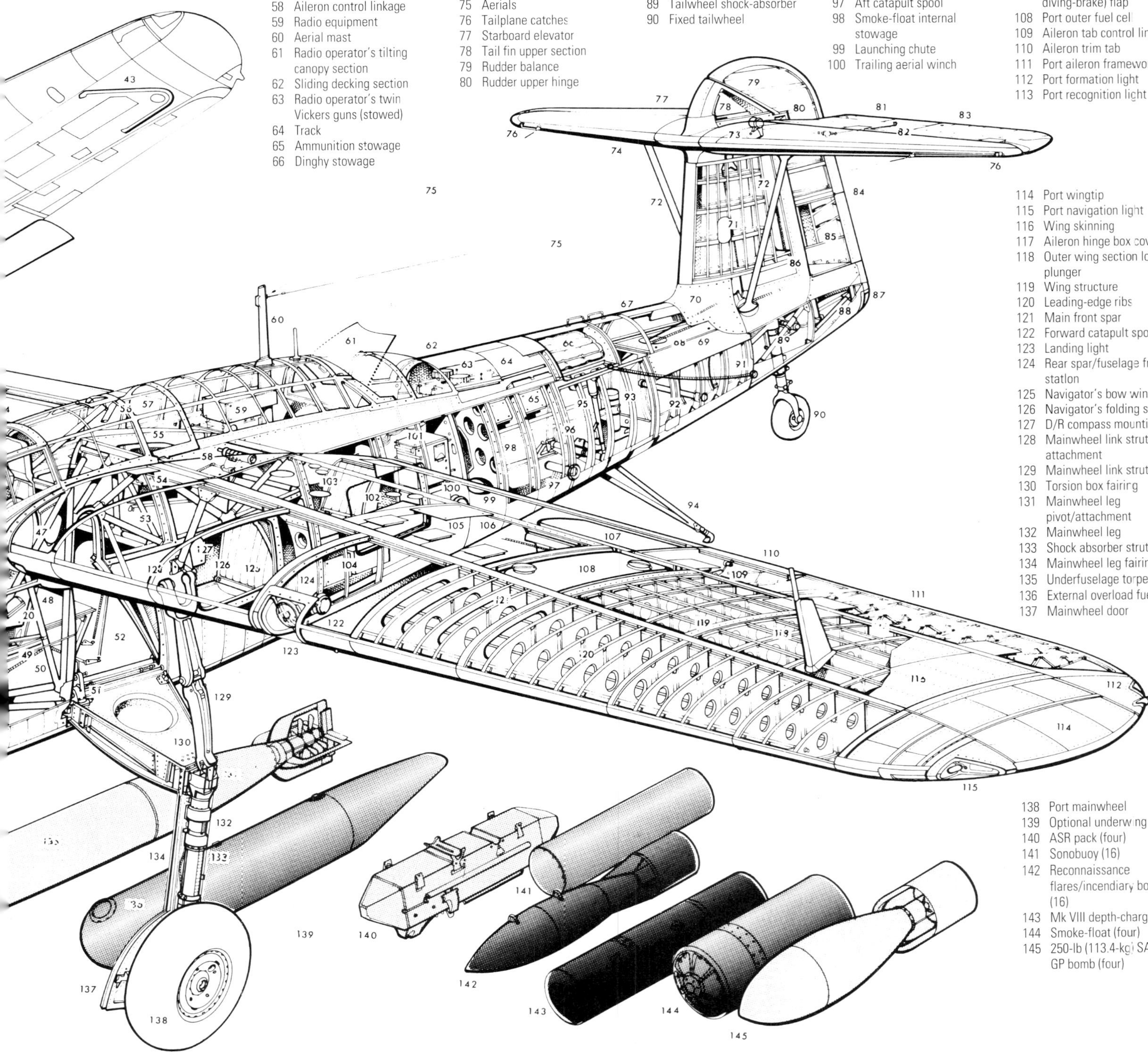

114 Port wingtip
115 Port navigation light
116 Wing skinning
117 Aileron hinge box covers
118 Outer wing section locking plunger
119 Wing structure
120 Leading-edge ribs
121 Main front spar
122 Forward catapult spool
123 Landing light
124 Rear spar/fuselage frame station
125 Navigator's bow window
126 Navigator's folding seat
127 D/R compass mounting
128 Mainwheel link strut pivot attachment
129 Mainwheel link strut
130 Torsion box fairing
131 Mainwheel leg pivot/attachment
132 Mainwheel leg
133 Shock absorber strut
134 Mainwheel leg fairing
135 Underfuselage torpedo
136 External overload fuel tank
137 Mainwheel door
138 Port mainwheel
139 Optional underwing stores,
140 ASR pack (four)
141 Sonobuoy (16)
142 Reconnaissance flares/incendiary bombs (16)
143 Mk VIII depth-charge (four)
144 Smoke-float (four)
145 250-lb (113.4-kg) SAP or GP bomb (four)

Fairey Barracuda

Used in the training role, this Barracuda Mk II operated with No. 785 Squadron. As a dedicated torpedo bomber reconnaissance training squadron the unit flew Barracudas from its base at Crail from April 1943 until after the end of the war.

Above: A Barracuda returns from a dive-bombing attack on the Tirpitz on 3 April 1944. The raids inflicted heavy damage on the German battleship, keeping it in harbour and away from Allied shipping.

Specification
Barracuda Mk II
Type: three-seat torpedo- and dive-bomber
Powerplant: one 1,640-hp (1223-kW) Rolls-Royce Merlin 32 inline piston engine
Performance: (without torpedo): maximum speed 240 mph (386 km/h) at 1,750 ft (535 m); cruising speed 205 mph (330 km/h) at 5,000 ft (1525 m); service ceiling 16,600 ft (5060 m); range 1,150 miles (1851 km) without bombs
Weights: empty 10,818 lb (4907 kg); maximum take-off 14,250 lb (6464 kg)
Dimensions: span 49 ft 2 in (14.99 m); length 39 ft 9 in (12.12 m); height 12 ft 3 in (3.73 m); wing area 414 sq ft (38.46 m²)
Armament: two 0.303-in (7.7-mm) machine-guns, plus one 1,620-lb (735-kg) torpedo, or up to 1,600 lb (726 kg) of bombs, or six 250-lb (113-kg) depth charges, or 1,640 lb (744 kg) of mines

Above: After it was hastily retired from service following VJ-Day, the Merlin-powered Barracuda Mk III re-entered front-line service with the Fleet Air Arm in December 1947, when No. 815 Squadron reformed at Eglinton, Northern Ireland.

Below: The Barracuda Mk II entered service in early 1943, replacing Albacores and Swordfish as the Fleet Air Arm's primary torpedo-bomber. This example, seen here in May 1943, with flaps/dive-brakes in the neutral cruising position, served as a test aircraft helping to develop operational procedures for the type.

Seen carrying its primary weapon, the single 1,620-lb (735-kg) torpedo, the Barracuda Mk II saw action in most of the Fleet Air Arm's operations from 1943. A total of 2,572 was built by Blackburn, Boulton Paul and Westland, as well as Fairey.

Barracudas made their mark when 42 aircraft dive-bombed the German battleship *Tirpitz* on 3 April 1944, inflicting heavy damage, and further attacks were made on the same target during the next four months.

The Barracuda squadrons of HMS *Illustrious*, Nos 810 and 847, introduced the type to the Pacific theatre in April 1944, supporting US Navy dive-bombers in an attack on Japanese installations in Sumatra. Barracudas flew from small escort carriers on anti-submarine patrols in European operations, using rocket-assisted take-off gear from the short decks. Most squadrons were disbanded soon after VJ-Day, or re-equipped with other aircraft, and after some shuffling within squadrons the last Barracudas in front-line service were replaced in 1953 by Grumman Avengers.

The Mk Vs never entered front-line service, being used by Nos 705, 744 and 753 Squadrons for training until 1950.

Fairey Battle

Battle Mk Is of No. 218 Squadron suffered heavy losses during the German invasion of France in May 1940. Survivors such as K9324 (centre) were later used overseas as part of the Empire Training Scheme.

When the Fairey Battle prototype flew on 10 March 1936, it represented a significant increase in performance over the Hawker Hart which it was designed to replace. However, when World War II began only three years later the type was already obsolete and the RAF was to learn, like the Luftwaffe with the Junkers Ju 87 Stuka, that it could only operate safely where air supremacy had been achieved.

Designed by Marcel Lobelle, the prototype **Fairey Day Bomber**, as it was then known, originated as the company's submission to Specification P.27/32 for a two-seat, single-engined monoplane bomber capable of carrying 1,000 lb (454 kg) of bombs for 1,000 miles (1609 km) at 200 mph (322 km/h). This performance was to be bettered by Fairey's aircraft, which was competing against design proposals from Armstrong Whitworth, Bristol and Hawker, but only the first's A.W.29 joined Fairey's prototype in receiving orders. Fairey's contender won the competition, but a first production contract for 155 aircraft, to the revised Specification P.23/35, had

Above: Fairey Battles of No. 88 Squadron are escorted by French Air Force Mohawks as they transit into enemy-held territory on a daylight bombing raid. During the Battle of France most of the the squadron's aircraft were lost.

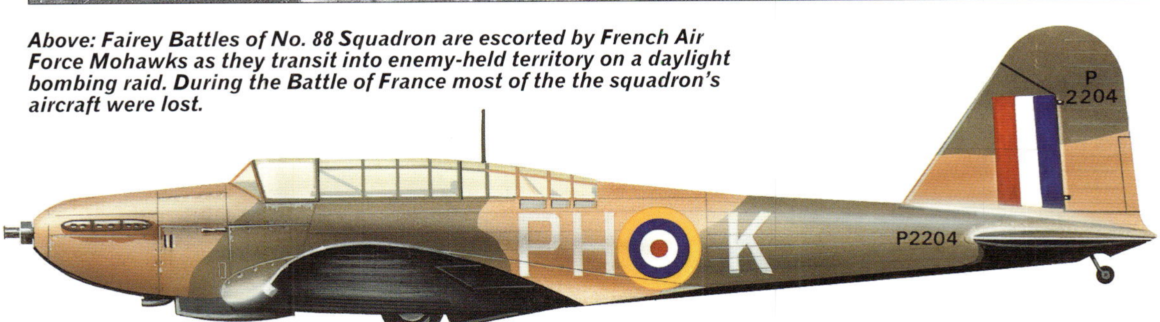

Heavy losses were inflicted on the Battles of No. 12 Squadron during their stay in France during the first nine months of the war. Initially used for reconnaissance and leaflet drops, the squadron was later tasked with bombing attacks against the rapidly advancing German army.

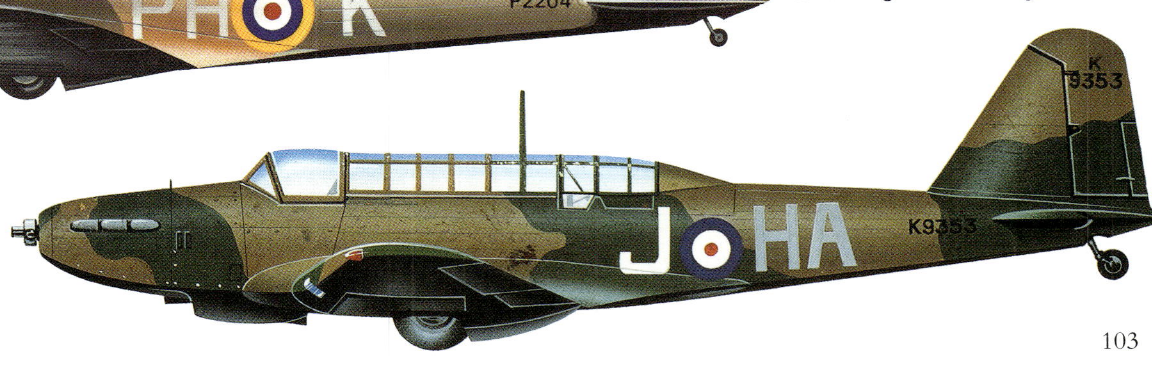

The Battle equipped 10 squadrons in Bomber Command's contribution to the AASF in France. Few returned intact, as they were called upon to fly perilous daylight attacks against the German army. K9353 was typical; it was originally issued to No. 218 Squadron at Boscombe Down early in 1939 and went to France in September. It went missing during the fighting on 13 May 1940.

Based at RAF Benson in November 1939, during the 'phoney war' period, this Battle Mk I operated with No. 63 Squadron. The unit provided operational training for Battle crews until 8 April 1940.

been placed in 1935 even before the prototype had flown. The Battle had accommodation for a crew of three comprising pilot, bomb-aimer/observer and radio operator/gunner. The first production aircraft was built, like the prototype, at Hayes and flew from the Great West Aerodrome (now part of Heathrow Airport), on 14 April 1937. It was used for performance trials during which it achieved 243 mph (391 km/h) at 16,200 ft (4940 m); the range of 1,050 miles (1690 m) was flown with maximum bomb load.

The second and subsequent production aircraft came from a production line established at a new purpose-built factory at Heaton Chapel, Stockport, and it was for the Battle that Rolls-Royce received its launching order for the famous 1,030-hp (768-kW) Merlin I engine, which powered the first 136 Fairey-built aircraft.

The aircraft's light alloy and stressed skin construction was a 'first' for Fairey, and the Battle proved to be extremely robust. In general it proved popular with the test pilots at the Aircraft and Armament Experimental Establishment at Martlesham Heath, and at the Royal Aircraft Establishment at Farnborough: it was said to be very easy to fly but the elevator was heavy on take-off; on the other hand, the Royal Aircraft Establishment considered the elevator over-light at low speeds. Engine-off stall was described as 'innocuous', but the accommodation came in for some criticism: although the pilot's cockpit was considered to be roomy and comfortable with reasonable forward vision, it could sometimes become extremely hot. The rear gunner, behind the pilot, had his own problems: the screen intended to protect him from the slipstream was badly designed and its shape deflected a downdraught into his face, while the rear vision was described as 'poor'.

By the end of 1937, 85 Battles had been built by Fairey, and the first squadron to receive the new bomber in May 1937 was No. 63 at Upwood, Huntingdonshire, with whom it replaced the Hawker Audax. Other squadrons which re-equipped that year were Nos 52, 88, 105 and 226.

As new orders for Battles were placed, production sub-contracts were awarded to Austin Motors at Longbridge, Birmingham. Meantime, the last 19 Battles of the initial Fairey order for 155 were provided with Merlin II engines, and these were fitted also to the Austin-built aircraft. The first Battle from the Longbridge factory flew in July 1938, and 29 had been completed there by the end of the year. By March the following year Austin was producing more than 30 Battles a month, but even then the programme was running late. After 60 Austin-built Battles had been completed, the Merlin II engine was introduced on the production line.

By the outbreak of World War II, No. 63 Squadron had adopted the code letters 'ON' and, along with the squadron's Avro Ansons, provided flying training for bomber crews. The rear cockpit screen, seen here in the raised position, deflected the slipstream into the gunner's face, making his job of aiming the Vickers 'K' machine-gun difficult.

Right: Life-expectancy of the three-man crew which flew Battles on daylight raids over advancing German troops and lines of communication was among the lowest of the war. On many raids over half the crews did not make it back to base. This crew from No. 218 (Gold Coast) Squadron prepare themselves for another daylight sortie.

Recognised as being obsolete before the war began, Battles equipped 17 squadrons that formed the first echelon of the ill-fated Advanced Air Striking Force in France. They were soon withdrawn for secondary duties in 1940. This example went to the A&AEE where it was fitted with target-towing equipment. Many others were similarly equipped as Battle TT.Mk 1s.

By the outbreak of World War II more than 1,000 Battles had been delivered, and aircraft of No. 226 Squadron were the first to be sent to France as part of the Advanced Air Striking Force. It was here that the Battle's inability to defend itself against enemy fighters became obvious. On armed daylight reconnaissance missions the type occasionally tangled with Messerschmitt Bf 109s, and although one of the latter was destroyed by a Battle's rear gunner in September 1940, the light bombers invariably suffered heavy casualties.

As the period of the so-called 'phoney war' came to an end, the Battle squadrons were thrown in on 10 May 1940 to try to stop the advancing German ground forces. Without fighter escort, and attacking from a height of only 250 ft (76 m) with delayed-action bombs, the Battles came under heavy ground fire, losing 13 of the 32 aircraft sent on the mission, while all the others were damaged. The next day seven out of eight were lost. On 12 May five Battles of No. 12 Squadron, flown by volunteer crews, attacked two vital road bridges over the Albert Canal: in the face of extremely heavy ground fire the attack was pressed home and one bridge seriously damaged, but at a cost of all five aircraft. The first RAF Victoria Crosses of World War II were awarded posthumously to Flying Officer D. E. Garland and his observer, Sergeant T. Gray, who led the formation.

Further heavy losses came on 14 May, when 35 of 63 Battles failed to return from attacks against bridges and troop concentrations. These losses marked the end of the Battle's career as a day bomber, and although a few remained in front-line service until late 1940, the

The Fairey Battle was rarely seen with spinners fitted because the rear of its fairing too easily chafed on the engine cowling. The latter was also difficult to remove. This converted Battle TT.Mk I served with No. 2 Anti-Aircraft Co-operation Unit based at Gosport. The unit flew a number of types, including Hawker Hectors and Blackburn Rocs.

One hundred of the later production Battles were produced as Battle T dual-control trainers with separate cockpits. This involved fairly extensive redesign of the control runs and the fuselage structure. Appearing in 1940, they were used to train prospective fighter pilots. Each cockpit was fitted with similar screens, sliding hoods and instrument/control layouts.

survivors were mostly diverted to other duties. The most important of these was training, and 100 were built as dual-control trainers with separate cockpits, while 266 target-towing variants were also supplied.

The last production aircraft, Austin-built, was a target-tug, and it was delivered on 2 September 1940. It brought total Battle production to 2,185 including the prototype, 1,156 being built by Fairey and 1,029 by Austin Motors.

Canada used a large number of Battles for training and target-towing in the Commonwealth Air Training Plan, the first being supplied to the Royal Canadian Air Force at Camp Borden in August 1939. They were the vanguard of 739 of these aircraft, this total including seven airframes for instructional purposes. The Royal Australian Air Force received four British-built Battles and assembled 360 in Australia, including 30 target-tugs, while other export customers were Belgium (16), Turkey (29), South Africa (several) and Eire, where an RAF aircraft which landed at Waterford in 1941 was interned and later taken over by the Air Corps.

A number of Battles were used as testbeds for such engines as the Napier Dagger and Sabre; Bristol Hercules and Taurus; Rolls-Royce Exe and Merlin XII; and Fairey Prince. Other Battles were used for experiments with various types of propellers.

Specification
Battle Mk I
Type: three-seat light bomber
Powerplant: one 1,030-hp (768-kW) Rolls-Royce Merlin I inline piston engine
Performance: maximum speed 257 mph (414 km/ h) at 20,000 ft (6100 m); cruising speed 210 mph (338 km/h); service ceiling 25,000 ft (7620 m); range 1,000 miles (1609 km) at 16,000 ft (4875 m) at 200 mph (322 km/h)
Weights: empty 6,647 lb (3015 kg); maximum take-off 10,792 lb (4895 kg)
Dimensions: span 54 ft 0 in (16.46 m); length 42 ft 4 in (12.90 m); height 15 ft 6 in (4.72 m); wing area 422 sq ft (39.20 m²)
Armament: one 0.303-in (7.7-mm) machine-gun in starboard wing and one Vickers 'K' gun in rear cockpit, plus bomb load of up to 1,000 lb (454 kg)

This Battle TT.Mk I target-tug served with a Service Flying Training School in Canada and was used as an aerial gunnery trainer. Broad black bands were applied over the basic yellow scheme to improve conspicuity in the air (there was no threat from hostile aircraft) and on the ground in the event of a forced-landing.

Although the Battle had been retired from front-line service by the RAF in 1940, the South African Air Force continued to operate the type as a bomber in Africa during 1941. This example served with No. 15 Squadron, SAAF, based at Algato, East Africa.

Early Battle Ts were not fitted with the separate cockpits of the later version. This example served with No. 8 Service Training Flying School at Moncton, Canada, training Commonwealth aircrew. A D/F loop is installed in the rear cockpit.

Fairey Firefly

Designed to Admiralty Specification N.5/40, which defined a requirement for a two-seat reconnaissance fighter, the Fairey Firefly represented a considerable advance on the earlier Fairey Fulmar, both in speed and firepower. A design team headed by H. E. Chaplin completed the submission in September 1939, and an order for 200 aircraft was placed on 12 June 1940. The first of four development aircraft was flown from Fairey's Great West Aerodrome on 22 December 1941, the pilot being Christopher Staniland, who also flew the second aircraft on 4 June 1942. The third machine was flown on 26 August, joining the test programme some six weeks after the crash of the second, and some minor changes resulted. These included a mass-balanced rudder and metal-skinned ailerons. Carrier trials were carried out aboard HMS *Illustrious* at the end of 1942.

The first aircraft from the Hayes production line was delivered in March 1943 powered by the 1,730-hp (1290-kW) Griffon IIB engine, although later machines had the 1,990-hp (1484-kW) Griffon XII. Other changes introduced during the **Firefly F.Mk I** production run included a deeper windscreen, fairings for the four 20-mm cannon mounted in the wings, and deletion of the two-man dinghy in the rear fuselage, in favour of individual K-type dinghies for pilot and observer. A total of 459 Firefly F.Mk Is was built, 327 by Fairey at Hayes and 132 under sub-contract by General Aircraft Ltd at Hanworth. The

Below: Firefly Mk 1 Z1881 was operating with No. 1770 Squadron at Grimsetter during the early part of 1944. The cannon were still without fairings at this time.

Above: The Fairey-Youngman drooping flaps were a distinguishing feature of the Firefly, although they were normally retracted in the cruise configuration.

Below: The first major action in which Fairey Fireflies took part was the successful attack on Japanese oil refineries in Sumatra. Fireflies of No. 1770 Squadron are shown here folding their wings on HMS Indefatigable after attacking Pangkalan Brandon on 4 January 1945.

Above: ***This was the third Firefly (Z1832) in the initial pre-production batch. The early Fireflies had a shallow screen, narrowing at the base, with a windscreen wiper. Later aircraft in the early batches had a much deeper windscreen.***

Left: ***Development of more compact radar equipment led to the NF.Mk I variant, a standard FR.Mk I in which the equipment was carried in a canister below the engine. DT933 was used by the A&AEE for trials work and thus became the prototype NF.Mk I.***

addition of ASH radar in a pod beneath the engine identified the **Firefly FR.Mk I**, of which 236 were built. A number of F.Mk Is were modified to FR.Mk I standard; these were designated **F.Mk IA** but did not enter service until after hostilities had ceased.

Fairey developed a night-fighter version, designated **NF.Mk II**, which had an 15-in (0.38-m) fuselage extension behind the engine firewall. This was necessary to adjust the centre of gravity, compensating for the weight of the AI Mk X radar equipment in the rear cockpit. However, problems with the Mk II's handling and with the AI radar led to the cancellation of the variant. Instead, the FR.Mk I was to form the basis of a Firefly night-fighter, this variant's ASH radar proving adaptable to the AI task. Thus, the planned 328-aircraft Mk II programme was cancelled in favour of modifications to FR.Mk Is on the production line, these emerging as **NF.Mk Is**, of which 140 were built. Most of the 37 NF.Mk IIs completed before cancellation were converted back to Mk I standard. Post-war conversions of the Mk I included the unarmed dual-control **T.Mk 1** pilot trainer, with a raised rear cockpit, which appeared in production form in September 1947; the **T.Mk 2** operational trainer, with two 20-mm cannon, first flown on 19 August 1949; and the **T.Mk 3** observer trainer of 1951, which retained the flush rear cockpit and was equipped for training observers in anti-submarine operations. A few target-tug **Firefly TT.Mk Is** were also converted.

Although 100 were ordered, the Griffon 61-engined **Firefly Mk III** was built only as a prototype in 1944, and development work was concentrated on the **Mk IV** which was powered by a 2,100-hp (1566-kW) Griffon 74 engine with a two-stage supercharger and driving a four-bladed propeller. This aircraft, with its so-called

This view of a later production Firefly Mk I day-fighter shows its raised windscreen and cockpit hood that gave a better view for the pilot. This was a great improvement for combat and while taking off and, more especially, for landing on a carrier deck.

Above: This dramatic view of the underside of a rocket-equipped Firefly Mk I as it approaches its carrier with wheels down shows its arrester hook and large landing flaps extended.

Left: The British Pacific Fleet markings seen on this Firefly Mk I came into use around May 1945. Here an aircraft from No. 1771 Squadron, FAA based aboard HMS* Implacable *returns from patrol. By this time in the war, the Allies had gained almost total air superiority in the region.

'universal' airframe, became the basis for the later **Mk 5** and **Mk 6**, the main post-war Firefly variants.

Fireflies entered service with No. 1770 Squadron at Yeovilton on 1 October 1943 and, embarked on HMS *Indefatigable*, were active in operations against the German battleship *Tirpitz* in Norway in July 1944, strafing anti-aircraft batteries protecting the ship. Further Firefly sorties followed in August, No. 1770 Squadron making reconnaissance flights over the *Tirpitz*.

In October, No. 1771 Squadron aboard *Implacable* flew armed reconnaissance and anti-shipping sorties along the Norwegian coast, but in these and the earlier actions against the *Tirpitz*, opportunities for the type to prove its capabilities in air-to-air combat were virtually non-existent. It was in the Pacific that the type was to score its first victories in the air.

HMS *Indefatigable* was transferred to the East Indies Fleet, and on 2 January 1945 Lieutenant D. Levitt of No. 1770 Squadron scored the type's first 'kill' when he shot down a Nakajima Ki-43 'Oscar'. Sub-Lieutenants Redding and Stott, of the same unit, claimed another 'Oscar' that same day. These victories occurred during softening-up operations in preparation for attacks later that month on Japanese oil refineries in Sumatra, during which rocket-firing Fireflies joined bomb-carrying Grumman Avengers in attacking the heavily defended installations.

In June 1945 Fireflies of No. 1771 Squadron, operating from HMS *Implacable*, took part in attacks in the Carolinas, while in July No. 1772's aircraft, from HMS *Indefatigable*, were flying strikes against shipping and ground targets in the Japanese home islands, becoming the first FAA aircraft to fly over the Japanese mainland. On 24 July, aircraft from No. 1772 Squadron became the first British aircraft to fly over Tokyo. During these actions, the Firefly gained a reputation for reliability and sturdiness that stayed with the aircraft during World War II and into the 1950s, when the type again saw action in the Korean War and over Malaya.

Night-fighter Fireflies were first issued to No. 746 Squadron, FAA (the Royal Navy's Night Fighter Interception Unit) in May 1943. Based at Ford, the NFIU flew alongside the RAF's FIU, developing night-fighter tactics. Flying from RAF Coltishall during late-1944, NFIU Fireflies undertook night patrols to counter V-1 flying bombs air-launched over the North Sea by Luftwaffe He111s.

Three FAA squadrons – Nos 1790, 1791 and 1792 – were ear-marked as night-fighter units to form up and join the growing British Pacific Fleet; No. 1790 received its first aircraft in January 1945 and, after joining HMS *Implacable*, reached the Fleet just prior to VJ-Day.

Specification

Firefly Mk I

Type: two-seat carrier-based fleet reconnaissance fighter/fighter-bomber
Powerplant: one 1,730-hp (1290-kW) Rolls-Royce Griffon IIB inline piston engine
Performance: maximum speed 316 mph (509 km/h) at 14,000 ft (4265 m); service ceiling 28,000 ft (8535 m); range 1,300 miles (2092 km)
Weights: empty 9,750 lb (4423 kg); maximum take-off 14,020 lb (6359 kg)
Dimensions: span 44 ft 6 in (13.56 m); length 37 ft 7 in (11.46 m); height 13 ft 7 in (4.14 m); wing area 328 sq ft (30.47 m^2)
Armament: four 20-mm cannon in wings, plus provision for eight 60-lb (27-kg) rocket projectiles or two 500-lb (227-kg) or 1,000-lb (454-kg) bombs on racks beneath the wings

Fairey Fulmar

Above: Equipping eight operational squadrons by mid-1941, the Fairey Fulmar was to play a vital and successful role in the shadowing of the German battleship* Bismarck. *Here a Fulmar lands on HMS* Victorious *after a patrol over the shipping lanes.

Warming up its Rolls-Royce Merlin VIII engine on the deck of HMS* Victorious*, this Fulmar Mk I displays an example of Fleet Air Arm 'nose art' which was often applied to operational aircraft. The Fulmar was the first eight-gun carrierborne fighter to serve with the Fleet Air Arm.

The Fleet Air Arm desperately needed a new aircraft to replace its antiquated biplanes, but the philosophy of the period dictated that if the Royal Navy was to get a high-performance fighter, a crew of two was desirable to cope with the growing sophistication of navigational aids. Inevitably, the extra size and weight imposed a performance penalty, but, until the arrival of the Hawker Sea Hurricane and Supermarine Seafire, the Fairey Fulmar was the best aircraft available.

Two prototypes of a light bomber to Specification P.4/34 had been flown, the first on 13 January 1937, and from them emerged, with comparatively few modifications, the Fulmar to Specification 0.8/38. The P.4/34 was smaller and lighter than the contemporary Fairey Battle, certainly better looking, and was stressed for dive-bombing. The second prototype was used as the flying mock-up of a fleet fighter, with certain changes to meet naval requirements and the 0.8/38 specification. An early stipulation that the Fulmar should be capable of operating with floats was dropped.

Within seven weeks of receiving the detailed specification, on 16 March 1938, Fairey confirmed to the Admiralty that a modified version of the P.4/34 would meet the requirements, and an initial order was placed for 127 aircraft to be known as the Fulmar. This was increased to 250 at the time of the Munich crisis in September 1938, but Fairey warned that production could not begin until its new factory at Heaton Chapel, Stockport, was completed.

While the P.4/34 had been powered by the 1,030-hp (768-kW) Rolls-Royce Merlin II, the initial production **Fulmar Mk I** was to have the 1,080-hp (805-kW) Merlin VIII, although in fact the first aircraft flew at Ringway on 4 January 1940 with a modified Merlin III. The first with the Merlin VIII engine flew on 6 April 1940 and, following the usual pattern, was submitted to the Aircraft and Armament Experimental Establishment at Boscombe Down for testing and then to HMS *Illustrious* for carrier trials. The pilots found the Fulmar viceless, manoeuvrable and pleasant to fly, although when fully equipped its longitudinal stability was said to be marginal. Not surprisingly, its performance in speed, rate of climb and ceiling came in for some criticism, but it should be remembered that when the original concept was evolved it was considered that as a carrier-based aircraft the Fulmar was unlikely to be pitted against land-based fighters of superior performance. Certainly it had the same eight-gun armament of the contemporary Hurricane and Spitfire, carried twice as much ammunition as the land-based fighters, and had an endurance of five hours (also double that of contemporary land-based fighters). In these circumstances the Fulmar, with the extra weight of its second crew member and wing-folding mechanism, could be considered to have a reasonable performance, and in any case was superior to the types it replaced, including the Blackburn Roc.

Once production began it proceeded apace and in the first three months six, 12 and 20 Fulmars were built, respectively, while by the fourth month (August 1940) the monthly rate of 25, agreed as the maximum, had been achieved; by the end of the year 159 Fulmars had been delivered.

The first squadron to receive Fulmars was No. 808 at Worthy Down in June 1940, embarking later in HMS *Ark Royal*. No. 806 Squadron at Eastleigh received 12 Fulmars in July to replace its Blackburn Skuas and Rocs, and the remaining squadron to get the new aircraft that year was No. 807, which formed at Worthy Down in

The Fulmar first saw action with the Fleet Air Arm defending the Malta convoys against the Italian Air Force in September-October 1940. This early production Fulmar Mk I served with No. 806 Squadron from June 1940. Soon afterwards it was embarked on HMS Illustrious .

September. As production increased so squadrons were formed or re-equipped: five in 1941 and six in 1942, but by 1943 the Fulmar was starting to be replaced by the Seafire. The last of 602 Fulmars built was delivered to the Fleet Air Arm in February 1943. Of this total, the first 250 were Mk Is, while subsequent aircraft were to **Mk II** standard. These had a 1,300-hp (969-kW) Merlin 30 engine, a new propeller, tropical equipment and various other changes. A useful weight reduction of 350 lb (159 kg) had been achieved, and although the Mk II was only a little faster than the Mk I, it had a much better rate of climb, enabling it to reach 15,000 ft (4570 m) in 12 minutes against 15 minutes for the earlier version.

Tests with a night-fighter model of the Fulmar began in 1941, following a series of night attacks on the Mediterranean Fleet by Italian air force torpedo-bombers. Installation of Air Interception (AI) radar Mark VI was carried out on a Fulmar Mk II at Lee-on-Solent, but the poor results led to a modified AI Mk IV being substituted. Extra drag and other problems held up the issue to front-line squadrons until February 1944, but this version was used from June 1942 to train night-fighter crews in preparation for the Fairey Firefly.

Around 100 Fulmar Mk IIs were converted to night-fighters, in more or less equal numbers for operational and training purposes. The arrival of a new lightweight, high-frequency wireless telegraphy set, in early 1942, enabled the Fulmars to operate effectively as long-range reconnaissance aircraft over the Indian Ocean.

Throughout its career the Fulmar, like most types, was subject to modifications to improve its fighting efficiency. Ammunition capacity was increased from 750 to 1,000 rounds per gun (three times that of the Hurricane) and tests of 0.5-in (12.7-mm) machine-guns in place of the standard 0.303-in (7.7-mm) weapons gave good results, but shortage of the former resulted in only a few of the final production aircraft being fitted with the larger-calibre weapons.

Perhaps the Fulmar's weakest point was its lack of rear-firing armament; in some cases the crew improvised with such weapons as the Thompson sub-machine gun or a Verey pistol, but it has been said that the most unusual weapon was a bundle of lavatory paper. Held together by an elastic band, this, when thrown into the slipsteam, scattered in all directions, causing the pursuers to break away in confusion.

The Fulmar figured briefly in the early stages of experiments to prove the feasibility of catapulting fighters from armed merchant ships. Intended to provide some protection for convoys, such an operation was invariably a one-way trip, as there was nowhere to land back on board. After combat the pilot had to bale out and hope to be picked up by one of the convoy. On 11 January 1941 a Fulmar of No. 807 Squadron was launched in this way from HMS *Pegasus*, but for future operations Hurricanes were used.

After serving in all theatres, the Fulmar ignominiously ended its front-line operational career on 8 February 1945, when a Mk II of No. 813 Squadron missed the arrester wire when landing back on HMS *Campania*, and was written-off in the subsequent argument with the safety barrier.

As the Firefly began to enter service in 1943, so the Fulmars were withdrawn until the only remaining example, by coincidence the first one built, ended its days with Fairey as a communications aircraft. Later, for a short time, it flew in its original colours before being grounded, and is now preserved in the Fleet Air Arm Museum at RNAS Yeovilton.

***Above:* Fulmar Mk II DR673 was fitted with the later Merlin XXX engine and tropical equipment. The first Mk II was flown in January 1941 and 350 were subsequently built before production of the Fulmar ceased in February 1943.**

***Left:* Fulmars of No. 806 NAS from HMS Illustrious shot down six Italian aircraft while providing fighter cover for the operation at Taranto in November 1940.**

***Below:* The Fulmar's lack of speed was largely due to the presence of the second seat for the navigator, but it must be remembered that, at the time, navigational aids were not sufficiently developed to ensure a single-seat fighter's safe return to its carrier in bad weather.**

Specification

Fulmar Mk I

Type: two-seat carrier-based fighter

Powerplant: one 1,080-hp (805-kW) Rolls-Royce Merlin VIII inline piston engine

Performance: maximum speed 247 mph (398 km/ h) at 9,000 ft (2745 m); service ceiling 21,500 ft (6555 m); patrol endurance 4 hours with reserves

Weights: empty 8,720 lb (3955 kg); maximum take-off 10,700 lb (4853 kg)

Dimensions: span 46 ft 5 in (14.15 m); length 40 ft 2 in (12.24 m); height 14 ft 0 in (4.27 m); wing area 342 sq ft (31.77 m^2)

Armament: eight 0.303-in (7.7-mm) machine-guns in wings

Fairey Gordon

When the time came to replace the ubiquitous Fairey IIIF, it was decided that the best replacement was in fact another IIIF, and the prototype **Gordon** was a conversion from a IIIF Mk IVM fitted with an Armstrong Siddeley Panther IIA radial engine of 525 hp (391 kW) in place of the IIIF's 570-hp (425-kW) Napier Lion. While this may sound an odd decision, the lower-powered Gordon was some 400 lb (181 kg) lighter when loaded and had a superior performance, particularly at take-off. Other changes were made in electrical, fuel and oil systems and in the mounting of the forward-firing machine-gun.

Ordered to Specification 18/30 for a two-seat day-bomber and general-purpose aircraft, the Gordon first flew on 3 March 1931 and 178 were built for the RAF before production ended in 1934.

First RAF production deliveries were in April 1931 to No. 40 Squadron at Upper Heyford, while the first overseas squadron to be equipped was No. 6 in the Middle East, a former Bristol Fighter unit. Aircraft from Nos 35 and 207 Squadrons formed part of the RAF reinforcement of the Middle East during the Abyssinian crisis of 1935.

Gordons were still serving with first-line squadrons at home and overseas in 1938, while others were in service on target-towing duties at the outbreak of World War II. The last surviving example was probably K2743, which was reported to be still on charge as late as September 1941.

Contemporary with the Gordon was the Fleet Air Arm's Fairey Seal which was, to all intents and purposes, a naval version operated on wheels or floats.

Specification
Gordon Mk I
Type: two-seat day bomber/general-purpose aircraft
Powerplant: one 525-hp (391-kW) Armstrong Siddeley Panther IIA radial piston engine
Performance: maximum speed 145 mph (233 km/h) at 3,000 ft (915 m); cruising speed 110 mph (177 km/h); service ceiling 22,000 ft (6705 m); range 600 miles (966 km)
Weights: empty 3,500 lb (1588 kg); maximum take-off 5,906 lb (2679 kg)
Dimensions: span 45 ft 9 in (13.94 m); length 36 ft 9 in (11.20 m); height 14 ft 2 in (4.32 m); wing area 438 sq ft (40.69 m²)
Armament: one forward-firing 0.303-in (7.7-mm) machine-gun and one aft-firing 0.303-in (7.7-mm) machine-gun

Seen over the Nablus Hills, Jordan in 1938, this Gordon Mk I was one of a number serving with the RAF Middle East HQ Flight as World War II loomed. By the outbreak of war the aircraft had been relegated to target-towing duties.

Fairey Seafox

One of the less glamorous but necessary tasks performed by Fleet Air Arm aircraft during World War II was the fleet spotting and reconnaissance undertaken by aircraft catapulted from capital ships.

Fairey tendered a biplane floatplane to meet the requirement of Specification S.11/32. With a metal monocoque fuselage and fabric-covered wings, the aircraft was accepted for service and a contract for 49 aircraft was placed in January 1936. Named **Seafox**, the design was powered by a Napier Rapier engine and was unusual in having the pilot stationed in an open cockpit while the observer/gunner was in an enclosed rear cockpit. This arrangement allowed the aircraft to be recovered onto the ship by crane after a catapult launch.

Production Seafoxes became available from April 1937 and, after exhaustive testing with the Royal Aircraft Establishment and the Marine Aircraft Experimental Establishment, were formed into catapult flights. At the outbreak of World War II Seafoxes equipped Nos 702, 713, 714, 716 and 718 Flights and in January 1940 these units were pooled to form No. 700 Squadron. In the first two years of the war Seafoxes equipped a number of cruisers and saw their first action against the German pocket battleship *Admiral Graf Spee* during the action in the River Plate in December 1939. Persued by the British cruisers HMS *Achilles*, *Ajax* and *Exeter*, the battleship was severely damanged thanks, in part, to the Seafox from HMS *Ajax* spotting for the guns. The pilot of the Seafox, Lt E. D. G. Lewin, received the DFC, which was the first Fleet Air Arm decoration of the war.

Seafox production had ended in 1938, but the type continued in front-line service until 1942 when it was replaced by the Vought-Sikorsky Kingfisher. Even then the Seafox served in the training role with Nos 753 and 754 Squadrons until July 1943.

Specification
Seafox Mk I
Type: two-seat spotter/reconnaissance floatplane
Powerplant: one 395-hp (295-kW) Napier Rapier VI inline piston engine
Performance: maximum speed 124 mph (200 km/h) at 5,860 ft (1785 m); cruising speed 106 mph (171 km/h); service ceiling 11,000 ft (3350 m); range 440 miles (708 km)
Weights: empty 3,805 lb (1726 kg); maximum take-off 5,420 lb (2458 kg)
Dimensions: span 40 ft 0 in (12.19 m); length 35 ft 6 in (10.82 m); height 12 ft 1 in (3.68 m); wing area 434 sq ft (40.32 m²)
Armament: one rearward-firing 0.303-in (7.7-mm) machine-gun

At anything approaching maximum weight, the under-powered Seafox took a long time to get airborne. Seafoxes served with a total of five catapult flights.

Fairey Seal

Developed from the Fairey IIIF and basically a three-seat predecessor to the RAF's Gordon Mk II, the Fairey **Seal** was one of a family of Fairey aircraft all related to the ubiquitous IIIF. Indeed, the Seal was originally designated Fairey IIIF Mk VI and differed from the earlier mark in having a 525-hp (391-kW) Armstrong Siddeley Panther IIA engine, a revised fin and rudder, Frise-type ailerons and a tailwheel replacing the tail-skid. The Seal was also the first Fairey aircraft to be fitted with the triangular frame arrester hook beneath the rear fuselage and was the first Fleet Air Arm type to utilise wheel brakes.

Deliveries of production Seals commenced in 1933 and the first batch was soon embarked aboard HMS *Courageous* with Nos 820 and 821 Squadrons of the Fleet Air Arm. Deliveries continued until 1935, with a total of six squadrons operating the type. Seals also served in twin-float-plane form with No. 702 Catapult Flight from various British warships and with the Base Training Squadron at Gosport.

The last squadron to equip with the Seal, No. 822 received the type in 1936 and by the end of 1938 all front-line squadrons had retired the type, replacing it with the Fairey Swordfish. Seals continued in the training role with the FAA until the outbreak of World War II, but the only wartime opertor was, ironically, the RAF. No. 273 Squadron operated Seals from its base in Ceylon on patrols over the Indian Ocean between August 1939 and April 1942.

Specification
Seal
Type: three-seat spotter-reconnaissance landplane/floatplane
Powerplant: one 525-hp (391-kW) Armstrong Siddeley Panther radial piston engine
Performance: maximum speed (landplane) 138 mph (222 km/h), (seaplane) 129 mph (208 km/h); service ceiling (landplane) 17,000 ft (5182 m), (seaplane) 13,900 ft (4237 m); endurance 4.5 hours
Weights: loaded (landplane) 6,000 lb (2722 kg), (seaplane) 6,400 lb (2903 kg)
Dimensions: (landplane) span 45 ft 9 in (13.94 m); length 33 ft 8 in (10.26 m); height 12 ft 9 in (3.88 m); wing area 443.5 sq ft (41.20 m²)
Armament: one forward-firing 0.303-in (7.7-mm) Vickers machine-gun and one rearwards-firing Lewis machine-gun, plus up to 500 lb (227 kg) of bombs

Seal K3577 was experimentally fitted with an Armstrong Siddeley Panther VI engine in a long-chord cowling. It also served as the prototype for the Gordon Mk III.

Fairey Swordfish

Having arrived at a stage of World War II when a biplane, other than the odd small-span Avro Tutor or de Havilland Tiger Moth, was a very rare sight, the appearance of a large and noisy biplane in the circuit created more than average interest. Despite appearances, this beautifully ugly aircraft was no anachronism, for the Fairey Swordfish, as it was named, had then still a vital role to play in World War II, a role for which it was so well engineered that it fought in the battle against the Axis from the very first moment of that conflict until victory for the Allies in Europe had been assured. In so doing, the Swordfish outlived and outfought aircraft which had been designed to replace it in service, and during this period created a record of machine achievement in association with human courage that makes pages of the Fleet Air Arm's history a veritable saga.

***Swordfish prepare for take-off from the flight deck of HMS* Eagle *off Mombasa in April 1941. The aircraft are from Nos 813 and 824 Squadrons, which carried out anti-submarine patrols. On 6 June 1941, Swordfish from these squadrons found and sunk the U-boat supply ship* Elbe.**

A batsman brings a Swordfish in to land on HMS* Smiter *in April 1945. Batsmen led a dangerous life on carriers, frequently making use of the back-up net. The job was made more hazardous by the narrowness of the escort carrier deck.

Approaching obsolescence in 1939, the Swordfish had originated from Fairey's private-venture **T.S.R.I** biplane of 1933. When this was destroyed in an accident during September of that year, its progress had been sufficiently worthwhile to warrant further development. When, therefore, the Air Ministry issued its Specification S.15/33, which called for a carrier-based torpedo-spotter-reconnais-

Shore-based, carrier-based and even catapulted from warships, the Swordfish was a very effective torpedo-bomber. These Swordfish Mk Is are carrying the standard 1,610-lb (730-kg) torpedo beneath the fuselage.

sance aircraft, Fairey submitted its layout for the improved **T.S.R.II** on which the design office had been working. This was to become the prototype of the Swordfish (K4190), first flown on 17 April 1934.

It differed from the T.S.R.I. by having a changed upper wing, slightly swept, to compensate for a fuselage which had been lengthened to improve the stability problems that had led to the loss of the T.S.R.I. Other changes brought the inclusion of an additional wing bay, and modification of the tail unit. Subjected to intensive testing, both in landplane and alternative floatplane form, the type was ordered into production in April 1935 with a first contract for 86 aircraft, to be named Swordfish.

The initial **Swordfish Mk I**, built to Air Ministry Specification S.38/34, was powered by a 690-hp (515-kW) Bristol Pegasus IIIM radial engine, driving a three-bladed, fixed-pitch metal propeller. The two-bay biplane wings were of all-metal construction, fabric-covered, with ailerons on both upper and lower wings, the biplane configuration and its structural integrity maintained by robust interplane struts, flying and landing wires. For shipboard stowage the wings could be folded about rear spar hinges.

The tail unit was entirely conventional, with a strut-braced tailplane, and fin and rudder of metal construction with fabric covering. The fuselage, with two open cockpits to accommodate the pilot forward, and crew of one or two aft, was also of metal construction, but covered by a combination of light alloy panels forward and fabric aft. Landing gear was of the fixed tailwheel type, with the individual main units each having an oleo shock-absorber. These were easily exchanged for an alternative float landing gear, consisting of two

A No. 818 Squadron Swordfish Mk II, one of the main Blackburn-built production batch, taxis aboard the escort carrier HMS* Tracker. *Swordfish were valuable weapons when deployed aboard the relatively small escort carriers, particularly in the North Atlantic.

Above: In the main, the Fleet Air Arm used the same air-to-surface weapons throughout the war. However, in 1943 a new weapon came into use that could be fitted onto any aircraft. This was the air-launched 'rocket projectile', and even the evergreen 'Stringbag' could carry four under each wing. These weapons were particularly effective against surfaced U-boats.

Left: A Blackburn-built Swordfish floatplane, V4367, is lowered over the side of HMS Malaya _with the engine already running and the crew aboard. With a full load, take-off was sluggish, but once on the 'step' the aircraft accelerated quickly to flying speed._

single-step light alloy floats, each provided with a small rudder to simplify directional control on the water.

Armament comprised one synchronised forward-firing 0.303-in (7.7-mm) Vickers machine-gun, one Vickers 'K' gun or Lewis gun in the aft cockpit, and mountings to carry one 18-in (0.46-m) 1,610-lb (730-kg) torpedo beneath the fuselage. Alternative weapon loads of the Mk I included one 1,500-lb (680-kg) mine, or two 500-lb (227-kg) bombs beneath the fuselage plus two 250-lb (113-kg) bombs on underwing racks, or one 500-lb (227-kg) bomb beneath the fuselage and one 500-lb (227-kg) bomb beneath each wing.

Swordfish Mk Is began to enter service with the FAA in July 1936, equipping first No. 825 Squadron as a replacement for the Fairey Seals which had first been allocated to squadrons some three years earlier. Next to go, before the end of 1936, were the Blackburn Baffins which had seen little service with Nos 811 and 812 Squadrons before their replacement, and also the Seals of No. 823 Squadron. When, in 1938, the Blackburn Sharks of Nos 810, 820 and 821 Squadrons were superseded (although they had seen even less service than the Seals), the FAA's torpedo-bomber squadrons had become equipped exclusively with the Swordfish.

At the beginning of World War II the Fleet Air Arm had 13 squadrons operational with the Swordfish, 12 of these squadrons at sea aboard the carriers HMS *Ark Royal*, *Courageous*, *Eagle*, *Furious* and *Glorious*, but the 'phoney' start to the war meant that these aircraft had virtually no fighting until the beginning of the Norwegian campaign in 1940. This, of course, was beneficial rather than detrimental to the Swordfish cause, giving all squadrons ample time in which to work up to a state of perfection. It was to prove of immense value when on 11 April torpedo-carrying Swordfish went into action for the first time from the carrier *Furious*. Two days later a catapulted Swordfish from HMS *Warspite* sank submarine *U-64*, the first U-boat sinking of the war to be credited to the FAA.

Fairey's production commitments were such that the growing contracts for Swordfish were becoming a little embarrassing, so continued construction was left in the capable hands of Blackburn Aircraft at Brough, Yorkshire, a company which had been concerned primarily with the design and manufacture of naval aircraft from its earliest days. Only a single example was built by Blackburn in 1940, but in the following year 415 were produced.

Before 1940 had ended, however, Swordfish had become involved in a different type of operation, under the guidance of the RAF's Coastal Command. This involved them in mine-laying operations and bombing attacks on the German-occupied Channel ports, carrying a crew of two and with auxiliary fuel tanks mounted in the rear cockpit. These tanks were essential to provide the necessary range, but could hardly be described as ideal additions to the gunner/observer's cockpit in a shooting war.

Also in 1940 came the supreme triumph of the Swordfish, the memorable attack on the Italian fleet at anchor in Taranto harbour, made after reconnaissance sorties had shown that six battleships, plus attendant cruisers and destroyers, were sheltering there. The attack, made by 21 Swordfish on the night of 11 November 1940, was launched in two waves, with an hour interval between them. All of the aircraft had long-range tanks in the rear cockpit, limiting crew to two in each aircraft, and of the total, four carried flares for target illumination, six had bombs, and 11 were armed with torpedoes. The first flares were dropped at 23.00, the aircraft of the initial wave going in through a protective umbrella of barrage balloons, a task so difficult that there was little time to consider the intense barrage of light and heavy fire being thrown at them. In spite of the conditions targets

Fairey Swordfish

Fairey Swordfish Mk II cutaway drawing key

1 Rudder structure
2 Rudder upper hinge
3 Diagonal brace
4 External bracing wires
5 Rudder hinge
6 Elevator control horn
7 Tail navigation light
8 Elevator structure
9 Fixed tab
10 Elevator balance
11 Elevator hinge
12 Starboard tailplane
13 Tailplane struts
14 Lashing down shackle
15 Trestling foot
16 Rear wedge
17 Rudder lower hinge
18 Tailplane adjustment screw
19 Elevator control cable
20 External bracing wires
21 Elevator fixed tab
22 Tailfin structure
23 Bracing wire attachment
24 Aerial stub
25 Bracing wires
26 Port elevator
27 Port tailplane
28 Tailplane support struts
29 Dinghy external release cord
30 Tailwheel oleo shock absorber
31 Non-retractable Dunlop tailwheel
32 Fuselage framework
33 Arrester hook housing
34 Control cable fairleads
35 Dorsal decking
36 Rod aerial
37 Lewis gun stowage trough
38 Aerial
39 Flexible 0.303-in (7.7-mm) Lewis machine-gun
40 Fairey high-speed flexible gun mounting
41 Type O 3 compass mounting points
42 Aft cockpit coaming
43 Aft cockpit
44 Lewis drum magazine stowage
45 Radio installation
46 Ballast weights
47 Arrester hook pivot
48 Fuselage lower longeron
49 Arrester hook (part extended)
50 Aileron hinge
51 Fixed tab
52 Starboard upper aileron
53 Rear spar
54 Wing ribs
55 Starboard formation light
56 Starboard navigation light
57 Aileron connect strut
58 Interplane struts
59 Bracing wires
60 Starboard lower aileron
61 Aileron hinge
62 Aileron balance
63 Rear spar
64 Wing ribs
65 Aileron outer hinge
66 Deck handling/lashing grips
67 Front spar
68 Interplane strut attachments
69 Wing internal diagonal bracing wires
70 Flying wires
71 Wing skinning
72 Additional support wire (fitted when underwing stores carried)
73 Wing-fold hinge
74 Inboard interplane struts
75 Stub plane end rib
76 Wing locking handle
77 Stub plane structure
78 Intake slot
79 Side window
80 Catapult spool
81 Drag struts
82 Cockpit sloping floor
83 Fixed 0.303-in (7.7-mm) Vickers gun (deleted from some aircraft)
84 Case ejection chute
85 Access panel
86 Camera-mounting bracket
87 Sliding bomb-aiming hatch
88 Zip inspection flap
89 Fuselage upper longeron
90 Centre cockpit
91 Inter-cockpit fairing
92 Upper wing aerial mast
93 Pilot's headrest
94 Pilot's seat and harness
95 Bulkhead
96 Vickers gun fairing
97 Fuel gravity tank (12.5-Imp gal/57-litre capacity)
98 Windscreen
99 Handholds
100 Flap control handwheel and rocking head assembly
101 Wing centre section
102 Dinghy release cord handle
103 Identification light
104 Centre-section pyramid strut attachment
105 Diagonal strengtheners
106 Dinghy inflation cylinder
107 Type C dinghy stowage
108 Aileron control linkage
109 Trailing-edge rib section
110 Rear spar
111 Wing rib stations
112 Aileron connect strut
113 Port upper aileron
114 Fixed tab
115 Aileron hinge
116 Port formation light
117 Wing skinning
118 Port navigation light
119 Leading-edge slot
120 Front spar
121 Nose ribs
122 Interplane struts
123 Pitot head
124 Bracing wires
125 Flying wires
126 Port lower mainplane
127 Landing ramp
128 Underwing bomb shackles
129 Underwing strengthening plate
130 Rocket launching rails
131 Four 60-lb (27-kg) anti-shipping rocket projectiles

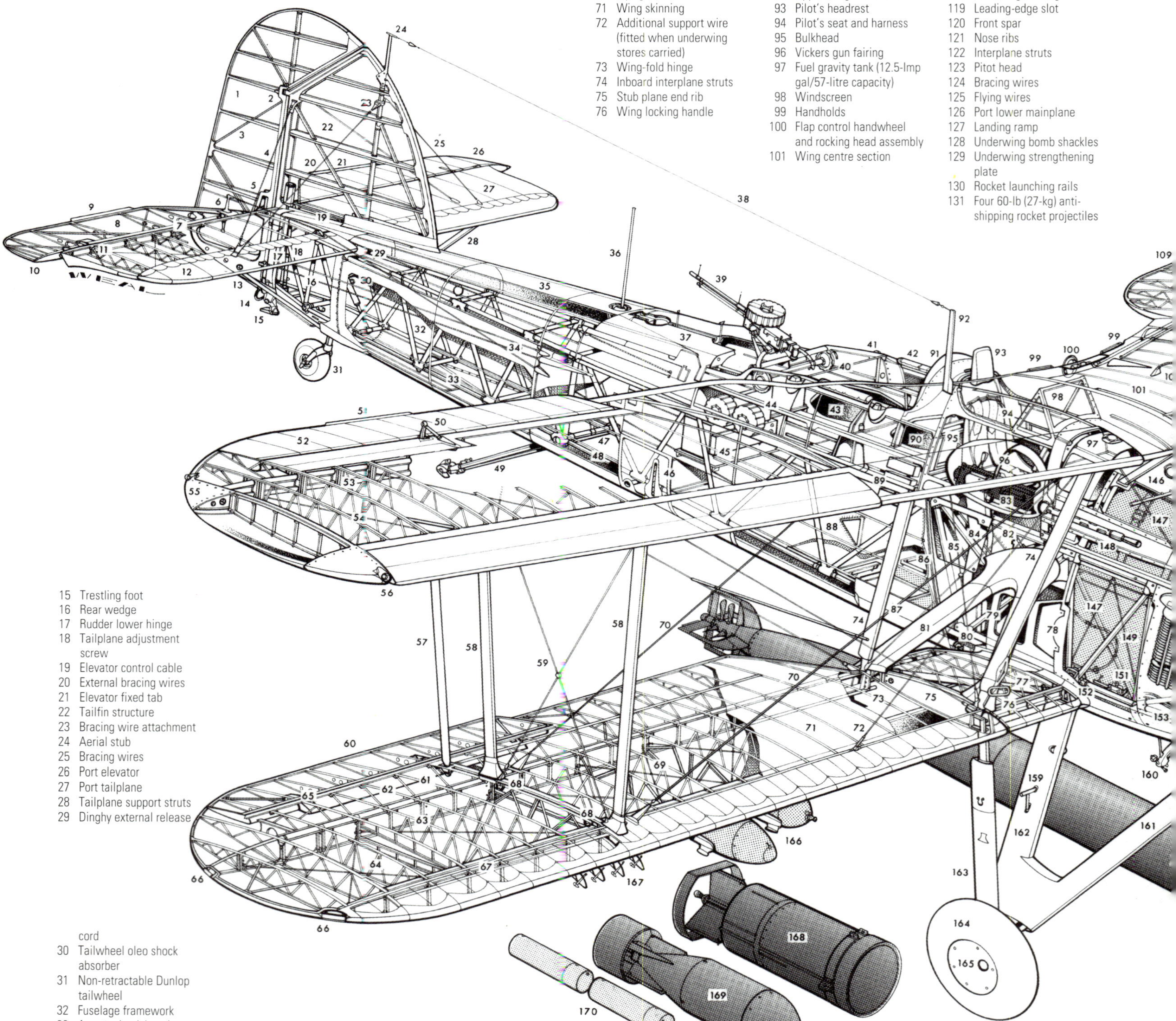

132 Three-bladed fixed-pitch Fairey-Reed metal propeller
133 Spinner
134 Townend ring
135 Bristol Pegasus IIIM (or Mk 30) radial engine
136 Cowling clips
137 Engine mounting ring
138 Engine support bearers
139 Firewall bulkhead
140 Engine controls
141 Oil tank immersion heater socket
142 Filler cap
143 Oil tank (13.75-Imp gal/62.5-litre capacity)
144 Centre-section pyramid struts
145 External torpedo sight bars
146 Fuel filler cap
147 Main fuel tank (155-Imp gal/705-litre capacity)
148 Vickers gun trough
149 Fuselage forward frame
150 Oil cooler
151 Fuel filter
152 Stub plane/fuselage attachment
153 Fuel feed lines
154 Dinghy immersion switch
155 Exhaust
156 Port Dunlop mainwheel
157 Jacking foot
158 1,610-lb (730-kg) 18-in (45.7-cm) torpedo
159 Access/servicing footholds
160 Torpedo forward crutch
161 Radius rod fairing
162 Undercarriage axle tube fairing
163 Undercarriage oleo leg fairing
164 Starboard mainwheel
165 Hub cover
166 Underwing bombs
167 Underwing outboard shackles
168 Depth charge
169 250-lb (113-kg) bomb
170 Anti-shipping flares

Above:** The escape of the* **Scharnhorst, Gneisenau** *and* **Prinz Eugen** ***was a tragic episode for the Swordfish. All six of the attacking aircraft were shot down, and 13 crew were killed. The Swordfish was subsequently used mainly on anti-submarine duties.

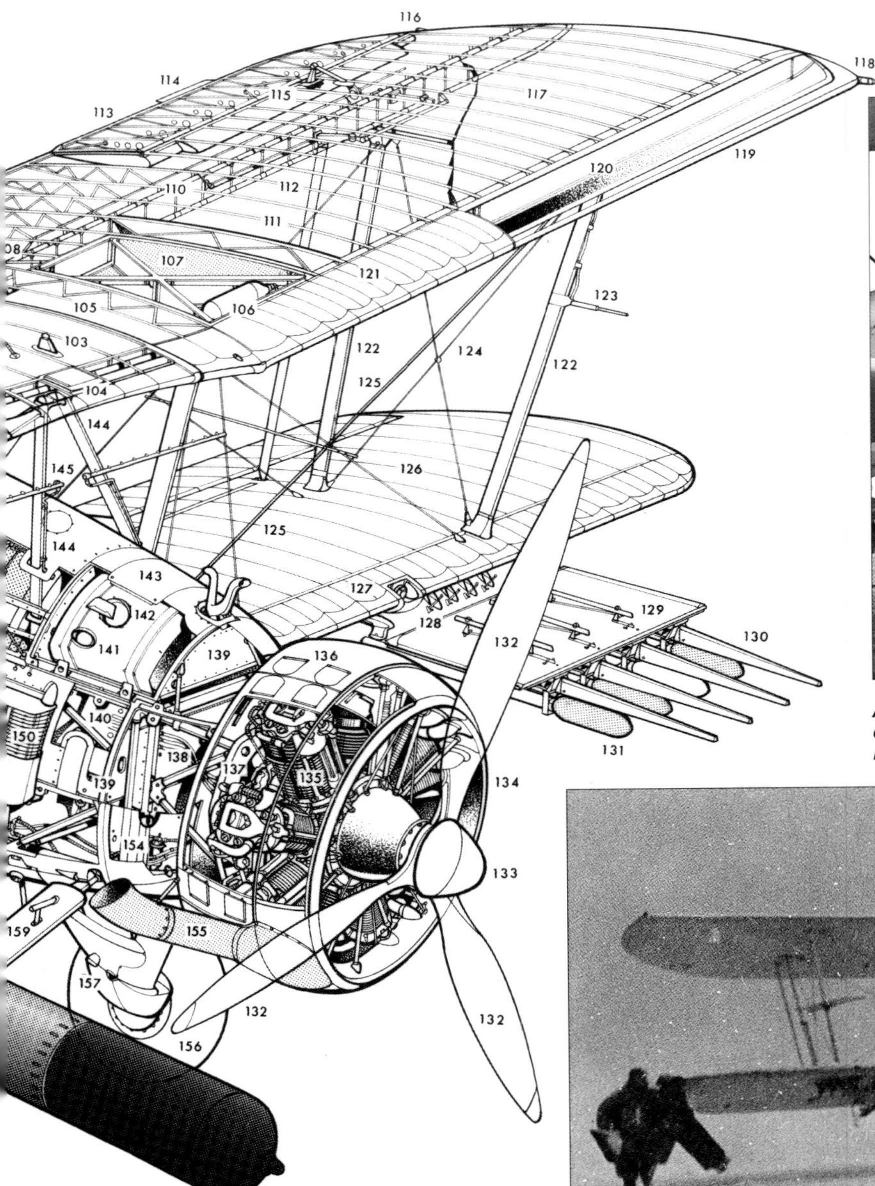

Above: Swordfish Mk II HS227 of No. 835 Squadron, on board the escort carrier HMS **Battler** ***(ex-US Navy*** **Breton*****) in 1943, receives adjustment to its 18-in (46-cm) torpedo.***

From August 1942, Swordfish did tremendous work on escort duties with convoys to Russia. There is no need to stress the frightful conditions in which the Swordfish were operated by day and night on these convoys. This aircraft runs up on the frozen deck of HMS **Fencer** ***in 1944.***

Fairey Swordfish

This Swordfish Mk I '5B' of No. 824 Squadron, Fleet Air Arm served aboard HMS Eagle in 1940. Much of the type's success was undoubtedly due to its lack of sophistication and inherent sturdiness, coupled with the fact that it operated primarily in an environment in which the fighter opposition was conspicuous by its absence.

Featuring a 'Wimpy' emblem on the front of its fuselage, Swordfish Mk II HS275 served with No. 1 Naval Air Gunnery School at Yarmouth, Nova Scotia in 1943. Swordfish operating in Canada usually had the aircraft code letter, in this case 'J', on a yellow square on the rear fuselage.

were being hit, and only one Swordfish was lost. The second wave also lost one of its number, but was also able to launch a concerted attack. Although initial debriefing suggested the entire operation to be a success, it needed reconnaissance confirmation to clarify the picture. When it came, the following day, it was realised that the Italian navy had been dealt a shattering blow: three battleships were damaged severely, two of them under water; a cruiser and two destroyers had been hit; and two auxiliary vessels had been sunk.

In the short space of one hour the balance of naval power in the Mediterranean had been irrevocably changed, confirming the belief of prophets such as the USA's 'Billy' Mitchell by demonstrating the potential of a force of 'obsolescent' aircraft to eliminate a naval fleet without any assistance from surface vessels. Those involved in this victorious achievement had come from Nos 813, 815, 819 and 824 Squadrons, all embarked on HMS *Illustrious* for this operation.

The last of the great torpedo attacks made by these aircraft came in

Above: These Swordfish Mk IIIs had Mk X air-to-surface vessel (ASV) radar in a radome between the undercarriage legs and under-wing bomb and rocket-launching rails. The radar installation greatly improved the Swordfish's chances of locating enemy shipping.

Night attack experiments were carried out by fitting a Leigh-Light under the port wing of the Swordfish, with the power pack mounted between the undercarriage legs. Although not used operationally, it was proposed that a pair of Swordfish acting as a hunter/killer team and equipped with ASV, rockets and a Leigh-Light be employed on U-boat attacks.

Above: Swordfish Mk III NR995/G was involved in RATO (rocket assisted take-off) trials. The RATO gear was jettisoned after use. Rockets were particularly useful for heavily laden Swordfish taking off from the short decks of MAC-ships. The 'G' after the serial denotes that regulations required a guard to stand watch over the aircraft, as the trial installation was secret.

Right: Swordfish HS533 was used to test an enclosed cockpit. A number of the type were subsequently fitted with canopies for training in Canada. The version was known unofficially in Canada as the Mk IV, but was more generally still referred to as the Mk II in the UK.

1942, when a futile attempt was made to prevent the German battle-cruisers *Gneisenau* and *Scharnhorst*, accompanied by the heavy cruiser *Prinz Eugen*, from making good their escape eastwards through the English Channel. Almost as a last resort, six Swordfish of No. 825 Squadron, led by Lieutenant Commander Esmonde, were detailed to make a torpedo attack, but as they approached the battleships with their escorting destroyers and umbrella of fighters overhead, it was clear to the crews that their task was hopeless. Despite such odds, however, Esmonde led his men into the attack. Immediately, they were met by a concentrated hail of anti-aircraft fire, and attacked from all angles by the defending fighters. Not a single Swordfish survived, and it was a miracle that five of the 18 crew members were rescued. All were subsequently decorated and the gallant leader, Esmonde, was posthumously awarded the Victoria Cross, the first to be given to a member of the FAA.

This experience gave confirmation, if any were needed, of the fact that it was no longer a practical proposition to deploy the Swordfish on torpedo attacks. Such operations called for a long, accurate approach if the weapon was to be successfully launched; but such an approach also provided the enemy with an excellent opportunity of destroying its attacker. This led to the redeployment of the Swordfish in an anti-submarine warfare (ASW) role, using as its weapons against these underwater vessels conventional depth charges and, for on-surface attack, the newly-developed rocket projectiles.

This led to development of the **Swordfish Mk II**, which entered service in 1943, and differed from the earlier version by having the lower wing strengthened and metal skinned so that it could carry and launch rocket projectiles. Early production Mk IIs retained the Pegasus IIIM engine, but later examples had the more powerful Pegasus XXX. The Swordfish Mk II was followed in the same year by what was to prove the final production version, the **Swordfish Mk III**, which mounted a radome carrying a scanner for its ASV (Air-to-Surface Vessel) Mk X radar between the landing gear main units; in other respects it was generally similar to the Mk II. There were, in addition to the three main production versions, a few examples converted from Mk IIs and provided with an enclosed cabin for operation in the much colder Canadian waters, these aircraft having the designation **Swordfish Mk IV**.

These changes were to bring new life to the old warrior which, at the peak of its deployment, equipped no fewer than 26 squadrons. Even at the beginning of 1945 no fewer than nine front-line squadrons were still operating their Swordfish successfully. The advent of the rocket projectile into the armoury of the Fleet Air Arm had been the responsibility of the Swordfish, which carried out suitability trials before the weapon was accepted as standard. With rockets and mines, these aircraft were to achieve unbelievable success in ASW operations, a highlight coming in September 1944 when Swordfish aboard the escort carrier HMS *Vindex*, then employed in escorting a convoy to north Russia, sank four U-boats in a single voyage.

The RAF also found the Swordfish valuable for maritime operations. In April 1940 No. 812 Sqn was assigned under RAF Coastal Command control, subsequently flying successful day and night mine-laying sorties in the English Channel and the North Sea. The squadron's Swordfish were also active in the Battle of France, making daylight bombing raids on enemy-held ports. Two RAF squadrons also operated the type. In October 1940 No. 202 Squadron in

Gibraltar received float-equipped Swordfish Mk Is and operated these on offensive patrols in the Straits of Gibraltar until January 1942. The only other RAF unit to be equipped with the type was No. 119 Squadron which, operating Swordfish Mk IIIs from bases in Belgium flew successful sorties in the North Sea against midget submarine between January and May 1945.

Production ended in 1944, after Fairey had built 692 and Blackburn 1,699, for a grand total of 2,391. On 21 May 1945 No. 836 Squadron the last first-line Swordfish squadron, was officially disbanded. Even then the Royal Navy was reluctant to lose such a doughty warrior and odd examples were to remain in use for several years.

In a remarkable career this valiant biplane had achieved a record that will remain indelibly endorsed in the history of air warfare, and especially that of the FAA. In five years of hard-fought war it had served as a torpedo-bomber for the British fleet, as a shore-based mine layer, as convoy protection from escort carriers, as a night-flying flare-dropper, as a rocket-armed anti-shipping and ASW aircraft, as well as for training and general utility duties.

Specification
Swordfish Mk II
Type: two/three-seat torpedo-bomber/reconnaissance biplane
Powerplant: one 750-hp (559-kW) Bristol Pegasus XXX radial piston engine
Performance: maximum speed (landplane) 138 mph (222 km/h), (seaplane) 128 mph (206 km/h) at 5,000 ft (1525 m); cruising speed (landplane) 120 mph (193 km/h); service ceiling (landplane) 10,700 ft (3260 m); maximum range (landplane) 1,030 miles (1658 km)
Weights: empty (landplane) 4,700 lb (2132 kg), (seaplane) 5,300 lb (2404 kg); maximum take-off (landplane) 7,510 lb (3406 kg), (seaplane) 8,110 lb (3679 kg)
Dimensions: span 45 ft 6 in (13.87 m); length (landplane) 35 ft 8 in (10.87 m), (seaplane) 40 ft 6 in (12.34 in); height (landplane) 12 ft 4 in (3.76 m), (seaplane) 14 ft 7 in (4.44 m); wing area 607 sq ft ($56.39 m^2$)
Armament: one forward-firing synchronised 0.303-in (7.7-mm) machine-gun in forward fuselage and one 0.303-in (7.7-mm) Lewis gun on Fairey high-speed mounting in aft cockpit, plus a torpedo of 1,610 lb (730 kg), or depth charges, mines or bombs up to 1,500 lb (680 kg), or up to eight rocket projectiles on underwing racks

Swordfish Mk IIs bedecked with invasion stripes begin a practice attack during a training flight. They were to be used for patrolling the Channel on D-Day and continued this duty until 1945.

Fokker T.VIIIW

Designed to Netherlands naval air service specifications, the Fokker T.VIIIW was one of the few aircraft to operate for both the Luftwaffe and the RAF during World War II. Built in three versions – the **T.VIIIWg** of wood/metal construction, the metal **T.VIIIWm** and the larger, mixed construction **T.VIIIWc** – an initial order of five for the Dutch navy was delivered in June 1939.

A subsequent order for 26 examples for operation in the East Indies was, in fact, delivered to home-based Dutch squadrons before the country was overrun by the advancing German army.

Under the confusion of the Dutch capitulation eight T.VIIIWs managed to escape, seven of them via France, despite attacks from German fighters. Arriving at Calshot, the aircraft and their crews were sent to Pembroke Dock where they formed the first non-British RAF unit of World War II: No. 320 (Dutch) Squadron. Here the aircraft were brought up to full RAF operational standards, were repainted in RAF camouflage and received RAF serial numbers. Small orange triangles on the nose and beneath the wing distinguishing them as belonging to a Dutch unit. From 20 June 1940 No. 320 was employed on convoy escort and air-sea rescue duties in the south-west approaches and the Irish Sea.

In October 1940 Pilot Officer Schaper of No. 320 Sqn was assigned to rescue a Dutch secret agent from occupied Holland. The mission was aborted at the first attempt due to fog. It did, however, alert German forces, and when the attempt was made the following night, 2,000 German soldiers were waiting. After landing on Tjeuke Lake the T.VIIIW was raked with machine-gun fire. Despite this, Schaper managed to get airborne in a zig-zag run and, despite being attacked by mistake by British Local Defence volunteers, he arrived at Felixstowe safely with the machine riddled with bullets. For his bravery he became the first Dutch pilot to receive the DFC. From early 1941 a lack of spares forced the T.VIIIWs to be placed into storage and they took no further part in the conflict.

Dutch T.VIIIWs came to England in 1940 after the German invasion of the Low Countries. Allotted RAF serials (AV958-965) they operated with Coastal Command's convoy patrols over the Western Approaches, alongside Ansons of No. 320 Squadron, from Pembroke Dock.

Specification
T.VIIIW
Type: general reconnaissance twin-float seaplane
Powerplant: two 450-hp (336-kW) Wright R-975-E-3 Whirlwind radial piston engines
Performance: maximum speed 177 mph (285 km/h); service ceiling 22,310 ft (6800 m); range 1,709 miles (2750 km)
Weights: empty 6,834 lb (3100 kg); maximum take-off 11,023 lb (5000 kg)
Dimensions: span 59 ft 1 in (18.00 m); length 42 ft 8 in (13.00 m); height 16 ft 5 in (5.00 m); wing area 473.63 sq ft ($44.00 m^2$)
Armament: one 0.31-in (7.9-mm) machine-gun on port side of fuselage, one similar weapon in rear cockpit plus 1,334 lb (605 kg) of bombs

General Aircraft Hamilcar

The Hamilcar, first flown in March 1942, was the biggest glider used by the Allies in World War II. It could carry a small tank, admitted via a ramp in the hinged nose.

Its success with the Hotspur encouraged General Aircraft to compete for Air Ministry Specification X.27/40, covering the design and construction of a large tank- or vehicle-carrying glider. This resulted in a contract for the design and manufacture of two prototypes of the G.A.L.49, the first making its maiden flight on 27 March 1942, and leading to the production of an additional 410 examples under the designation **Hamilcar Mk I**.

These aircraft were all-wood structures, except for the control surfaces which had wooden framing and fabric covers. Configuration was that of a high-wing, cantilever monoplane, with pneumatically actuated, single-slotted, trailing-edge flaps and slotted ailerons. The configuration was chosen, of course, to ensure that the wing centre-section structure in no way interfered with the loading of tanks or vehicles through the swing-nose of the fuselage. For the same reason, the crew of two was accommodated in a flight compartment high on the fuselage and directly above the wing leading-edge. Access to this compartment was gained via a ladder mounted within the fuselage, through a hatch in its upper surface, and along a walkway provided on top of the wing centre-section. The tail unit was conventional, and the tailwheel type landing gear had main units comprising side Vees hinged to the fuselage and tied by long oleo-pneumatic shock-absorbers. These could be deflated to bring the fuselage nose down for the loading or unloading of tanks or vehicles. Large underfuselage ash skids, mounted on rubber blocks, were provided for emergency landing in rough terrain after the main landing gear units had been jettisoned. Largest and heaviest of the transport gliders used by the Allies during World War II, it was also the first British glider to carry a tank into action, and was able to accommodate a 7-ton (7.1-tonne) Tetrarch tank or two Universal Carriers. It could, of course, carry any other cargo load up to a maximum of 17,600 lb (7983 kg), including a variety of Allied tracked and wheeled vehicles.

In 1944, to meet the requirements of Air Ministry Specification X.4/44, General Aircraft designed a powered version of the glider. This was generally similar to the Hamilcar Mk I, except for the installation of two 965-hp (720-kW) Bristol Mercury 31 radial piston engines in nacelles on the wing leading-edges, plus the associated controls, instruments and fuel installation. One hundred of these were ordered as conversions from the Hamilcar Mk I after a prototype, first flown in February 1945, had shown the conversion to be practical. Intended for deployment in the Pacific theatre, only 22 (including prototypes) had been completed before VJ-Day brought contract cancellation. None of these powered gliders, designated **Hamilcar Mk X**, was used operationally.

A fleet of Halifaxes and Stirlings towed more than 70 Hamilcar Mk Is during the Normandy landings, and 28 were used at Arnhem in September 1944. A total of 412 Hamilcars was built, including 22 by General Aircraft. The cockpit enclosure was located above the fuselage to give maximum cargo space in the main hold.

Specification
Hamilcar Mk I
Type: tank-carrying or cargo glider
Powerplant: none
Performance: maximum towing speed 150 mph (241 km/h); stalling speed 65 mph (105 km/h)
Weights: empty 18,400 lb (8346 kg); maximum take-off 36,000 lb (16329 kg)
Dimensions: span 110 ft 0 in (33.53 m); length 68 ft 0 in (20.73 m); height 20 ft 3 in (6.17 m); wing area 1,657.5 sq ft (153.98 m²)

General Aircraft Hotspur

A Hotspur Mk I commences its glide following release from a glider-tug. This variant was 17 miles (27 km) short of meeting the specified gliding performance from 20,000 ft (6096 m). Only 20 Hotspurs were used operationally, with over 1,000 dual control trainers being used by the Glider Training Schools.

Designed to meet the requirement of Air Ministry Specification 10/40 for an assault glider, the General Aircraft G.A.L.48 design was launched into production with an initial order for 400. These, designated **Hotspur Mk I**, were of all-wood construction and had plywood skins. The mid-set cantilever monoplane wing had wide-span split trailing-edge flaps, and fuselage and tail unit were quite conventional structures. Landing gear comprised two main units, with twin wheels mounted on a rubber-in-compression shock strut, a tail skid, and a long central skid on rubber blocks for rough terrain landing when the main units had been jettisoned. Accommodation included a nose compartment with tandem seating, and small cabins fore and aft of the wing to seat six combat troops.

Testing of the Mk I was to show that its design performance of a full-load glide of 100 miles (161 km) from a 20,000-ft (6096-m) point of release could not be achieved and, as a result, only 20 were used operationally. They were, however, to become the standard trainer of the Glider Pilot Regiment, and subsequently more than 1,000 were built, mostly by furniture manufacturer Harris Lebus of Tottenham, London, to equip Nos 1, 2, 3, 4 and 5 GTS (Glider Training Schools). The later **Hotspur Mk II** gliders all had their wing span reduced 16 ft 0 in (4.88 m) by comparison with that of the Mk I, and the Mk II was distinguished by the introduction of dual controls, and in having flaps and ailerons modified. Final production version was the **Hotspur Mk III**, which introduced complete duplication of flying controls and instruments for the pupil pilot. Structural differences included an externally braced tail unit.

Troops disembark from Hotspur Mk II BT671 during a training exercise in the UK. Dual controls were introduced with the Mk II, as were modifications to the flaps and ailerons.

Specification
Hotspur Mk I
Type: eight-seat training glider
Powerplant: none
Performance: maximum towing speed 130 mph (209 km/h); maximum gliding speed 90 mph (145 km/h); landing speed 56 mph (90 km/h); maximum gliding range following launch at 20,000 ft (6096 m) 83 miles (134 km)
Weights: empty 1,661 lb (753 kg); maximum take-off 3,598 lb (1632 kg)
Dimensions: span 61 ft 11 in (18.87 m); length 39 ft 4 in (11.99 m); height 10 ft 10 in (3.30 m); wing area 272 sq ft (25.27 m^2)

Gloster Gladiator

Left: Although largely replaced in Fighter Command at the outbreak of war by the far superior Hurricane and Spitfire, the Gladiator operated overseas with the RAF in France, Malta and Norway, with great distinction.

Below: The Gladiator was in effect an adaptation of the Gauntlet, with flaps on the upper and lower wings, single-leg cantilever landing gear and an enclosed cockpit. It was the last RAF biplane fighter.

The inability of the British manufacturers to produce by the mid-1930s a Bristol Bulldog replacement, to the admittedly demanding Air Ministry Specification F.7/30, led to further orders for Gloster Gauntlets to equip additional squadrons proposed under the 1935 RAF expansion scheme. Although design studies for monoplane fighters were showing considerable promise, Gloster's designer H.P. Folland conducted a detailed examination of the Gauntlet design to define the extent to which performance might be improved. The wings were redesigned as single-bay units with strengthened main spars, and the landing gear was replaced by internally-sprung wheel assemblies mounted on cantilever struts. Both changes considerably reduced drag, promising a 10-15 mph (16-24 km/h) increase in maximum speed, and the 250-mph (402-km/h) target seemed attainable with an uprated Mercury engine then being developed by Bristol.

A prototype was built as a private venture, with the company designation **SS.37**, and flown in September by the company's chief test pilot, Flt Lt P. E. G. Sayer. With a Mercury IV engine installed a maximum speed of 236 mph (380 km/h) was recorded, and this was increased to 242 mph (389 km/h) after fitting a 645-hp (481-kW) Mercury VIS in November 1934. With the Gauntlet's two fuselage-mounted Vickers Mk III machine-guns supplemented by two underwing Lewis guns, the SS.37 met another of the requirements of F.7/30, and it was flown to Martlesham Heath early in 1935 for official evaluation.

Gloster's design was submitted to the Air Ministry in June 1935 and Specification F.14/35 was written around it, accompanied by an order for 23 aircraft, the name Gladiator being announced on 1 July. The 840-hp (626-kW) Mercury IX was specified, and other changes included an enclosed cockpit, minor landing gear modifications, a revised tail unit, and the fitting of improved Vickers Mk V guns.

The first production batch of 23 **Gladiator Mk I**s, delivered in February and March 1937, carried Lewis guns under the wings, as did the first 37 of the second order, for 100 aircraft. All of this second batch were fitted with a universal armament mounting under each wing, capable of accepting any Vickers or Lewis gun or, indeed, the licence-built Colt-Browning which was installed in fuselage and wing positions in the majority of aircraft delivered in 1938. A third order, for 28 machines, brought the RAF's Gladiator Mk I procurement to 231 aircraft, some of which were converted to Mk II standard.

The Royal Air Force later received 252 new **Gladiator Mk II**s, built to Specification F.36/37, with an 830-hp (619-kW) Mercury VIIIA engine fitted with automatic mixture control, electric starter and a Vokes air filter in the carburettor intake. Thirty-eight Gladiator Mk IIs were fitted with arrester hooks and transferred to the Fleet Air Arm in December 1938, these being an interim replacement for Hawker Nimrods and Ospreys until the delivery of 60 fully navalised **Sea Gladiators**. These latter aircraft had an arrester hook, catapult points and a ventral dinghy stowage fairing. Gladiator production was to total 746, with orders from Belgium, China, Eire, Greece, Latvia, Lithuania, Norway and Sweden covering 147 Mk Is and 18 Mk IIs.

Gladiators were first issued in February 1937 to No. 72 Squadron at Church Fenton, and although most of the squadrons that received the type had been re-equipped with Hawker Hurricanes or Supermarine Spitfires by September 1939, some of their aircraft had been re-issued to home-based auxiliary units, four of which were fully operational when war broke out. Two of them, Nos 607 and 615 Squadrons, were posted to France in November 1939 as part of the Advanced Air Striking Force. No. 263 Squadron, together with No. 804 Squadron, Fleet Air Arm, participated in the Norwegian campaign while the handful of aircraft of Hal Far Fighter Flight, and of No. 261 Squadron, took part in the defence of Malta between April and June 1940. In the Middle East, Gladiators saw service during the war with Nos 6, 33, 80, 94, 112 and 127 Squadrons and with No. 3 Squadron, Royal Australian Air Force. In addition to No. 804 Squadron, Fleet Air Arm

Above: A Gladiator Mk II awaits delivery to No. 33 Squadron in Egypt. Between March and October 1940 the squadron's Gladiators fought with success in North Africa, claiming several air combat victories against Italian opponents. This aircraft has been adapted for desert conditions, as evidenced by the box-shaped sand filter fitted beneath the engine.

Below: This Gladiator Mk I wears the RAF fighter camouflage carried at the outbreak of World War II. The Gladiator equipped a number of home-based front-line units at this time, but when the Battle of Britain began most had been sent abroad or retired to secondary duties.

Below: During the spring of 1940 No. 615 Squadron was based in France as part of the British Expeditionary Force with Gladiator Mk IIs. During the 'Phoney War' in early spring the squadron saw little action, and by the time the Battle of France began the squadron had re-equipped with the Hawker Hurricane Mk I.

As a concession to modern design, the Gladiator featured a sliding canopy for the pilot, although most RAF pilots at the time preferred to fly with the canopy open. This Gladiator joined No. 615 Squadron in May 1939 and took up its war station at Croydon in September of that year. In October the squadron re-equipped with Gladiator Mk IIs and crossed the Channel to France in November 1939 as part of the Air Component of the BEF.

Gloster Gladiator

As the RAF did not want to commit too many modern fighters to France, its contribution to the BEF included two squadrons of Gladiators (Nos 607 and 615). N2304 had transferred to No. 615 Squadron from No. 605, and fought in the campaign in the markings shown. It was one of the few Gladiators to survive and return to the UK, and it subsequently served with No. 16 (Army Co-operation) Squadron.

Gloster Sea Gladiator N5519 'R' was one of the famous Sea Gladiators which repelled attacks during the frantic early defence of Malta in June 1940. They were later named Faith, Hope and Charity by a local journalist in a wildly romanticised account of their actions. There were actually four Sea Gladiators on the island and they were flown by RAF pilots.

Sea Gladiator units included Nos 769, 801, 802, 805, 813 and 855 Squadrons. After withdrawal from first-line service, the Gladiator continued in RAF use for communications and liaison. At least five RAF Coastal Command units (No. 521 Squadron and Nos 1403, 1560, 1561 and 1562 Flights) used a handful of Gladiators on meteorological reconnaissance duties until 1944.

Specification

Gladiator Mk II
Type: single-seat biplane fighter
Powerplant: one 830-hp (619-kW) Bristol Mercury IX radial piston engine
Performance: maximum speed 257 mph (414 km/ h) at 14,600 ft (4450 m); service ceiling 33,500 ft (10211 m); range 440 miles (708 km)
Weights: empty 3,444 lb (1562 kg); maximum take-off 4,864 lb (2206 kg)
Dimensions: span 32 ft 3 in (9.83 m); length 27 ft 5 in (8.36 m); height 11 ft 7 in (3.53 m); wing area 323 sq ft (30.01 m^2)
Armament: four forward-firing 0.303-in (7.7-mm) machine-guns

Left: N5519 was one of the famous trio of Sea Gladiators which later 'named' Faith, Hope and Charity, that served with the Malta Fighter Flight before joining No. 261 Squadron.

Below: A Fleet Air Arm Sea Gladiator, with hook down, approaches a carrier showing the dinghy stowage fairing between the undercarriage struts. Eight squadrons received Sea Gladiators.

Gloster Meteor

A line-up of No. 616 Squadron Meteor F.Mk Is and F.Mk IIIs is seen at RAF Colerne, prior to the unit moving to Europe in January 1945. The squadron had been the first to equip with the Meteor in July 1944.

The only Allied turbojet-powered aircraft to see action during World War II, the Gloster Meteor was designed by George Carter, whose preliminary study was given Air Ministry approval in November 1940 under Specification F.9/40. Its twin-engined layout was determined by the low thrust produced by the turbojet engines then available. On 7 February 1941 an order was placed for 12 prototypes, although only eight were actually built. The first of these was fitted with Rover W.2B engines, each of 1,000 lb (4.45 kN) thrust, and taxiing trials were carried out at Newmarket Heath, commencing in July 1942. Delays in the production of flight-standard engines meant that the fifth airframe, with alternative de Havilland-developed Halford H.1 engines of 1,500 lb (6.67 kN) thrust was the first to fly on 5 March 1943.

Modified W.2B/23 engines then became available and were installed in the first and fourth prototypes. On 13 November the third prototype made its maiden flight at Farnborough, powered by two Metrovick F.2 engines in underslung nacelles, and in the same month the second aircraft flew, initially with Power Jets W.2/500 turbojets. The sixth aircraft later became the prototype **F.Mk II**, with two 2,700-lb (12.00-kN) thrust de Havilland Goblin engines, and was flown on 24 July 1945. The eighth, with Rolls-Royce W.2B/37 Derwent Is, was flown on 18 April 1944.

Twenty Gloster **G.41A Meteor Mk I**s comprised the first production batch, these being powered by W.2B/23C Wellands and incorporating minor airframe improvements, including a clear-view canopy. After a first flight on 12 January 1944 the first Mk I was delivered to the United States in February, in exchange for a Bell YP-59A Airacomet, the first American jet aircraft. Others were used for airframe and engine development, and the 18th later became the Trent Meteor, the world's first turboprop-powered aircraft, which was flown on 20 September 1945.

The first operational jet fighter squadron was No. 616, based at Culmhead, Somerset, which was equipped with Spitfire Mk VIIs when its first two Meteor F.Mk Is arrived on 12 July 1944. On 21 July the squadron moved to Manston, Kent, receiving more Meteors on 23 July to form a detached flight of seven. The first operational sorties were flown on 27 July, and on 4 August, near Tonbridge, Flying Officer Dean destroyed the first V-1 flying bomb to be claimed by a jet fighter, using the Meteor's wingtip to tip it over into a spin after the aircraft's four 20-mm cannon had jammed. On the same day, Flying Officer Roger shot down a V-1 near Tenterden.

Conversion to Meteors was completed towards the end of August, and the autumn was spent preparing for operations on the continent. Between 10 and 17 October, however, four Meteors were detached to Debden, to take part in an exercise with the USAAF 2nd Bombardment Division and 65th Fighter Wing, to enable defensive tactics against the Luftwaffe's Messerschmitt Me 163 and Me 262 fighters to be devised. The first **Meteor F.Mk III**s were delivered to Manston on 18 December, and on 17 January the squadron moved to Colerne, Wiltshire, where the remaining Mk Is were replaced. On 20 January 1945 one flight of No. 616's Meteors joined No. 84 Group, 2nd Tactical Air Force in Belgium, and in March No. 504 became the second Meteor F.Mk III unit to operate on the other side of the English Channel.

The Meteor F.Mk III had increased fuel capacity and a sliding bubble canopy in place of the sideways-opening hood of the Mk I.

Left: Meteor F.Mk I EE223 was the eighth prototype aircraft and the first to be powered by Derwent I engines. They were installed in short-chord nacelles that were standard features of the series production F.Mk IIIs.

Specification
Type: single-seat day-fighter
Powerplant: (F.I): two 1,700-lb (7.56-kN) thrust Rolls-Royce W.2B/23C Welland turbojets
Performance: maximum speed 415 mph (668 km/h) at 10,000 ft (3050 m); service ceiling 40,000 ft (12190 m)
Weights: empty 8,140 lb (3692 kg); maximum take-off 13,795 lb (6257 kg)
Dimensions: span 43 ft 0 in (13.11 m); length 41 ft 3 in (12.57 m); height 13 ft 0 in (3.96 m); wing area 374 sq ft (34.74 m^2)
Armament: four 20-mm cannon

Above: A detachment of Meteor F.Mk IIIs from No. 616 Squadron operated from B.58 (Melsbroek), Belgium in February-March 1945 to continue operations against the remnants of the German flying-bomb offensive.

Left: Deliveries of the more reliable Welland-powered Meteors to the RAF commenced in December 1944. No. 616 Squadron joined the 2nd Tactical Air Force in Holland, commencing ground-attack missions on 16 April 1945.

Grumman Avenger/Tarpon

Destined to become the principal torpedo-bomber used by the US Navy and, eventually, the FAA, in the Pacific war theatre, the Avenger was truly an example of 'the right aircraft at the right time'. Its design originated from a Bureau of Aeronautics requirement circulated in March 1939, and the prototype **XTBF-1** first flew on 7 August 1941. Production contracts had by then already been placed, and the first combat mission was flown on 4 June 1942. Early experience was inauspicious, but problems were successfully overcome and production demands led to a second source being provided by Eastern Aircraft Division, set up by General Motors. British Avengers came from both Grumman and Eastern Aircraft production.

Delivery of the Grumman torpedo-bombers to the Royal Navy began in August 1942, the name **Tarpon Mk I** being allocated; this was changed to **Avenger TR.Mk I** in January 1944 to conform to US Navy nomenclature. Provided through Lend-Lease, the 627 Mk I aircraft were US Navy **TBF-1B** or **TBF-1C** models; the -1B designation was specific to the Lend-Lease version of the **TBF-1**, while the -1C had extra fuel in a bomb-bay tank and underwing tank provision, plus two 0.5-in (12.7-mm) wing guns.

No. 832 Squadron was selected to put the Tarpon into service, embarking for the US in December 1942 to equip at NAS Norfolk. To help overcome an initial shortfall of aircraft, the US Navy transferred 25 TBF-ls for use by this squadron for the first few months of 1943, and they were in action from May onwards, making a sweep in the Coral Sea that month and then operating from USS *Saratoga* to support the landings in the Solomons. Returning to the UK in HMS *Victorious*, No. 832 Sqn was at Hatston with British Tarpon Mk Is by September 1943, but soon returned to the Far East, which would continue to be the principal area of operations for the Avenger.

Meanwhile, Nos 845, 846 and 850 Squadrons of the Fleet Air Arm had all re-equipped on the new torpedo-bomber in the US, at Quonset, Norfolk or Squantum. Nos 832 and 845 participated in the major attack on the Japanese naval base at Surabaya in May 1944. Before the war ended, further FAA squadrons were operating in the Far East, including Nos 820, 849, 854 and 857 with the British Pacific Fleet aboard HMS *Indefatigable*, *Victorious*, *Illustrious*, *Indomitable* and *Formidable*. On 24 July 1945, Avengers of No. 848 Squadron from *Formidable* made the first attack by British warplanes on the Japanese mainland.

Nearer home, Avengers flying from escort carriers and home bases flew anti-submarine patrols and mine-laying sorties. Escort duty was performed on convoys to Russia, and, in the build-up to D-Day, Avengers flew anti-shipping strikes in the English Channel from April 1944 onwards.

The FAA inventory of Avenger Mk Is was supplemented, from mid-1944, by delivery of 108 **Avenger TR.Mk IIs**, these differing

Above: Avenger Mk Is of No. 846 Squadron fly in formation during a training flight in December 1943. The squadron was formed on 1 April 1943 for service from escort carriers.

Left: Eight squadrons of carrierborne and home-based Fleet Air Arm Avengers conducted operations in Scandinavian waters. This Mk II was attached to No. 856 Sqn aboard HMS Premier *in 1944.*

A total of 402 Grumman TBF-1Bs (Avenger Mk Is) was acquired by the Royal Navy, with No. 832 Squadron being the first unit to receive the type in January 1943. They were initially operated from escort carriers or shore bases on anti-submarine patrols. This aircraft served with No. 846 Squadron from Macrihanish in western Scotland.

During the D-Day invasion this Avenger Mk II (TBM-1) operated from Royal Naval Air Station Donibristle. It features invasion stripes on the wings and rear fuselage, which were added as an aid to identification of Allied aircraft.

from the Mk Is only in that they came from the Eastern Motors line as **TBM-1** or **TBM-1C**s. Finally came 50 **Avenger TB.Mk III**s, which were **TBM-3E** versions with the R-2600-20 engine in place of the earlier -8, and APS-4 radar in an underwing pod. Planned delivery of 130 more Mk IIIs was cancelled with the end of the war, but delivery was made to the UK of 76 reconditioned ex-US Navy Avengers; these, however, went straight into storage and saw no service.

Specification
Tarpon Mk I
Type: three-seat torpedo-bomber and anti-submarine aircraft
Powerplant: one 1,850-hp (1380-kW) Wright GR-2600-8 Cyclone radial piston engine
Performance: maximum speed 259 mph (417 km/h) at 11,200 ft (3414 m); cruising speed 171 mph (275 km/h); service ceiling 23,000 ft (7010 m); normal range 1,020 miles (1642 km)
Weights: empty 10,600 lb (4808 kg); loaded 16,300 lb (7394 kg)
Dimensions: span 54 ft 2 in (16.51 m); length 40 ft 0 in (12.19 m); height 15 ft 8 in (4.78 m); wing area 490 sq ft (45.52 m^2)
Armament: two forward-firing 0.5-in (12.7-mm) machine-guns in wings, one similar weapon in dorsal turret and one 0.3-in (7.62-mm) machine-gun in ventral position plus one 1,921-lb (871-kg) torpedo or up to 2,000 lb (907-kg) of bombs

Above: The Avenger's large wing area provided good lift. This example is carrying a drop tank beneath each wing during tests with the A&AEE.

Right: This Avenger flew with No. 848 Squadron on HMS Formidable while operating with the British Pacific Fleet from early 1945 (note the Far East national insignia). The unit was flying strike missions in the East China Seas during April that year.

Grumman Goose

Designed primarily for the civil market, the Grumman **G-21** was an eight-seat amphibian that first flew on 29 May 1937. It quickly attracted the attention of the US Navy, Marine Corps and Coast Guard, and all three services, as well as, eventually, the USAAC, had ordered examples by 1939.

The G-21 was also chosen to serve with Britain's Fleet Air Arm, which concluded that it was a suitable aircraft for the training of observers, and an order was placed for 50 by the British Purchasing Commission. Passage of the Lend-Lease Act resulted in this order being absorbed into the new arrangements before deliveries began in March 1942. These aircraft were designated **Goose Mk IA** and were used almost exclusively by No. 749 Squadron at Piarco, in Trinidad, as the observer training squadron of No. 1 Observer School. Only 44 of the batch were delivered, one being diverted to Bolivia and five to the USAAC (in exchange for five Beechcraft AT-7s supplied to the Fleet Air Arm).

Five more of the Grumman amphibians were delivered in 1944, these being US Navy **JRF-5**s, whereas the Goose Mk IAs were **JRF-6B**s, a Navy designation specific to the Lend-Lease model. Consequently, three of the aircraft were designated **Goose Mk I** for delivery to the FAA, while the other two became **Goose Mk II**s and were allocated to the British Air Commission to operate in the staff transport role, rather than as trainers, in the US and Canada.

Two other examples of the Grumman aircraft saw service with the RAF. One, having been on the British civil register, was presented to Britain by a US organisation for ASR duty and was used for a time in this role by the Sea Rescue Flight in Egypt before being passed to the RAAF. The other served at Air Transport Auxiliary headquarters in 1942, later passing to No. 24 Squadron at RAF Hendon and then to the Metropolitan Communications Squadron.

Specification
Goose Mk I
Type: utility amphibian flying-boat
Powerplant: two 450-hp (335-kW) Pratt & Whitney R-985-AN-6 radial piston engines
Performance: maximum speed 201 mph (323 km/h) at 5,000 ft (1524 m); cruising speed 191 mph (307 km/h); service ceiling 21,300 ft (6492 m); range 640 miles (1030 km)
Weights: empty 5,425 lb (2461 kg); maximum loaded 8,000 lb (3629 kg)
Dimensions: span 49 ft 0 in (14.94 m); length 38 ft 6 in (11.73 m); height 16 ft 2 in (4.93 m); wing area 375 sq ft (34.84 m^2)
Armament: none

The Goose was supplied under Lend-Lease to both the RAF and the Fleet Air Arm. The latter used it for observer training in the West Indies. The RAF had a number for search and rescue use and one for use by the Air Transport Auxiliary.

Grumman Hellcat

Above: Painted midnight blue overall, JX822 was a Fleet Air Arm Hellcat Mk II used by the A&AEE at Boscombe Down for weapons trials. Here it is carrying two 1,000-lb (454-kg) bombs of British origin. Anti-shipping attacks by the FAA began in April 1944 off Norway.

Left: A Hellcat of No. 1839 Squadron is brought to a halt by the barrier aboard HMS **Indomitable*****, on return from a strike while operating in the Far East. Little damage resulted from the encounter with the wire.***

From total production of 12,275 examples of the Grumman **F6F**, Britain received 1,182 aircraft through Lend-Lease contracts, making this the second most numerous US aircraft used by the Fleet Air Arm (after the Corsair). The F6F had been evolved by Grumman during 1940 to provide a naval fighter with better all-round performance than the F4F Wildcat, obtained by a combination of improved aerodynamics and a more powerful engine – the Pratt & Whitney R-2800. A prototype was first flown on 26 June 1942, and service use with the US Navy of the **F6F-3** production version began in January 1943, with the name Hellcat.

Deliveries of the F6F-3 to Britain began almost at the same time, with the first aircraft handed over in March 1943 – by which time the originally proposed name of Gannet had been abandoned in favour of **Hellcat F.Mk I**. A total of 252 of this mark was allocated to Britain. Powered by the R-2800-10 engine, the Hellcat Mk I had an armament of six wing-mounted 0.5-in (12.7-mm) machine-guns. Early aircraft were shared between test establishments, training units and the

Above: These Hellcats of No. 800 Squadron were flown by Dutch pilots during the final Fleet Air Arm operations in the Mediterranean, which took place in September 1944. The carrier, HMS **Emperor*****, is seen here anchored at Grand Harbour, Malta.***

Right: Hellcat Mk II JV270 (coded 7-C) is from No. 1840 Squadron, which was based onboard HMS **Indefatigable** ***for a raid on the*** **Tirpitz** ***in June 1944. The aircraft, named*** **Ivy*****, is fitted with rocket rails and was from a batch of 225 Lend-Lease Hellcat Mk I/IIs .***

Above: As part of the force for **Operation Tungsten** *– the attack on the* **Tirpitz** *– Hellcats based aboard* **HMS Emperor** *are dispatched as a snow squall sweeps across the deck in April 1944. Despite severe weather conditions, the Hellcats flew fighter escort duties as well as strafing the ship with their machine-guns.*

Below: **HMS Emperor** *dispatches a No. 800 Squadron aircraft. The carrier was operating off the south coast of France, providing air cover for the landings there in August 1944. Hellcats also served on this carrier in both Norwegian and Far East operations.*

first two operational squadrons, Nos 800 and 804 at RNAS Eglinton in Co. Derry. After spending most of 1943 working-up on the new type, both these squadrons embarked on HMS *Emperor* in December, as part of No. 7 Naval Fighter Wing, bound for the US on convoy-protection duty which brought no active contact with the enemy.

Returning to Britain in February 1944, *Emperor* was ready to join other ships of the Home Fleet in March for the attack on the *Tirpitz* in the Kaarfjord, Norway (Operation Tungsten). This brought the Hellcat Mk Is their first taste of action, when contact was made with a mix of Focke-Wulf Fw 190As and Messerschmitt Bf 109Gs, in which three 'kills' were claimed for the loss of one Hellcat. For the next two months, strikes were made against shipping off Norway. In June 1944, No. 800 Sqn absorbed No. 804, but the expectation of participation in D-Day landings came to nought and instead *Emperor* took the Hellcats to the Mediterranean to support the invasion of the south of France in August – this proving to be the Royal Navy's final major operation in the Mediterranean area.

By this time, deliveries were well under way of the **Hellcat F.Mk II**, equivalent of the **F6F-5** variant with the R-2800-10W engine with water injection and a number of progressive improvements. The Hellcat Mk II could carry two 1,000-lb (454-kg) bombs on racks close inboard under the wing, for which reason the designation **FB.Mk II** was sometimes used by the squadrons, though not adopted officially. Designations that are confirmed were **Hellcat FR.Mk II** and **PR.Mk II** for aircraft, respectively armed and

The high-set cockpit of the Hellcat was designed to give good all-round vision, and an unusual feature of the aircraft was the 3° of down-thrust in the engine installation, giving it a tail-down attitude in flight. This Hellcat Mk I served with No. 1839 Squadron in the Far East before being transferred to No. 735 Sqn. Like most other Lend-Lease aircraft, the Hellcats were returned to the USA after the end of hostilities, but odd examples were still to be seen at Royal Navy air stations for a number of years after the war, while a number were dumped at sea.

unarmed, that were modified by Blackburn Aircraft – either in the UK or at Roosevelt Field in the US – to have one vertical and two oblique F.24 cameras in the rear fuselage. Within the overall total of 930 Hellcat Mk IIs supplied to Britain, some 85 were to **F6F-5N** standard and designated **Hellcat NF.Mk II** as night-fighters. These had two 20-mm cannon replacing two of the wing machine-guns and AN/APS-6 radar in a small radome on the starboard wing leading edge.

Hellcat F.Mk IIs were in the hands of No. 800 Sqn by the time this veteran user of the Grumman fighter embarked for service in the Far East, which it reached, in *Emperor*, in July 1944. Most operational use of British Hellcats was made in the Far Eastern theatre, action against Japanese targets commencing in late August 1944 when Nos 1839 and 1844 Sqns from HMS *Indomitable* flew cover and photo-reconnaissance missions during strikes on targets in the Netherlands East Indies. As No. 5 Fighter Wing, these two squadrons saw further action in the area through January 1945, including successful combat with Japanese aircraft, before joining the British Pacific Fleet in the East China Seas.

Other squadrons with Hellcat Mk IIs, mostly on escort carriers, were busy elsewhere in the Far East: No. 800 Sqn, for example, helped in the recapture of Rangoon; Nos 804 and 805 Sqns operated over Malaya and Sumatra; No. 885 Sqn provided fighter cover over the British Pacific Fleet; No. 888 Sqn operated with PR.Mk IIs in Ceylon; No. 896 Sqn fought over the Malayan Peninsula, as did No. 898 Sqn although it was too late to see action. At least four further FAA squadrons had equipped, or were re-equipping, on the Hellcat when the war with Japan ended; they were disbanded before reaching the combat zones. In the rapid post-war run-down, most of the Hellcat squadrons in the Fleet Air Arm were quickly stood down and their aircraft returned to the US Navy, although No. 892 and No. 888 Sqns remained active, respectively, with Hellcat NF.Mk IIs and PR.Mk IIs until April and August 1946.

Above: The Hellcat was also flown by the Fleet Air Arm in the Far East, seeing the last days of combat in Malayan waters. The unusual way in which the main undercarriage folded backwards into the wing is illustrated in this view.

Specification
Hellcat F.Mk II
Type: single-seat carrierborne fighter
Powerplant: one 2,000-hp (1491-kW) Pratt & Whitney R-2800-10W Double Wasp radial piston engine
Performance: maximum speed 371 mph (597 km/h) at 17,200 ft (5243 m); service ceiling 36,700 ft (11186 m); range 1,040 miles (1674 km)
Weights: empty 9,212 lb (4178 kg); maximum take-off 13,753 lb (6238 kg)
Dimensions: span 42 ft 10 in (13.06 m); length 33 ft 7 in (10.24 m); height 14 ft 5 in (4.39 m); wing area 334 sq ft (31.03 m^2)
Armament: six wing-mounted 0.5-in (12.7-mm) machine-guns plus six 60-lb (27-kg) rocket projectiles or two 1,000-lb (454-kg) bombs

Below: An FAA Hellcat Mk I with No. 800 Squadron is seen on the deck of HMS Emperor as the ship approaches dock. The carrier sailed into Singapore harbour on 10 September 1945 to restore British rule.

Grumman Martlet/Wildcat

Above: An early Martlet Mk II catches a deck wire with its arrester hook whilst landing on HMS Indomitable *during convoy escort duty in the summer of 1942.*

Right: Diverted from a French order, the Martlet Mk Is had fixed wings and first entered Fleet Air Arm service with No. 804 Squadron in July 1940, replacing Sea Gladiators. Armament consisted of four machine-guns in the wings, while power came from Wright Cyclone engines.

Below: Martlet Mk IIs are seen massed on the deck of HMS Formidable. *The Martlet replaced the Sea Gladiator and Fairey Fulmar as the Fleet Air Arm's premier fighter.*

Developed in competition with the Brewster XF2A-1 (Buffalo) to provide the US Navy with its first single-seat fighter monoplane, the **XF4F-2** flew for the first time on 2 September 1937. To overcome some early problems, particularly associated with the Pratt & Whitney R-1830-SC-G Twin Wasp engine, this prototype was extensively revised as the **XF4F-3** and flown on 12 February 1939 with an improved version of the R-1830. The first of what would become a long series of US Navy contracts was placed in August 1939.

Before deliveries of the Navy's **F4F-3**s could begin, both France and the UK had placed contracts for the Grumman **G-36A** and **G-36B**, respectively. The French order, for 81 plus the equivalent of 10 complete airframes in spares, was for a fixed-wing carrier-based version, with an armament of two 7.5-mm Darne guns in the fuselage and four in the wings; powerplant was a Wright R-1820G-205A engine. Britain's order for 109 was for a folding-wing version with the Pratt & Whitney R-1830-S3C4-G engine and British or US machine-guns. None of the G-36As had been dispatched by the time France

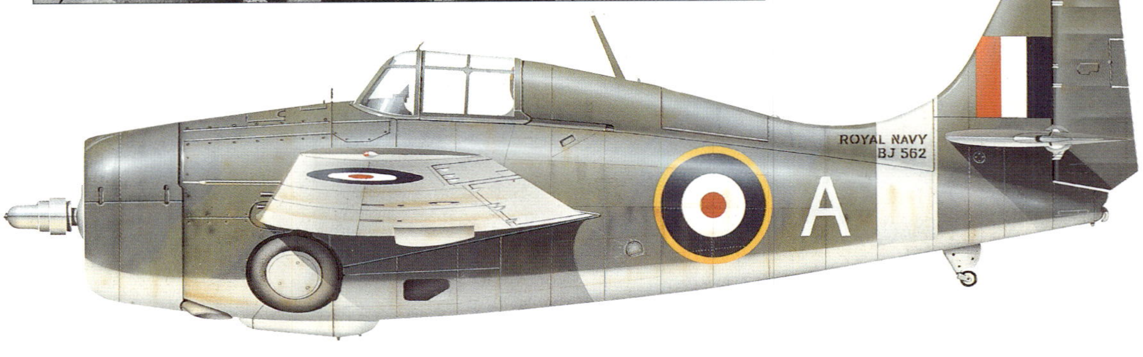

A pair of Martlet Mk Is from No. 804 Squadron achieved the first combat success with the type on Christmas Day, 1940. This Mk I was delivered for service with No. 804 Sqn at Skeabrae in October 1940. Early versions bought by the British government were named Martlet – those provided under Lend-Lease (Mks III-VI) were named Wildcat.

For the Allied landings in North Africa (Operation Torch) at the end of 1942 certain squadrons of British aircraft were painted in American markings. This Wildcat Mk IV of No. 888 Squadron, flown by S/L Fleet, shot down a Heinkel He 111 in November 1942 sharing the 'kill' with another Wildcat from the squadron.

Martlet Mk II AM974 is seen here in the markings of No. 881 Squadron when flying from HMS Illustrious in the vicinity of Madagascar during May 1942. In July 1943, during operations from HMS Furious off the coast of Norway, pilot Squadron Leader Lindsay 'shared' a Blohm und Voss BV 138 with another No. 881 Squadron Martlet.

collapsed; consequently, Britain took over the full quantity of 91 (in the event the 'spares' were provided as completed aircraft after 10 of the earlier deliveries were lost at sea when en route). These fixed-wing aircraft were given the British designation **Martlet Mk I**, being delivered with four 0.5-in (12.7-mm) wing guns but none in the fuselage. The first examples reached the UK in August 1940 and No. 804 Squadron at Hatston was nominated to be the first to fly the new aircraft – replacing Sea Gladiators. Combat initiation followed on 25 December 1940 with the destruction of a Junkers Ju 88 off Orkney.

The British-ordered **Martlet Mk II**s began to arrive in the UK in April 1941, but the first 10 were 'non-standard' with fixed wings and were redesignated **Martlet Mk III** in July 1941 as a result. The definitive folding-wing Mk IIs were delivered between August 1941 and early 1942, 36 to the UK and 54 direct to Karachi or China Bay for service in the Far East. Martlet Mk IIs were urgently needed for service aboard the small escort carriers, and No. 802 Squadron took the new type to sea for the first time in July 1941 in HMS *Audacity*, and in HMS *Argus* in August. The following month, the squadron was again in *Audacity* escorting a convoy to Gibraltar and claimed the destruction of a Focke-Wulf Fw 200 Condor. The whole squadron was lost, however, when *Audacity* was sunk by a U-boat in December 1941. For the next two years, the Martlet Mk IIs saw intensive service, flying at various times with 10 different FAA front-line squadrons from as many as nine different carriers. Among these were Nos 890 and 892 Squadrons, which worked-up at NAS Norfolk in the summer of 1942 using 16 (or more) F4F-3s temporarily on loan from the US Navy. These Martlet squadrons were engaged, in particular, in providing air cover for Arctic convoys to Murmansk in 1942/43.

Another batch of Martlets passed into British service in the Middle East in April 1941, and – like the 10 fixed-wing aircraft in the UK – were given the designation Martlet Mk III. These came from a batch

Above: Martlet Mk II AM997 of No. 888 Squadron sits on a temporary hard-standing area at La Senia in 1943 after assisting with the North African landings. During this operation the squadron shot down two enemy aircraft with its Martlets. The unit disbanded in November 1943, reforming with Hellcats in June 1944.

Below: The Martlet was very compact, making it ideal for service aboard the Royal Navy's smaller escort carriers. The type saw action in most major FAA areas of operation, including the Mediterranean and Far East. Among new features introduced by the Martlet were tail-down take-offs and the stinger-type arrester hook.

Above: A Martlet Mk II of No. 806 Squadron, Fleet Air Arm is waved down on to the deck of HMS Indomitable during operations in support of the Malta convoys in August 1942.

Left: Shown after modification at the Brough factory of Blackburn Aircraft, this heavily armed Wildcat Mk IV is equipped with three rocket projectiles beneath each wing.

Below: HMS Atheling _was one of the carriers in the early build-up of the British fleet in the Indian Ocean. It served as a fighter escort carrier in this theatre, equipped with the Wildcat Mk IVs from No. 890 Squadron._

(of 95) **F4F-3A**s that were folding-wing aircraft with R-1830-90 engines with single-stage two-speed superchargers (whereas the F4F-3 had a two-stage version of the R-1830). The first 30 F4F-3As were released by the US Navy for use by the Greek Air Force, but were still at sea when Greece fell, and were consequently offloaded at Gibraltar and taken over by the Royal Naval Fighter Unit that was then flying from land bases in the Western Desert, particularly in the hands of No. 805 Squadron. In the Western Mediterranean, No. 806 Squadron was aboard HMS *Indomitable* for Operation Pedestal in August 1942 and Nos 882, 888 and 893 Squadrons supported the Operation Torch landings in Algeria. Martlet Mk IIs in the hands of Nos 881 and 882 Sqns aboard HMS *Illustrious* appeared in the Indian Ocean for the first time in May 1942, when Operation Ironclad was mounted to take control of Madagascar.

Passage of the Lend-Lease act allowed Britain to receive further batches of Martlets, starting in mid-1942 with 220 **Martlet Mk IV**s. Designated **F4F-4B** by the USN for contractual purposes, these had the Pratt & Whitney R-1830 Twin Wasp engine, folding wings and six 0.5-in (12.7-mm) machine-guns in the wings (all earlier marks having had only four wing guns). In January 1944, the US Navy name Wildcat was adopted in place of Martlet, applied retrospectively to all earlier mark numbers. Britain then received 312 **Wildcat Mk V**s, which were built by Eastern Aircraft Division of General Motors as the **FM-1** and differed from the Mk IV in having only four wing guns (but with a greater quantity of ammunition). Finally came 370 **Wildcat Mk VI**s, these being also Eastern Motors-built (as the **FM-2**), but powered by the Wright R-1820-56 Cyclone engine, and having a taller fin and rudder. The later Wildcats were fitted to carry, underwing close in to the fuselage (i.e., inboard of the wing fold), two 250-lb (113-kg) bombs or two 48-Imp gal (220-litre) drop tanks. Trial installations were made of a six-rocket installation under the wings, using either British Mk I rails or US Mk V zero-length launchers, but these weapons were not used operationally on Wildcats.

Wildcat Mk III AX733, one of the first provided under Lend-Lease, was delivered to the Royal Naval Air Station at Donisbristle in Scotland for FAA service. Mk IIIs were not equipped with folding wings and were therefore used for land-based operations. This example was flown by Sub-Lieutenant Walsh of No. 805 Sqn in the Western Desert during the autumn of 1941.

Serving with No. 819 Squadron, this Wildcat Mk V was based aboard HMS Activity _during the early months of 1944. Pilot, Sub-Lieutenant Yeo claimed a share of a Junkers Ju 88 downed on 30 March of that year._

This Wildcat Mk V served with No. 813 Squadron in the spring of 1945. Embarked on HMS Vindex, _escorting a north Russian convoy, the squadron managed to down three Junkers Ju 88s in February, of which Sub-Lieutenant Fleischman-Allen claimed one flying this aircraft. Note the two-tone grey finish that, late in the war, became the standard Royal Navy camouflage._

Shortly after D-Day a new version of the Wildcat, the Mk VI, began to equip FAA squadrons. It was equivalent to the US Navy's FM-2, and could be easily distinguished from earlier Wildcats by its modified tail design, with a much taller fin and rudder giving improved manoeuvrability and handling. This example carries long-range drop tanks beneath the wings.

Reinforced with the Lend-Lease deliveries, the British Wildcat force was able to make a major contribution in the Battle of the Atlantic, with a dozen squadrons aboard the escort carriers from April 1943 until September 1944 to fly defence sorties and to strafe surfaced U-boats. In a generally similar role, four other squadrons flew from escort carriers in the Indian Ocean but, both there and in the Atlantic, the Wildcats were largely out of service by the time the war ended.

Specification
Martlet Mk II
Type: single-seat carrierborne fighter
Powerplant: one 1,200-hp (895-kW) Pratt & Whitney R-1830-S3C4-G Twin Wasp radial piston engine
Performance: maximum speed 315 mph (507 km/h); cruising speed 260 mph (418 km/h); service ceiling 28,000 ft (8534 m); range 1,150 miles (1851 km)
Weights: empty 4,649 lb (2109 kg); maximum take-off 8,152 lb (3698 kg)
Dimensions: span 38 ft 0 in (11.58 m); length 28 ft 9 in (8.76 m); height 9 ft 3 in (2.82 m); wing area 260 sq ft (24.15 m^2)
Armament: six wing-mounted 0.5-in (12.7-mm) machine-guns

Wildcat Mk VI JV377 was one of 227 Mk VIs delivered. This version saw a return to the Wright Cyclone powerplant, which incorporated a turbocharger and developed 1,350 hp (1007 kW). Serving with No. 882 Squadron the aircraft was involved in a formation sweep off Norway on 26 March 1945 which managed to down four Messerschmitt Bf 109Gs. The Mk VI was the last Wildcat variant supplied for British service.

Handley Page H.P.50 Heyford

As the last of the RAF's biplane heavy bombers, the Handley Page Heyford was remarkable in appearance. The aircraft's relatively streamlined fuselage was attached to the upper wings, instead of the lower wings as on a conventional biplane. With the lower wing below the fuselage, the bomb load had to be stowed in a thickened centre-section of the lower wing.

The prototype, designated **H.P.38**, first flew in June 1930 and a production order for 15 **Heyford Mk I**s was placed in 1932. Following a successful introduction into service an additional order was placed for 23 **Heyford Mk IA**s, which introduced the more powerful Rolls-Royce Kestrel IIIS engine with four-bladed propellers.

The main production variant was the **Heyford Mk III** of which 70 were produced between September 1935 and July 1936. Faster and able to carry a larger bomb load, this version eventually equipped 11 bomber squadrons before more modern monoplane types began to replace it in service in 1937.

At the outbreak of World War II, the last frontline Heyford squadron (No. 166) replaced its Heyfords with Whitleys. However, Heyford Mk IIIs continued to serve with the RAF in the first months of war as trainers. Allocated to No. 3 and No. 4 Bombing Schools at Aldergrove and West Freugh, respectively, they helped train bomber aircrews until mid-1940. Two Heyfords remained on RAF strength, being used as glider tugs for secret experiments with Hotspur Mk I gliders until July 1941. One of these was believed to be stored in an airworthy condition as late as August 1944.

Specification
Heyford Mk III
Type: four-seat heavy bomber
Powerplant: two 640-hp (477-kW) Rolls-Royce Kestrel VI inline piston engines
Performance: maximum speed 154 mph (248 km/h) at 13,000 ft (3962 m); service ceiling 21,000 ft (6401 m); range 920 miles (1481 km)
Weights: empty 10,200 lb (4627 kg); maximum take-off 17,000 lb (7711 kg)
Dimensions: span 75 ft 0 in (22.86 m); length 58 ft 0 in (17.68 m); height 17 ft 6 in (5.33 m); wing area 1,470 sq ft (136.56 m^2)
Armament: three 0.303-in (7.7-mm) machine-guns in nose, fuselage and ventral 'dustbin' positions plus up to 3,500 lb (1588 kg) of bombs

One of the first batch of 20 Heyford Mk IIIs, this aircraft survived a forced landing near York in 1936 and went on to serve with No. 4 Bombing and Gunnery School during the the first six months of World War II.

Handley Page H.P.52 Hampden/ H.P.53 Hereford

In September 1932 the Air Ministry issued Specification B.9/32 for a twin-engined bomber, for which both Handley Page and Vickers tendered. Each was awarded a contract and the resulting prototypes, the **H.P.52** and the Vickers 271, flew within a week of one another, the former on 21 June 1936 and the 271, later known as the Wellington, on 15 June. Considering that they shared the same specification, the two types could hardly have been more different, Handley Page going for an extremely slim 'pod and boom' fuselage, with three manually-operated gun positions, while Vickers adopted a portly fuselage with power-operated turrets and manual beam guns. In the event, the Wellington was to remain in service in the night-bomber role for just over a year longer than its rival.

This rare colour photograph of Hampden Mk I AT137 was taken in May 1942 after its squadron, No. 455 Sqn, RAAF, had transferred to RAF Coastal Command. No. 455 was the first Australian bomber squadron to form in Britain, and from April 1942 to December 1943 used its Hampdens as torpedo-bombers.

First delivered to RAF Finningley in January 1940, this Hampden Mk I was flown by No. 106 Squadron. Between September 1940 and March 1941 No. 106's Hampdens flew 1,230 operational sorties, losing 55 aircraft.

Below: No. 185 Squadron received Hampdens in June 1939 and by the outbreak of war was operating the type from Cottesmore as a bomber trainer. The need for suitable types to train bomber crews resulted in many Hampdens being used in this role. On 5 April 1940 the squadron was absorbed into No. 14 OTU.

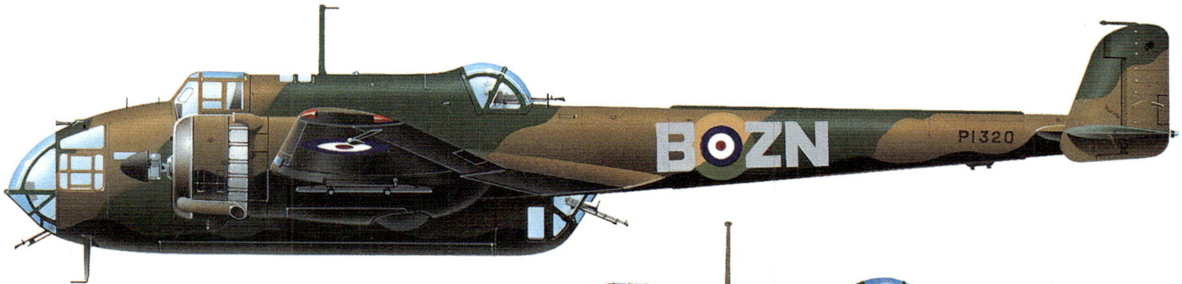

Carrying the markings of No. 106 Squadron, this Hampden of No. 5 Group was based at Finningley in April 1940. The Mk I carried a crew of four. It was armed with three 0.303-in (7.7-mm) Vickers machine-guns and could carry a 4,000-lb (1814-kg) bombload.

No. 420 'Snowy Owl' Squadron was the fourth RCAF bomber squadron to be formed overseas. Serving from RAF Waddington as a night-bomber unit from December 1941, No. 420 Squadron operated the Hampden until August 1942.

Handley Page H.P.52 Hampden/H.P.53 Hereford

Above: Built by English Electric at Preston, Lancashire, this Hampden Mk I, AE148, was flown by No. 16 Operational Training Unit from RAF Upper Heyford, training night-bomber crews. Part of No. 6 Group, the OTU was formed in April 1940 and had a total of 38 Hampdens and Heyfords when at peak strength.

Right: The Lincolnshire bomber airfields had begun the war operating the Hampden as this was the standard equipment of No. 5 Group from mid-1939. Here, the crews of No. 50 Squadron are seen with their aircraft. In March 1940 the unit became the first in Bomber Command to attack a German land target, when it bombed a seaplane base on the island of Sylt.

In spite of an antiquated appearance, the **Hampden Mk I**, as it was subsequently named, had several remarkable characteristics. With the use of Handley Page leading-edge slats it was able to land at only 73 mph (117 km/h), while its maximum speed of 254 mph (409 km/h) was higher than either the Wellington or Whitley, and it could carry 4,000 lb (1814 kg) of bombs for 1,200 miles (1931 km), compared with the Wellington's 4,500 lb (2041 kg) load over the same distance.

Following an order for 180 Hampdens placed on 15 August 1936, to the new Specification B.30/36, the production prototype flew in 1937. Simultaneously with the first contract, another was placed for 100 aircraft with Napier Dagger engines; responsibility for their manufacture, under the name **H.P.53 Hereford**, was given to Short Brothers and Harland in Belfast.

In May 1938 the first genuine production aircraft from the Handley Page line was flown at Radlett, and on 24 June the type was chris-

Above: Hampdens of No. 44 Squadron fly in formation over their base at RAF Waddington. The squadron flew Hampdens until the end of 1941, when it became the first to convert to the Lancaster.

Right: This torpedo-carrying Hampden TB.Mk I was flown by No. 489 Squadron, RNZAF. The unit flew maritime patrols in the North Sea and the Atlantic Ocean.

Hampden TB.Mk Is of No. 489 Squadron, RNZAF fly along the east coast of Scotland while based at Wick and Leuchars from September 1942 to October 1943.

Below: A total of 1,217 operational Hampden Mk I sorties was flown by No. 408 'Goose' Squadron, RCAF. This total included participation in the first '1,000 bomber' raid on Germany and the 'Gardening for Victory' minelaying operation.

tened officially by the Viscountess Hampden. The build up of the RAF was now in full swing and on 6 August 1938 further orders were placed: English Electric at Warton was contracted to build 75, and in Canada a British mission negotiated for 80 more to be constructed by a consortium named Canadian Associated Aircraft Ltd.

Following trials at the Aircraft and Armament Experimental Establishment, Martlesham Heath, and the Central Flying School at Upavon, deliveries to the RAF began in September 1938, with the first batch of Hampdens going to No. 49 Squadron at Scampton Lincolnshire, replacing Hawker Hinds. No. 49 Sqn was part of No. 5 Group, which eventually was completely equipped with Hampdens; by the end of the year 36 were in service. When World War II broke out in September 1939 10 squadrons were using the type: Nos 7 and 76 at Finningley; Nos 44 and 50 at Waddington; Nos 49 and 83 at Scampton; Nos 61 and 144 at Hemswell; with Nos 106 and 185 in reserve, the former in the process of moving from Evanton to Cottesmore where No. 185 Sqn was already based.

Early operations in the daylight reconnaissance role were uneventful, but on 29 September the Hampden's shortcomings were vividly highlighted when five out of 11 aircraft in two formations were destroyed by German fighters when they were reconnoitring the Heligoland Bight area, within sight of the German coast. Not long after this it was decided to operate in future under cover of darkness, and some leaflet dropping missions were carried out.

The sub-contracted Hampdens began to come off the production lines in 1940, the first English Electric aircraft flying on 22 February and the first Canadian Hampden in August.

Like the Avro Manchester, the Handley Page H.P.52 Hereford was basically a good airframe with a bad engine. The prototype Hereford, a modified Hampden, was flown in June 1937 with two 955-hp (712-

Used as a crew trainer with one of the RAF's Operational Training Units (OTUs), this Hampden, X3015, has its armament removed for its new role. The Hampden was retired as a night-bomber in mid-September 1942, but 144 aircraft continued as torpedo-bombers until December 1943.

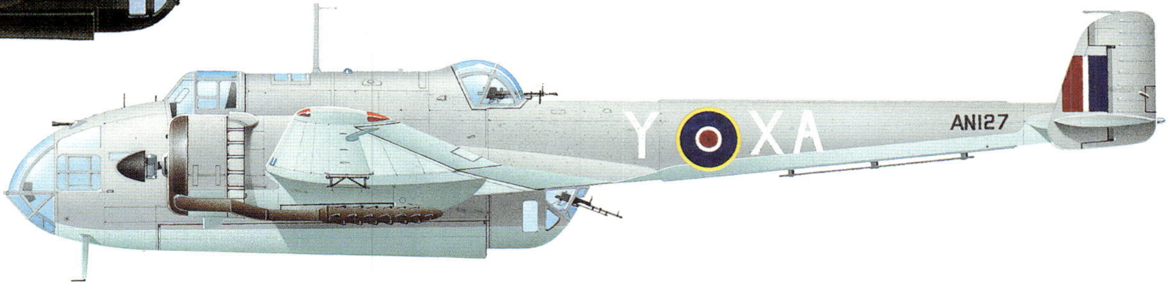

This Canadian-built Hampden TB.Mk I of No. 489 Squadron, RNZAF was based at Wick in 1942. It is shown in the Coastal Command sea grey camouflage on the upper surfaces with sky blue on the under surfaces.

Above: The Hampden was faster than both the Whitley and the Wellington and could carry over twice the bombload of the Blenheim. It had a shorter front-line career than these types, primarily because of its poor defensive armament.

Left: Hampden Mk I P1333 is loaded with 250-lb (113-kg) bombs during mid-1940. This example flew with No. 49 Squadron, which became the first Bomber Command squadron to be equipped with the type on 20 September 1938.

kW) Napier Dagger VIII H-type engines, and Short Brothers and Harland was contracted to build an initial batch of 100 aircraft, a number later increased to 152. The first of these production aircraft from the Belfast line flew on 17 May 1939.

Tests at the Aircraft and Armament Experimental Establishment, Martlesham Heath, showed the Hereford's performance to be almost the same as that of the Hampden, but there the similarity ended. The engines were unreliable, overheating on the ground and cooling too rapidly when airborne, while the very high pitched exhaust note proved uncomfortable for the crews.

One or two Herefords served alongside Hampdens in operational squadrons for a very short time but were soon relegated to a training role, primarily with No. 16 Operational Training Unit (OTU) at Upper Heyford, to where the first deliveries were made on 7 May 1940. Another Hereford unit was No. 14 OTU at Cottesmore, which had begun to operate the type as No. 185 Squadron; it was retitled No. 14 OTU in April 1940. One Hereford was used by the Torpedo Development Unit at Gosport, and at least 19 Herefords were subsequently re-engined and converted to Hampden standard.

By the winter of 1939-40, the Hampden had found its most useful role – as a minelayer. Aircraft from five squadrons sowed mines in German waters on the night of 13/14 April 1940, just after the German invasion of Norway, and by the end of the year No. 5

The first production Hereford (L6002) was flown for the first time at the end of 1939. Differences from the Hampden included longer engine nacelles for the Napier Dagger VIII engines, modifications to the nose and gunner's cupola, and outer wings with marked dihedral. The 152 production Herefords served almost exclusively in secondary roles.

A line-up of the unpopular Dagger-engined Herefords awaits allocation to OTUs. The engines were very unreliable, overheating on the ground and cooling too quickly in the air, resulting in frequent engine seizures and subsequent loss of the aircraft.

Group's Hampden squadrons had flown 1,209 minelaying sorties and delivered 703 mines, losing 21 aircraft in the operations – a loss rate of less than 1.8 per cent, which was considered acceptable.

The Norwegian campaign, however, once again showed the Hampden's 'Achilles heel': because of its inadequate defensive armament the type suffered heavily at the hands of German fighters when used as a day-bomber.

Bomber Command's first Victoria Cross was awarded to Flight Lieutenant R. A. B. Learoyd, a pilot of No. 49 Squadron, following an attack by five Hampdens on the Dortmund-Ems Canal on the night of 12 August 1940. Just over a month later a second VC was won, by an air gunner of No. 83 Squadron, Sergeant John Hannah who, at 18 years of age, was the youngest RAF recipient of the award. Later that month Hampdens and Armstrong Whitworth Whitleys took part in the RAF's first raid on Berlin, and the Hampden continued to support the night bombing offensive until September 1942 when, on the night of 15/16, aircraft of the RCAF's No. 408 Squadron attacked Wilhelmshaven in the Hampden's final sorties with Bomber Command.

From April 1942, Hampdens had begun to transfer to Coastal Command for torpedo-bombing operations (as the **Hampden TB.Mk I**), a task for which experiments had been carried out at the Torpedo Development Unit, Gosport. The first two squadrons in this role were Nos 144 and 455, the latter an RAAF unit, and detachments from both squadrons went to northern Russia for convoy protection operations. Thirty-two Hampdens from the two squadrons left Sumburgh in the Shetlands on 4 September 1942, but nine were lost in the crossing, including two which crashed in Norway and one which crashed on landing in Russia. The squadrons subsequently handed over their Hampdens to the Russians before leaving for the UK on 23 October. No. 455 Squadron was the last operational unit with Hampdens, continuing to operate from Sumburgh, and sinking a U-boat on 4 April 1943, before re-equipping with Bristol Beaufighters at the end of the year.

The Hampden remained little changed throughout its production run. Two aircraft were experimentally fitted with Wright R-1820 Cyclone engines under the designation **H.P.62 Hampden Mk II**, but this powerplant was not adopted for service.

In all, 1,432 Hampdens were built, 502 of them by Handley Page, 770 by English Electric and 160 in Canada. A total of 152 Herefords was built by Short Brothers and Harland with several being converted to Hampdens.

Specification
Hampden Mk I
Type: four-seat medium bomber
Powerplant: two 1,000-hp (746-kW) Bristol Pegasus XVII radial piston engines
Performance: maximum speed 254 mph (409 km/h) at 13,800 ft (4206 m); cruising speed 167 mph (269 km/h); service ceiling 19,000 ft (5791 m); range 1,885 miles (3034 km) with 2,000 lb (907 kg) of bombs
Weights: empty 11,780 lb (5343 kg); maximum take-off 18,756 lb (8508 kg)
Dimensions: span 69 ft 2 in (21.08 m); length 53 ft 7 in (16.33 m); height 14 ft 11 in (4.55 m); wing area 668 sq ft (62.06 m²)
Armament: two forward-firing and twin 0.303-in (7.7-mm) machine-guns in dorsal and ventral positions, plus up to 4,000 lb (1814 kg) of bombs

Handley Page H.P.54 Harrow

Specification B.3/34 ushered in the era of the monoplane bomber for the Royal Air Force by asking, as it did, for modern twin-engined designs to replace the Handley Page Heyford and the Vickers Virginia.

The **H.P.54** was less original in concept than Armstrong Whitworth's Whitley , featuring a high wing and fixed landing gear. It was intended initially as an interim bomber trainer and later, when the more advanced bombers were in quantity production, as a transport aircraft. A hundred were ordered as the **Harrow** before the prototype first flew on 10 October 1936.

The first 39 Harrows built were **Mk I**s with 850-hp (634-kW) Bristol Pegasus X engines, but the following 61 aircraft were **Mk II**s with Pegasus XX engines of 925 hp (690 kW), giving an extra 10 mph (16 km/h).

No. 214 Squadron at Feltwell was the first unit to receive Harrows in January 1937, and by the end of that year four other squadrons had re-equipped with the new bomber. Harrow production terminated after 100 examples in late 1937, but aircraft remained in service until the final stages of World War II.

A novel use of the Harrow was as an aerial minelayer when, in October 1940, No. 420 Flight was formed to carry out experiments under the codename Pandora. These aircraft carried Long Aerial Mines (LAMs), which consisted of many small explosive charges suspended from parachutes with a 2,000-ft (610-m) length of piano wire trailing below. They were to be launched in the path of a bomber stream, and, on contact, the charges were released, sliding down the wires to explode on contacting the enemy bomber. Three months of trial proved the idea to be impractical, although four or five kills were achieved.

No. 271 Sqn was formed in March 1940 to operate in the transport role. Equipped with a number of types, including Harrows, the squadron flew many different transport missions and research flights including air sickness tests with airborne troops. In February 1944, the Harrows supported the Allied forces in northwest Europe. A month later the Harrows were formed into the Harrow Ambulance Flight and two of the Harrows evacuated wounded from the Arnhem operation in September 1944.

Seven of the flight's Harrows were lost in the 1945 New Year's Day attack by the Luftwaffe on 2nd Tactical Air Force bases in Europe. This was essentially the end of the Harrow's war, and the flight re-equipped with Dakotas in May 1945.

Specification
Harrow Mk II
Type: four- or five-seat bomber/20-seat transport
Powerplant: two 925-hp (690-kW) Bristol Pegasus XX radial piston engines
Performance: maximum speed 200 mph (322 km/h) at 10,000 ft (3048 m); cruising speed 163 mph (262 km/h) at 15,000 ft (4572 m); service ceiling 22,800 ft (6949 m); range 1,250 miles (2012 km)
Weights: empty 13,600 lb (6169 kg); maximum take-off 23,000 lb (10433 kg)
Dimensions: span 88 ft 5 in (26.95 m); length 82 ft 2 in (25.04 m); height 19 ft 5 in (5.92 m); wing area 1,090 sq ft (101.26 m²)
Armament: four 0.303-in (7.7-mm) machine-guns plus up to 3,000 lb (1361 kg) of bombs

After use as interim bombers, some Harrows were converted into transports. This example joined No. 271 Squadron in 1940.

Handley Page H.P.57 Halifax

Based at RAF Middleton St George, No. 76 Squadron was the second unit to fly the Halifax Mk I operationally. This aircraft was photographed with Pilot Officer Chris Cheshire (brother of the famous Leonard Cheshire) at the controls, after it had flown four missions. It was shot down during an attack on Berlin on 12/13 August 1941. Except for the front and rear gunners, the crew parachuted clear and became prisoners of war.

Second of the four-engined heavy bombers to enter service with the RAF, in November 1940, the Handley Page Halifax was one of the famous triad comprised of the Halifax, Avro Lancaster and Short Stirling which mounted Bomber Command's night-bombing offensive against Germany. In conjunction with the daylight attacks for which the USAAF had accepted responsibility, this round-the-clock battering of German targets was to reach its peak in 1944, causing almost unbelievable devastation. But although it entered service more than a year ahead of the Lancaster, the Halifax was always somewhat overshadowed in the bombing role by the achievement of the superb Avro design. This was largely the result of the latter aircraft's apparent capability to carry ever-increasing bomb loads without serious degradation of its performance and handling capabilities, and in fact the Lancaster had flight and handling characteristics well above average. The Halifax, however, was to score over the Lancaster in its multi-role capability for, in addition to its deployment as a heavy night-bomber, it was equally at home when employed as an ambulance, freighter, glider-tug, personnel transport and maritime reconnaissance aircraft.

This early Halifax Mk I Series III, with beam gun hatches and no mid-upper turret, was flown by No. 10 Squadron. It was delivered in time for the squadron's first daylight bombing raid from RAF Leeming on 18 December 1941. The crew abandoned this aircraft while on a mission early in 1942, after becoming lost and low on fuel over Keld, North Yorks.

The origin of the Halifax stemmed from an Air Ministry requirements of 1935 for a twin-engined bomber, to which Handley Page submitted a design identified as the H.P.55. This proved to be unsuccessful, Vickers being awarded a contract for what was to appear in mid-1942 as the Warwick. About a year later the Air Ministry issued a new specification, P.13/36, which called for a medium/heavy bomber to be powered by a 24-cylinder engine known as the Vulture, which Rolls-Royce then had under development. Design proposals from Avro and Handley Page (H.P.56) were selected for prototype construction, that from Avro leading first to the Manchester, which was to fly with the high-powered but under-developed Vulture engine. Presumably, Handley Page had an ear rather closer to the ground than Avro. for the company soon had grave doubts that the Vulture engine would emerge as a reliable production powerplant, and set about the task of redesigning the H.P.56 to take four Rolls-Royce Merlins instead. It was, of course, no easy task, but while the overall configuration was not greatly changed, the **H.P.57** design which was submitted to the Air Ministry for approval was for a considerably

This early Halifax Mk II with improved armament, more powerful Merlin XX engines and a higher all-up weight was flown by the first of the Canadian Halifax units, No. 405 Squadron. Serialled W7710 and named Ruhr Valley Express, it was based at RAF Topcliffe in the autumn of 1942. The aircraft did not survive long, failing to return from a bombing mission on 2 October 1942.

***Above:** Halifax Mk II W7676 flew with No. 35 (Madras Presidency) Squadron operating from RAF Linton-on-Ouse in May 1942. The higher weight of the B.Mk II, combined with the increased drag of the new dorsal turret, seriously affected the performance of this variant. This aircraft was lost on a raid in August 1942.*

larger and heavier aircraft. On 3 September 1937 Handley Page was awarded a contract for the manufacture of two prototypes of the H.P.57, with construction beginning in early 1938. When the first of these was nearing completion, it was realised that the company's airfield at Radlett, Hertfordshire, was too restricted for the first flight of such a large aircraft, and it was decided instead to use the nearest non-operational RAF airfield, which was at Bicester in Oxfordshire. Thus, final assembly was carried out in one of Bicester's hangars, and it was from there that the first flight was made on 25 October 1939.

As then flown, the H.P.57 was a mid-wing cantilever monoplane of all-metal construction, the wing featuring automatic leading-edge slots, but these were to be deleted on production aircraft as the Air Ministry required that the wing leading edges should be armoured and provided with barrage balloon cable-cutters. Handley Page slotted trailing-edge flaps were fitted, and the large-span ailerons were fabric-covered. The tail unit comprised a large high-mounted tailplane and rudder assembly with twin endplate fins and rudders. The fins of the prototypes and of production aircraft built until early 1943 were of triangular shape, the apex facing forward. The fuselage was a deep, slab-sided all-metal structure with considerable internal volume, and it was this feature which was to provide the later versions with a multi-role capability. Accommodation was provided for a crew of seven, including three gunners to man nose, beam and tail positions, but armament and turrets were not fitted for these early flights. Landing gear was of the retractable tailwheel type, and the powerplant comprised four Rolls-Royce Merlin engines. For its primary role as a bomber, a variety of weapons could be carried in a 22-ft (6.71-m) long bomb bay in the lower fuselage, supplemented by two bomb compartments in the wing centre-section, one on each side of the fuselage.

***Above:** This Halifax B.Mk II Series I (Special) had its guns removed from the nose and dorsal positions to give less drag and hence better flight performance. Built in 1942 by the London Aircraft Production Group, it served with No. 10 Squadron.*

***Below:** It was not until July 1941 that the British public was given information about the existence of the Handley Page Halifax bomber. The announcement followed a successful attack on the German battleship* Scharnhorst *at La Pallice. The first Halifax raid was made on 10/11 March by aircraft from No. 35 Squadron, the first Halifax unit.*

First becoming operational in March 1941, the Halifax served with Bomber Command until the end of the war. This B.Mk II was flown by No. 78 Squadron at RAF Middleton St George in the summer of 1942.

Handley Page H.P.57 Halifax

Unusual construction
One of the Halifax's unusual features was the use of split assembly for its construction. Separate sections, such as the outer wings, rear fuselage, tail units and cockpit/nose, were manufactured independently, making it possible for more people to be involved and for the components to be constructed more quickly. It also allowed the bomber to be broken down for road transportation and repair. Although the first 50 Halifaxes had leading-edge wing slats, the Air Ministry requirement to fit barrage balloon cutters in the front of the wings necessitated deletion of the slats on subsequent aircraft.

Squadron service
This early production Halifax Mk I (L9530) is shown with the squadron markings ('MP') and individual letter 'E' of No. 76 (Bomber) Squadron. It was first equipped with the type at RAF Linton-on-Ouse on 1 May 1941, moving to RAF Middleton St George a month later. It has the standard camouflaged upper surfaces and black undersides.

Handley Page H.P.57 Halifax

Powerplants
As an early production Halifax Mk I, this aircraft was powered by four 1,280-hp (954-kW) Rolls-Royce Merlin X in-line engines, driving three-bladed, constant-speed, compressed wood propellers giving a top speed of 265 mph (426 km/h). After the 75th aircraft, 1,390-hp (1037-kW) Merlin XXs were fitted, but other modifications restricted its performance. It was not until the Halifax B.Mk III, re-engined with four 1,615-hp (1204-kW) Bristol Hercules XVI engines and de Havilland Hydromatic propellers, that there was a marked improvement in speed to 282 mph (454 km/h), bombload to 13,000 lb (5897 kg) and range to 2,350 miles (3782 km).

This Halifax B.Mk II Series IA was built by English Electric at Preston in 1943., It carries the codes of No. 78 Squadron that operated the Halifax from March 1942. The unit was based at RAF Breighton when this photograph was taken in September 1943. This aircraft has the larger area, rectangular-shaped fin and rudder, introduced to overcome control problems at low speeds.

Handley Page Halifax B.Mk I

The Halifax was the third of the RAF's heavy bombers to enter service in World War II and remained in service with Bomber Command through to VE-Day. The aircraft illustrated, L9530, was one of the very first batch (L9485-L9534) to be produced and was delivered in the winter of 1940-41. It carries the markings of No. 76 Squadron, Bomber Command, based at RAF Middleton St George.

Specification
Halifax B.Mk III
Type: seven-seat long-range heavy bomber
Powerplant: four 1,615-hp (1204-kW) Bristol Hercules XVI radial piston engines
Performance: maximum speed 282 mph (454 km/h) at 13,500 ft (4115 m); long-range cruising speed 215 mph (346 km/h); service ceiling 24,000 ft (7315 m); range with maximum bomb load 1,030 miles (1658 km)
Weights: empty 38,240 lb (17345 kg); maximum take-off 65,000 lb (29484 kg)
Dimensions: span 104 ft 2 in (31.75 m); length 70 ft 1 in (21.36 m); height 20 ft 9 in (6.32 m); wing area 1,275 sq ft (118.45 m^2)
Armament: one 0.303-in (7.7-mm) machine-gun on flexible mount in nose and eight 0.303-in (7.7-mm) machine-guns (four each in dorsal and tail-turrets) plus up to 13,000 lb (5897 kg) of bombs

Armament
The Halifax B.Mk I was fitted with Boulton Paul power-operated turrets in the nose and tail, housing two 0.303-in (7.7-mm) Browning machine-guns in the nose and four in the tail. Two Vickers 0.303-in (7.7-mm) 'K' guns could be aimed by hand through beam hatches. The maximum bombload consisted of six 1,000-lb (454-kg), two 2,000-lb (907-kg) and six 500-lb (227-kg) bombs, all carried on racks in the fuselage bomb-bay.

Flight Sergeant D. Cameron and his crew pose in front of their damaged Halifax from No. 158 Squadron. The damage was caused by a 'friendly' bomb which hit the aircraft while on a mission from RAF Lissett in 1943. After being repaired the aircraft was returned to service.

Left: This Halifax B.Mk II Series IA of No. 35 Squadron was fitted with the later 'D'-type fins and H2S ground-mapping radar under the fuselage.

Handley Page H.P.57 Halifax

This Halifax B.Mk III of No. 171 (Special Duties) Squadron was used for 'Mandrel' (radio countermeasures) operations with No. 100 Group, North Creake in 1945. These missions were directed against the German early warning radar to set up a jamming screen which helped to obscure Allied aircraft movements.

With the superstitious name* Friday the 13th*, this Halifax B.Mk III, LV907 of No. 158 Squadron, was based at RAF Lissett. This aircraft became the first Halifax to complete 100 missions and went on to survive the war with 128 sorties, the highest number for the type.

An interesting feature of this design was its method of construction, each major unit breaking down into several assemblies. The wing, for example, comprised five sections, and the very considerable thought which had been given to this system of fabrication was to pay enormous dividends in subsequent large-scale production, and in the simplification of transport, maintenance and repair. The second prototype made its first flight on 18 August 1940 followed just under two months later by the first production example, by then designated **Halifax Mk I**, and this was powered by 1,280-hp (954-kW) Rolls-Royce Merlin X engines. Armament of these early production aircraft consisted of two and four 0.303-in (7.7-mm) machine-guns in nose and tail turrets respectively. Full designation of the first production version was **Halifax B.Mk I Series I**, and these began to equip the RAF's No. 35 Squadron during November 1940. It was this unit that, in early March 1941, was the first to use the Halifax operationally, in an attack on Le Havre, and a few days later the Halifax became the first of the RAF's four-engined bombers to make a night attack against a German target, when bombs were dropped on Hamburg. The Halifax was used for the first time in a daylight attack against Kiel on 30 June 1941, but it did not take long to discover that the aircraft's defensive armament was inadequate for daylight use, and by the end of 1941 the Halifaxes were used only by night in the bombing role.

This resulted in the provision of better armament for later versions, but there were two variants of the Mk I to appear before that: the **B.Mk I Series II** was stressed for a higher gross weight, and the **B.Mk I Series III** had standard fuel capacity increased by almost 18 per cent. Late-production examples introduced Merlin XX engines, which, although having the same take-off rating as the Merlin X, provided 1,480 hp (1104 kW) at their optimum altitude. Early deployment of the Halifax had confirmed that this new four-engined bomber had much to offer, but although contracts for large-scale construction very quickly exceeded the productive capacity of the Handley Page factories at Cricklewood and Radlett, pre-war plans had been made for alternative sources of supply. The establishment of four new production lines was made easier by the unit method of construction which had been adopted for the Halifax, and the first of these sub-contract aircraft to fly, on 15 August 1941, came from the English Electric Company, which had earlier been involved in manufacture of Handley Page's Hampden medium bomber. The other three lines were those of Fairey at Stockport, Rootes Securities at Speke and the London Aircraft Production Group. This last organisation was an interesting set-up, with rear fuselages being built by Chrysler Motors, forward fuselages and components by Duplex Bodies and Motors, inner wing sections by Express Motor and Body Works, and outer wing sections by Park Royal Coachworks; the extensive works of the London Passenger Transport Board were responsible for the construc-

Above: A prototype for the Halifax B.Mk III, this aircraft was fitted with the experimental rectangular 'D' fins, a modified nose, a smaller and squatter Mk VIII four-gun dorsal turret and Bristol Hercules engines.

Left: Assigned to No. 346 Squadron of the Free French Air Force, this Halifax B.Mk VI was based at RAF Elvington in 1945. It took part in the final mass Halifax operation of the war, the attack on Wangerooge on 25 April 1945. The aircraft survived until February 1949, when it was scrapped at RAF High Ercall.

tion of many components and fittings, final erection and testing at Leavesden.

The Halifax Mk I was followed into service by the **B.Mk II Series I**, which introduced a Boulton Paul twin-gun dorsal turret, and an increase of 15 per cent in standard fuel capacity; the powerplant, initially Merlin XXs, was later changed to the Merlin 22 of equal power output. These changes, plus others introduced after the prototypes had made their first flights, had resulted in a steady increase in gross weight. As there had been no surplus engine power from the outset, the result was that operational performance was being eroded by enhanced operational capability. This can be accepted during wartime conditions provided that the rate of attrition remains fairly constant. In the case of the Halifax Mk II the dorsal turret represented 'the last straw', and steps were taken immediately to improve the performance of these aircraft.

The resulting **B.Mk II Series IA** had a performance increase of some 10 per cent in both maximum and cruising speeds, which had been achieved by efforts to reduce both weight and drag. The nose turret was deleted, the nose acquiring a streamlined Perspex fairing; the dorsal turret was replaced by one which housed four instead of two guns, but which had a more shallow profile and created less drag; the aerial mast, fuel jettison pipes, and all possible equipment were deleted; new engine cooling radiators enabled the cross-sectional area of the engine nacelles to be reduced; the astrodome was of improved aerodynamic form; fuselage length increased by 1 ft 6 in (0.46 m); and the engines, initially Merlin 22s, were changed later to Merlin 24s which offered 1,620 hp (1208 kW) for take-off. News of these impending changes brought in-service adoption of those improvements which could most easily be introduced by squadron personnel. These included removal of the nose turret, dorsal turret and fuel jettison pipes, although only some aircraft had all of these modifications: the resulting Halifaxes were known as **B.Mk II Series I (Special)**. A later change introduced retrospectively to all aircraft then in service involved replacement of the triangular fins by larger units of rectangular shape. This came after extensive testing – following some inexplicable losses of fully loaded aircraft – had shown that it was possible for the Halifax to enter an inverted and uncontrollable spin.

The last major production version was the **Halifax B.Mk III**, the first of the bombers to introduce Bristol Hercules VI or XVI radial engines, which offered 1,615 hp (1204 kW) for take-off. Wing span was also extended by 5 ft 4 in (1.63 m), the resulting increase of 25 sq ft (2.32 m^2) in wing area improving the aircraft's operational ceiling. The first of the production Mk IIIs flew on 29 August 1943, and when this version entered squadron service in February 1944 it was found to have definite performance advantages.

Other bomber versions included the **B.Mk V** which, in **Series I (Special)** and **Series IA** variants, was virtually identical to the equivalent B.Mk IIs except for a change from Messier to Dowty landing gear. The **B.Mk VI**, with Hercules 100 engines which could develop 1,675 hp (1249 kW) for take-off and 1,800 hp (1342 kW) at 10,000 ft (3050 m), was virtually the last of the bombers, for the **B.Mk VII** was essentially the same, differing only in a reversion to Hercules XVI engines as the Hercules 100 was in short supply. Both the Mk VI and VII had a pressurised fuel system, plus small-particle filters over the engine intakes, as it had been envisaged that they would be used in the Pacific theatre after the war in Europe ended.

From their first introduction into operational service, Halifax bombers were in continuous use by Bomber Command, equipping at their peak usage no fewer than 34 squadrons in the European theatre, and four more in the Middle East. Two flights were in early use in the

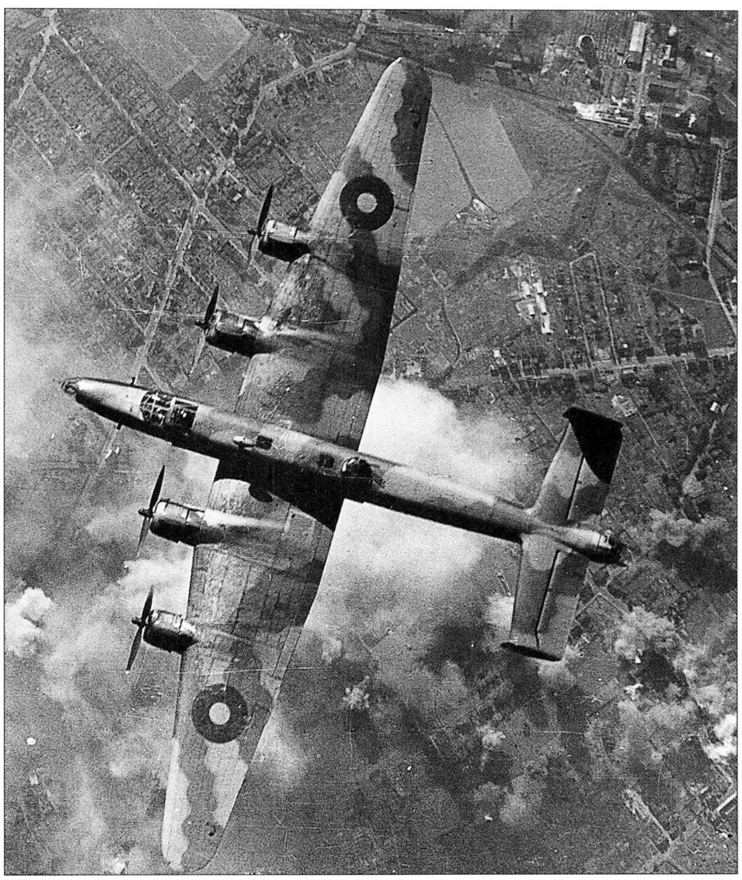

Left: The extra power from the four Bristol Hercules XVI engines and improved streamlining of the Mk III restored the Halifax's performance and permitted an all-up-weight of 65,000 lb (29483 kg). However, much of the additional weight was required for extra fuel to increase range. This late-production aircraft has extended, rounded wingtips.

Below: This Halifax B.Mk III, LL599, was flown by No. 462 Squadron, Royal Australian Air Force, based at RAF Driffield, Yorkshire. This photograph was taken over the North Sea at the start of a daylight raid early in October 1944. The aircraft was lost in a collision with a Lancaster over Essex later in this month.

Handley Page H.P.57 Halifax

Fastest of all the Halifax variants, this B.Mk VI was powered by the 1,800-hp (1342-kW) Bristol Hercules 100 and was in almost all respects superior to the earlier versions. This example was operated by No. 158 Squadron from RAF Lissett in April 1945.

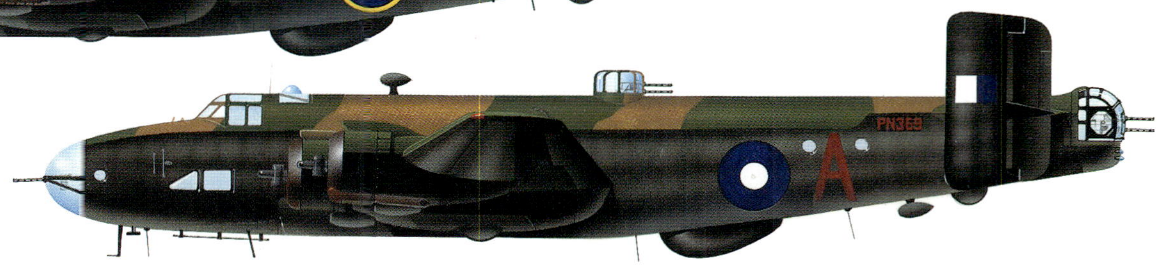

This Halifax B.Mk III (Special) of No. 1341 Flight was based at Digri, India in May 1945. It was fitted with advanced listening and recording equipment to monitor enemy radio transmissions. Some of the additional HF and VHF whip aerials can be seen on the underside of the fuselage.

Far East, and following VE-Day a number of squadrons operating with Halifax Mk VIs flew their aircraft out for co-operation with the Allied forces fighting in the Pacific theatre. The Halifax was involved in the first Pathfinder operations in August 1942; was the first RAF aircraft to be equipped with the highly secret H2S blind bombing radar equipment; was extensively involved in daylight attacks on German V-1 sites; and between 1941 and 1945 flew 75,532 sorties during which 227,610 tons (231263 tonnes) of bombs were dropped on European targets.

The Halifax was also operated by nine squadrons of the RAF's Coastal Command for anti-submarine, meteorological and shipping patrols, the aircraft being converted from standard bombers and specially equipped, taking the designations **GR.Mk II**, **GR.Mk V** or **GR.Mk VI** according to the bomber version from which they were derived. Similarly, RAF Transport Command acquired **C.Mk III**, **C.Mk VI** and **C.Mk VII** Halifaxes as casualty, freight and personnel transports. Little known in wartime was the work of Nos 138 and 161 (Special Duties) Squadrons which had the task of dropping special agents and/or supplies by parachute into enemy territory.

Based at RAF St David's in 1943, this Halifax GR.Mk II Series 1 (Special) of No. 502 Squadron, Coastal Command has ASV Mk III radar fitted for anti-submarine patrols and the location of enemy shipping.

Below: Airspeed Horsas and General Aircraft Hamilcar gliders are seen lined up at RAF Tarrant Rushton shortly before D-Day. Halifax Mk V glider-tugs of Nos 298 and 644 Squadrons are prepared on either side of the runway to tow the gliders to their destinations.

One other vital use of the Halifax was by the Airborne Forces, for, under the designations **A.Mk III**, **A.Mk V** and **A.Mk VII**, equivalent bomber versions were converted to serve for the deployment of paratroops or as glider-tugs. The Halifax was, in fact, the only aircraft capable of towing the large General Aircraft Hamilcar glider, a capability first proven in February 1942. Soon after that date the Halifax tug made its operational debut when two Airspeed Horsas were hauled across the North Sea to attack the German heavy water plant in south Norway. They were subsequently to tow Horsas from Britain to North Africa in preparation for the invasion of Sicily, and were involved in this action as well as in airborne forces operations in Normandy, at Arnhem and during the final crossing of the Rhine.

Although withdrawn from Bomber Command immediately after VJ-Day, the Halifax GR.Mk VI continued to serve with Coastal Command after the war, as did the A.Mk VII with transport squadrons at home and overseas. Post-war versions included the **C.Mk VIII** which could accommodate an 8,000-lb (3629-kg) detachable cargo pannier beneath the fuselage, and the **A.Mk IX** troop-carrier and supply-dropper for use by airborne forces. When production of these two versions ended, amounting to some 230 aircraft, a total of about 6,200 Halifaxes had been built, and examples remained in RAF service until late 1947.

This Handley Page masterpiece acquired the affectionately bestowed nickname of 'Halibag', an affection which most probably stemmed from its punishment-absorbing get-you-home durability. A typical example was one Halifax Mk III which, in July 1944, was coaxed back to base after losing half of its tail assembly to accurately placed German flak, and there must be many crews who still retain their own stirring, and grateful, memories of this bomber.

Below: Formed at Tarrant Rushton in November 1943 with Halifax Mk Vs, No. 298 Squadron was involved with supply dropping and glider-tug training from February 1944. This example, trailing a tow rope, prepares to 'take up the slack' before getting airborne with a glider.

Hawker Fury/Nimrod

Designed by Sidney Camm, the Hawker Fury was the first in-service RAF fighter to exceed 200 mph (322 km/h). Entering service in 1931, the **Fury Mk I** was a single-seat all-metal fabric-covered biplane powered by a Rolls-Royce Kestrel IIA engine. Such was the excellence of the design that it won every RAF fighter challenge between 1933-35.

In 1932 design work began on a new version of the Fury which featured the more powerful Kestrel VI engine. Designated **Fury Mk II**, the aircraft served as a front-line fighter between 1936-38 before being relegated to the training role. At the outbreak of war small numbers remained in service with the Flying Training Schools; however, by mid-1940 the Fury had been retired from RAF service. A number of ex-RAF examples served operationally with the South African Air Force in East Africa from 1940-42.

Bearing a distinct resemblance to the Fury, the Nimrod fighter equipped frontline FAA units between 1932-39. The **Nimrod Mk II** saw wartime service as a trainer with No. 757 and No. 759 Squadrons.

This Nimrod Mk II served aboard HMS **Furious** *with No. 801 Squadron, FAA in the late 1930s. A number of front-line Nimrods were relegated to training units during the early part of World War II.*

This ex-RAF Fury Mk I served with No. 43 Squadron of the South African Air Force. South African Furies saw combat against Italian opposition in East Africa.

Specification
Fury Mk II
Type: single-seat fighter/trainer
Powerplant: one 640-hp (477-kW) Rolls-Royce Kestrel VI inline piston engine
Performance: maximum speed 223 mph (359 km/h) at 16,500 ft (5029 m); service ceiling 29,500 ft (8992 m); range 270 miles (435 km)
Weights: empty 2,734 lb (1240 kg); maximum take-off 3,609 lb (1637 kg)
Dimensions: span 30 ft 0 in (9.14 m); length 26 ft 9 in (8.15 m); height 10 ft 2 in (3.10 m); wing area 252 sq ft (23.41m^2)
Armament: two forward-firing 0.303-in (7.7-mm) machine-guns

Hawker Hart family

Designed as a light day-bomber under the Air Ministry Specification 12/26, the Hawker **Hart** was the first of a prolific series of inter-war biplanes designed by Sidney Camm. Powered by a Rolls-Royce Kestrel engine, the Hart entered RAF service in 1930 and was found to have excellent performance, being not only faster than the RAF's existing bombers but also outperforming its fighters. Production was carried out by Gloster, Armstrong Whitworth and Vickers, as well as the parent company, resulting in a total of 937 examples for the RAF.

Serving at home, in the Middle East and in Africa, the Hart provided valuable service in the inter-war period, and by the outbreak of war some 500 were still in RAF service. Apart from brief front-line service in the Middle East, the Hart's wartime role was restricted to training (with the Flying Training Schools) and communications.

In 1938 around 250 Harts were transferred to the South African Air Force and these were used operationally against the Italian forces in Africa. However, by 1943 both the RAF's and the SAAF's Harts had been declared obsolete.

The exceptional performance of the Hart, which caused great embarrassment to the Air Ministry, prompted the development of a two-seat fighter variant. Ordered into production under Specification 6/32, the **Demon**, as it was named, was also powered by the Rolls-Royce Kestrel engine, but differed from the Hart in having two forward-firing Vickers machine-guns and a Lewis machine-gun in a modified aft cockpit on a flexible mount. This gun was replaced in later

Above right: A pilot stands in front of a Hawker Audax operated by No. 11 Service Flying Training School at Little Rissington. The Audax remained in RAF service in a variety of secondary roles until 1944.

Right: The Hawker Osprey could be equipped with either float or wheeled undercarriage. This example undertakes a catapult launch from a ship of the Home Fleet. By the outbreak of war the majority of Ospreys had been relegated to shore-based secondary duties.

Right: Many of the Hart family were converted for wartime use as target- or glider-tugs. Visible to the rear of this Hector, operated by a Glider Operational Training Unit, is the tow rope which was attached to a Hotspur glider. The Hector continued in this role until April 1943.

Below: This Demon was one of a number which were converted for the target-tug role. Painted yellow with black stripes, it was fitted with a towing bar enabling a target drogue to be flown behind the aircraft. A limited number of Demons operated at Castle Camps in this role in 1940-41 until they were replaced by the Hawker Henley.

models by a Frazer-Nash armour-protected gun mounting and was known as the **Turret Demon**. The aircraft entered service in 1931 and a total of 234 examples was delivered to the RAF, equipping front-line fighter squadrons until 1938. By the outbreak of World War II the Demon had been replaced in front-line service, but a number of examples were adapted for target-towing and served in this role at Castle Camps in Cornwall and Langham, Norfolk until the end of 1941. The last Demon was believed to have still been in service as a 'hack' for a repair depot at Wooton Turn, Oxfordshire in 1944.

Early in 1931, Hawker began adapting the Hart to replace the Armstrong Whitworth Atlas in the army co-operation role. Named **Audax**, the aircraft retained the Hart's engine and armament but featured lengthened exhaust manifolds to prevent glare from obstructing the pilot's view, and had a message pick-up hook mounted on the undercarriage spreader bar. Entering RAF service with No. 4 (AC) Squadron, Audaxes served at home and abroad throughout the 1930s, and at the outbreak of war around 400 were still in serviceable condition. Wartime operational service was restricted to No. 237 Squadron which flew border patrols against the Italians in East Africa and No. 4 FTS which operated its Audaxes in Persia during the Iraqi uprising of 1941. Many home-based examples were converted into glider-tugs for Hotspur gliders as well as being used in the training and station 'hack' roles. The last RAF examples were not retired from service until 1944.

With the successful introduction of the Hart into RAF service, Hawker adapted the design to fulfil a Fleet Air Arm Requirement for a fleet spotter/reconnaissance aircraft. The prototype Hart, after completing its trials with the RAF, was adapted to the naval requirements and underwent evaluation in 1930. Modifications from the basic Hart included folding wings, interchangeable float/wheeled undercarriage and strengthening of the structure to withstand catapult accelerations. Named **Osprey**, production of this navalised version began in 1932 and for the next six years the type saw extensive shore- and ship-based operations with the Royal Navy. By mid-1938 the Osprey had been replaced in front-line service (mainly by the Fairey Seafox) but continued to be used as target-tugs for naval air-to-air and anti-aircraft gunnery practice. Also used for training, these last remaining Ospreys flew with Nos 755, 758, 759 and 780 Squadrons in these roles until the type was retired early in 1943.

By 1933 the Westland Wapitis of No. 30 Squadron in Iraq were reaching the end of their service lives and the Air Ministry again turned to the Hart design as a replacement. Designed as a general-purpose machine capable of policing the area from the air, the Hawker **Hardy** incorporated features from both the Hart and the Audax. A production Hart was modified to carry a tropical survival kit and water containers, the engine was fitted with a tropical filter and a message pick-up hook was attached to the undercarriage. A total of 47 production examples was built and the first examples entered service with No. 30 Squadron at Mosul in late 1934. At the outbreak of war the aircraft had been transferred to No. 6 Squadron in Palestine and early in 1940 four examples were detached to No. 237 (Rhodesia) Squadron in East Africa, where they flew dive-bombing, army co-operation and field reconnaissance sorties against Italian forces. They were withdrawn from service after the Battle of Karen in 1941.

In 1935 the Air Ministry identified a need for an interim replacement for the Hart before modern monoplane bombers such as the Fairey Battle and Bristol Blenheim became available. Such was the excellence of the Hart that Hawker tendered an improved version called the **Hind**. Fitting the more powerful Rolls-Royce Kestrel V engine enhanced performance, and other improvements included a cut-down rear cockpit to improve the field-of-fire, a superior prone bomb-aiming position for the observer/gunner and a tailwheel replacing the tail skid. By the spring of 1937 over 300 Hind bombers equipped around 20 Bomber Command squadrons; however, by the autumn of that year more modern types began to appear and the Hind began to be withdrawn from front-line service. A desperate need for suitable training aircraft resulted in 124 of these bombers being sent in 1938 to the General Aircraft company for conversion to dual-control trainers and it was these, along with 20 production Hind trainers, which were to play a vital role training the bomber crews which went on to fly the RAFs heavy bombers. Hinds continued in the training role until 1941 although the type continued in RAF service in other secondary roles, such as glider-towing and communications, until early 1943.

Similar to Bomber Command's needs for an improved version of the Hart, the RAF's army co-operation squadrons required an improved version of the Audax. A lack of Rolls-Royce engines resulted in the aircraft being powered by a Napier Dagger engine, giving the aircraft a less streamlined appearance. The aircraft adopted the other improvements incorporated into the Hind as well as the addition of a message pick-up hook beneath the fuselage. A production order was placed in 1935 and the name **Hector** was adopted. During the next three years Hectors operated with seven army co-operation squadrons but by the outbreak of World War II the type had been relegated for service with the Auxiliary Air Force. The only wartime operational sorties by the Hector were flown by No. 613 Squadron, RAuxAF which made dive-bombing attacks from Manston against enemy troops attacking Calais in May 1940. The squadron also dropped supplies to beleagured Allied ground forces during the following month. By mid-1940 the Hector had been relegated to glider-towing duties for Hotspur gliders with No. 38 Group training units, and continued in this role until 1942.

Specification
Hind
Type: two-seat light bomber/trainer
Powerplant: one 640-hp (477-kW) Rolls-Royce Kestrel V inline piston engine
Performance: maximum speed 186 mph (299 km/h) at 16,400 ft (4999 m); service ceiling 26,400 ft (8047 m); range 430 miles (692 km)
Weights: empty 3,251 lb (1475 kg); maximum take-off 5,298 lb (2403 kg)
Dimensions: span 37 ft 3 in (11.35 m); length 29 ft 7 in (9.02 m); height 10 ft 7 in (3.23 m); wing area 348 sq ft (32.33 m²)
Armament: one 0.303-in (7.7-mm) forward-firing machine-gun and one 0.303-in (7.7-mm) Lewis gun in rear cockpit, plus up to 500 lb (227 kg) of bombs

In November 1941 this Hind, L7189, was serving with No. 1 FTS (Flying Training School) as a dual-control trainer. The aircraft was from the last batch of 70 examples built by the Hawker company in 1937. By the following January the aircraft had been withdrawn from use and was allocated to a maintenance unit as an instructional airframe.

Hawker Henley

In February 1934, the Air Ministry detailed the requirement for a light bomber which could also be deployed in a close-support role. High performance was required, with a maximum speed of around 300 mph (483 km/h), and the contenders were Fairey, Gloster and Hawker Aircraft.

With only a modest requirement in respect of bomb load, it seemed logical to the Hawker design team to evolve an aircraft somewhat similar in size to the Hurricane. Thus the **Henley**, as this aircraft was to become known, had outer wing panels and tailplane that were built from identical jigs. The other common area was the powerplant, for with no great difference in size the Rolls-Royce Merlin, then being developed and already selected for installation in the Hurricane, offered the best power to weight ratio. Landing gear was of the retractable tailwheel type, the cantilever fabric-covered monoplane wing was mid-set, and accommodation was provided for a pilot and an observer/air gunner.

The prototype did not fly until 10 March 1937, powered by a Merlin 'F' engine. Subsequently, this aircraft was provided with light alloy stressed-skin wings and a Merlin I engine, and testing was to confirm the excellence of its overall performance. It was at this point that the Air Ministry decided it no longer had a requirement for a light bomber, and the Henley was ordered into production as a target-tug, with 200 to be built under sub-contract by Gloster Aircraft. Modifications included a propeller-driven winch to haul in the drogue cable after air-to-air firing sorties.

Designated **Henley Mk III**, production aircraft entered service first with Nos 1, 5 and 10 Bombing and Gunnery Schools, as well as with the Air Gunnery Schools at Barrow, Millom and Squires Gate. It was soon discovered that unless restricted to an unrealistically low tow speed, the rate of engine failure was unacceptably high. This resulted in the Henley's withdrawal from this role, and its relegation to an even less suitable task, that of towing larger drogue targets with anti-aircraft co-operation units and squadrons. The number of engine failures increased and several Henleys were lost in accidents which resulted after the engine cut out and the drogue could not be released quickly enough.

This situation was brought to an end in mid-1942, with the Henleys withdrawn from service as Boulton Paul Defiants were adopted for target-towing, and purpose-built Miles Martinets came into use.

Specification
Henley TT.Mk III
Type: two-seat target tug
Powerplant: one 1,030-hp (768-kW) Rolls-Royce Merlin II or III inline piston engine
Performance: maximum speed (with air-to-air target) 272 mph (438 km/h) at 17,500 ft (5335 m), (with ground-to-air target) 200 mph (322 km/h); service ceiling 27,000 ft (8230 m); range 950 miles (1529 km)
Weights: empty 6,010 lb (2726 kg); maximum take-off 8,480 lb (3846 kg)
Dimensions: span 47 ft 11 in (14.60 m); length 36 ft 5 in (11.10 m); height 14 ft 8 in (4.47 m); wing area 342 sq ft (31.77 m²)

Designed as a light bomber, the Henley saw service as a high-speed target-tug. Like most target-tugs, yellow/black stripes were applied to the underside.

Hawker Hurricane

Few members of the British public could have been aware that a significant new fighter aircraft had joined the ranks of the RAF when, in December 1937, the first production examples of the Hawker **Hurricane Mk I** were delivered to No. 111 Squadron at RAF Northolt. It was not until two months later, during February 1938, that this news became common, and exciting, knowledge when banner headlines announced, on 11 February, that one of these new Hurricane fighters had more than lived up to its name on the previous afternoon. Piloted by Sqn Ldr J. W. Gillan, commanding officer of No. 111 Squadron, this aircraft had been flown from Turnhouse, Scotland, to Northolt, a distance of 327 miles (526 km), in 48 minutes at an average speed of almost 409 mph (658 km/h).

The impact of this news story was not then diluted by the information that such a high speed had been recorded only because of an exceptionally fast tail wind. This bald, unadulterated statement of fact achieved maximum effect, doubtlessly intended, and served the dual purpose of, firstly, encouraging the British people by intimating that a new and revolutionary fighter was available for the defence of the country and, secondly, providing propaganda for consumption by the German people and their leaders, propaganda which sought to offset the achievements of the German Bf 109 designed by Willy Messerschmitt. This latter aircraft had created headlines of its own in the summer of 1937, winning climb, dive, speed and team race competitions, as well as the international Circuit of the Alps race, at the international flying meeting held at Zurich in late July. But having regard to the fact that a Bf 109, with a specially supercharged engine, had captured the world speed record for landplanes on 11 November

In September 1939 Nos 1 and 73 Squadrons moved to France as the Hurricane Wing of the Advanced Air Striking Force. Both squadrons of Hurricane Mk Is were instructed to remove their squadron identity codes, although the third aircraft is still carrying No. 73's 'TP' code.

Below: A Hurricane Mk I of RAF Fighter Command is put through its paces in early 1938. Low-visibility national markings were introduced after the Munich Crisis of that year.

Based at Lille/Seclin during the Battle of France, Hurricanes from 'B' Flight of No. 87 Squadron are seen at dispersal in May 1940. The smoke bomb was used to simulate a gas attack on the airfield.

Wing armament
Production Hurricane Mk Is were armed with eight licence-built Colt Browning 0.303-in (7.7-mm) machine-guns. The rate of fire was 1,200 rounds per minute per gun with a total ammunition capacity of 2,660 rounds.

Hawker Hurricane Mk IA

This Hurricane Mk IA from No. 87 Squadron formed part of 60 Wing of the Air Component of the British Expeditionary Force which was dispatched to France at the outbreak of World War II. Seeing intense action during the Battle of France, the squadron's Hurricanes suffered heavy losses while tasked with escorting army co-operation Lysanders in May 1940.

Specification
Hurricane Mk I
Type: single-seat fighter
Powerplant: one 1,030-hp (768-kW) Rolls-Royce Merlin II or III inline piston engine
Performance: maximum speed 318 mph (512 km/h); service ceiling 33,400 ft (10180 m); range 440 miles (708 km)
Weights: empty 4,670 lb (2118 kg); loaded 6,600 lb (2994 kg)
Dimensions: span 40 ft 0 in (12.19 m); length 31 ft 5 in (9.58 m); height 13 ft 1 in (3.99 m); wing area 258 sq ft (23.97 m^2)
Armament: eight 0.303-in (7.7-mm) Browning machine-guns in outer wings

Structure
All marks of Hurricanes had a round-section steel and Duralumin tube fuselage structure with a fabric covering. Early examples of the Hurricane were fitted with fabric-covered outer wing panels although later marks featured all-metal wings.

Camouflage
Hurricanes dispatched with the BEF carried the standard RAF day- fighter topside scheme of matt Dark Earth and Dark Green which was introduced in 1937. The underside is painted in one of the many variations on the 'Black and White' pattern which was used on and off on UK-based aircraft and Middle East Hurricanes between 1938 and 1941.

Hawker Hurricane

Based at Croydon and Debden, No. 85 Squadron was part of No. 11 Group, which participated in the fiercest fighting of the Battle of Britain. This Hurricane Mk I appears in the standard scheme worn by RAF fighters during the battle.

No. 85 Squadron was one of Fighter Command's most successful units during the Battle of Britain. During August 1940 the squadron claimed 44 enemy aircraft for the loss of only eight Hurricanes and two pilots.

1937, at a speed of 379.38 mph (610.55 km/h) it is doubtful if Germans would have believed or been impressed by the British news.

The subject of all this excitement, the Hurricane, stemmed back as far as 1933 when Hawker's chief designer, Sydney Camm, discussed with the Air Ministry's Directorate of Technical Development the prospects for a monoplane fighter. Despite the fact that monoplane racing seaplanes involved in the Schneider Trophy contests had achieved speeds of up to 340 mph (547 km/h), and that the Italian Macchi MC.72 monoplane seaplane had established a world speed record of 423.82 mph (682.07 km/h) on 10 April 1933, the British Air Ministry then had little confidence in the integrity of the monoplane structure.

Hawker Aircraft decided to design a monoplane fighter based on the Fury biplane, using as its powerplant the Rolls-Royce Goshawk engine. As development of the design progressed, the Goshawk became supplanted by the Rolls-Royce P.V.12, a private venture engine which led directly to the Merlin, and Hawker began construction of a prototype around which the Air Ministry Specification F.36/34 had been drawn up. As first flown on 6 November 1935, this prototype had retractable tailwheel-type landing gear, a strut-braced tailplane, conventional Hawker-structure fuselage with fabric covering, a new two-spar monoplane wing covered with fabric, and a powerplant comprising a 990-hp (738-kW) Rolls-Royce Merlin 'C' engine driving a two-bladed fixed-pitch propeller.

Official trials began in February 1936, when the most optimistic high-speed performance predictions were comfortably exceeded, and on 3 June 1936 an initial order for 600 production aircraft was issued to Hawker. At the end of the month the new fighter was named the Hurricane. Hawker had in fact anticipated the production contract, and plans for the construction of 1,000 examples had already been initiated when the Air Ministry order was received. This, however, called for installation of the Merlin II engine, causing some delay as it was necessary to redesign related items such as controls, mountings and nose cowlings, but Hawker's advance preparations made possible the first flight of a production Hurricane Mk I on 12 October 1937.

As mentioned at the beginning of this entry, the Hurricane Mk I began to enter service with No. 111 Squadron at Northolt, Middlesex, which had one flight operational in December 1937 and was completely re-equipped by the end of the following month. Soon afterwards, Nos 3 and 56 Squadrons became equipped, and by the end of 1938 about 200 Hurricanes had been delivered to the RAF's Fighter Command. The early production aircraft differed little from the prototype, except for the installation of the 1,030-hp (768-kW) Merlin II engine. The aircraft initially had individual exhaust stubs for each of the engine's 12 cylinders, but triple ejector exhaust manifolds on each side were soon to become the standard. Other early variations were to be found in the propeller installation, the Watts two-bladed propeller being replaced first by a de Havilland three-bladed variable-pitch unit and later by a de Havilland or Rotol three-bladed constant-speed type.

No doubts existed that the Hurricane was anything but an important and essential aircraft to reinforce the expansion of the RAF, and plans were made in late 1938 for additional construction to be undertaken by Gloster Aircraft at Hucclecote, Gloucestershire. This latter

Hurricanes from No. 56 Squadron scramble to repel another German bombing raid against the airfields of No. 11 Group, Fighter Command. The squadron flew daily operations during the Battle of Britain from their base at North Weald until 1 September 1940.

Below: Two late production Hurricane Mk Is of No. 501 Squadron depart for another sortie on 15 August 1940. During the height of the Battle of Britain the squadron was flying up to four sorties a day against attacking German bomber formations. Both these aircraft were lost in heavy fighting during the day this photograph was taken.

Ground crew finish preparing a 'bombed-up' Hurricane Mk IIB as the pilot, wearing a 'Mae West', approaches his aircraft on the island of Malta. Among successful bombing missions flown by Hurricanes from Malta was No. 185 Squadron's raid on the seaplane base at Syracuse, Greece in July 1941.

Below: A number of Hurricane squadrons served in the Middle East during the early war years. These Mk Is from No. 237 Squadron are seen departing their base at Mosul, Iraq in May 1942. At this time the squadron mainly flew tactical reconnaissance sorties in the defence of the oilfields.

company's first production aircraft was to make its initial flight on 27 October 1939, and in little over 12 months Gloster had completed 1,000 Hurricanes, a figure that was to reach 1,850, plus 1,924 by Hawker, before later versions superseded the Hurricane Mk I in production. Before that happened, however, the fabric-covered wing had been replaced by one with metal stressed skin, and other progressively introduced improvements had included the Merlin III engine, a bullet-proof windscreen, and some armour protection for the pilot.

Despite the pressure of its production programme for the RAF, Hawker had found time and space to cope with modest production orders covering 24 aircraft and a production licence for Yugoslavia, followed by aircraft for Belgium, Iran, Poland, Romania and Turkey; Belgium also negotiated a production licence for construction to be carried out by Avions Fairey, but only two Belgian-built Hurricanes had been completed and flown before the German invasion. Arrangements were also completed for Hurricanes to be built in Canada by the Canadian Car and Foundry Co., the first production aircraft flying on 9 January 1940. Canadian aircraft were at first generally similar to the British-built Hurricane Mk I, but later differed by having the Packard-built Merlin engine.

At the outbreak of World War II 19 RAF squadrons were fully equipped with Hurricanes, and within a short time Nos 1, 73, 85 and 87 Squadrons had been dispatched to bases in France. Not inappropriately, a Hurricane of No. 1 Squadron was the first RAF aircraft to destroy a German machine over the Western Front in World War II. This victory came on 30 October 1939 when Pilot Officer P. W. Mould shot down a Dornier Do 17 over Toul, but in this 'phoney' period of the war these squadrons had comparatively little to do until the German push westward in May 1940. Immediately, six more Hurricane squadrons were flown to France, followed shortly after by two more squadrons, but these were an inadequate number to stem the flood of German arms, armour and aircraft. Post-Dunkirk accounting showed that almost 200 Hurricanes had been lost, destroyed or so severely damaged that they had to be abandoned. It represented a major disaster for the RAF, for this number of aircraft amounted to

Part of the first consignments of Hurricane Mk Is to be shipped to North Africa, these aircraft are seen on the long flight from the port of Takoradi in West Africa (where they were assembled) to Egypt. These aircraft were yet to be fitted with the Vokes tropical filter.

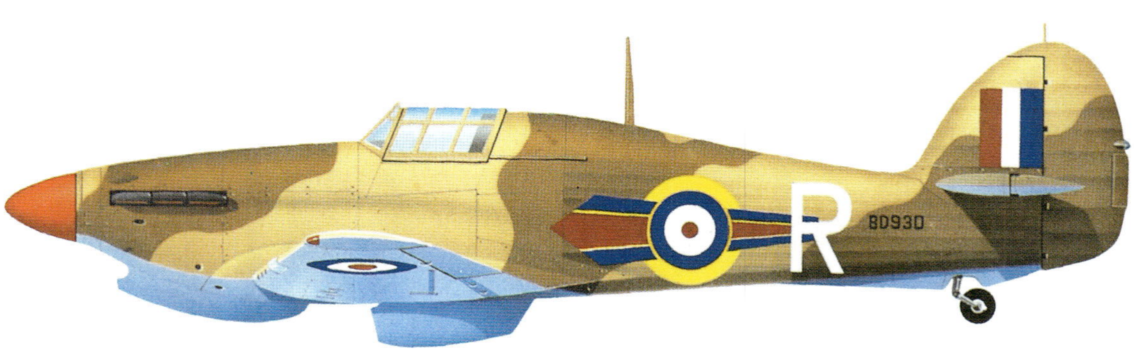

After seeing extensive combat in the Battle of France and the Battle of Britain, No. 73 Squadron took its Hurricanes to the Western Desert in November 1940. Fitted with a tropical filter, and unofficially adorned with a peacetime squadron flash on the fuselage, this Hurricane Mk IIB flew day and night sorties when based in Egypt in 1942.

A Hurricane Mk IIB of No. 402 Squadron is seen carrying two 250-lb (113-kg) bombs. After working up to operational standard with the Air Fighting Development Unit, the squadron made its first bombing raid against Berck-sur-Mer airfield in November 1941.

about a quarter of its total strength in first-line fighters.

Fortunately for the UK, and the RAF, the anticipated invasion of the British Isles by Germany failed to materialise, and there was a breathing space during which the squadrons of Fighter Command were able to reinforce their numbers. On 8 August 1940, which is regarded officially as the opening date of the Battle of Britain, the RAF could call upon 32 squadrons of Hurricanes and 19 squadrons of Supermarine Spitfires. Despite the debacle at Dunkirk and the resulting fighter famine in Britain, three Hurricane squadrons were transferred overseas. These comprised No. 261 Squadron sent to support the island of Malta, and Nos 73 and 274 Squadrons which, suitably 'tropicalised' by the substitution of a larger coolant radiator and a small-particle filter for the engine air intake (to minimise sand ingestion), began operations in the Western Desert.

It had been appreciated at an early date that the basic Hurricane had considerable development potential, leading first to the introduction of a Merlin XX engine in a Hurricane Mk I airframe under the designation **Hurricane Mk IIA Series 1**. Generally similar, except for a slightly lengthened fuselage, was the **Hurricane Mk IIA Series 2**, this representing an interim change on the production lines to make possible the installation of newly-developed and interchangeable wings. Thus, with a wing housing no fewer than 12 0.303-in (7.7-mm) machine-guns and with provision for the carriage of two 250-lb (113-kg) or two 500-lb (227-kg) bombs beneath the wings, the designation became **Mk IIB**. The **Hurricane Mk IIC** was generally similar, but the 12 wing-mounted machine-guns were replaced by four 20-mm cannon. When the Hurricane's life as a fighter had virtually come to an end, in 1942, the introduction of yet another wing was to rejuvenate this remarkable aircraft as the **Hurricane Mk IID**. The new wing carried two 40-mm

At the outbreak of World War II the UK lacked suitable night-fighting aircraft. When the Germans turned to night attacks in October 1940, No. 85 Squadron's Hurricanes were hastily blackened and fitted with flame-damping exhausts for this role.

Hawker Hurricane Mk IIC cutaway

1 Starboard navigation light
2 Starboard wingtip
3 Aluminium alloy aileron
4 Self-aligning ball-bearing aileron hinge
5 Aft wing spar
6 Aluminium alloy wing skinning
7 Forward wing spar
8 Starboard landing light
9 Rotol three-bladed constant-speed propeller
10 Spinner
11 Propeller hub
12 Pitch-control mechanism
13 Spinner back plate
14 Cowling fairings
15 Coolant pipes
16 Rolls-Royce Merlin XX liquid-cooled 12-cylinder Vee engine
17 Cowling panel fasteners
18 'Fishtail' exhaust pipes
19 Electric generator
20 Engine forward mounting feet
21 Engine upper bearer tube
22 Engine forward mount
23 Engine lower bearer tubes
24 Starboard mainwheel fairing
25 Starboard mainwheel
26 Low-pressure tyre
27 Brake drum (pneumatic brakes)
28 Manual-type inertia starter
29 Hydraulic system
30 Bearer joint
31 Auxiliary intake
32 Carburettor air intake
33 Wingroot fillet
34 Engine oil drain collector/breather
35 Fuel pump drain
36 Engine aft bearers
37 Magneto
38 Two-stage supercharger
39 Cowling panel attachments
40 Engine RPM indicator drive
41 External bead sight
42 Removable aluminium alloy cowling panels
43 Engine coolant header tank
44 Engine firewall (armour-plated backing)
45 Fuselage (reserve) fuel tank, capacity 28 Imp gal (127 litres)
46 Exhaust glare shield
47 Control column
48 Engine bearer attachment
49 Rudder pedals
50 Control linkage
51 Centre-section fuel tank
52 Oil system piping
53 Pneumatic system air cylinder
54 Wing centre-section/front spar girder construction
55 Engine bearer support strut
56 Oil tank (port wingroot leading edge)
57 Dowty undercarriage ram
58 Port undercarriage shell
59 Wing centre-section girder frame
60 Pilot's oxygen cylinder
61 Elevator trim tab control wheel
62 Radiator flap control lever
63 Entry footstep
64 Fuselage tubular framework
65 Landing lamp control lever
66 Oxygen supply cock
67 Throttle lever
68 Safety harness
69 Pilot's seat
70 Pilot's break-out exit panel
71 Map case
72 Instrument panel
73 Cockpit ventilation inlet
74 Reflector gunsight
75 Bullet-proof windscreen
76 Rear-view mirror
77 Rearward-sliding canopy
78 Canopy frame
79 Canopy handgrip
80 Plexiglas canopy panels
81 Head/back armour plate
82 Harness attachment
83 Aluminium alloy decking
84 Turnover reinforcement
85 Canopy track
86 Fuselage framework cross-bracing
87 Radio equipment (TR9D/TR133)
88 Support tray
89 Removable access panel
90 Aileron cable drum
91 Elevator control lever
92 Cable adjusters
93 Aluminium alloy wing/fuselage fillet
94 Ventral identification and formation-keeping lights
95 Footstep retraction guide and support rail
96 Radio equipment (R3002)
97 Upward-firing recognition apparatus
98 Handhold
99 Diagonal support
100 Fuselage fairing
101 Dorsal identification light
102 Aerial mast
103 Aerial lead-in
104 Recognition-apparatus cover panel
105 Mast support
106 Wire-braced upper truss
107 Wooden fuselage fairing formers
108 Fabric covering
109 Radio antenna
110 All-metal tailplane structure
111 Static and dynamic elevator balance
112 Starboard elevator
113 Fin metal leading edge
114 Fabric covering
115 Tail fin structure
116 Diagonal bracing struts
117 Built-in static balance
118 Aerial stub
119 Fabric-covered rudder
120 Rudder structure
121 Rudder post
122 Rear navigation light

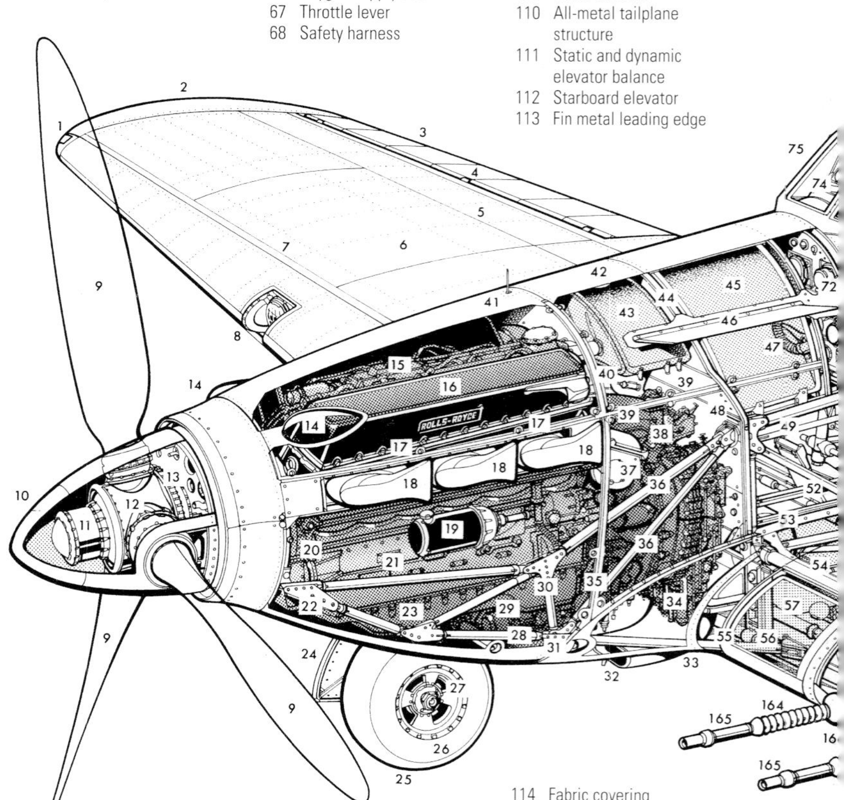

Hawker Hurricane

In the spring of 1942 No. 1 Squadron was equipped with Hurricane Mk IICs under the leadership of Sqn Ldr J. A. F. MacLachlan. During this period the squadron flew highly successful intruder night sorties over France, attacking enemy aircraft as they took off or landed at their own bases.

Hawker Hurricane Variants

F.36/34 prototype: one aircraft with 764-kW (1,025-hp) Merlin C engine
Hurricane Mk I: original production model with 768-kW (1,030-hp) Merlin II or III engine, eight Browning 7.7-mm (0.303-in) guns; early aircraft with fabric-covered wings, later metal-clad (total 2,719)
Canadian Hurricane Mk I: built by Canadian Car and Foundry Co. in Montreal, 1940; Merlin III engine and DH propellers, batch included Hillson BiMono slip-wing Hurricane (total 40)
Hurricane Mk IIA Series 1: introduced 883-kW (1,185-hp) Merlin XX two-stage supercharged engine; eight-gun wing; some converted from Mk Is
Hurricane Mk IIA Series 2: introduced provision for wing stores on Universal wing; some converted from Mk I
Hurricane Mk IIB: introduced 12-Browning gun wing and bomb-tank shackles for 227-kg (500-lb) bombs (approximately 3,100 built by Hawker, Gloster and Austin, plus conversions from other variants)
Hurricane Mk IIC: introduced four 20-mm cannon armament in 1941; bomb and drop tank provision; world-wide service (approximately 3,400 built by Hawker, Gloster and Austin, plus many conversions)
Hurricane Mk IID: introduced pair of 40-mm Vickers or Rolls-Royce anti-tank guns plus two Brownings in 1942; many tropicalised (approximately 800 built; plus many conversions)
Hurricane Mk IV: introduced 954-kW (1,280-hp) Merlin 24 or 27 engine and Universal wing to carry alternative rockets, drop tanks, bombs or anti-tank guns in 1942; many tropicalised (approximately 2,000 built, plus numerous conversions)
Hurricane Mk V: two prototypes (KZ193 and NL255, converted Mk IVs) with ground-boosted Merlin 32 engine and four-bladed Rotol propeller
Canadian Hurricane Mk X: Packard Merlin 28 engine; about 100 with eight-gun wing, remainder with Mk IIB wing; many converted to Mk IIC wing (total 489 built in 1940-41)
Canadian Hurricane Mk XI: 150 aircraft with 12-gun or four-cannon armament; majority shipped to Soviet Union in 1942-43
Canadian Hurricane XII: 248 aircraft with Hurricane IIC modifications, included single ski-equipped example
Canadian Hurricane XIIA: Packard Merlin 29 engine; 150 mostly to Soviet Union and Burma

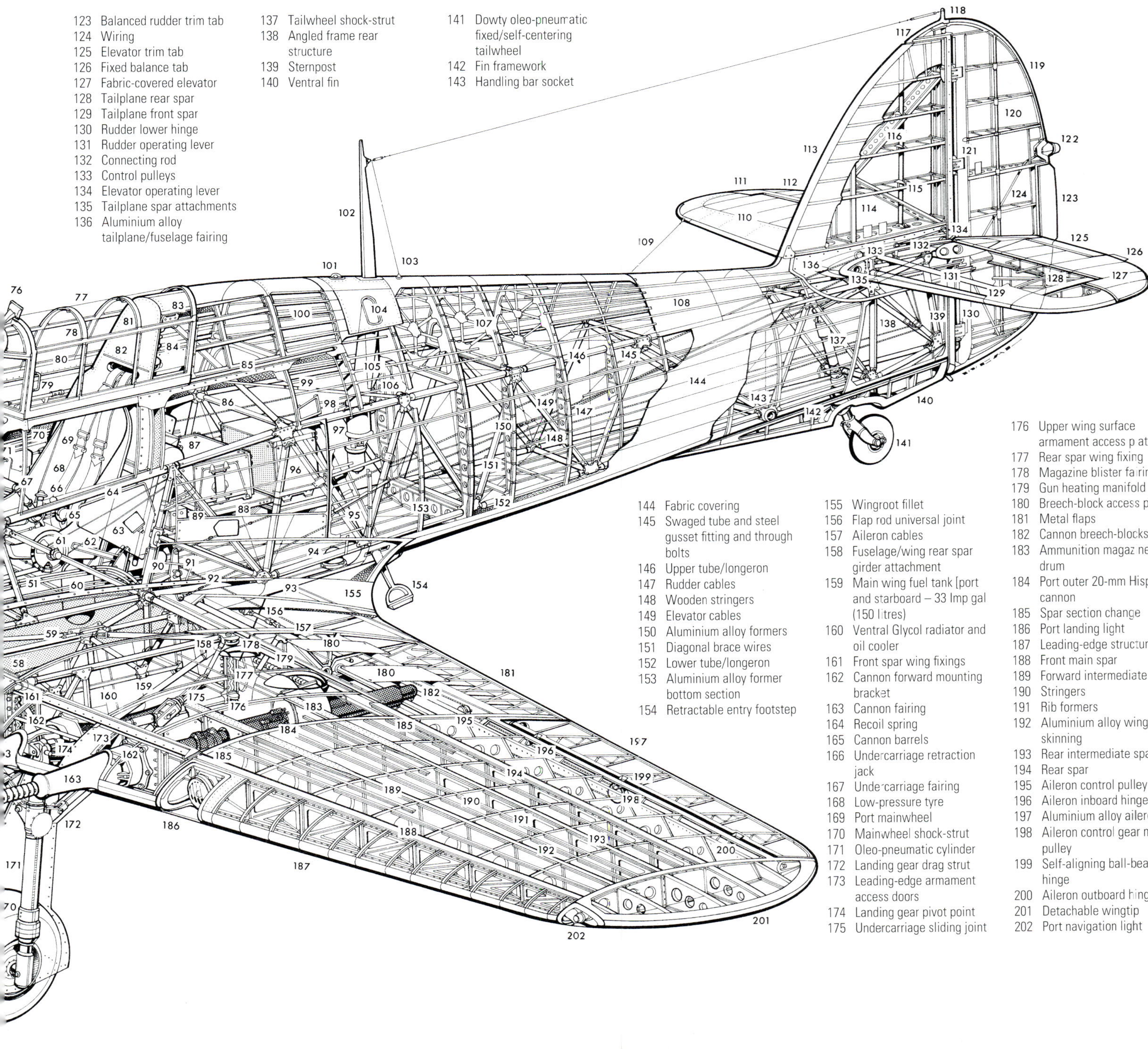

123 Balanced rudder trim tab
124 Wiring
125 Elevator trim tab
126 Fixed balance tab
127 Fabric-covered elevator
128 Tailplane rear spar
129 Tailplane front spar
130 Rudder lower hinge
131 Rudder operating lever
132 Connecting rod
133 Control pulleys
134 Elevator operating lever
135 Tailplane spar attachments
136 Aluminium alloy tailplane/fuselage fairing
137 Tailwheel shock-strut
138 Angled frame rear structure
139 Sternpost
140 Ventral fin
141 Dowty oleo-pneumatic fixed/self-centering tailwheel
142 Fin framework
143 Handling bar socket
144 Fabric covering
145 Swaged tube and steel gusset fitting and through bolts
146 Upper tube/longeron
147 Rudder cables
148 Wooden stringers
149 Elevator cables
150 Aluminium alloy formers
151 Diagonal brace wires
152 Lower tube/longeron
153 Aluminium alloy former bottom section
154 Retractable entry footstep
155 Wingroot fillet
156 Flap rod universal joint
157 Aileron cables
158 Fuselage/wing rear spar girder attachment
159 Main wing fuel tank [port and starboard – 33 Imp gal (150 litres)
160 Ventral Glycol radiator and oil cooler
161 Front spar wing fixings
162 Cannon forward mounting bracket
163 Cannon fairing
164 Recoil spring
165 Cannon barrels
166 Undercarriage retraction jack
167 Undercarriage fairing
168 Low-pressure tyre
169 Port mainwheel
170 Mainwheel shock-strut
171 Oleo-pneumatic cylinder
172 Landing gear drag strut
173 Leading-edge armament access doors
174 Landing gear pivot point
175 Undercarriage sliding joint
176 Upper wing surface armament access plates
177 Rear spar wing fixing
178 Magazine blister fairings
179 Gun heating manifold
180 Breech-block access plates
181 Metal flaps
182 Cannon breech-blocks
183 Ammunition magazine drum
184 Port outer 20-mm Hispano cannon
185 Spar section change
186 Port landing light
187 Leading-edge structure
188 Front main spar
189 Forward intermediate spar
190 Stringers
191 Rib formers
192 Aluminium alloy wing skinning
193 Rear intermediate spar
194 Rear spar
195 Aileron control pulley
196 Aileron inboard hinge
197 Aluminium alloy aileron
198 Aileron control gear main pulley
199 Self-aligning ball-bearing hinge
200 Aileron outboard hinge
201 Detachable wingtip
202 Port navigation light

Five Hurricane Mk IICs of No. 94 Squadron fly in formation from their base at El Gamil, Egypt in mid-1942. The first, third and fourth aircraft have had their outboard cannon removed to reduce weight.

Rolls-Royce B.F. or Vickers Type S anti-tank guns, plus one harmonised 0.303-in (7.7-mm) machine-gun for each anti-armour weapon to assist in aiming. The Hurricane Mk IID 'tank-buster' was to prove a potent weapon, highly effective against German armour in North Africa and when opposing more lightly armoured Japanese fighting vehicles in Burma.

The success of these wing variations led to the final production version, the **Hurricane Mk IV** (early examples of this version were designated **Mk IIE**), which introduced the 1,620-hp (1208-kW) Merlin 24 or 27 engine, and a Universal wing to make the Mk IV a highly-specialised ground-attack aircraft. This wing carried two 0.303-in (7.7-mm) machine-guns to assist in sighting the other weapons, which could include two 40-mm anti-tank guns, two 250-lb (113-kg) or 500-lb (227-kg) bombs, or smoke curtain installations, ferry or drop tanks, or eight rocket projectiles with 60-lb (27-kg) warheads. This last weapon, first proposed in late 1941, had been tested on a Hurricane in February 1942. When used operationally on the Hurricane Mk IV, this was the first of all Allied aircraft to deploy air-to-ground rockets, leading to newspaper headlines which claimed that the Hurricane 'packed a punch equivalent to the broadside from a destroyer'. Such firepower meant that the little Hurricane was a giant in capability, extending its operational life beyond the end of World War II, for it was not until January 1947 that the RAF's last Hurricane squadron, No. 6, received replacement aircraft.

Hurricane production in Canada, like that in Britain, had grown considerably in proportions from the initial line of Hurricane Mk Is. The introduction of the 1,300-hp (969-kW) Packard-built Merlin 28 engine and Hamilton Standard propellers brought a designation change to **Hurricane Mk X**. This model was generally similar to the British-built Mk IIB with the 12-gun wing, and while small numbers of these were supplied to Britain, the majority were retained for use by the Royal Canadian Air Force. The **Hurricane Mk XI** which followed was developed specifically for RCAF requirements, but differed from the Mk X primarily in having RCAF rather than RAF military equipment. The major production version from Canadian sources was the **Hurricane Mk XII**, this introducing the 1,300-hp (969-kW) Packard-built Merlin 29. Initially, this was provided with the 12-gun wing; subsequently, the four-cannon and Universal wings became available. The final land-based version to emanate from Canada was the **Mk XIIA**, identical to the Mk XII except for having an eight-gun wing.

In addition to the Hurricanes which went to other countries before the war, wartime production was to supply almost 3,000 of these aircraft to Russia, although as a result of convoy shipping losses not all reached their destination. Other wartime deliveries, most made at a time when it was difficult to spare a single aircraft, went to Egypt (20), Finland (12), India (300), Irish Air Corps (12), Persia (1) and Turkey

Fitted with a Universal wing, the Hurricane Mk IV could carry bombs, drop tanks, rocket projectiles or, as seen here, two 40-mm anti-tank cannon. This weapon was used to good effect against German armour in North Africa and Italy.

Tropicalisation
Hurricanes operating in the Western Desert were fitted with Vokes filters to protect the ventral radiator and oil cooler from sand and dust. The filter also proved useful for aircraft operating in the Soviet Union and the Far East.

Hawker Hurricane Mk IIC

Attached to No. 94 Squadron, this Hurricane was one of three donated to the RAF by Lady Rachel MacRobert in memory of her three sons who had been killed flying for the RAF. The squadron reformed at Aden in 1939 and spent the entire war in the Middle East and Mediterranean theatres, operating Hurricanes between May 1941 and May 1944.

Improved armament
The Hurricane Mk IIC replaced the eight Browning 0.303-in (7.7-mm) machine-guns, fitted to earlier versions, with either two or four Oerlikon or Hispano 20-mm cannon. The more destructive firepower provided by the cannon proved particularly useful in the ground-attack role. The capacity was 364 rounds and firing bursts were kept short, not only to preserve ammunition, but also beacuse the longer burst resulted in a noticeable degradation in airspeed due to the effects of recoil.

Powerplant
The Hurricane Mk IIC was fitted with the more powerful 1,280-hp (955-kW) Rolls-Royce Merlin XX engine. The additional power compensated for the extra weight of the cannon armament and allowed the aircraft to carry two 250-lb (113-kg) or two 500-lb (227-kg) bombs, or a pair of 44-Imp gal (200-litre) drop tanks. The engine drove a Rotol RS5/2 or /3 three-bladed constant-speed propeller.

Desert markings
RAF fighter aircraft in the Western Desert normally wore a camouflage scheme of Dark Earth, Middle Stone and Azure Blue in the same overall pattern as Europe-based aircraft. The presentation of code letters was less strictly enforced; the individual code letter of 'P' of this aircraft being preceded with 'O' instead of the full squadron identity 'GO'.

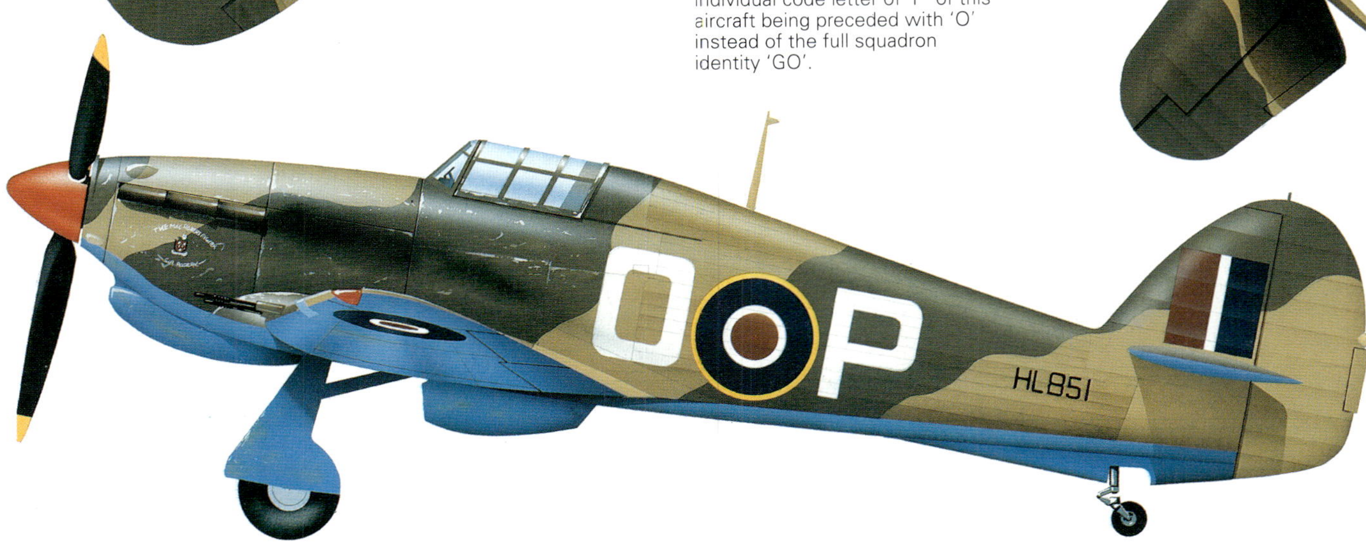

Hawker Hurricane

(14), and total production in Britain and Canada amounted to more than 14,000 aircraft.

Undoubtedly one of the great fighter aircraft of World War II, it is difficult to highlight the capabilities of this remarkable aircraft without using a host of tired adjectives or clichés. In the Battle of Britain Hurricanes destroyed more enemy aircraft than all other defences, air or ground, combined. Even this statement must be put in perspective, for there was an early appreciation that the maximum speed of the Hurricane put it at a distinct disadvantage when confronted by the Messerschmitt Bf 109. Consequently, the Spitfires tangled with the Bf 109s, enabling the Hurricanes to battle the German bombers which sought initially to destroy the RAF's fighter airfields and Britain's vital radar installations. 'Hurri-bombers' fought from Malta, carried out anti-shipping operations in the English Channel, and caused havoc to Axis columns in the Western Desert. Tank-busting Hurricanes ranged far and wide in practically every operational theatre. One fighter flown by Flt Lt J. B. Nicholson of No. 249 (Fighter) Squadron during the summer of 1940, helped earn for its gallant pilot the only Victoria Cross to be awarded to a member of Fighter Command. This occurred on 17 August when, with his Hurricane badly damaged and wreathed in flames, the wounded and severely burnt Nicholson succeeded in destroying the attacking Messerschmitt Bf 110 before baling out, to be rescued and survive his wounds.

It is not really surprising, therefore, that for many years after the end of World War II, a lone Hurricane had the honour of leading the RAF fly-past over London, flown each year to commemorate victory in the Battle of Britain.

Above: As the Japanese swept westwards through Asia, the first Hurricanes arrived in January 1942 and actively took part in the defence of Singapore. Hurricanes continued to operate in the theatre until the end of the Pacific War. This 'Hurri-bomber' makes an attack on the Tiddim Road in Burma during mid-1944.

Left: The Hurricane demonstrated its durability during operations with No. 1 Wing, RAF in northern Russia. Despite the freezing temperatures and primitive conditions, the Hurricanes gave an excellent account of themselves against the numerically superior Luftwaffe.

Below: In October 1943, No. 42 Squadron, which was already based in the Far East, received 'tropicalised' Hurricane Mk IICs and Mk IVs. It operated the type during the Allied advance through Asia until it received by the Republic Thunderbolt in July 1945. This Mk IV is camouflaged to prevent detection at a forward airstrip in spring 1945.

Fitted with a tropical filter, this Hurricane Tac R.Mk IIC flew photogrpahic reconnaissance sorties over Southeast Asia. The camera window is located on the lower port side of the fuselage. The light-coloured tail band was painted on all Hurricanes operating in Burma during the last six months of the war.

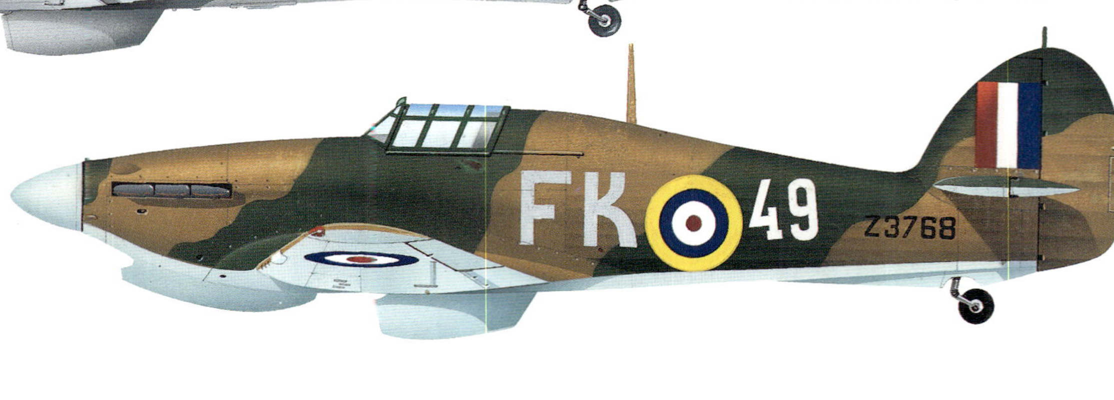

With the Germans advancing through western Russia in the summer of 1941, two squadrons of Hurricane Mk IIBs were sent to help the Soviet defence. This example, from No. 134 Squadron, was based at Vaenga, North Russia in September 1941. Originally bound for North Africa, it is fitted with a tropical filter.

Hawker Sea Hurricane

Top: Featuring catapult spools, an arrester hook and naval radio, the Sea Hurricane Mk IB was a conversion of the RAF's Hurricane Mk I. This Gloster-built example has exhaust glare shields fitted forward of the windscreen. Sea Hurricane Mk IBs saw intensive action in the Mediterranean theatre during 1942.

Above: A Sea Hurricane Mk IA is launched at dawn from the bow-mounted catapult of a merchant ship. Tasked with on-the-spot fighter defence, the pilots of the catapult-launched Sea Hurricanes were forced to ditch or bale out at the end of a sortie and hope to be picked up by a passing ship. The system only achieved limited success during 1941.

The early success of the Hawker Hurricane fighter in RAF service meant that the Royal Navy was keen to acquire numbers of these aircraft to help in the Battle of the Atlantic which, in early 1940, was depicted statistically by a steeply rising graph of shipping losses. A large proportion of such losses resulted far from shore, in areas where land-based aircraft could not provide air cover for Allied convoys. Thus, German long-range patrol aircraft were able to range freely, spotting convoys far out at sea, and calling in and directing U-boat packs to attack them.

An interim measure gave birth to the 'Hurricat', a converted Hurricane carried by CAM-ships (Catapult Aircraft Merchantmen). Mounted on and launched from a catapult at the ship's bows, the Hurricane was flown off on what was usually a one-way flight: after providing defence for the convoy there was nowhere for the FAA or RAF pilot to land, which meant that he was obliged to bale out, or ditch his aircraft as near as possible to the convoy, hoping that he would be picked up. The provision of long-range drop tanks beneath the wings, introduced in August 1941 after the CAM-ships had been provided with more powerful catapults for the higher gross weight, improved the situation a little.

Hurricanes converted for the above role needed only the addition of catapult spools, and 50 Mk I landplanes so modified were designated **Sea Hurricane Mk IA**s. They were followed by about 300 Mk Is converted to **Sea Hurricane Mk IB** configuration, these having catapult spools plus a V-frame arrester hook; in addition, 25 Hurricane Mk IIA Series 2 aircraft were similarly modified as Sea Hurricane Mk IBs or Hooked Hurricane Mk IIs. Their initial role was a considerable improvement on CAM-ship deployment, for from October 1941 they began to go to sea aboard MAC-ships, these being large merchant ships which had received the addition of a small flight deck. They carried on deck (for there was no hangar accommodation) a small

Right: A Sea Hurricane Mk IA stands ready on the bow catapult of a CAM-ship. The catapult is angled slightly away from the bow to give the pilot a chance to escape from the path of the ship should the aircraft not gain sufficient airspeed and ditch after launch.

Hawker Sea Hurricane

Above: Deck crew service Sea Hurricanes in the hangar of a Royal Navy aircraft-carrier. The nearest aircraft is having its machine-gun ports covered with doped fabric to prevent ingestion of foreign objects.

number of fighter and ASW aircraft, which were able to operate from and to the mini-carriers. **Sea Hurricane Mk IC**s, introduced in February 1942 were, once again, conventional Mk I conversions with catapult spools and arrester hook: they had, however, the four-cannon wing of the land-based Hurricane Mk IIC. Last of the Sea Hurricanes from British sources was the **Mk IIC**, which was intended for conventional carrier operations and, consequently, was without catapult spools. They also introduced to navy service the Merlin XX engine, and carried FAA radio equipment. Last of all the Sea Hurricane variants was the **Mk XIIA**, of which a small number were converted from Canadian-built Hurricane Mk XIIs, and these were used operationally in the North Atlantic and Mediterranean, operating with some success mostly from light carriers and the ubiquitous escort carriers.

Specification

Sea Hurricane Mk IIC

Type: single-seat carrier-based fighter

Powerplant: one 1,280-hp (954-kW) Rolls-Royce Merlin XX inline piston engine

Performance: maximum speed 342 mph (550 km/h) at 22,000 ft (6706 m); maximum cruising speed 292 mph (470 km/h) at 20,000 ft (6096 m); long-range cruising speed 212 mph (341 km/h); service ceiling 35,600 ft (10851 m); range with internal fuel 460 miles (740 km); range with maximum internal and external fuel 970 miles (1561 km)

Weights: empty 5,880 lb (2667 kg); maximum take-off 8,100 lb (3674 kg)

Dimensions: span 40 ft 0 in (12.19 m); length 32 ft 3 in (9.83 m); height 13 ft 1 in (3.99 m); wing area 257.5 sq ft (23.92 m²)

Armament: four 20-mm forward-firing cannon

Above: With its wide-track undercarriage the Hurricane was more suitable for navalisation than Britain's other premier fighter of the early war years, the Spitfire. These Mk IBs are refuelled on deck before another sortie.

Above: With its arrester hook extended, a Sea Hurricane Mk IB approaches the deck of its carrier. The aircraft's long nose and bouncy undercarriage made carrier landings a tricky operation.

Left: This trio of tatty-looking Sea Hurricanes from No. 760 Squadron, Fleet Air Arm, are all fitted with different propellers. The nearest has a Rotol unit, the middle a de Havilland and the farthest a Jablo-Rotol 11-ft 3-in (3.43 m) propeller.

Hawker Tempest

One of the first units to receive the Tempest was No. 501 (RAuxAF) Squadron, to which these Mk V Series II aircraft belong. The squadron was in action against flying bombs only three days after converting to the Tempest in August 1944 and specialised in night interceptions – the commanding officer alone accounted for six V-1s.

The Hawker Typhoon proved a disappointment in its intended role as an interceptor, although it was to distinguish itself later as a fighter-bomber, particularly when armed with rocket projectiles. Its rate of climb and performance at altitude were relatively poor, and in 1941 it was suggested that remedial action might be taken in the form of a new, thinner wing, elliptical in planform. The radiator was to be moved from beneath the engine to the wing leading edges, and the Napier Sabre EC.107C was selected. As the new wing would be some 5 in (0.13 m) thinner than that of the Typhoon, the inclusion of an additional fuselage fuel tank was needed to replace the lost wing-tank capacity.

The design study, originally referred to as the **Typhoon Mk II**, was submitted to the Air Ministry, and on 18 November 1941 two prototypes were ordered. There were major changes, however, compared with the earlier aircraft, resulting in the name change to Tempest in early 1942. After cancellation of the Hawker Tornado programme, the alternative engine installations planned for that aircraft were, instead, applied to the Tempest. Thus the two original prototypes became the **Tempest Mk I** with a Sabre IV and **Tempest Mk V** with a Sabre II, and four more were ordered. Two **Tempest Mk II**s were to have the 2,520-hp (1879-kW) Bristol Centaurus, and two **Tempest Mk III**s the Rolls-Royce Griffon IIB, becoming **Tempest Mk IV**s when re-engined with the Griffon 61. Only one

Tempest Mk Vs of No. 3 Squadron are serviced between sorties, under sunny skies at Newchurch, soon after the D-Day invasion in June 1944. The aircraft carried black and white identification stripes around the wings and the rear fuselage.

EJ783 was one of the second batch of Tempest Mk V Series IIs, allocated to No. 274 Squadron in late 1944. It carried invasion stripes only on the underside of the fuselage and not around the wings, to assist in maintaining camouflage from enemy fighters flying above. Later in the year, No. 274 Squadron was renumbered as No. 174.

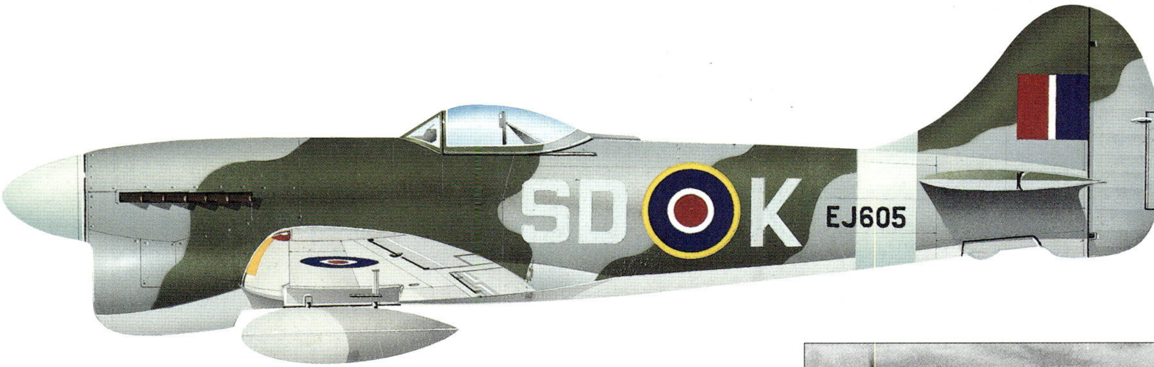

Specialising in night operations against V-1 flying-bombs, No. 501 Squadron received the Tempest Mk V in August 1944. It continued with this task until the squadron was disbanded in April 1945.

Griffon-engined aircraft was completed, in fact, as one of the prototype Hawker Furies.

Before any of the prototypes could be flown, however, the Air Ministry placed contracts for 400 Tempest Mk Is, although these were later transferred to other versions. The prototype Tempest Mk I, its lines not spoilt by the beard radiator of the Typhoon, was flown on 24 February 1943, and later achieved a maximum speed of 466 mph (750 km/h) at 24,500 ft (7470 m) with the Sabre IV's supercharger in FS (high) gear. The engine programme suffered from technical problems and delays, however, and the Tempest Mk I was dropped.

The first of the Tempest prototypes to fly had been that of the Mk V, flown by Philip Lucas on September 1942. Retaining the Typhoon's chin radiator, it was fitted originally with a standard Typhoon tail unit, but the lengthened fuselage necessitated the addition of a fairing to the leading edge of the fin, and an increase in tailplane chord. The first of 805 Tempest Mk Vs was flown from Langley on 21 June 1943, one of the initial production batch of 100 Series I aircraft which had four 20-mm British Hispano Mk II cannon, whose barrels protruded from the leading edge of the wing. The remaining Tempest Mk Vs had short-barrelled Mk V cannon, completely contained in the wings. In 1945, one Mk V was fitted with a 40-mm 'P' gun under each wing, similar to the 40-mm cannon installation of the Hawker Hurricane Mk IID. After the war had ended some were converted for use as **TT.Mk 5** target-tugs.

An order for 500 of the Centaurus-powered Tempest Mk II was placed in October 1942, once again before the first flight of the prototype. This first flight took place on 28 June 1943, the aircraft being powered by a Mk IV engine, which was superseded by the 2,520-hp (1879-kW) Mk V in the production aircraft that were built under sub-contract by the Bristol Aeroplane Company at its Weston-super-Mare factory. The first Bristol-built aircraft flew on 4 October 1944, but only 36 were completed before production was transferred back to Hawker, the parent company manufacturing a further 100 **F.Mk II** fighters and 314 **FB.Mk II** fighter-bombers with underwing racks for bombs or rockets.

The third and last production version of the Tempest was the **F.Mk VI** with the 2,340-hp (1745-kW) Napier Sabre V engine, the result of a trial installation in the Tempest Mk V prototype which was first flown in this configuration on 9 May 1944. Increased radiator frontal area necessitated the transfer of carburettor intakes to the wings, and the installation of an additional oil cooler in the starboard wing-root. Intended for service in the Middle East, 142 tropicalised Tempest Mk VIs were built. As in the case of the Mk V, some were converted as **TT.Mk 6** target-tugs.

RAF service commenced in April 1944, when 50 Tempest Mk Vs were delivered to Newchurch, Kent, where the first Tempest Wing was formed within No. 85 Group, under the command of Wing Commander R. P. Beamont, DSO, DFC. The component squadrons were Nos 3 and 486 Squadrons, Royal New Zealand Air Force, joined by No. 56 Squadron in June. The wing was active during the build-up to the Normandy invasion, but on 13 June the first V-1 flying bomb fell at Swanscombe in Kent, and the Tempests were among aircraft tasked to combat the menace. Their success can be measured by the fact that of 1,847 bombs destroyed by fighters between June 1944 and March 1945, 258 were disposed of by No. 3 Squadron and kills confirmed for No. 480 Squadron totalled 223½. Top-scoring Tempest pilot against V-1s was Squadron Leader J. Berry of No. 501 Squadron at Hawkinge, with 61⅓. Until the end of war in Europe, Tempest Mk Vs flew 'cab rank' patrols in support of ground forces, moving up to airfields in France and Belgium as the Germans fell back. In addition, they engaged in combat the Luftwaffe's Messerschmitt Me 262 jet fighters, 20 of which were destroyed before VE-Day.

An echelon of Tempests flies from the busy RAF Central Fighter Establishment (CFE) at West Raynham in 1945, from where most of the RAF's trials and evaluations with fighter aircraft were conducted. All the aircraft shown here are Mk V Series IIs – SN328, SN108 and EJ884. The nearest aircraft, SN328, has eight of the lengthened rocket rails fitted.

Although plans were made for 50 Tempest Mk IIs to be sent to the Far East in May 1945, to operate with Tiger Force against the Japanese, the war in the Pacific ended before these aircraft were ready for service. Wing Commander Beamont was to have commanded the wing, and it was he who flew the leading aircraft in the Victory Fly Past over London on 8 June 1946, No. 54 Squadron at Chilbolton having re-equipped with the Mk II in November 1945.

Specification

Tempest Mk V

Type: single-seat fighter/fighter-bomber
Powerplant: one 2,180-hp (1626-kW) Napier Sabre IIA inline piston engine
Performance: maximum speed 426 mph (686 km/h) at 18,500 ft (5639 m); service ceiling 36,500 ft (11125 m); maximum range 1,530 miles (2462 km)
Weights: empty 9,000 lb (4082 kg); maximum take-off 13,540 lb (6142 kg)
Dimensions: span 41 ft 0 in (12.50 m); length 33 ft 8 in (10.26 m); height 16 ft 1 in (4.90 m); wing area 302 sq ft (28.06 m²)
Armament: four 20-mm cannon, plus two 500-lb (227-kg) or two 1,000-lb (454-kg) bombs, or rocket projectiles

Two Tempests tuck up their undercarriage on take-off in July 1944 for a fighter sweep over the Caen area in northern France. The Tempest's performance enabled it to gain a good ratio of kills against the Me 262 jet fighter.

Hawker Typhoon

Although, figuratively speaking, the Hawker Typhoon was little more than an unreliable breeze in its early days, there is no doubt that by the summer of 1944 it had become one of the strongest forces in the RAF's inventory.

Design of this aircraft had been initiated in 1937 by Sydney Camm, who anticipated that the Air Ministry would shortly be seeking a successor to the Hawker Hurricane. Nevertheless, this interest probably came a little earlier than even he had expected with the issue of Air Ministry Specification F.18/37. This called for a 12-gun interceptor to be powered by either a Rolls-Royce Vulture or a Napier Sabre, both 24-cylinder engines, and with much of the basic design work completed it was decided to proceed with the final design of two fighters. One was to be powered by the Vulture: this ultimately became known as the Tornado but, like other Vulture-engined projects, was to become the subject of extensive redesign when further development of the Vulture engine was abandoned by Rolls-Royce.

The Sabre-engined version was to become known as the Typhoon and it, in its turn, was to suffer serious development problems, primarily as a result of its chosen powerplant. This, however, was to survive the teething troubles, for the Napier company was able to devote more effort to its development than Rolls-Royce could spare for the Vulture, for the latter was committed to the production and improvement of the Merlin engine in unprecedented numbers. The Merlin had to have every priority, for so much depended on it.

As testing of the two Typhoon prototypes was underway in the spring of 1941, the first major production order was placed for 250 Typhoon Mk Is. Hawker sub-contracted this order to Gloster Aircraft, of which this Mk IA was the fifth production example to fly.

The Typhoon prototype was flown for the first time on 24 February 1940, but encountered indifference in official circles. This was inevitable, of course, in the traumatic period of the war in which its early flight programme took place, for within 10 weeks of the prototype's first flight the Germans had started their attack against western Europe. Within no time at all the UK had its back to the wall, and the only interest shown by the Air Ministry was for the manufacture and delivery of every possible example of the Hurricane, Supermarine Spitfire and Merlin engine. This was considered essential to mount a spirited defence against the anticipated invasion of Britain, which then seemed the inevitable corollary to German occupation of the Low Countries and France.

Adding to the difficulties of the times, and selection of a powerplant which was then both unorthodox and new, Hawker was discovering a few problems of its own. The first major one came on 9 May 1940, for a routine test of the first prototype nearly ended in disaster when the fuselage suffered a structural failure in flight, and there was a loss of

***Left:** In September 1941 No. 56 (Fighter) Squadron introduced the Typhoon to operational service. However, it became increasingly evident that the aircraft had many major problems, of which the most serious was a structural failure of a rear fuselage joint, costing the lives of a number of RAF and test pilots.*

***Below:** Funded by the 'Fellowship of the Bellows' of Brazil, these nine Typhoon Mk IBs were handed over to No. 193 Squadron by the Brazilian Ambassador. The squadron flew the Typhoon between January 1943 until August 1945, and from D-Day flew almost entirely ground-attack sorties from bases in the continent as the Allies advanced eastwards.*

Although the machine-gun-armed Mk IA was the first variant to enter service, it was the four-cannon-armed Mk IB which became the definitive model. It used the cannon with great effect to supplement bombs and rocket projectiles in the ground-attack role.

a month before investigation and remedial action put the prototype back on the flight line. This aircraft had a 12 machine-gun wing, and was to be designated in production form as the **Typhoon Mk IA**, the first production example being flown on 27 May 1941. This aircraft had been built by Gloster Aircraft at Hucclecote, the company having been given responsibility for construction of the Typhoon from the outset, with the parent company scheduled to manufacture only a token batch.

A little over three weeks before this latter event, on 3 May 1941, the second prototype had been flown. This had different armament, the wing housing four 20-mm cannon, and production aircraft in this configuration were to be designated **Typhoon Mk IB**. Early production aircraft were almost entirely Mk IAs, with occasional Mk IBs coming off the line, but ultimately the cannon armament was regarded as the more important and was produced in greater numbers.

In this form the Typhoon was a cantilever low-wing monoplane of all-metal construction, the wing having Frise-type ailerons and split trailing-edge flaps. The fuselage was of what had then become standard Hawker construction, with the centre-region built up of steel tubes and the aft fuselage a monocoque stressed-skin structure. The tail unit was a conventional cantilever structure, and the wide-track

Armed with eight rocket projectiles, this Typhoon Mk IB of No. 257 Squadron departs for a raid on German radio installations near Boulogne. This example features the improved single-piece sliding cockpit canopy which replaced the earlier 'greenhouse' hood.

Hawker Typhoon Mk IB cutaway

1 Starboard navigation light
2 Starboard aileron
3 Fixed trim tab
4 Aileron hinge control
5 Landing lamp
6 Ammunition boxes
7 Starboard 20-mm Hispano Mk II cannon
8 Split trailing-edge flaps
9 Starboard main fuel tank, capacity 40 Imp gal (182 litres)
10 Self-sealing leading-edge fuel tank, capacity 35 Imp gal (159 litres)
11 Cannon barrel fairings
12 Rocket launcher rails
13 60-lb (27-kg) ground attack rockets
14 Main undercarriage leg fairing
15 Starboard mainwheel
16 de Havilland four-bladed propeller
17 Air intake
18 Propeller pitch change mechanism
19 Spinner
20 Armoured spinner backplate
21 Coolant tank, capacity 7¼ Imp gal (33 litres)

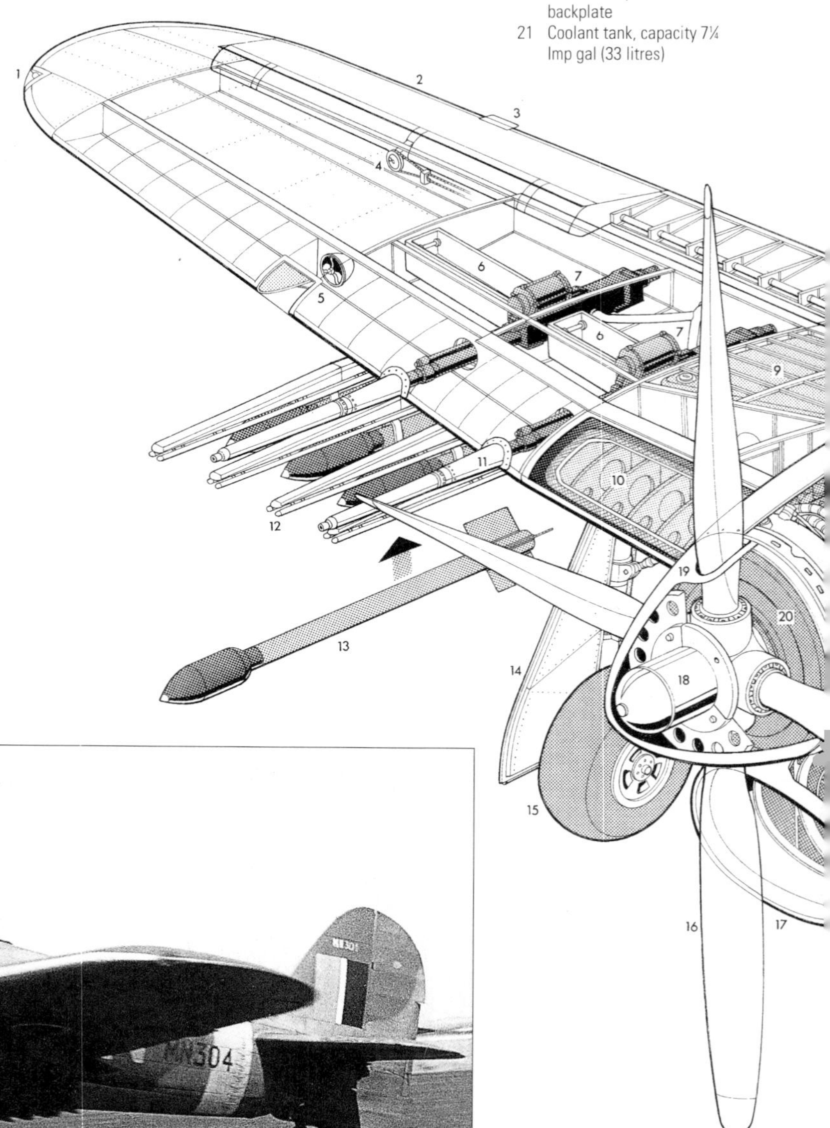

Hawker Typhoon

Featuring the 'car door' style access on the starboard side of the fuselage, this Typhoon Mk IB served with No. 3 Squadron from West Malling during May and June 1943. During this period the squadron flew ground-attack sorties, Rhubarbs and night intruder missions.

22 Supercharger ram air intake
23 Oil radiator
24 Coolant radiator
25 Radiator shutter
26 Engine mounting block
27 Tubular steel engine support framework
28 Exhaust stubs
29 Napier Sabre II, 24-cylinder flat H engine
30 Engine cowlings
31 Cartridge starter
32 Engine compartment fireproof bulkhead
33 Oxygen bottle
34 Gun heating air duct
35 Hydraulic reservoir
36 Footboards
37 Rudder pedals

47 Forward fuselage steel tube construction
48 Pilot's seat
49 Safety harness
50 Back and head armour plate
51 Pneumatic system air bottle
52 Rearward-sliding canopy cover
53 Aft fuselage joint
54 Canopy rails
55 Radio transmitter/receiver
56 Fuselage double frame
57 Whip aerial
58 Fuselage skinning
59 Starboard tailplane
60 Starboard elevator
61 Elevator trim tab
62 Fin leading edge

63 Fin construction
64 Rudder sternpost
65 Fabric-covered rudder construction
66 Rudder trim tab
67 Tail navigation light
68 Elevator trim tab
69 Port tailplane construction
70 Tailplane spar attachments
71 Tailwheel hydraulic jack
72 Forward-retracting tailwheel
73 Dowty oleo-pneumatic tailwheel strut
74 Tailplane spar fixing double bulkhead
75 Tailplane attachment joint strap
76 External strengthening fishplates

77 Elevator mass balance
78 Elevator cross shaft
79 Cable guides
80 Tailplane control cables
81 Rear fuselage frame and stringer construction
82 Wingroot fillet
83 Spar root pin joints
84 Undercarriage door hydraulic jack
85 Mainwheel door
86 Main undercarriage bay

93 20-mm Hispano Mk II cannon
94 Ammunition feed drum
95 Ammunition boxes, 140 rounds per gun

105 Gun camera
106 Camera port
107 Landing lamp
108 1,000-lb (454-kg) bomb

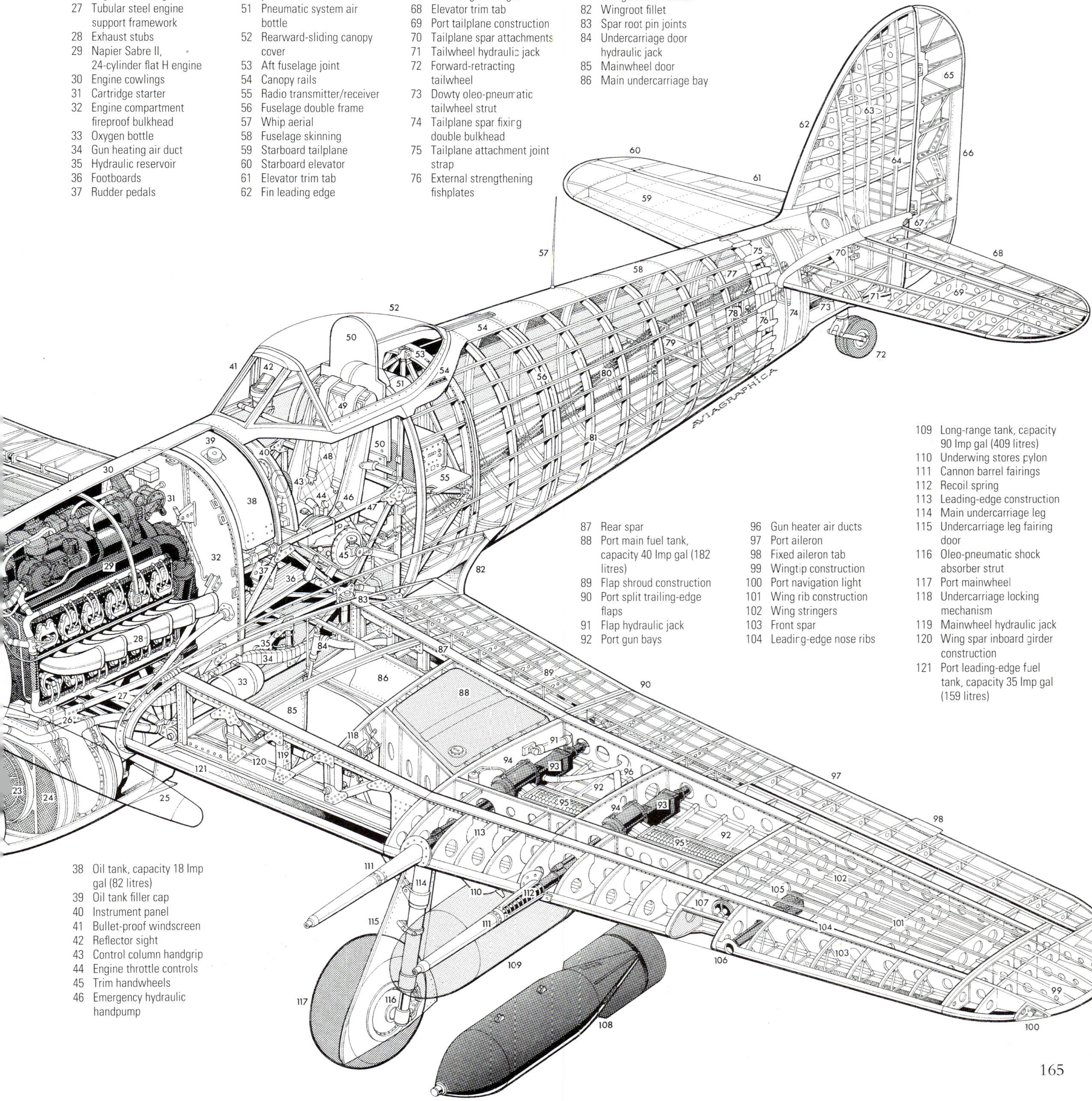

109 Long-range tank, capacity 90 Imp gal (409 litres)
110 Underwing stores pylon
111 Cannon barrel fairings
112 Recoil spring
113 Leading-edge construction
114 Main undercarriage leg
115 Undercarriage leg fairing door
116 Oleo-pneumatic shock absorber strut
117 Port mainwheel
118 Undercarriage locking mechanism
119 Mainwheel hydraulic jack
120 Wing spar inboard girder construction
121 Port leading-edge fuel tank, capacity 35 Imp gal (159 litres)

87 Rear spar
88 Port main fuel tank, capacity 40 Imp gal (182 litres)
89 Flap shroud construction
90 Port split trailing-edge flaps
91 Flap hydraulic jack
92 Port gun bays

96 Gun heater air ducts
97 Port aileron
98 Fixed aileron tab
99 Wingtip construction
100 Port navigation light
101 Wing rib construction
102 Wing stringers
103 Front spar
104 Leading-edge nose ribs

38 Oil tank, capacity 18 Imp gal (82 litres)
39 Oil tank filler cap
40 Instrument panel
41 Bullet-proof windscreen
42 Reflector sight
43 Control column handgrip
44 Engine throttle controls
45 Trim handwheels
46 Emergency hydraulic handpump

Hawker Typhoon

Due to major problems with the structure and Napier Sabre powerplant, the Typhoon underwent many hours of test and development trials. This Mk IB had its serial obscured by the wartime censor.

Below: Carrying a 500-lb (227-kg) bomb beneath each wing, this Mk IB served with No. 181 Squadron. During the summer of 1943 the squadron used this weapon on many dive-bombing raids against German airfields in France.

landing gear of the retractable tailwheel type. In its later developed form for ground-attack, the pilot had the protection of armour fore and aft, plus a bullet-proof windscreen.

The first production examples began to enter RAF service in September 1941, initially with No. 56 (Fighter) Squadron, and Typhoons were delivered also to the Air Fighting Development Unit. Away from the Gloster factory, it was soon discovered that the Typhoon's problems had by no means been eradicated. As increasing numbers were delivered to the RAF, there was a corresponding escalation of the accident rate. This was not confined to service units, however, for a number of Gloster's test pilots were killed in accidents, and it was suggested at the Air Ministry that the type should be withdrawn from service.

This did not happen, however, for Hawker was able to discover the cause of the problem: fatigue failure at a rear fuselage joint had been responsible for the loss of the complete tail unit of an alarming number of aircraft. But even the elimination of this failing was not to represent the end of the aircraft's teething troubles, for high-speed buffeting and aileron reversals were being experienced, together with continuing engine failures. But by the end of 1942 the worst was over, and the RAF was able to take a less jaundiced look at its new interceptor.

However enthusiastic pilots might be about this or that aspect of the Typhoon's capabilities, there was unanimous agreement that it had an abysmal rate of climb and very disappointing high-altitude performance. The Typhoon's forte was high speed at low altitude, for in this segment of the flight envelope it was supreme among all Allied fighters. These factors had encouraged its deployment in a low-level interception role in late 1941, when German use of the high-speed Focke-Wulf Fw 190 to make hit-and-run attacks against Britain's south and east coast military installations and strategic targets was becoming rather more than a nuisance. The Typhoon quickly showed its capability in this role when No. 609 Squadron took its aircraft to RAF Manston in November 1941, and within a week had destroyed four Fw 190s.

This early and highly successful use of the Typhoon in a low-level role was to encourage further development along the same lines, despite the fact that at that time the cause of mounting Typhoon losses had not been determined. Once this problem was out of the way, and the early and unreliable Sabre I engine replaced by the much improved

Above: Ground crew add their own personal message to a 500-lb bomb beneath the wing of a Typhoon Mk IB from No. 245 (Northern Rhodesia) Squadron. In the spring of 1944 the squadron's Typhoons made numerous raids against German V-1 launch sites (codename Noball) as well as flying interdiction and bomber escort sorties.

Right: This Typhoon from No. 175 Squadron is being bombed up for a Rhubarb attack sortie with two short-tail 500-lb (227-kg) bombs. Although still fitted with the 'car door' style cockpit canopy, this aircraft does have the smoothly-faired cannon barrels which were introduced to increase the aircraft's maximum speed by reducing the effects of drag.

Wing structure
The Typhoon's wing was built around an immensely strong two-spar structure allowing the aircraft to carry up to 2,000-lb (907-kg) of bombs. The Mk IB's armament consisted of four 20-mm Hispano cannon, each with 140 rounds held in boxes outboard of the cannon.

Hawker Typhoon Mk IB

Part of the fifth production batch of 800 aircraft built by Gloster Aircraft, this Mk IB served with No. 193 Squadron in 1944-45. During this period the squadron was almost entirely engaged on tactical bombing and rocket-attack sorties in support of the advancing Allied armies. The squadron operated the Typhoon until it disbanded at Hildesheim, Germany on 31 August 1945.

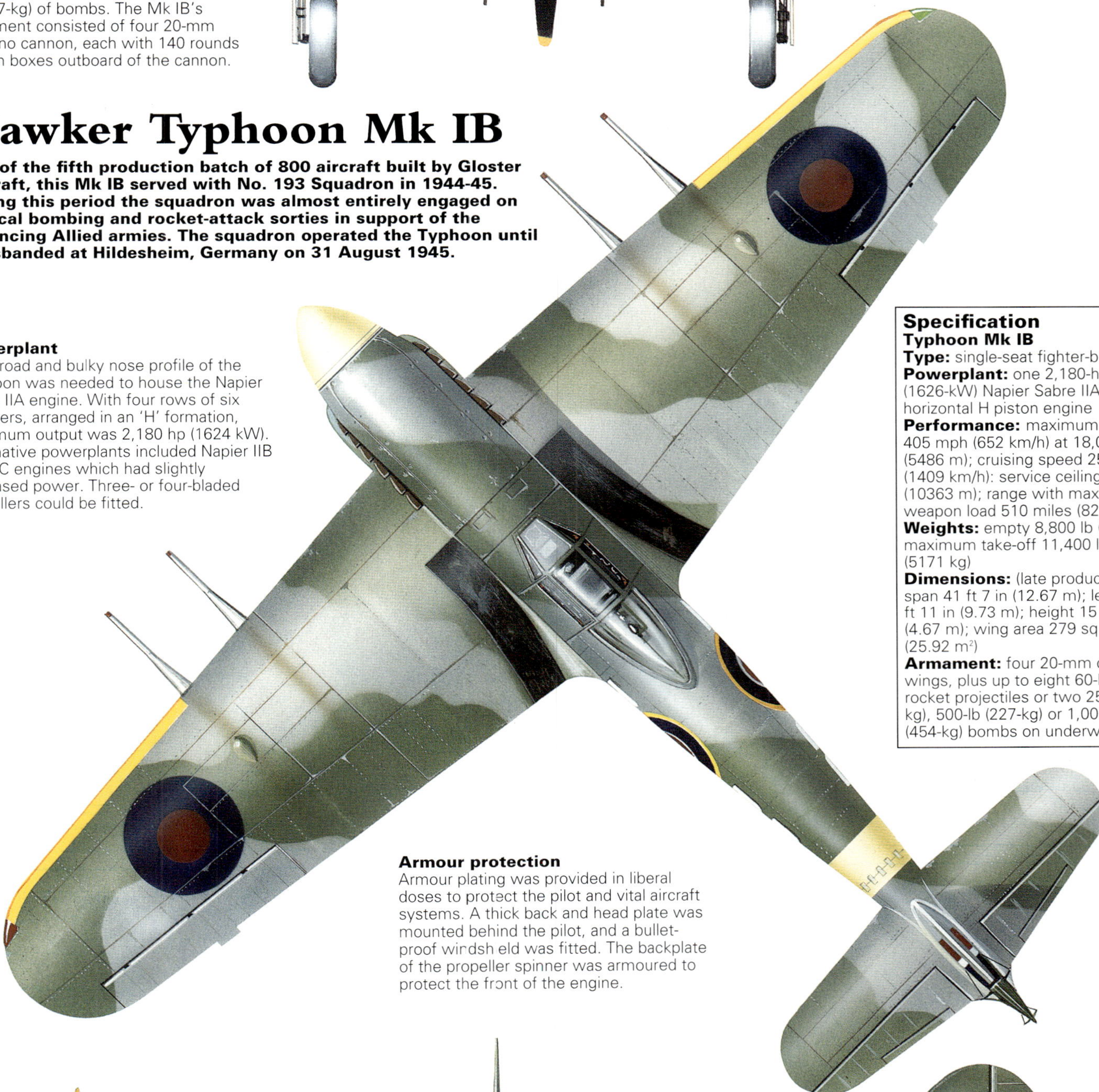

Powerplant
The broad and bulky nose profile of the Typhoon was needed to house the Napier Sabre IIA engine. With four rows of six cylinders, arranged in an 'H' formation, maximum output was 2,180 hp (1624 kW). Alternative powerplants included Napier IIB and IIC engines which had slightly increased power. Three- or four-bladed propellers could be fitted.

Specification
Typhoon Mk IB
Type: single-seat fighter-bomber
Powerplant: one 2,180-hp (1626-kW) Napier Sabre IIA horizontal H piston engine
Performance: maximum speed 405 mph (652 km/h) at 18,000 ft (5486 m); cruising speed 254 mph (1409 km/h): service ceiling 34,000 ft (10363 m); range with maximum weapon load 510 miles (821 km)
Weights: empty 8,800 lb (3992 kg); maximum take-off 11,400 lb (5171 kg)
Dimensions: (late production): span 41 ft 7 in (12.67 m); length 31 ft 11 in (9.73 m); height 15 ft 4 in (4.67 m); wing area 279 sq ft (25.92 m²)
Armament: four 20-mm cannon in wings, plus up to eight 60-lb (27-kg) rocket projectiles or two 250-lb (113-kg), 500-lb (227-kg) or 1,000-lb (454-kg) bombs on underwing racks

Armour protection
Armour plating was provided in liberal doses to protect the pilot and vital aircraft systems. A thick back and head plate was mounted behind the pilot, and a bullet-proof windshield was fitted. The backplate of the propeller spinner was armoured to protect the front of the engine.

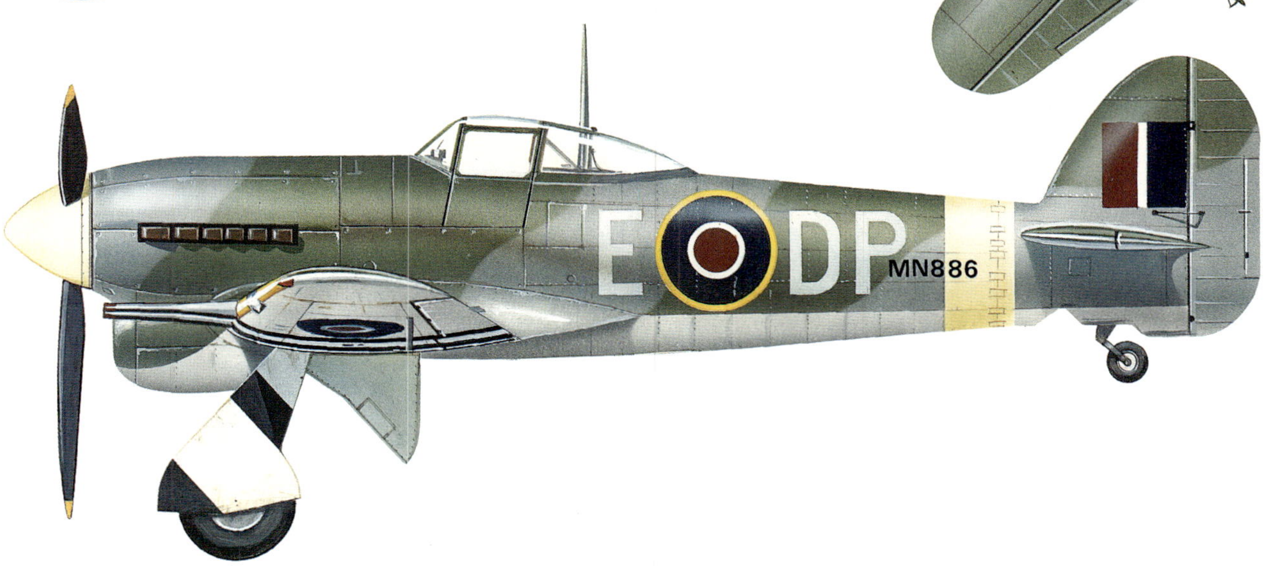

Fitted with the clear-view hood, this Typhoon Mk IB served with No. 128 Squadron. This unit operated the Typhoon from November 1942 until the close of the war in Europe, and was heavily involved in close air support operations during the Allied advance in Europe.

2,180-hp (1626-kW) Sabre IIA, it became possible to utilise the growing potential of this aircraft to the full. By the end of 1942 the Typhoon could no longer be regarded purely as a defensive aircraft, for it had become equipped to serve most effectively in an offensive role, thanks to its ability to carry two 250-lb (113-kg), 500-lb (227-kg), or 1,000-lb (454-kg) bombs on underwing racks. These weapons, in conjunction with four wing-mounted 20-mm cannon, were to make the Typhoon an important fighter-bomber, and towards the end of 1942 No. 609 Squadron pioneered the use of these aircraft in a night-intruder role. From that period, used primarily by day, but also by night, Typhoons in service with Nos 174, 181, 245 and 609 Squadrons ranged over France and the Low Countries, playing havoc with German communications. Their low-level, high-speed capability provided a considerable degree of immunity from both German fighters and ground weapons.

During 1943, following an extended series of trials and development, the Hurricane had become the first Allied aircraft to be armed with rocket projectiles, using them operationally for the first time on 2 September 1943. Similarly equipped, the Typhoon was to realise its full potential, and by the end of 1943 was operating in conjunction with fighter-bomber squadrons based along Britain's south coast, their combined efforts limiting very considerably German coastal shipping. Even more effective were the low-level attacks which these units mounted almost continuously in the early months of 1944 – before D-Day – using the most efficient combination of rockets, bombs and guns to harass German communications by day and night. The aim was not only to attack and eliminate the trains or vehicles moving on rail or road, but also to destroy or damage bridges, tunnels and major junctions. At the height of this campaign up to 150 locomotives were being destroyed each month, and in their first few months of such operations No. 609 Squadron accounted for 100 locomotives for the loss of only two aircraft. The resulting chaotic conditions on D-Day, when it was only with extreme difficulty that the Germans could move troops and essential supplies in the areas behind the Normandy beach-heads, were to prove just how successful this cross-Channel interdiction had been.

There was to be little change in the Typhoon during the last year of war in Europe, other than progressive improvements in the installed powerplant. As mentioned above, the Sabre I had been displaced by the Sabre IIA, and this in turn was to be followed by the 2,200-hp (1641-kW) Sabre IIB, and finally the 2,260-hp (1685-kW) Sabre IIC. Propellers could be either three- or four-bladed units of the constant-speed type, supplied by de Havilland or Rotol. Variants were meagre in number, comprising a single **NF.Mk IB** night-fighter converted from a fighter-bomber in late 1941, and equipped with AI Mk VI interception radar, and a small quantity of tactical reconnaissance aircraft. These latter, produced in two versions during 1944, were both designated **Typhoon FR.Mk IB**. One carried two vertical cameras and retained its full four-cannon armament, the other substituted a forward facing ciné recorder for the port inner cannon. When production ended in 1944, more than 3,200 Typhoons had been built, all but about 20 by Gloster Aircraft. They had all been delivered to the RAF, but some were allocated for use by RCAF and RNZAF units operating alongside the RAF in Europe.

By D-Day, utilisation of the Typhoon was at its peak, with no fewer than 26 squadrons serving in the 2nd Tactical Air Force, and these were to play a significant role in the break-out from Caen. Their contribution to the German debacle at the Falaise gap was monumental. With no danger from German fighters, the Typhoon destroyed columns of troops and machinery almost at will.

Such had become the capability of the Typhoon, a type which was so unreliable at the time of its operational debut that it had almost been withdrawn from service. None, however, was to remain in operational use for any considerable time after VE-Day, having been replaced by Hawker Tempests.

As the Allied forces advanced at an increasing rate, Typhoons operated from former German-held airfields in France, Belgium and Germany. This Typhoon Mk IB receives attention from the 2nd Tactical Air Force Repair and Salvage Unit at an airfield which had been wrecked by the Germans before their hurried departure.

Built in early 1944 by Gloster Aircraft, which by then was producing an average of one Typhoon a day, this rocket-armed Mk IB served with No. 247 Squadron. During a hectic period of fighting in mid-1944, when based at Coulombes in France, the squadron flew 410 offensive sorties in one month.

Lockheed Hudson

From 1939 until 1944, the Lockheed Hudson was the standard Coastal Command shore-based aircraft, used by many squadrons for anti-submarine and shipping patrols, and strikes. This Hudson Mk III from No. 48 Squadron operated from Stornoway, Skitten, Wick and Sumburgh in Scotland for patrols over the North Atlantic during 1941-42.

At short notice, for a visit by the British Purchasing Commission in April 1938, the Lockheed company prepared a mock-up to show how its Model 14 twin-engined civil transport might be adapted for military use – perhaps as a navigation trainer. The Commission, however, saw wider possibilities for this B14 project as a maritime reconnaissance aircraft (a successor for the Avro Anson), and thus was born the Hudson – Lockheed's first warplane. As the **Model B14L** and, later, **Model 214**, the design was finalised: a low/mid-wing monoplane with characteristic twin fins and rudders, a Boulton Paul dorsal turret, two forward-firing guns, a four-man crew including navigator/bomb-aimer in the extreme nose, and up to 3,300 lb (1500 kg) of bombs in the fuselage. Later, there would be provision for a fifth crewman and ventral and beam guns.

An initial order was placed on 23 June 1938 for 200 B14Ls, with an option on 250 more. The first of these flew on 10 December 1938 and, with Wright GR-1820-G102A Cyclone engines, was representative of the **Hudson Mk I**. Deliveries began in February 1939 and, with some aircraft going to No. 1 OTU for crew training, No. 224 (GR) Squadron became the first to equip on the type. From Leuchars, in Scotland, this squadron was flying patrols over the North Sea from the first day of the war. It was soon joined by No. 223 Squadron at Leuchars, followed by Nos 220 at Thornaby, No. 206 at Bircham Newton and No. 269 at Wick, all in Coastal Command. From early

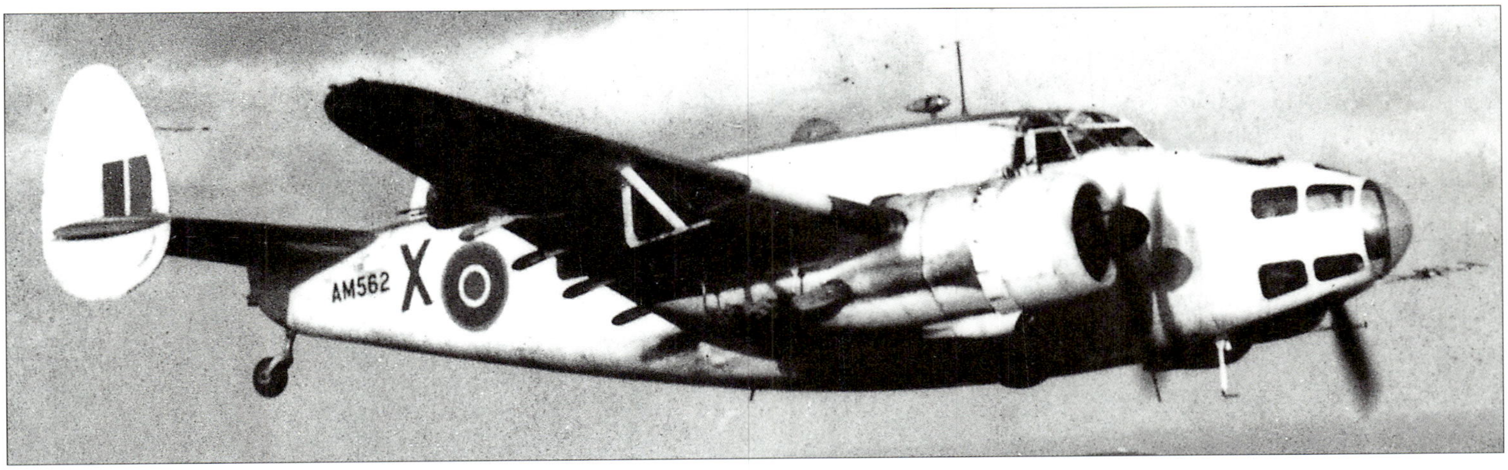

Above: Three-hundred and fifty Hudson Mk Vs were delivered to the RAF from July 1941. This version was powered by two 1,200-hp (895-kW) Pratt & Whitney Twin Wasp engines in place of the 900-hp (671-kW) Wright Cyclones of the earlier marks. This example served with No. 5 Operational Training Unit (OTU).

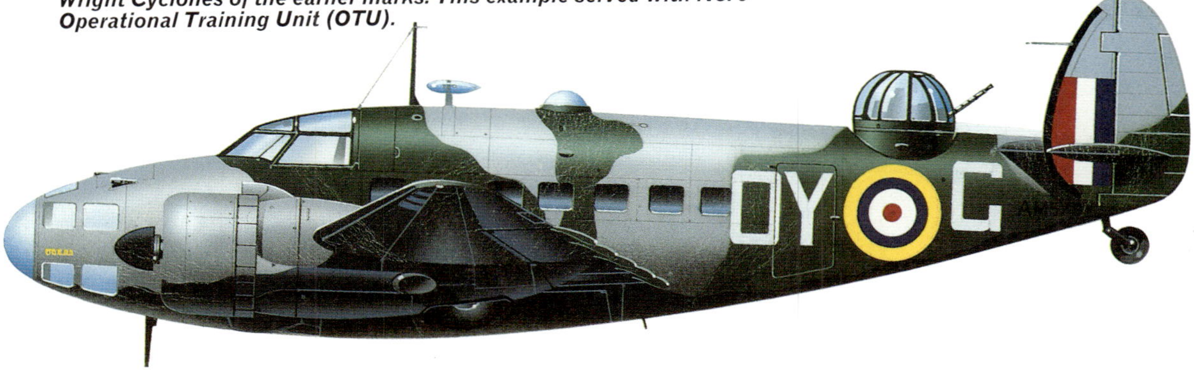

Hudson Mk V AM579 'OY-G' operated with No. 48 Squadron Coastal Command, based at Stornoway in the Outer Hebrides in early 1942. During this period the Hudsons operated over the North Sea, attacking shipping off the Norwegian coast. The squadron received its first Hudson Mk IIIs and Mk Vs in September 1941, and the definitive Mk VI version was delivered in November 1942.

Lockheed Hudson

This long-range Hudson Mk III, V9158, was engaged on air-sea rescue duties during 1942 with No. 279 Squadron based at Sturgate. Among specialised equipment carried was a ventrally-mounted Mk 3 airborne lifeboat, designed by the celebrated yachtsman Uffa Fox.

In August 1941 Coastal Command adopted a colour scheme of matt white applied to the vertical surfaces and gloss white applied to the undersurfaces of its aircraft. The upper surfaces were painted in a dark green/ocean grey camouflage. This Hudson Mk VI served with Coastal Command in late 1942.

1940 onwards, ASV Mk I radar began to appear on the Hudson Mk Is, of which Lockheed built a total of 351; from this total, the RAF diverted 28 to the RCAF and two to the RAAF. A few Hudson Mk Is served as six-passenger transports with No. 24 Squadron, and others made an important contribution to the work of the Photographic Development Unit in Europe and the Middle East.

The **Hudson Mk II** had some structural improvements, and flush riveting and/or spot welding on exterior surfaces for better aerodynamic performance. Only 20 were delivered to the RAF, followed by 428 **Hudson Mk III**s. The latter introduced the GR-1820-G205A engines in the Mk II airframe, and ventral and beam guns became standard. The first 187 became **Hudson Mk III(SR)** after the introduction of additional wing tanks, resulting in the subsequent 241 becoming **Hudson Mk III(LR)**. Following the introduction of Lend-Lease, the USAAC gave the designations **A-28** and **A-29** to variants of the Lockheed 214 for contractual purposes. Deliveries included 420 A-29s and 384 **A-29A**s, the latter with convertible troop interiors. Those that entered RAF service were designated **Hudson Mk IIIA** and were similar to the Hudson Mk III(LR), but many of these Lend-Lease supplies went to Commonwealth Air Forces.

Further British contracts had already covered 30 **Hudson Mk IV**s, which switched to Pratt & Whitney R-1830-SC3G engines, and 409 **Hudson Mk V**s, with these engines and all the definitive features of the Mk III. Through Lend-Lease, the RAF finally received 450 Lockheed **A-28A**s, which it designated **Hudson Mk VI**.

Delivery of all these aircraft (and others direct to the RAAF, including the **Hudson Mk IVA** version) allowed the Coastal Command squadrons already mentioned to maintain a high level of activity. They were joined in 1941 by four more – Nos 53, 59, 500 and 608 Squadrons converting from Blenheims – and by newly-formed No. 320 Squadron with Dutch personnel plus the Canadian-manned No. 407 Squadron. Finally, in 1942, No. 42 Sqn joined the Hudson force, which was now operating also from bases in the Far East, Iceland and Gibraltar. Combat effectiveness was enhanced in 1943 with the addition of eight 60-lb (27-kg) rocket projectiles carried underwing.

From late 1940 onwards, Hudsons also operated in the troop transport role in the Middle East (Nos 163, 217 and 267 Squadrons) and in India (Nos 194 and 353 Squadrons). No. 161 Sqn in Europe and No. 357 Sqn in India flew Hudsons on special duties in support of agents and guerrillas behind enemy lines. Later, as the Hudson was replaced in the front-line squadrons, No. 269 Sqn added meteorological reconnaissance to its duties, and Nos 517, 519, 520 and 521 Sqns continued in this role up to the end of the war. For air-sea rescue, No. 251 Squadron used Hudsons equipped to carry an airborne lifeboat.

Specification
Hudson Mk VI
Type: five-seat maritime general reconnaissance aircraft
Powerplant: two 1,200-hp (895-kW) Pratt & Whitney R-1830-S3C4-G Twin Wasp radial piston engines
Performance: maximum speed 261 mph (420 km/h) at 15,000 ft (4572 m); service ceiling 27,000 ft (8230 m); range 2,160 miles (3476 km); endurance 6 hours 55 mins
Weights: empty 12,929 lb (5864 kg); loaded 18,500 lb (8391 kg)
Dimensions: span 65 ft 6 in (19.96 m); length 44 ft 4 in (13.51 m); height 11 ft 11 in (3.63 m); wing area 551 sq ft (51.19 m^2)
Armament: twin 0.303-in (7.7-mm) machine-guns in fixed forward and dorsal turret and one 0.303-in (7.7-mm) machine-gun in ventral position, and option of two 0.303-in (7.7-mm) machine-guns in beam positions, plus up to 1,000 lb (454 kg) of bombs or depth charges

An uncoded Hudson Mk VI of No. 608 Squadron is seen carrying ASV Mk II search radar and four rockets on rails underneath each wing. Rockets were used successfully by Hudsons against U-boats in the Mediterranean.

Lockheed Lodestar

Closely related to the Model 14 civil transport – which provided the basis for the RAF's Hudson – Lockheed's **Model 18** combined a new, lengthened fuselage with the same wings, tail unit and (in the first model) engines. Named the Lodestar, a prototype flew on 21 September 1939, and the first production example on 2 February 1940. With seats for 14 passengers, and a crew of three, the Lodestar quickly attracted BOAC's attention, and on behalf of the airline the British Purchasing Commission ordered nine Model 18-07 Lodestars to operate principally on the trans-Africa route, from 1941 onwards.

The BOAC fleet was quickly supplemented by 16 more aircraft purchased (through the RAF) on the civil market in the US and South Africa, and embracing **Models 18-07**, **18-10**, **18-14**, **18-40** and **18-50**, with various engines and accommodation differences. Eventually, most of these were brought up to a common **Model 18-56** standard, with Wright R-1820-87 engines. As well as the African routes, these transports were used to fly supplies into Malta and to operate the hazardous link between Scotland and Sweden.

During 1943, five of the BOAC aircraft were returned to the RAF to operate as **Lodestar Mk I**s. Meanwhile, a Lend-Lease contract for 25 aircraft had been arranged, comprising 10 impressed (in the US) Model 18-07s, called **C-59** by the USAAF and **Lodestar Mk IA** by the RAF, and 15 impressed Model 18-56s, called **C-60** by the USAAF and **Lodestar Mk II** by the RAF. Of these, the first three Mk IAs were retained by the USAAF; the remainder served primarily with Nos 117, 173, 267 Squadrons in the Middle East. A further Lend-Lease contract was to provide another 67 Lodestar Mk IIs, but only one aircraft in this later batch came to the UK; some, at least, of the balance remained in USAAF service.

Specification
Lodestar Mk II
Type: general transport and ambulance aircraft
Powerplant: two 1,200-hp (895-kW) Wright R-1820-87 Cyclone radial piston engines
Performance: maximum speed 266 mph (428 km/h) at 17,150 ft (5227 m); cruising speed 200 mph (322 km/h); service ceiling 30,100 ft (9174 m); maximum range 2,500 miles (4023 km)
Weights: empty 12,500 lb (5670 kg); maximum take-off 21,000 lb (9525 kg)
Dimensions: span 65 ft 6 in (19.96 m); length 49 ft 10 in (15.19 m); height 11 ft 11 in (3.63 m); wing area 551 sq ft (51.19 m²)

This Lodestar Mk II was supplied under Lend-Lease and was operated by No. 173 Squadron. The unit was tasked with VIP transport duties in the Middle East from July 1942.

Lockheed Ventura

Given the early operational success of the Hudson, which had evolved to meet a specific British requirement, Lockheed's interest in development of an improved variant was logical. Combining the operational aspects of the Hudson with the somewhat larger size of the Lockheed Model 18 Lodestar civil transport, the new aircraft was entrusted to the company's Vega division, where the prototype of the **Model 37** first flew on 31 July 1941. Compared with the Hudson, the new aircraft had a deeper, wider and longer fuselage, a ventral two-gun position, more powerful engines and an enlarged bomb-bay which would accommodate a 22-in (56-cm) torpedo. Provision was made for two 500-lb (227-kg) bombs, depth charges or fuel tanks under the wings.

The British Purchasing Commission placed two contracts for the new aircraft, to total 675. These eventually appeared as the **Ventura B.Mk I** (188) and the **Ventura B.Mk II** (160), with the remainder diverted to the US Navy and the RCAF. The Ventura Mk II was distinguished by the change from the commercial R-2800-S1A4G engines to the military R-2800-31. Further quantities were included in Lend-Lease supplies, but not all plans came to fruition: the **Ventura B.Mk IIA** would have been the same as the B.Mk II, and the **Ventura B.Mk IV** was to have been the US Navy **PV-1** in the day-bomber role.

Right: Additional 'muscle' for Coastal Command was provided by the Ventura GR.Mk II in late 1943 after the type's withdrawal from bombing duties.

Below: The late model Ventura GR.Mk V was based on the US Navy's PV-1 maritime patrol bomber. This example carries long-range tanks beneath the wings.

None of these was delivered; nor was the **Ventura GR.Mk III**, which would have been powered by Wright R-2600-13 Cyclones in place of the usual Pratt & Whitney engines. A Lend-Lease requisition for 550 GR.Mk IIIs was abandoned and the RAF serial numbers for all but the first 18 were re-allocated. There is, however, no evidence that even the first 18 were completed or delivered. Thus, the only other variant actually to reach the RAF was the **Ventura GR.Mk V**, which was the same as the intended B.Mk IV but adapted for the general reconnaissance role with Coastal Command; 228 were supplied.

At first seen by the RAF as a potential replacement for the Blenheim Mk IV in the night intruder role, the Ventura B.Mk I began to enter service with No. 21 Squadron in May 1942, but a switch to day operations was made before the first sortie on 3

November 1942, flying from Methwold. Two more squadrons, No. 464 (RAAF) and No. 487 (RNZAF), were equipped with Venturas at Feltwell.

The operational success of the Ventura in this role was marginal and heavy losses were suffered by the three squadrons. Such operations ended in September 1943, after which time use of the Ventura in the UK was limited to crew training at OTUs, some transport flights and meteorological duties (with No. 519 Squadron at Wick and No. 521 Squadron at Langham).

The introduction of the Ventura GR.Mk V, based on the US Navy's PV-1 maritime patrol bomber, brought the aircraft a new career, flying from a variety of bases in the Middle East. First to operate in this GR role was No. 13 Squadron in Tunisia, but the principal users became No. 500 Sqn of the RAF along with No. 459 Sqn, RAAF, and Nos 17, 22 and 27 of the SAAF. Primarily flying patrols, these squadrons also engaged in some anti-shipping strikes and attacks on airfields. Briefly, late in 1943, No. 624 Sqn in Algeria used Ventura Mk IIs for agent and supply drops to resistance forces in Italy and southern France.

More than half of all the RAF Venturas were assigned to the SAAF, for use by those squadrons flying the type in North Africa, and by other units in South Africa itself. The Ventura remained in service with the SAAF for many years after the war had ended.

This Ventura Mk II, AE939 'SB-G', of No. 464 Squadron, RAAF, was based at Feltwell in late 1942. Heavy losses forced Bomber Command to withdraw the Ventura Mk II from operations after a year.

Specification
Ventura B.Mk II
Type: five-seat light bomber
Powerplant: two 2,000-hp (1491-kW) Pratt & Whitney GR-2800-S1A4-G Double Wasp radial piston engines
Performance: maximum speed 300 mph (483 km/h); cruising speed 260 mph (418 km/h); service ceiling 25,000 ft (7620 m); range 950 miles (1529 km)
Weights: empty 17,250 lb (7824 kg); loaded 26,000 lb (11793 kg)
Dimensions: span 65 ft 6 in (19.96 m); length 51 ft 3 in (15.62 m); height 11 ft 11 in (3.63 m); wing area 551 sq ft (51.19 m²)

No. 21 Squadron received Venturas in mid-1942 and used them on daylight operations, leading to the daring raid on the Philips plant at Eindhoven on 6 December 1942. However, the type was not really suited to this type of operation. AE924 was based at Methwold in mid-1943.

Martin 162 Mariner

Continuing a long line of patrol flying-boats designed and built for the US Navy, Glenn Martin's **XPBM-1** flew on 18 February 1939, providing a modern alternative to the highly successful Consolidated PBY Catalina. In the event, the Mariner – as the Martin product was named in due course – did not see such large-scale production or service as the 'Cat', but it was destined to remain in service for a decade or more after the war ended.

A batch of 35 **Mariner GR.Mk Is** was allocated to the RAF through Lend-Lease, comprising examples of both the **PBM-3C** and the **PBM-3S**, the latter being the more specialised long-range anti-submarine version. Both could carry ASV radar in a large dorsal fairing just aft of the cockpit, but the -3S dispensed with dorsal and tail turrets in favour of greater range. Of the aircraft allocated to the RAF, 28 were received, and seven were undelivered. The designation **Mariner GR.Mk II** was reserved for the lightened anti-submarine version but was not used in practice.

Testing of one of the first Mariners at the MAEE at Helensburgh showed the aircraft to have good handling on water and a reasonable performance. In the air, however, elevator control was reported to be heavy, and aileron response slow. For these and other reasons the Mariner found little favour with the RAF and in the end no operational use was made of these flying-boats. However, before this decision was made, No. 524 Squadron was formed at Oban, on 20 October 1943, to operate the type.

All of the Mariners had arrived in the UK by January 1944 and 10 were delivered to No. 524 Squadron, but the decision not to use the type led to the squadron's disbandment by the end of the year. A few other Mariners were acquired by No. 45 Group in Canada, but all were returned to the US during 1944 or early in 1945.

Above: Mariner JX117 is seen 'beached' at Beaumaris in Anglesey. It was at this base that Saunders-Roe prepared the flying-boats, after delivery to the UK, for service with the RAF.

Left: Ten Mariners were delivered to No. 524 Squadron at Oban, but the squadron had disbanded by the end of 1944 and all the aircraft were returned to the US.

Specification
Mariner GR.Mk I
Type: maritime patrol/transport flying-boat
Powerplant: two 1,700-hp (1268-kW) Wright R-2600-12 Cyclone radial piston engines
Performance: maximum speed 211 mph (340 km/h); cruising speed 147 mph (237 km/h); service ceiling 19,800 ft (6035 m); range 2240 miles (3605 km)
Weights: empty 33,175 lb (15048 kg); loaded 58,000 lb (26308 kg)
Dimensions: span 118 ft 0 in (35.97 m); length 79 ft 10 in (24.33 m); height 28 ft 10 in (8.79 m); wing area 1,400 sq ft (130.06 m²)

Martin Maryland

Unsuccessful in a USAAC fly-off to select a new light bomber (the Douglas A-20 Havoc was the contest winner), the Martin **167** had flown in prototype form on 14 March 1939, with the Army designation **XA-22**. Looked at, but rejected, by the British Purchasing Commission, the Martin 167 would have been consigned to obscurity had it not been for France's desperate need for ground-attack/light bombers in 1939. Orders were placed for two batches of Martin **167F-3**s, totalling 215 aircraft. The three-crew aircraft were armed with four FN-Browning 0.3-in (7.62-mm) forward-firing machine-guns, and two each in a ventral position and a semi-retractable dorsal turret; a 1,200-lb (544-kg) internal bombload was supplemented by 560 lb (254 kg) under the wings.

With the collapse of French resistance in June 1940, Britain agreed to take over the remainder of the French order (50 aircraft) and confirmed an outstanding option for a further 150, which were built as the Martin **167B-4** and powered by Pratt & Whitney R-1830-SC3G engines. These were designated **Maryland Mk I** and **Maryland Mk II**, respectively. An additional 32 Marylands joined the RAF, and were presumably aircraft that had already been delivered to France in the Middle East and 'escaped' to Britain.

Starting in the autumn of 1940, the RAF used Marylands initially to equip No. 22 Squadron as a stop-gap for the Bristol Beaufort in the GR role. Before becoming operational, however, the Marylands were transferred to No. 431 Flight (which became No. 69 Squadron in January 1941) to fly in the strategic reconnaissance role from Malta. Such missions were flown successfully over enemy ports and airfields in Sicily, Libya and Italy throughout 1941 and 1942. Taking advantage of the forward-firing armament, No. 69 Squadron also flew its Marylands as night-fighters and on daylight patrols to intercept Luftwaffe transports supplying North Africa.

In the bomber role, Maryland Mk IIs were used by Nos 39 and 203 Sqns in the Western Desert, replacing Blenheims from the beginning of 1941 and early 1942, respectively. No. 233 Squadron served as the training unit for Marylands, and also used the type operationally in the Western Desert on strategic reconnaissance until January 1942. A few ex-French Marylands reached No. 8 Squadron in Aden, where they were also used for reconnaissance during the later months of 1940. Three Maryland Mk Is went to No. 771 Sqn, FAA, and one of these flew the sortie on 22 May 1941 that discovered that the *Bismarck* had put to sea, leading to the destruction of this German battleship.

Some 75 Marylands were transferred by the RAF to the SAAF, and these were used by several of the South African squadrons operating in the Western Desert, and by one in the coastal reconnaissance role in Madagascar.

Making a useful contibution to the Allies during the 1941 campaign in North Africa, the Maryland Mk I was a fast, long-range reconnaissance aircraft that was also employed as a light bomber.

Specification
Maryland Mk II
Type: four-seat light bomber/ reconnaissance aircraft
Powerplant: two 1,200-hp (895-kW) Pratt & Whitney R-1830-S3C4-G Twin Wasp radial piston engines
Performance: maximum speed 278 mph (447 km/h) at 11,800 ft (3597 m); service ceiling 31,000 ft (9449 m); maximum range 1,800 miles (2897 km)
Weights: empty 11,213 lb (5086 kg); loaded 16,809 lb (7624 kg)
Dimensions: span 61 ft 4 in (18.69 m); length 46 ft 8 in (14.22 m); height 15 ft 0 in (4.57 m); wing area 539 sq ft (50.07 m^2)
Armament: four forward-firing 0.303-in (7.7-mm) Browning machine-guns in wings and single 0.303-in (7.7-mm) Vickers K machine-guns in dorsal and ventral positions, plus up to 2,000 lb (907 kg) of bombs

Above: Martin Marylands were used for aerial reconnaissance of enemy ports and to report on shipping movements in the Mediterranean. It was a Maryland flown from Malta by Pilot Officer Warburton that spotted the Italian fleet at Taranto in November 1940.

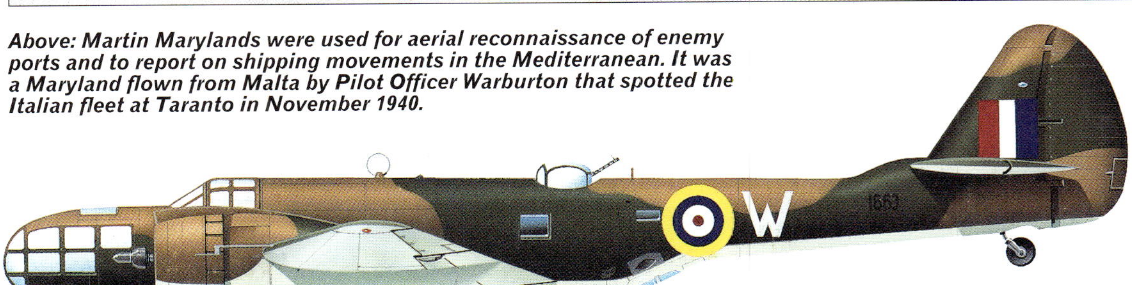

This Maryland Mk II of No. 24 Squadron, South African Air Force was based at Fuka, Egypt during May 1941. From 23 May, the squadron was one of three allocated to operations over Crete. Bostons replaced the Marylands in November 1941.

After the fall of France, the RAF took over the French order for Martin 167 reconnaissance bombers, known as the Maryland in RAF service. AR707, fitted with an Armstrong Whitworth turret, served on Malta with No. 431 Flight in 1941.

Martin 179 Marauder

This Marauder Mk III of No. 39 Squadron was based in southern Italy and flew with the Balkan Air Force. A total of 200 B-26Fs and 150 B-26Gs was supplied to the RAF under this designation.

Unusual in winning a USAAC production contract before construction and evaluation of a prototype, the Martin **B-26** emerged as one of the most significant medium bombers of World War II. First flown on 25 November 1940, the B-26 suffered more than its fair share of development problems both before and after its entry into service during 1941. These problems, and the urgent re-equipment needs of the US Army Air Force notwithstanding, provision was soon made for the supply of B-26s to Britain through Lend-Lease.

With no clear operational requirement for an aircraft like the B-26 in Europe, the RAF opted to deploy the Martin bomber in the Middle East. The initial supply comprised 52 **Marauder Mk I**s, of which three came to the UK for evaluation and the remainder were delivered direct to the Middle East from August 1942 onwards. These were of **B-26A** standard, with R-2800-9 or -39 engines and armament comprising a 0.5-in (12.7-mm) machine-gun in the nose, and two each in dorsal and tail turrets. The internal bomb-load could be supplemented by a 2,000-lb (908-kg) torpedo under the fuselage. The 19 **Marauder Mk IA**s were **B-26B-4**s with R-2800-43 engines and tropical filters; otherwise generally similar to the Mk Is, these were also sent straight to the Middle East, where No. 14 Squadron had converted from Blenheims to Marauders in Egypt to engage in maritime reconnaissance, mine-laying and anti-shipping strikes, often carrying torpedoes. Operational use began in November 1942, and the first successful torpedo attacks were made in January 1943. As the year progressed, long-range reconnaissance became one of the Marauder's primary missions, and considerable success was also achieved in intercepting and shooting down German and Italian transport aircraft supplying North Africa from Italy.

More B-26s reached the Middle East in 1943, comprising 100 **Marauder Mk II**s, these being **B-26C-30**s, which featured four 'package' guns on the forward fuselage sides, and a longer-span wing. These aircraft were used almost exclusively to equip Nos 12 and 24 Squadrons of the SAAF in Libya and Italy. Finally, in the second half of 1944, came 350 **Marauder Mk III**s, which comprised a mix of **B-26F** and **B-26G** models, the principal new feature of which was an increase in wing incidence angle to produce some handling benefits; provision for torpedo carriage was removed.

The Marauder Mk IIIs were used to reinforce the SAAF squadrons in Italy and to form two more, Nos 21 and 30, making No. 3 Wing an all-Marauder unit. A second RAF unit, No. 39 Squadron, also converted to the Marauder, to join No. 25 Sqn SAAF in providing support for Tito's partisan forces in Yugoslavia. These two squadrons flew from December 1944 to the end of the war, the last mission being flown by No. 25 Sqn on 4 May 1945. Thereafter, the Marauder was taken rapidly out of RAF and SAAF service, and the aircraft were scrapped where they stood, the USAAF declining the opportunity to have them returned to the US.

From a South African squadron of the Desert Air Force, this Marauder egresses the target area after a raid on the Dvar rail yards in Yugoslavia, during early 1944.

Specification
Marauder Mk III
Type: six-seat medium bomber
Powerplant: two 2,000-hp (1491-kW) Pratt & Whitney R-2800-43 Double Wasp radial piston engines
Performance: maximum speed 305 mph (491 km/h) at 15,000 ft (4572 m); cruising speed 274 mph (441 km/h); service ceiling 28,000 ft (8534 m); range 1,200 miles (1931 km)
Weights: empty 24,000 lb (10886 kg); loaded 37,000 lb (16783 kg)
Dimensions: span 71 ft 0 in (21.64 m); length 57 ft 6 in (17.53 m); height 20 ft 0 in (6.10 m); wing area 664 sq ft (61.69 m^2)
Armament: two 0.5-in (12.7-mm) machine-guns in nose and dorsal and tail turrets and provision for four 0.5-in (12.7-mm) machine-guns in forward fuselage, plus up to 4,000 lb (1814 kg) of bombs

Serving as a torpedo-bomber, this Marauder Mk IA belonged to No. 14 Squadron, based at Fayid, Egypt in late 1942. Air strikes and British submarines inflicted severe losses on Axis convoys between Italy and North Africa. The motto under the cockpit reads 'Dominion Revenge'.

Martin 187 Baltimore

A Baltimore Mk III of No. 15 Squadron, SAAF drops its bomb load over the railway station at Sulmona, Italy, in 1944. RAF and South African Air Force Baltimores flew operations throughout the campaign in Italy.

Although generally considered to have been developed to meet a British requirement, the Baltimore originated, in fact, as the Martin **187F** for France, designed to succeed the large numbers of Martin 167F (Maryland) bombers ordered by the Armée de l'Air. A letter of intent for 400 Martin 187Fs was written by France on 18 May 1940 – too late for any of these aircraft to be built as ordered.

The British Purchasing Commission therefore took over the entire commitment, and the aircraft was refined in certain details, as the Martin **187B-1**, to conform with British standards of equipment and armament. In overall configuration, the aircraft to which the RAF gave the name Baltimore was similar to the Maryland, using the same wing but a deepened fuselage that allowed direct communication between crew members, and more powerful engines in the shape of Wright GR-2600-A5B5 Double Cyclones.

Once fitted with workable dorsal gun positions, this Baltimore Mk II operated with No. 70 OTU in the training role. The Baltimore had good handling characteristics, as well as excellent performance.

No prototype was built as such, the first aircraft to fly, on 14 June 1941, being the first of 50 **Baltimore Mk I**s. This and the next aircraft were lost at sea en route to the UK on 29 April 1942, the first of no fewer than 41 lost in this way from the initial order for 400. Those first two aircraft had, however, been held back in the US for development testing, and later production aircraft were in Britain by October 1941 for evaluation at the A&AEE and other establishments. Service use of the Baltimore was restricted exclusively to the Mediterranean area, where No. 223 Squadron became the first to operate the type, converting from Marylands in early 1942, and commencing bombing operations in May. At about the same time, No. 69 Squadron received Baltimore Mk Is in Gibraltar for shipping reconnaissance and anti-submarine patrols, and Nos 55 and 203 Squadons also converted to Mk Is in Egypt during 1942.

Deliveries continued, meanwhile, with 100 **Baltimore Mk II**s, which had two Vickers 0.303-in (7.7-mm) hand-operated machine-guns in the dorsal position, whereas the Mk Is had only a single dorsal gun. To complete the original French/British purchase, 250 **Baltimore Mk III**s were delivered, up to November 1943, featuring a twin-gun Boulton Paul dorsal turret. These additional supplies allowed further squadrons to be equipped, with operations in the North African campaign remaining the priority. Other squadrons to fly the later Baltimore marks in Egypt, Libya and Palestine included No. 13 (from late 1943), No. 52 (from February 1943), No. 454, RAAF (from March 1943), No. 459, RAAF (from July 1944) and No. 680 (from early 1944). Most of these squadrons moved on through Italy as the war progressed, giving close support to the advancing ground forces, and some remained in action right up to the end of World War II.

With passage of the Lend-Lease Act, further quantities of Baltimores

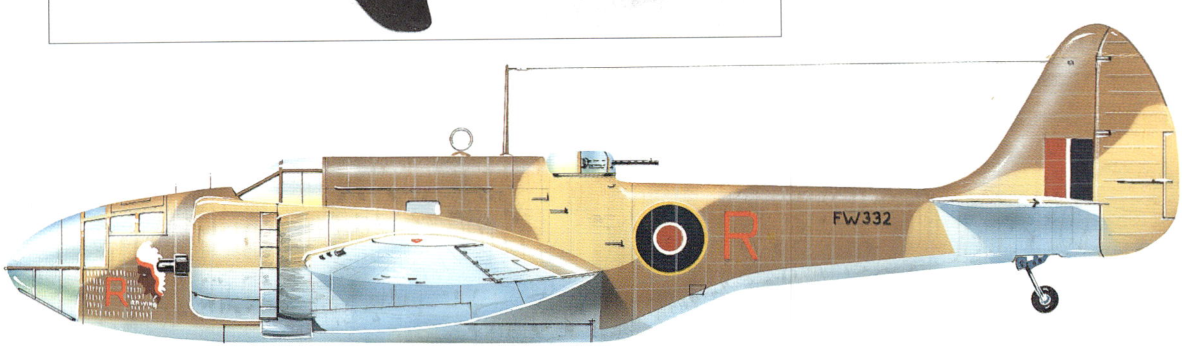

The Baltimore was an American light bomber designed to European specifications. It was fast and was armed with up to 14 0.303-in (7.7-mm) machine-guns, as well as being able to carry a 2,000-lb (907-kg) bomb load. This example is a Mk V, which was the most numerous (600) of the variants in the total of 1,575 built.

Fitted with an experimental under-fuselage pannier, this Baltimore Mk V was the sixth from last of the 600 Mk Vs delivered to the RAF when it arrived in May 1944. All Baltimore-equipped squadrons were operational in the Mediterranean theatre.

A Baltimore Mk IIIA from No. 69(GR) Squadron receives attention in revetments on Malta's Luqa airfield in 1943. The squadron's role was maritime reconnaissance.

were funded for Britain, under the USAAF designation **A-30**. The 281 **Baltimore Mk IIIA**s (Martin **187B-2**) were substantially the same as the Mk IIIs; a few repossessed for miscellaneous duties with the USAAF were known as **RA-30**s. Then came 294 **Baltimore Mk IV**s (**A-30A**) in which a Martin dorsal turret replaced the Boulton Paul turret of the Mk III/IIIA, and 600 **Baltimore Mk V**s (**A-30B**), which differed only in having US government-funded equipment in place of certain British items.

The designation **Baltimore GR.Mk VI** was reserved for a version for Coastal Command, but this did not materialise. Fourteen Baltimore Mk IVs/Vs were transferred to FAA units in the Mediterranean and were used by No. 728 Squadron, a Fleet Requirements Unit, during the last few months of the war and beyond. At Eastleigh, Kenya, No. 249 Sqn became, in October 1945, the last RAF squadron to convert to the Baltimore, flying Mk IVs and Vs until February 1946.

Specification
Baltimore Mk III
Type: four-seat light/medium bomber
Powerplant: two 1,660-hp (1238-kW) Wright GR-2660-A5B Cyclone radial piston engines
Performance: maximum speed 302 mph (486 km/h) at 11,000 ft (3353 m); service ceiling 24,000 ft (7315 m); range 950 miles (1529 km)
Weights: empty 15,200 lb (6895 kg); loaded 23,000 lb (10433 kg)
Dimensions: span 61 ft 4 in (18.69 m); length 48 ft 6 in (14.78 m); height 17 ft 9 in (5.41 m); wing area 539 sq ft (50.07 m²)
Armament: four 0.303-in (7.7-mm) machine-guns in wings, two 0.303-in machine-guns in dorsal turret, two 0.3-in (7.62-mm) machine-guns in ventral position and provision for four rearward-firing 0.3-in (7.7-mm) machine-guns plus up to 2,000 lb (907 kg) of bombs

Miles M.9, M.19, M.24, M.27 Master

By the mid-1930s the RAF had begun to take delivery of its first high-performance monoplanes, and it became clear that a trainer with similar performance characteristics would be required. F. G. Miles therefore designed a low-wing monoplane trainer around the 745-hp (556-kW) Rolls-Royce Kestrel XVI engine used in the Hawker Fury and Hart biplanes. Rolls-Royce had acquired a large financial interest in Phillips & Powis, primarily to ensure a continuing market for the Kestrel engine, and the new aircraft acquired the same name. Of wooden construction, this trainer was of exceptionally clean design, and Miles duly submitted it to the Air Ministry. It was turned down as being premature but Miles, undeterred, pressed on with construction as a private venture. The Kestrel flew first on 3 June 1937 and proved to have exceptional performance, with a top speed of almost 300 mph (483 km/h), a mere 20 mph (32 km/h) less than the Hawker Hurricane, which had an engine giving an additional 350 hp (261 kW).

With the failure of another trainer project which had been ordered by the Air Ministry, and with nothing else in prospect, an official

The Master reversed the trend towards stressed-skin metal aircraft structures, being of wooden construction, which had production advantages. This Mk IA had a taller, improved windscreen.

The Master Mk II, fitted with an 870-hp (649-kW) Bristol Mercury XX radial engine, was introduced because of dwindling stocks of the Rolls-Royce Kestrel. Another distinguishing feature of the Mk II was its appreciably shorter wing span, which reduced stress on the centre section of the Master's gull-shaped wing.

order was placed on 11 June 1938 to Specification 16/38. This was for the **M.9** development of the Kestrel, to be named **Master**, and the £2 million contract was then the largest ever awarded by the Air Ministry for a training aircraft.

The Ministry demanded a considerable number of modifications to the Kestrel design to meet its requirements. Changes were made to the windscreen, cabin top, rear fuselage and tail unit, the radiator was moved back from its position beneath the engine to below the wing centre-section, and the engine was changed to the derated 715-hp (533-kW) Kestrel XXX. Not surprisingly, the changes were made at a considerable cost to performance, the **Master Mk I** having a top speed 70 mph (113 km/h) below that of the Kestrel; even so, it was still the best training aircraft of its day, and had handling characteristics similar to those of the Hurricane and Supermarine Spitfire. Like the Kestrel, it was of wooden construction, covered with plywood.

The first of 900 **M.9A** Master Mk Is flew on 31 March 1939, but only seven had entered service by the outbreak of World War II. A sliding canopy soon replaced that of hinged design fitted on early aircraft, and in 1942 the round wingtips were removed in favour of square-cut tips, reducing the span by 3 ft 2 in (0.97 m) to 39 ft (11.89 m). A popular feature with pilots was the provision of a hand control box of Miles design: mounted on the port side of the cockpit, this incorporated controls for throttle, mixture, propeller, landing gear, trailing-edge flaps, landing lights, and elevator and rudder trim tabs, all easily accessible to the left hand.

A number of Master Mk Is were converted to single-seat configuration and equipped with six 0.303-in (7.7-mm) Browning machine-guns at the time of the Battle of Britain. Intended for use in dire emergency, none of these **M.24 Modified Master Mk I**s was, however, used in anger. In addition to use in a training role, Master Mk Is were also attached to squadrons for ferrying pilots.

Before the Master Mk I entered production, Miles was asked by the Air Ministry to modify an airframe to take the 870-hp (649-kW) Bristol Mercury XX engine as stocks of the Rolls-Royce Kestrel, then no longer in production, were unlikely to be adequate to meet total production requirements. With the Miles designation **M.19**, the Mercury-engined Master made its first flight in November 1939 and undertook service trials during the same month. In this form it became the M.19 **Master Mk II**, and was 16 mph (26 km/h) faster than its predecessor.

At this point the Ministry found that there were no stocks of Mercury engines available, so another powerplant, the 825-hp (615-kW) Pratt & Whitney Wasp Junior, was installed in a modified airframe and flown as the **M.27 Master Mk III** in 1940. This was some 10 mph (16 km/h) slower than the Master Mk II, but was otherwise satisfactory. By the time it had completed its trials, however, the Ministry had discovered stocks of Mercury engines, so the Master Mk II and Mk III were both put into production. Assembly lines at Woodley and South Marston built the Mk II, while the Mk III was only built at the latter factory. A total of 1,698 Master Mk IIs was built, plus 602 Mk IIIs, before the two production lines became occupied with other types: Miles Martinets at Woodley and Spitfires at South Marston. By the time production had been completed, 1,748 Master Mk IIs and 602 Master IIIs (excluding prototypes) had been built for the RAF.

All variants of the Master had an instructor's seat in the rear cockpit, which could be raised to provide a better view over the head of the pupil in the front seat for take-off and landing. Interconnected with the seat-raising mechanism was a hinged panel in the cockpit canopy which was raised automatically to provide a windscreen for the instructor.

Master Mk IIs were used for a variety of experiments in addition to their normal training role. One was fitted with underwing rockets to assess its suitability as an armed trainer, and in 1942 a requirement arose to replace the Hawker Audax and Hector biplane in the light glider-tug role. Within five days of the request being made by the Air Ministry, Miles delivered a Master Mk II for service trials; it had been modified to incorporate a towing hook in the rear fuselage with a release mechanism in the cockpit. The trials were completely successful and a number of other airframes were similarly converted to tow Hotspur gliders.

In addition to the RAF orders, a number of Master Mk IIs were supplied to overseas military customers, including 26 to Egypt, 18 to Turkey, and one to Portugal. One aircraft was transferred to the US Air Force, and one Master Mk III went to the Irish Air Corps. Many Master Mk IIs were shipped to South Africa.

The Master Mk III was powered by the smaller-diameter Pratt & Whitney Twin Wasp Junior engine, which gave a better forward view. The Master was the most significant British-designed trainer to serve with the RAF during World War II. This test aircraft is fitted with rocket projectiles beneath the wings.

Specification

Master Mk II

Type: two-seat advanced trainer
Powerplant: one 870-hp (649-kW) Bristol Mercury XX radial piston engine
Performance: maximum speed 242 mph (389 km h) at 6,000 ft (1829 m); service ceiling 25,100 ft (7650 m); range 393 miles (632 km)
Weights: empty 4,293 lb (1947 kg); maximum take-off 5,573 lb (2528 kg)
Dimensions: span 39 ft 0 in (11.89 m); length 29 ft 6 in (8.99 m); height 9 ft 3 in (2.82 m); wing area 235 sq ft (21.83 m²)
Armament: provision for one fixed forward-firing Vickers 0.303-in (7.7-mm) machine-gun and practice bombs

This Master Mk I, N7408, is painted in the standard RAF Training Command colours during service in 1940. This initial version was powered by a derated 715-hp (533-kW) Rolls-Royce Kestrel XXX engine, which was available from surplus stock. The intended Merlin engine was not fitted as it was in too much demand for front-line types.

Miles M.14 Magister

Following the success of the Miles Hawk Trainer, the Air Ministry produced Specification T.40/36 for a development of the Hawk to be built as an elementary trainer for the RAF. The new aircraft was to make history as the first low-wing trainer adopted by that service, and it also cut across the contemporary Air Ministry policy to use only metal aircraft, by being of wooden construction with plywood covering.

Changes to the basic design of the Hawk Trainer included larger cockpits and provision of blind flying equipment, and production began as the **M.14 Magister** on 20 March 1937.

Deliveries to the RAF began in May 1937, and early production aircraft were virtually identical to the prototype. Early problems were encountered when a series of crashes followed failure to recover from a spin. The prototype, which had been flown to the A&AEE, Martlesham Heath, for spinning trials, was lost in this way on its first flight from the test establishment, the pilot escaping by parachute.

Modifications to cure the problem included the raising of the position of the tailplane, the redesign of the rear fuselage and decking, and the fitting of anti-spin strakes. When these did not prove sufficient a new rudder of increased area and higher aspect ratio was fitted, and this cured the fault. The modifications were incorporated in all subsequent Magisters, these being designated **M.14A**.

Production ran from 1937 to 1941, and at its peak reached 15 per week. The Air Ministry contract covered 1,229 aircraft, but some of these were exported.

In RAF service the Magister proved an excellent trainer, its low-wing layout being particularly useful for fighter pilot training, and several RAF Magisters were used for experimental purposes during the war. When a German invasion of Britain was expected, in June 1940, racks to carry eight 25-lb (11-kg) bombs were fitted to about 15 aircraft.

Magisters served with many Elementary Flying Training Schools, the Central Flying School and in all RAF commands; the type also saw service with the British Army and Fleet Air Arm. With the army its work included glider pilot-training and co-operation with ground forces. Many Magisters were used as squadron 'hacks', and for communications duties, and also some 40 Fighter Command squadrons each had a Magister on strength.

Specification
Magister Mk I
Type: two-seat elementary trainer
Powerplant: one 130-hp (97-kW) de Havilland Gipsy Major I inline piston engine
Performance: maximum speed 132 mph (212 km/h) at 1,000 ft (305 m); cruising speed 123 mph (198 km/h); service ceiling 18,000 ft (5486 m); range 380 miles (612 km)
Weights: empty 1,286 lb (583 kg); maximum take-off 1,900 lb (862 kg)
Dimensions: span 33 ft 10 in (10.31 m); length 24 ft 8 in (7.52 m); height 6 ft 8 in (2.03 m); wing area 176 sq ft (16.35 m²)

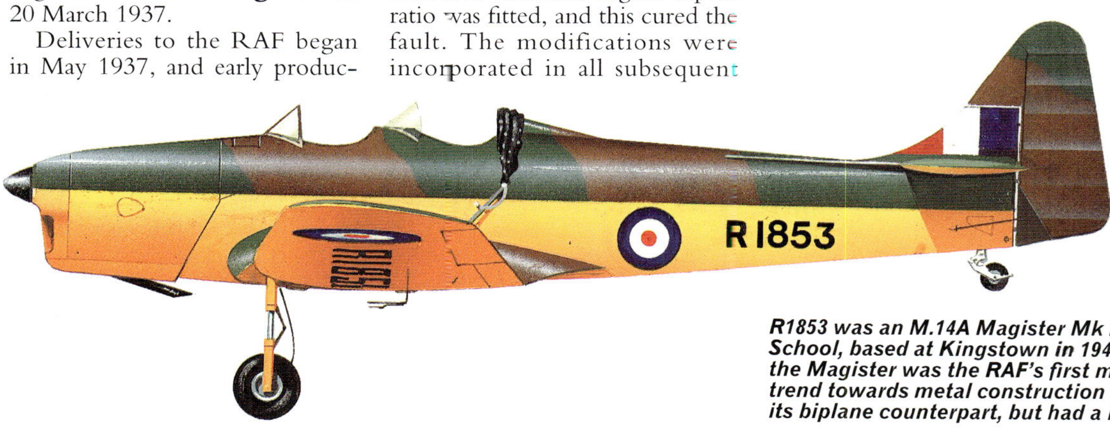

R1853 was an M.14A Magister Mk I of No. 15 Elementary Flying Training School, based at Kingstown in 1940. A contemporary of the Tiger Moth, the Magister was the RAF's first monoplane trainer, but reversed the trend towards metal construction by being all wood. It was faster than its biplane counterpart, but had a lower landing speed.

Miles M.16 Mentor

Developed from the Miles M.7 Nighthawk, the **M.16 Mentor** was produced to meet Air Ministry Specification 38/37 for a three-seat cabin communications monoplane with a 200-hp (149-kW) de Havilland Gipsy Queen I engine. Among its other duties, the Mentor was to be capable of carrying out instrument and radio training by day or night. Full dual controls were specified, together with blind-flying instruments, landing lights and radio.

The prototype first flew on 5 January 1938, proving to be heavier and more sluggish than the Miles M.7 Nighthawk which had preceded it, but was submitted for service trials, and orders for 45 were placed for supply to the RAF. Deliveries had been completed by mid-1939.

Like the Magister, the Mentor was provided with anti-spin strakes and, following the prototype's testing, a taller rudder similar to that of the Magister was fitted. A total of 42 Mentors was available for service when the war began and they were used by the RAF for communications and training by No. 24 Squadron, Station Flights and other UK-based units. Only one Mentor survived the war, being sold to a civil owner in 1947, but this aircraft was destroyed in a crash on 1 April 1950.

Specification
M.16 Mentor
Type: three-seat training and communications aircraft
Powerplant: one 200-hp (149-kW) de Havilland Gipsy Six 1 inline piston engine
Performance: maximum speed 156 mph (251 km/h) at sea level; service ceiling 13,800 ft (4206 m)
Weights: empty 1,978 lb (897 kg); maximum take-off 2,710 lb (1229 kg)
Dimensions: span 34 ft 10 in (10.61 m); length 26 ft 2 in (7.98 m); height 9 ft 8 in (2.95 m); wing area 181 sq ft (16.81 m²)

The de Havilland Gipsy Six-powered Mentor was produced before the war, and 45 were delivered to the RAF for communications duties. They equipped No. 24 Squadron based at Hendon, and various station flights.

Miles M.25 Martinet

The two-seat Martinet TT.Mk 1 was the first aircraft type to join the RAF which had been designed from the outset as a target-tug. Based on the Master trainer, a total of 1,700 was built.

For a number of years, target-towing for the British services was carried out by obsolete aircraft adapted for the purpose, but in 1941 F. G. Miles was approached by the Air Ministry with a request to evolve an aircraft specifically for this purpose. Specification 12/41 was issued, and the prototype **M.25** flew on 24 April 1942.

The **Martinet**, as this excellent tug aircraft became named, was based on the Miles Master Mk II but had a longer nose than the trainer, this being necessary to compensate for the weight of target-towing equipment which considerably altered the position of the centre of gravity; the cockpit enclosure also differed, and the winch could be either wind-driven or motorised. Stowage was provided for six flag and sleeve drogue targets. Construction followed normal Miles practice, with a wooden structure covered in plywood.

As Martinet production began the type superseded the Master on the line at Woodley, and between 1942 and 1945 more than 1,700 were built. They continued to serve for some years after the war until replaced by faster aircraft.

In 1943 the Air Ministry awarded a contract to Miles for a radio-controlled pilotless version of the Martinet. Built to Specification Q.10/43 under the Miles designation **M.50**, this variant was known as the **Queen Martinet**, and following successful tests with the prototype a production contract for 65 was awarded, which began to enter service during 1946.

Another version of the standard Martinet was a glider-tug, in which the standard target-towing gear was replaced by somewhat heavier equipment to make it suitable for its new role. Apart from deletion of the winch, the only external difference was removal of the lower part of the rudder to prevent it from fouling the tow cable.

Specification

Type: two-seat target-tug
Powerplant: one 870-hp (649-kW) Bristol Mercury XX or XXX radial piston engine
Performance: maximum speed 240 mph (386 km/h) at 5,800 ft (1768 m); cruising speed 199 mph (320 km/h) at 5,000 ft (1524 m); range 694 miles (1117 km)
Weights: empty 4,640 lb (2105 kg); maximum take-off 6,750 lb (3062 kg)
Dimensions: span 39 ft 0 in (11.89 m); length 30 ft 11 in (9.42 m); height 11 ft 7 in (3.53 m); wing area 242 sq ft (22.48 m^2)

Miles M.38 Messenger

At the private request of certain army officers in June 1942, George Miles designed and built the prototype of an air observation post (AOP) aircraft. The requirements were an ability to carry two people, a radio, armour plating and other military equipment. At the same time, it had to be suitable for operation from small, tree-surrounded fields in all weathers, be maintained in the field by unskilled staff, and have the capability of being flown by pilots of limited experience.

George Miles took the prototype M.28 fuselage and its engine, to which he added a larger one-piece wing with non-retractable external aerofoil flaps, and a large tailplane with endplate fins and rudders; a third central fin and rudder was added later. To produce the required ground angle for the short landing and take-off characteristics, a stalky, fixed landing gear was adopted, and the powerplant was given a fine-pitch propeller.

Within three months of the initial approach, George Miles flew the prototype **M.38** on 12 September 1942, subsequently allowing an AOP squadron to test fly it. The M.38 was an instant success, proving capable of fulfilling all of the army's requirements. At this juncture officialdom stepped in and, not for the first time, Miles was reprimanded for not obtaining government authority before building the aircraft. So strong was the feeling of the Ministry of Aircraft Production on this matter that the M.38 was not ordered for the AOP squadrons yet, in the following year, Miles received a small production order for the type to be used for VIP communications work under the name **Messenger**. A total of 21 was built, 11 at Reading and 10 at Newtonards, Northern Ireland. Among the VIPs to receive personal Messengers were Field Marshal Sir Bernard Montgomery and Marshal of the RAF Lord Tedder.

In 1944 one Messenger was fitted with a 150-hp (112-kW) Blackburn Cirrus Major engine and retractable flaps, under the designation M.48, but the modification had little effect on performance and was not taken any further.

Nineteen of the 21 Messengers survived the war, and were released for civil use.

Specification

Type: four-seat liaison and VIP communications aircraft
Powerplant: one 140-hp (104-kW) de Havilland Gipsy Major inline piston engine
Performance: maximum speed 116 mph (187 km/h); cruising speed 95 mph (153 km/h); service ceiling 14,000 ft (4267 m); range 260 miles (418 km)
Weights: empty 1,518 lb (689 kg); maximum take-off 1,900 lb (862 kg)
Dimensions: span 36 ft 2 in (11.02 m); length 24 ft 0 in (7.32 m); height 9 ft 6 in (2.90 m); wing area 191 sq ft (17.74 m^2)

The Messenger was primarily produced to meet the requirements of the army for use as an air observation post. Twenty-one were built for light VIP liaison and communications duties with the RAF.

North American Harvard

These Harvard Mk Is are from No. 2 Service Flying Training School at RAF Brize Norton in 1940. This SFTS was formed on 3 September 1939 with 31 Harvards on charge. The initial version was distinguished by its curved rudder.

One of the best-known, and certainly most-utilised, advanced trainers of World War II (and the first post-war decade), the Harvard was a member of the extensive North American **NA-16** family. This originated as a prototype with open tandem cockpits and a fixed undercarriage, but was soon developed to have a long transparent cover over the cockpits, and a retractable undercarriage. In this guise, the type was adopted by the US Army Air Corps as a basic combat and, later, advanced trainer and by the US Navy as a scout trainer; at the same time, orders were placed by a number of foreign air forces for basically similar aircraft.

Among the early customers were both Britain (with an order for 400) and France (for 450). The British aircraft (**NA-49**) were named **Harvard Mk I** and began to arrive in the UK at the end of 1938. Characterised by rounded wingtips and a rounded trailing edge to the rudder, the Harvard Mk Is introduced a new sound in British skies that would readily identify the Harvard wherever it flew – a high-pitched snarl said to be caused by the high propeller tip speeds. Harvard Mk Is entered service with No. 12 FTS at Grantham early in 1939 and thereafter at numerous other Flying Training Schools.

After the fall of France, Britain took over the French order for 450 **NA-76**s, which it designated **Harvard Mk II**s. These introduced the blunt wingtips and straight-edged rudder that would feature on all subsequent marks. With the introduction and expansion of training schools for RAF and Commonwealth pilots in Canada, South Africa and Southern Rhodesia, all but 50 of the French Harvard Mk IIs went directly to these schools, as did all but 20 of a further British contract for 600 Harvard Mk IIs. A large proportion of the subsequent allocation of the North American trainers to Britain through Lend-Lease contracts was similarly delivered direct to the Commonwealth training schools.

The first Lend-Lease version was the **Harvard Mk IIA**, 747 of which were built (as the **AT-6C**) by North American; this was similar to the Harvard Mk II, with a wooden rear fuselage and R-1340-AN1 engine. A switch from 12-volt to 24-volt electrics and a fabric-covered steel-tube rear fuselage brought a change of designation to **AT-6D**, of which the British equivalent was the **Harvard Mk III**; 532 were supplied, including 20 for the Fleet Air Arm, which also received a considerable number of Harvard Mk IIAs and **Mk IIB**s on transfer from the RAF. The Harvard Mk IIB was similar to the Mk IIA but came from the Noorduyn production line in Canada, from where some 2,700 were delivered. A few adapted as target-tugs took the official designation of **Harvard TT.Mk IIB**.

For the whole of World War II, the great majority of RAF pilots took their advanced training on the Harvard, and more than 5,000 of all marks reached British or Commonwealth flying schools. As the numbers proliferated, a few became station 'hacks' or were adopted for other special duties (even achieving, post-war, an operational role against terrorists in Kenya and Malaya), and close to 1,000 remained in RAF service when the war ended.

Specification
Harvard Mk IIB
Type: two-seat advanced trainer
Powerplant: one 550-hp (410-kW) Pratt & Whitney R-1340-49 Wasp radial piston engine
Performance: maximum speed 205 mph (330 km/h) at 5,000 ft (1524 m); cruising speed 170 mph (274 km/h); service ceiling 23,000 ft (7010 m); range 750 miles (1207 km)
Weights: empty 4,158 lb (1886 kg); loaded 5,250 lb (2381 kg)
Dimensions: span 42 ft 10 in (13.06 m); length 29 ft 0 in (8.84 m); height 11 ft 8 in (3.56 m); wing area 253 sq ft (23.50 m²)

The Harvard was one of the first US aircraft ordered by the British Purchasing Commission for the RAF in June 1938. The Harvard Mk I was the RAF version of the USAAC's BC-1 of 1937, and the initial contract for 200 (serials N7000 to N7199) was completed before the war. This aircraft, with a gas patch on its upper rear fuselage, was the 34th to be received and served with No. 2 SFTS from 1939.

In wartime Fleet Air Arm trainer markings, this Lend-Lease Harvard Mk IIA was one of 747 AT-6Cs built by North American and supplied to Britain. Most of the Mk IIAs initially served with the RAF, but a number were subsequently transferred to the Navy, continuing in use as advanced trainers.

North American Mitchell

Widely regarded as one of the best all-round light/medium bombers of World War II, and certainly one of the most popular with the crews who flew it for its docile handling and all-round performance, the Mitchell was a relative late-comer to RAF service. Based on a private-venture prototype first flown in January 1939, North American offered its **NA-62** design to meet a USAAC requirement and obtained an order 'off-the-drawing board' for 162 **B-25**s in September 1939. The first of these, effectively the Mitchell prototype, flew on 14 August 1940, and service introduction of the developed **B-25A** began in mid-1941.

Provision for the delivery of the new bomber to Britain was made during 1942 through Lend-Lease, with an initial allocation of 23 **B-25B**s that took the RAF name **Mitchell Mk I**. Three of these came to the UK for evaluation at the A&AEE with the remainder being used to set up No. 111 (Coastal) Operational Training Unit at Nassau/Oakes Field in the Bahamas. The purpose of this OTU, which began work in November 1942, was to train general reconnaissance crews, being one of 11 OTUs planned in early 1942 for the training of bomber crews outside of the UK, but the only one actually set up.

Operational use of the type by the RAF had to await the arrival in the UK of the first of an eventual total of 543 **Mitchell Mk II**s, starting in mid-1942. The Mitchell Mk II was the equivalent of the USAAF **B-25C** and **B-25D** (virtually identical models built, respec-

Top: Only three RAF Mitchell Mk Is were delivered to the UK, the remainder going to No. 111 OTU in the Bahamas. FK161 is seen here during evaluation at the Aeroplane and Armament Experimental Establishment at Boscombe Down.

Above left: The 2nd Tactical Air Force struck at German communications, headquarters, supply depots and armour concentrations. The main bomber type used was the B-25. This Mitchell Mk II of No. 98 Squadron, based at RAF Foulsham, was photographed before D-Day.

Left: Mitchell Mk IIs were first delivered to Nos 98 and 180 Squadrons at RAF West Raynham in September 1942, and flew their first operation on 22 January 1943, mounting an attack on oil refineries in Belgium.

Below: A total of 316 B-25Js was delivered to the RAF as the Mitchell Mk III, being used principally by the 2nd Tactical Air Force. This aircraft, HD378, was one of the first batch to be delivered.

North American Mitchell

Right: This Mitchell Mk II, coded 'EV-W', is from No. 180 Squadron, which was based at Foulsham from October 1942 until August 1943. The aircraft carries nine bomb silhouettes, each recording a raid over enemy territory with No. 2 (Bomber) Group.

Below: Mitchell Mk IIs from No. 320 (Dutch) Squadron line-up at Melsbroek towards the end of 1944. No. 320 Sqn became the third Mitchell squadron formed within No. 2 Group, after transferring from Coastal Command to re-equip with the light bomber in March 1943.

tively, at Inglewood and Kansas City). Externally similar to the B-25B, they featured later engines, an autopilot and a higher gross weight. Armament comprised a single or twin nose-mounted 0.5-in (12.7-mm) machine-gun, with two similar weapons each in dorsal and ventral turrets. Later, some Mk IIs acquired the beam gun positions developed for later B-25 variants such as the **B-25H**, and a single 0.5-in (12.7-mm) gun in the tail.

Deliveries to Britain concluded with 316 **Mitchell Mk III**s, these being equivalent to the **B-25J**; some 50 of this total were diverted to the RCAF. This model, built at North American's Kansas City plant, was the most-produced of all Mitchell versions. With bombing as its primary mission, it retained the transparent nose and bomb-aimer's position of the earlier models used by the RAF – whereas the preceding **B-25G** and H models for the USAAF had a 'solid' nose mounting a 75-mm cannon. Two B-25Gs, thus armed, were included in the supplies to Britain, and underwent evaluation at the A&AEE. On the B-25J, the dorsal turret was moved forward to a location just aft of the cockpit, ventral guns were abandoned, and waist hatches provided for two 0.5-in (12.7-mm) machine-guns, one each side. Two more 'fifties' were in a power-operated tail mounting, and there were four forward-firing package guns on the front fuselage sides, plus three more in the nose itself. Typically, the Mitchell Mk II carried six 500-lb (227-kg) or three 1,000-lb (454-kg) bombs.

Wearing invasion stripes, this Mitchell Mk II from the 2nd TAF flies over the target during an attack on the rail bridge at Deventer, Holland in the autumn of 1944.

The Mitchell Mk IIs and, progressively, Mk IIIs were used to equip, primarily, four UK-based medium-bomber squadrons, of which the first two, Nos 98 and 180, began to equip on the new type in September 1942. The first operation was flown on 22 January 1943, from Foulsham, and from then on these squadrons flew intensively against enemy communications centres and airfields as part of the 'softening-up' in preparation for D-Day. With the formation of 2nd Tactical Air Force, these squadrons were joined at Dunsfold by No. 320 (Dutch) Squadron, which flew its first raid on 17 August 1943, by which time No. 226 Sqn at Swanton Morley had already converted to the Mitchell and was similarly engaged within 2nd TAF up to D-Day.

Following the invasion of Europe, these four squadrons moved to the continent, to operate from airfields in Belgium, the Netherlands, France and, eventually, Germany up to the war's end. No. 305 Sqn, having also converted to the type in September 1943, flew only 16 missions on Mitchells, and No. 342 (French) Sqn had an equally brief experience on the type between March and May 1945.

No use was made by the RAF of the Lend-Lease Mitchells outside of Europe, but five or six B-25Cs were used for armed reconnaissance over Burma, Siam and Malaya during 1943. These were survivors of the Mitchells supplied to the Netherlands East Indies Air Force, added to a heterogenous collection of equipment used by Nos 681 and 684 Sqns (formed out of No. 3 PRU) in that area and retained at least until the end of 1943.

Specification
Mitchell Mk II
Type: five-seat medium bomber
Powerplant: two 1,700-hp (1268-kW) Wright GR-2600-13 Double-Row Cyclone radial piston engines
Performance: maximum speed 292 mph (470 km/h) at 15,000 ft (4572 m); cruising speed 210 mph (338 km/h); service ceiling 26,700 ft (8138 m); range 1,230 miles (1979 km)
Weights: empty 16,000 lb (7257 kg); loaded 26,000 lb (11793 kg)
Dimensions: span 67 ft 7 in (20.57 m); length 54 ft 1 in (16.48 m); height 15 ft 10 in (4.83 m); wing area 610 sq ft (56.67 m²)
Armament: two 0.5-in (12.7-mm) machine-guns in dorsal and ventral positions and one 0.3-in (7.62-mm) gun in nose, plus normal bomb load of 4000 lb (1814 kg)

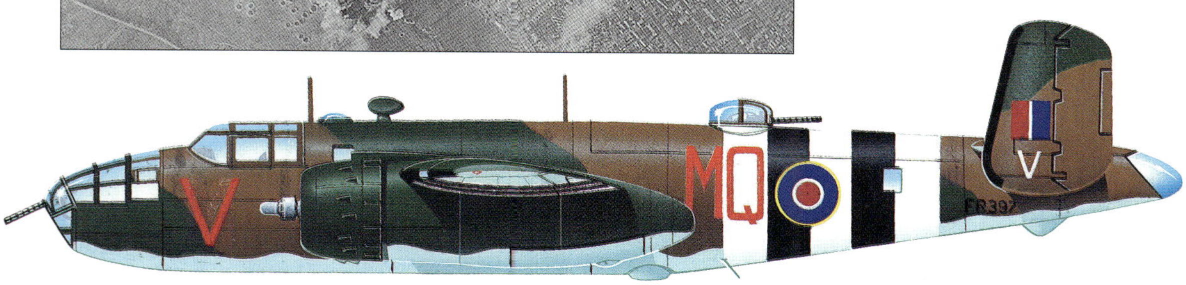

This Mitchell Mk II of No. 226 Squadron was based at Gilze Rijen, Netherlands in late 1944, operating in support of the advancing Allied armies in the tactical support role. The D-Day invasion markings were retained due to pressure of operations which prevented their removal.

Serving with No. 320 (Dutch) Squadron, No. 2 Group, this Mitchell Mk II was based at RAF Dunsfold in April 1944. The Mitchells of the Dutch units were very active during the run-up to D-Day in June 1944.

North American Mustang

***Above:** This early Mustang Mk I, AG528 of No. 400 Squadron based at RAF Odiham, undertook low-level tactical reconnaissance with RAF Army Co-operation Command from mid-1942. The aperture for the oblique camera is visible behind the cockpit. Mustang Mk Is were the first RAF single-engined fighters to fly over Germany, in October 1942.*

***Left:** The Mustang Mk IA differed from the initial Allison-engined version, having four wing-mounted 20-mm cannon. In November 1943 all of the Army Co-operation Command's Mustangs came under 2nd Tactical Air Force control and on D-Day still served with Nos 168, 414 and 430 Squadrons at Odiham and Nos 2 and 268 Squadrons at Gatwick.*

***Below:** After disposing of its Kittyhawks and moving to Italy, No. 260 Squadron received Merlin-engined Mustang Mk IIIs in the spring of 1944. Capable of carrying two 1,000-lb (454-kg) bombs, the aircraft were flown on fighter-bomber missions for the rest of the war over Italy and Yugoslavia.*

The outstanding fighter of World War II, a design that was to prove indispensable and little short of a war-winner, the Mustang was conceived to a British requirement. A prototype was designed and built in the space of 102 days and first flew on 26 October 1940. Powered by the ubiquitous Allison V-1710, production variants of this aircraft, the North American **NA-73X**, entered RAF service in early 1942 and, somewhat belatedly, joined the ranks of the USAAF the following year.

The story of the Mustang in RAF service began in late 1939, when the British Purchasing Commission (BPC), while placing orders for war matériel in the US, enquired of North American Aviation (NAA) whether it would build Curtiss P-40s under licence to fill an RAF order. Unenthusiastic, NAA reacted by suggesting that it could design and build a better aircraft. Although the company had not built a fighter before, the BPC was sufficiently impressed with its proposal to sign a contract for a prototype in May 1940. Before it had flown, an order for 320 production aircraft had been placed.

The NA-73X outperformed any contemporary American fighter, largely due to a number of innovative features, including its NACA laminar-flow wing and the radiator air intake situated aft of the wing. The latter not only ensured maximum radiator efficiency, but reduced drag, ensuring high performance from the all-metal airframe. This was designed using simple shapes that were easily, and thus quickly, constructed. The Allison V-1710 hampered the aircraft's performance above 13,000 ft (3962 m), but was the only suitable powerplant available; it was not until the Rolls-Royce Merlin was installed in the Mustang that it was transformed into an outstanding machine.

No. 26 Squadron became the first of 14 UK-based Army Co-operation Command squadrons to be equipped with the **Mustang Mk I**, in February 1942. Given the Allison engine's shortcomings, it was

Fitted with a Rolls-Royce Merlin engine, this Mustang Mk X, carrying test markings, underwent evaluation with the A&AEE at Boscombe Down and the Air Fighting Development Unit in February 1942.

decided that the Mustang in its original form was unsuitable as a day fighter, but would make an admirable co-operation machine with which to replace Lysanders and Tomahawks. To this end, Mustang Mk Is were fitted with an F.24 oblique camera behind the cockpit for tactical reconnaissance work. The Mk I's armament of two 0.5-in (12.7-mm) machine-guns in the lower forward fuselage, plus one in each wing alongside two 0.3-in (7.62-mm) guns, was retained.

Reconnaissance of the northern coast of occupied Europe was undertaken (including Dieppe during the ill-fated Allied raid of August 1942) and later nuisance raids on ground targets were carried out, especially once the Mustang squadrons came under the control of the 2nd Tactical Air Force (TAF) in late 1943. During one such raid in October 1942, Mustangs became the first single-engined RAF fighter (if one discounts PR Spitfires) to fly over Germany during an attack on the Dortmund-Ems canal. From mid-July 1942, the first of 150 **Mustang Mk IA**s were replacing some of the oldest Mk Is. These

FR409 was one of the three lightweight XP-51F experimental fighters. It was an extensive redesign in which loaded weight was reduced to 9,060 lb (4110 kg) through simplification of the structure, the deletion of some equipment and the use of new materials, including plastics. Only one aircraft was supplied to the RAF for evaluation.

differed in having four wing-mounted 20-mm cannon in place of the machine-guns of the Mk I.

Five of the Mk I/IA squadrons were still operational on D-Day and the type was also employed as trials aircraft; several were used during the development of rocket projectile launch rails, while one aircraft was fitted with a pair of 40-mm Vickers 'S' guns.

The first Mustangs in USAAF service were ground-attack **A-36A**s, fitted with six 0.5-in (12.7-mm) guns, divebrakes and racks for two 500-lb (227-kg) bombs. One was delivered to the RAF for evaluation, as the **Mustang Mk I (Dive Bomber)**, but the type was not adopted. However, six ex-USAAF A-36As (with cameras installed) served with No. 1437 Flight in the Mediterranean during late 1943, while eight camera-equipped, early-model P-51s (**F-6A**s) were assigned to Nos 14 and 225 Squadrons in North Africa in 1943, for tactical reconnaissance and bomber escort duties.

Fifty **Mustang Mk II**s were delivered to supplement the Mk I/IA fleet and replace 57 earlier aircraft taken over by the USAAF. These had re-rated engines, retained cannon armament and introduced the bomb-carrying capability of the A-36A. The Mk II's wings were also 'plumbed' to allow the carriage of wing drop tanks. Two squadrons in the 2nd TAF (the first, No. 2 Squadron, in May 1944) and one in North Africa were equipped with the mark. These were among the last Allison-engined Mustangs built and served the RAF (with the remaining Mk I/IAs) until VE-Day.

During 1942 Ronnie Harker, a Rolls-Royce test pilot, had occasion to fly a Mustang Mk I and came away convinced that the already excellent aircraft could be improved by the installation of a Merlin engine with two-stage supercharging, as being prepared for the Spitfire Mk VIII/IX. Investigations by Rolls-Royce were sufficiently encouraging for the RAF to supply five Mk I airframes for re-engining trials. The RAF was primarily interested in the 'Merlin-Mustang' as a fighter optimised for medium altitude, i.e. between 10,000 ft (3048 m) and 20,000 ft (6096 m).

The five aircraft were initially fitted with Merlin 65s (a variation on

Mustang Mk I AG470 was from the first batch of 320 Allison-engined examples delivered in 1942. This aircraft served with No. 414 Squadron, RCAF, at RAF Middle Wallop and carried a small maple leaf badge on the engine cowling.

This Mustang Mk III of No. 112 Squadron was based in Italy in early 1945. The distinctive shark-mouth insignia was applied during the war to various RAF aircraft and differed from type to type, as well as among individual aircraft.

Allison engine
The 1,150-hp (858-kW) Allison V-1710-39 Vee-12 engine fitted to the Mustang Mk I performed well at low evel but very poorly at higher altitudes. Unable to compete with the Bf 109 at dogfighting heights, the Mk I was restricted to the army co-operation role.

North American Mustang Mk I

Based at RAF Gatwick with No. 26 Squadron, AM101 was the 364th Mustang Mk I for the RAF. The squadron commenced operations in January 1942 flying fighter sweeps, photographic reconnaissance sorties and night fighter-bomber raids against railway targets in France.

Armament
The Mustang Mk I had the original four 0.5-in (12.7-mm) and four 0.3-in (7.62-mm) machine-guns that had been originally stipulated by the RAF. Later, the Mk IA was fitted with 20-mm cannon for army support missions in the co-operation role.

Cockpit
The cockpit was well laid out with all controls within easy reach of the pilot. A false panel between the pilot's seat and the radiator allowed residual heat from the radiator in to warm the cockpit. An oblique F24 camera was fitted on the port side behind the cockpit canopy for the photographic reconnaissance role.

Radiator
The liquid-cooled engine had its coolant radiator far back under the rear fuselage in the most efficient position, and it was installed in a long profiled duct with a variable exit shutter. Instead of creating drag, the heated air could behave like a jet-propulsion unit and help to push the fighter along.

Wing structure
The Mustang Mk I featured new aerodynamics, including a laminar-flow one-piece wing with the thickest section further back than on previous fighters. Fuel was contained in two tanks in the centre-section and a further tank in the fuselage. All production Mustangs had underwing hardpoints for the carriage of weapons or drop tanks.

North American Mustang

Above: With its distinctive bubble canopy and long-range tanks, this Mustang Mk IV was flown by No. 19 Squadron for long-range bomber escort duties.

Right: Mustang Mk I AG633 flew with No. II(AC) Squadron based at Sawbridgworth in July 1942. Army Co-operation Command's Allison Mustangs were used for long-range cross-Channel missions from October 1942.

the Merlin 61 tuned to produce maximum power at 21,000 ft/6400 m) and redesignated **Mustang Mk X**. The biggest outward change to the Mk X was a 'chin' intake under the engine, this housing the carburettor air intake and the intercooler radiator, the latter a new feature with the two-stage engine. The repowered aircraft exceeded expectations; a top speed of 433 mph (696 km/h) was attained by the second conversion during testing at the end of 1942. Rolls-Royce drew up plans to carry out 500 Merlin conversions for the RAF, but was thwarted by the lack of production facilities in the UK. Besides, NAA had meanwhile been working on a 'Merlin-Mustang' of its own, using Packard-built engines.

Known as the **P-51B** (or **P-51C** if built at NAA's Dallas factory), the first production Mustang with a V-1650 engine (as the Packard Merlin was known) entered USAAF service in the second half of 1943. The P-51B/C differed from the Mustang Mk X in having a much neater and aerodynamic intercooler radiator installation, in the existing ventral oil cooler intake, and thereby had an improved top speed of 453 mph (729 km/h).

Mustang Mk III was the designation applied to 274 P-51Bs and 636 P-51Cs delivered to the RAF, the first of which entered service in late 1943 with No. 65 Squadron. Twelve other units were also issued with Mk IIIs, the aircraft performing escort duties for RAF daylight bombing raids during 1944/45. Other roles included fighter-reconnaissance, ground-attack and anti-Diver (V-1 flying bomb) patrols. One of the least known of RAF Mustang operators was No. 617 ('Dambusters') Squadron, which utilised at least one Mk III in the pathfinding role. A number of Mustang Mk III units joined 2nd TAF in 1943 and saw service on the Continent after D-Day, while the following year four squadrons employed the type in Italy and the Balkans. Many were fitted with the distinctive, bulged Malcolm Ltd cockpit canopy, for much improved pilot visibility.

If the war in Europe had continued, many Spitfire units would have re-equipped with the Mustang Mk IV long-range fighter. This example served in Italy with No. 93 Squadron shortly after the end of the war. Note the dorsal fin fairing added to this version.

The RAF's last large-scale Mustang deliveries comprised examples of the main Mustang production variants, the **P-51D** (281 aircraft) and Dallas-built **P-51K** (595 aircraft) which introduced a number of refinements, including the 'teardrop' cockpit canopy and redesigned rear fuselage. Armed with six 0.5-in (12.7-mm) machine-guns, the P-51D/K was able to carry two 1,000-lb (454-kg) underwing bombs. Known in the RAF as the **Mustang Mk IV**, the variant entered service from February 1945 with four squadrons in Italy and seven UK-based units. Several other units flew the variant post-war.

Finally, single examples of the experimental lightweight **XP-51F**, **XP-51G** and the **P-51H** were sent to UK for evaluation at RAE Boscombe Down towards the end of the war; had the G-model been ordered by the RAF, it would have become the **Mustang Mk V**.

Specification
Mustang Mk III
Type: single-seat fighter/fighter-bomber
Powerplant: one 1,680-hp (1253-kW) Packard-built Rolls-Royce Merlin V-1650-7 inline piston engine
Performance: maximum speed 442 mph (711 km/h) at 24,500 ft (7468 m); service ceiling 42,500 ft (12954 m); maximum range 1,710 miles (2752 km)
Weights: empty 7,000 lb (3175 kg); loaded 9,500 lb (4309 kg)
Dimensions: span 37 ft 1 in (11.30 m); length 32 ft 3 in (9.83 m); height 8 ft 8 in (2.64 m); wing area 235 sq ft (21.83 m²)
Armament: four 0.5-in (12.7-mm) machine-guns in wings plus provision for up to 1,000 lb (454 kg) of bombs

As commanding officer of No. 133 Wing, RAF, Wing Commander Stanislaw Skalski applied his own initials 'SS' to his aircraft in lieu of unit codes. Wearing D-Day invasion stripes, the aircraft has Skalski's 21 kills are represented by Iron Crosses beneath the cockpit canopy. No. 133 was the Mustang wing of No. 84 Group of the 2nd TAF.

Piloted by Sqn Ldr D. Westenra, this Mustang Mk III was from No. 65 Squadron. This unit was one of the most successful Mk III operators, mounting long-range fighter sweeps and escort sorties deep into Europe and Scandinavia.

Northrop N-3PB

In common with several other European nations, Norway became acutely aware during 1939 of the need to expand its fighting forces and its defensive capability. One consequence of this realisation was the dispatch of a purchasing commission to the USA, and early in 1940 this team placed an order with the (reformed) Northrop company for 24 N-3PB patrol-bomber floatplanes, designed specifically to meet the Norwegian requirement.

Powered by a Wright R-1820-G205A radial engine, the three-seat N-3PB could carry a torpedo or bombs between the two large floats, and was armed with four 0.5-in (12.7-mm) and two 0.3-in (7.62-mm) machine-guns. Before deliveries could begin, German forces had begun the occupation of Norway, in April 1940. Consequently, the first six N-3PBs went in March 1941 to 'Little Norway', the Norwegian flying training school set up at Island Airport, Toronto.

The remaining 18 N-3PBs were shipped aboard the freighter *Fjordheim* from Canada to Reykjavik in April-May 1941 to equip No. 330 Sqn, which by agreement with Britain would come under RAF operational control (within RAF Coastal Command) but in all other respects would be Norwegian. Divided into three flights at Reykjavik, Akureyvi and Budareyvi, the N-3PBs were flying convoy escorts and anti-submarine patrols from 23 June onwards. The N-3PBs continued to operate into 1942 in this way, and made a number of attacks on U-boats. None of these resulted in a kill, but one submarine was damaged and, watched by the crew of the attacking N-3PB, the U-boat surrendered to a destroyer.

Of only limited operational capability in the role that was thrust upon them, the Northrop floatplanes were replaced by Catalinas progressively through the second half of 1942. Operations had reached a peak in May of that year, in which month N-3PBs flew 118 sorties.

Specification
N-3PB
Type: three-seat floatplane patrol-bomber
Powerplant: one 1,100-hp (820-kW) Wright GR-1820-G205A radial piston engine
Performance: maximum speed 257 mph (414 km/h) at 1,000 ft (305 m); service ceiling 24,000 ft (7315 m); range 1,000 miles (1609 km)
Weights: empty 6,190 lb (2808 kg); maximum take-off 10,600 lb (4808 kg)
Dimensions: span 48 ft 11 in (14.91 m); length 36 ft 0 in (10.97 m); height 12 ft 0 in (3.66 m); wing area 377 sq ft (35.02 m²)
Armament: four forward-firing 0.5-in (12.7-mm) machine-guns in wings and one 0.3-in machine-gun in dorsal and ventral positions, plus up to 2,000 lb (907 kg) of bombs

N-3PB seaplanes were flown from Iceland on convoy escort and maritime reconnaissance duties by No. 330 Squadron from 1941.

Percival Proctor

Developed from the pre-war Vega Gull, 15 of which had been acquired by the Royal Air Force for communications duties and for the use of overseas air attachés, the Percival Proctor was designed to Air Ministry Specification 20/38 as a communications and radio training aircraft. The prototype made its first flight on 8 October 1939, and was the first of more than 1,100 military examples to be produced during the war years for the RAF and Fleet Air Arm.

The initial production version was the **P.28 Proctor Mk I** (247 built), a three-seat communications aircraft, followed by the **P.30 Proctor Mk II** (175) and **P.34 Proctor Mk III** (437), both of which were radio trainers without dual controls. Named originally Preceptor, and designed to Specification T.9/41, the **P.31 Proctor Mk IV** had a longer, deepened fuselage to accommodate four, including trainee radio operators who were provided with operational standard equipment. The increase in capacity made this an effective communications aircraft, and many were later fitted with dual controls. An experimental Proctor Mk IV with a 250-hp (186-kW) de Havilland Gipsy Queen engine was used as a personal transport by Air Vice Marshal Sir Ralph Sorley. Some 258 Proctor Mk IVs were built and powered by the 210-hp (157-kW) Gipsy Queen II engine.

Most Proctors built during the war were manufactured under sub-contract by F. Hills and Sons of Manchester, the result of the involvement of the Percival factory at Luton with sub-contract manufacture of Airspeed Oxfords and de Havilland Mosquitoes. Hills built 25 Mk Is, 100 Mk IIs, 487 Mk IIIs and 250 Mk IVs.

At the end of World War II, more than 200 Proctor Mk Is, Mk IIs and Mk IIIs were prepared for disposal to civil buyers, but some Mk IVs remained in service with communications squadrons until 1955.

Specification
Type: three/four-seat radio trainer and communications aircraft
Powerplant: one 210-hp (157-kW) de Havilland Gipsy Queen II inline piston engine
Performance: maximum speed 160 mph (257 km/h), cruising speed 140 mph (225 km/h) at 3,000 ft (914 m); service ceiling 14,000 ft (4267 m); range 500 miles (805 km)
Weights: empty 2,370 lb (1075 kg); maximum take-off 3,500 lb (1588 kg)
Dimensions: span 39 ft 6 in (12.04 m); length 28 ft 2 in (8.59 m); height 7 ft 3 in (2.21 m); wing area 202 sq ft (18.77 m²)

First flown in October 1939, the Percival Proctor was developed from the pre-war Vega Gull. It served as a radio trainer and as a three-seat light communications aircraft. This Mk II served with the Fleet Air Arm.

Percival Q.6 Petrel

Virtually all of the Percival Q.6s built flew with either the RAF or Royal Navy during the war, performing communications and liaison duties.

Edgar Percival's first twin-engined aircraft was the Type Q, designed as a Q.4 four-seat executive transport with a crew of two, and powered by de Havilland Gipsy Major engines; or as a six-seat **Q.6** feederliner with 205-hp (153-kW) Gipsy Six engines. Only the Q.6 was built, and the prototype was first flown at Luton by Captain Percival on 14 September 1937.

Of wooden construction with plywood and fabric covering, the aircraft initially had fixed tailwheel type landing gear, the main units in streamlined fairings beneath the engine nacelles. The Q.6 entered production in 1938, and 27 aircraft were completed, including four with retractable landing gear. The first of the latter was used for landing gear trials at Martlesham Heath in June 1938, and after completion of these tests, although built to the order of Captain P. G. Taylor, the renowned Australian pilot and navigator, the aircraft was delivered not to him but to Vickers-Armstrong Ltd.

Government users included Egypt, with two camouflaged aircraft, while the Royal Air Force received seven new Q.6s, to which the service name **Petrel** was applied. The Petrel was ordered under Air Ministry Specification 25/38 for communications duties and the last of the RAF order was delivered in March 1940. By May 1940 the nine civil-registered Q.6s which were based in Great Britain had been impressed for use by the RAF and the Royal Navy, serving with station flights and communications squadrons. Two aircraft were impressed at Heliopolis in February 1940 and December 1941.

One Q.6 was used by Vickers as a civil aircraft throughout the war, but in 1946 four impressed machines which had survived hostilities were assembled with many other requisitioned aircraft at No. 5 Maintenance Unit at Kemble for sale to civil buyers. Three of the seven RAF Petrels also found their way onto the British civil register in 1946 and 1947.

Specification
Petrel Mk I
Type: four/six-seat communications aircraft or feederliner
Powerplant: two 205-hp (153-kW) de Havilland Gipsy Six inline piston engines
Performance: maximum speed 195 mph (314 km/h); cruising speed 175 mph (282 km/h); service ceiling 21,000 ft (6401 m); range 750 miles (1207 km)
Weights: empty 3,500 lb (1588 kg); maximum take-off 5,500 lb (2495 kg)
Dimensions: span 46 ft 8 in (14.22 m); length 32 ft 3 in (9.83 m); height 9 ft 9 in (2.97 m); wing area 278 sq ft (25.83 m²)

Republic Thunderbolt

Above: RAF Thunderbolts flew operations exclusively in the Far East from 1944. White recognition bands were applied to prevent attacks by Allied pilots who may have mistaken them for Nakajima Ki-44s or Ki-84s.

With a total production run of 15,683 examples, the Republic **P-47** came second only to the Curtiss P-40 family in terms of US fighter production quantities during World War II. Within that total, the run of 12,602 P-47Ds singled out this particular variant of the 'Jug' as the most-produced of any single model of a US fighter. Perhaps surprisingly, therefore, RAF use of the Thunderbolt was relatively modest, deliveries totalling 825 and deployment being limited almost exclusively to the Burma theatre.

Influenced by early combat reports from the air war in Europe, Republic designers sketched in 1940 an advanced single-seat fighter that was characterised by its large size and great weight. The design philosophy dramatically contrasted with that of other companies that sought to achieve operational effectiveness through light weight. The

Right: This early example of the Thunderbolt Mk I was delivered to the RAF in spring 1944. It is seen here undergoing tests with the A&AEE carrying auxiliary fuel tanks. The aircraft was sent for operational service in the Far East in August 1944.

Above: Thunderbolt Mk IIs of No. 30 Squadron mount a patrol from their base at Chittagong over Burma in late 1944. The squadron had replaced its Hurricane Mk IICs with Thunderbolt Mk Is in July and received the Thunderbolt Mk II in September of that year. In January 1945 the squadron switched to bombing and napalm attacks.

Left: This Thunderbolt Mk I belonged to the 'Ace of Spades' Flight of No. 73 OTU based at Fayid in the Middle East. The unit trained Thunderbolt pilots on their way to Burma for operational service. The Thunderbolt is believed to have had the lowest loss per sortie rate of any World War II RAF combat aircraft – only seven were known to have been lost to enemy anti-aircraft fire.

XP-47B, first flown on 6 May 1941, was powered by the massive Pratt & Whitney twin-row air-cooled radial engine, with a turbo-supercharger located under the rear fuselage, and weighed in at 12,000 lb (5443 kg). In the proposed production form, armament was to comprise eight wing-mounted 0.5-in (12.7-mm) machine-guns – following European trends – and weight would go up to 15,000 lb (6804 kg).

Initial USAAF orders covered the **P-47B** and **P-47C** versions, but the RAF had to wait for the **P-47D** before Lend-Lease supplies could begin. The P-47D designation covered several sub-variants that introduced progressive improvements; range was increased by use of a centreline drop tank that could be replaced by a 500-lb (227-kg) bomb, while wing pylons could carry two tanks or two 1,000-lb (454-kg) bombs. Eventually, two or three rocket projectiles could be carried under each wing as well as a 500-lb (227-kg) bomb, vindicating the heavyweight, high-power design philosophy.

Deliveries to the RAF began in mid-1944 and comprised 240 **Thunderbolt F.Mk I**s and 590 **Thunderbolt F.Mk II**s (of a

Above: As Thunderbolt Mk Is began to arrive in the Far East during the latter part of 1944, they generally replaced Hurricanes in the fighter-bomber role. These Mk Is, carrying auxiliary fuel tanks, taxi past a squadron of Hurricanes at an airstrip in Burma.

This P-47D-30 Thunderbolt Mk II belonged to No. 79 Squadron based at Wangjing, Burma in November 1944. It is painted with the medium and dark blue national insignia adopted in Southeast Asia to avoid confusion with the red 'meatball' of the Japanese aircraft. Theatre stripes appear on the wings, fin and tailplane.

Republic Thunderbolt

Above: No. 134 Squadron (coded 'GQ') re-equipped with Thunderbolt Mk I/IIs in August 1944 and commenced operations in December 1944, covering the landings at Rangoon in April 1945. The squadron moved back to India in June 1945 and was renumbered No. 131.

planned total of 1,098). The Mk Is were the so-called 'razorback' variants with the original built-up rear fuselage into which the cockpit canopy faired, whereas the Mk IIs were the USAAF's **P-47D-25** version with a 'bubble' canopy and cut-down rear fuselage. A few Thunderbolts came to the UK for test and evaluation, but the bulk of deliveries, continuing to July 1945, were made direct to India – where Thunderbolts were to operate – or to Egypt for the use of No. 73 Operational Training Unit (OTU) to train pilots destined to serve with the operational squadrons.

The conversion of RAF squadrons in India (then flying Hurricanes) to Thunderbolts began in May 1944, and Nos 30, 79, 146 and 261 Squadrons were flying the Republic fighters by the late summer – by which time Thunderbolt Mk IIs were already reaching all four squadrons. The first operational sorties were made on 14 September 1944 by No. 261 Squadron, when Mk Is and Mk IIs made an armed reconnaissance sortie over the Chudwin river; two days later No. 146 Squadron joined No. 261 Squadron in a bombing and strafing attack south of Imphal.

Nos 30 and 79 Squadrons went into operation over the Arakan, joined later by No. 135 Squadron. These became employed mostly on offensive reconnaissance and Rhubarb missions, but on 4 November, No. 30 Squadron was able to claim the first victory in an air-to-air engagement. Four more Thunderbolt squadrons were operational by the end of 1944 – three over the Arakan and one more in central Burma – and a final two Hurricane squadrons converted in March and April 1945. Action continued at a high rate through to the end of the war, and No. 60 Squadron continued to fly Thunderbolt Mk IIs in Singapore until October 1946.

Thunderbolts in Burma flew 'cab-rank' patrols, directed by ground visual control posts. With their 500-lb (227-kg) bombs and heavy armament they caused considerable damage to the Japanese ground forces and their long supply lines.

The 'teardrop' canopy of the P-47D-25 Thunderbolt Mk II gave the pilot much improved all-round vision. The Mk II was involved in little air-to-air combat, concentrating instead on ground attack.

Specification
Thunderbolt Mk II
Type: single-seat fighter-bomber
Powerplant: one 2,300-hp (1715-kW) Pratt & Whitney R-2800-59 Double Wasp radial piston engine
Performance: maximum speed 427 mph (687 km/h); service ceiling 36,500 ft (11125 m); maximum range 1,970 miles (3170 km)
Weights: empty 10,000 lb (4536 kg); loaded 14,600 lb (6622 kg)
Dimensions: span 40 ft 9 in (12.42 m); length 36 ft 2 in (11.02 m); height 12 ft 8 in (3.86 m); wing area 308 sq ft (28.61 m^2)
Armament: eight 0.5-in (12.7-mm) machine-guns in wings plus provision for up to 2,000 lb (907 kg) of bombs

Saro A.27 London

Between the two World Wars the flying-boat reigned supreme for coastal patrol work with the RAF, and the Saro London, together with its contemporary, the Supermarine Stranraer, were the last of the biplane flying-boats to see service before replacement by the Short Sunderland. Twenty-nine Londons were still in service at the outbreak of World War II.

The prototype London, built to Specification R.24/31, flew in 1934 and the type was ordered into production in the following March. Deliveries began in 1936 and the first 10 aircraft were designated **London Mk I**s. Construction Nos 11 to 48 (the final production London) were all **London Mk II**s, which differed in having 915-hp (682-kW) Bristol Pegasus X engines, driving four-bladed propellers, in place of the Mk I's 820-hp (611-kW) Pegasus IIIs with two-bladed propellers.

First service deliveries, between April and September 1936, were to No. 201 Squadron, replacing Supermarine Southamptons at Calshot; further batches were delivered in October 1936 to No. 204 Squadron at Mount Batten, Plymouth, also replacing Southamptons. More were delivered to the same squadron at Mount Batten the following year to replace Blackburn Perths, and in 1938 the London Mk IIs supplanted Supermarine Scapas of No. 202 Squadron in Malta.

No. 204 Squadron used five Londons on a long-distance training flight to New South Wales, Australia and back between December 1937 and May 1938. They were fitted with external overload fuel tanks to increase their range to 2,600 miles (4184 km).

Nos 201, 202 and 240 Squadrons were still operating Londons in first-line service at the outbreak of World War II, flying patrols over the Straits of Gibraltar and the North Sea. They were eventually retired early in 1941 when they were replaced by the Consolidated Catalina. At this time a number of the Londons were transferred to the Royal Canadian Air Force.

Specification
London Mk II
Type: six-seat general reconnaissance flying-boat
Powerplant: two 915-hp (682-kW) Bristol Pegasus X radial piston engines
Performance: maximum speed 155 mph (249 km/h) at 6,250 ft (1905 m); cruising speed 129 mph (208 km/h); service ceiling 19,900 ft (6066 m); range 1,100 miles (1770 km)
Weights: empty 11,100 lb (5035 kg); maximum take-off 18,400 lb (8346 kg)
Dimensions: span 80 ft 0 in (24.38 m); length 56 ft 10 in (17.32 m); height 18 ft 9 in (5.72 m); wing area 1,425 sq ft (132.38 m²)
Armament: three 0.303-in (7.7-mm) Lewis guns (one each in nose, dorsal and tail positions), plus up to 2,000 lb (907 kg) of bombs

K5910 entered service as a London Mk I in 1936 for maritime patrol. It was later converted to Mk II standard and is seen here with No. 240 Squadron at Sullom Voe in late 1939. It was fitted with long-range tanks behind the cockpit.

Saro S.36 Lerwick

Designed to Specification R.1/36, the Saro **S.36 Lerwick** was intended to serve alongside the Short Sunderland in RAF Coastal Command. The first three aircraft were used for trials, completed in 1938, and these revealed that the Lerwick was unstable on the water and in the air.

The deficiencies were sufficient, in the opinion of the pilots and crews who flew the machine, to render it unfit for service use, and a series of modifications was made, including the fitting of auxiliary fins; these improved the performance, but were subsequently replaced by a larger fin and rudder.

Trials continued and revealed that the Lerwick had a vicious stall and its performance in roll and yaw was still not satisfactory. However, as the war had by now begun and aircraft were required urgently, production started and the type first entered service with No. 209 Squadron at Oban towards the end of 1940, replacing Short Singapores. One aircraft was soon lost, sinking on 6 December, and another went just over three months later.

The last of 21 Lerwicks was delivered to the RAF in May 1941, the same month in which No. 209 Squadron re-equipped with Consolidated Catalinas. A few Lerwicks served with No. 4 Operational Training Unit at Invergordon, and three others carried out service trials with No. 240 Squadron. The type was withdrawn from operational service in May 1941 and declared obsolete the following year as soon as adequate numbers of more acceptable patrol flying-boats became available from home production and Lend-Lease.

Specification
Lerwick Mk I
Type: six-seat reconnaissance flying-boat
Powerplant: two 1,375-hp (1025-kW) Bristol Hercules II radial piston engines
Performance: maximum speed 216 mph (348 km h) at 4,000 ft (1219 m); cruising speed 166 mph (267 km/h); service ceiling 14,000 ft (4267 m)
Weight: maximum take-off 33,200 lb (15059 kg)
Dimensions: span 80 ft 10 in (24.64 m); length 63 ft 8 in (19.40 m); height 20 ft 0 in (6.10 m); wing area 845 sq ft (78.50 m²)
Armament: seven 0.303-in (7.7-mm) machine-guns (one in nose turret, two in dorsal turret and four in tail turret), plus up to 2,000 lb (907 kg) of bombs

A Lerwick Mk I of No. 209 Squadron takes off at Castle Archdale in 1941. The aircraft was not a success and was replaced by the Catalina in April 1941.

Short S.19 Singapore

The Singapore Mk IIIs filled a gap in Coastal Command's long-range anti-shipping patrol capabilities before more capable types, such as the Sunderland, became available.

Largest of the RAF's pre-war biplane flying-boats still in service at the outbreak of World War II, the Short **S.19 Singapore Mk III** was powered by two tractor and two pusher Rolls-Royce Kestrel engines, mounted in back-to-back pairs.

Development of the Singapore's basic design began with the **Mk I** of 1926, and was followed by the **Mk II** of 1930, which did not go into production. The Mk III was Short's submission to Specification R.3/33; four development aircraft were ordered and the first flew in July 1934. This batch underwent trials at the Marine Aircraft Experimental Establishment, Felixstowe, and, following the completion of these, a production order was issued against a new specification, R.14/34. Contracts followed in batches, and production ceased with the 37th aircraft in June 1937.

The four development aircraft were delivered to squadrons for operational training, and the first production Singapore Mk III flew in March 1935. Deliveries began to No. 230 Squadron at Pembroke Dock in April 1935, and other Singapore Mk IIIs went to Nos 203, 205 and 209 Squadrons.

Nineteen Singapores were still in service at the outbreak of World War II with Nos 203 and 205 Squadrons. The last operations were flown by No. 205 Sqn in October 1941 before the squadron received the Consolidated Catalina.

No. 203 Squadron had maintained a long-range reconnaissance role in the Persian Gulf with Singapore Mk IIIs from 1935. K6907 joined the squadron early in 1936. It remained in service until March 1940, when No. 203 re-equipped with Blenheims.

Specification
Singapore Mk III
Type: six-seat general reconnaissance flying-boat
Powerplant: four 560-hp (418-kW) Rolls-Royce Kestrel inline piston engines
Performance: maximum speed 145 mph (233 km/h) at 2,000 ft (610 m); cruising speed 105 mph (169 km/h); service ceiling 15,000 ft (4572 m); range 1,000 miles (1609 km)
Weights: empty 18,420 lb (8355 kg); maximum take-off 27,500 lb (12474 kg)
Dimensions: span 90 ft 0 in (27.43 m); length 76 ft 0 in (23.16 m); height 23 ft 7 in (7.19 m); wing area 1,834 sq ft (170.38 m²)
Armament: three 0.303-in (7.7-mm) Lewis guns (one each in nose, dorsal and tail positions) plus up to 2,000 lb (907 kg) of bombs

Short S.25 Sunderland

Above: First entering service in August 1941, the Sunderland Mk II had improved armament. This aircraft, W6050, was the first produced by Short & Harland, seen at Queen's Island on 24 April 1942 before its first flight.

Just as the Short S.23 C-class 'Empire' flying-boat marked a startling advance on all previous civil transport aircraft in Imperial Airways, so its military derivative, the Sunderland, marked an equally great advance on marine aircraft in the RAF. Sometimes nicknamed 'The Pig' by its crews, it was dubbed 'The Flying Porcupine' by Luftwaffe pilots who tried to attack it. When the last of these well-loved flying-boats was retired from the RAF on 20 May 1959, it had set a record of 21 years' continuous service in the same oceanic duty. It had also performed many other remarkable feats.

The Sunderland had its origins in a 1933 Air Ministry specification, R.2/33, calling for a new maritime reconnaissance flying-boat to replace the Short Singapore Mk III biplane then just coming off the production line at the Rochester works of Short Brothers. The same company's chief designer, Arthur (later Sir Arthur) Gouge, immediately began to prepare a tender to the new requirement. He was already well advanced with planning a new civil transport flying-boat. Almost alone among British designers, Gouge realised that the all-metal stressed-skin monoplanes being built in the USA and Germany were

Right: A formation of early Sunderland Mk Is is seen just prior to the outbreak of World War II. Coastal Command was one of the success stories of the RAF, particularly in the Battle of the Atlantic, where it played a decisive part in the demise of the U-boat threat to Allied shipping convoys.

Short S.25 Sunderland

This Sunderland Mk I of No. 10 Squadron, RAAF, on patrol from Mount Batten in 1942, had the two dorsal gunners' turrets provided early in the war. By February 1943, Coastal Command had nine squadrons of Sunderlands.

Below: Stripped of armament and fitted with bench-type seats, ex-RAF BOAC Sunderland Mk IIIs flew passenger, freight and mail services between Poole, Dorset, and West Africa from January 1943.

Below: In February 1944 No. 230 Squadron flew Sunderlands to Assam, where they were the first flying-boats to operate from the monsoon-swollen flood waters of the River Brahmaputra. They operated evacuation flights, bringing out injured Chindits.

superior aircraft; he designed the S.23 as a stressed-skin cantilever monoplane with a smooth skin and paid the greatest attention to the reduction of drag. It was an ideal basis for the new RAF 'boat, the **S.25**.

Gouge made his submission in 1934, the specified armament being a 37-mm Coventry Ordnance Works gun in a bow cockpit or turret and a single Lewis machine-gun in the extreme tail. Compared with the civil S.23, the military version had a completely new hull of much deeper cross-section, and a long nose projecting ahead of a flight deck quite near the wing. When construction was well advanced it was decided to alter the armament to a nose turret with one machine-gun and a tail turret with four, a complete reversal of original thoughts on firepower. The shift in centre of gravity could only be countered by moving back the wing or altering the planform so that taper was mainly on the leading edge. The first prototype, K4774, now named Sunderland, was completed with the original wing, basically similar to that of the C-class transport, and flown without armament by J. Lankester Parker from the River Medway on 16 October 1937. After preliminary trials it went back into the factory to have the 'swept-back' wing fitted, flying again on 7 March 1938.

Powered by 1,010-hp (753-kW) Bristol Pegasus XXII engines, more powerful than those of the civil machine, the Sunderland was far more capable in the maritime patrol role than any previous RAF aircraft. Fuel was housed in six vertical drum tanks between the spars with a capacity of 2,025 Imp gal (9206 litres), later increased to 2,552 Imp gal (11602 litres) by four further cells aft of the rear spar. In the original **Sunderland Mk I** the normal crew was seven, accommodated basically on two decks with comprehensive provision for prolonged habitation, with six bunks, galley with cooking stove, workshops and stowage for a considerable quantity of equipment including four rifles and three spare propeller blades. At the upper level it was possible to walk aft from the two-pilot flight deck past the cubicles of the radio operator (left) and navigator (right) and through the deep front spar into the domain of the flight engineer, who had extensive instrument panels inside the wing centre-section.

The main offensive load, comprising up to 2,000 lb (907 kg) of bombs, depth charges, mines or other stores, was hung beneath the centre-section on carriers running on lateral tracks. In combat, large side hatches were opened beneath the wing and the weapons run out under the wings by a drive motor which cut out when the bomb carriages had reached full travel on each side. Defensive armament was concentrated in a Nash and Thompson FN.13 hydraulic tail turret, with four of the new Browning 0.303-in (7.7-mm) guns. In the bows was an FN.11 turret with a single VGO (Vickers gas-operated)

This is Sunderland Mk I N9029 'NM-V' of No. 230 Squadron, Coastal Command. This was the first unit to fly the type when it re-equipped in the summer of 1938. Operating in the Mediterranean from May 1940, it was used during the Battle for Crete, flying from RAF Suda Bay.

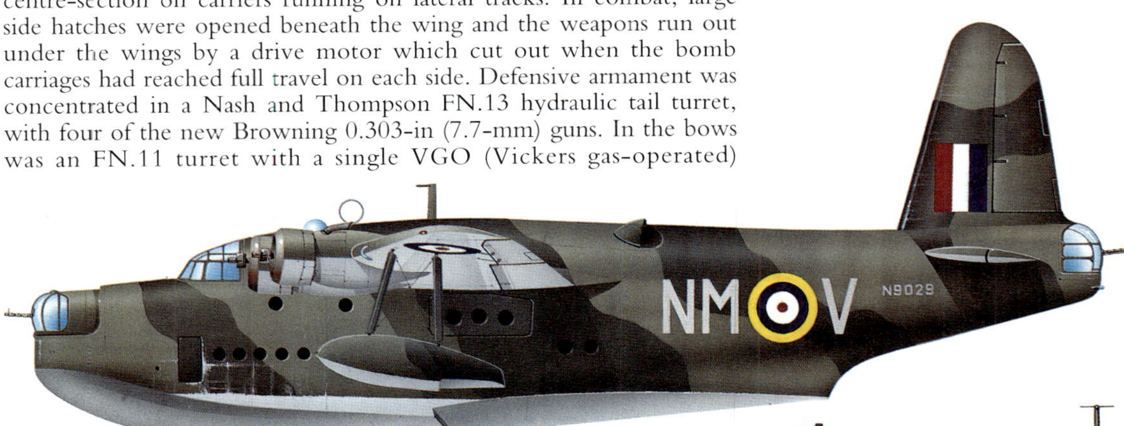

Sunderland Mk II T9807 is seen here in the markings of No. 201 Squadron at Castle Archdale, Co. Fermanagh in 1941. Improved defensive armament was a feature of the Mk II and this example is also fitted with the early ASV aerials. It remained with the squadron until 1944.

Short S.25 Sunderland

machine-gun with a winching system for retracting the turret aft so that the big anchor could be passed out through a bow hatch.

Despite its great bulk the hull was well shaped, and drag was actually lower than for the much smaller biplane Singapore Mk III. Wing loading was, of course, in the order of twice that common on RAF aircraft of the mid-1930s, but Gouge's patented flaps (which had broad chord and rotated aft about a part-cylindrical upper surface) provided increased area and added 30 per cent more lift for landing. Hydrodynamically, a new feature was the bringing of the planing bottom to a vertical knife-edge at the rear (second) step, thereafter sweeping the bottom line smoothly up and back to the tail. Flight-control surfaces were fabric-covered and driven manually, with no servotab assistance, but the Sunderland responded admirably to powerful control demands. A twin-wheel beaching chassis could be attached under the main spar and at the rear of the planing bottom.

RAF service began in June 1938 when the second production Mk I (L2159) was ferried out to No. 230 Squadron at Seletar, Singapore. About 40 were in service at the outbreak of war, and by late 1941 the total output of the Mk I had risen to 90, of which 15 were built by a second-source supplier, a works set up at the Denny shipyard at Dumbarton and run by Blackburn. From late 1939 until 1942 Sunderlands were camouflaged, though in their harsh environments paint flaked off rapidly. Early home-based units, such as Nos 204, 210 and 228 Sqns, plus No. 10 Sqn of the RAAF which arrived to collect its aircraft and stayed in the UK for the next six years, were intensively in action from the first day of the war. Successes against U-boats were at first non-existent, but rescues of torpedoed crews gave the aircraft a good reputation, starting on 18 September 1939 when two of No. 228

U-boat U-426 was sunk after a depth-charge attack by Sunderland Mk III U-Uncle of No. 10 Squadron, RAAF, on 8 January 1944. The squadron flew anti-submarine patrols from RAF Mount Batten for much of the war.

Most of the aircraft on Malta were vulnerable to enemy air attacks. This Sunderland Mk I of No. 228 Squadron was caught in one of the many raids by Axis aircraft on Kalafrana harbour in the winter of 1940. The unit moved to a better protected location at Aboukir in March 1941.

Short Sunderland Mk III cutaway key

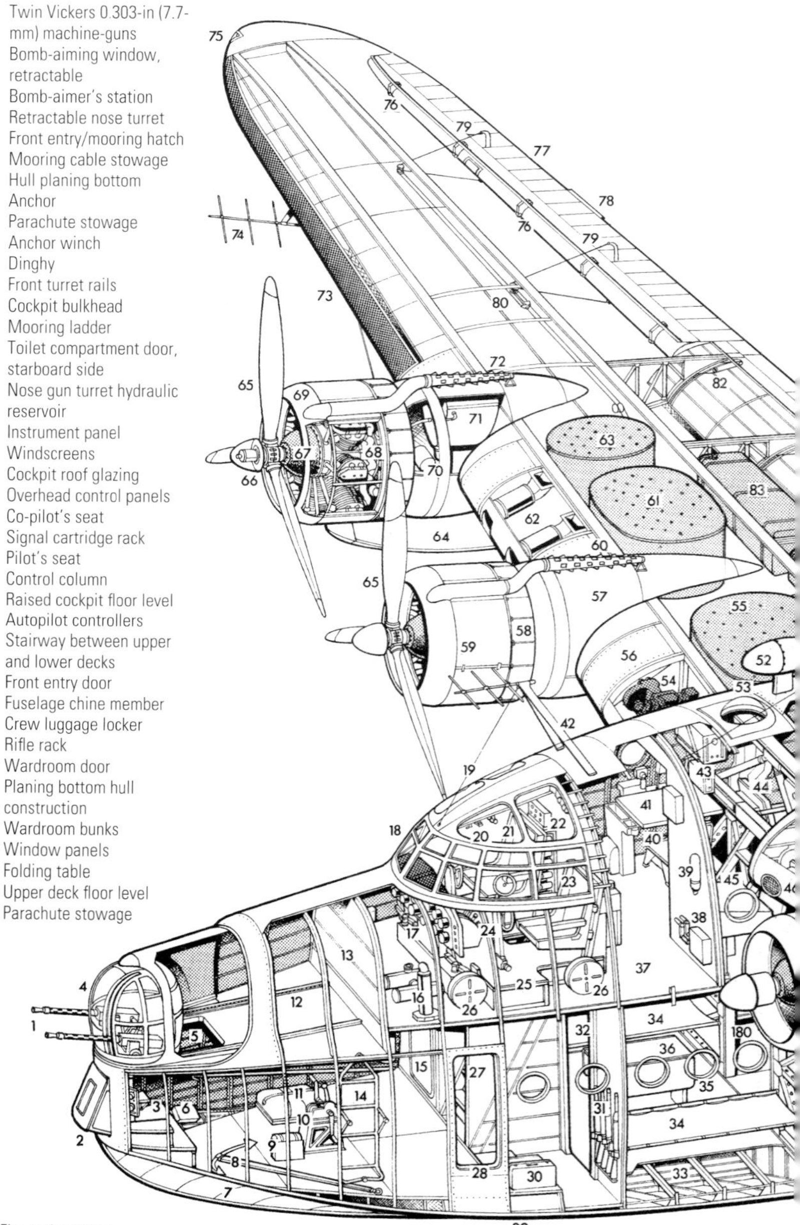

1 Twin Vickers 0.303-in (7.7-mm) machine-guns
2 Bomb-aiming window, retractable
3 Bomb-aimer's station
4 Retractable nose turret
5 Front entry/mooring hatch
6 Mooring cable stowage
7 Hull planing bottom
8 Anchor
9 Parachute stowage
10 Anchor winch
11 Dinghy
12 Front turret rails
13 Cockpit bulkhead
14 Mooring ladder
15 Toilet compartment door, starboard side
16 Nose gun turret hydraulic reservoir
17 Instrument panel
18 Windscreens
19 Cockpit roof glazing
20 Overhead control panels
21 Co-pilot's seat
22 Signal cartridge rack
23 Pilot's seat
24 Control column
25 Raised cockpit floor level
26 Autopilot controllers
27 Stairway between upper and lower decks
28 Front entry door
29 Fuselage chine member
30 Crew luggage locker
31 Rifle rack
32 Wardroom door
33 Planing bottom hull construction
34 Wardroom bunks
35 Window panels
36 Folding table
37 Upper deck floor level
38 Parachute stowage
39 Fire extinguisher
40 Navigator's seat
41 Chart table
42 Forward ASV radar aerial mast
43 Navigator's instrument panel
44 Flight engineer's aft facing seat
45 Radio operator's station
46 Air intake duct
47 Wing/fuselage attachment main frames
48 Wingroot rib cut-outs
49 Air conditioning plant
50 Engineer's control panels
51 Carburettor de-icing fluid tank
52 D/F loop aerial
53 Astrodome observation hatch
54 Auxiliary Power Unit
55 Forward inner fuel tank, 529-Imp gal (2405-litre) capacity
56 Fold-down, leading-edge maintenance platform

A Coastal Command Sunderland drops three depth charges during a low-level run over a submerged U-boat in the Bay of Biscay, sometime in 1943. When the U-boats were on the surface they were attacked using the Sunderland's nose armament, followed up by depth charges as soon as they dived beneath the surface.

57 Starboard inner engine nacelle
58 Cowling air flaps
59 Detachable engine cowlings
60 Flame suppressor exhaust pipe
61 Forward inner fuel tank 325-Imp gal (1477-litre) capacity
62 Oil coolers
63 Forward outer fuel tank, 132-Imp gal (600-litre) capacity
64 Starboard wing tip float
65 De Havilland three-bladed, constant-speed propeller, 12-ft 9-in (3.89-m) diameter
66 Propeller hub pitch change mechanism
67 Engine reduction gearbox
68 Bristol Pegasus XVIII nine-cylinder radial engine, 1,065 hp (795 kW)
69 Exhaust collector ring
70 Oil filter
71 Oil tank, 32-Imp gal (145-litre) capacity
72 Flame suppressor exhaust pipe
73 Leading edge de-icing
74 Starboard ASV aerial array
75 Starboard navigation light
76 Aileron hinges
77 Starboard aileron
78 Fixed tab
79 Aileron control horns
80 Control cable runs
81 Starboard 'Gouge-type' trailing-edge flap
82 Flap guide rails
83 Rear outer fuel tank, 147-Imp gal (668-litre) capacity
84 Flap jack
85 Rear inner fuel tank, 111-Imp gal (505-litre) capacity
86 Pitot tubes
87 Aerial mast
88 Observation window
89 Propeller de-icing fluid tank
90 Windscreen de-icing fluid tank
91 Bomb carriage traversing drive motor
92 Smoke floats and flame floats
93 Tailplane control cable runs
94 Reconnaissance flares
95 Turret fairing
96 Mid upper gun turret, offset to starboard
97 Twin Browning 0.303-in (7.7-mm) machine-guns
98 Fuselage skin plating
99 Spare propeller blade stowage
100 Fire extinguisher
101 Rear entry door
102 Maintenance platform stowage
103 Observation window
104 Fuselage frame and stringer construction
105 ASV Mk II search radar aerial array
106 Leading edge de-icing
107 Starboard tailplane
108 Starboard elevator
109 Fin root attachments
110 Fin construction
111 Leading-edge de-icing
112 Fin tip construction
113 Fabric-covered rudder construction
114 Rudder tabs
115 Tail gun turret
116 Four Browning 0.303-in (7.7-mm) machine-guns
117 Elevator tab
118 Fabric-covered elevator construction
119 Port tailplane construction
120 Leading-edge de-icing
121 Tailplane spar fixing fuselage double frames
122 Tail fuselage fabric draught screen
123 Smoke and flame floats
124 Handrail
125 Tail fuselage walkway
126 Reconnaissance flare chute, stowed
127 Mooring shackle
128 Tow bar
129 Rear beaching trolley
130 Camera stowage
131 Dinghy paddles
132 Distress flares
133 Emergency ration container
134 Dinghy stowage
135 Crew luggage locker
136 Tool locker
137 Bilge keel construction
138 Rear fuselage deck level
139 Crew rest bunks
140 Trailing-edge wingroot fillet
141 Reconnaissance camera mounting
142 Ditching flare chutes
143 Ladder to upper deck level
144 Rear wardroom
145 Twin bunks
146 Fuselage bomb door, open
147 Retractable bomb carriage
148 Four 100-lb (45.4-kg) bombs
149 Bomb store and loading room: maximum bomb load, 2,000 lb (907 kg)
150 Port flap shroud
151 Port 'Gouge-type' trailing-edge flap
152 Fabric-covered aileron construction
153 Aileron tab, fixed
154 Trailing-edge lattice ribs
155 Wingtip construction
156 Port navigation light
157 Rear spar
158 Wing rib construction
159 Front spar
160 Leading-edge de-icing
161 Port ASV radar aerial
162 Wingtip float construction
163 Float support struts
164 Diagonal wire bracing
165 Wing spar girder construction
166 Landing lamps
167 Leading-edge rib construction
168 Diagonal wire-braced wing ribs
169 Fold-down, leading-edge maintenance platform
170 Engine nacelle construction
171 Engine mounting ring
172 Port outer engine nacelle
173 Oil cooler intakes
174 Oil coolers
175 Exhaust shroud heat exchangers
176 Port inner engine nacelle
177 Emergency escape hatch
178 Ice chest
179 Drogue container
180 Gallery compartments, port and starboard
181 Watertight trailing aerial socket
182 Main beaching gear leg strut
183 Twin beaching wheels

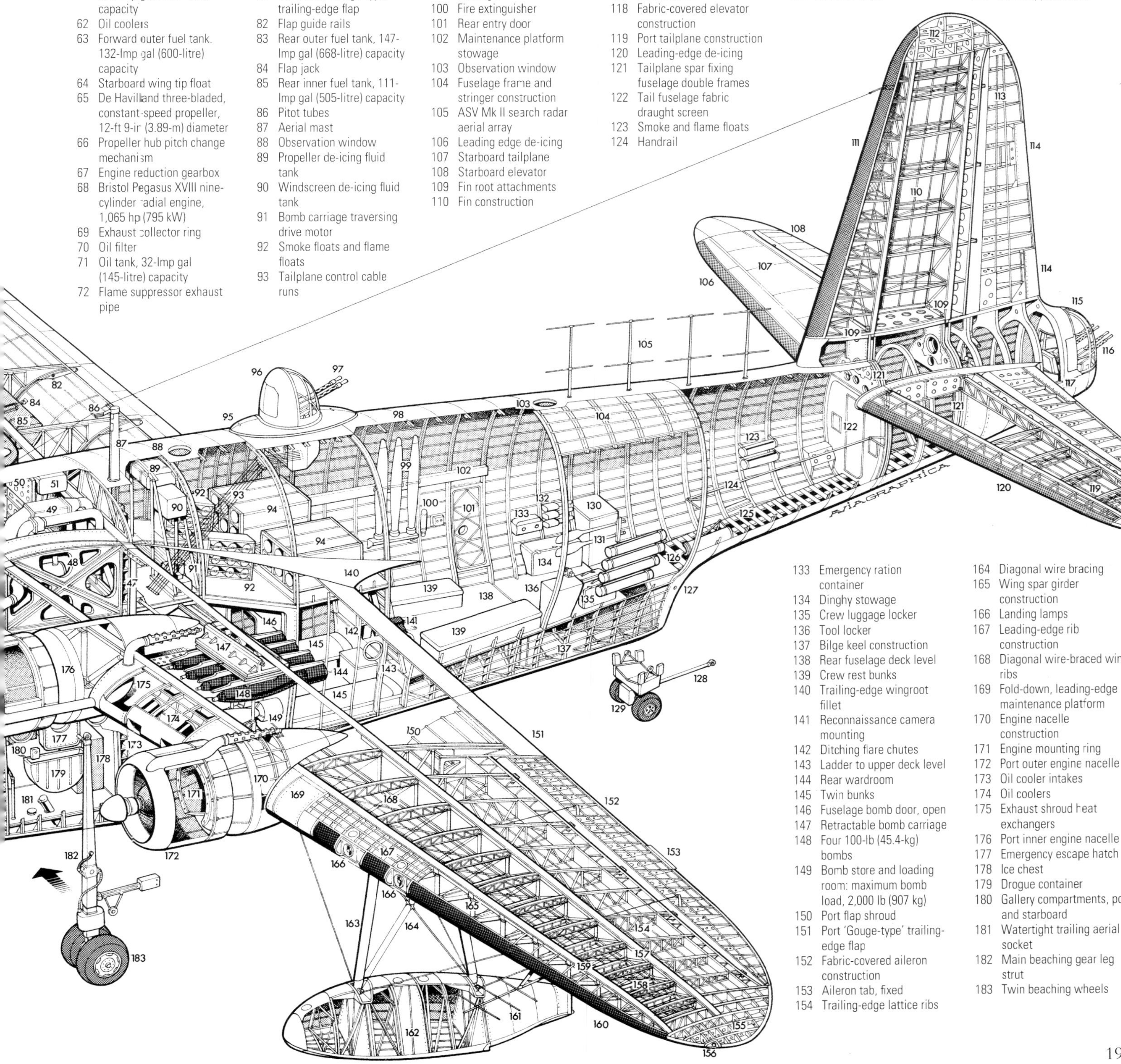

Short Sunderland Mk III

The Short Sunderland Mk III was the version of the flying-boat built in the largest numbers for the RAF. NJ188 was one of a number built by the Blackburn Aircraft Co. Ltd at Dumbarton. It was issued to No. 330 (Norwegian) Squadron, comprised of Norwegian personnel who had escaped to Britain, and served with the RAF until 1945 as 'WH-C', in the markings shown. It was then re-engined with Twin Wasps as a GR.Mk V, but did not enter service and was eventually converted again as a civil Sandringham, operating with BOAC and later Qantas.

Layout
The Sunderland had a double-deck layout, with the entrance door and wardroom below the flight deck and the galley situated between the main frames under the wing. The bow compartment also contained the bomb-sight and forward-hinged bomb-aimer's window, above which was the bow turret. This was retractable aft by means of a chain gear to make an open mooring cockpit, with a folding double bollard for towing. Despite its mammoth proportions and ruggedness in structural design, the Sunderland was not intended for operation in heavy seas or ocean waters. Its true element was coastal waters and sheltered harbours.

Radar
From October 1941, the Mk III had ASV Mk II radar, which covered the upper rear of the hull with distinctive 'Porcupine' matched dipole Yagi homing aerials in groups of four along with dipole-equipped horizontal poles under the outer wings. A Botha-type two-gun dorsal turret took the place of the original open gun mountings.

Armament
The Sunderland Mk III had 18 machine-guns, the greatest number of guns carried by any regular British service aircraft. The Germans gave it the respectful nickname 'Fliegende Stachelschwein' (Flying Porcupine). The bombs or depth charges were fitted to a mobile bomb rack which was wound out under the wing from the fuselage.

Captained by Flt Lt A. Lywood, this Sunderland Mk I of No. 230 Squadron flew reconnaissance missions for the Mediterranean Fleet. Flying this aircraft, Lywood reported Italian fleet movements which led to the Battle of Cape Matapan.

This Sunderland Mk III of No. 201 Squadron was based at Castle Archdale, Northern Ireland in 1945. The white finish was found to be the best camouflage for surface viewing (as seen by U-boats) and so became the standard finish for all maritime reconnaissance units of Coastal Command from early 1943.

Design
Because of revised armament, there was a substantial rearward shift of the centre of gravity and this was offset by the sweeping-back of the wings through 4¼°. Fuel was housed in six (later 10) vertical drum tanks between the spans with a total capacity of 2,025 Imp gal (9206 litres). Wing loading was in the order of twice that common on RAF aircraft of the mid-1930s. Designer Arthur Gouge's patented flaps (which had a broad chord and rotated aft about a part-cylindrical upper surface) provided increased area. Flight control surfaces were fabric-covered and driven manually. The Pegasus XVIII engines of the Mk III were run almost continuously at combat rating, with a consequent deterioration of service life.

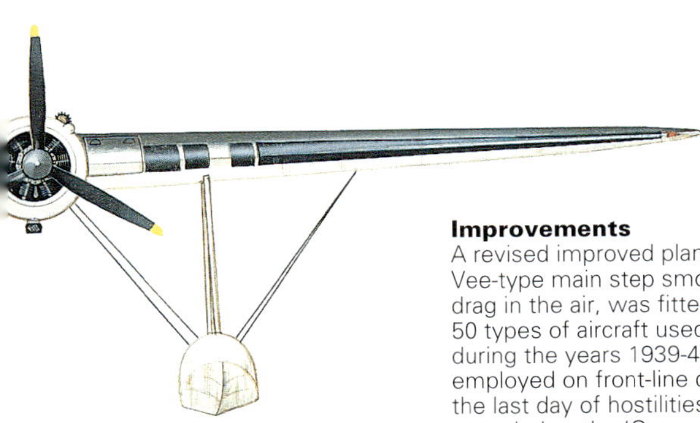

Improvements
A revised improved planing bottom, with the Vee-type main step smoothly faired to reduce drag in the air, was fitted to the Mk III. Of some 50 types of aircraft used by Coastal Command during the years 1939-45, the only one actually employed on front-line duties from the first to the last day of hostilities was the Sunderland, regarded as the 'Queen of the Boats'.

Specification
Sunderland Mk III
Type: long-range reconnaissance and anti-submarine flying-boat
Powerplant: four 1,066-hp (794-kW) Bristol Pegasus XVIII nine-cylinder radial piston engines
Performance: maximum speed 212 mph (341 km/h); service ceiling 15,000 ft (4570 m); range 3,000 miles (4828 km) at 145 mph (233 km/h); endurance 20 hours
Weights: empty 33,000 lb (14969 kg); maximum take-off 58,000 lb (26308 kg)
Dimensions: span 112 ft 10 in (34.39 m); length 85 ft 4 in (26.01 m); height (on beaching chassis) 32 ft 2 in (9.79 m); wing area 1,487 sq ft (138.14 m²)
Armament: one 0.303-in (7.7-mm) Vickers GO machine-gun in nose turret, two 0.303-in (7.7-mm) Browning machine-guns in mid-upper turret, four similar Brownings in tail turret, optional second nose-turret gun, four fixed Brownings firing ahead and twin 0.5-in (12.7-mm) Brownings fired from waist hatches; assorted ordnance to total load of 4,960 lb (2250 kg) housed in hull and cranked out under wings prior to attack

Squadron's aircraft had the whole crew of 34 from the *Kensington Court* in hospital an hour after their ship sank off the Scilly Isles.

By 1940 Sunderlands were being improved in various ways, notably by the addition of two VGO guns aimed from hatches at the rear of the upper deck on each side, with the front part of each hatch opening into the slipstream to give the gunner a calmer area for aiming. Other changes included the progressive addition of a second gun to the nose turret, replacement of the bracket-type de Havilland propellers by 12 ft 6 in (3.81 m) constant-speed propellers with spinners, addition of pulsating rubber-boot de-icers to the wings and tail and, from October 1941, ASV Mk II radar which covered the upper rear of the hull with matched dipole Yagi aerials in groups of four and added long dipole-equipped horizontal poles under the outer wings to give azimuth (homing) guidance. At the 150 mph (241 km/h) speeds which were hardly ever exceeded on patrol, these prominent arrays had little effect on performance.

Though the defensive armament was actually quite light, and contained no gun greater than rifle calibre, the Sunderland soon gained the great respect of the enemy. On 3 April 1940 a Sunderland off Norway was attacked by six Junkers Ju 88s, shot one down, forced another to land immediately, and drove the rest off. Later, another was attacked by eight Ju 88s over the Bay of Biscay and shot down three (confirmed by the convoy it was escorting).

In late 1941 production switched to the **Sunderland Mk II**, with Pegasus XVIII engines with two-speed superchargers and, in the last few examples of this mark, improved armament in a twin Browning nose turret, two more Brownings in an FN.7 dorsal turret on the right side of the hull at the trailing edge, and four Brownings in an FN.4A tail turret with ammunition doubled to 1,000 rounds per gun. Only 43 of this mark were produced, 15 of them at a third source, the Short & Harland company at Queen's Island, Belfast (later the home of the parent company). This limited production resulted from the fact that in June 1941 a Mk I had begun testing an improved planing bottom, with the Vee-type main step smoothly faired to reduce drag in the air. This hull led to the designation **Sunderland Mk III**, and it succeeded the Mk II from December 1941. No fewer than 461 were delivered, 35 coming from a fourth assembly shop on Lake Windermere. The Mk III was effectively the standard wartime boat, and its exploits were legion in all theatres.

In the Mediterranean, Sunderlands were called upon to undertake many dangerous missions, none worse than the prolonged evacuation from Crete when many trips were made with as many as 82 armed passengers in addition to the crew, which by this time had grown to 10. A Sunderland made the necessary visual reconnaissance of Taranto before the Fleet Air Arm attack of 11 November 1940. Over the Atlantic the Sunderland shared with the Consolidated Catalina the main effort against U-boats, but when the latter received Metox passive receivers tuned to ASV Mk II they received ample warning of the presence of British aircraft and kills dropped sharply. The RAF response was the new ASV Mk III, operating in the band well below 50 cm and with the aerials neatly faired into blisters under the outer wings. When thus fitted, the Sunderland became a **Mk IIIA**.

The U-boat sensors could not pick up this radar, and once again, in early 1943, kills became frequent. The response of the U-boats was to fit batteries of deadly flak, typically one or two 37-mm and two quadruple 20-mm cannon, and fight it out on the surface. The odds were then heavily against the flying-boat, which needed forward-firing firepower. Curiously, although the bow was ideally arranged for it, really heavy forward-firing armament was never fitted to the Sunderland, nor was the Leigh light, although many aircraft received four fixed 0.303-in (7.7-mm) Brownings, firing straight ahead, together with a pilot gunsight. The one thing these guns did sometimes succeed in doing was to knock out the U-boat gunners as

Short S.25 Sunderland

they ran from the conning-tower hatch the few metres to their guns.

In addition, heavier lateral armament became common, to combat the more numerous and more heavily armed Luftwaffe long-range fighters. Although the latter's cannon always gave a considerable edge in stand-off range, Sunderlands did at least fit locally contrived installations of single VGOs or Brownings from the escape hatches in the galley compartments. This became a standard fit in late 1943, at which time Short also added an installation of one or two of the much more effective 0.5-in (12.7-mm) Brownings from upper rear hatches behind the trailing edge. Thus, the number of guns rose in a year from five to 18, believed to be the greatest number of guns carried by any regular British service aircraft.

In late 1942 severe shortage of equipment by BOAC, the national civil airline, resulted in six Sunderland Mk IIIs being stripped of all armament and put into joint BOAC/RAF service between Poole and Lagos (West Africa) and Calcutta (India). BOAC investigated the engine installation and cruising angle of attack to such effect that mean cruising speed, which had seldom bothered the RAF, was improved by more than 40 per cent. Spartan bench seats for seven passengers, the main payload being mail, gradually gave way in the BOAC 'Hythe' class to an excellent airline interior for 24 passengers (16 with sleeping accommodation), plus 6,500 lb (2950 kg) of mail, and the engines were modified to Pegasus 38 (later 48) standard. By 1944 the number of civil Sunderland Mk IIIs had grown to 24, and after the war the Hythes, eventually totalling 29, were supplemented by a complete civil rebuild, the S.26 Sandringham – which went into production as a basic transport for BOAC (as the 'Plymouth' class) and its airlines.

The increasing demands made on the military Sunderland, especially after the start of warfare in the Pacific, led in 1942 to Specification R.8/42 for a more powerful long-range flying-boat, to which Short Brothers responded with the Hercules-engined **Sunderland Mk IV**. This grew so different from the Sunderland, with an improved hull, new tail and completely revised armament, that it was renamed the **Seaford Mk I**. Surprisingly, this saw only brief post-war service, but formed the basis for the civil Solent. The need for more power remained, and in early 1944 the decision was taken simply to re-engine a Mk III with Pratt & Whitney R-1830-90B Twin Wasps, similar to the engine used in the Catalina and Dakota and many other types and already in widespread RAF service. The 14-cylinder engine conferred a substantial improvement in climb, ceiling and engine-out performance, yet had hardly any effect on range, although cruising speed tended to be slightly higher. Operationally, the US-engined machine had a great advantage in being able to cruise with two engines out on one side, whereas the Sunderland Mk III in this state lost height steadily.

After trials in March 1944 the Twin Wasp Sunderland was accepted for production as the **Mk V**, with de Havilland Hydromatic propellers without spinners. ASV Mk III was fitted as standard, and in the course of 1944 Rochester, Belfast and Dumbarton all switched to the Mk V, respectively building 47, 48 and 60. This version entered service with No. 228 Sqn in February 1945. A further 33 were produced by conversion from Mk IIIAs. In August 1945 large contracts were cancelled, the last Sunderland coming from Belfast in June 1946, where, as at Dumbarton, dozens of new 'boats were packed with new military equipment and deliberately sunk shortly after the end of the war.

***Above:** In January 1945 No. 230 Squadron's long-serving Sunderland Mk IIIs were replaced by the Mk V version. Fitted with the more powerful Pratt & Whitney Twin Wasp engine, the Mk Vs remained in service with the squadron until February 1957.*

***Below:** This Sunderland Mk III served with No. 230 Squadron after the unit returned to the Far East in February 1944. A year later No. 230 Sqn moved to Burma, where this photograph was taken, to attack Japanese shipping. The aircraft is painted in Pacific theatre markings.*

***Right:** No. 230 Squadron was one of the original recipients of the Mk I in 1938, when it was based at Seletar. In April 1942 it received its first Mk III, and by January 1943 had replaced all of the remaining Mk IIs. ML868 was a Blackburn-built Mk III equipped with ASV II radar, here flying over Burma near the end of the war in the Far East.*

The Sunderland joined the Catalina in the Indian Ocean in 1943 to fly maritime patrols. ML868 'H' flew with No. 230 Squadron, operating from bases in Ceylon, India, Burma and East Africa during 1944 and 1945. After the war, this aircraft took part in the British North Greenland expedition. The 'goalpost' radar aerials are clearly visible above and on the side of the fuselage, and under the wingtips.

Short S.29 Stirling

Above: A flight of No. 1651 Heavy Conversion Unit Stirlings flies over Little Thetford, Cambs on 29 April 1942. All three aircraft subsequently came to grief. Aircraft 'G' (N6096) was lost on the Hamburg raid of 29 July 1942, while 'S' (N3676)and 'C' (N6069) both crashed on take-off, the former at Waterbeach on 30 July 1942 and the latter on 20 April 1943.

The Stirling was used extensively on night raids during 1941-42. This bomb trolley carries the load for one aircraft, ready to be winched up into the fuselage and wingroot bomb bays of N6101 at Waterbeach in 1942.

The Short S.29 Stirling was the RAF's first four-engined monoplane bomber to enter service, and the first to be used operationally in World War II. Ironically, since it was also the first to be withdrawn from service, it was the only one of the three bombers to be designed from the outset with four engines, both the Avro Lancaster and Handley Page Halifax originating as twin-engined projects.

Specification B.12/36 drew submissions from Armstrong Whitworth, Short and Supermarine, and two prototypes were ordered from each of the two latter companies. In the event, the Supermarine aircraft were destroyed in an air raid before completion, so Short's design was left with a clear field. An initial production order for 100 was given to Short's at Rochester, and another 100 were ordered from Short & Harland's new Belfast factory. It was decided to build a half-scale wooden research aircraft, powered by four 90-hp (67-kW) Pobjoy Niagara engines, to test the aerodynamic qualities of the design, and this flew at Rochester on 19 September 1938. It was later re-engined with 115-hp (86-kW) Niagaras and made well over 100 flights before being scrapped in 1943.

It was only natural that, as Britain's pre-eminent flying boat builder, Short should consider using the Sunderland wing design, but an Air Ministry requirement that the span should not exceed 100 ft (30.48 m), so that the aircraft could be housed in standard RAF hangars, meant that the wing had to be shortened, and the high

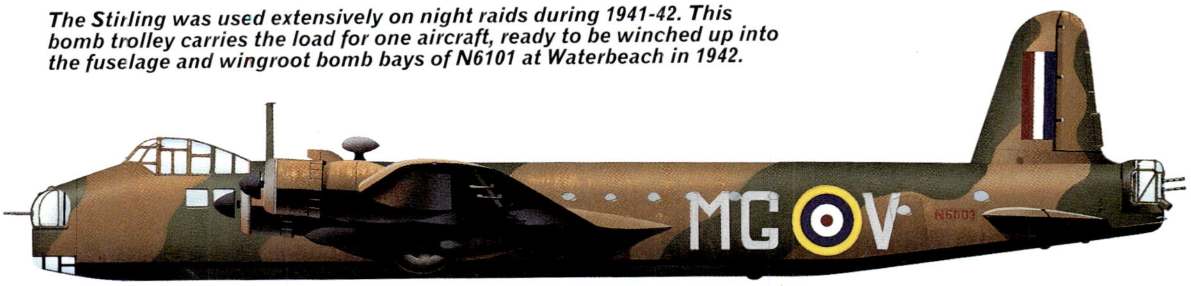

This Stirling Mk I Series 1 of No. 7 Squadron was based at RAF Oakington, in early 1941. The aircraft was operational with this squadron until December, when it joined the training circuit with No. 26 Conversion Flight and then No. 1651 (Heavy) Conversion Unit.

With the black camouflage extended to include the tail fin, this Stirling Mk I Series 2 of No. 149 Squadron flew from Mildenhall in early 1942. Transferred to training duties with No. 1657 (Heavy) Conversion Unit, it was shot down over Britain on 7 September 1943 by a German intruder.

Left: A late-model Stirling Mk I Series III with a dorsal turret from No. 218 Squadron is seen taking off from Downham Market bound for Germany in late 1943. Its undercarriage and flaps are being retracted as it climbs out at an indicated airspeed of 150 mph (241 km/h).

Below: Late-production Stirling Mk Is of No. 7 Squadron, fitted with Frazer-Nash FN 50 mid-upper turrets, are fuelled and prepared for operations at Oakington in 1942. The squadron, the first to be equipped with Stirlings in August 1940, received Mk IIIs in August 1943.

altitude performance suffered accordingly.

The prototype Stirling made its first flight on 14 May 1939, but was written off when a brake seizure caused the landing gear to collapse on landing; hardly an auspicious start to its career. Seven months later the second prototype flew, powered like the first with 1,375-hp (1025-kW) Bristol Hercules II engines. The first production Stirling, flown on 7 May 1940, had 1,595-hp (1189-kW) Hercules XIs, and deliveries to the RAF began in August 1940, when No. 7 Squadron at Leeming began to replace its Wellingtons with the first of the new four-engined bombers. The **Stirling Mk I** was 'blooded' on the night of 10/11 February 1941, when three aircraft from No. 7 Squadron attacked oil storage tanks at Rotterdam.

Stirling orders then stood at 1,500 aircraft, and contracts for manufacture were extended to cover Austin Motors at Longbridge, Birmingham, and Rootes at Stoke-on-Trent; Stirling production eventually spread to more than 20 factories, but was initially very slow as priority had been allocated to fighter construction. Another factor which held up early production was the destruction of a number of Stirlings on the assembly lines, when the Rochester and Belfast factories were bombed in August 1940.

However, production eventually got into its stride, and by the end of 1941 more than 150 Stirlings had been completed. In service the Stirling was to prove popular with its crews and very manoeuvrable – a useful attribute when it was attacked by German fighters, and one which earned it the contemporary nickname 'the fighter bomber'. One Stirling of No. 218 Squadron, returning from a night raid in June 1942, survived attacks from four German night-fighters and destroyed three, before returning battered but safe to its base.

Plans to build Stirlings in Canada were made in 1941, but although a contract for 140 was placed it was later cancelled. This was to have been the **Stirling Mk II**, powered by 1,600-hp (1193-kW) Wright Cyclone R-2600 engines, and two prototypes were built as conversions from Mk Is. They were followed by three production aircraft, but this variant was not adopted as the supply of Hercules engines was proving sufficient for requirements.

The **Stirling Mk III** had 1,635-hp (1219-kW) Hercules VI or XVI engines; apart from their minimal extra power, the main advantage of this powerplant was that it was far easier to maintain. The Mk III was given a new dorsal turret, of flatter profile, to replace the angular model of the Mk I, and some internal changes were made.

Stirling production peaked at 80 aircraft a month by mid-1943, and the last to be built as bombers were completed in the autumn of 1944.

As deliveries of the Halifax and Lancaster built up, so the Stirlings

This early-production Stirling Mk I Series 1, with No. 7 Squadron in late 1940, was fitted with the underpowered Hercules II radial engine and equipped with Frazer-Nash nose and tail turrets, but no dorsal turret.

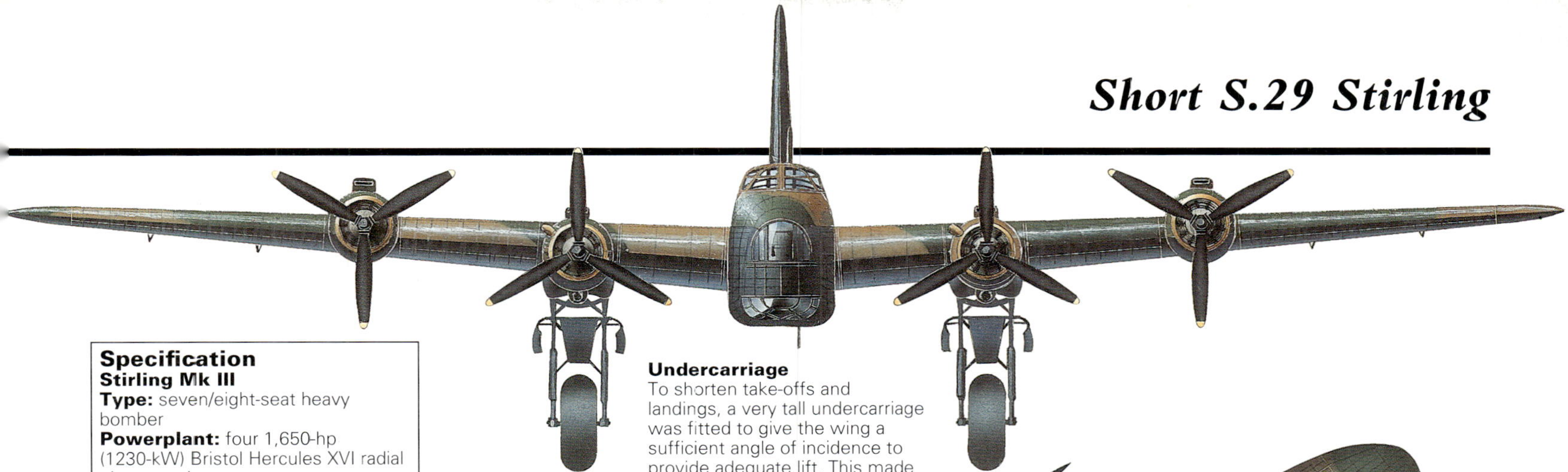

Specification
Stirling Mk III
Type: seven/eight-seat heavy bomber
Powerplant: four 1,650-hp (1230-kW) Bristol Hercules XVI radial piston engines
Performance: maximum speed 270 mph (435 km/h) at 14,500 ft (4420 m); ceiling 17,000 ft (5182 m); range 2,010 miles (3235 km) with 3,500 lb (1588 kg) of bombs or 590 miles (950 km) with 14,000 lb (6350 kg) of bombs
Weights: empty 43,200 lb (19595 kg); maximum take-off 70,000 lb (31751 kg)
Dimensions: span 99 ft 1 in (30.20 m); length 87 ft 3 in (26.59 m); height 22 ft 9 in (6.93 m); wing area 1,460 sq ft (135.63 m²)
Armament: eight 0.303-in (7.7-mm) machine-guns (two each in nose and dorsal turrets, and four in tail turret), plus up to 14,000 lb (6350 kg) of bombs

Undercarriage
To shorten take-offs and landings, a very tall undercarriage was fitted to give the wing a sufficient angle of incidence to provide adequate lift. This made taking-off and landing very tricky as the aircraft had a tendency to swing violently unless carefully handled.

Wings
The Stirling was the only one of three RAF wartime four-engined heavy bombers that was designed as such from the outset. Although it was a good, stable aircraft in flight and surprisingly manoeuvrable, its weight was supported by a wing of short span owing to the design requirement that the aircraft could be housed in the standard pre-war hangars, which had 100-ft (30.48-m) door openings. The wing area was the chief limiting factor that resulted in the Stirling's poor operational altitude when loaded.

Bomb load
While a Stirling could carry as many as 25,500 lb (11567 kg) of bombs and deliver them over a short range, it was unable to accommodate the larger bombs that the Lancaster could accept. It had seven fuel tanks in each wing and a total capacity of 2,254 Imp gal (10247 litres), sufficient to give a radius of 900 miles (1448 km) from base in favourable weather conditions.

Short Stirling Mk I

The first of the RAF's four-engined heavy bombers to enter service, the Short Stirling eventually equipped seven squadrons in No. 3 Group, with airfields in the Cambridge-Huntingdon area. The first, No. 7, started to receive Stirlings in August 1940, and this unit took the new bomber on its first operation on the night of 10-11 February 1941 to attack an oil storage depot at Rotterdam. This Stirling Mk I Srs 1, N3641 'MG-D', was the first to join No. 7 Squadron.

Wheels
The main wheels of the Stirling had the largest British tyre, manufactured by Dunlop, on an operational aircraft during World War II. The aircraft suffered from troublesome undercarriage retraction motors which proved inadequate for the task they were required to undertake.

Short S.29 Stirling

***Right:** As a result of its high wing loading, the Stirling had a high rate of roll and was manoeuvrable enough to out-turn the Ju 88 night-fighter during dogfights. This Stirling of No. 15 Squadron is seen with Hurricane fighters on 7 July 1941.*

***Below:** A Stirling Mk V of No. 46 Squadron conducts an air test in 1945. The propeller spinners were sometimes used in conjunction with cooling fans, fitted under the cowlings of Mk IVs and Mk Vs, to help prevent overheating.*

began to be withdrawn for other tasks. They had two main drawbacks an inability to attain the operating altitude of around 20,000 f (6100 m) achieved by the newer bombers, and a bomb bay which could not be adapted to carry the ever larger bombs that were being designed. Bomber Command's last operational Stirling sortie was flown by No. 149 Squadron, on 8 September 1944, and at the peak of their use 13 squadrons had been equipped in the bombing role (Nos 7, 15, 75, 90, 101, 149, 166, 199, 214, 218, 513, 622 and 623). Total production of bomber versions amounted to 1,759, of which 712 were Mk Is and 1,047 Mk IIIs.

From the beginning of 1944 the Stirling's main role became that of glider-tug and transport with RAF Transport Command, under the designation **Mk IV**. Two Stirling Mk IIIs served as prototypes for the new version, and were first flown in 1943. Retaining the Mk III's engines, the Mk IV had nose and dorsal turrets removed and the apertures faired over. Glider-towing equipment was fitted in the rear fuselage, but the tail turret was retained.

The Stirling proved efficient in its new roles, with Nos 190 and 622 Squadrons from Fairford and Nos 196 and 299 from Keevil, towing Airspeed Horsa gliders to Normandy on D-Day, 6 June 1944. Stirling Mk IVs were also used for the airborne landings at Arnhem and the March 1945 attack across the Rhine. Other squadrons to use this version included Nos 138, 161, 171, 295, 570, 620 and 624.

As a glider-tug, the Stirling Mk IV could cope with one Hamilcar or two Horsas in the assault role, or up to five Hotspurs on a ferry flight or for training. Less well known were the operations of Nos 138 and 161 (Special Duties) Squadrons, flying for the Special Operations Executive (SOE) from Tempsford, near Cambridge. They had the task of supplying arms to the Resistance in occupied countries, and No. 624 Sqn engaged in similar work in the Mediterranean area, operating from Blida in North Africa. Total production of the Mk IV was 450.

Wearing its recently applied invasion stripes (three white and two black), a Stirling Mk IV of No. 295 Squadron at RAF Harwell takes off with a Horsa glider on tow on 6 June 1944, to head across the Channel for the D-Day landings in Normandy.

Short Stirling Mk III cutaway drawing key

1 Starboard wingtip navigation light
2 Formation light
3 Starboard aileron
4 Aileron control horns
5 Outboard No. 6 fuel tank, capacity 81 Imp gal (568 litres)
6 Outboard No. 5 fuel tank, capacity 164 Imp gal (745.5 litres)
7 Starboard outer engine nacelle
8 De Havilland three-bladed propellers
9 Propeller hub pitch-change mechanism
10 Starboard inner engine nacelle
11 Oil cooler
12 Carburettor air intake
13 Flame suppressor exhaust pipe
14 Inboard No. 4 fuel tank, capacity 254 Imp gal (1155 litres)
15 Dinghy stowage
16 Gouge-type trailing-edge flap
17 Flap guide rails
18 Flap screw Jack
19 Inboard dinghy stowage
20 Trailing-edge No. 1 fuel tank, capacity 80 Imp gal (364 litres)
21 Trailing-edge No. 2 fuel tank, capacity 63 Imp gal (286 litres)
22 Inboard No. 2 fuel tank, capacity 331 Imp gal (1505 litres)
23 Main undercarriage wheel bay
24 Inner wing auxiliary fuel tanks, capacity 219 Imp gal (996 litres)
25 Aerial mast
26 Identification beacon
27 Cockpit canopy construction
28 Pilot's escape hatch
29 Cockpit roof control panel
30 Windscreen panels
31 Co-pilot's seat
32 Seat back armour plate
35 Pilot's seat
34 Control column
35 Rudder pedals
36 Instrument panel
37 Nose gun turret, Frazer-Nash FN5
38 Two 0.303-in (7.7-mm) Browning machine-guns
39 Forward identification light
40 Bomb aimer's window
41 Bomb sight
42 Bomb aimer's control panel
43 Ballast weight stowage box
44 Prone position couch
45 Pitot tubes
46 Parachute stowage
47 Nose section joint frame
48 Ventral escape hatch
49 Access steps
50 Brake system air bottles
51 Flight deck floor level
52 Cockpit heater pipe
53 Auto pilot controls
54 Dinghy stowage
55 Navigator's chart table
56 Engineer's control panel
57 Cabin side windows
58 Dinghy and parachute pack stowage
59 Main floor/bomb bay longeron

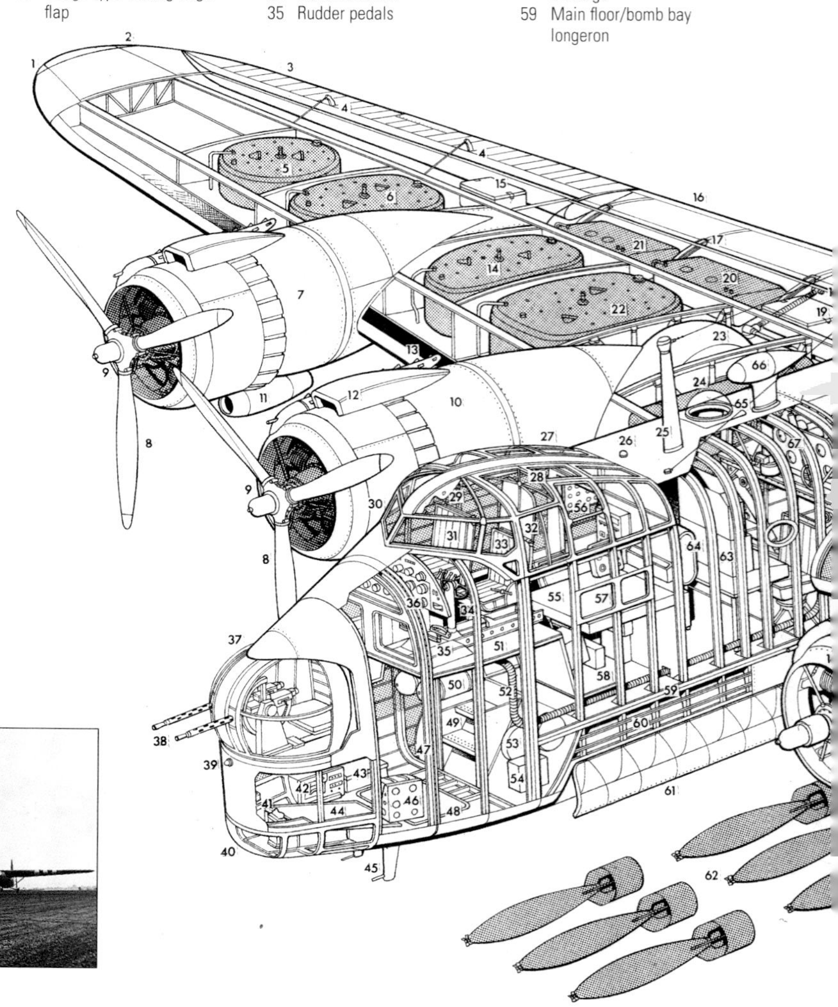

Short S.29 Stirling

***Left:* A crew from No. 149 Squadron retire to the crew room at Mildenhall in early 1942. The aircraft, W7455 'OJ-B', survived bombing operations with this unit and two other squadrons, only to be shot down by an enemy night intruder over Great Thurlow.**

***Below:* Perhaps the best known Stirling of the early war years, N6086 was allocated to No. 15 Squadron on 15 September 1941. The aircraft bears the coat of arms of the MacRobert family and the legend 'MacRobert's Reply'.**

60 Forward end of bomb bay
61 Bomb doors
62 Total bomb load, 14,000 lb (6350 kg)
63 Radio operator's station
64 Water tank
65 Astrodome observation hatch
66 D/F loop aerial fairing
67 Oxygen bottles
68 Fuselage/wing spar frame
69 Centre-section access panel
70 Batteries
71 Leading-edge No. 7 fuel tank, capacity 154 Imp gal (700 litres)
72 Port wing bomb bay auxiliary fuel tanks, capacity 219 gal (995.5 litres)
73 Crew rest bunk
74 Flap drive motor
75 Oxygen bottles
76 De-icing fluid tank
77 Electrical system junction boxes
78 Sliding door to rear fuselage
79 Rear fuselage joint frame
80 Whip aerial
81 Kite aerial stowage
82 Cabin roof escape hatch
83 Ladder
84 Upper turret ammunition boxes
85 Mid upper gun turret, Frazer-Nash FN7
86 Two 0.303-in (7.7-mm) Browning machine-guns
87 Turret fairings
88 Gun turret mechanism
89 Gunner's access ladder
90 Gunner's seat
91 Tail gun turret ammunition boxes
92 Flame floats
95 Flare launcher chutes
94 Reconnaissance flares
95 Ammunition tracks to rear turret
96 Rear fuselage frame construction
97 Master compass
98 Starboard tailplane
99 Starboard elevator
100 Aerial cable
101 Fin construction
102 Rudder hinges
103 Fabric-covered rudder construction
104 Rudder servo tab
105 Tail navigation light
106 Rudder trim tab
107 Tail gun turret, Frazer-Nash FN 20A
108 Four 0.303-in (7.7-mm) Browning machine-guns
109 Rear formation light
110 Tail turret access doors
111 Tailplane double frames
112 Elevator trim tab
115 Fabric-covered elevator construction
114 Port tailplane construction
115 Tail undercarriage doors
116 Twin tailwheels
117 Retraction mechanism
118 Tail gunner's access ladder
119 Toilet
120 Rear fuselage walkway
121 Entry door
122 Combined parachute and dinghy stowage (spares)
125 Ventral escape hatch
124 Ammunition feed bolt
125 Ventral 0.303-in (7.7-mm) machine-gun
126 Radio aerial
127 Aft end of bomb bay
128 Wingroot trailing-edge fillet
129 Flap housing construction
130 Port main undercarriage retraction motor
131 Rear spar girder construction
132 Port main undercarriage wheel bay
133 Undercarriage retraction gearbox and screw jack
134 Dinghy stowage
135 Flap screw jack gearbox
136 Port No. 1 fuel tank, capacity 180 Imp gal (363.7 litres)
137 Port No. 3 fuel tank, capacity 63 Imp gal (286 litres)
138 Flap guide rails
139 Port Gouge-type flap
140 Outboard dinghy stowage
141 Port fabric-covered aileron
142 Aileron control horns
143 Aileron trim tab
144 Wingtip construction
145 Formation light
146 Port navigation light
147 Outer wing ribs
148 Leading-edge nose ribs
149 Retractable landing/taxiing lamps
150 Wing skin/fuel tank access panels
151 Watertight ribs between fuel tank bays
152 Engine nacelle support structure
153 Engine support struts
154 Engine mounting ring
155 Front cowling support struts
156 Port mainwheel
157 Main undercarriage leg strut
158 Main undercarriage doors
159 Mudguard
160 Undercarriage tie-beam
161 Undercarriage leg knee joint pivot
162 Front spar girder construction
163 Wing rib construction
164 Oil tank, capacity 55 Imp gal (150 litres)
165 Engine accessories
166 Cooling air exit flaps
167 Flame suppressor exhaust pipe
168 Carburettor air intake
169 Exhaust pipe collector ring
170 Bristol Hercules XVI radial engine
171 Propeller reduction gearbox
172 Oil cooler intake

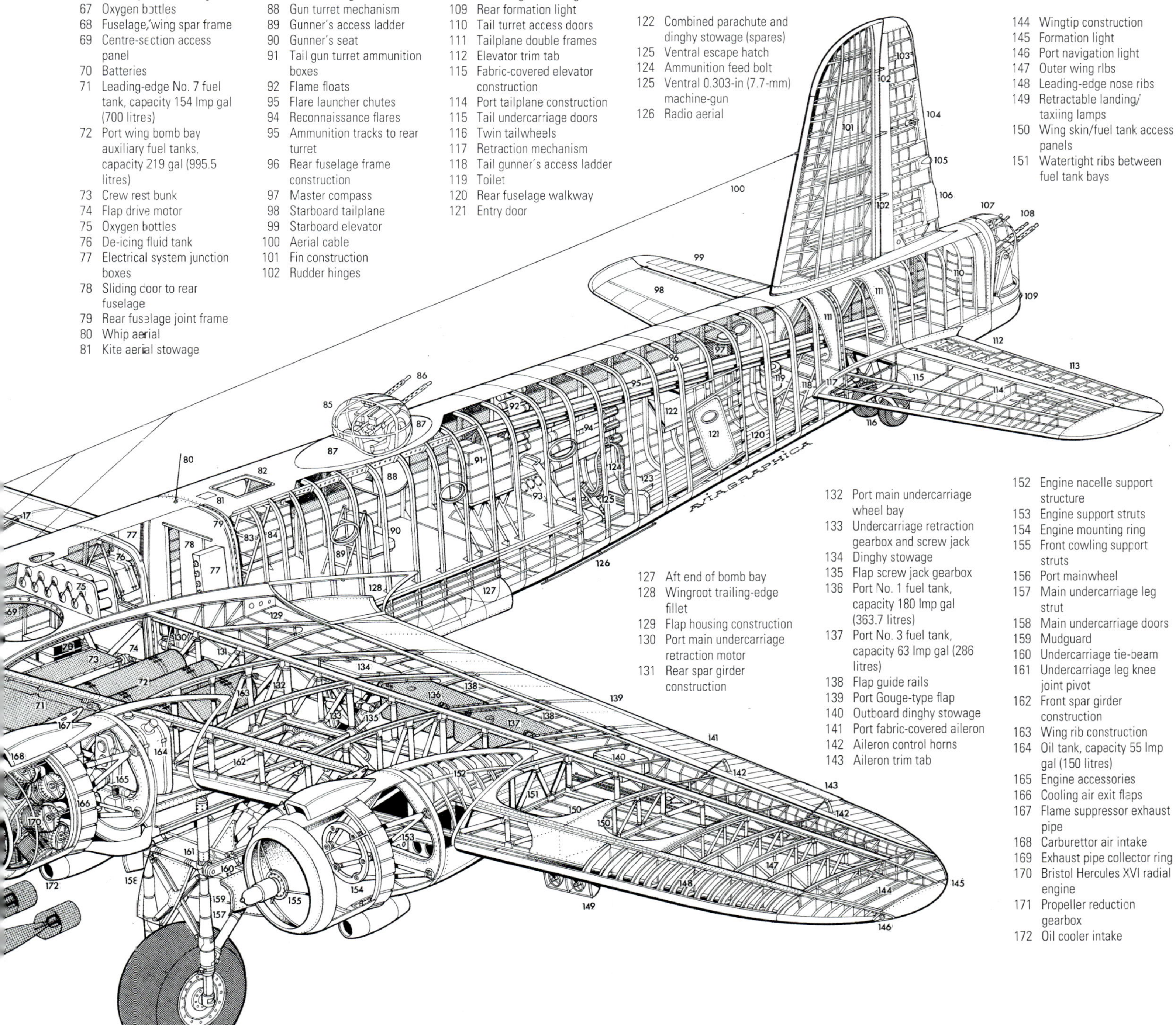

Short S.29 Stirling

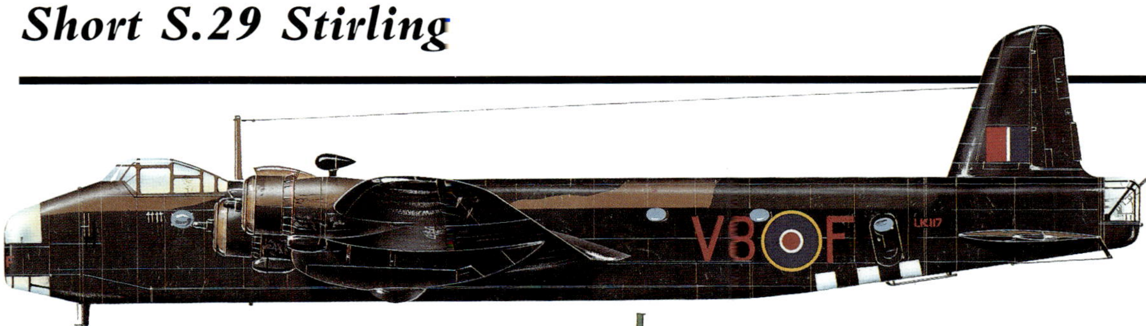

This Stirling, 'V8-F' of No. 570 Squadron, was based at RAF Harwell in 1944. The Squadron carried out 22 glider-towing sorties to Arnhem, followed by 58 resupply missions, for the loss of 11 aircraft.

This Stirling Mk I Series 2 of No. 7 Squadron operated with No. 8 Group Pathfinder Force from Oakington, in the summer of 1943. The aircraft is fitted with the H_2S bombing radar.

The last production version was the **Mk V** unarmed transport, first flown from Rochester in August 1944. It could carry up to 40 troops (20 if they were fully equipped paratroops), or 12 stretchers and 14 seated casualties. The lengthened nose hinged open, and there was a large loading door in the right-hand side of the rear fuselage with portable loading ramps. Two jeeps with trailers, or a jeep with a field gun, trailer and ammunition could be carried.

Production of the Stirling Mk V was undertaken at Belfast, and ended with the 160th aircraft in November 1945. Stirling Mk Vs served with Nos 46, 48, 158, 242 and 299 Squadrons until Avro Yorks replaced them.

Official figures for the RAF Stirling show that they made 18,440 sorties, dropped 27,821 tons (28268 tonnes) of bombs and laid 20,000 mines, for the loss of 769 aircraft.

The prototype Stirling Mk V, LJ530, was converted on the Rochester production line and flown in August 1944. Specifically designed for cargo and entirely unarmed, it could carry two jeeps with trailers, or a single jeep with a six-pounder field gun, trailer, ammunition and crew. With a large loading door, it was intended for use in the Far East campaign in support of the 'Tiger Force'.

Sikorsky Hoverfly

First flown in September 1939, the Sikorsky VS-300 was the basis for development of the world's first truly practical helicopter, built for the USAAF as the **XR-4**. Thirty pre-production **YR-4A**s and **YR-4B**s were followed by full production of 100 **R-4B**s for the USAAF. From this total, Britain received two YR-4As in 1943, and five YR-4Bs in 1944, plus 45 of the definitive R-4Bs – well below a requested 240. The name **Gadfly** was used initially, and perhaps unofficially, before **Hoverfly Mk I** was adopted for all the British R-4 variants.

The Hoverfly seated two side-by-side, with dual controls but had little margin to carry anything more than the two occupants. Nevertheless, the potential for anti-submarine patrols was evaluated by British pilots aboard the merchantman *Daqhestan* on a transatlantic convoy in January 1944, while the training of Service pilots (RAF, RN and Army) began in March 1944 at the US Coast Guard base at Floyd-Bennett Field, using RAF Hoverflies. When this school disbanded, 11 Hoverflies made a 350-mile (563-km) cross-country flight in formation to Norfolk, Virginia, to embark on HMS *Thane*, bound for the UK. General Aircraft Ltd became responsible in Britain for the introduction of the Hoverfly into RAF and RN service, establishing a training school at Hanworth.

Operational deployment of the Hoverfly Mk I began during 1944 with both the RAF and the FAA. No. 529 Sqn, already conversant with the Cierva Rota, evaluated the Hoverfly, as did a rotary-wing flight set up by the AFEE at Beaulieu, while No. 43 OTU at Andover formed a helicopter training flight. The RN Hoverflies, mostly fitted with floats in place of wheels, were flown by No. 771 Squadron at Whetstone in the Orkneys and, later, Portland. Much experience of helicopter operations continued to be gained with the Hoverfly Mk Is until 1950.

The designation **Hoverfly Mk II** applied to the much developed Sikorsky **R-6A**, with a more streamlined fuselage around the same basic transmission and rotor system as the R-4. Britain requested 150 of these through Lend-Lease, but received just 28, delivered between July and September 1945 and thus too late for wartime service.

The Hoverfly Mk I was the British version of the Sikorsky R-4 and was the first type of helicopter to be used by the RAF. A total of 45 production examples was delivered to the RAF during the latter stages of World War II.

Specification
Hoverfly Mk I
Type: two-seat training and rescue helicopter
Powerplant: one 180-hp (134-kW) Warner R-550-1 radial piston engine
Performance: maximum speed 75 mph (121/km/h); service ceiling 8,000 ft (2440 m); range 130 miles (209 km)
Weights: empty 2,020 lb (916 kg); maximum take-off 2,535 lb (1150 kg)
Dimensions: main rotor diameter 38 ft 0 in (11.58 m); length 48 ft 2 in (14.68 m); height 12 ft 5 in (3.78 m); rotor disc area 1,134 sq ft (105.35 m^2)

Stinson Reliant

Between December 1939 and September 1940, 14 examples of the Reliant high-wing cabin monoplane were impressed for service in the UK; a 15th was added at the end of 1942. All previously on the British civil register, these were of five different models, similar in configuration but differing in detail and powerplant and identified as the **SR-5**, **SR-7B**, **SR-8**, **SR-9** and **SR-10**. Several of the Reliants served with No. 1 Camouflage Unit at Baginton and later Hendon – a unit that existed to advise military and industrial establishments on camouflage of their facilities from the air – while others were used by the Air Transport Auxiliary and elsewhere.

In the US, some 47 Reliants were similarly impressed for military use, but production under a wartime US Army Air Force contract was undertaken only to meet a Lend-Lease contract to provide 500 aircraft to Britain, for use by the Fleet Air Arm. Designated **AT-19** for contractual purposes, these four-seat cabin monoplanes were named **Reliant Mk I** and served as radio/navigation trainers or for communications duties.

Delivery of the Reliants to the UK began in late 1943 and continued throughout 1944, some also being shipped from the US direct to the Far East. Records show Reliants were on the strength of as many as 26 Fleet Air Arm training and ancillary squadrons, and the use made of this type in the communications role was clearly significant in the closing year or so of the war, although little publicised. Overseas, No. 752 Squadron was a major user of the Reliant in its capacity as No. 1 Observer's School, based at Piarco in Trinidad.

Within a few months of the war's end, 415 Reliants were returned to NAS Norfolk, where they were taken on charge by the US Navy for administrative purposes only, being then sold off in mid-1946 by the War Assets Administration for civilian use.

Specification
Reliant Mk I
Type: four-seat navigation/radio trainer and communications aircraft
Powerplant: one 290-hp (216-kW) Lycoming R-680 radial piston engine
Performance: maximum speed 141 mph (227 km/h); service ceiling 14,000 ft (4267 m); range 810 miles (1303 km)
Weights: empty 2,810 lb (1275 kg); maximum take-off 4,000 lb (1814 kg)
Dimensions: span 41 ft 11 in (12.78 m); length 30 ft 0 in (9.14 m); height 8 ft 7 in (2.62 m); wing area 258.5 sq ft (24.01 m²)

Some 500 military versions of the Stinson Reliant were transferred to the Royal Navy under Lend-Lease. They were used for navigation training and communications duties with 26 second-line squadrons and units.

Stinson Sentinel

With the usefulness of light aircraft with STOL performance having been well demonstrated by such aircraft as the Stinson (Vultee) Model 74 Vigilant, the US Army Air Corps was ready by 1940 to encourage the development of a lighter, less costly aircraft to operate in the air observation post role and as a 'runabout'. Stinson offered a **Model 75B** based on the two-seat Vultee Voyager and then further developed the military version as the **Model 76**, which first flew on 28 June 1941.

To save on strategic materials, the Model 76 combined a metal fuselage with wooden wings and tail, and was powered by a 175-hp (130-kW) Lycoming engine that was already widely available for civilian use. After small modifications to the leading-edge slots and the tailplane, the Model 76 proved to be extremely docile, with the ability to operate into and out of field lengths of about 650 ft (200 m). At first designated by the USAAC as the **O-62** in the Observation category, the Model 76 became the **L-5 Sentinel**, and the Army bought some 3,600 examples up to November 1945.

Quickly becoming known as the 'Flying Jeep', the L-5 was the most-used, and most versatile, of any of the light utility aircraft operated by the Allies during World War II. British use, nevertheless, was relatively modest, limited to the Lend-Lease supply of 100 aircraft, made up of 40 **Sentinel Mk I**s that were equivalent to the basic L-5, and 60 **Sentinel Mk II**s, which were **L-5B**s. The latter were distinguished by having a long downward-opening hatch in the starboard fuselage side, aft of the observer's door, to allow the loading of a stretcher-borne casualty, or 200 lb (91 kg) of cargo. Provision was also made for operation on floats, but it is thought that none of the RAF's Sentinels was so equipped.

The 100 Sentinel Mk Is and Mk IIs were delivered between August 1944 and January 1945, and all went directly to the Far East, operating in the India-Burma theatre. Two of the RAF squadrons engaged in supply dropping missions to support army units in Burma, Nos 117 and 194, each added Sentinels to their basic equipment of Dakotas, and the latter unit, in particular, formed a casualty-evacuation flight with Sentinel Mk IIs. Other principal users of the Sentinel included No. 221 Group Communications Flight, providing detachments from its Imphal base; No. 224 Group Communications Flight from Cox's Bazaar and Akyab; and No. 231 Group Communications Flight at Alipore.

Specification
Sentinel Mk I
Type: two-seat light liaison and observation aircraft
Powerplant: one 185-hp (138-kW) Lycoming O-435-1 flat-four piston engine
Performance: maximum speed 130 mph (209 km/h); service ceiling 15,800 ft (4816 m); range 420 miles (676 km)
Weights: empty 1,550 lb (703 kg); maximum take-off 2,020 lb (916 kg)
Dimensions: span 34 ft 0 in (10.36 m); length 24 ft 1 in (7.34 m); height 7 ft 11 in (2.41 m); wing area 155 sq ft (14.40 m²)

The RAF received 100 Sentinels (60 Mk Is and 40 Mk IIs). Their operational use was mainly with No. 194 Squadron in Burma, used from January 1945 for casualty evacuation from jungle airstrips.

Stinson Vigilant

The use of unarmed two-seat lightplanes for observation and army co-operation duties was a relatively new concept for the British Army in 1939, although the US Army had already recognised the value of such aircraft, as had the German Army, with its experience of the Fieseler Fi 156 Storch.

Aircraft such as the Hawker Audax and the Westland Lysander, although useful in some roles, had their limitations and the Army was soon actively seeking a small lightplane to fulfil the observation and support role.

This search eventually led to the introduction of the Auster series, but meanwhile the rather larger and more powerful Stinson **O-49** (later, Vultee **L-1**), developed for the US Army Air Corps during 1940 attracted British attention. A contract was placed for 96 Vigilant **O-49A**s, these being USAAC L-1As, with deliveries starting in November 1941, but in the event only nine of these aircraft reached Britain (of which four were damaged in transit). Four more were designated **Vigilant Mk I**s, equivalent to the L-1, and were part of a planned batch of 100, probably on a Lend-Lease contract.

Five of the delivered Vigilants were evaluated at the A&AEE during 1942, and the Army's first AOP unit, No. 651 Squadron, formed a Combined Operations Flight at Old Sarum at the end of 1941 to assess the value of the L-1s. The Austers soon arrived to make the Vigilants superfluous, however, and little further use was made of these aircraft, although they lingered on as 'hacks' at miscellaneous Army units. Six more Vigilants, transferred from USAAF stocks in February 1943, were used by Western Desert Communication Flight.

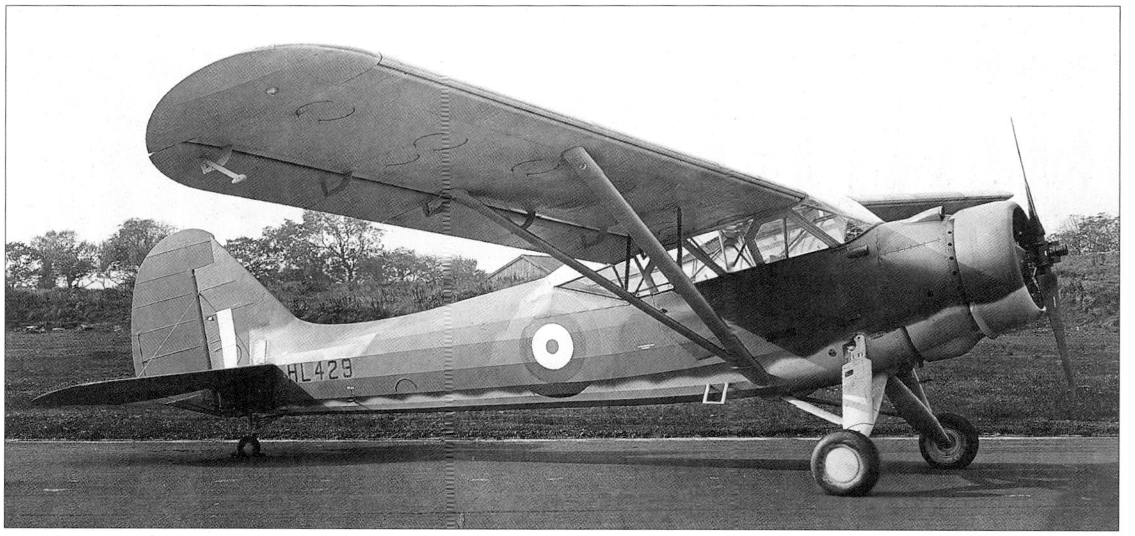

Specification
Vigilant Mk I
Type: two-seat liaison and observation aircraft
Powerplant: one 295-hp (220-kW) Lycoming R-860-9 radial piston engine
Performance: maximum speed 122 mph (196 km/h); service ceiling 12,800 ft (3901 m); range 280 miles (451 km)
Weights: empty 2,670 lb (1211 kg); maximum take-off 3,400 lb (1542 kg)
Dimensions: span 50 ft 11 in (15.52 m); length 34 ft 3 in (10.44 m); height 10 ft 2 in (3.10 m); wing area 329 sq ft (30.56 m^2)

The RAF obtained 15 Vigilants in 1941-42 for light liaison and air observation duties. They were evaluated by the A&AEE and subsequently used briefly by No. 651 (AOP) Squadron at Larkhill and Old Sarum.

Supermarine Sea Otter

The last of Supermarine's biplane amphibians, the Sea Otter was intended as a replacement for the Supermarine Walrus, designed to fulfil the requirements of Specification S.7/38. The Sea Otter had an improved all-metal hull, with better hydrodynamic performance which, with the additional benefit of cleaner lines and a more powerful 855-hp (638-kW) Bristol Mercury XXX engine, endowed the aircraft with the ability to lift heavier loads off the water (at a maximum overload weight of 10,830 lb/4912 kg), and to operate over greater distances from base. The prototype made its first flight in August 1938 and Specifications S.14/39 and S.12/40 were written to cover development and modifications – including shorter wingtip float struts, a deeper engine nacelle for the tractor power unit, and trials with various types of propeller.

Supermarine developed the Sea Otter in 1938 as a successor to the Walrus, but it did not go into service until 1943. The 290 aircraft were mainly used for air-sea rescue.

Production aircraft were the responsibility of Saunders Roe at East Cowes, Isle of Wight, who built 290 Sea Otters between 30 July 1943, when the first machine flew, and July 1946. The air-sea rescue **Sea Otter Mk II** entered service with RAF Coastal Command squadrons towards the end of 1943, the last biplane type to enter the RAF inventory. Bases included Beccles and Martlesham Heath in East Anglia, Hawkinge in Kent and St Eval in Cornwall. In addition, Sea Otters flew with the air-sea rescue service during the 1944-45 Burma campaign.

Sea Otter Mk Is entered service with the Fleet Air Arm in November 1944 when six were delivered to Lee-on-Solent, later embarking in the escort carrier HMS *Khedive* with No. 1700 Squadron which, by the end of the war, had been assigned to the East Indies Fleet, based at Trincomalee, Ceylon. No. 1701 Squadron, formed in February 1945, was attached to the Pacific Fleet based in Australia and later in Hong Kong, while Mediterranean duties were undertaken by No. 1702 Squadron which formed in the summer of 1945.

Specification
Sea Otter Mk I
Type: three-/four-seat carrier-based or shore-based communications or air-sea rescue amphibian
Powerplant: one 855-hp (638-kW) Bristol Mercury XXX radial piston engine
Performance: maximum speed 150 mph (241 km/h) at 5,000 ft (1524 m); cruising speed 100 mph (161 km/h); service ceiling 16,000 ft (4877 m); maximum range 725 miles (1167 km)
Weights: empty 6,805 lb (3087 kg); maximum take-off 10,000 lb (4536 kg)
Dimensions: span 46 ft 0 in (14.02 m); length 39 ft 5 in (12.01 m); height 16 ft 2 in (4.93 m); wing area 610 sq ft (56.67 m^2)
Armament: one 0.303-in (7.7-mm) Vickers 'K' gun in a bow position, and two similar weapons amidships

Supermarine Seafire

Following the success of the Hawker Sea Hurricane in carrier-borne operations, the decision was taken to go ahead with a naval version of the Supermarine Spitfire. A Spitfire Mk VB, fitted in late 1941 with an arrester hook beneath the fuselage, was flown on to HMS *Illustrious* for compatibility trials. While the Spitfire's narrow-track landing gear made it more difficult to operate aboard carriers than the Hurricane, the concept was proved and work began on converting a number of existing Spitfires, the name Seafire being chosen for the modified aircraft.

Air Service Training at Hamble undertook the conversion in 1942, and others were modified by Supermarine on the production line. About 140 Spitfire Mk Vs were involved, and were designated **Seafire Mk IB**s. Additionally, 48 new Seafire Mk IBs were built by Cunliffe-Owen Aircraft.

All Seafire Mk IBs had fixed wings, some being clipped as on the Spitfire Mk VB, and the type of wing fitted depended on the mark of Spitfire converted. The B wing had two 20-mm cannon and four 0.303-in (7.7-mm) machine-guns, while the **Mk IC** could have four 20-mm cannon; the latter was not common, however, because of the weight penalty imposed by the heavier armament and ammunition.

Following the Mk IB came 372 **Seafire Mk IIC**s, similar to the earlier mark but using the C wing and having provision for catapult spools. This variant was built in two versions, by Supermarine (262) as the **F.Mk IIC** and by Westland (110) as the **L.Mk IIC**, the latter being a low-altitude version. A sub-variant, the **LR.Mk IIC**, carried F.24 cameras for photo-reconnaissance work.

Seafire Mk IIC deliveries began in June 1942, when 12 were received by No. 807 Squadron. These, together with Seafires delivered to No. 801 Squadron in September, were embarked on HMS *Furious* until February 1943, participating in the Allied invasion of North Africa in November 1942. By the end of 1942 six squadrons had received Seafires, the others being Nos 808, 880, 884 and 887. During 1943 Nos 809, 886, 894, 895, 897 and 899 Squadrons were equipped, while Nos 833, 834, 842 and 879 Squadrons operating from escort carriers each received six Seafires.

The next variant, the **Seafire Mk III**, introduced a manually folding wing, folding upwards from just inboard of the cannon, with the wingtips folding downwards. This enabled Seafires to be moved on carrier lifts, and made deck handling easier. The Seafire Mk III prototype was a converted Mk IIC, and the new mark went into production in 1943, a total of 1,220 being built between November 1943 and July 1945, 870 by Westland and 350 by Cunliffe-Owen .

The Seafire Mk III was built in three versions, fighter (**F.Mk III**), low-altitude fighter (**L.Mk III**) and low-altitude reconnaissance (**LR.Mk III**), the last having vertical and oblique cameras like the LR.Mk IIC. A 30-Imp gal (136-litre) flush-fitting drop tank could be fitted beneath the fuselage to increase the range from 465 to 725 miles (748 to 1167 km).

Above: Seafire Mk IIC MB240 served with No. 880 Squadron from HMS* Indomitable *in March 1943. Forming Force H with HMS* Formidable, Indomitable *carried 28 Mk IICs of Nos 880 and 899 Squadrons and 12 L.Mk IICs of No. 807 Squadron during Operation Husky (the invasion of Sicily).

Above: A Seafire Mk II approaches the arrester wires of a Royal Navy carrier in the Mediterranean. The 6-ft (1.83-m) long 'A-frame' arrester hook was located midway down the fuselage.

Below: After being used as the development aircraft for the L.Mk IIC, MA970 became the prototype F.Mk III. The main improvement was the fitting of the folding wing mechanism allowing more easy stowage aboard the carriers. A four-bladed propeller was also fitted to take advantage of the power from the Rolls-Royce Merlin 55 engine.

Left: Seafire L.Mk IICs from No. 880 Squadron provided support for the Allied landings in North Africa from HMS **Argus** *in the autumn of 1942, before joining HMS* **Furious** *for operations during the landings in Sicily in 1943.*

Below: During the spring and early summer of 1943 these Seafire Mk IBs of No. 885 Squadron provided air cover for the landings in Sicily and Salerno. The aircraft were based aboard HMS **Formidable.**

Not surprisingly, considerable numbers of Seafires took part in operations in the Mediterranean. In September 1943 the Allied forces landed in the Gulf of Salerno, naval air support being provided by the fleet carriers HMS *Formidable* and *Illustrious* and four escort carriers, operating eight Seafire squadrons totalling 76 aircraft; additionally, the repair and maintenance carrier HMS *Unicorn* was pressed into temporary service and had three squadrons of Seafires with a total of 30 aircraft.

With only a light wind blowing and the carriers operating 1,000 yd (915 m) apart, conditions for the Seafires were unfavourable and an unusually large number of deck-landing accidents occurred. Many propeller tips were damaged when the Seafires' noses dipped slightly as the hooks picked up the arrester wires, and on the escort carrier HMS *Hunter* 19 such incidents in three days exhausted the ship's stock of

Above: In November 1944 No. 894 Squadron re-equipped with 24 Seafire L.Mk IIIs and sailed for Ceylon aboard HMS **Indefatigable.** *During January 1945 the Seafires provided fighter escort for the Allied attacks on Japanese oil installations in Sumatra. This example hits the crash barrier after the starboard undercarriage leg collapsed. The Seafire's fragile, narrow-track main landing gear caused many such accidents.*

Right: For operations from the short flight decks of Royal Navy carriers, two Seafire Mk IICs were modified for trials with rocket-assisted take-off gear (RATOG). Although the trials were successful, the system was never used operationally during the war due to the disadvantages of using it on a deck crowded with aircraft and personnel.

Not originally designed as a naval aircraft, the Seafire suffered from a number of shortcomings. Landings were particularly difficult with the aircraft's narrow-track undercarriage and fairly weak landing gear. This example was one of a large number which suffered landing accidents during Avalanche – the Allied assault on Salerno in 1943.

spare propellers. The only course of action was to crop the damaged propellers, and 6 in (0.15 m) were cut off each blade, an effective remedy which subsequently became standard practice.

Seafire Mk III deliveries began in March 1944 to No. 899 Squadron at Belfast, and in July the squadron embarked on the escort carrier HMS *Khedive* for the Mediterranean, its 26 Seafires joining Nos 807, 809 and 879 Squadrons of No. 4 Naval Fighter Wing at Malta. All took part in the invasion of southern France in August 1944.

Meanwhile, other Seafire squadrons had seen active service in the Allied invasion of northern France in June 1944, with Nos 808, 885, 886 and 897 Squadrons operating from shore bases alongside two Spitfire squadrons as part of the 2nd Tactical Air Force. The Seafires returned to Fleet Air Arm command the following month.

By 1945, Seafires were operational in the Far East, eight squadrons flying from six carriers. By VJ-Day 12 Seafire squadrons were in first-line service, eight of them with Mk IIIs and four with Mk IICs. All were powered by various marks of Rolls-Royce Merlin engine giving between 1,340 and 1,640 hp (999 and 1223 kW).

As the powerplant of the Spitfire changed from the Merlin to the Rolls-Royce Griffon, it was a natural progression for the Seafire to be similarly equipped, and three prototypes were built to Specification N.4/43, all flying in 1944. This first Griffon variant was designated the **Seafire Mk XV**, and production orders were placed for 384, Westland building 250 and Cunliffe-Owen 134. Increased fuel capacity in internal wing tanks was provided, and from the 51st aircraft a new 'sting'-type arrester hook was mounted at the bottom of the rudder, replacing the V-type hook used on earlier Seafires. Rocket-assisted take-off gear was standardised from the 75th aircraft. No. 802 Squadron at Arbroath was the first to receive Seafire Mk XVs, in May 1945.

A later variant, the **Seafire Mk XVII**, was basically a refined version of the Mk XV with a clear-view bubble canopy, a cut-down rear fuselage and greater fuel capacity, with a 33-Imp gal (150-litre) tank in the rear fuselage, but this version did not enter service until after the war had ended.

Above: With significant right rudder input to counteract the Merlin engine's torque, a Seafire Mk IIC takes off from the deck of HMS* Indomitable *during operations in the Mediterranean.

Left: In October 1942 Seafire Mk IIC MB156 was embarked aboard HMS* Formidable *in support of the Torch landings in North Africa. On 8 November this aircraft, along with MB146, attacked a French Vichy Martin 167 light bomber. The aircraft was last seen descending in flames and thus became the first Seafire kill of the war.

Specification
Seafire Mk III
Type: single-seat carrier-based fighter
Powerplant: one 1,470-hp (1096-kW) Rolls-Royce Merlin 55 inline piston engine
Performance: maximum speed 352 mph (566 km/h) at 12,250 ft (3735 m); cruising speed 218 mph (351km/h) at 20,000 ft (6100 m); service ceiling 33,800 ft (10300 m); range 465 miles (748 km), or 725 miles (1167 km) with drop tank
Weights: empty 5,400 lb (2449 kg); maximum takeoff 7,100 lb (3221 kg)
Dimensions: span 36 ft 8 in (11.18 m); length 30 ft 0 in (9.14 m); height 11 ft 2 in (3.40 m); wing area 242 sq ft (22.48 m2)
Armament: two 20-mm cannon and four 0.303-in (7.7-mm) machine-guns in wings, plus provision for 500 lb (227 kg) of bombs

Supermarine Spitfire

Above: Six Spitfire Mk Is from No. 65 Squadron formate for the camera just before the outbreak of World War II. The nearest aircraft was flown by Flying Officer Robert Stanford Tuck, who became one of the first RAF pilots to claim five victories in the Battle of Britain.

The prototype Spitfire, K5054, first flew on 5 March 1936 from Eastleigh airfield near Southampton. After flight trials had been completed in October 1938, the aircraft was used as a 'high-speed hack', and also in the development of the 'Speed Spitfire'.

If asked to name a British aircraft of World War II, many people would pick the Spitfire. The subject of constant development, the Supermarine design was the RAF's most capable fighter of the period, in production and front-line service throughout.

Having designed a monoplane fighter, to Specification F.7/30, which failed to win orders (losing to the Gloster Gladiator biplane), Supermarine's chief designer, Reginald Mitchell, set about developing a new aircraft, the **Type 300**, this time as a private venture. It was to be powered by Rolls-Royce's latest engine, another private venture appropriately known as the PV.12. Rated initially at 1,000 hp (746 kW), it offered an excellent power-to-weight ratio. It also shared with Mitchell's airframe a great deal of development potential, something that was to be exploited to the full during the upcoming war.

The Type 300's design benefitted a good deal from Mitchell's s uccesses in creating the Schneider Trophy-winning S.6B seaplane racers. It was an all-metal design (apart from its control surfaces), with a distinctive elliptical wing planform and an eight machine-gun armament. However, it was the development of the PV.12 engine (soon

Pilot Officer Crelin 'Bogle' Bodie of No. 66 Squadron flew this Spitfire Mk I during the Battle of Britain in September 1940. Bodie achieved significant success during the war claiming five victories and nine probables as well as five shared 'kills'. The aircraft was not so fortunate, flying for only one week during the battle before being badly damaged in a forced landing.

On 27 August 1941 Pilot Officer W. Dunn of No. 71 'Eagle' Squadron became the first American ace of the war when he downed two Bf 109Fs in this Mk IIA. During the same sortie his aircraft was damaged and he suffered wounds that kept him in hospital for four months.

Supermarine Spitfire Mk I

Based at Rochford and Hornchurch during the Battle of Britain, K9953 was flown by the commanding officer of No. 74 Squadron, Sqn Ldr D. F. 'Sailor' Malan. This South African-born ace was instrumental in modifying Fighter Command tactics.

Poison panel
Fearing that the German arsenal might include poison gas as in World War I, a gas detection square was painted on the upper surface of the port wing. The panel was designed to change colour if gas was present in the air.

Camouflage
Wearing the standard Dark Earth/Dark Green colour scheme adopted by the Spitfire at its introduction into service, this aircraft has its serial number painted out for security reasons.

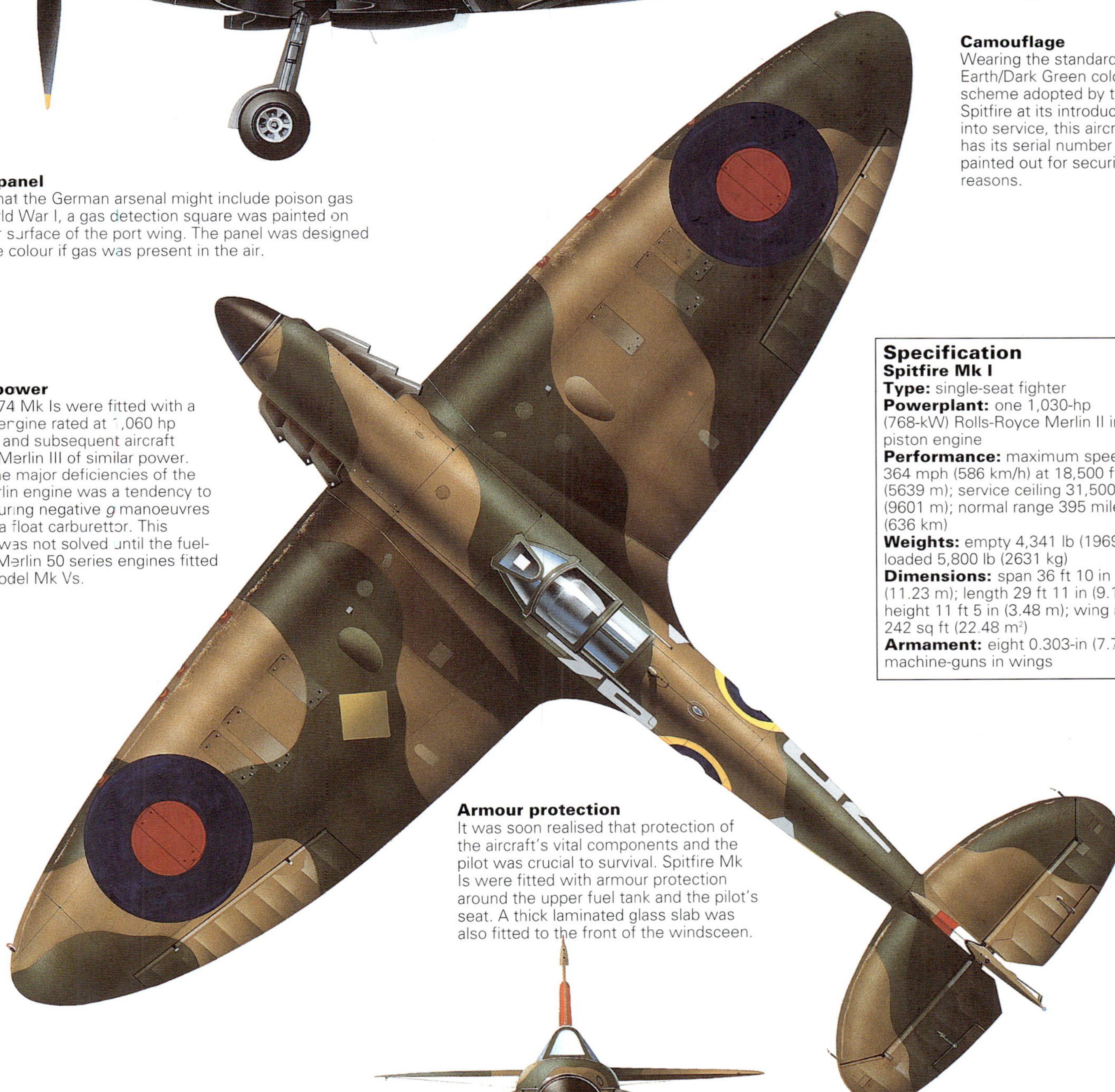

Merlin power
The first 74 Mk Is were fitted with a Merlin II engine rated at 1,060 hp (790 kW) and subsequent aircraft having a Merlin III of similar power. One of the major deficiencies of the early Merlin engine was a tendency to cut out during negative *g* manoeuvres as it had a float carburettor. This problem was not solved until the fuel-injected Merlin 50 series engines fitted to late-model Mk Vs.

Specification
Spitfire Mk I
Type: single-seat fighter
Powerplant: one 1,030-hp (768-kW) Rolls-Royce Merlin II inline piston engine
Performance: maximum speed 364 mph (586 km/h) at 18,500 ft (5639 m); service ceiling 31,500 ft (9601 m); normal range 395 miles (636 km)
Weights: empty 4,341 lb (1969 kg); loaded 5,800 lb (2631 kg)
Dimensions: span 36 ft 10 in (11.23 m); length 29 ft 11 in (9.10 m); height 11 ft 5 in (3.48 m); wing area 242 sq ft (22.48 m^2)
Armament: eight 0.303-in (7.7-mm) machine-guns in wings

Armour protection
It was soon realised that protection of the aircraft's vital components and the pilot was crucial to survival. Spitfire Mk Is were fitted with armour protection around the upper fuel tank and the pilot's seat. A thick laminated glass slab was also fitted to the front of the windsceen.

Armament
The standard armament for the Spitfire Mk I comprised eight 0.303-in (7.7-mm) machine-guns. This rifle-calibre weapon was insufficient against aircraft with armour protection and self-sealing fuel tanks, with many hits being required to achieve a kill.

Flying in battle formation, these Spifire Mk Is operated with No. 610 'County of Chester' Squadron during the Battle of Britain. The larger fuselage roundels and squadron code letters on the sides of the fuselage had been introduced in June 1940.

A flight of Spitfires from No. 616 Squadron 'scrambles' from its base at Kenley. On 18 August 1940, 10 days after the Luftwaffe assault began, 348 Spitfires were on strength, representing about one third of Fighter Command's modern single-engined fighters.

named Merlin) that was to be the most important catalyst in Spitfire development.

Given the rapid advances in monoplane fighter design in Germany, it was clear to the RAF that it needed a new home defence interceptor. Impressed with the Type 300, the Air Ministry drew up a specification (F.37/34) around the design and ordered 310 production examples in June 1936.

A prototype flew in March 1936, the first production **Spitfire Mk I**s reaching No. 19 Squadron at Duxford in August 1938. These first aircraft were fitted with a Merlin II rated at 1,060 hp (791 kW) and driving a two-bladed, fixed-pitch wooden propeller. Armament was eight 0.303-in (7.7-mm) Browning machine-guns.

By the time war had broken out, a total of 1,960 Spitfires was on order, of which 306 Mk Is had been delivered. The Spitfire saw action for the first time on 16 October 1939, when Nos 602 and 603 Squadrons engaged Luftwaffe bombers off the coast of Scotland. Both units were successful in downing German aircraft – the Spitfire's first aerial victories. Nineteen squadrons operated the type by mid-1940; almost a third of these aircraft were lost covering the withdrawal from Dunkirk during May.

As production was stepped up, improvements to the basic Mk I were introduced, the most important of which was a three-bladed, variable-pitch, constant-speed propeller. The other innovation was in the type's armament. The inadequacies of the rifle-calibre machine-guns fitted to the Spitfire were well-known. Something with more firepower was required to down enemy aircraft fitted with self-sealing fuel tanks and armour plating. Accordingly, two Hispano 20-mm cannon were tested.

The Battle of Britain raged during the summer of 1940, the Spitfire and more numerous Hawker Hurricane bearing the brunt of the Luftwaffe's onslaught. During the battle a small number of cannon-armed aircraft, known as **Spitfire Mk IB**s (the machine-gun-armed aircraft became **Mk IA**s), were issued to No. 19 Squadron and, though their guns were initially prone to jamming, they performed well enough to convince the Air Ministry that cannon armament was worth incorporating in future Spitfire orders.

A few **Spitfire Mk IIA**s were also delivered at around this time, the first to No. 611 Squadron in August 1940. These introduced the Merlin 12, which produced an extra 110 hp (82 kW) and was faster than the Mk I. Most were Mk IIAs; some had two cannon and four machine-guns in what had become known as the the 'B' wing – hence **Mk IIB**. Small numbers of Mk IIs were modified with a wing-mounted fuel tank as **Mk IIA(LR)** long-range escort aircraft; others were equipped with air-sea rescue equipment as **Mk IIC**s (later **ASR.Mk II**s).

By January 1941 RAF Fighter Command had begun offensive fighter sweeps over France. During the spring No. 452 Squadron, RAAF, flew these sorties, as well as Circus and Ramrod attack missions in an attempt to lure the Luftwaffe into battle.

After escaping from Czechoslovakia and downing seven enemy aircraft whilst flying for the French air Force, Flight Lieutenant A. Vybiral joined No. 312 Squadron. He flew this Spitfire Mk II in November 1941, and later became commanding officer of the squadron.

Early the following year, as the RAF went on the offensive, Spitfires became involved in sweeps over France, aimed at luring Luftwaffe fighters into action. It was at this time that the first **Spitfire Mk V**s were delivered to No. 92 Squadron. The Mk V combined many of the improvements promised by the stillborn **Mk III** with its Merlin XX engine and, as it was based on the Mk I, was easier to produce. Its Merlin 45 offered 1,515 hp (1130 kW) at 11,000 ft (3353 m) and a much improved performance.

A few **Mk VA**s were built, though most were **Mk VB**s. By the end of 1941, 46 squadrons within Fighter Command were equipped with Spitfires, some with the **Mk VC**. This variant had appeared in October and featured the 'Universal' or 'C' wing, which could be configured to carry either 'A' and 'B' armament or four 20-mm cannon. Its airframe was strengthened to better cope with the extra weight of the Merlin 45-series engine.

The Mk V was the first Spitfire variant to serve overseas. Examples were rushed to Malta to help defend this strategically important Mediterranean island in March 1942 and were soon being issued to units in North Africa, where Hurricane and Kittyhawk squadrons were suffering at the hands of Luftwaffe Bf 109Fs. No. 145 Squadron in May was the first unit to receive the mark. The Mediterranean theatre saw the first use of the Spitfire as a fighter-bomber, Mk VCs being converted to carry a 250-lb (113-kg) bomb under each wing, or a 500-lb (227-kg) device under the fuselage. Other Mk Vs served in the defence of Australia, while a small number were also shipped to the Far East.

A low-level version, the **LF.Mk V**, was introduced in the second half of 1942. Most were fitted with the 'B' wing, often 'clipped' (i.e. reduced in span) to increase roll rate at low altitude. LF.Mk Vs were employed in large numbers by Fighter Command over Europe and in the Mediterranean.

The **Mk VI** was a variation on the Mk V with a pressurised cockpit for high-altitude operations. In the event, the threat from high-altitude bombers failed to materialise and only 100 were built.

During 1942, the Luftwaffe's new Focke-Wulf Fw 190 fighter became an increasing problem. This aircraft outperformed the Spitfire Mk V and a countermeasure was urgently needed. Meanwhile, Rolls-Royce had developed the Merlin 60, with its two-stage supercharger offering almost 42 per cent more power at 30,000 ft (9144 m) and adding just 9 in (22.9 cm) in length and 200 lb (90.7 kg) in weight to the Merlin 45. The Merlin 61 (the fighter variant) could be accommodated in a Spitfire airframe with minimal structural change. Those changes that were necessary were confined to the fitting of a four-bladed propeller to absorb the extra power and a new underwing radiator for the engine's intercooler. The performance gains made with the new engine were spectacular: a Spitfire fitted with a Merlin 61 attained a maximum speed of 414 mph (666 km/h) at 27,200 ft (8291 m), had a much improved climb rate and an estimated service ceiling of 41,800 (12741 m).

Three new Spitfire variants were equipped with Merlin 60 series engines – **Mks VII**, **VIII** and **IX**. The Mk VIII was intended to replace the Mk V as the standard production Spitfire fighter variant

In February 1941 the third major production fighter version of the Spitfire appeared, the Mk V. The more powerful Merlin 45 engine gave the aircraft significantly improved performance over the Mk II. The most produced variant was the Mk VB, which was armed with two 20-mm cannon and four 0.303-in (7.7-mm) machine-guns.

This dramatic photograph does not show the engine catching fire but rather the characteristic exhaust flames sometimes expelled by the Merlin engine during start-up. The Merlin became the most successful Allied inline engine of the war.

No. 92 Squadron was the top-scoring RAF unit of World War II. This aircraft was converted from a Mk I to a Mk VB by Rolls-Royce in April 1941, before joining No. 92 later in the month. On 22 June the aircraft was shot down by a Bf 109 over the English Channel.

This rare air-to-air wartime colour photograph features a Spitfire Mk VB. This aircraft was the personal mount of the commander of No. 222 Squadron, RAF, some time in late 1941/early 1942 while based at North Weald.

Below: After forming in England in December 1941, No. 417 Squadron was deployed to Egypt in April 1942. From October of that year the squadron flew Spitfire Mk VBs and Mk VCs on offensive sorties, until victory in North Africa was accomplished in May 1943.

and, to cope with the extra power and weight of its engine, had a redesigned and strengthened fuselage. To build these new machines, production lines needed to be retooled – a prolonged process. It was for this reason that the Mk IX entered service first, with No. 64 Squadron at Hornchurch in July 1942. The Mk IX was effectively (and in some cases, literally), a Mk VC re-engined with a Merlin 61. There were few airframe modifications to compensate, and, although the aircraft was easier and quicker to build, pilots were warned not to overstress its airframe. Though it was intended as an interim variant, the Mk IX went on (with its Parkard Merlin-engined equivalent, the **Mk XVI**) to be the most numerous of all Spitfire marks.

With the Mk IX in service, the need for the Mk VIII became less urgent. Production did not get into full swing until mid-1943 and, in the event, all Mk VIIIs would be sent overseas. No. 145 Squadron based in Malta, was the first unit to re-equip with the type, in June 1943. Others were issued to RAF and USAAF units in Italy, the RAAF in the southwest Pacific and the RAF and Indian Air Force in the CBI theatre. They served until the end of the war.

All were fitted with the 'Universal' or 'C' wing which, on the Mk VIII, contained two 20-mm cannon and four machine-guns, with few exceptions. The more robust fuselage and wings of the variant allowed a 500-lb (227-kg) bomb to be carried on a centreline rack, with a 250-lb (114-kg) bomb under each wing. Some examples were fitted with a 'low-level' variant of the Merlin 60 (the Merlin 66, the supercharger of which 'cut in' at lower altitude) and were known as **LF.Mk VIII**s; those with 'high-altitude' Merlin 70s were **HF.Mk VIII**s.

One early production aircraft was fitted with a cut-down rear fuselage and 'teardrop' canopy, greatly improving rearward visibility for the pilot. Successful tests led to the adoption of this feature on most production Spitfires (of Mks IX, **XIV**, XVI) after the early spring of 1945. Other changes introduced on the Mk VII/VIII/IX family were a broad-chord rudder, gyro gunsight and extra fuel tanks in the rear fuselage. The Spitfire was plagued by its lack of range throughout its service life; belly-mounted fuel tanks were commonly carried in service by Spitfires from Mk V onwards.

The Mk VII was a high-altitude version of the Mk VIII, to replace the Mk VI. Like the latter it featured cabin pressurisation and extended wingtips. As it was intended for combat at 40,000 ft (12192 m), it car-

From May 1942, No. 81 Squadron formed part of the Hornchurch Wing with Spitfire Mk VBs and was involved in fighter sweeps over France. These aircraft carry the standard temperate RAF fighter camouflage scheme applied from the spring of 1942.

The commanding officer of No. 91 Squadron, Squadron Leader Robert Oxspring, flew this Spitfire Mk VC during the spring/summer of 1942. Of Oxspring's 13 kills, three were achieved while flying Spitfire Mk Vs. This aircraft later flew glider-tug trials flights at the A&AEE.

Fitted with an Aboukir tropical filter, this Spitfire Mk VB was the personal aircraft of Wing Commander Ian Gleed in the spring of 1943. One of the RAF's most famous pilots of the North African campaign, Gleed gained 13 kills and three shared before he was shot down and killed by Bf 109Gs in April 1943.

Above: Adapted for combat at lower levels, the Spitfire LF.Mk VB was fitted with a Merlin 45 engine designed to give maximum power at these heights. The majority of LF.Mk VBs had 'clipped' wings which increased the rate of roll and improved performance by 5 mph (8 km/h).

Right: Armed with four 20-mm Hispano cannon, these Spitfire Mk VCs of No. 2 Squadron, SAAF, fly in line-astern over the Adriatic. With little fighter opposition during the Italian campaign, Spitfire units spent much of their time on ground-attack sorties carrying 500-lb (227-kg) bombs.

The leading Fighter Command ace of the war was J. E. 'Johnnie' Johnson. He claimed the first of his 34 kills in a Spitfire Mk I on 15 January 1941 and his last was a Bf 109 shot down on 27 September 1944. He is seen here in August of that year with his black Labrador, Sally.

Flying operationally with Nos 65, 452 and 602 Squadrons, B. E. F. 'Paddy' Finucane achieved 26 kills and six shared flying Spitfire Mk Is, Mk IIs and Mk Vs between August 1940 and July 1942. He was killed when he ditched in the English Channel after being hit by anti-aircraft fire.

Below: Both RAF and SAAF Spifire squadrons participated in the Italian campaign. These bomb-laden Mk VCs of No. 2 Squadron, SAAF, overfly the Sangro River on their way to attack another Italian target.

riedextra internal fuel in the fuselage and wing leading-edges. The threat from high-altitude bombers and reconnaissance aircraft had failed to increase as expected during 1943, so the first Mk VIIs did not enter service until May. In all, just 140 were built, the first examples re-equipping No. 124 Squadron at North Weald.

As mentioned above, the Mk IX entered service in mid-1942 from bases in the UK, initially as a fighter. A number were also sent to North Africa in December pending the arrival of Mk VIIIs, to counter Fw 190s and Bf 109Gs in the Mediterranean. Early examples were fitted with the 'B' wing, though most had the 'C' wing installed, almost always with two cannon and four machine-guns, as the **Mk IXC**; later production aircraft were **Mk IXE**s, the 'E' wing having two cannon and two 0.5-in (12.7-mm) Browning machine-guns. As with the Mk VIII, there were **LF.Mk IXC** and **HF.Mk IXC** versions with engines optimised for low-level and high-altitude operations, respectively.

Small numbers of Mk IXs were modified for specialised roles.

Spitfire Mk Vs were also active in the southwest Pacific and Far East campaigns. This Mk VC with a Vokes tropical filter was flown by Squadron Leader Eric Gibbs, OC of No. 54 Squadron, based at Darwin, Australia in the spring of 1943. Gibbs became the squadron's leading ace in Australia with five kills and one shared.

The subject of this excellent colour photograph is a Spitfire Mk VB of No. 316 'City of Warsaw' Squadron. Significant numbers of Mk VBs and Mk VCs received 'clipped' wings for service in both the European and Mediterranean theatres.

Spitfire fighter variants (Merlin-engined)

Spitfire Mk I: 1,567 built, most as Mk IAs, some late-production aircraft as Mk IB; Merlin II/III engine
Spitfire Mk II: 921 built; Merlin 12 engine
Spitfire Mk IIA(LR): about 60 conversions from Mk IIA for long-range escort duties with 40 Imp-gal (182-litre) fuel tank under port wing.
Spitfire Mk IIC/ASR.Mk II: about 50 conversions from Mk IIA/B; Merlin XX engine
Spitfire F.Mk V: 6,478 built, including 94 Mk VA, 3,925 Mk VB, 2,459 Mk VC; Merlin 45-series engines; aircraft with 'low-level Merlin 45M/50M/55M engines were LF.Mk Vs (mainly LF.Mk VBs, often with 'clipped' wings)
Spitfire F.Mk VI: 100 built; high-altitude version of Mk VB; Merlin 47 engine; 'C' wing armament
Spitfire F.Mk VII: 140 built; high-altitude version of Mk VIII; Merlin 64 engine; some aircraft had Merlin 71 as HF.Mk VII; 'C' wing armament
Spitfire F.Mk VIII: 1,658 built; strengthened airframe to take Merlin 61/63 engine; 'C' wing; some aircraft had 'low-level' Merlin 66 (LF.Mk VIII) or Merlin 70 (HF.Mk VIII)
Spitfire F.Mk IX: 5,656 built, plus 56 conversions from Mk V by Rolls-Royce; Merlin 60 series engine, including Merlin 61 (F.Mk IXC), Merlin 66 (LF.Mk IXC/E) and Merlin 70 (HF.Mk IXC); small number converted to FR.Mk IXC with oblique cameras and reduced armament
Spitfire F.Mk XVI: 1,054 built; Packard Merlin 266-engined equivalent of Mk IX; early examples Mk XVIC, though most Mk XVIE

Spitfire fighter variants (Griffon-engined)

Spitfire F.Mk XII: 100 built; Griffon II/III/IV engine; 'C' wing
Spitfire F.Mk XIV: 957 built; Griffon 61 engine; early examples Mk XIVC, though most Mk XIVE; late production to FR.Mk XIVE standard with oblique camera
Spitfire Mk 21: 120 built; redesigned 'definitive' Spitfire variant with completely new wing; Griffon 61/64 engine; four 20-mm cannon

Spitfire PR variants

Spitfire PR.Mk IA: two aircraft; two wing-mounted 5-in cameras
Spitfire PR.Mk IB: one 8-in camera, extra fuel in fuselage
Spitfire PR.Mk IC/Mk III: 'long-range' aircraft with two 8-in cameras and extra fuel in wing
Spitfire PR.Mk ID/Mk IV: 229 built; 'extra-super-long-range' aircraft; Merlin 45 engine; two cameras (8-in or 20-in) and large integral wing fuel tankage
Spitfire PR.Mk IE/Mk V: one known conversion from PR.Mk IC; low-level 'dicing' aircraft; two oblique cameras in wings
Spitfire PR.Mk IF/Mk VI: 15 built, plus a number of conversions from PR.Mk IB/C aircraft; 'super long-range' aircraft; two cameras (8-in or 20-in) and second wing fuel tank
Spitfire PR.Mk IG/Mk VII: low-level 'dicing' aircraft; one oblique and two vertical cameras; eight Browning 0.303-in (7.7-mm) machine-guns
Spitfire PR.Mk IX: 15 conversions from F.Mk IX; two vertical cameras; armament deleted
Spitfire PR.Mk X: 16 aircraft; PR.Mk XI variant with pressurised cabin
Spitfire PR.Mk XI: 471 aircraft; long-range aircraft to replace all previous models; Merlin 61/66/70 engine; one oblique and two vertical cameras and integral wing fuel tanks
Spitfire PR.Mk XIII: 26 conversions from PR.Mk VIIs and Mk I/V fighters; 'dicing' aircraft to replace PR.Mk VII; Merlin 32 engine; one oblique and two vertical cameras; four Browning 0.303-in (7.7-mm) machine-guns
Spitfire PR.Mk XIX: 225 aircraft; Griffon 61 engine; one oblique and two vertical cameras and integral wing fuel tanks; most aircraft with pressurised cabin

Spitfire F.Mk IXC cutaway

1 Starboard wingtip
2 Navigation light
3 Starboard aileron
4 Browning 0.303-in (7.7-mm) machine-guns
5 Machine-gun ports (patched)
6 Ammunition boxes (350 rounds per gun)
7 Aileron control rod
8 Bellcrank hinge control
9 Starboard split trailing-edge flap
10 Aileron control cables
11 Cannon ammunition box (120 rounds)
12 Starboard 20-mm Hispano cannon
13 Ammunition feed drum
14 Cannon barrel
15 Rotol four-bladed constant-speed propeller
16 Cannon barrel fairing
17 Spinner
18 Propeller hub pitch control mechanism
19 Armoured spinner backplate
20 Coolant system header tank
21 Coolant filler cap
22 Rolls-Royce Merlin 61 liquid-cooled Vee 12-cylinder engine
23 Exhaust stubs
24 Forward engine mounting
25 Engine bottom cowling
26 Cowling integral oil tank, 5.6-Imp gal (25-litre) capacity
27 Extended carburettor air intake duct
28 Engine bearer struts
29 Main engine mounting member
30 Oil filter
31 Two-stage supercharger
32 Engine bearer attachment
33 Suppressor
34 Engine accessories
35 Intercooler
36 Compressor air intake scoop
37 Hydraulic reservoir
38 Hydraulic system filter
39 Armoured firewall/fuel tank bulkhead
40 Fuel filler cap
41 Top main fuel tank, 48-Imp gal (218-litre) capacity
42 Back of instrument panel
43 Compass mounting
44 Fuel tank/longeron attachment fitting
45 Bottom main fuel tank, 37-Imp gal (168-litre) capacity
46 Rudder pedal bar
47 Sloping fuel tank bulkhead
48 Fuel cock control
49 Chart case
50 Trim control handwheel
51 Engine throttle and propeller controls
52 Control column handgrip
53 Radio controller
54 Bulletproof windscreen
55 Reflector gunsight
56 Pilot's rear view mirror
57 Canopy framing
58 Windscreen side panels
59 Sliding cockpit canopy cover
60 Headrest
61 Pilot's head armour
62 Safety harness
63 Pilot's seat
64 Side entry hatch
65 Back armour

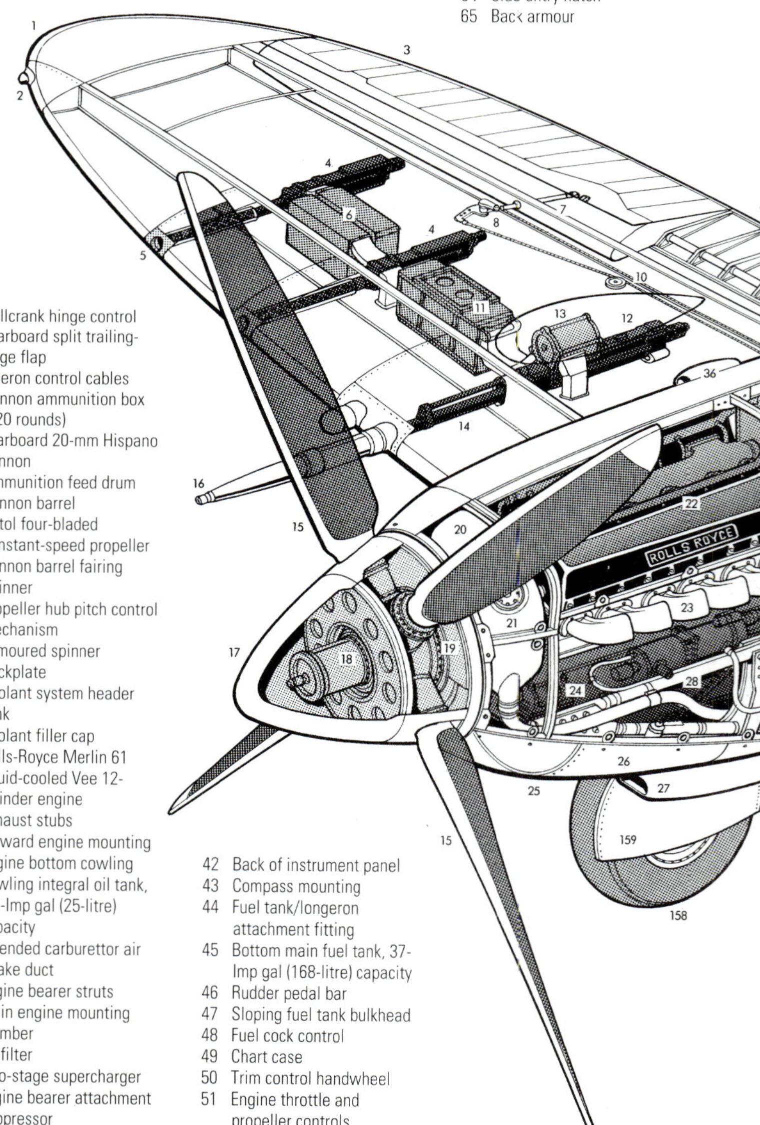

The Spitfire Mk VIII, along with the Mk VII and Mk IX, featured the Merlin 61 engine giving a marked increase in performance. This Mk VII was flown in Southeast Asia by Flight Lieutenant W. Goold, who shot down one and damaged two Ki-43 'Oscars' in this aircraft on 18 May 1944.

One of the most famous wartime RAF pilots, J. E. 'Johnnie' Johnson was the highest-scoring Spitfire ace of the war with 34 destroyed plus seven shared. He gained 12 of these kills plus five shared while flying this Mk IX, EN398, which carries his personal code 'JE-J'.

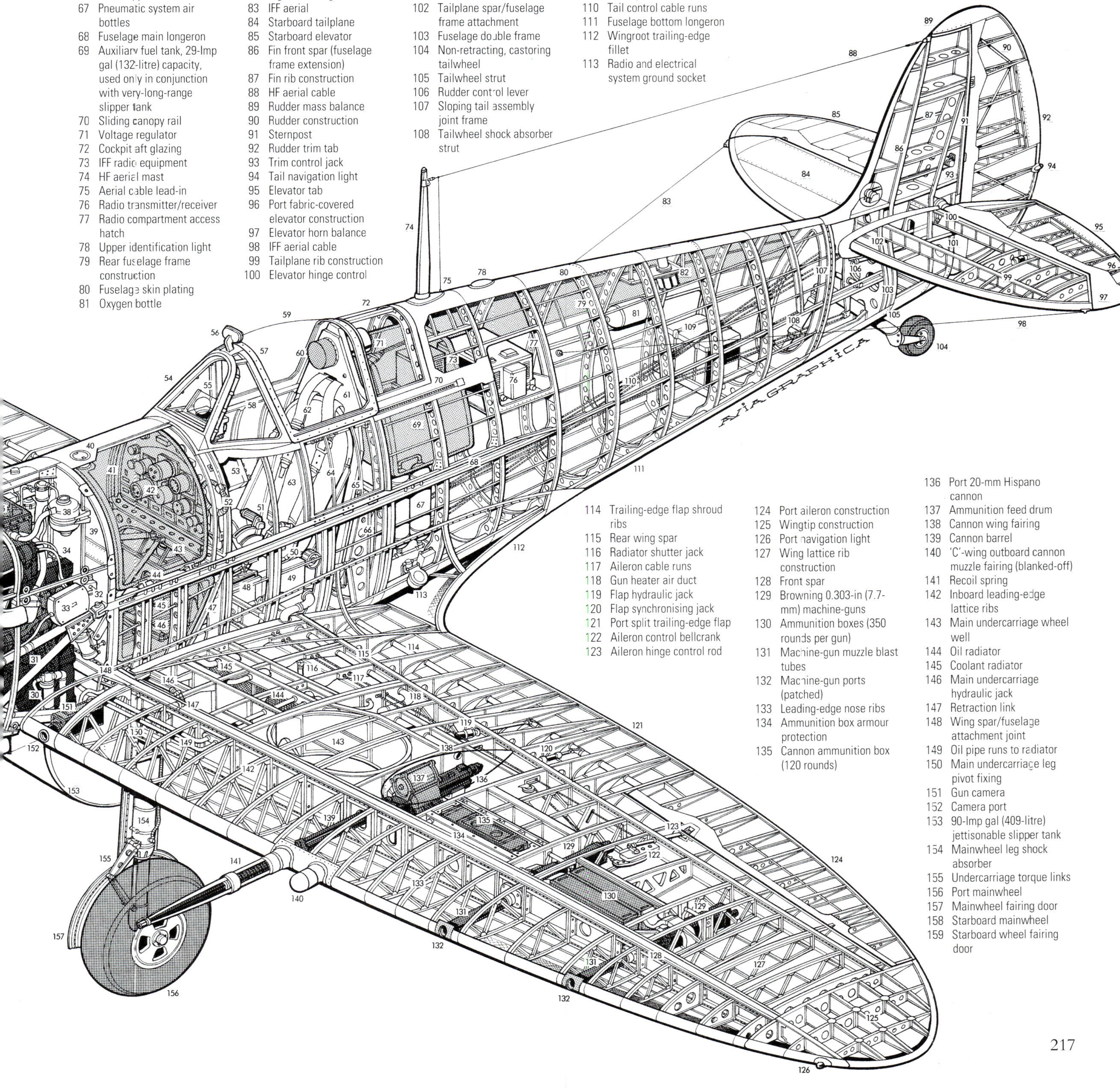

66 Seat support frame
67 Pneumatic system air bottles
68 Fuselage main longeron
69 Auxiliary fuel tank, 29-Imp gal (132-litre) capacity, used only in conjunction with very-long-range slipper tank
70 Sliding canopy rail
71 Voltage regulator
72 Cockpit aft glazing
73 IFF radio equipment
74 HF aerial mast
75 Aerial cable lead-in
76 Radio transmitter/receiver
77 Radio compartment access hatch
78 Upper identification light
79 Rear fuselage frame construction
80 Fuselage skin plating
81 Oxygen bottle
82 Signal cartridge launcher
83 IFF aerial
84 Starboard tailplane
85 Starboard elevator
86 Fin front spar (fuselage frame extension)
87 Fin rib construction
88 HF aerial cable
89 Rudder mass balance
90 Rudder construction
91 Sternpost
92 Rudder trim tab
93 Trim control jack
94 Tail navigation light
95 Elevator tab
96 Port fabric-covered elevator construction
97 Elevator horn balance
98 IFF aerial cable
99 Tailplane rib construction
100 Elevator hinge control
101 Rudder control rod
102 Tailplane spar/fuselage frame attachment
103 Fuselage double frame
104 Non-retracting, castoring tailwheel
105 Tailwheel strut
106 Rudder control lever
107 Sloping tail assembly joint frame
108 Tailwheel shock absorber strut
109 Battery
110 Tail control cable runs
111 Fuselage bottom longeron
112 Wingroot trailing-edge fillet
113 Radio and electrical system ground socket
114 Trailing-edge flap shroud ribs
115 Rear wing spar
116 Radiator shutter jack
117 Aileron cable runs
118 Gun heater air duct
119 Flap hydraulic jack
120 Flap synchronising jack
121 Port split trailing-edge flap
122 Aileron control bellcrank
123 Aileron hinge control rod
124 Port aileron construction
125 Wingtip construction
126 Port navigation light
127 Wing lattice rib construction
128 Front spar
129 Browning 0.303-in (7.7-mm) machine-guns
130 Ammunition boxes (350 rounds per gun)
131 Machine-gun muzzle blast tubes
132 Machine-gun ports (patched)
133 Leading-edge nose ribs
134 Ammunition box armour protection
135 Cannon ammunition box (120 rounds)
136 Port 20-mm Hispano cannon
137 Ammunition feed drum
138 Cannon wing fairing
139 Cannon barrel
140 'C'-wing outboard cannon muzzle fairing (blanked-off)
141 Recoil spring
142 Inboard leading-edge lattice ribs
143 Main undercarriage wheel well
144 Oil radiator
145 Coolant radiator
146 Main undercarriage hydraulic jack
147 Retraction link
148 Wing spar/fuselage attachment joint
149 Oil pipe runs to radiator
150 Main undercarriage leg pivot fixing
151 Gun camera
152 Camera port
153 90-Imp gal (409-litre) jettisonable slipper tank
154 Mainwheel leg shock absorber
155 Undercarriage torque links
156 Port mainwheel
157 Mainwheel fairing door
158 Starboard mainwheel
159 Starboard wheel fairing door

Flown by No. 94 Squadron, this Spitfire Mk IX spent its operational life in North Africa and the Mediterranean. One of its major duties was to counter Luftwaffe Fw 190s.

Below: No. 241 Squadron received Spitfire Mk IXs at the end of 1943, flying tactical reconnaissance, escort and ground-attack sorties until the end of the Italian campaign.

No. 16 Squadron operated a few FR.Mk IXC fighter-reconnaissance machines after D-Day. These carried oblique cameras, and had their two cannon removed to save weight.

In September 1944 the Mk XVI entered service. This had an identical airframe to the Mk IX but was fitted with a Packard-built Merlin 266 (equivalent to the 'low-level' Merlin 66). Mk XVIs served exclusively in Europe, many units equipped with the type (as well as many of those equipped with the Mk IX) taking on a fighter-bomber role. Most were built with the 'E' wing, which was often 'clipped' to improve roll rate. Both the Mk IX and XVI were able to carry the bomb load of a Mk VIII.

As early as 1939, Supermarine had been looking at possible engine alternatives to the Merlin. Among them was the Rolls-Royce Griffon, a derivative of the 'R' racing engine fitted to Supermarine's pre-war S.6B floatplanes. With a capacity one third larger than that of the Merlin, the Griffon offered a sizeable increase in power, but accomplished this in an engine that was only 3 in (7.62 cm) longer than the Merlin and just 600 lb (272 kg) heavier.

A 'Griffon-Spitfire' prototype, the **Mk IV**, flew in November 1941. This was effectively a modification of the Merlin-engined Mk III, but fitted with a 1,735-hp (1294-kW) Griffon IIB. Impressed by the performance of the new aircraft, the Air Ministry ordered the Mk IV into production, with modifications, as the **Mk XX**, though its designation was to change to **Mk XII** before it entered service. The Spitfire Mk XII used what was essentially a Mk V and Mk VIII airframe, with 'C' wing armament and 'clipped' wings. Its role was

Above: With excessive demands being placed on the Royal Navy aircraft-carriers, an alternative to ferrying Spitfires by ship out to the Mediterranean was sought. This Mk VC was fitted with a huge 170-Imp gal (773-litre) belly tank and a 290-Imp gal (132-litre) auxiliary tank in the rear fuselage, giving a range of 1,100 miles (1770 km).

Below: Floatplane trials were carried out with one Spitfire LF.Mk IXB with a view to using such a layout in the Far East. Although it was only 30 mph (48 km/h) slower than the land-based version, the idea was abandoned. Three Spitfire Mk Vs had been similarly converted in 1943.

Left: Designed to counter the percieved threat of high-altitude Luftwaffe bombers, the Spitfire Mk VI featured a pressurised cabin, extended wingtips and a Merlin 47 engine optimised for high-altitude performance. The aircraft did not live up to expectations and only two squadrons were fully equipped with the variant.

Modified canopy
On either side of the cockpit canopy bulged blisters were fitted to give improved vision to the rear and below. A small cross on a circle, etched on the canopy blister on the port side, served as a sight for the oblique camera.

Armament
Unlike later PR Spitfire models, the PR.Mk IG operated at low level and therefore retained the fighter's armament of eight 0.303-in (7.7-mm) machine-guns in the wings for self-defence.

Supermarine Spitfire PR.Mk IG

Built as a Mk I fighter, this aircraft (R7059) was converted by Heston Aircraft Ltd to the low-altitude reconnaissance role as a PR.Mk IG. In May 1941 it was delivered to No. 1 Photographic Reconnaissance Unit (PRU) flying from St Eval, Cornwall. Later in the month PR.Mk IGs were redesignated PR.Mk VII.

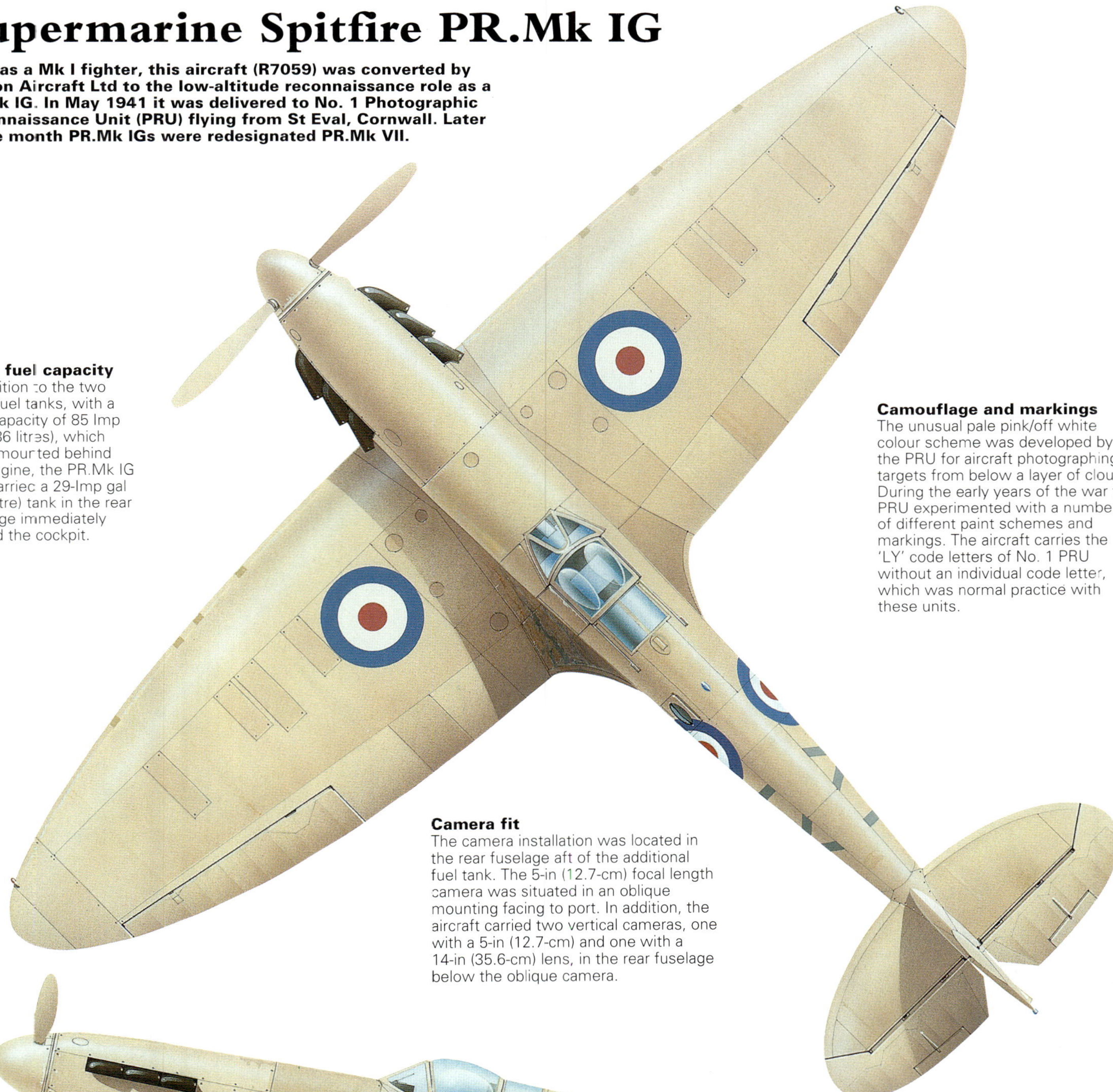

Extra fuel capacity
In addition to the two main fuel tanks, with a total capacity of 85 Imp gal (386 litres), which were mounted behind the engine, the PR.Mk IG also carried a 29-Imp gal (132-litre) tank in the rear fuselage immediately behind the cockpit.

Camouflage and markings
The unusual pale pink/off white colour scheme was developed by the PRU for aircraft photographing targets from below a layer of cloud. During the early years of the war the PRU experimented with a number of different paint schemes and markings. The aircraft carries the 'LY' code letters of No. 1 PRU without an individual code letter, which was normal practice with these units.

Camera fit
The camera installation was located in the rear fuselage aft of the additional fuel tank. The 5-in (12.7-cm) focal length camera was situated in an oblique mounting facing to port. In addition, the aircraft carried two vertical cameras, one with a 5-in (12.7-cm) and one with a 14-in (35.6-cm) lens, in the rear fuselage below the oblique camera.

Supermarine Spitfire

Right: A formation of No. 610 Squadron Spitfire Mk XIVs is seen over Kent in September 1944. Based at Lympne, the squadron was mainly involved in anti-Diver (V-1 interception) operations and long-range fighter sweeps over Germany.

Below: The Spitfire Mk XII was the first production variant to be fitted with the Rolls-Royce Griffon engine. Selected by the RAF to counter the low-level 'tip and run' raid by Luftwaffe Fw 190s and Bf 109s, 100 examples were ordered. All production examples featured 'clipped' wings which improved speed and roll rate at lower altitudes.

that of a low-level interceptor, countering Fw 190 and Bf 109G fighter-bombers carrying out raids on coastal targets in southern England.

Mk XIIs entered service in February 1943 with No. 41 Squadron. No. 91 Squadron followed in April and was the only other unit so-equipped. As well as defensive patrols, low-altitude sweeps over Europe were also undertaken.

Mk XIVs followed the Mk XII into service in the spring of 1944 as another interim type, pending the arrival of the definitive 'Griffon-Spitfire', the **Mk 21**. It featured a Griffon 61 with a two-stage supercharger to improve performance at altitude, a strengthened fuselage, a five-bladed propeller and, initially, the 'C' wing. A 'teardrop' canopy and the 'E' wing were features of later production aircraft; many of these aircraft had 'clipped' wings. A considerable number were completed as **FR.Mk XIVE**s for the low-level tactical reconnaissance role, with an oblique camera installed behind the cockpit.

Nos 91, 322 and 610 Squadrons were the first units equipped with the Mk XIV, which entered service in the south of England in time to counter V-1 'flying bomb' attacks on London. After D-Day many served as fighter-bombers in Europe. Plans were in hand to ship Mk XIVs to the Far East but, although a number of aircraft arrived, none was operational before the war ended.

Very similar to the Mk XIV, the **Mk XVIII** had a strengthened fuseslage and greater fuel capacity, but was just too late for war service. The 'definitive' Mk 21, with a new wing and other changes, was plagued by handling problems and though No. 91 Squadron was operational with the type from March 1945, it saw little action before VE-Day.

As the latest Spitfire variants entered squadron service, older marks were relegated to training and other duties. Advanced flying and operational training, fighter affiliation and target-towing were typical tasks for these aircraft. The Air Fighting Development Unit also employed

With an identical airframe to the Mk IX, the Mk XVI differed in having a licence-built Packard Merlin 66 engine. This late production LF.Mk XVI from No. 74 Squadron features the 'teardrop' canopy and cut-down rear fuselage. Based in Belgium during the spring of 1945, this example carries a bomb beneath each wing for ground-attack duties.

All-round vision
This FR.Mk XIV features the cut-down rear fuselage introduced early in 1945 which, in association with the 'bubble' canopy, gave the pilot a much improved field-of-view to the rear and below.

Specification
Spitfire F.Mk XIVE
Type: single-seat fighter
Powerplant: one 2,050-hp (1529-kW) Rolls-Royce Griffon 65 inline piston engine
Performance: maximum speed 439 mph (707 km/h) at 24,500 ft (7468 m); service ceiling 43,000 ft (13106 m); normal range 395 miles (636 km)
Weights: empty 6,376 lb (2892 kg); loaded 8,475 lb (3844 kg)
Dimensions: span 36 ft 10 in (11.23 m); length 32 ft 8 in (9.96 m); height 11 ft 8 in (3.56 m); wing area 242 sq ft (22.48 m^2)
Armament: two 20-mm Hispano cannon plus two 0.5-in (12.7-mm) machine-guns mounted in the wings

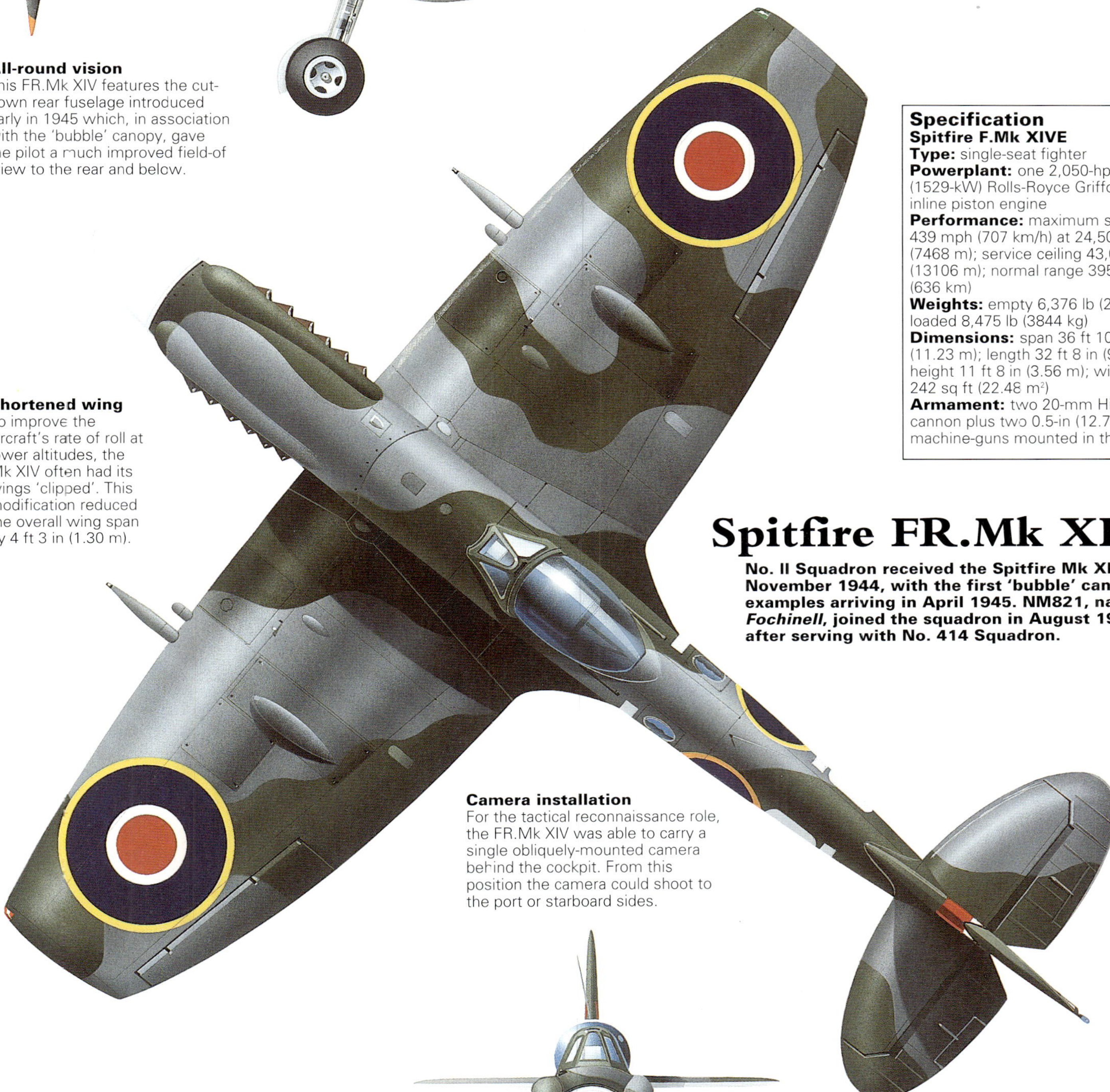

Shortened wing
To improve the aircraft's rate of roll at lower altitudes, the Mk XIV often had its wings 'clipped'. This modification reduced the overall wing span by 4 ft 3 in (1.30 m).

Spitfire FR.Mk XIVE

No. II Squadron received the Spitfire Mk XIVE in November 1944, with the first 'bubble' canopy examples arriving in April 1945. NM821, named *Fochinell*, joined the squadron in August 1945 after serving with No. 414 Squadron.

Camera installation
For the tactical reconnaissance role, the FR.Mk XIV was able to carry a single obliquely-mounted camera behind the cockpit. From this position the camera could shoot to the port or starboard sides.

Wing armament
The first production Mk XIVs were fitted with the four-cannon version of the 'C' wing. Later aircraft, such as this example, had the 'E' wing with two 20-mm Hispano cannon and two 0.5-in (12.7-mm) Browning machine-guns.

Left: *Built in the largest numbers of all the wartime photographic Spitfires, the unarmed PR.Mk XI was based on the Mk IX airframe. The excellent 60 (later 70) Series Merlin engine gave the aircraft outstanding speed and altitude performance, making interception highly unlikely.*

Below: Wearing invasion stripes, this PR.Mk XI belonged to No. 541 Squadron. The 'U' (Universal) camera installation on the underside of the fuselage allowed a variety of sensors or cameras to be fitted.

older model Spitfires for tactical training. The Fleet Air Arm employed Spitfire Mk Is, IIs and Vs as advanced trainers and equipped Mk Vs with arrester hooks for carrier training.

Other Spitfires were modified, often in the field, for specialised front-line roles, including the high-altitude interception of Junkers Ju 86 bombers and reconnaissance aircraft, for which a Mk VC in Egypt and two Mk IXs in the British Isles were modified by lightening their airframes and removing part of their armament. Perhaps the oddest of all Spitfire modifications was the fitting of floats. Three Mk Vs and a Mk IX were converted to floatplanes for use as waterborne interceptors. Though the Mk Vs were shipped to Egypt in 1943, they saw no action.

Of all the Spitfires, the least-known are perhaps the photo-reconnaissance variants. Yet it was these aircraft that were the most important strategic reconnaissance machines of the European theatre, and with the Mosquito made up the bulk of the Allies' camera-equipped assets.

Once the Air Ministry recognised the need for a fast reconnaissance platform, it persuaded RAF Fighter Command to part with two Spitfire Mk Is. These became the first of a whole family of 'PR' Spitfires. The first of the two Spitfire **PR.Mk IA**s – unarmed, with a 5-in focal length, vertically-mounted camera in each wing – flew the first Spitfire PR mission on 18 November 1939. Taking off from a base at Seclin, near Lille, the sortie photographed Aachen from 33,000 ft (10058 m), proving the concept.

However, the Mk IA, little changed from the standard Spitfire Mk I fighter, had its limitations. Thus, the **PR.Mk IB** and 'long-range' **PR.Mk IC** were introduced, with more fuel tanks in the wings and fuselage and extra cameras. By May these aircraft were tracking the progress of the German army as it advanced across Europe.

The 'super long-range' **PR.Mk IF**, with a radius of action some 100 miles better than the Mk IC, followed in July, but it was the **PR.Mk ID** 'extra-super-long-range' aircraft of late 1940 that had the greatest range. With its specially constructed wing housing 114-Imp gal (518 litres) of fuel, this variant was able to cover much larger areas; sorties with the Mk ID took the aircraft to the Baltic, Norway and France's Mediterranean coast. Over 200 were built, the Mk ID becoming the most important type in the PRUs in 1941/42.

The need for close-up photographs and photographs below the

Below: Fitted with an Aboukir tropical filter, this PR.Mk IV was dispatched to the Middle East aboard the* Amot Elkerk. *Reassembled at Takoradi on the Gold Coast, the aircraft was dispatched to Egypt for service with No. 2 PRU.

Above: The PR.Mk XIX was the definitive Griffon-powered PR Spitfire. Note the auxiliary belly tank.

To counter the high-altitude Junkers Ju 88R bombers which were invulnerable to the RAF's standard fighters, the Special Service Flight was formed at Northolt. This is one of two Mk IXs which were specially modified with all armour, armament and non-essential equipment removed apart from two 20-mm cannon.

As the war was drawing to a close No. 91 Squadron became the first unit to receive the F.Mk 21, in January 1945. This variant had a new wing which allowed an increase in maximum speed. Here two Mk 21s flank an F.Mk 22, which did not enter service until after the end of the war.

cloud base in bad weather prompted the development of the **PR.Mk IE** in mid-1940. Low-altitude PR flying ('dicing') required the use of an oblique camera in each wing. Only one Mk IE was produced, but was followed by the **PR.Mk IG**, another 'low-level' variant and the last PR Spitfire to be based upon the Mk I fighter. The Mk IG retained the eight 0.303-in (7.7-mm) machine-guns and sported one extra fuel tank and three cameras.

Soon the system for designating these aircraft would also change. The PR.Mk IC became the **Spitfire PR.Mk III**, the PR.Mk ID became the **PR.Mk IV** and so on. Surviving PR.Mk IAs and Mk IBs were converted to later variants, 1941 saw the introduction of the uprated Merlin 45 engine, which was soon being fitted to new PR aircraft (beginning with the PR.Mk ID); existing machines were re-engined with the new powerplant.

The threat posed to RAF fighters by the Luftwaffe's Fw 190s and Bf 109Gs also led to new PR Spitfire variants. As an interim measure, a small batch of **PR.Mk IX**s was converted from Mk IX fighters (and therefore retained only standard fighter fuel capacity), entering service in November 1942 for service over western Europe. The purpose-built **PR.Mk XI** soon followed, based on the Mk VIII fighter, but utilising the wing of the PR.Mk IV (Mk ID). Range could be improved further by fitting a 90-Imp gal belly fuel tank. Camera equipment consisted of an oblique camera behind the cockpit and two vertical cameras, of varying size, in a 'universal' mounting in the lower, rear fuselage.

In all, 471 Mk XIs were built from December 1942, replacing all the earlier, unarmed PR Spitfires, including those in the Middle East. Others were deployed to the Far East. In Europe, until the advent of the Luftwaffe's first jet fighters in early 1944, the Mk XI was virtually immune from interception.

The **PR.Mk X** followed the Mk XI into service in 1943. Effectively a pressurised version of the Mk XI, only 16 examples were built and service use was limited.

Meanwhile, the armed 'dicing' **PR.Mk VII**s were replaced by the **PR.Mk XIII** from early 1943. With the same camera fit as a Mk VII and four 0.303-in (7.7-mm) machine-guns, the Mk XIII remained in use until the Spitfire FR.Mk XIV entered service.

In May 1944, the Griffon-engined **PR.Mk 19** was introduced. Though based on the Mk XIV fighter, most Mk XIXs were pressurised and all had integral wing fuel tanks. In all, 225 were built, for service in Europe, the Mediterranean and the Far East.

Supermarine Stranraer

Air Ministry Specification R.24/31 called for a twin-engined general-purpose coastal reconnaissance flying-boat, and Supermarine's submission was a biplane known originally as the **Southampton Mk V**, although it clearly owed more to its immediate predecessor, the Scapa, than to the 1925-vintage Southampton. Of all-metal construction, with fabric-covered wings, the **Stranraer** was larger than the Scapa, with an extra bay in the wings and a lengthened fuselage with an open gun position in the tail.

The prototype Southampton Mk V, renamed Stranraer in August 1935, was powered by two Bristol Pegasus IIIM engines, each driving two-bladed wooden propellers, but these were replaced by Pegasus Xs with three-bladed Fairey-Reed metal propellers for production machines. In August 1935 17 were ordered to Specification R.17/35, and a further six in May of the following year. In 1936 No. 228 Squadron at Pembroke Dock was the first Royal Air Force squadron to receive the Stranraer, and the type was still in service at the outbreak of war in September 1939. Nos 201 and 209 Squadrons at Invergordon used the aircraft until the summer of 1940, when they were re-equipped respectively with Sunderlands and Saro Lerwicks.

The Stranraer was also built under licence by Canadian Vickers, the initial Royal Canadian Air Force order for seven aircraft being later increased to 40. Production began in 1938, and eight were in the RCAF inventory when the war started. The last Canadian-built Stranraer was delivered in 1941.

The RCAF's No. 5 (General Reconnaissance) Squadron received its first Stranraers in November 1938 and, after redesignation as a bomber reconnaissance squadron on 31 October 1939, operated Canadian anti-submarine patrols from bases in Nova Scotia. No. 4 Squadron, in British Columbia, performed a similar role and was later joined by Nos 6, 7 and 9 Squadrons, the last being the ultimate unit to retire its Stranraers which were withdrawn in April 1944 on replacement by Consolidated Cansos. The Stranraer was used briefly by No. 117 (Auxiliary) Squadron in the autumn of 1941, and from October 1941 to November 1942 by No. 13 Operational Training Squadron to train flying-boat crews.

Specification
Stranraer Mk I
Type: six-seat general reconnaissance flying-boat
Powerplant: two 875-hp (652-kW) Bristol Pegasus X radial piston engines
Performance: maximum speed 165 mph (266 km/h) at 6,000 ft (1829 m); cruising speed 105 mph (169 km/h); service ceiling 18,500 ft (5639 m); range 1,000 miles (1609 km)
Weights: empty 11,250 lb (5103 kg); maximum take-off 19,000 lb (8618 kg)
Dimensions: span 85 ft 0 in (25.91 m); length 54 ft 10 in (16.71 m); height 21 ft 9 in (6.63 m); wing area 1,457 sq ft (135.36 m^2)
Armament: three 0.303-in (7.7-mm) Lewis guns (one each in nose, dorsal and tail positions) plus up to 1,000 lb (454 kg) of bombs

Stranraer K7295 from No. 240 Squadron flew from Pembroke Dock and Stranraer during 1940-41. It was one of 15 which remained in service with Nos 209 and 240 Squadrons in September 1939.

Supermarine Walrus

A Walrus is launched from the catapult of HMS **Ameer**. *From 1944 onwards the Walrus was gradually superseded by the Sea Otter, but some remained in service with No. 1700 Squadron at Sembawang until June 1946.*

Designed by R. J. Mitchell, and produced by Supermarine as a private venture, the **Seagull Mk V** was a very different flying-boat from its similarly named predecessor, the Seagull Mk III. It had a hull of metal instead of wood, a pusher rather than a tractor powerplant, an enclosed cockpit for the crew of two, and was stressed for catapult launch from warships. The prototype Seagull Mk V was flown by chief test pilot J. 'Mutt' Summers on 21 June 1933, and 24 were ordered for the Royal Australian Navy. The first aircraft sailed with HMAS *Australia* in September 1936, the second was allocated to HMAS *Sydney*, while others were issued to No. 1 Seaplane Training Flight and No. 101 Flight.

The prototype was flown to the Marine Aircraft Experimental Establishment at Felixstowe on 29 July 1933, for Air Ministry trials, and 12 aircraft were ordered to Specification 2/35 in May 1935, being given the name Walrus in August. The first two were completed in March 1936, and initially delivered to Felixstowe; others were used for pilot training at Calshot and observer training at Lee-on-Solent

Further orders for the **Walrus Mk I**, with the 620-hp (462-kW) Bristol Pegasus IIM2 engine, were placed in 1936 to Specification 37/36. A total of 287 was built by Supermarine before production was transferred to Saunders Roe Ltd at East Cowes, Isle of Wight, thus enabling the Supermarine factory to concentrate on Spitfire production. When production ceased in January 1944, Saunders Roe had built 453 **Walrus Mk II**s with 775-hp (578-kW) Bristol Pegasus VI engines, a wooden hull, and a tail wheel replacing the skid of the Mk I.

The third production Walrus was possibly the first to be allocated to a specific ship, serving aboard HMS *Achilles*, then with the Royal Navy's New Zealand Division. Interestingly, after it had been transferred to the Royal New Zealand Navy, *Achilles* and its sister ship HMNZS *Leander* unloaded five aircraft in New Zealand in 1942, to equip the Seaplane Training Flight of the Royal New Zealand Air Force, preparing pilots for conversion to Catalinas.

In the UK the Admiralty had equipped many of its battleships, battle-cruisers and cruisers with the Walrus by the time war broke out, and in January 1940 these catapult flights were combined as No. 700 Squadron, Fleet Air Arm. This was gradually run down during 1943, and finally disbanded on 24 March 1944. Not all Fleet Air Arm operations were from ships, however, and by 10 September 1939 No. 710 Squadron was flying coastal patrols from Freetown, Sierra Leone, watching for German commerce raiders.

Affectionately known as the 'Shagbat', the Walrus was used by the Royal Navy for ship-to-shore communication flights, spotting for its parent ship's guns, and in an attack role using its capacity to carry 760 lb (345 kg) of bombs or depth-charges on underwing racks.

Late in 1941 the RAF began to form specialist air-sea rescue squadrons, and the Walrus became the mainstay of many of these life-saving units. Four Middle East and seven home-based squadrons flew the type and, of these, No. 277 alone rescued 598 survivors. Landings were often made in mine-infested waters or under enemy fire, and the Walrus established an enviable reputation for reliability and its ability to withstand damage.

Specification
Walrus Mk II
Type: four-seat spotter-reconnaissance or air-sea rescue aircraft
Powerplant: one 775-hp (578-kW) Bristol Pegasus VI radial piston engine
Performance: maximum speed 135 mph (217 km/h) at 4,750 ft (1450 m); cruising speed 95 mph (153 km/h) at 3,500 ft (1065 m); service ceiling 18,500 ft (5640 m); range 600 miles (966 km)
Weights: empty 4,900 lb (2223 kg); maximum takeoff 7,200 lb (3266 kg)
Dimensions: span 45 ft 10 in (13.97 m), folded 17 ft 11 in (5.46 m); length 37 ft 3 in (11.35 m); height 15 ft 3 in (4.65 m); wing area 610 sq ft (56.67 m^2)
Armament: one 0.303-in (7.7mm) Vickers 'K' or Lewis machine-gun in bow position, and one or two similar weapons on flexible mount in midships position, plus up to 760 lb (345 kg) of bombs or depth charges on underwing racks

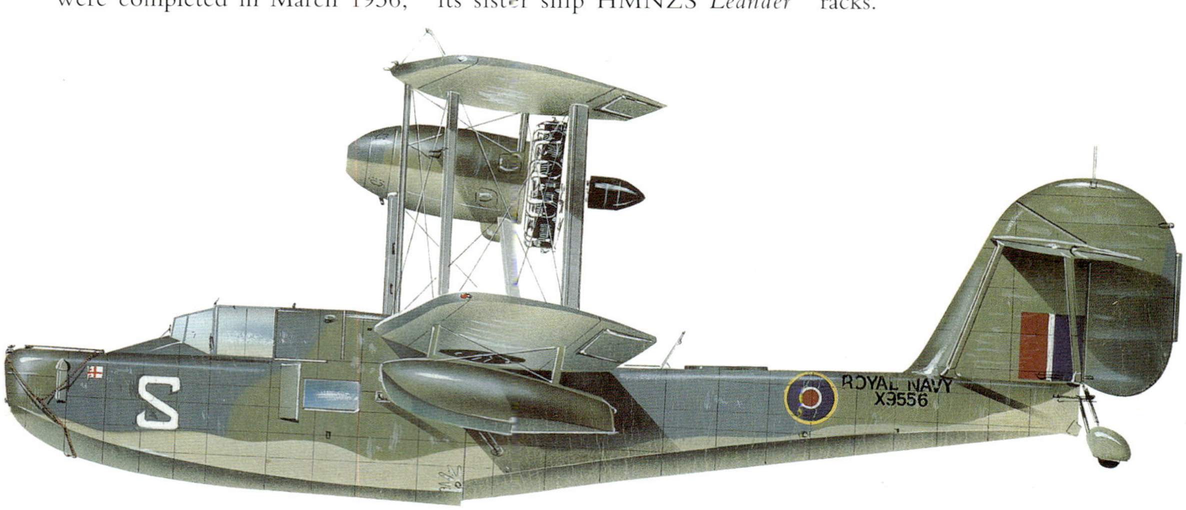

This Walrus Mk I served with No. 700 Squadron FAA, based on HMS **Belfast** *in 1943. The squadron operated as a pool, headquarters and training unit for catapult aircraft embarked on battleships and cruisers from January 1940.*

Taylorcraft Aeroplanes (England) Auster

MZ105 was built as an Auster AOP.Mk III, but was temporarily converted to a Mk II, seen here with yellow prototype markings. Only two Auster Mk IIs, powered by 130-hp (97-kW) Lycoming 0-290 engines, were built due to a shortage of the American engines.

In 1936 the Taylorcraft Aviation Company was formed in the USA to design and manufacture lightplanes for private use. The most successful pre-war aircraft to emanate from this company were designated Models B, C, and D, and in November 1938 Taylorcraft Aeroplanes (England) Ltd was established at Thurmaston, Leicestershire, to build these aircraft under licence.

Six American-built Model As were imported into Britain, followed by one Model B, and these were typical of the aircraft to be built by the new company. Of braced high-wing monoplane layout, with a fabric-covered wing of composite wood and metal construction, the aircraft featured a fuselage and tail unit both of welded steel tube with fabric covering. Accommodation within the enclosed cabin was for two persons, seated side by side, and landing gear was of basic non-retractable tailwheel type, with main unit shock-absorption by rubber bungee. Powerplant of the imported Model As was one 40-hp (30-kW) Continental A-40 flat-four engine, and the Model B differed by having a 50-hp (37-kW) A-50 engine from the same manufacturer.

The British-built equivalent to the Model A was designated originally **Model C**, but this was soon to become redesignated **Plus C**, reflecting the improved performance resulting from installation of a 55-hp (41-kW) Lycoming O-145-A2 engine. Including the prototype, 23 Plus Cs were built. With a 90-hp (67-kW) Cirrus Minor 1 engine, the designation changed to **Plus D**, and nine civil aircraft were completed as such before the outbreak of World War II.

Of the 32 British-built aircraft mentioned above, 20 of the Plus Cs and four of the Plus Ds were impressed for service with the RAF. The Plus Cs, re-engined with the Cirrus Minor for RAF use, became redesignated **Plus C.2**. Most of these aircraft were used by No. 651 Squadron for evaluation of their suitability for deployment in AOP and communications roles. This led to an initial order for 100 generally similar aircraft for military use under the designation **Auster Mk I**.

Other than provision of split trailing-edge flaps to improve short-field performance, Austers were to change little throughout the war. During this time more than 1,600 were built for service use under the designations Auster Mk I, **Mk III**, **Mk IV** and **Mk V**, the Auster Mk I entering service with No. 654 Squadron in August 1942. Only two **Auster Mk II**s, with 130-hp (97-kW) O-290 engines, were built because of a shortage of the American powerplant. This led to the Auster Mk III, basically identical to the Auster Mk I, but with a 130-hp (97-kW) Gipsy Major I engine. The 470 Auster Mk IIIs were followed by 254 Auster Mk IVs, which reverted to the Lycoming engine, and introduced a slightly larger cabin to provide space for a third seat. The major production version was the Auster Mk V, of which approximately 800 were built, and this differed from the Auster Mk IV by introducing blind-flying instrumentation .

At the height of their utilisation, Austers equipped Nos 652, 653, 657, 658, 659, 660, 661, 662, 664 and 665 Squadrons of the 2nd Tactical Air Force, and Nos 651, 654, 655, 656, 663, 666, 671, 672 and 673 Squadrons of the Desert Air Force. They were used also in small numbers by associated Canadian and Dutch squadrons. Their initial deployment in an operational role was during the invasion of Algeria, and they were to prove an indispensable tool in the Sicilian and Italian campaigns. Just three weeks after D-Day, these unarmed lightplanes were in the forefront of the action as the Allied armies advanced into France.

Some 800 of the Lycoming-powered Auster Mk V variant were built. It differed from the Auster Mk IV by introducing blind-flying instrumentation, and featured a slightly larger cabin to provide space for a third seat.

This Auster Mk I of No. 651 Sqn was based at RAF Dumfries in the autumn of 1942, before being shipped to North Africa. In Algeria the squadron provided support for the 1st Army. It was replaced by the Auster Mk III in August 1943.

Specification
Auster Mk V
Type: light liaison/observation aircraft
Powerplant: one 130-hp (97-kW) Lycoming 0-290-3 flat-four piston engine
Performance: maximum speed 130 mph (209 km/h) at sea level; cruising speed 112 mph (180 km/h); normal range 250 miles (402 km)
Weights: empty 1,100 lb (499 kg); maximum take-off 1,850 lb (839 kg)
Dimensions: span 36 ft 0 in (10.97 m); length 22 ft 5 in (6.83 m); height 8 ft 0 in (2.44 m); wing area 167.0 sq ft (15.51 m²)

Vickers 132/266 Vildebeest/Vincent

The prototype Vickers Type 132 first flew in April 1928, powered by a 460-hp (343-kW) Bristol Jupiter VIII engine. After competitive trials against the Blackburn Beagle at the A&AEE, the powerplant was considered unacceptable and was replaced with the Armstrong Siddeley Panther. This arrangement was even worse and it was not until the 660-hp (492-kW) Bristol Pegasus was fitted that the type, by then named **Vildebeest Mk I**, was accepted for service.

RAF deliveries began in 1933 and the first squadron to receive the type was No. 100 Squadron.

The more powerful Pegasus IIM3-engined **Mk II** was ordered in December 1933 but, after only 30 had been built, it was replaced on the production line by the **Mk III**. This variant had a redesigned rear cockpit to accommodate a third crew member. Production examples were delivered to Nos 22 and 36 Sqns in 1935-36. The final production variant was the **Mk IV** powered by the Bristol Perseus engine. The first examples were delivered to No. 42 Sqn in 1937 and these were still in service at the outbreak of war flying east coast convoy patrols. At this time about 100 Vildebeests of various marks were still in RAF service. The last front-line operations were flown by Nos 36 and 100 Sqns shortly before Singapore fell to the Japanese in 1942.

A need to replace the Westland Wapiti and Fairey IIIF general-purpose biplanes led the Air Ministry to order a modified version of the Vildebeest for the role. Modifications included a long-range fuel tank in place of the torpedo, message pick-up gear and pyrotechnics.

Initial production deliveries of the **Vincent** were made to No. 8 Sqn in Aden in late 1934 and a total of 171 examples was produced for the RAF. A number of Vildebeests were also converted to Vincent standard and more than 80 were still in service at the outbreak of war. No. 244 Sqn Vincents flew front-line operations in Iraq during 1941, before being replaced by Bristol Blenheims.

Torpedo-armed Vildebeest Mk IVs, such as these pre-war examples, were used against Japanese shipping in the Far East.

Specification
Vincent Mk I
Type: three-seat general-purpose biplane
Powerplant: one 660-hp (492-kW) Bristol Pegasus IIM3 radial piston engine
Performance: maximum speed 142 mph (229 km/h); service ceiling 17,000 ft (5182 m); range 1,250 miles (2012 km) with long-range tank
Weights: empty 4,229 lb (1918 kg); maximum take-off 8,100 lb (3674 kg)
Dimensions: span 49 ft 0 in (14.94 m); length 36 ft 8 in (11.18 m); height 17 ft 9 in (5.41 m); wing area 728 sq ft (67.63 m²)
Armament: one forward-firing 0.303-in (7.7-mm) machine-gun and one Lewis gun in aft cockpit, plus up to 1,000 lb (454 kg) of bombs

No. 47 Squadron Vincents were used in the army co-operation role in Eritrea from May to December 1941.

Vickers 246 Wellesley

Like many other successful aircraft, the Vickers Wellesley started life as a private venture. Its most radical feature was the use for the first time in a heavier-than-air craft of the geodetic construction devised by Barnes Wallis, to give maximum strength for minimum weight.

The origin of the Wellesley was somewhat unusual, stemming from Specification G.4/31 for a general-purpose biplane. Vickers built a biplane to this specification, and this aircraft flew on 16 August 1934; on 19 June 1935 the company flew its private venture monoplane, which had been designed to meet the same specification. Comparison of the performance of the two aircraft showed the monoplane to be far superior, and the proposed order for 150 biplanes was changed to 96 monoplanes, these to be named Wellesley.

The first production aircraft, to the new Specification 22/35, flew at Brooklands on 30 January 1937, and was delivered to the RAF on 18 March for trials at the A&AEE, Martlesham Heath. The second Wellesley went to No. 76 Squadron at Finningley for service trials, and this unit was the first to be re-equipped with the new aircraft. Further production orders followed, and a total of 176 Wellesleys was built. Other UK squadrons to receive the type included Nos 35, 77, 148 and 207, and more than 100 served overseas with Nos 14, 45, 47 and 223 Squadrons in Aden, Asmara, East Africa, Egypt, Nairobi, Sudan and Transjordan.

In 1938 a world long-distance record flight of 7,162 miles (11526 km), made in just over 48 hours, was established by two Wellesleys of the RAF Long Range Development Flight: their route was from Ismailia, Egypt, to Darwin, Australia. A third aircraft reached Kupang, but with fuel getting low it was considered prudent for it to land there; after refuelling it completed the flight to Darwin.

Wellesley Mk Is had separate canopies for the two cockpits, but the **Wellesley Mk II** featured a continuous canopy. Novel features were the extremely long-span wing and the underwing bomb carriers with a capacity of up to 1,000 lb (454 kg) each. These were also each capable of carrying two 250-lb (113-kg) depth charges, and Wellesleys were used for anti-submarine patrols in 1942 by No. 47 Squadron operating from Egypt.

Wellesleys had been replaced in Bomber Command by Handley Page Hampdens, Armstrong Whitworth Whitleys and Vickers Wellingtons by the outbreak of World War II, and those still overseas were replaced between 1941 and 1944 by

Wellesley K7718 was attached to No. 76 Squadron based at RAF Finningley just prior to the outbreak of war. The Wellesley was largely obsolete by the start of hostilities, but played a small part in Middle East and North African operations.

Vickers 246 Wellesley

Specification
Wellesley Mk I
Type: two-seat general-purpose bomber
Powerplant: one 950-hp (708-kW) Bristol Pegasus XX radial piston engine
Performance: maximum speed 228 mph (367 km/h) at 19,680 ft (5998 m); cruising speed 188 mph (303 km/h); service ceiling 33,000 ft (10058 m); range 1,110 miles (1786 km)
Weights: empty 6,369 lb (2889 kg); maximum take-off 11,100 lb (5035 kg)
Dimensions: span 74 ft 7 in (22.73 m); length 39 ft 3 in (11.96 m); height 12 ft 4 in (3.76 m); wing area 630 sq ft (58.53 m^2)
Armament: one 0.303-in (7.7-mm) forward-firing machine-gun and one Vickers gun in rear cockpit, plus up to 2,000 lb (907 kg) of bombs

Above: The Wellesley's high-aspect-ratio wing of nine to one is clearly demonstrated in this photograph of a production Mk I.

Right: The Wellesley, like the Wellington, was of geodetic construction. This formation of Mk Is is carrying bomb containers beneath the wings.

Bristol Blenheims, Bristol Beauforts and Martin Marylands. Notable wartime efforts were the bombing of Addis Ababa by Wellesleys of No. 223 Squadron from Perin Island in August 1940, the bombing of Massana by No. 14 Squadron from Port Sudan in June 1940, and shipping reconnaissance by No. 202 Group into 1941.

Vickers 264 Valentia

A descendent of the famous Vickers Vimy bomber, the Valentia was derived in the early 1930s from the need to improve the performance of the Victoria, which in its original Mk III production form had first entered service in 1925. The Victorias were equipped with Napier Lion engines, long-serving and reliable powerplants which had originated in 1917 with a take-off rating of about 300 hp (224 kW). The evolutionary process of development had almost doubled this rating, for the Lion XIBs that powered the Type 169 Victoria Mk V each produced a maximum of 570 hp (425 kW).

The Bristol Pegasus radial engine was chosen for trial installation in a Victoria Mk V, and this led to an initial order for 11 Pegasus-powered aircraft which became designated Victoria Mk VI.

Testing of a trial conversion, powered by 660-hp (492-kW) Pegasus IIL3 engines, brought the decision that this basic powerplant should be introduced retrospectively for in-service aircraft, as well as being used for new production machines. Thus Victoria Mk Vs with the new engines installed, but without structural strengthening, were designated Victoria Mk VI. New production aircraft (28 built) and conversions (54), which included both the new engines and improved structural strength, became designated **Valentia Mk I**.

Equipped to accommodate a crew of two and a total of 22 troops, Valentias first entered service with No. 70 Squadron in the Middle East during 1934, and in the following year No. 216 Squadron began to receive these improved aircraft. They remained in operational use with these so-called Bomber Transport squadrons until 1940 and 1941, respectively. A version with Pegasus IIM3 engines, which offered improved high altitude/temperature performance, was supplied in 1938 for service with one flight of No. 31 Squadron which was then based at Lahore, India. Valentias of this squadron took part in the evacuation of Habbaniyah during the Iraqi rebellion of 1941.

Specification
Valentia Mk I
Type: troop transport
Powerplant: two 635-hp (474-kW) Bristol Pegasus IIM3 radial piston engines
Performance: maximum speed 120 mph (193 km/h) at 5,000 ft (1524 m); service ceiling 16,250 ft (4953 m); range 800 miles (1287 km)
Weights: empty 10,994 lb (4987 kg); maximum take-off 19,500 lb (8845 kg)
Dimensions: span 87 ft 4 in (26.62 m); length 59 ft 6 in (18.14 m); height 17 ft 9 in (5.41 m); wing area 2,178 sq ft (202,34 m^2)
Armament: up to 2,200 lb (998 kg) of bombs on underwing racks

When World War II started, the bomber force in the Middle East comprised two squadrons of Vickers Valentias, biplanes that doubled as troop transports. K3611 shown here served with No. 216 Squadron and was used on night bombing raids in 1940 before being relegated to transport duties. It later moved to India and served with No. 31 Squadron until it crashed in Persia in August 1941.

Vickers 271 Wellington

Left: The Vickers B.9/32 prototype K4049 made its first flight, piloted by J. 'Mutt' Summers, at Brooklands on 15 June 1936. It was written off in a crash the following April. It preceded the production Wellington bomber, which became almost a total redesign, benefiting substantially from the contemporary Warwick.

Above: A formation of Wellington Mk Is of No. 9 Squadron from RAF Stradishall is seen during exercises in 1939. The squadron flew Wellingtons until August 1942, when its Mk IIIs were replaced by Lancasters.

Wellington Mk I fuselages are seen in the erecting shop at Weybridge in 1939, showing clearly their 'basket weave' geodetic construction. Another feature was the engine nacelles that were completely external to the wing structure.

Building upon the experience gained from Barnes Wallis's geodetic structural concept, which had been used in the airframe of the Wellesley, Vickers adopted such construction when tendering for a prototype contract to Air Ministry Specification B.9/32. This called for an aircraft capable of delivering a bomb load of 1,000 lb (454 kg) and with a range of 720 miles (1159 km). These requirements were surpassed by the Vickers proposal, which was for a mid-wing medium day-bomber with two Rolls-Royce Goshawk engines and retractable landing gear, able to carry more than 4,500 lb (2041 kg) of bombs, and having a maximum range of 2,800 miles (4506 km).

The prototype B.9/32, with two 915-hp (682-kW) Bristol Pegasus X engines and a Supermarine Stranraer fin and rudder assembly, was completed at Weybridge in May 1936. It was first flown by Vickers chief test pilot, J. 'Mutt' Summers, on 15 June. Later that month, it was exhibited at the 1936 Hendon Air Display, with nose and tail cupolas covered to prevent details of its still-secret construction method being revealed. After initial manufacturer's testing the aircraft was flown to the Aircraft and Armament Experimental Establishment at Martlesham Heath for official trials. Near there, on 19 April 1937, with tests almost concluded, the prototype crashed after elevator overbalance in a high-speed dive resulted in inversion and structural failure.

On 15 August 1936, however, the Air Ministry had placed an order for 180 **Wellington Mk I**s to Specification B.29/36. These were required to have a redesigned and slightly more angular fuselage, a revised tail unit, and hydraulically operated Vickers nose, ventral and tail turrets. The first production Wellington Mk I was flown on 23 December 1937, powered by Pegasus X engines. In April 1938, however, the 1,050-hp (783-kW) Pegasus XVIII became standard for the other 3,052 Mk Is of all variants built at Weybridge, or at the Blackpool and Chester factories which were established to keep pace with orders.

Initial Mk Is totalled 181, of which three were built at Chester. These were followed by 187 **Mk IA**s with Nash and Thompson turrets and strengthened landing gear with larger main wheels. Except for 17 Chester-built aircraft, all were manufactured at Weybridge. The most numerous of the Mk I variants was the **Mk IC**, which had Vickers 'K' or Browning machine-guns in beam positions (these replacing the ventral turret), improved hydraulics, and a strengthened bomb bay beam to allow a 4,000-lb (1814-kg) bomb to be carried. Of this version 2,685 were built (1,052 at Weybridge, 50 at Blackpool and 1,583 at Chester), 138 of them being delivered as torpedo-bombers after successful trials at the Torpedo Development Unit, Gosport.

Many of the improvements incorporated in the Mks IA and IC were developed for the **Mk II**, powered by 1,145-hp (854-kW) Rolls-Royce Merlin X engines as an insurance against Pegasus supply problems. The prototype was a conversion of the 38th Mk I, and made its first flight on 3 March 1939 at Brooklands. Although range was reduced slightly, the Wellington Mk II offered improvements in speed, service ceiling and maximum weight, the last rising from the 24,850 lb (11272 kg) of the basic Mk I to 33,000 lb (14969 kg). Weybridge built 401 of this version.

With the **Wellington Mk III** a switch was made to Bristol Hercules engines, the prototype being the 39th Mk I airframe with Hercules HEISMs, two-stage superchargers and de Havilland propellers. After initial problems with this installation, a Mk IC was converted to take two 1,425-hp (1063-kW) Hercules III engines

Wellington Mk III X3763 operated with No. 425 (Alouette) Squadron, an RCAF-manned unit based at RAF Dishforth in September 1942. The Wellingtons were replaced by Halifaxes towards the end of 1943.

In April 1940 No. 37 Squadron was flying Wellington Mk IAs from RAF Feltwell. The squadron had mounted its first offensive Wellington mission within seven hours of the outbreak of war against German shipping. In November 1940 the squadron moved to the Middle East.

driving Rotol propellers. Production Mk IIIs had 1,590-hp (1186-kW) Hercules XIs, and later aircraft were fitted with four-gun FN.20A tail turrets, doubling the firepower of the installation in earlier marks. Two were completed at Weybridge, 780 at Blackpool and 737 at Chester.

The availability of a number of 1,050-hp (783-kW) Pratt & Whitney Twin Wasp R-1830-S3C4-G engines, ordered by but not delivered to France, led to development of the **Wellington Mk IV**. The prototype was one of 220 Mk IVs built at Chester, but on its delivery flight to Weybridge carburettor icing caused both engines to fail on the approach to Brooklands, and the aircraft made a forced landing at Addlestone. The original Hamilton Standard propellers proved very noisy and were replaced by Curtiss propellers.

For high-altitude bombing Vickers was asked to investigate the provision of a pressure cabin in the Wellington: the resulting **Mk V** was powered by two turbocharged Hercules VIII engines. Service ceiling was increased from the 23,500 ft (7165 m) of the Mk II to 36,800 ft (11215 m). The cylindrical pressure chamber had a porthole in the lower nose position for the bomb-aimer, and the pilot's head projected into a small pressurised dome which, although offset to port, provided little forward or downward view for landing. Two prototypes were built in Vickers's experimental shop at Foxwarren, Cobham, to Specification B.23/39, and one production machine, to B.17/40, was produced at the company's extension factory at Smith's Lawn, Windsor Great Park.

The **Wellington Mk VI** was a parallel development, with 1,600-hp (1193-kW) Merlin 60 engines and a service ceiling of 38,500 ft (11735 m), although the prototype had achieved 40,000 ft (12190 m). Wellington Mk VI production totalled 63, including 18 re-engined Mk Vs, all assembled at Smith's Lawn. Each had a remotely controlled FN.20A tail turret, and this was locked in position when the aircraft was at altitude.

Intended originally as an improved Mk II with Merlin XX engines, the **Wellington Mk VII** was built only as a prototype, and was transferred to Rolls-Royce at Hucknall for development flying of the Merlin 60 engine.

First Wellington variant to be developed specifically for Coastal Command was the **Wellington GR.Mk VIII**, a general reconnaissance/torpedo-bomber version of the Pegasus XVIII-engined Mk IC. Equipped with ASV (Air to Surface Vessel) Mk II radar, it was identified readily by the four dorsal antennas and the four pairs of transmitting aerials on each side of the fuselage. A total of 271 torpedo-bombers for daylight operation was built at Weybridge, together with 65 day-bombers, and 58 equipped for night operation with a Leigh searchlight in the ventral turret position. In these last aircraft the nose armament was deleted and the position occupied by the light operator.

The designation **Mk IX** was allocated to a single troop-carrying conversion of a Wellington Mk IA, but the **Mk X** was the last of the bomber variants and the most numerous. It was based on the Mk III, but had the more powerful 1,675-hp (1249-kW) Hercules VI or XVI engine with downdraught carburettor, and was distinguished externally from earlier marks by the long carburettor intake on top of the engine cowling. Internal structural strengthening, achieved by the use

Above: This trio of Wellington Mk ICs from No. 311 (Czechoslovak) Squadron was based at RAF Honington in late 1940. The white section of the fuselage roundel has been painted out to reduce its brightness when caught by searchlights.

Right: No. 75 (New Zealand) Squadron, which first received Wellington Mk Is in July 1939, took part in the second RAF bombing raid of World War II. As the first Commonwealth squadron to be formed in Bomber Command, No. 75 flew the Wellington between July 1940 and October 1942.

Vickers 271 Wellington

Wellingtons of Nos 109 and 156 Squadrons were introduced into the Pathfinder Force in August 1942. A 4,000-lb (1814-kg) 'blockbuster' bomb is shown being loaded onto a Wellington Mk III with Type 423 modification, at RAF Mildenhall.

Specification
Wellington Mk III
Type: long-range night-bomber
Powerplant: two 1,500-hp (1119-kW) Bristol Hercules XI radial piston engines
Performance: maximum speed 235 mph (378 km/h) at 15,500 ft (4724 m); service ceiling 19,000 ft (5791 m); range 1,540 miles (2478 km) with 4,500-lb (2041-kg) bomb load
Weights: empty 18,650 lb (8459 kg); maximum take-off 29,500 lb (13381 kg)
Dimensions: span 86 ft 2 in (26.26 m); length 60 ft 10 in (18.54 m); height 17 ft 5 in (5.31 m); wing area 840 sq ft (78.04 m²)
Armament: eight 0.303-in (7.7-mm) machine-guns (two in nose, four in tail turret, and two in beam positions), plus up to 4,500 lb (2041 kg) of bombs

Above: With guns no longer fitted, this aged Wellington Mk IA (N2887) underwent conversion as an interim transport (Mk XV) for second-line duties with RAF Transport Command in 1942. The majority of Wellington Mk Is which were converted became Mk XVIs. It was struck off charge on 26 April 1945.

The Vickers Wellington – universally nicknamed 'Wimpy' – was the primary RAF heavy bomber used for operations in North Africa. This Mk IC warms up on a desert landing strip in 1942. Air-cooled engines had an advantage over inline powerplants in the dusty conditions, possessing greater serviceability and reliability.

Wellington B.Mk III cutaway drawing key

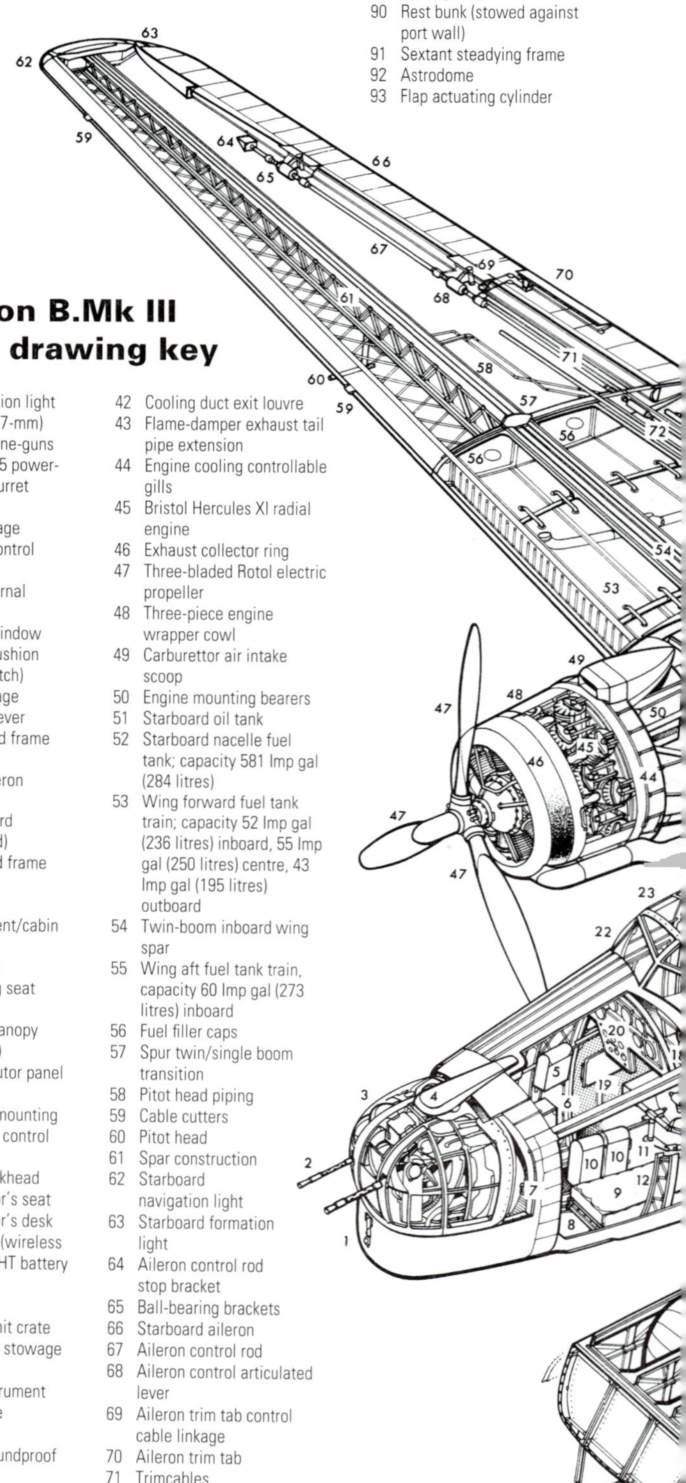

1 Forward navigation light
2 Two 0.303-in (7.7-mm) Browning machine-guns
3 Frazer-Nash FN.5 power-operated nose turret
4 Turret fairing
5 Parachute stowage
6 Bomb-aimer's control panel
7 Nose turret external rotation valve
8 Bomb-aimer's window
9 Bomb-aimer's cushion (hinged entry hatch)
10 Parachute stowage
11 Rudder control lever
12 Fuselage forward frame
13 Camera
14 Elevator and aileron control levers
15 Bomb-bay forward bulkhead (canted)
16 Cockpit bulkhead frame
17 Pilot's seat
18 Control column
19 Nose compartment/cabin step
20 Instrument panel
21 Co-pilot's folding seat
22 Windscreen
23 Hinged cockpit canopy section (ditching)
24 Electrical distributor panel
25 Aerial mast
26 R.3003 controls mounting
27 Tail unit de-icing control unit
28 Armour-plate bulkhead
29 Wireless operator's seat
30 Wireless operator's desk
31 Motor-generator (wireless installation) and HT battery stowage
32 Bomb-bay doors
33 TR.9F wireless unit crate
34 Aldis signal lamp stowage
35 Navigator's desk
36 Navigational instrument and map stowage
37 Navigator's seat
38 Folding doors (soundproof bulkhead)
39 Fire extinguisher (on leading-edge fuselage frame)
40 Flying-controls locking bar ('nuisance bar') stowage
41 Wing inboard geodetic structure
42 Cooling duct exit louvre
43 Flame-damper exhaust tail pipe extension
44 Engine cooling controllable gills
45 Bristol Hercules XI radial engine
46 Exhaust collector ring
47 Three-bladed Rotol electric propeller
48 Three-piece engine wrapper cowl
49 Carburettor air intake scoop
50 Engine mounting bearers
51 Starboard oil tank
52 Starboard nacelle fuel tank; capacity 581 Imp gal (284 litres)
53 Wing forward fuel tank train; capacity 52 Imp gal (236 litres) inboard, 55 Imp gal (250 litres) centre, 43 Imp gal (195 litres) outboard
54 Twin-boom inboard wing spar
55 Wing aft fuel tank train, capacity 60 Imp gal (273 litres) inboard
56 Fuel filler caps
57 Spur twin/single boom transition
58 Pitot head piping
59 Cable cutters
60 Pitot head
61 Spar construction
62 Starboard navigation light
63 Starboard formation light
64 Aileron control rod stop bracket
65 Ball-bearing brackets
66 Starboard aileron
67 Aileron control rod
68 Aileron control articulated lever
69 Aileron trim tab control cable linkage
70 Aileron trim tab
71 Trimcables
72 Aileron control rod joint
73 Fuel jettison pipe
74 Flap operating shaft
75 Flap links
76 Flap trailing edge
77 Aileron control rod adjustable joint
78 Dinghy stowage
79 Flotation gear CO_2 bottles
80 Fuel lines
81 D/F loop fairing
82 Dorsal identification light
83 Handgrips
84 Oxygen cylinders
85 'Floating'-spar centre section carry-through
86 Reconnaissance flares
87 Wing forward pivot fixing
88 Spar/rib pick-up
89 Spar aperture
90 Rest bunk (stowed against port wall)
91 Sextant steadying frame
92 Astrodome
93 Flap actuating cylinder
94 Flame float/sea marker stowage
95 Flap synchronising mechanism
96 Parachute stowage
97 Reconnaissance flare launching tube

Wellington Mk I L4235 was serving with No. 38 Squadron at RAF Marham at the outbreak of war. The squadron received its first Mk Is in November 1938 and operated the type in various marks until early 1942.

Fitted with a Leigh Light for night operations and ASV Mk III radar in a ventral 'dustbin' housing, the Wellington GR.Mk XIV was based on the Mk X airframe. This aircraft served with No. 304 Squadron on anti-submarine patrols in the English Channel and North Atlantic ocean.

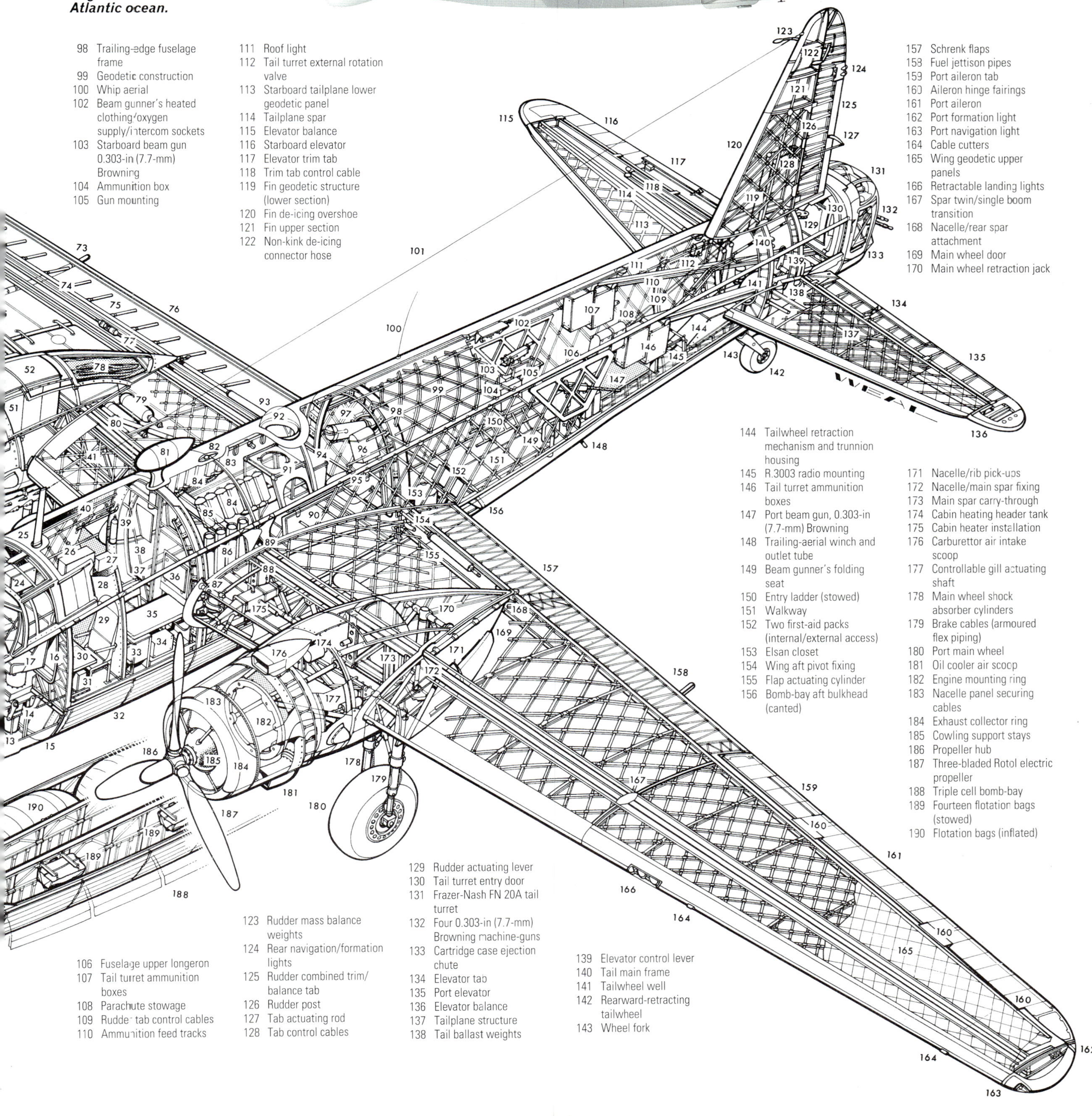

98 Trailing-edge fuselage frame
99 Geodetic construction
100 Whip aerial
102 Beam gunner's heated clothing/oxygen supply/intercom sockets
103 Starboard beam gun 0.303-in (7.7-mm) Browning
104 Ammunition box
105 Gun mounting
106 Fuselage upper longeron
107 Tail turret ammunition boxes
108 Parachute stowage
109 Rudder tab control cables
110 Ammunition feed tracks
111 Roof light
112 Tail turret external rotation valve
113 Starboard tailplane lower geodetic panel
114 Tailplane spar
115 Elevator balance
116 Starboard elevator
117 Elevator trim tab
118 Trim tab control cable
119 Fin geodetic structure (lower section)
120 Fin de-icing overshoe
121 Fin upper section
122 Non-kink de-icing connector hose
123 Rudder mass balance weights
124 Rear navigation/formation lights
125 Rudder combined trim/balance tab
126 Rudder post
127 Tab actuating rod
128 Tab control cables
129 Rudder actuating lever
130 Tail turret entry door
131 Frazer-Nash FN 20A tail turret
132 Four 0.303-in (7.7-mm) Browning machine-guns
133 Cartridge case ejection chute
134 Elevator tab
135 Port elevator
136 Elevator balance
137 Tailplane structure
138 Tail ballast weights
139 Elevator control lever
140 Tail main frame
141 Tailwheel well
142 Rearward-retracting tailwheel
143 Wheel fork
144 Tailwheel retraction mechanism and trunnion housing
145 R.3003 radio mounting
146 Tail turret ammunition boxes
147 Port beam gun, 0.303-in (7.7-mm) Browning
148 Trailing-aerial winch and outlet tube
149 Beam gunner's folding seat
150 Entry ladder (stowed)
151 Walkway
152 Two first-aid packs (internal/external access)
153 Elsan closet
154 Wing aft pivot fixing
155 Flap actuating cylinder
156 Bomb-bay aft bulkhead (canted)
157 Schrenk flaps
158 Fuel jettison pipes
159 Port aileron tab
160 Aileron hinge fairings
161 Port aileron
162 Port formation light
163 Port navigation light
164 Cable cutters
165 Wing geodetic upper panels
166 Retractable landing lights
167 Spar twin/single boom transition
168 Nacelle/rear spar attachment
169 Main wheel door
170 Main wheel retraction jack
171 Nacelle/rib pick-ups
172 Nacelle/main spar fixing
173 Main spar carry-through
174 Cabin heating header tank
175 Cabin heater installation
176 Carburettor air intake scoop
177 Controllable gill actuating shaft
178 Main wheel shock absorber cylinders
179 Brake cables (armoured flex piping)
180 Port main wheel
181 Oil cooler air scoop
182 Engine mounting ring
183 Nacelle panel securing cables
184 Exhaust collector ring
185 Cowling support stays
186 Propeller hub
187 Three-bladed Rotol electric propeller
188 Triple cell bomb-bay
189 Fourteen flotation bags (stowed)
190 Flotation bags (inflated)

Wellington Mk IC

The Vickers Type 415 Wellington Mk IC had a redesigned hydraulic system, a 24-volt electrical system and the substitution of beam guns in the midship position for the unsatisfactory ventral turret. The Pegasus XVIII-powered bomber set the standard for subsequent marks in the early war years.

Tail unit
On the production Wellington Mk I the tailplane was raised by 6 in (15 cm) to account for the deeper fuselage. The tail fin and rudder were redesigned into a taller and thinner structure giving the rear of the aircraft a distinctive appearance.

Systems
The rising operational requirements of the Wellington led to the Mk IC being fitted with a new hydraulic system using VSG pumps combined with a 24-volt electrical system required to operate the directional radio (DR) compass.

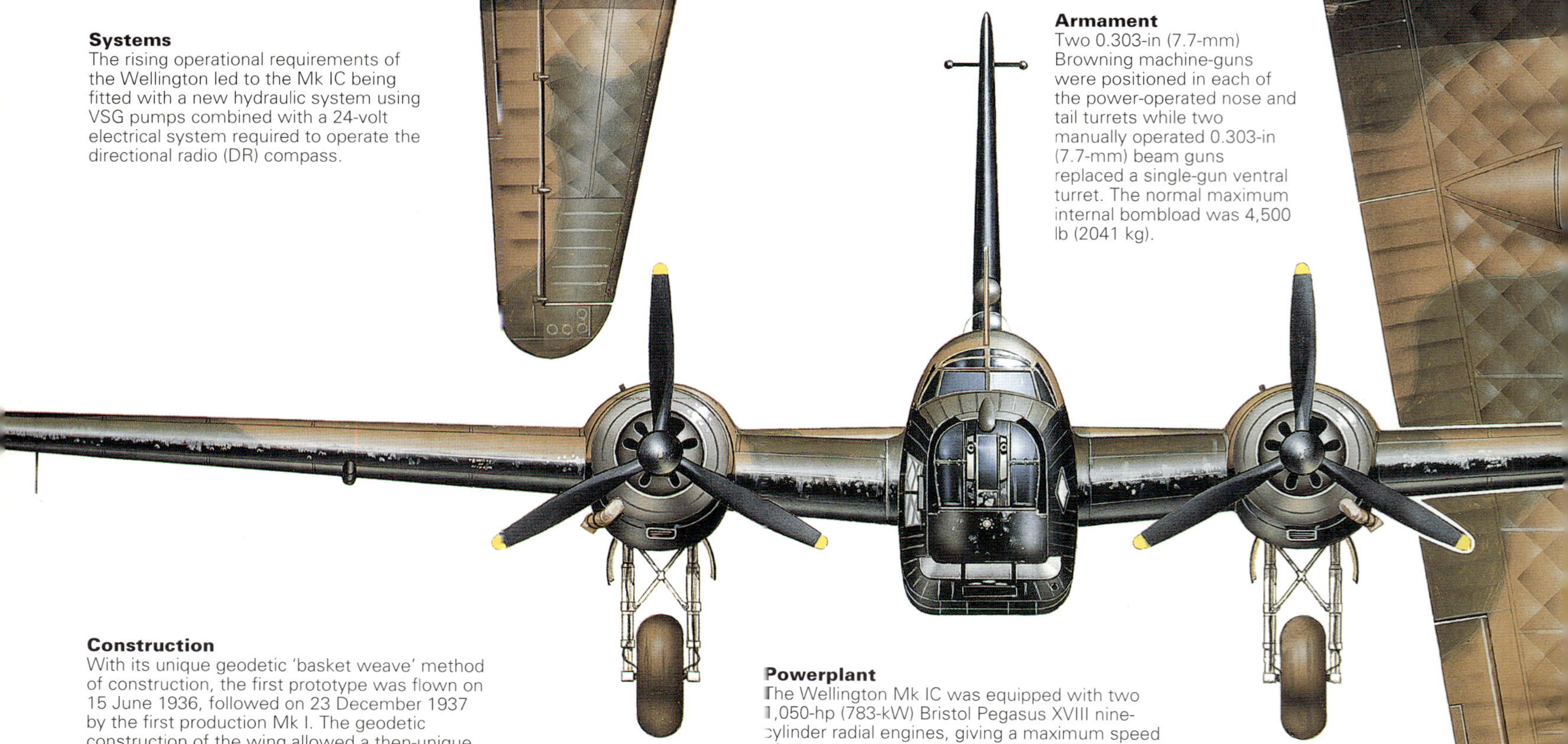

Armament
Two 0.303-in (7.7-mm) Browning machine-guns were positioned in each of the power-operated nose and tail turrets while two manually operated 0.303-in (7.7-mm) beam guns replaced a single-gun ventral turret. The normal maximum internal bombload was 4,500 lb (2041 kg).

Construction
With its unique geodetic 'basket weave' method of construction, the first prototype was flown on 15 June 1936, followed on 23 December 1937 by the first production Mk I. The geodetic construction of the wing allowed a then-unique method of stowing the fuel in the space outboard of the engine nacelles. Aircraft were built at Chester and Blackpool, as well as at the main Weybridge factory.

Powerplant
The Wellington Mk IC was equipped with two 1,050-hp (783-kW) Bristol Pegasus XVIII nine-cylinder radial engines, giving a maximum speed of 235 mph (378 km/h) at 15,500 ft (4724 m).

of newly-developed light alloys, allowed maximum take-off weight to rise to 36,000 lb (16329 kg). Production was shared between Blackpool and Chester, with totals of 1,369 and 2,434, respectively. After withdrawal from first-line service with Bomber Command, Mk Xs were among many Wellingtons flown by Operational Training Units. After the war a number were converted by Boulton Paul Aircraft as **T.Mk 10** crew trainers, with the nose turret faired over.

Making use of the experience gained with the Wellington VIII torpedo-bombers, the **GR.Mk XI** was developed from the Mk X, using the same Hercules VI or XVI engines. It was equipped initially with ASV Mk II radar, although this was superseded later by centimetric ASV Mk III. This latter equipment had first been fitted to the **GR.Mk XII**, which was a Leigh Light-equipped anti-submarine version. Weybridge built 105 Mk XIs and 50 Mk XIIs, while Blackpool and Chester respectively assembled 75 Mk XIs and eight Mk XIIs, but with 1,735-hp (1294-kW) Hercules XVII engines. Weybridge was responsible for 42 Mk XIIIs and 53 **Mk XIV**s, Blackpool for 802 XIIIs and 250 Mk XIVs, and Chester for 538 Mk XIVs.

A transport conversion of the Mk I, the **C.Mk IA**, was further developed as the **C.Mk XV**, while the **C.Mk XVI** was a similar development of the Mk IC. They were unarmed, as were the last three basic versions which were all trainers. The **T.Mk XVII** was a Mk XI converted by the RAF for night-fighter crew training with SCR-720 AI (Airborne Interception) radar in a nose radome. Eighty externally similar aircraft, with accommodation for instructor and four pupils and based on the Mk XIII, were built at Blackpool as **T.Mk XVIII**s. Finally, RAF-converted Mk Xs for basic crew training were designated **T.Mk XIX**s. In total, 11,461 Wellingtons were built, including the prototype, and the last was a Blackpool-built Mk X handed over on 25 October 1945.

The fourth production Wellington Mk I was the first to reach an operational squadron, arriving at Mildenhall in October 1938 for No. 99 Squadron. Six squadrons of No. 3 Group (Nos 9, 37, 38, 99, 115 and 149) were equipped by the outbreak of war, and among units working up was the New Zealand Flight at Marham, Norfolk, where training was in progress in preparation for delivery to New Zealand of 30 Wellington Mk Is. The flight later became No. 75 (NZ) Squadron, the first Dominion squadron to be formed in World War II. Sergeant James Ward of No. 75 later became the only recipient of the Victoria Cross while serving on Wellingtons, the decoration being awarded for crawling out on to the wing in flight to extinguish a fire, during a sortie made on 7 July 1941.

On 4 September 1939, the second day of the war, Wellingtons of Nos 9 and 149 Squadrons bombed German shipping at Brunsbuttel. Wellingtons in tight formation were reckoned to have such outstanding defensive firepower as to be almost impregnable, but after maulings at the hands of pilots of the Luftwaffe's JG 1, during raids on the Schillig Roads on 14 and 18 December, some lessons were learned. Self-sealing tanks were essential, and the Wellington's vulnerability to beam attacks from above led to introduction of beam gun positions. Most significantly, operations switched to nights.

Wellingtons of Nos 99 and 149 Squadrons were among aircraft dispatched in Bomber Command's first attack on Berlin, which took place on 25/26 August 1940; and on 1 April 1941, a Wellington of

This Wellington Mk IV (LL) operated from RAF Chivenor in 1944. Note the radar scanner 'chin' housing under the nose, and the extended under-fuselage Leigh Light.

Wellington Mk VI W5798, on air test in February 1942, was the third of 20 machines ordered as Mk Vs and completed as Mk VIs. However, the high-altitude pressurised Mk VI bomber, with its strangely shaped nose, failed to reach operational service.

This Wellington T.Mk XVIII was converted from a Mk XIII and fitted with a Mosquito NF.Mk 30 radar dome which housed a radar scanner for training night-fighter crews. The radio operator/navigator's compartment was redesigned to accommodate four pupils and an instructor.

No. 149 Squadron dropped the first 4,000-lb (1814-kg) 'blockbuster' bomb during a raid on Emden. Of 1,046 aircraft which took part in the Cologne raid during the night of 30 May 1942, 599 were Wellingtons. The last operational sortie by Bomber Command Wellingtons was flown on 8/9 October 1943.

There was, however, still an important role for the Wellington to play with Coastal Command. Maritime operations had started with the four DWI Wellingtons: these had been converted by Vickers in the opening months of 1940 to carry a 52-ft (15.85-m) diameter metal ring, which contained a coil that could create a field current to detonate magnetic mines. Eleven almost identical aircraft, with 48-ft (14.63-m) rings, were converted by W. A. Rollason Ltd at Croydon, and others on site in the Middle East.

No. 172 Squadron at Chivenor, covering the Western Approaches, was the first to use the Leigh Light-equipped Wellington Mk VIIIs operationally, and the first attack on a U-boat by such an aircraft at night took place on 3 June 1942, with the first sinking recorded on 6 July. From December 1941 Wellingtons were flying shipping strikes in the Mediterranean, and in the Far East No. 36 Squadron began anti-submarine operations in October 1942.

In 1940 the entry of the Italians into World War II resulted in Wellingtons being sent from Great Britain to serve with No. 205 Group, Desert Air Force. No. 70 Squadron flew its first night attack on 19 September, against the port of Benghazi, and as the tide of war turned during 1942 and 1943, units moved into Tunisia to support the invasions of Sicily and Italy, operating from Italian soil at the close of 1943. The last Wellington bombing raid of the war in southern Europe took place on 13 March 1945, when six aircraft joined a Consolidated Liberator strike on marshalling yards at Treviso in northern Italy.

In the Far East, too, Wellingtons served as bombers with No. 225 Group in India, Mk ICs of No. 215 Squadron flying their first operational sortie on 23 April 1942. Equipped later with Wellington Mk Xs, Nos 99 and 215 Squadrons continued to bomb Japanese bases and communications until replaced by Liberators in late 1944, when the Wellington units were released for transport duties.

After the war the Wellington was used principally for navigator and pilot training by Air Navigation Schools and Advanced Flying Schools until 1953.

Above: This Wellington C.Mk XVI, belonging to No. 24 (Commonwealth) Squadron, Ferry Command, appears to be fitted with standard nose and tail turrets. In fact, these were painted on in an attempt to camouflage the transport's lack of defensive armament.

Right: Used as a transport by BOAC during the war, this Wellington C.Mk IA was named **Duke of Rutland**. ***The accommodation provided was austere but practical.***

Vickers 284 Warwick

***Above:** Vickers Warwick GR.Mk V PN811 was flown by No. 179 Squadron on anti-submarine duties from St Eval in Cornwall between January 1944 and June 1946. The squadron achieved a probable U-boat kill in February 1945.*

***Left:** This Warwick Mk III transport, with a large pannier attached below the fuselage, served with Nos 525 and 167 Squadrons at Lyneham, Holmsley South and Blackbushe between August 1944 and November 1946.*

The failure of the Rolls-Royce Vulture engine effectively killed both the Vickers Warwick and the Avro Manchester, but at least the latter entered service and was subsequently the basis of the highly successful Lancaster. The Warwick, on the other hand, flew in prototype form with Vultures, but teething troubles were so prolonged that the Warwick had been superseded by the new four-engined bombers before it could enter production.

Designed to Specification B.1/35, and intended to be complementary to the Wellington, the Warwick got off to a bad start because of policy changes and some doubts on the form of geodetic construction. It was not until 13 August 1939 that the Vulture-powered prototype flew. The unreliability of this engine compelled a change, and the second prototype flew with a Bristol Centaurus powerplant in April 1940.

Delay in delivery of these engines in quantity necessitated another change of powerplant, this time to American Pratt & Whitney Double Wasps of 1,850 hp (1380 kW), and in this form the **Warwick Mk I** entered production, the first aircraft flying from Brooklands on 1 May 1942. By then it was far too late to consider the aircraft as a bomber and in January 1943 the decision was made to convert the type for air-sea rescue work, carrying an airborne lifeboat beneath the fuselage. This became the **Warwick ASR.Mk I**, and the first three were delivered in August 1943 to No. 280 Squadron at Langham, Norfolk, where they replaced Ansons.

Early Warwick ASR.Mk Is, known as Stage A aircraft, carried a Mk I lifeboat and Lindholme rescue equipment; later versions (Stage B aircraft) had provision for ASV radar and a Frazer-Nash tail turret, but had no camera mounting. The final (Stage C) version could be operated at higher all-up weights. Total production of ASR Warwicks amounted to 275, and 16 **B.Mk Is** were also built.

A BOAC requirement for a long-range transport led in 1942 to an order for 14 Warwick transports. Designated **C.Mk Is**, these came from the Weybridge production line, with nose and tail turrets replaced by blunt fairings, and all military equipment removed. The first Warwick C.Mk I flew on 5 February 1943, powered by Pratt & Whitney Double Wasp R-2800s, and following tests at Boscombe Down the type entered service with BOAC on its Middle East routes. The Warwick C.Mk Is served with the airline until 1944, when they were transferred to RAF Transport Command and operated by No. 167 Squadron at Holmsley South.

A further transport development was the **Warwick Mk III**, which was basically similar to the C.Mk I but had a large, fixed ventral pannier. In cargo configuration a 6,710-lb (3044-kg) payload could be carried, or alternatively 24 men and equipment; in a VIP role eight to 10 passengers could be accommodated. One hundred Warwick Mk IIIs were built and served mainly in the Mediterranean area with Nos 46 and 47 Groups of RAF Transport Command, before being withdrawn in 1946.

Bristol Centaurus engines became available in 1943, and the opportunity was taken to develop the Warwick in the general-reconnaissance role as the **GR.Mk II**; 133 were built to serve with Coastal Command squadrons at home and in the Middle and Far East. The GR.Mk II had a single nose gun in place of the two-gun turret of earlier versions, and a mid-upper turret was added.

The last production Warwick was the **GR.Mk V**, generally similar to the GR.Mk II, but with beam guns in place of the mid-upper turret. A radar scanner beneath the nose also housed the Leigh Light, an airborne searchlight intended primarily for anti-submarine operations.

The first GR.Mk V flew at Brooklands in April 1944, and service trials were carried out at Hullavington. Deliveries began to No. 179 Squadron at St Eval in 1945 and 212 were built, but was too late to see much service.

Specification
Warwick GR.Mk II
Type: seven-seat general reconnaissance aircraft
Powerplant: two 2,500-hp (1864-kW) Bristol Centaurus VI radial piston engines
Performance: maximum speed 262 mph (422 km/h) at 2,000 ft (610 m); service ceiling 19,000 ft (5791 m); range 3,050 miles (4908 km)
Weights: empty 31,125 lb (14118 kg); maximum take-off 51,250 lb (23247 kg)
Dimensions: span 96 ft 9 in (29.49 m); length 68 ft 6 in (20.88 m); height 18 ft 6 in (5.64 m); wing area 1,006 sq ft (93.46 m^2)
Armament: six 0.303-in (7.7-mm) machine-guns (one each in nose and dorsal turrets, and four in tail turret), plus up to 12,250 lb (5557 kg) of bombs

The Warwick ASR.Mk I version was specifically built for air-sea rescue duties, in which capacity it served with 10 Coastal Command squadrons. An airborne lifeboat is seen underneath this aircraft.

Vought Chesapeake

Yet another of the types of US aircraft that came to Britain as a result of French orders that were unfulfilled at the time of the June 1940 Armistice, the **Chesapeake Mk I** was designed to be a carrier-based scout-bomber. This category of aircraft was much favoured by the US Navy, which had ordered a prototype **XSB2U-1** in 1934 and had gone on to buy 169 production examples in **SB2U-1**, **-2** and **-3** versions, named **Vindicator**.

For service aboard its aircraft-carriers, the French Navy had ordered two batches of **V-156** dive-bombers, these being similar to the USN's SB2U-1. The second batch, comprising 50 aircraft, came to Britain following the fall of France, deliveries being complete by November 1941.

Erected at No. 37 Maintenance Unit at Burtonwood, the Chesapeakes were used for a time by No. 728 Squadron based at RNAS Arbroath, before being assigned to No. 811 Squadron which was nominated to operate them in the torpedo-bomber-reconnaissance role.

The unit received 14 examples plus two Sea Hurricanes on 14 July 1941. However, the take-off performance of the Chesapeake was found to be too poor for operation from escort carriers, as planned, and interest in the type for front-line service with the Navy soon waned. Thereafter, the Chesapeakes were distributed among several Fleet Air Arm training and support units, these including Nos 770, 771, 772 and 776 Fleet Requirements Units, and Nos 778, 781, 784, 786 and 787 Squadrons for training and role development purposes. All were out of service before the end of 1943.

Specification
Chesapeake Mk I
Type: two-seat carrier-based or shore-based dive-bomber
Powerplant: one 825-hp (615-kW) Pratt & Whitney R-1535-SB4G Twin Wasp Junior radial piston engine
Performance: maximum speed 250 mph (402 km/h) at 7,500 ft (2286 m); cruising speed 220 mph (354 km/h); service ceiling 26,500 ft (8077 m); maximum range 1340 miles (2157 km)
Weights: empty 5,600 lb (2540 kg); maximum take-off 9763 lb (4428 kg)
Dimensions: span 42 ft 0 in (12.80 m); length 34 ft 0 in (10.36 m); height 10 ft 3 in (3.12 m); wing area 305 sq ft (28.33 m²)
Armament: one 0.5-in (17.7-mm) and two 0.303-in (7.7-mm) forward-firing machine-guns plus one 0.5-in (12.7-mm) machine-gun in an aft position plus up to 1,500 lb (680 kg) of bombs

No. 811 Squadron based at Lee-on-Solent received 14 Chesapeake torpedo bombers in July 1941, but they proved unsuitable for operations from escort carriers, and were soon replaced by the Fairey Swordfish.

Vought Corsair

The best US Navy fighter to see combat in World War II, and one of that conflict's most significant warplanes, the **F4U Corsair** grew from a US Navy requirement first set out early in 1938. Designed to make use of the powerful new Pratt & Whitney R-2800 Double Wasp engine, the **XF4U-1** prototype was first flown on 29 May 1939, and quickly demonstrated outstanding performance. By the middle of 1941, the Navy had placed contracts for nearly 600 of the distinctive new single-seat deck-landing fighter, characterised by the inverted gull, upward-folding wings in which were housed six 0.5-in (12.7-mm) machine-guns. To help meet escalating Navy production demands, Brewster and Goodyear were brought into the manufacturing programme to make variants of the **F4U-1** known as the **F3A-1** and **FG-1**, respectively. Service introduction, with both the US Marine Corps and US Navy, was under way by the autumn of 1942.

Although early operational experience showed that the Corsair was not the easiest aircraft to land on a carrier deck, Britain was more than willing to receive supplies of the new fighter as soon as they became available through the provisions of the Lend-Lease Act, from early

The Corsair appeared operationally for the first time in Fleet Air Arm service during the* Tirpitz *raids on 3 April 1944. No. 1834 Squadron operated from HMS* Victorious*, providing fighter cover for the Barracuda torpedo bombers.

1943 onwards. The first 95 aircraft were of the early-production F4U-1 type with the so-called 'bird-cage' cockpit canopy, and were designated **Corsair Mk I**. To handle the introduction of the new type, the Fleet Air Arm set up a procedure for forming and working-up of squadrons in North America, either at Quonset or at Brunswick, and then shipping the complete unit with its pilots to the UK in an escort carrier. The first unit so formed was No. 1830 Squadron, commissioned on 1 June 1943 and attached to HMS *Illustrious*.

Three more units, Nos 1831, 1833 and 1834, formed in July, Nos 1835 and 1836 in August, No. 1837 in September and No. 1838 in October. Further squadrons were formed at regular intervals through 1944 and the final two in February and April 1945 to bring the FAA Corsair force to a total 19 squadrons. This steady build-up depended on the flow of additional batches of aircraft, with the Corsair Mk Is followed by 510 **Corsair Mk IIs**. These introduced the raised,

Top: With 8 in (0.20 m) 'clipped' from each wing and the wingtip squared-off, the Corsair could fit in the below-decks stowage on small carriers. Despite this reduction in wing area, the Corsair was cleared for carrier operations as soon as a curving landing pattern had been devised to keep the deck in view.

Above: This formation of six Corsair Mk IIs is from No. 738 Naval Air Squadron. This unit formed at Quonset Point, Rhode Island, USA on 1 February 1943, with a variety of aircraft supplied under Lend-Lease, including Corsairs. It provided advanced carrier landing training for RN pilots trained at US Navy air stations.

Left: British Fleet Air Arm Corsairs were almost immediately deployed aboard carriers from their introduction in 1943, when carrier flying by Corsairs was still prohibited in the US Navy. A total of 2,012 Corsairs was supplied under Lend-Lease to the Royal Navy.

This early production Corsair Mk I flew with No. 1835 Naval Air Squadron based at Brunswick, Maine in late 1943. The aircraft has the 'flat-top' metal-reinforced canopy of the F4U-1 and an 8-in (20-cm) reduction of the wingtip to allow stowage in the hangar decks of escort carriers.

Right: Corsair Mk II JT228 was delivered to No. 1833 Squadron in September 1943 with whom it received the code '6A'. Aircraft bound for Fleet Air Arm duties were 'worked up' in the USA before being shipped to the UK aboard escort carriers.

Below: The predominant feature of the Vought Corsair was the distinctive 'inverted-gull' wing, with engine cooling intakes in the leading edges of the wingroots. Both features are easily identified in this head-on view.

'blown' cockpit canopy; later Mk IIs also had provision to carry either a drop tank or a bomb beneath the starboard and, eventually, also the port wing. The final 150 Mk IIs lacked internal wing leading-edge tanks and were thus the equivalent of the US Navy's **F4U-1D** variant, but were not separately designated in British use.

For deployment of the Corsair Mk Is and Mk IIs aboard the Royal Navy's escort carriers, it became necessary to 'clip' the wing span by 16 in (40 cm) to allow the aircraft to be stowed with wings folded in the below-deck hangars. Operating from HMS *Victorious*, No. 1834 Squadron took its Corsair Mk IIs into action for the first time on 3 April 1944, providing fighter cover (in company with Wildcat, Hellcat and Seafire squadrons) for the Barracudas engaged in attacking the *Tirpitz* at Kaarfjord, Norway. Further attacks on *Tirpitz* in July and August saw Nos 1841 and 1842 Squadrons also using Corsairs, flying from HMS *Formidable*. The operational debut of the Corsair in the Pacific area had meanwhile occurred on 19 April 1944, when Nos 1830 and 1833 Squadrons, in HMS *Illustrious*, provided escort for Barracudas making an attack on Sabang. From this time on, Corsairs

No fewer than 19 Fleet Air Arm squadrons received Corsairs, with a total of 1,977 being built for the Royal Navy. On this Corsair Mk II the long-range fuel tank, attached beneath the fuselage, has burst into flames after coming adrift following a heavy landing.

Vought Corsair

Above: Most of the Fleet Air Arm Corsairs were of the FG-1 type made by Goodyear. This clipped-wing FG-1D was equivalent to the F4U-1D and was allocated the British designation Corsair Mk IV.

Above: Wearing Pacific theatre markings, this Corsair Mk IV was from No. 1846 Squadron which embarked aboard HMS *Colossus* for the Far East in February 1945. The squadron joined the 14th Carrier Air Group in June but saw no action and was disbanded at the end of July.

Below: The Corsair added a new dimension to Fleet Air Arm operations. Each aircraft in this formation had provision for two 1,000-lb (454-kg) bombs while still retaining excellent performance for attack and defence. These aircraft are from the 6th Naval Fighter Wing (Nos 1841 and 1842 Naval Air Squadrons).

were frequently in action in the Far East. The aircraft of Nos 1830 and 1833 Squadrons were credited with the destruction of 13 Nakajima Ki-44 'Tojo' Army fighters during an attack on oil refineries at Pelembang on 24 January 1945, and in the period from 26 March to 14 April that year, these two units were responsible for flying some 20 per cent of the 2,000 odd sorties flown from the four large aircraft-carriers serving with the British Pacific Fleet.

Further deliveries of Corsairs came from the Brewster and Goodyear production lines. More than half of all Brewster production of the F3A-1 came to Britain, comprising 430 **Corsair Mk III**s.

At the same time, Goodyear was delivering 857 **Corsair Mk IV**s (with another 120 cancelled at the war's end). Of the latter total, the first 400 were to FG-1 standard, with the remainder having the same underwing provision for bombs or fuel tanks as the **FG-1D**.

In July and August 1945, Corsair squadrons Nos 1834 and 1836 (in HMS *Victorious*) and Nos 1841 and 1842 (in HMS *Formidable*) carried the war to the Japanese mainland in a series of strikes in the Tokyo area. It was in the course of one of these actions, against Shiogama on 9 August, that the Fleet Air Arm's second VC of the war was won, by Lt R. H. Gray of the Royal Canadian Volunteer Reserve. Pressing home an attack on a destroyer, he was shot down and killed – but not before he had scored a direct hit that sank the destroyer.

With the end of the war in the Pacific, the Corsair quickly disappeared from the FAA inventory; by the end of 1945, only four squadrons still flew the type, and of these, the final two, Nos 1831 and 1851, stood down on 13 August 1946.

Specification
Corsair Mk IV
Type: single-seat carrier-based or shore-based fighter or fighter-bomber
Powerplant: one 2,250-hp (1678-kW) Pratt & Whitney R-2800-8 Double Wasp radial piston engine
Performance: maximum speed 415 mph (668 km/h) at 19,500 ft (5944 m); cruising speed 261 mph (420 km/h); service ceiling 34,000 ft (10363 m); maximum range 1,562 miles (2514 km)
Weights: empty 9,100 lb (4128 kg); maximum take-off 12,100 lb (5488 kg)
Dimensions: span 39 ft 8 in (12.09 m); length 33 ft 4 in (10.16 m); height 15 ft 1 in (4.60 m); wing area 305 sq ft (28.33 m^2)
Armament: four 0.5-in (12.7-mm) forward-firing machine-guns in the wings plus up to 2,000 lb (907 kg) of bombs

Corsair Mk IV KD345 served with No. 1850 Squadron aboard HMS *Vengeance* off Japan in August 1945. It retains the US Navy high-gloss blue overall finish, with white codes and serial, along with British Pacific theatre identification markings.

Vought Kingfisher

Designed, like the Curtiss SO3C (see Seamew), to replace biplane scouts serving aboard ships of the US Fleet, the **VS-310** first flew as a landplane in March 1938 and as a single-float seaplane on 19 May that year. Placed into production, and entering service in August 1940, the **OS2U-1 Kingfisher** became the first catapult-launched monoplane in its category.

As a potential replacement for the elderly Supermarine Walrus and the little-used Fairey Seafox biplanes serving in the scouting role aboard British ships, the OS2U was requested by the Admiralty and a batch of 100 was allocated through Lend-Lease channels. As the **Kingfisher Mk I**, these aircraft began to arrive in Britain in May 1942, entering test programmes in the landplane configuration at the A&AEE and as a floatplane at the MAEE. Generally satisfactory results were recorded and plans proceeded to issue the type for service aboard armed merchant cruisers, and for training. The Kingfisher seated pilot and observer in tandem and could carry two 250-lb (113-kg) depth charges in addition to single forward-firing and aft cockpit machine-guns.

To furnish aircraft for the merchant cruisers, as well as the light cruisers HMS *Emerald* and *Enterprise*, No. 703 Squadron was formed in June 1942 at Lee-on-Solent, and continued in this role until May 1944, when the last shipboard Kingfishers were brought ashore. To train FAA pilots in seaplane operations, Nos 764 and 765 Squadrons used Kingfishers respectively at Lawrenny Ferry, near Pembroke Dock, and Sandbanks, at Poole Harbour in Dorset. A few others were flown in South Africa by No. 726 Squadron at Durban and No. 789 Squadron, an FRU, at Wingfield, Cape Town. All of the Kingfishers were withdrawn from Fleet Air Arm service before the end of 1944.

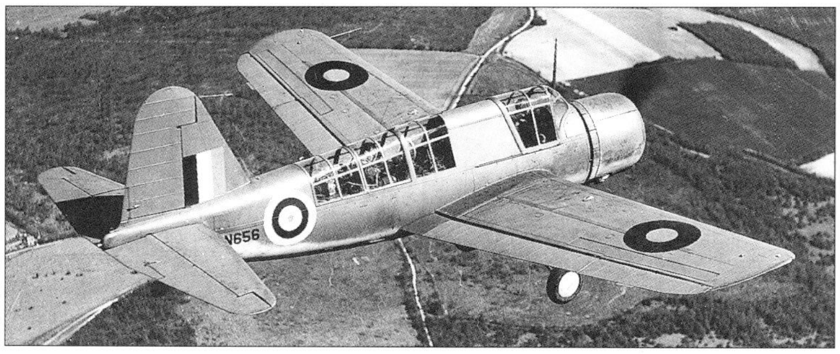

Kingfisher Mk I, FN656, was from a batch of 100 supplied, after evaluation at the A&AEE, in May 1942. The type was produced in both land and seaplane versions.

Deliveries of the Kingfisher were mainly to the Middle East, South Africa and Jamaica. In the UK, the type served with two Fleet Air Arm second-line squadrons.

Specification
Kingfisher Mk I (floatplane)
Type: two-seat reconnaissance aircraft
Powerplant: one 450-hp (336-kW) Pratt & Whitney R-985-SB3 Wasp Junior radial piston engine
Performance: maximum speed 171 mph (275 km/h); cruising speed 152 mph (245 km/h); service ceiling 18,000 ft (5486 m); range 900 miles (1448 km)
Weights: empty 3,335 lb (1513 kg); loaded 4,980 lb (2259 kg)
Dimensions: span 35 ft 11 in (10.95 m); length 33 ft 8 in (10.26 m); height 14 ft 8 in (4.47 m); wing area 262 sq ft (24.34 m^2)
Armament: two 0.3-in (7.62-mm) machine-guns (one forward-firing and one in aft cockpit) plus up to 240 lb (109 kg) of bombs

Vultee Vengeance

Like the Lockheed Hudson, the Vengeance owed its existence to the British Purchasing Commission, there having been no prior interest shown by the US Army Air Corps, nor even a prototype built, when the first British orders were placed in September 1940 for 200 **V-72** single-engined dive-bombers to be built by Vultee, and a further 200 built under licence by Northrop. The latter took the designation **Vengeance Mk I** while those built by Vultee – the first to be delivered – were **Vengeance Mk II**s. Later, orders were placed for 300 more Vengeance Mk IIs and then, on Lend-Lease contracts, Northrop built a further 200 as **Vengeance Mk IA**s (USAAC **A-31**) and Vultee built 100 **Vengeance Mk III**s, also A-31s.

Very small differences distinguished these marks, which were powered by a 1,600-hp (1193-kW) Wright Cyclone R-2600 engine, had an armament of four wing-mounted 0.3-in (7.62-mm) Browning guns, two more in the rear cockpit and a bomb-bay to carry 1,000 lb (454 kg) of bombs. Few of these aircraft reached Britain; those that entered the RAF's inventory were for the most part shipped direct to India, to equip RAF or Indian Air Force squadrons there. Large numbers, however, were also diverted to the RAAF in Australia, or retained by the USAAF (to serve as V-72s) after December 1941.

In India, No. 82 Squadron became the first to fly the Vengeance, at first on anti-submarine patrols over the Bay of Bengal starting in November 1942. By the end of the year, Nos 45, 84 and 110 Squadrons of the RAF, as well as the first IAF unit, were flying Vengeances, and in March 1943 ground-attack and dive-bombing sorties began against Japanese targets in Burma. No. 84 Squadron soon moved to Ceylon, but the other three squadrons continued to operate at high intensity in the Burma area, the effectiveness of the Vengeance being enhanced by fitting British 0.303-in (7.7-mm) machine-guns in the rear cockpit in place of the unreliable American weapons at first fitted.

With No. 84 Squadron back

This Vengeance, undergoing trials with the A&AEE, is fitted with the standard RAF underwing bomb carriers for 250-lb (113-kg) bombs, in addition to its internal load of two 500-lb (227-kg) bombs.

from Ceylon, all four RAF Vengeance squadrons, as well as those of the IAF, saw major action through late 1943 and the first half of 1944, taking part in the battles in the Arakan and around Imphal. For almost all of this operational period – which effectively came to an end in July 1944 – the squadrons were using Vengeance Mk I, Mk IA and Mk II variants, with a few Mk IIIs arriving mid-1943.

Meanwhile, the USAAF had backed development of an improved V-72, for Lend-Lease and its own possible use, as the **A-35**. This had some aerodynamic improvements, more powerful engine (R-2600-13 or -8) and improved armament of four (in **A-35A**) or six (**A-35B**) 0.5-in (12.7-mm) wing guns and a single gun of this calibre in the rear cockpit, with the bomb load increased to a maximum 2,000 lb (907 kg). Through Lend-Lease, the RAF was allocated 562 A-35Bs, which it designated **Vengeance DB.Mk IV** (104 Series 1s with the -13 engine and 458 Series 2s with the -8 engine).

By the time delivery of the Vengeance Mk IVs began, the RAF no longer needed these aircraft in the dive-bombing role, and the great majority were converted by Cunliffe Owen to serve as target-tugs with the designation **Vengeance TT.Mk IV**, with a Type B.Mk IIB winch. In this role, they served with 10 squadrons in the UK. More than 100 Vengeances were transferred by the RAF to the Fleet Air Arm for service as target-tugs, in 1944/45, including some Mk IIs as well as Mk IVs. One other role briefly performed by Vengeance Mk IIIs was that of smoke-laying during combined operations, in the hands of No. 1340 Flight, in India during early 1945.

Specification
Vengeance Mk I
Type: two-seat dive-bomber
Powerplant: one 1,600-hp (1193-kW) Wright R-2600-A5B Cyclone radial piston engine
Performance: maximum speed 275 mph (443 km/h) at 11,000 ft (3353 m); cruising speed 235 mph (378 km/h); service ceiling 22,500 ft (6858 m); maximum range 1,400 miles (2253 km)
Weights: empty 9,725 lb (4411 kg); maximum take-off 14,300 lb (6486 kg)
Dimensions: span 48 ft 0 in (14.63 m); length 39 ft 9 in (12.12 m); height 15 ft 4 in (4.67 m); wing area 332 sq ft (30.84 m²)
Armament: four forward-firing 0.3-in (7.62-mm) machine-guns and two 0.3-in (7.62-mm) machine-guns in rear cockpit, plus up to 2,000 lb (907 kg) of bombs

A Vengeance Mk II of No. 84 Squadron takes off in Ceylon in the summer of 1943. Persistent rumours of the return of the Japanese Carrier Strike Force from Singapore led to the unit being placed on readiness, but in the event nothing materialised. Much practice dive-bombing in co-operation with Royal Navy warships was done at this time.

Waco Hadrian

Paralleling British interest in troop-carrying gliders, the US Army Air Force began the development of such aircraft in 1941, to meet two separate specifications. One was for a small transport glider, the other for a larger 15-seat glider. Of some eight designs considered, only two reached quantity production, both by Waco and comprising the smaller CG-3A used for training, and the **CG-4A**, which became the first US troop glider operated in World War II.

A massive production programme, embracing 16 companies, allowed the USAAF to provide large numbers of the Waco gliders to the RAF, although only 24 of these came to Britain. As the **Hadrian Mk I**, these gliders were used from February onwards at the A&AEE, and by No. 21 Heavy Glider Conversion Unit at Brize Norton for pilot training. The designation **Hadrian Mk II** was used for all subsequent deliveries to the RAF, these gliders going directly to India in preparation for their use by airborne forces in planned operations against Japanese-occupied territory. For this purpose, some 700 Hadrian Mk IIs were dispatched from the US to India; and, after the war in Europe ended, over 1,000 more were transferred from US stocks in the UK for shipment to the Far East – an activity that was brought to an end when Japan capitulated.

Six squadrons – Nos 668, 669 and 670 in the No. 343 (Fatchjang) Wing and Nos 671, 672 and 673 in No. 344 Wing – were to have operated the Hadrian, but in the event no airborne assaults were mounted. Two examples of the larger, but similar, Waco CG-13A were also tested in Britain, and four were shipped to India, but not used.

Specification
Hadrian Mk II
Type: cargo and troop-carrying glider
Performance: maximum towing speed 150 mph (241 km/h); normal towing speed 120 mph (193 km/h)
Weights: empty 3,750 lb (1701 kg); maximum take-off 9,000 lb (4082 kg)
Dimensions: span 83 ft 8 in (25.50 m); length 48 ft 8 in (14.83 m); height 12 ft 7 in (3.84 m); wing area 852 sq ft (79.15 m²)

Hadrians were first supplied to the RAF in 1943, and 129 were in action (towed by Dakotas) in the Allied invasion of Sicily in July 1943. This prototype Hadrian made aeronautical history by becoming the first glider ever to have been towed across the Atlantic, in an actual flying time of 28 hours.

Westland Lysander

Above: Based at Heliopolis in Egypt, a formation of three No. 6 Squadron Lysanders passes over a ship navigating its way through the Suez Canal in the spring of 1941. During this period the squadron was involved in reconnaissance of the advancing German forces.

Left: A maintenance job is undertaken 'literally in the field' for No. 13 Squadron Lysander Mk II L4767. The winter of 1939-40 was very severe, and the squadrons in France had great difficulty keeping their aircraft flying. This aircraft has sunk into the soft ground at Mons-en-Chausseé.

Below: In early 1940 the prototype Lysander was used for a trial installation of two 20-mm cannon, with 60-round ammunition drums, for attacks on German invasion barges. One was mounted above each wheel fairing, positioned so that the shells just cleared the propeller arc. The proposal was never adopted operationally.

British army co-operation aircraft used between the wars were largely conversions of existing airframes. In 1934, however, the Air Ministry issued Specification A.39/34, for a new aircraft to replace the Hawker Hector biplane which was then used for the purpose. In June 1935 Westland tendered for, and won, a contract covering two prototypes which the company designated **P.8**, the name Lysander being adopted subsequently. The first prototype underwent taxiing trials at Yeovil on 10 June 1936, before being taken by road to Boscombe Down, where it made its first flight on 15 June, in the course of which it returned to Yeovil. Minor modifications were made and the prototype was shown at the SBAC Display at Hatfield at the end of June, and on 24 July it went to the Aircraft and Armament Experimental Establishment at Martlesham Heath for a week to undertake handling evaluation.

A production order for 144 aircraft was placed in September, and the second prototype flew on 11 December 1936, spending much of its time at Martlesham Heath before going to India in 1938, for tropical trials with No. 5 Squadron. Deliveries to the RAF began in June 1938, when No. 16 Squadron at Old Sarum received its first aircraft to replace the Hawker Audax then in service. The School of Army Co-operation was also based at Old Sarum, and its pilots received instruction on the Lysander from squadron personnel.

During 1939, 66 **Lysander Mk I**s were completed: of these, No. 16 Squadron received 14, the School of Army Co-operation nine, while other deliveries were made to No. 13 Squadron at Odiham, No.

A Lysander Mk I drops supplies to Allied troops in the Egyptian desert. The container, released from under the stub wings, dropped to earth by parachute, usually behind enemy lines to Special Operations troops or local partisans. This technique was also used in Europe, mostly at night.

Lysander Mk IIs of No. 225 Squadron based at Odiham formate for the camera in early 1940. The stub wings on which light bombs could be carried are clearly visible attached to the undercarriage fairing.

26 at Catterick and No. 4 at Wimborne, the Lysanders in all cases replacing Hawker Hectors. On the outbreak of war there were seven Lysander squadrons, the others being No. II, and the Auxiliary Air Force's squadrons Nos 613 and 614. By this time most of the home-based squadrons had replaced their 890-hp (664-kW) Bristol Mercury XII-powered Mk Is with **Lysander Mk IIs**. These had the 905-hp (675-kW) Bristol Perseus XII engine, which offered a slightly better performance at altitude. Many of the Mk Is were sent overseas, for service in Egypt, India and Palestine. A total of 116 Mk Is was followed on the production line by 442 Mk IIs, and it was with this latter mark that Nos II, 4, 13 and 26 Squadrons moved to France in 1940.

As the German attack began, No. 4 Squadron moved to Belgium, but such was the fury of the onslaught that 11 Lysanders were lost between 10 and 23 May, some being eliminated on the ground. One of the squadron's Lysander crews destroyed a Bf 110 during a running battle with six Messerschmitts and managed to return to base; on 22 May an aircraft of No. II Squadron accounted for a Henschel Hs 126 with its front gun and a Junkers Ju 87 with the rear gun. By then the end of French resistance was near, and the Lysander squadrons were withdrawn to the UK, although some sorties were still made over the battle area to drop supplies to Allied forces. One of these sorties was decimated when, of 16 Lysanders and Hectors sent out on a supply sortie over Calais, 14 aircraft and crews failed to return. In all, some 118 Lysanders and 120 crew members were lost over France and Belgium between September 1939 and May 1940, almost 20 per cent of the aircraft sent out from the UK.

The heavy fighting on the continent, and severe losses incurred by army co-operation units, indicated that the old concept of this type of operation was outdated, particularly when air superiority had not been achieved. Accordingly, Lysanders were withdrawn from the UK-based squadrons, which began to re-equip in early 1941 with Curtiss P-40 Tomahawks.

Overseas, Lysanders had replaced Audaxes in No. 208 Squadron in Egypt in April 1939, and the squadron's new aircraft saw action in the Western Desert alongside Hawker Hurricanes of the same squadron which were being used for tactical reconnaissance. The squadron later took part in the Greek campaign, its Lysanders being replaced by Tomahawks in 1942.

No. 6 Squadron at Ramleh, Palestine, operated a variety of aircraft, and was using Hawker Hardies and Gloster Gauntlets when it received

The Lysander Mk II was the standard army co-operation aircraft used by the RAF in the Air Component of the BEF, initially with Nos II, 4, 13 and 26 Squadrons although 16 squadrons were eventually equipped with the type. The Lysander was an easy target for marauding German fighters and many were destroyed both in the air and on the ground. R1999 served with No. 225 Squadron.

In February 1942 No. 161 Squadron became the second Special Duties squadron to be established. It was responsible for Lysander (and Hudson) aircraft operating into France. Lysander V9367 was a Mk IIIA (SD) which flew with the squadron from February 1942 until December 1943. Finished in matt black, the aircraft was equipped with a 150-Imp gal (682-litre) auxiliary fuel tank and a ladder.

Under instruction from ground personnel, a No. 208 Squadron Lysander Mk I picks up a message in the Western Desert. The message was attached to a rope between two poles. Retrieval was achieved by a message hook attached to the top of the starboard main undercarriage leg.

its Lysanders in February 1940. These were supplemented and later replaced, in 1942, by various marks of Hurricane and Bristol Blenheim Mk IVs.

In September 1941 No. 28 Squadron at Ambala, India, was the first squadron in the area to receive Lysanders, replacing Audaxes. The squadron subsequently took its new aircraft to Burma, and operated in ground-attack, bombing and tactical reconnaissance roles before being withdrawn to India in March 1942; in December of that year it converted to Hurricanes, becoming a fighter squadron. The last squadron to use Lysanders in action was No. 20, in Burma during late 1943, before receiving Hurricanes as replacements.

Although withdrawn from first-line service, Lysanders continued in operation for a variety of other roles as target-tugs, air-sea rescue aircraft and, least publicised at the time, with the Special Operations Executive. Nos 138 and 161 Squadrons, using a mixed bag of aircraft which included Lysanders, maintained contact with resistance groups in occupied Europe, dropping supplies and agents, and bringing agents back to the UK. It was in these night operations in occupied territory that the Lysander really came into its own, being able to use its remarkable short landing and take-off capabilities to the utmost in the small fields marked out by the resistance. **Lysander Mk III**s and **Mk IIIA**s were used for this work, 367 of the former and 347 of the latter being built, powered by the 870-hp (649-kW) Bristol Mercury XX or XXX engines.

Final production variant was the **TT.Mk IIIA** target-tug, of which 100 were built. Figures for total Lysander production vary, as a number of aircraft were cancelled, but around 1,650 were built, including 225 under licence in Canada.

A batch of 26 Mk IIs was supplied to the Turkish air force, 20 to Egypt, six to the Irish Air Corps, nine to Finland, eight to Portugal and several to France. Three went to the USAF, and others to the South African Air Force. Several Lysanders were used for experimental purposes, the most unusual being a tandem-wing conversion with twin fins and rudders and a Boulton Paul gun turret mock-up. This was intended as a home defence beach strafer, but fortunately was not needed. Another Lysander was fitted with a completely new wing designed by Blackburn. Intended for research purposes only, this Steiger wing was swept forward 9°, and used full-span slats and flaps to provide high lift. At the end of the war Canada was the only country to have a large Lysander population, some of which remained in service until the early 1960s.

Specification
Lysander Mk III
Type: two-seat army co-operation aircraft
Powerplant: one 870-hp (649-kW) Bristol Mercury XX or XXX radial piston engine
Performance: maximum speed 212 mph (341 km/h) at 5,000 ft (1524 m); service ceiling 21,500 ft (6553 m); range 600 miles (966 km)
Weights: empty 4,365 lb (1980 kg); maximum take-off 6,318 lb (2866 kg)
Dimensions: span 50 ft 0 in (15.24 m); length 30 ft 6 in (9.30 m); height 14 ft 6 in (4.42 m); wing area 260 sq ft (24.15 m^2)
Armament: two forward-firing 0.303-in (7.7-mm) machine-guns in wheel spats, two 0.303-in (7.7-mm) guns on mounting in rear cockpit, plus light bombs on stub wings attached to spats

Westland Wallace

With the success of its Wapiti assured, Westland went ahead with a private venture development in 1931. Designated **P.V.6**, the prototype was of all-metal construction, and of generally similar configuration to the Wapiti. However, the fuselage was lengthened by 1 ft 8 in (0.51 m), and spatted landing gear, wheel brakes, and a cowled 655-hp (488-kW) Bristol Pegasus IV engine were introduced.

Duly impressed by a much improved performance, the Air Ministry ordered 12 Wapitis converted to the new standard against Specification 19/32. The name Wallace was chosen for the new type. The **Wallace Mk I** aircraft were fitted with 570-hp (425-kW) Bristol Pegasus IIM3 engines and were delivered to No. 501 Squadron at Filton in early 1933. Another 56 Wapitis were converted to Wallace Mk I standard, and in 1935 the **Wallace Mk II** appeared with an enclosed cabin and 680-hp (507-kW) Pegasus IV engines.

Contracts for 75 Wallace Mk IIs to Specification G.31/35 were placed in June 1935, and a further 29 were ordered the following February, the last Wallace leaving Westland's factory in October 1936.

Most Wallaces served with Auxiliary Air Force Squadrons Nos 501, 502, 504, 608 and 610, while others replaced Hawker Horsleys at Biggin Hill with the Anti-Aircraft Co-operation Flight.

As more modern types entered service the Wallaces began to be withdrawn, but around 83 were still in service at the outbreak of World War II. Many of these had been converted to target-tugs, and they continued to serve in this role until about 1943, fulfilling an important if unglamorous role until finally replaced by monoplane types capable of performing more comparably with later combat aircraft.

Specification
Wallace Mk II
Type: two-seat general-purpose biplane
Powerplant: one 680-hp (507-kW) Bristol Pegasus IV radial piston engine
Performance: maximum speed 158 mph (254 km/h) at 15,000 ft (4572 m); cruising speed 135 mph (217 km/h); service ceiling 24,100 ft (7346 m); range 470 miles (756 km)
Weights: empty 3,840 lb (1742 kg); maximum take-off 5,750 lb (2608 kg)
Dimensions: span 46 ft 5 in (14.15 m); length 34 ft 2 in (10.41 m); height 11 ft 6 in (3.51 m); wing area 488 sq ft (45.34 m^2)
Armament: one 0.303-in (7.7-mm) forward-firing machine-gun and one Lewis gun in rear cockpit, plus up to 580 lb (263 kg) of bombs

Among the RAF Wallaces that served in the war years was this aircraft (K4344) which was operated by the Gunnery Research Unit (GRU). It was based at Exeter from June 1940 to April 1944 for armament testing.

Westland Wapiti

The first Westland design to achieve quantity production, the Wapiti was built to replace the ageing de Havilland DH.9A; when, in 1926, the Air Ministry decided to invite competitive tenders for this new aircraft, it was stipulated that as many DH.9A parts as possible should be used.

Westland had built over 400 DH.9As and rebuilt more than another 150, so were well placed to produce a successor. The prototype Wapiti, flown in early 1927, had standard DH.9A wings, ailerons, interplane struts and tail unit, with a new wider and deeper fuselage than that of the original de Havilland aircraft. Powerplant was the 420-hp (313-kW) Bristol Jupiter VI. Early tests indicated that a larger fin and rudder were needed, and when these had been fitted the prototype went to the A&AEE, Martlesham Heath, for trials.

A first batch of 25 **Wapiti Mk I**s was ordered to Specification F.26/27, these being required for service trials with No. 84 Squadron in Iraq, and intended to replace its DH.9As. They had the Jupiter VI engine, and the wings and rear fuselage were of wooden construction. Ten **Mk II**s followed, and all-metal construction was featured from this mark, which had the 460-hp (343-kW) Jupiter VI. The **Wapiti Mk IIA**, introduced in 1931, had the 550-hp (410-kW) Jupiter VIII, and a batch of 35 similarly powered **Mk V**s followed. The last RAF version was the **Wapiti Mk VI** trainer which was introduced in 1932. Wapiti production ended in August 1932, after 517 had been constructed for the RAF.

At the outbreak of World War II, Wapitis remained in use in India with Nos 5, 27 and 60 Squadrons, while others were serving in the RCAF and SAAF.

Specification
Wapiti Mk IIA
Type: two-seat general-purpose biplane
Powerplant: one 550-hp (410-kW) Bristol Jupiter VIII radial piston engine
Performance: maximum speed 135 mph (217 km/h) at 5,000 ft (1525 m); cruising speed 110 mph (177 km/h); service ceiling 20,600 ft (6280 m); range 360 miles (579 km)
Weights: empty 3,180 lb (1442 kg); maximum take-off 5,400 lb (2449 kg)
Dimensions: span 46 ft 5 in (14.15 m); length 32 ft 6 in (9.91 m); height 11 ft 10 in (3.61 m); wing area 468 sq ft (43.48 m^2)
Armament: one 0.303-in (7.7-mm) machine-gun firing forward on side of fuselage and one Lewis gun in rear cockpit, plus up to 580 lb (263 kg) of bombs

The Wapiti Mk IIA was used by No. 5 Squadron from Fort Sandeman in north west India during the first year of the war. This Mk IIA was retained by Westland for trials.

Westland Whirlwind

After a long series of rather staid biplanes, the choice of Westland to produce a high-speed fighter must have seemed somewhat unlikely, but the company tendered against Specification F.37/35, and in January 1939 won a production contract for 200 aircraft.

The first of two prototype Westland Whirlwinds flew on 11 October 1938, but the Air Ministry lowered a security curtain around the new fighter which was not to be raised until August 1941. This caused considerable amusement, since a French technical paper had published drawings in 1938, and there was every reason to suppose that the Germans knew about the Whirlwind.

The new type was interesting on several accounts: it was the RAF's first twin-engined fighter, and had low-altitude performance that was better than that of any contemporary single-seat fighter. Furthermore, its four 20-mm nose-mounted cannon gave a weight of fire of 600 lb (272 kg) per minute, which conferred firepower superior to that of any other fighter in the world.

Production deliveries began to No. 263 Squadron at Drem in July 1940, and the squadron settled down to eliminate the inevitable bugs in a new airframe and engine – the Rolls-Royce Peregrine. Troubles were also experienced with the cannon, but the squadron scored its first confirmed success with the destruction of an Arado Ar 196 floatplane on 8 February 1941, although a Whirlwind pilot was lost.

Deliveries were slow, as a result of a shortage of engines, and only eight Whirlwinds had been received by the RAF by the end of 1940. No. 137 was the second (and only other) squadron to be equipped with Whirlwinds; it was formed at Charmy Down on 20 September 1941 with a nucleus of No. 263 Squadron personnel.

While the new fighter proved to have excellent performance at low altitude, it was at a distinct disadvantage when fighter-against-fighter

The Westland Whirlwind was the first single-seat twin-engined fighter to see RAF service. Its existence was a closely guarded secret in the early days of the war. Unfortunately, reliability problems with the Rolls-Royce Peregrine engines meant that only two RAF squadrons – Nos 263 and 137 – operated Whirlwinds before they were finally withdrawn from operations in July 1943.

Westland Whirlwind

Whirlwinds were found to have admirable performance at low level, and with their long-range capability proved to be excellent bomber escorts. One of 114 produced, this Whirlwind was retained by Westland and assumed the civil indentity G-AGOI after the end of the war.

combat began to move to higher altitudes, and it was necessary to restrict Whirlwind operations to a lower level where, for a time, the type proved useful for light bombing operations and fighter sweeps.

It had become obvious by 1940 that the Whirlwind had its drawbacks, engine unreliability being high on the list, while high landing speed restricted the number of airfields it could use. The initial order for 200 was cut to 112, and a second order for 200 was cancelled, with the last production aircraft off the line flying in January 1942. In June 1943 No. 137 Squadron was re-equipped with rocket-firing Hawker Hurricane Mk IVs, while No. 263 gave up its Whirlwinds for Hawker Typhoons in December of that year.

The Whirlwind first entered service with No. 263 Squadron on 6 July 1940, but due to delays in engine deliveries it was not until December that the squadron became operational. This trio of Whirlwinds is seen over the south of England on a sortie from its base at Colerne in February 1942.

Some experimental work had taken place with Whirlwinds: the second prototype undertook night-fighting trials with No. 25 Squadron, a Blenheim Mk IF unit, between May and July 1940; the first prototype was tested with an armament of 12 Browning 0.303-in (7.7-mm) machine-guns; and another had a 37-mm cannon installed.

One Whirlwind survived the war, being used under civil markings as a Westland hack during 1946-47, before being dismantled in the latter year.

Specification
Whirlwind Mk I
Type: single-seat long-range fighter-bomber
Powerplant: two 885-hp (660-kW) Rolls-Royce Peregrine inline piston engines
Performance: maximum speed 360 mph (579 km/h) at 15,000 ft (4572 m); service ceiling 30,300 ft (9235 m); range 800 miles (1287 km)
Weights: empty 8,310 lb (3769 kg); maximum take-off 11,388 lb (5166 kg)
Dimensions: span 45 ft 0 in (13.72 m); length 32 ft 9 in (9.98 m); height 11 ft 7 in (3.53 m); wing area 250 sq ft (23.23 m²)
Armament: four 20-mm cannon in nose, plus up to 1,000 lb (454 kg) of bombs

Whirlwind Mk I P6969 of No. 263 Squadron was based at RAF Exeter in 1941. Innovative features of the Whirlwind included the mounting of coolant radiators within wing centre-section ducts, which helped to reduce drag. The 'bubble' canopy gave excellent all-round visibility.

Impressed Aircraft

Aeronca Chief

Only one Aeronca Chief was impressed during the war. Originally on the civil register in India as VT-ALN, the aircraft carried the unofficial serial Z2003. In 1941 it began liaison duties with No. 221 Group Communications Flight in India then served with the Bengal Com. Flight until it was withdrawn after an accident in February 1943.

Airspeed AS.4 Ferry

AS.4 Ferry G-ABSI was impressed in April 1940 from Portsmouth, Southsea and Isle of Wight Aviation Ltd. Allocated the serial AV968, it served with the Halton Station Flight between July and November 1940.

Of the two AS.4 Ferrys impressed into service, only one, G-ABSI (AV968) was allocated to flying duties. The other example, G-ACFB (DJ715) was dismantled and used by No. 1037 ATC Sqn. AV968 was also later used as an instructional airframe with No. 474 Sqn ATC.

Armstrong Whitworth A.W.15 Atalanta

Three BOAC and two Indian National Airways Atalantas were impressed for service in the Middle and Far East. Three of the aircraft were used to fly reinforcements to Shaibah during the Iraq rebellion. All five examples later served with No. 101(GR) Squadron in Madras on coastal patrols before they were withdrawn in August 1942.

Allocated the British serial no. DG454,* Aurora *was one of five A.W.15s impressed into Indian Air Force service in April 1941. Serving with No. 101 Sqn, the aircraft was destroyed after a forced landing in April 1942.

Armstong Whitworth A.W.27 Ensign

Twelve Ensigns were used by National Air Communications from September 1939 to June 1940. Three examples (G-ADSX, 'DSZ and 'DTA) were destroyed during the evacuation of France. Two other examples were used by No. 24 Sqn at Hendon before the surviving aircraft were returned to BOAC at the end of 1940.

Avro 619 Five

Owned by Air Service Training Ltd, G-ABBY was the only Avro Five to see wartime service. It joined No. 11 Air Observer's Navigation School (AONS) when it was formed in November 1939 serving with this unit until early 1941. The aircraft was scrapped in March of that year after its Certificate of Airworthiness had expired.

Avro 638 Club Cadet

Differing from the earlier Avro Cadet in having unstaggered wings which could be folded, a single Club Cadet was impressed in July 1942. Originally G-ACHP, the aircraft was allocated the serial HM570, and was used throughout the war by Saunders-Roe for communications duties. Post-war the aircraft reassumed its civil identity.

Avro 641 Commodore

Of the six Commodores completed, two survived to be impressed into service. G-ACUG was used by the headquarters of the Training Ferry Pilot's Pool at White Waltham with the identity DJ710. G-ACZB was impressed in August 1941 as HH979 and was used for communications at RAF Cranwell and No. 6 MU.

Impressed in August 1941, G-ACZB served in the communications role until it was transferred to No. 51 OTU. It was withdrawn in August 1942.

Bellanca Pacemaker

A six-seat high-winged monoplane, the Pacemaker was an American design of the early 1930s. Imported into the UK from Italy in 1932, G-ABNW survived to be impressed into service as DZ209 in July 1941. The aircraft was the sole example of its type in the UK.

Owned by Cunliffe-Owen aircraft at the time of its impressment, G-ABNW was briefly used by the Admiralty before returning to RAF service at the end of 1942 for use with No. 5 MU. It was finally struck off charge in March 1943.

Blackburn B-2

A side-by-side two-seat training biplane, the Blackburn B-2 was a sturdy machine with an Alclad-covered fuselage for increased durability. Three examples were bought by the Air Ministry and at the outbreak of war these, along with around 30 civil examples, were transferred to No. 5 Elementary Flying Training School at Brough. The aircraft retained their civil identities but were camouflaged and carried RAF roundels. After serving with this unit until early 1942 the surviving B-2s were reallocated to various Air Training Corps squadrons as instructional airframes.

Boeing 247

On arrival in the UK, DZ203 was allocated to the Telecommunications Flying Unit for use by the Telecommunications Research Establishment. It carried camouflage markings throughout the war.

Originally owned by National Air Transport, followed by United Airlines and Inland Airlines, the only example of the Boeing 247 to operate from the UK was bought by the British Purchasing Commission in 1941. Allocated the serial no. DZ203, the aircraft survived the war and continued to serve with the RAF until early 1946.

British Aircraft Company Drone de Luxe

Derived from the BAC VII glider, the Drone de Luxe was powered by a tiny Carden Ford engine. Two examples were flying during the war. One was used by No. 609 Sqn for communications and, with the addition of a 12-bore shotgun, for hunting wild geese! The other example, G-AEKM, was used by the Development Unit and the Airborne Forces Experimental Establishment at Ringway.

British Klemm/BA Eagle/Eagle 2/Double Eagle

Seven Eagle and Eagle 2s were impressed into service in 1941. A low-wing cabin monoplane with accommodation for a pilot and two passengers, the Eagle was unusual for an aircraft of the 1930s in having retractable landing gear. Two six-seat Double Eagles were impressed: one for communications (ES949) and one for ground instruction.

British Klemm/BA Swallow

The Klemm L-25 first appeared on the British civil market in 1929 and from 1933 the aircraft was licence-built at Hanworth by the British Klemm company. Four were impressed into RAF service, one being used for training and the others as instructional airframes. The Swallow was a modified version of the L-25C. Four were converted to gliders for experiments and others were used for training or ground instruction.

Swallow 2 G-AFGE was allocated the serial BK894 in February 1941 and was converted at Hanworth as a glider for experiments with the RAE.

Cessna C-34 Airmaster

A single four-seat C-34 Airmaster was impressed in October 1941. Originally registered as G-AEAI, it was allocated the serial HM502 and was used briefly by the Station Flight at Hucknall before transfer to No. 27 MU for disposal. It was acquired by Dowty Equipment Ltd for spares to keep its own C-34 (G-AFBY) airworthy.

Comper CLA.7 Swift

At least four CLA.7 Swifts saw active service during the war years. G-ABPE was used by the CO of No. 25 Sqn and was painted in night-fighter black camouflage with roundels and code letters 'ZK'. Another example was used by No. 247 Sqn as a station 'hack' in 1940-41. G-ABUU was used by the Air Defence Cadet Corps and the ATC.

de Havilland DH.60 Moth

As one of the most successful inter-war light aircraft, many examples of the DH.60 Moth were on the British civil register at the outbreak of war. Around 150 examples were impressed for service with the RAF and Royal Navy in a number of different roles including communications, instructional airframes and decoy duties.

G-AAAA was one of at least 40 DH.60s which were released to Sound City Films for decoy purposes. Many others were used by various communications and maintenance units, mainly from 1940-42.

de Havilland DH.80A Puss Moth/DH.85 Leopard Moth

Over 50 Puss Moths were impressed for service with the RAF and the Royal Navy. With accommodation for three, they were used for a wide range of duties including station 'hacks', communications for the ATA and the TFPP along with various maintenance units and schools of technical training. All of the 45 Leopard Moths impressed were used for army co-operation and communications duties. The majority were allocated initially to various Anti-Aircraft Co-operation Units (AACUs) and a number survived the war to return to the civil register.

Impressed in July 1940, G-ACLL (AW165) had a varied military career serving with the Station Flight Ringway, Nos 6 and 7 AACUs and the AFEE before being retired for disposal to No. 5 MU in September 1945.

de Havilland DH.83 Fox Moth

A light transport capable of carrying four passengers, the Fox Moth was impressed into RAF service for use in the communications role. Of the 15 on the British register at the start of the war, 11 were impressed, serving with various maintenance units and the air transport auxiliary. One example (G-ACIY) was allocated to the Royal Naval Air Service at Lee-on-Solent as DZ213.

de Havilland DH.84 Dragon

A twin-engined transport aircraft, the Dragon was the first in a successful series of feederliner types from the de Havilland company. Fifteen of the 20 examples impressed served with AACU units flying night missions to help improve ground defences. Of the other five examples, four saw service with No. 24 Sqn on communications duties and one was used by No. 3 School of General Reconnaissance.

de Havilland DH.86

Designed as a high-speed mail and passenger airliner for the Australian government, the DH.86 could carry 10 passengers and a crew of two. Both the Fleet Air Arm and the RAF operated impressed examples during the war. No. 782 Sqn, FAA operated three examples from Donibristle and No. 24 Sqn, RAF flew two examples on VIP duties.

de Havilland DH.87 Hornet Moth

Designed for the civilian market to replace the Moth Minor, a large number of Hornet Moths were on the civil register at the outbreak of war. Approximately 65 examples were impressed and were used by a wide variety of units including Flying Training Schools, photographic units, communications flights, and Coastal Patrol Flights (CPFs).

G-AFDT was used by No.6 CPF for Scarecrow patrols before going to Lundy & Atlantic Coast Airlines, and thence to No. 73 Wing and No. 529 Squadron. It survived the war and was bought by Cardiff Aeroplane Club.

de Havilland DH.90 Dragonfly

A smaller and more streamlined version of the DH Rapide, the Dragonfly was an expensive aircraft and only 67 were built. Of these, 14 were impresssed into service between January 1940 and January 1941. The type was used primarily by AACU and ATA units, although a number of examples were later used by communications flights.

de Havilland DH.91 Albatross

Orignally G-AEVW, 'Franklin' became AX904 and joined No. 271 Sqn in October 1940. It served on the Icelandic route until a brake failure while landing at Reykjavik in April 1942 caused the undercarriage to collapse.

A total of seven DH.91s was built, of which five served pre-war as airliners for Imperial Airways and two were used as transatlantic mailplanes. The five airliners were not impressed but were used by BOAC during the war on the Bristol to Shannon service. The two mailplanes (G-AEVV and G-AEVW) were impressed in September 1940 and were allocated to No. 271 Sqn on the Icelandic passenger and mail service. Both were withdrawn after landing accidents.

de Havilland DH.94 Moth Minor

After serving as a test aircraft at Boscombe Down G-AFTH was used for communications by de Havilland until October 1942 when it was impressed into service as HM585 for service with Woodley Com. Flight.

Of the 34 DH.94s impressed into service during the war, 26 served with No. 22 (Army Co-operation) Group for *ab initio* glider training. Other examples were used for communications with a variety of units, including No. 24 Sqn, and for training with Service Flying Training Schools and Elementary Flying Training Schools. Many examples ended their flying careers with Maintenance Units in 1943-44.

Desoutter Mk I and Mk II

Basically a licence-built Koolhoven FK 41, the Desoutter was a three-seat cabin monoplane which was in production in the late 1920s and early 1930s. Five examples were impressed and these aircraft were used on communications duties. G-AAPS (ES946) was used as a station 'hack' at RAF Turnhouse before being used, along with G-AAZI, (HM507) by SHQ, RAF Tempsford.

G-AANB was impressed in December 1941 as HM508. Serving with No. 81 OTU at Whitchurch Heath, then No. 27 OTU at RAF Lichfield, it was withdrawn from flying duties and allocated to No. 5 MU in August 1943.

Dornier Do 17/22

Upon the German invasion of Yugoslavia in April 1941, a number of Yugoslav military aircraft escaped to Greece. Among the aircraft were two Do 17Kas and eight Do 22/Sees. Allocated RAF serials, the aircraft operated under the control of No. 230 Sqn until, in March 1942, No. 2 (Yugo) Sqn formed as an independent unit operating from Aboukir.

Douglas DC-2

Acquired by the British Purchasing Commission in America, 22 DC-2s were impressed into RAF service from American Airlines, Delta Air Lines, Pan Am and TWA. The first 12, allocated serials DG468-479, served in the Far East with No. 31 Sqn. Two further allocations of four and six served in the Middle East with No. 267 and No. 117 Sqns.

Fairchild 91

One example of this single-engined eight-seat amphibian was bought in the US by the British Air Ambulance Corps. Named *Wings of Mercy*, the aircraft was originally intended for air-sea rescue service in the English Channel, but it was diverted to the Middle East and served in that theatre between November 1941 and May 1943.

Owned by Panair do Brasil, PP-FAP was acquired in 1941 and delivered to the Sea Rescue Flight at Heliopolis with the serial HK832. It served until May 1943, when it sank after hitting a submerged object.

Focke-Wulf Fw 200

In May 1940 a Danish Fw 200 (OY-DAM) was seized by the British at Shoreham as the Germans invaded Denmark. Taken over by BOAC, it had little use due to the restriction on operating enemy types, and in January 1941 was impressed as DX177. It was allocated to the ATA but was damaged beyond repair in a landing accident in July 1941.

Fokker F.XXII/F.XXXVI

Built for KLM in 1934, two F.XXIIs and one F.XXXVI were purchased by Scottish Aviation in 1939 as navigation trainers. At the outbreak of war all three were operated by No. 12 E&RFTS, carrying camouflage, with small black registration letters. The two F.XXIIs were impressed into service as HM159 and HM160 in October 1941 and served with No. 24 Sqn on transport duties.

The two F.XXIIs and the F.XXXVI are seen at Prestwick Airport in January 1940 while serving with No. 1 Air Observer's Navigation School.

Ford 5AT-0 Trimotor

The only remaining Trimotor on the British register at the outbreak of war was G-ACAE. Able to accommodate 16 passengers, the aircraft was impressed in April 1940 as X5000 and served with No. 271 Sqn on freight and passenger supply flights until September 1940, when it was damaged beyond repair during a forced landing in Northern Ireland.

Foster Wikner GM.1 Warferry

Eight high-winged cabin monoplane Warferries were impressed during the war. Five were operated by the ATA from White Waltham in 1941. Another two were operated by No. 24 Sqn and were later joined by one of the ATA aircraft. Two examples survived the war, serving with various communications units.

General Aircraft Monospar ST-4/-6/-10/-12/-25

This series of twin-engined light transport aircraft were found to be particularly useful in the anti-aircraft co-operation role. Three ST-4s, one ST-6, one ST-10, two ST-12s and 13 ST-25s were impressed during 1940 and all but one served with No. 6, No. 7 or No. 8 AACUs. By the end of 1942 most had been retired as instructional airframes.

General Aircraft GAL 42/45 Cygnet/Owlet

The single GAL 45 Owlet was impressed in May 1941 and was delivered to No. 23 Sqn, as a trainer for Boston crews, as G-AGBK. In October 1941 the Owlet was transferred to No. 51 OTU with the military serial DP240.

A two-seat training aircraft intended for the civilian market, the Cygnet/Owlet was designed with twin fins and, unusually for the time, tricycle undercarriage. Six examples were impressed and were used for training Boston pilots with Nos 23, 24, 85 and 88 Sqns, being one of the few tricycle undercarriage aircraft available. The aircraft later served with various station flights, OTUs and the ATA.

Grumman Widgeon

A single G-44A Widgeon was acquired from the American civil register in the spring of 1942. In May of that year it was allocated to West Africa Command at Lagos, via No. 107 MU. It served in this theatre throughout the war before being withdrawn from use in July 1945.

Handley Page H.P.42

At the outbreak of war three H.P.42Ws were used by the NAC for ferrying supplies and personnel to France. However, it was the four H.P.42Es based in the Middle East that were earmarked for official impressment. One of these was destroyed on the return trip, presumably over the Arabian Sea. The remaining three – G-AAUC, G-AAUE and G-AAXF – were allocated the serials AS981, AS982 and AS983, respectively, in June 1940. Allocated to No. 271 Sqn for transport duties, all three had been withdrawn from use by December 1940 after forced landings or, in the case of AS982, destruction by gale-force winds. *Horatius* was destroyed when it returned from France to find Exeter airport covered in fog. The aircraft diverted to Tiverton and made a downwind forced landing on the golf links due to a fuel shortage. The aircraft hit trees upon landing and was written off.

Harlow PC-5A

By 1939 Hindustan Aircraft had begun licence-building the PC-5A at its Bangalore factory. At the outbreak of war the five examples which were under construction were taken over by the Indian Air Force and allotted the serials DR423-427. Subsequent units to use the type included No. 155 Sqn which operated DR423, No. 22 AACU with DR425 and No. 225 Group Com. Flight which used DR426.

Heston Type I Phoenix Srs II

G-AESV was used for trials of blind approach equipment in 1941. The aircraft survived the war and was sold to Heston Aircraft Co. in 1946.

Three examples of this relatively high-performance, high-winged, six-seat monoplane were impressed into service in March 1940. All three were initially delivered to No. 24 Sqn at Hendon, for communications duties. G-AEMT (X9393) later served with No. 4(C) FPP, while G-AESV (X2891) served as a research aircraft with various units. G-AEYX subsequently served with No. 4(C) FPP and No. 116 Sqn before returning to No. 24 Sqn for the use of General Spaatz.

Koolhoven FK 43

Already impressed into Dutch army service by the outbreak of war, a single FK 43 escaped the German invasion and arrived in the UK in May 1940. Impressed into RAF service, it served with Nos 277, 320 and 510 Sqns as well as a number of different station flights, and survived the war to return to Holland in 1945.

Lockheed Model 10/12/18

First in a series of highly successful twin-engined airliners, the Model 10 Electra was in widespread use at the outbreak of war. Eleven were impressed into service. Five (including four ex-British Airways examples) were allocated to No. 24 Sqn, and three ex-Yugoslav and one ex-US example were used for various duties in the Middle East including photographic reconnaissance. Two other examples, impressed from the British register, served with test units and the ATA. The RAF took over nine Model 18-07 aircraft (originally intended for BOAC) in 1940, and later received more from America. Most of the Lodestars saw service in Africa and the Middle East, including Persia Comms. Flight.

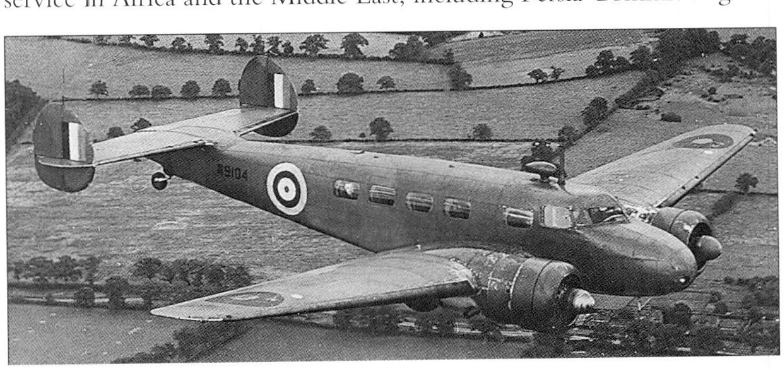

A former British Airways aircraft, W9104 made its last flight with a civil registration in March 1940, before being overhauled for RAF service.

Messerschmitt Bf 108

Bf 108 DK280 lived an exciting life, suffering a collapsed undercarriage on landing in 1942 and an engine failure in 1944 that led to its destruction.

Designed as a luxury four-seat touring aircraft, two examples of the Bf 108 were on the British register in September 1939. These, along with an example which was used by the German Embassy and was abandoned by its staff, were impressed for service and were used by No. 41 Group, various station flights and No. 24 Sqn for light communications.

Miles M.2/M.3

A total of seven Miles M.2s and 11 M.3s was impressed for service at home, in the Middle East and in the Far East. Serving with a variety of communications flights and maintenance units, the aircraft also provided valuable service with the ATA. Five Falcons were based at Aden during 1942-43, with the serials 38, 42, 43, 44 and 48.

Miles M.11/M.12

About 20 assorted Miles M.11 and M.12 aircraft were taken into RAF service, mostly as station flight and communications aircraft. A very high proportion were written off in the course of their wartime careers. One of the more fortunate was G-AEVG, which served as DP854 with RAF Northolt's station flight. It was transferred to Andover's station flight in 1942, and then to No. 8 MU to await reallocation. After the war the aircraft was eventually purchased by W. A. Strauss, and after equipping the machine with a long-range fuel tank he flew the aircraft to Australia. It was then reregistered as VH-EVG, and was sold to a new owner.

Miles M.17 Monarch

Only 11 of these aircraft were ever produced due to the need to produce Magisters; of these, five were impressed. One was used by Camille Gutt, co-owner of Miles Aircraft. Although he was Finance Minister to the Belgian government following liberation, private flying was banned. To overcome this, the serial TP819 was given to the aircraft which was attached to the Allied Flight of the M.C.S.

Morane Saulnier MS.406

A few MS.406s flew to Egypt from Syria in June and July 1940. Nos 826 and 827 arrived at Amriya in June, and left for Ismailia in company with a No. 80 Sqn Gladiator. The MS.406s received RAF camouflage and serials at Heliopolis, becoming AX674 and AX675, respectively. In service with No. 2 French (Fighter) Flight, the aircraft flew patrols over Alexandria, but the pair did not serve for long. AX674 was damaged in a landing accident and its engine transferred to AX675, which itself was struck off charge in 1942. No. 891 escaped to Egypt from Ryak, and became AX684. It was finally struck off in April 1942.

Parnall Heck

This Parnall Heck was based at Tolworth, but later delivered to RAF Turnhouse where it was used by No. 17 Group Communications Flight.

The Air Ministry purchased six Heck IIs, one of which was used to test the gun-sight installation in the Spitfire and Hurricane. During the war, this aircraft, K8853, was used by Andover and Heston communications flights. One Mk III Heck was built as a trainer before the war to an Air Ministry specification. It flew with a class 'B' registration until the outbreak of war, when it was reregistered G-AFKF.

Percival P.3 Gull Six/P.10 Vega Gull

Developed from the Gull Four, the Gull Six and Vega Gull had DH Gipsy Six engines. Later Vega Gulls were produced to an Air Ministry specification. A few went to the Army and Royal Navy, but most were used by RAF station flights. X1033 was used by No. 3 EFTS prior to impressment, and eventually served with Aboukir Station Flight. It was destroyed there when the pilot lost control in a steep climbing turn.

Vega Gull G-AEYC was delivered to RAF Ternhill's station flight in 1939, and had a long and successful wartime career with Training Command and the Air Ministry. It flew on until an engine fire in 1960 ended its days.

Piper J-4A Cub Coupé

G-AFSZ was used by the Wiltshire School of Flying, and was loaned to No. 651 Squadron in 1941. The aircraft survived the war and was sold to Rice Caravans in December 1945, but was crashed by another owner in 1962.

Twenty one J-4As were impressed, mostly from flying clubs, and used by the ATA and various maintenance units and detached flights. Typical of the Cub Coupé's fate was the G-AFVL of the Wiltshire School of Flying, which became BT441 and was loaned to No. 651 Squadron.

Potez 29

A few Potez 29s arrived at Heliopolis from Syria in September 1940, and were sent on to Haifa with British serials, No. 54 becoming AX678 and No. 99 becoming AX679. Both served with the detachment at Fort Lamy, but AX678 soon became unserviceable and was struck off in June 1941 and AX679 was written off after being overturned by a gust of wind at Ma'an in December 1940.

Potez 63

Six Potez 63s were impressed by the RAF, including No. 699 (later AX673) and No. 670 (later AX672). Both were destroyed in accidents within a year after beginning service with No. 2 French (Fighter) Flight. AX670 swung off the runway and hit a sand bank in September 1940 and was soon struck off, and AX673 caught fire soon after take-off and was totally destroyed in the subsequent forced landing and fire. No. 691 was given the RAF serial AX691 and was struck off in 1941.

Rogojarski SIM-XIV-H Srs 1

In total, nine seaplanes of the Yugoslav Naval Air Service fled to the Allies following the German occupation of the country. A single Yugoslav SIM-XIV-H was used by No. 2 (Yugo) Sqn as No. 157 after fleeing the German invasion of Yugoslavia and arriving at Heliopolis in June 1941. The aircraft was used for anti-submarine patrols, but ran into a sandstorm which brought it down after fuel starvation had stopped the engines. Three of the four crew were killed, the observer surviving after swimming to shore. A second SIM-XIV-H may have escaped with AX716 and been used as a source of spares.

Savoia Marchetti S.79

Four Yugoslav S.79s arrived at Heliopolis in April 1941, carying gold. The aircraft were given the serials AX702-705, and converted for desert operations, three serving with No. 117 Squadron and one (AX705) serving with No. 2 PRU at Heliopolis. AX703 was destroyed when it crash-landed near Takoradi in November 1941 after one engine failed; the aircraft could not fly on two. AX705 was also damaged in a crash-landing at Heliopolis in 1942.

Short S.16 Scion/S.22 Scion Senior

The Scion was a small short-range airliner with five passenger seats, and most of those impressed were taken from local airlines such as Yorkshire Airways and Southend Flying Services. The majority were used by No. 110 (AAC) Wing, but W7419 was transferred to RAF Waddington and used as a transport by OC No. 5(B) Group.

G-ACUW (later AV891) belonged to Lundy & Atlantic Coast Air Lines before delivery to No. 110 (AAC) Wing. The aircraft crashed after stalling and spinning close to the ground on a training flight in November 1940.

Short S.20

G-ADHJ retained its civil registration despite being impressed into RAF service. In former times the aircraft had been used for carrying heavy mail loads with the assistance of its lower half, the S.21 Maia.

A single Short S.20, Mercury, formerly the upper half of the Short-Mayo composite, was taken into RAF service in 1940 for training pilots in a newly formed No. 320 Dutch Seaplane Squadron. When the unit converted to Hudsons in October 1940 it returned to Felixstowe and thence to Short Bros, and was then scrapped.

Short S.23/S.26

Two of the famous 'C'-class Imperial Airways flying-boats were impressed after two S.30s were lost in Norway. *Clio* (G-AETY, later AX659) was destroyed in 1941 following a crash due to engine failure. *Cordelia* (G-AEUD, later AX660) served briefly with No. 430 Squadron before being returned to BOAC, flying until 1946.

Clio was one of two S.23 flying-boats impressed into RAF service. ASV radar masts are visible on the rear fuselage, as is the Bolton Paul rear gun turret installed by Shorts as part of the conversion process for military service. The aircraft also carried depth charge racks.

Spartan Cruiser/Executive

Three Spartan Cruisers were impressed from Scottish Airways and delivered to No. 6 AACU in 1940, but all suffered from deterioration and were soon unairworthy. Eight Executives were impressed by the USAAF and lent to the RCAF, and one, formerly used by the King of Iraq, was used by No. 1 PRU under the serial AX666.

Stampe SV.4

A single Stampe SV.4 was used by two Belgian pilots to escape to Britain in 1941. The aircraft was taken to Hendon and given the serial MX457 in August 1942, and transferred to the Allied Flight. It was transferred with the flight to No. 510 Squadron in October 1942 and stayed with the unit until the end of the war, when it was returned to Belgium, where it found its way on to the civil register in 1948.

Stinson Voyager

A pair of Stinson Voyagers was impressed, X1050 being loaned from the manufacturers and X5324 from Brian Allen Aviation. X1050 made a brief visit to France in May 1940, returning shortly before the Germans invaded. The aircraft was used by a number of units including No. 43 OTU and No. 70 Group Comm. Flt. It survived the war.

Tipsy Trainer

Five Tipsy Trainers were impressed in the UK, beginning with G-AFEI in 1940 with the final example being G-AFPK in 1944. Their exact use is unknown, but the type was a light two-seat sport aircraft and civil examples were generally used as trainers. G-AGBM was used by the ATA at White Waltham until 1942 when it was sent to No. 5 MU. Eventually it was sold to a private owner in 1945 and crashed in Belgium in 1948. One example was impressed from the civil register in India. Originally VT-AKQ, it became MA930 and was used by the Communications Flight Bengal during late 1942 to early 1943. The aircraft was destroyed after flying into trees in March 1943.

Waco YKC/ZGC-7

A pair of Wacos was purchased from Egyptian owners by the British Army in Egypt, for use by the Long Range Desert Group. The ZGC-7 became AX695 and the YKC became AX697, and both received service paint schemes after permission was reluctantly granted by headquarters. Major Prendergast flew one, and Trooper Barker the other, flying the unit CO around for communications and even flying in support of LRDG patrols to deliver spares and evacuate wounded personnel. Their final fate is unknown, but they were probably withdrawn and scrapped when the LRDG was disbanded in 1944.

Westland Wessex

The Westland Wessex was a tri-motor design derived from the Westland IV. A high-winged monoplane, it was powered by three Armstrong-Siddeley Genet Major engines. Accommodation for four passengers was provided in a glazed cabin. Both G-AAGW and G-ACHI were ex-Imperial Airways aircraft, which were sold to Air Pilots Training Ltd in 1935 (which was subsequently renamed Air Service Training Ltd in 1940). Used by No. 3 E&RFTS, the two aircraft were later used by No. 11 AONS when this unit was formed at Hamble. The pair was withdrawn from use when their certificates of airworthiness expired in 1940.

G-AAGW was one of two Wessexes sold by Imperial Airways to Air Pilots Training Ltd, eventually ending up with No. 3 E&RFTS as navigation trainers and finally transferred to No. 11 AONS at Hamble in 1939.

Zlin 212 Tourist

The Zlin 212 was a light two-seat tandem design powered by a Walther engine. Little is known about VT-ALU, alias MA926, which was impressed in 1942. Even its service history and owner were not recorded. The aircraft was struck off in 1943.

INDEX

Page numbers in **bold** refer to sections with technical artworks or cutaway illustrations.

INDEX

Picture acknowledgments

The following organisations have kindly supplied photographs for this book:

Aerospace Publishing
Royal Air Force Museum
Imperial War Museum
Rolls-Royce
British Aerospace